# Time Out
# New York

**Penguin Books**

PENGUIN BOOKS

Published by the Penguin Group
Penguin Books Ltd, 27 Wrights Lane, London W8 5TZ, England
Penguin Books USA Inc., 375 Hudson Street, New York, New York 10014, USA
Penguin Books Australia Ltd, Ringwood, Victoria, Australia
Penguin Books Canada Ltd, 10 Alcorn Avenue, Toronto, Ontario, Canada M4V 3B2
Penguin Books (NZ) Ltd, 182-190 Wairau Road, Auckland 10, New Zealand

Penguin Books Ltd, Registered Offices: Harmondsworth, Middlesex, England

First published 1990
Second edition 1992
Third edition 1994
Fourth edition 1996
Fifth edition 1997
10 9 8 7 6 5 4 3 2 1

Colour reprographics by Precise Litho, 34–35 Great Sutton Street, London EC1
Mono reprographics printed and bound by William Clowes Ltd, Beccles, Suffolk NR34 9QE

## Edited and designed by

Time Out Magazine Limited
Universal House
251 Tottenham Court Road
London W1P OAB
Tel: 0171 813 3000
Fax: 0171 813 6001
Email: guides@timeout.co.uk
http://www.timeout.co.uk

## Editorial

**Managing Editor** Peter Fiennes
**Editor** Caroline Taverne
**Consultant Editor** Steve Ellman
**Copy Editors** Phil Harriss, Nicholas Royle
**Researchers** Ben Gibberd, Maria Weisbin
**Indexer** Jackie Brind

## Design

**Art Director** Warren Beeby
**Associate Art Director** John Oakey
**Art Editor** Paul Tansley
**Designer** Mandy Martin
**Design Assistant** Wayne Davies
**Picture Editor** Catherine Hardcastle
**Picture Researcher** Michaela Freeman

## Advertising

**Group Advertisement Director** Lesley Gill
**Sales Director** Mark Phillips
**Advertisement Sales (New York)** Time Out New York Partners, LP

## Administration

**Publisher** Tony Elliott
**Managing Director** Mike Hardwick
**Financial Director** Kevin Ellis
**Marketing Director** Gillian Auld
**Production Manager** Mark Lamond
**Accountant** Catherine Bowen

## Features in this guide were written and researched by:

**Introduction** Steve Ellman. **Essential Information** Frank Broughton, Steve Ellman. **Getting Around** Frank Broughton, Steve Ellman. **Accommodation** Kathy Passero. **New York by Season** Frank Broughton, Steve Ellman, Sue Stemp. **Architecture** Frank Broughton, Steve Ellman. **History** Frank Broughton, Robert W Snyder, Mary Trewby. **New York Today** Steve Ellman. **New York by Neighbourhood** Frank Broughton, Steve Ellman. **Eating & Drinking** Brandon Holley, Milena Damjanov, Adam Sachs. **Shopping & Services** Gia Kourlas. **Museums** Sue Nelson, Linda Yablonsky. **Art Galleries** Linda Yablonsky. **Media** Frank Broughton, Steve Ellman. **Spoken Word** Barbara Aria. **Cabaret** Frank Broughton, Eric Myers, Jill Pearlman. **Clubs** Adam Goldstone. **Film** Steve Talty. **Music** Robert Kemp, Ken Smith. **Theatre** Gerald Newman. **Dance** Gia Kourlas. **Sport & Fitness** Frank Broughton, Steve Ellman. **Gay & Lesbian New York** Cathay Che. **Children** Barbara Aria. **Business** Frank Broughton, Steve Ellman, Kathy McFarland. **Students** Frank Broughton, Kathy McFarland. **Trips Out of Town** Frank Broughton, Kathy McFarland. **Survival** Steve Ellman.

## The editors would like to thank the following:

Margaret M Danek, Cath Phillips, Jim Weisbin, Cyndi Stivers and the staff of *Time Out New York*.

**Maps by** JS Graphics, Hill View Cottage, 17 Beadles Lane, Old Oxted, Surrey RH8 9JG; maps on pages 344 and 346 reproduced by kind permission of the Metropolitan Transportation Authority.

**Photography by** Andrew Kist except for: page 69 AKG; 34 Kirk Condyles/Impact Visuals; 35, 37, 40, 61, 64, 65, 71, 73, 75, 77, 283, 297, 298, 300, 301, 305, 307, 309, 311 Corbis; 63(b) Hulton Getty; 82 Mary Levin/ Impact Visuals; 79 Magnani/Frank Spooner Pictures; 51 Arnhel de Serra; 54(b) Wurts Bros/Otis Elevator Company. Pictures on pages 20(b), 21, 49, 106(b), 189, 190, 214, 215, 220, 234, 239, 240, 241, 249, 254, 258, 261, 268, 269, 306 were supplied by the featured establishments.

# Contents

# About the Guide

The *Time Out New York Guide* is one of an expanding series of city guides that also includes London, Paris, Amsterdam, Rome, Prague, San Francisco, Los Angeles and Miami. They're produced by the company responsible for *Time Out*, London's definitive arts and entertainment magazine – this edition with help from its New York counterpart, *Time Out New York*.

Our team of resident writers aims to provide you with all the information you'll need to take on the world's most exciting city and win. The guide has been completely updated for this fifth edition: many chapters have been rewritten from scratch, all have been thoroughly revised and new features have been added, including a series of colour maps of Manhattan and New York City.

## CHECKED & CORRECT

Above all, we've tried to make this book as useful as possible. Addresses, telephone numbers, transport details, opening times, admission prices and credit card details are all included in our listings. And, as far as possible, we've given up-to-date details of facilities, services and events, all checked and correct at the time we went to press. But owners and managers can change their arrangements at any time. Before you go out of your way, it's always best to telephone and check opening times, dates of exhibitions, admission prices and other details.

## PRICES

The prices we've given should be treated as guidelines, not gospel. Fluctuating exchange rates and inflation can cause prices, in shops and restaurants especially, to change rapidly. If, however, you find things have changed beyond recognition, ask why – and then write to let us know. We aim to give the best and most up-to-date advice, so we always appreciate feedback. The average price quoted in the restaurant chapter is for a three course meal without alcohol or tip.

## CREDIT CARDS

The following abbreviations have been used for credit cards: **AmEx**: American Express; **DC**: Diners' Club; **Disc**: Discover; **JCB**: Japanese credit cards; **MC**: Mastercard (Access); **V**: Visa (Barclaycard). Virtually all shops, restaurants and attractions will accept dollar travellers' cheques issued by a major financial institution (such as American Express).

## TELEPHONE NUMBERS

All telephone numbers in this guide are written as dialled from Manhattan. Therefore we have included the '1' and the three-figure dialling code you need to dial if calling a location off the island. The code for Brooklyn, Queens, Staten Island and the Bronx is 718; for Long Island it's 516 and 201 or 908 for New Jersey. If you want to phone a Manhattan number from anywhere off the island, prefix the number listed with 1-212. Numbers preceded by 1-800 can be dialled free of charge from anywhere within the United States.

## RIGHT TO REPLY

In all cases the information we give is impartial. No organisation has been included because its owner or manager has advertised in our publications. We hope you enjoy the *Time Out New York Guide*, but we'd like you to let us know if you don't. We welcome tips for places that you think we should include in future editions and also take notice of your criticism of our choices. There's a reader's report card at the back of this book.

There's an on-line version of this guide, together with weekly events listings for New York and other international cities, at: http://www.timeout.co.uk.

# Introduction

On a bright day, the towers of New York glisten in the distance like some lost city of legend. You glimpse them off and on as you cross the outer boroughs on your way in from the airport, like intimations of a great beast over the horizon. When you reach the river crossings and get your first close-up look at the island of Manhattan – that slender capsule of land and the inconceivable tons of steel and concrete that cover it – the sight is, inevitably, breathtaking.

That density of structure and activity constrains the city's residents. It's a pressure cooker. The native New Yorker, every so often, absolutely has to get out of town and everyone who can afford it has a summer or weekend retreat.

The visitor, however, can translate that density into accessibility. This lodestone city compresses time as well as space. Because so many distinct and intriguing cultures, landmarks and neighbourhoods stand cheek by jowl in a few square miles, your days here take on a kaleidoscopic quality.

Work your way up from the steel canyons of Wall Street (where the nearby Staten Island ferry and the World Trade Center offer stunning views) to Chinatown or Little Italy for lunch. Head east towards East Village grunge or west to SoHo chic. A few more blocks brings you to the classic bohemia of Greenwich Village and the budding gallery district of Chelsea. And that's just lower Manhattan. You're minutes by public transport from the midtown Theater District, the great expanse of Central Park and the heart of black America, Harlem. All this can be done in one day, and that's just only borough out of five.

The phrase 'New York minute' usually refers to the pace and intensity from which the natives suffer (and of which they boast). It shows most clearly in the fixity of purpose with which they stride the avenues or dart through the traffic with shopping bags, backpacks and briefcases held close. If time is money, the typical New Yorker has a miser's mentality. The tourist, by comparison, has the Midas touch, graced with the one asset that is in chronically short supply here.

The super-dense minutes of a New York holiday provide more information and stimulation per second than those of any other city. Don't be put off by that velocity. Underneath the surface toughness, New York's whole purpose is in bringing people together – with the things of this world and with each other. That's all it has done for the past 300 years. The first whites took this foothold on

the continent for the furs of the interior. In later centuries the city became the great point of transfer for all the products of the New World. But New York's pre-eminent commodity has always been people, 'tired, poor, huddled masses' of them.

In its brusque way, consequently, the city is user-friendly. No one can live here happily without some curiosity about their fellow creatures. Though they may not always be free to indulge it, even the most harried of New Yorkers practise tolerance. The mayor's famous 'quality of life' campaign may seek to smooth out the city's rough edges; an invasion of superstores and chain stores may threaten the small entrepreneur; rude Times Square may give way to the tender mercies of Disney – but this city still has too much raw vitality and taste for innovation to ever be homogenised. If only by necessity, the city's unacknowledged motto remains 'different strokes...'.

You'll get the most out of New York if you put on a little of that hard veneer make-up. Down these mean streets a tourist must go. The richest experience of the city comes when you treat it as a round-the-clock assertiveness training class. The natives respect directness. They may not cater to your every whim, but they won't delay your quest. They're on one of their own.

New York may be decried for breeding a crushing anonymity, and it can do that: you're just one more face in the crowd. And yet, that cloak of invisibility is ultimately liberating. That is another of Gotham's great virtues. Because you're an unknown, you're free to re-invent yourself. New Yorkers do it all the time. It may be this monster city's greatest appeal.

André Breton once said, 'I wish I could change my sex as easily as I change my clothes'. After a night on this town you'll see how many New Yorkers have realised that surrealist desire. Most visitors' dreams will be more prosaic – and even more possible. Whatever they are, discover New York and discover yourself. *Steve Ellman*

# Essential Information

*Essential tips for conquering the Naked City.*

For more detailed advice on surviving the urban jungle, *see chapter* **Survival**; for information about the abbreviations used in this guide, *see page vi* **About the Guide**.

## Visas

Under the Visa Waiver Program, citizens of the UK, Japan, Australia, New Zealand and all West European countries (except for Portugal, Greece and the Vatican City) do not need a visa for stays of less than 90 days (business or pleasure), as long as they have a passport that is valid for the full 90-day period and a return ticket. An open standby ticket is acceptable.

Canadians and Mexicans do not need visas but must have legal proof of their residency. All other travellers must have visas. Full information and visa application forms can be obtained from your nearest US embassy or consulate. In general, send in your application at least three weeks before you plan to travel. Visas required more urgently should be applied for via the travel agent booking your ticket.

**US Embassy Visa Information Line**
*(Recorded information in the UK 0891 200 290.)*

## Immigration & Customs

Standard immigration regulations apply to all visitors, which means you may have to wait (up to an hour) when you arrive at Immigration. During your flight, you will be handed an immigration form and a customs declaration form to be presented to an official when you land.

You may be expected to explain your visit, so be polite and be prepared. You will usually be granted an entry permit to cover the length of your stay. Work permits are hard to get, and you are not permitted to work without one (*see chapter* **Students**).

US Customs allow foreigners to bring in $100 worth of gifts ($400 for returning Americans) before paying duty. One carton of 200 cigarettes (or 100 cigars) and one litre of liquor (spirits) is allowed. No plants, fruit, meat or fresh produce can be taken through customs. For more detailed information, contact your nearest US embassy or consulate.

## Insurance

It's advisable to take out comprehensive insurance before arriving: it's almost impossible to arrange in the US. Make sure that you have adequate health cover, since medical expenses can be high.

## Banks & Foreign Exchange

Banks are open from 9am to 3pm Monday to Friday. You need photo identification, such as a passport, to change travellers' cheques. Many banks will not exchange foreign currency, and the bureaux de changes, limited to tourist-trap areas, close at around 6pm or 7pm. It's best to arrive with some dollars in cash and use travellers' cheques like cash (possible in most restaurants and larger stores – but ask first and be prepared to show ID). In an emergency, most big hotels offer 24-hour change facilities but charge extortionate commission and give atrocious rates.

### Currency

A dollar ($) is 100 cents (¢). A cent is copper and more likely to be called a 'penny'. Then there are nickels (5¢), dimes (10¢)

and quarters (25¢), which are all silver. Paper money is all the same size and colour so make sure you dispense the right denomination. Occasionally you might get a silver dollar or a two-dollar note in change. These are quite unusual and worth keeping.

### Credit Cards
Bring plastic if you have it, because that's the American way. It's essential for things like car hire and booking hotels and handy for buying tickets over the phone. Get a personal identification number (PIN) from your credit company before you travel and you can use Access or Visa to draw cash from all of the city's cashpoints ('ATMs') labelled with the appropriate symbol. Just watch out for those handling fees.

**American Express Travel Service**
*65 Broadway, between Rector Street & Exchange Place (493 6500). Subway 1, N or R to Rector Street.* **Open** 8.30am-5.30pm Mon-Fri.
Will change money and travellers' cheques and offer other services such as poste restante. Phone for the location of other branches.

**Chequepoint USA**
*22 Central Park South (750 2400). Subway N or R to 59th Street.* **Open** 8am-11pm Mon-Fri; 9.30am-8pm Sat; 9.30am-7pm Sun.
Foreign currency, travellers' cheques and bank drafts.
**Branches**: 609 Madison Avenue, at 58th Street (750 2255); 1568 Broadway, at 47th Street (869 6281); 708 Seventh Avenue, at 47th Street (262 1030).

**People's Foreign Exchange**
*19 West 44th Street, Suite 306 (944 6780). Subway B, D, F or Q to 42nd Street.* **Open** 9am-6pm Mon-Fri; 10am-3pm Sat, Sun.
Free foreign exchange on banknotes and travellers' cheques.

**Thomas Cook Currency Services**
*29 Broadway, at Morris Street (757 6915/1-800 287 7362). Subway 4 or 5 to Bowling Green.* **Open** 9am-5pm Mon-Fri.
A complete foreign exchange service is offered. There are seven branches in JFK Airport, all open 8am-9pm daily (718 656 8444), in addition to those listed below.
**Branches**: 41 East 42nd Street; 1590 Broadway; 511 Madison Avenue (all branches 757 6915/1-800 287 7362).

## Disabled Access

New York is one of the most challenging cities for a disabled visitor, but there is support and guidance close by. The Society for the Advancement of Travel for the Handicapped, which promotes travel for the disabled worldwide, is based in New York City. This non-profitmaking group was founded in 1976 to gather information and to educate people about travel facilities for the disabled. Membership is $45 a year ($30 for students and senior citizens) and includes access to an information service and a quarterly newsletter. Write or phone SATH, 347 Fifth Avenue, Suite 610, New York, NY 10016 (447 7284/fax 725 8253).

Another useful resource is the HAI (Hospital Audiences Inc) guide to New York's cultural institutions, *Access for All*. The book lets you know how accessible each place really is, and includes information on the height of telephones and water fountains, hearing and visual aids, passenger loading zones and alternative entrances.

HAI also has an audio description service for the blind and visually impaired for theatre performances. The program, called Describe! ($5), consists of pre-recorded audio cassettes with a description of the theatre, the sets, characters, costumes and special effects. It also offers a live service during performances: phone 575 7660 for more information.

The Theater Development Fund's Theater Access Program (TAP) arranges sign language interpretation for Broadway shows. Phone 221 1103 (voice) or 719 4537 (TDD). Hands On does the same for Off-Broadway performances. Phone 627 4898 (voice/TDD). For more information on facilities for the disabled, *see chapter* **Survival**.

## Time & Dates

New York is on Eastern Standard Time, which extends from the Atlantic coast, across to the eastern side of Lake Michigan and south to the Georgia coast: this is five hours behind Britain, six hours behind France and 17 behind New Zealand. Clocks are put forward one hour in early April and back one hour at the end of October. Going from the east coast to the west, Eastern Standard Time is one hour ahead of Central Time (from Manitoba to Texas), two hours ahead of Mountain Time (Alberta to Arizona and New Mexico) and three hours ahead of Pacific Time (California).

In the US, dates are written in the order of month, day, year; so 2.5.98 is the fifth of February, not the second of May.

## Electricity

Rather than the standard 220-240V, 50-cycle AC used in Europe, the US uses a 110-120V, 60-cycle AC voltage. Except for dual-voltage, flat-pin plug shavers, you will need to run any European appliances via an adaptor, available at airport shops, pharmacies and department stores.

## Safety

Statistics on New York's crime rate, particularly violent crime, have nosedived in the past few years, though bad things still happen to good people. More than ever, most of it is what Americans refer to as 'black on black' crime, happening late at night in poor outlying 'ghetto' neighbourhoods. Don't arrive thinking you need an armed guard to accompany you wherever you go: it is highly unlikely that you will ever be troubled.

Use common sense about flashing your money and valuables around. Avoid lonely and poorly lit streets and, if necessary, walk in the opposite direction to the traffic so no one can kerb-crawl you. In the extreme, walk down the centre of the street: muggers prefer to hang back in doorways and shadows. If the worst happens and you find

citysearch.com

*Views from the inside.*

Don't order the salmon.

yourself threatened, hand over your wallet or camera at once (your attacker will be as anxious to get it over with as you are) and then phone the police as soon as you can (dial 911 from any pay phone).

Beware of pickpockets and street hustlers – especially in busy tourist areas like Times Square – and don't be seduced by card sharps or other tricksters you may come across. A shrink-wrapped camcorder for 50 bucks might well turn out to be brick when you open the box.

As a rule, if you look comfortable rather than lost you should deter wrongdoers. Make sure you know exactly where you are and where you're going when in any of the following areas: west of Eighth Avenue; east of Avenue A; anywhere above 96th Street; anywhere off the island of Manhattan. That's not to say that these are dangerous areas, just that everywhere else should be wholly unproblematic.

## Smoking

New Yorkers are the target of some of the strictest anti-smoking laws on the planet. As well as in most eating establishments (you can smoke at the bar in some), smoking is outlawed in taxis, buses and the subway, in banks, hotel lobbies, public toilets, cinemas, sports arenas and other public places. Now could be the time to quit.

## Telephones

Public payphones are easy to find. Most of them work, but the Nynex ones are the best: those from other phone companies tend to be poorly maintained. If someone's left the handset dangling, it's a helpful sign that something's wrong. Phones take any combination of silver coinage: local calls usually cost 25¢ for about four minutes. The ringing tone is long; the engaged tone is short and higher pitched.

The Manhattan code is 212, but you don't need to dial it unless you're off the island (for example at the airport). In this guide, all seven-figure numbers are Manhattan numbers. We have included the area code and the 1 you need to dial first for all other numbers.

If you want to phone long distance or make an international call from a payphone, you need to go via one of the long-distance companies. In New York, most payphones automatically link up with AT&T. Make the call either by dialling 0 for an operator or by dialling direct (cheaper). To find out how much a call will cost, dial the number first and a voice will tell you how much money to deposit.

You can pay for calls with your credit card. There's a different access number for each phone company: look in the Yellow Pages under Telephone Companies, but beware of the hazards involved. There is little regulation, and some renegade firms charge unannounced and outlandish

rates. The best way of making calls is with a phone card ($4-$50), available from large stores such as 7-11 and Payless Drug.

**Operator assistance** dial 0
**Directory enquiries** (local) dial 411 (free from payphones)
**International calls** dial 011 + country code (UK 44; New Zealand 64; Australia 61)
**Long-distance directory enquiries** dial 1 + area code + 555 1212 (long-distance charges apply)
**Collect calls** (reverse charges) dial 0 followed by the area code and number, or dial 1-800 COLLECT; for calls to the UK dial 1-800 445 5667.

## Tax & Tipping

You'll be hard pressed to find anything more expensive in New York than in Europe, but you will have to account for a few extras. Sales tax (8.25 per cent) is added to the price of most purchases, but is absent from price tags. In addition, there's a lot of tipping to do. Waiting staff get 15-20 per cent (as a rough guide, double the sales tax on your bill) and cabbies 15 per cent. But don't forget to tip bartenders ($1 a round), hairdressers (10-15 per cent), hotel doormen ($1 for hailing a cab) and porters ($1 per bag), and remember that the person who delivers your Chinese food probably receives no wage at all ($2 is considered a good tip).

## Tourist Information

Hotels are usually full of maps, leaflets and free tourist magazines, which give advice about entertainment and events. Be aware that advice from hotels is not always impartial. Plenty of other magazines (including the weekly *Time Out New York*) offer entertainment and practical information (*see* chapter **Media**).

### New York Convention & Visitors Bureau
*2 Columbus Circle, at West 59th Street & Broadway (397 8222). Subway 1, 9, A, B, C or D to Columbus Circle.* **Open** 9am-6pm Mon-Fri; 10am-3pm Sat, Sun.

A barrage of leaflets on all manner of things: free, helpful advice on accommodation and entertainment, coupons for discounts and free maps. The phone number gives you access to either a multilingual human or a huge menu of recorded information. In addition to the main office there are booths at World Trade Center 2, JFK Airport International Arrivals Building, Grand Central Station and Penn Station.

## When to Visit

The climate is at its sublime best in spring and early summer (April-June), when the Atlantic sea breezes are still fighting off the inevitable humidity that can make July and August insufferably hot; and in autumn or 'fall' (September-November), when the heat subsides in readiness for the extremely cold winter round the corner.

Summer temperatures will often reach the 90s (31°C), but even below this the humidity makes it feel much hotter. At the same time, air-conditioned buildings are cool to the point of cold, so wear layers. The converse problem occurs in winter, when outside may be well below freezing and inside has the dry burnt air of some far-off central furnace.

In terms of things to do, New York is alive throughout the year, but during the summer the parks and plazas and other public places are especially busy with free entertainment. At the same time, indoor diversions take a break and the museum, gallery and concert calendar slows to a halt. The American summer officially lasts from Memorial Day (end of May) to Labor Day (beginning of September), and most New Yorkers will try to leave the heat of the city as often as possible. Springtime has the most parades and is when the shops are full of the newest bargains, while late summer and fall have the most festivals. Winter can be bitterly cold, but is the busiest time for cultural activities. Christmas is a very special time in the city, with unmissable street decorations, ice-skating, roaming Santas and a wonderland in every shop window. *See chapter* **New York By Season** for more information

# Divided by a common language

Forget **queuing** and get **in line**. Take the **elevator** and not the **lift**, and remember **fags** are only for smoking if you're a homophobic gunman. **WASPS** are White Anglo Saxon and Protestant, while **JAPs** are Jewish American Princesses. **Buppies** are black yuppies and **guppies** are gay ones. **Jocks** are sporty types, named after their straps. A **hero** is a French bread sandwich, also a sub (after 'submarine'). **Takeaway** food is **to go** or **delivered**. A **schmear** is the spreading of cream cheese that you ask for on your bagel. A **soda** is any flavour of fizzy drink, while soda is **seltzer**. Malt **liquor** is just strong beer. If someone's **pissed** they're not necessarily drunk. A **bum** is a tramp, and so your bum is your **butt** or your **tush** or **fanny**. And whatever you do, don't forget your euphemisms when asking for the toilet. **Bathroom**, **washroom**, **restroom** or (no lies) **comfort station** are sufficiently removed from reality for American ears. Get it wrong, of course, and you're a **schmuck**.

# Getting Around

*As New Yorkers will explain, when a traffic light flashes 'Walk', you walk; 'Don't Walk' means you should run.*

New York is a collection of boroughs, but for most visitors it means Manhattan, an island only 13.4 miles (22km) long and 2.3 miles (4km) at its widest. The roads above 14th Street are laid out in a grid pattern, which makes finding your way around relatively simple. The avenues run north/south and are numbered from east to west (with Lexington, Park and Madison between Third and Fifth). Sixth Avenue is also known as the Avenue of the Americas. There are four short avenues around the East Village that are lettered A to D.

The cross streets run east/west (Fifth Avenue marks the dividing line between east and west; the lower the building number the closer it is to Fifth Avenue) and are numbered from the south. Most streets are one-way: traffic flow on even-number streets tends to be eastwards; on odd-number streets it's usually westwards.

The major exception to the grid rule is Broadway, an old Indian trail that was well established when the grid was laid down in the 1800s. It runs north/south, then cuts diagonally downtown from the west to the East Side.

Downtown streets, below 14th Street, are more confusing, since they were built on before the grid pattern was established; here you will need a map.

## Information

Information on subways and buses is available by phoning the **Metropolitan Transport Authority's helpline** on 1-718 330 1234 (1-718 330 4847 for non-English speakers). The phone line is staffed from 6am to 9pm daily and offers recorded information at other times. Alternatively, you can phone the New York Convention & Visitors Bureau Information Center (397 8222) for instructions on the best way to get between any two places in the city.

## To & From the Airport

'If the Martians landed they'd better not use JFK or they'd be two hours late getting into the city'. The same joke could be applied to Newark and LaGuardia, New York's other two airports.

Though using public transport is the cheapest method, the links are poor and frustrating to use. The private bus services are usually the best budget option. **Gray Line** runs a minibus service from each of the three airports to any address in midtown (between 23rd and 63rd Streets) from 7am to midnight; the wait at the airport is never more than 20 minutes. On the outward journey, it picks up at several hotels (you must book in advance). Call 757 6840 or 1-800 315 3006 for details. Or take a **Carey Bus**, operating between 6am and midnight, with stops at Grand Central Terminal, the Port Authority terminal (both on 42nd Street) and a host of midtown hotels. Call 1-718 632 0500 for recorded details. For a full list of these and other transport services between New York City and its three airports call **1-800 AIR RIDE**, a touch-tone menu of recorded information provided by the Port Authority.

A **yellow cab** is the most effortless method to get from plane to hotel, though by no means the cheapest: the trip to Manhattan is now a flat-rate $30, plus tip and bridge tolls. It's actually cheaper to book a 'private hire' taxi or limousine to meet you (arrange it before you fly or call from the airport). This will cost around $25 plus tolls and tip. **Tel Aviv** (777 7777) aims to pick you up from any airport three minutes after you call. For a little more you can order a 'stretch' limo and arrive in true style.

### John F Kennedy Airport

*(1-718 244 4444)*
There's a subway link from JFK (extremely cheap at $1.50), but this involves waiting for a shuttle bus to Howard Beach station and then more than an hour's ride into Manhattan. **Gray Line** minibus $16; **Carey Bus** $13; **yellow cab** $30.

### LaGuardia Airport

*(1-718 476 5000)*
Seasoned New Yorkers take a 20-minute ride on the **M60** bus ($1.50) to 125th Street in Harlem (not a good place to be

## 'You can't get there from here'

The trick to asking directions in New York is to deliver your question within earshot of at least two people. One of them will be completely wrong, but the inevitable debate (sometimes involving the entire bus, subway carriage or street-corner) will ensure that the issue is hammered out sufficiently for you to know where to head. The arguments sparked by your innocent enquiry may well continue long after you have left.

at night), where you can get off at Lexington Avenue subway station for the 4, 5 and 6 trains or Lenox Avenue for the 2 and 3. Otherwise **Gray Line** $13; **Carey Bus** $10; **yellow cab** $25-$35.

### Newark Airport

The **New Jersey Transit bus** company goes to the Port Authority bus terminal (41st Street and Eighth Avenue). The fare is $7 and buses leave every 10-15 minutes (information 629 8767). Various hotels also offer a minibus shuttle. **Yellow cab** $35.

## The Subway

Much maligned, but actually clean, efficient, heated, air-conditioned and far safer than most people will tell you, the subway is easily the fastest way to get around during daylight hours. It runs all night, but with sparse service and fewer riders it's advisable (and usually quicker) to take a cab after seven or eight in the evening. Entry to the system is with a MetroCard or a token costing $1.50. You can buy both from a booth inside the entrance to a station and can use both on buses as well. Staff won't accept notes bigger than $20. Once through the turnstile you can travel anywhere on the network. If you're planning to use the subway a lot, it's worth buying a magnetic-strip MetroCard. These can be used by any number of passengers, start at $6 for four trips, and can be topped up to a total of $80. They can be bought in selected stores as well as subway stations.

Trains are known by letters and numbers and are colour-coded according to which line they run on. 'Express' trains run between major stops, 'local' trains stop at every station. Check on the map (available free at all stations from the token booth) before you board; for a subway map of Manhattan, *see page 346*. Stations are usually named after the street they're on, so they're easy to find. Entrances are marked with a green globe (a red globe marks an entrance that is not always open). It's worth knowing that some stations don't have connecting walkways, so there are separate entrances to the uptown and downtown platforms. Feel free to ask advice: New York subway etiquette assumes that no-one has a clue where they're going or even which train they're on, and directions will be gladly given.

To ensure safety, don't wear flashy jewellery, keep your bag with the opening facing you and board the train from the off-peak waiting area marked at the centre of every platform. This is monitored by video and is where the conductor's car will stop.

## Buses

Buses are fine if you aren't in a hurry. If your feet hurt from walking around, a bus is a good way of continuing your street-level sightseeing. They're white and blue with a route number and a digital destination sign. The fare is $1.50, either with a token or MetroCard (the same ones that you buy for the subway) or in change (no notes are accepted). Express buses operate on some routes; these cost $4. If you're travelling on a bus going up- or downtown and want to continue your journey crosstown (or vice versa) ask the driver for a 'transfer' when you get on – you'll be given a ticket for use on the second stage. Again, you can rely on other passengers for advice, but bus maps are available from all subway stations. Almost all buses are now equipped with wheelchair lifts.

## Taxis

Once you start using cabs in New York you begin to wish they were this cheap everywhere in the world. Yellow cabs are hardly ever in short supply, except in the rain and at around 4 or 5pm, when rush hour gets going and when many cabbies – inexplicably – change shifts. They have a light on to show they're available, and will stop if you stick your arm out. Jump in first and then tell the driver where you're going. Cabs carry up to four people for the same price: $2 plus 30¢ per fifth of a mile, with an extra 50¢ charge after 8pm. This makes an average fare for a three-mile (4.5km) ride about $5 to $7, depending on the traffic and time of day. Unfortunately, some cabbies will know the city as poorly as you do, so it helps if you know where you're going. Tip 10-15 per cent or round the fare up to the nearest dollar plus one. The cab number and driver's number are on a sign on the dashboard if you have a problem. There's also a meter number on the receipt. If you wish to complain or trace lost property, phone the Taxi and Limousine Commission on 302 8294 (9am-5pm Mon-Fri). Late at night, cabbies stick to fast-flowing routes and reliably lucrative areas. Try the Avenues and the key east/west streets (Canal, Houston, 14th, 23rd, 42nd, 59th, 86th). Bridge and tunnel exits are also good for a steady flow from the airports, and passengerless cabbies will usually head for nightclubs and big hotels. Otherwise, try one of the following:

**Chinatown**: Chatham Square, where Mott Street meets the Bowery, is an unofficial taxi stand; or try the Bowery at Canal Street, where you can hail one coming off the Manhattan Bridge.

**Financial District**: Not the most nocturnal of neighbourhoods; try the Vista Hotel or World Trade Center 1. There may be a queue but there'll certainly be a cab.

**Lincoln Center**: The crowd will head towards Columbus Circle for a cab. Those in the know go west to Amsterdam Avenue.

**Lower East Side**: Katz's Deli (corner of Houston & Ludlow Streets) is a cabbies' hangout; otherwise try Delancey Street, where cabs come in over the Williamsburg Bridge.

*Manhattan gridlock: time to buy a bike or take a hike.*

**Midtown**: Penn Station and Grand Central attract cabs through the night, as does the Port Authority building (42nd & Eighth) and Times Square.

**SoHo**: If you're west, try Sixth Avenue; east, the gas station on Houston at Broadway.

**TriBeCa**: Cabs here (many arriving from the Holland Tunnel) head up Hudson Street. Canal Street is also a good bet.

### Car Service Companies

The following companies will pick you up anywhere in the city, at any time of day or night: **All City Taxis** (1-718 402 2323); **Bell Radio Taxi** (691 9191); **Communicar** (1-718 457 7777); **Sabra** (777 7171); **Tel Aviv** (777 7777).

## Driving

A car is useless in Manhattan. Drivers are among the worst in the world and taking to the streets, not to mention finding a place to park, is not for the faint-hearted. Don't bother hiring a car unless you are planning a trip out of town; if you do, restrict your driving to evening hours, when traffic is less heavy and on-street parking plentiful. Even then, keep your eyes on the road and be prepared for anything. Car hire is much cheaper on the city's outskirts and in neighbouring states such as New Jersey and Connecticut. Book ahead for weekends, and note that street parking is very restricted, especially in the summer. Don't ever park within 15 feet (5m) of a fire hydrant and make sure you read the parking signs. Unless there are meters, most streets have 'alternate side parking' – i.e. one side is out of bounds for certain hours on alternate days. The New York City Department of Transportation (442 7080) provides information on daily changes to parking regulations.

Most New York authorities will be happy for you to drive on a UK licence for a limited time, though an international one (available in the UK from the AA or RAC) is better. All car hire companies listed below add sales tax. They also offer a 'loss damage waiver' (LDW). This is expensive – almost as much as the rental itself – but without it you are responsible for the cost of repairing even the slightest damage. If you pay with an AmEx card or a gold Visa or Mastercard the LDW may well be covered by them; it might also be covered by a reciprocal agreement with a motoring organisation. Personal liability insurance is optional but recommended (but check whether your holiday or home insurance covers it already). You will invariably need a credit card to rent a car and usually have to be over 25. If you know you want to rent a car before you travel, ask your travel agent or airline if they can offer any good deals.

### Avis

*(1-800 331 1212).* **Open** 24 hours daily. **Rates** from $55 a day unlimited mileage; special weekend rates. **Credit** AmEx, DC, Disc, MC, V.

### Budget Rent-a-Car

*(807 8700).* **Open** *city* 7am-12am, *airport* 5am-2am, daily. **Rates** from $60 a day unlimited mileage; special weekend rates. **Credit** AmEx, DC, Disc, JCB, MC, V.

### Enterprise

*(1-800 325 8007).* **Open** 8am-9pm Mon-Sat; 9am-9pm Sun. **Rates** from $35 a day off Manhattan; around $60 a day on the island; unlimited mileage restricted to New York, New Jersey and Connecticut. **Credit** AmEx, DC, Disc, MC, V.

We highly recommend this cheap and reliable service. The most accessible branches off Manhattan are Hoboken

**BLUE MAN GROUP**

ASTOR PLACE THEATRE • 434 LAFAYETTE ST. (CHARGE BY PHONE) 212-254-4370 212-307-4100

# For wheels

New York's love affair with the automobile makes for nonexistent parking, horrendous traffic jams and environmental degradation. Mass transit is indirect and occasionally chaotic. Simple pragmatism – and a taste for thrills and/or recreation – have spurred a growing interest in a broader spectrum of wheels.

Bicycles would seem to be a sensible form of transport in a city as compact and flat as this. Cross-town races between automobile, subway and bicycle invariably show the bicyclist as winner. What's more, it's estimated that the 80,000 current daily riders spare the city thousands of tons of air pollutants each year.

While certain parts of town are inherently bike-friendly (notably Central Park and Prospect Park) there are only a hundred miles of designated bicycle path in the city. And since space is New York's most valued commodity, cyclists have had to fight for their right to pedal.

Official attitudes have been ambivalent at best. Former Mayor Ed Koch became a supporter after a visit to Beijing provided a vision of masses on wheels. He instituted an innovative bike lane along Sixth Avenue in Manhattan but, legend has it, soured on the concept after visiting Governor Hugh Carey's limousine was struck by a cyclist on the roadway.

The explosion of commercial bicycle messenger services in the 1980s did much to colour the debate. The stereotypical messenger was thought of as young, and of questionable

ethnicity. But while this supposed menace to pedestrian life resulted in a 1987 midtown bicycle ban, cyclists were well enough organised by that time to overturn it in court. They continue to organise and demonstrate for freedom of wheel, and have since been joined on the streets by an army of rollerbladers.

If you're planning to get around by bicycle or blade you'll find no shortage of rental shops: *see chapters* **Shopping & Services** *and* **Sport & Fitness**. Stick to the parks and other prime biking areas to begin with. Dealing with New York traffic requires a judicious blend of bravery and responsibility, since a certain amount of aggression is required to win a comfortable share of road space. A helmet is always advisable and (mandatory for cyclists of 14 and under). Transportation Alternatives, an organisation campaigning for city cycling and safe streets (629 3311) is an excellent source for maps and other information.

---

(PATH train to 34th Street) and Greenwich (Metro-North to Grand Central). Agents will collect you from the station.

## Further Afield

Don't ask for single or return tickets, but for one-way and round-trip. All long-distance trains depart from Penn Station (Amtrak 1-800 872 7245). Commuter rail services that operate within the immediate metropolitan area include Metro-North (532 4900/1-800 638 7646); the Long Island Railroad (1-718 217 5477; and NJ Transit (1-201 762 5100/1-800 772 2222). *See chapter* **Trips Out of Town** for more information.

### Grand Central Terminal
*42nd Street at Park Avenue. Subway 4, 5, 6 or 7 to Grand Central Station.*
Home to Metro-North, which runs trains to more than 100 stations throughout New York State and Connecticut.

### PATH Trains
PATH (Port Authority Trans Hudson) trains run from six

stations in Manhattan to various places across the river in New Jersey (including Hoboken, Jersey City and Newark). The system is fully automated and costs $1 for each journey. You need change or a crisp dollar bill to put in the machines. Trains run 24 hours a day, but you can face a very long wait outside commuter hours. Manhattan PATH stations are marked on the subway map. For more information call 1-800 234 PATH.

### Penn Station
*West 34th Street, between Seventh & Eighth Avenues (582 6875). Subway A, C or E to Penn Station.*
Long Island Rail Road, New Jersey Transit and Amtrak (long-distance) trains depart from here.

### Greyhound Trailways
*(1-800 231 2222).* **Open** 24 hours daily. **Credit** AmEx, Disc, MC, V.
Long-distance bus travel.

### Port Authority Bus Terminal
*Eighth Avenue & West 41st Street (564 8484). Subway A, C, E or K to 42nd Street.*
The number listed above gives information and times on almost all bus transport out of New York. Be warned that the area around the terminal is notoriously dodgy.

**How to get from Peoria to Pretoria.**

© 1997 AT&

 AND **I 800 CALL ATT**® GETS YOU FROM
THE U.S. TO THE WORLD.

It's all within your reach.

# Accommodation

*Stay calm or stay wild – where to rest your head in the city that never sleeps.*

*The **Gramercy Park Hotel** – a dependable midtown option. See page 23.*

First, the good news: thanks to favourable exchange rates, a booming economy, a six per cent drop in occupancy taxes and a much-touted reduction in crime, tourists are once again flocking to the Big Apple. Now, the bad news: although there are plans to open ten hotels over the next decade, until then finding a hotel in Manhattan – especially a reasonably priced one – is getting tougher. Occupancy and rates are at an all-time high, and during peak travel times like the Christmas holidays, Gotham is practically sold out. If you don't have friends with tiny walk-up studios where you can borrow floor space (forget about spare bedrooms in Manhattan), your best bet is to look for weekend discounts, family specials, business rates and other special promotions. After all, this is New York: there's always a deal if you're sharp enough to find it. The more flexible you are about arrival and departure dates, the better the rate you're likely to root out. Check with reservation agencies, too; they can often help when everyone else tells you there's no room at the inn.

On a more positive note, hoteliers are gearing up for the competition ahead by rolling out a cornucopia of unusual amenities and services to woo travellers – from futuristic fitness centres with herbal wraps and aromatherapy, to four-star restaurants and personal attachés. So at least you'll get a few perks for those extra dollars you're shelling out. Better yet, a new trend towards boutique hotels (*see page 28*) and rentable private apartments (*page 32*) offers a change of pace from the behemoths towering over Times Square.

Finally, a word of warning: taxes aren't included in the rates quoted. Even though they've been scaled down, at 6.25 per cent plus a $2 per night occupancy tax they can still come as a shock at checkout. Also, though many hotels now offer free local telephone calls and minimum surcharges, it's best to ask about the policy before using the phone. And watch out for hidden costs like mini-bars, faxes, in-room safes and gift shop purchases. Chances are you'll find toothpaste and other essentials for a third the cost at a drug store across the street.

For more information contact, the Hotel Association of New York City, 437 Madison Avenue, NY 10022 (754 6700; website www. hanyc.org), or write to the New York Convention & Visitors Bureau at 2 Columbus Circle, NY 10019, to ask for a copy of its accommodation booklet.

*1-800 numbers can be called toll-free from within the US.*

# The best hotels for...

## Art lovers

The **SoHo Grand** (*above and p21*) in the heart of Manhattan's art community. Works by local artists fill the guest rooms (and the doormen look like bouncers).

## Backpackers, budget-watchers & bohemians

More hostel than hotel, the economical **Gershwin** (*above and p31*) pays homage to pop art, with Warhols and Lichtensteins in the lobby.

## Celebrity spotting

If you don't spot a star at the **Waldorf-Astoria** (*p20*), take heart in knowing you're standing in the same lobby where glitterati have gathered for decades.

## Executive travellers

The **Millennium Hilton** (*p19*) offers a prime location in the Financial District, and rooms with fax machines. The new **Trump International Hotel & Tower** (*p20*) provides everything from personalised business cards and stationery to cellular phones.

## Exercise fanatics

The **Barbizon** (*p23*) recently added a state-of-the-art fitness centre with a three-floor spa, acupuncture and hot-rock therapy. **The New York Palace** (*see p19*) offers aromatherapy and personal televisions with headphones at every treadmill.

## Gourmets

The place to dine this year is the **New York Palace** (*p19*), new home the famous Le Cirque. Equally fabulous is the **Trump International Hotel & Tower**'s Jean-Georges, the newest from four-star chef Jean-Georges Vongerichten (*p20*).

## History buffs

The **Algonquin** (*p23*), where Dorothy Parker et al swapped bon mots at the Round Table. Or the **Chelsea Hotel** (*above and p27*), whose venerable door is surrounded by plaques dedicated to Mark Twain, Thomas Wolfe and other famous ex-residents.

## Hopeless romantics

At the cosy **Inn at Irving Place** (*above and p28*), it's easy to forget you're in the twentieth century, not to mention the Big Apple. All fireplaces and four-posters.

## Million-dollar deals

Media moguls and other power-brokers gather nightly at 5757, the ultra-chic piano bar at the **Four Seasons** (*p19*). Aspiring gossip columnists hang out at the bar and take notes.

## Model gazing

Elle Macpherson celebrated her birthday in the bar at **Morgans** (*p20*); or try the **44** at the **Royalton** or the **Whiskey Bar** at the **Paramount** (*p20*). For a glimpse of supermodels-to-be, try the **Franklin** (*p28*).

## HOTEL RESERVATION AGENCIES

These companies block-book reservations in advance and can therefore offer reduced rates on hotel rooms. Discounts cover most price ranges from economy upwards and although some agencies claim savings of up to 65 per cent, around 20 per cent is more likely. If you already know where you'd like to stay it's worth calling a few agencies before booking, in case the hotel is on their list. If you're simply looking for the best deal, mention the part of town you'd like to stay in and the approximate rate you're willing to pay and see what's available. The following agencies work with selected hotels in New York and are free of charge. A few require payment by credit card or personal cheque ahead of time, but most let you pay directly at the hotel.

### Accommodations Express

*Sixth Floor, 801 Asbury Avenue, Ocean City, New Jersey (08226 3625/1-800 444 7666/1-609-391 2100).*

### Central Reservations Service

*11420 North Kendall Drive, Miami, Florida 33176 (1-305 274 6832/1-800 950 0232).*

### Hotel Reservations Network

*8140 Walnut Hill Lane, Suite 1010, Dallas, Texas 75231 (1-800 964 6835/96 HOTEL/e-mail www.180096hotel).*

### Express Hotel Reservations

*3800 Arapahoe, Boulder, Colorado 80303 (1-303 440 8481/1-800 356 1123/e-mail www.express-res.com).*

### Quikbook

*381 Park Avenue South, NY 10016 (1-800 789 9887/ 1-212 779-ROOM/fax 1-212 779 6120/web site: www. quikbook.com).*

## Only the Best Will Do

### Four Seasons

*57 East 57th Street, NY 10022, between Park & Madison Avenues (758 5700/fax 758 5711). Subway 4, 5, 6 to 59th Street; N or R to Lexington Avenue.* **Rates** *single* $440-$525; *double* $490-$575; *suite* $825-$5,000. **Credit** AmEx, DC, JCB, MC, V.

Two years after it opened in 1993, the Four Seasons was voted best hotel in New York by *Condé Nast Traveler*. The Art Deco-style rooms are the largest in the city, bathrooms are made from Florentine marble and the tub fills in just 60 seconds. This honey coloured limestone building is also the tallest hotel in town, so views over Manhattan are superb. The lobby is where *Absolutely Fabulous* filmed Edina's search for the perfect doorknob. Guests can get suitably wasted on one of 14 types of Martini served in the Fifty Seven Fifty Seven bar.
**Hotel services** *Air-conditioning. Babysitting. Bar. Car park. Conference facilities. Currency exchange. Disabled: access, rooms. Fax. Laundry. Multi-lingual staff. Restaurants. Spa & fitness rooms.* **Room services** *Cable TV. Fax. Hair dryer. Mini-bar. Radio. Refrigerator. Room service. Safe. VCR.*

### Hotel Carlyle

*35 East 76th Street, NY 10021, between Park & Madison Avenues (744 1600/fax 800 227 5737/fax 717 4682). Subway 6 to 77th Street.* **Rates** *single* $300-$475; *double* $330-$505; *suite* $500-$1,600. **Credit** AmEx, DC, MC, V.
The sumptuous Carlyle is one of the Big Apple's most

luxurious hotels, with whirlpools in every bathroom and a private entrance foyer for each of the apartment-style rooms. Since it opened in 1930, the hotel has attracted numerous famous guests – especially those who desire privacy. Service is so discreet that two members of the Beatles stayed here after the group split without either knowing the other was there. Cabaret entertainers perform in the Café Carlyle (Woody Allen plays on Monday nights) and there's the enduring appeal of Ludwig Bemelmans' murals in his namesake bar.
**Hotel services** *Air-conditioning. Babysitting. Bar. Beauty salon. Cable TV. Conference facilities. Currency exchange. Fax. Fitness centre. Laundry. Multi-lingual staff. Restaurant.* **Room services** *Cable TV. Fax. Hair dryer. Mini-bar. Radio. Refrigerator. Room service. Safe. VCR.*

### Millennium Hilton

*55 Church Street, at Fulton & Dey Streets (693 2001/ 1-800 835 2220/fax 571 2316). Subway 1, 9, N or R to World Trade Center/Courtland Street.* **Rates** *single* $250-$335; *double* $250-$360; *junior suite* from $295; *suite* $450-$900. **Credit** AmEx, DC, Disc, JCB, MC, V.
This 58-storey black skyscraper next to the World Trade Center is pitched firmly at corporate clients. Each room has a fax, and facilities are high-tech – including a glass-enclosed swimming pool to relax in after a hard day at the office. The upper floors have superb views of New York Harbour and Brooklyn Bridge.
**Hotel services** *Air-conditioning. Bar. Car park. Conference facilities. Currency exchange. Disabled: rooms. Fax. Fitness centre. Laundry. Multi-lingual staff. Restaurant.* **Room services** *Cable TV. Fax. Hair dryer. Mini-bar. Radio. Refrigerator. Room service. Safe. VCR.*

### New York Palace

*455 Madison Avenue, NY 10022, at 50th Street (888 7000/1-800 697 2522/fax 303 6000). Subway E or F to Fifth Avenue/53rd Street.* **Rates** *single/double* from $275; *tower room* from $475; *suite* $800-$1,900. **Credit** AmEx, DC, Disc, JCB, MC, V.
Look out from the central lobby and it's hard to believe you're in New York. There's a leafy courtyard and a view of St Patrick's cathedral across the street. Things look just as good inside. The Palace was once the Villard Houses, a cluster of mansion homes designed by Stanford White. Rooms are elegant and luxurious, and there's a wonderful club-like feel to the place. The Palace's newest claim to fame is **Le Cirque 2000**, Sirio Maccioni's celebrated French restaurant recently relocated here, converting the erstwhile Gold Room into a stunning bar with an enormous neon sculpture.
**Hotel services** *Air-conditioning. Babysitting. Bar. Car park. Conference facilities. Disabled: access, rooms. Fax. Laundry. Restaurant.* **Room services** *Cable TV. Hair dryer. Mini-bar. Radio. Refrigerator. Room service. VCR.*

### Pierre

*795 Fifth Avenue, NY 10021, at 61st Street (838 8000 1-800 332 3442/fax 940 8109). Subway N or R to Fifth Avenue.* **Rates** *single* from $375; *double* from $415; *suite* from $540. **Credit** AmEx, DC, JCB, MC, V.
Once Salvador Dali's favourite hotel, the Pierre has been seducing guests since 1929 with its superb service and discreet, elegant atmosphere. Even if a room here is out of your price range, try and take afternoon tea in the magnificently opulent Rotunda – its setting is on a par with the Ritz in London. Rooms at the front overlook Central Park and it's just one block away from some of the most famous designer stores on Fifth Avenue – naturally.
**Hotel services** *Air-conditioning. Babysitting. Bar. Beauty salon. Car park. Conference facilities. Currency exchange. Fax. Fitness centre. Laundry. Restaurant. Theatre desk. Valet packing/unpacking.* **Room services** *Cable TV. Hair dryer. Mini-bar. Radio. Refrigerator on request. Room service. Safe. VCR & fax on request.*

## Plaza Hotel

*768 Fifth Avenue, NY 10019, at 59th Street (759 3000/ 1-800 228 3000/fax 759 3167). Subway N or R to Fifth Avenue/59th Street.* **Rates** *single/double $265-$575; suite $450-$15,000.* **Credit** AmEx, Disc, DC, JCB, MC, V.

Ivana Trump may no longer run the Plaza (*pictured opposite*), smack in the middle of Fifth Avenue's most expensive shopping strip, but it still bears her inimitable stamp of style. Apart from the delightful Tiffany ceiling in the famous Palm Court, there's the 1,500sq ft (140 sq m) Frank Lloyd Wright Suite, where the architect stayed while designing the Guggenheim Museum. The furniture is a mixture of reproduction designs and originals, commissioned by the Trumps after researching the Wright archives.

**Hotel services** *Air-conditioning. Bar. Beauty salon. Car park. Conference facilities. Fax. Fitness centre. Laundry. Multi-lingual staff. Restaurant.* **Room services** *Cable TV. Dual-line phones. Hair dryer. Mini-bar. Radio. Room service. Safe. VCR on request. Voice mail.*

## UN Plaza – Park Hyatt

*One United Nations Plaza, NY 10017, at East 44th Street (758 1234/1-800 228 9000/fax 702 5051). Subway 4, 5, 6 or 7 to Grand Central.* **Rates** *single/double $270-$300; suite $500-$850.* **Credit** AmEx, Disc, DC, JCB, MC, V.

The lobby may be on the ground floor, but the rooms go from the 28th floor upwards. As the name suggests, the hotel is a revenue-earning enterprise for the United Nations and is in an interesting glass-walled building.

**Hotel services** *Air-conditioning. Babysitting. Bar. Car park. Conference facilities. Currency exchange. Disabled: rooms. Fax. Fitness centre & indoor pool. Laundry. Multi-lingual staff.* **Room services** *Cable TV. Fax on request. Hair dryer. Mini-bar. Radio. Refrigerator. Room service. Safe.*

## Trump International Hotel & Tower

*1 Central Park West, NY 10023, at Columbus Circle (299 1000/fax 299 1150). Subway 1, 9, A, C, B, D to Columbus Circle.* **Rates** *suite $325-$900.* **Credit** AmEx, DC, MC, V.

'The Donald's' latest project is an impressive new addition to the New York hotel scene. The striking glass and steel skyscraper towers over Columbus Circle, just steps from Central Park. Inside all is subdued elegance, from the small but tasteful marble lobby to the 168 suites equipped with fax machines, Jacuzzis and floor-to-ceiling windows. Each guest is assigned a personal attaché to cater to his or her whims, and a chef will come to your room to cook on request. Better yet, head downstairs to **Jean-Georges**, the new restaurant from four-star chef Jean-Georges Vongerichten of Jo Jo and Vong fame (*see chapter* **Restaurants**). Special summer rates are available.

**Hotel Services** *Air-conditioning. Bar. Cellular phones. Conference facilities. Fax. Fitness Centre. Restaurant.* **Room Services** *Cable TV. CD player. Computer on request. Fax. Hair Dryer. Mini-bar. Refrigerator. Room service (24 hours). VCR.*

## Waldorf-Astoria

*301 Park Avenue, NY 10022, at 50th Street (355 3000/ 1-800 924 3673/fax 872 7272). Subway 6 to 51st Street.* **Rates** *single $290-$315; double $315-$390; suite $515-$950.* **Credit** AmEx, DC, Disc, JCB, MC, V.

The famous Waldorf salad made its début at the hotel's opening in 1931. At the time, this was the world's largest hotel and it has been associated with New York's high society ever since. Several years later, the Astoria Hotel was built and later connected to the Waldorf by a walkway which became known as Peacock's Alley, such was the posturing and promenading. There's a magnificent 148,000-piece Art Deco mosaic in the lobby that was hidden for more than 30 years. The four-storey Grand Ballroom houses numerous charity balls

and political bashes. Incidentally, the Presidential Suite is so named because of its guests. Get the picture?

**Hotel services** *Air-conditioning. Babysitting. Bar. Beauty salon. Car park. Conference facilities. Fax. Fitness centre with steam rooms. Laundry. Multi-lingual staff. Restaurant.* **Room services** *Cable TV. Fax in tower rooms. Hair dryer. Mini-bar. Radio. Room service.*

# Sleek & Chic

## Morgans

*237 Madison Avenue, NY 10016, between 37th & 38th Streets (686 0300/1-800 334 3408/fax 779 8352). Subway 4, 5, 6 or 7 to Grand Central.* **Rates** *single $205-$405; double $230-$475; suite from $395.* **Credit** AmEx, Disc, DC, JCB, MC, V.

Morgans is an understated hotel, designed by Schrager and Rubell and named in honour of JP Morgan, whose nearby home, the Pierpont Morgan Library, was converted to a museum in 1924. The hotel has a cosy residential feel. The new industrial-chic Morgans Bar is a favourite late-night haunt for the stand-and-model crowd; Elle Macpherson recently celebrated her birthday here.

**Hotel services** *Air-conditioning. Babysitting. Bar & café. Conference facilities. Fax. Fitness centre & spa. Laundry. Multi-lingual staff. Restaurant.* **Room services** *Cable TV. Hair dryer. Mini-bar. Refrigerator. Room service. VCR on request.*

## Paramount

*235 West 46th Street, NY 10036, between Broadway & Eighth Avenue (764 5500/1-800 225 7474/fax 575 4892). Subway N or R to 49th Street.* **Rates** *single/double $135-$225; suite $295-$475.* **Credit** AmEx, DC, Disc, JCB, MC, V.

The Phillipe Starck-designed Paramount (*below*), like the Royalton, is chic almost beyond belief. It's an astoundingly

modern and stylish hotel, with a cavernous, windowless lobby inspired by the great transatlantic liners, and multi-coloured lifts that give a weather report on each floor. Rooms feature Vermeer's Lacemaker silkscreen headboards and stainless steel bathrooms, although they're smallish, and some guests say they're beginning to fray around the edges. There's a Dean & DeLuca shop and an espresso bar in the lobby, and the Whiskey Bar is still a good spot for model-spotting.
**Hotel services** *Air-conditioning. Bar. Business centre. Conference facilities. Currency exchange. Fax. Fitness centre. Laundry. Multi-lingual staff. Non-smoking floors. Restaurants.* **Room services** *Cable TV. Room service. VCR.*

### Royalton

*44 West 44th Street, NY 10036, between Fifth & Sixth Avenues (869 4400/1-800 635 9013/fax 869 8965). Subway B, D or F to 42nd Street.* **Rates** *single from $275; double from $295; suite from $475.* **Credit** AmEx, DC, JCB, MC, V.

Like Morgans, this is a Rubell-Scrager production, but the Starck interiors are more likely to remind visitors of the Paramount. Waitresses in satin mini-dresses serve fashionable young things in the lobby (*pictured*), and the restaurant (called **44**) has some of the most sought-after tables in town. So many of the regulars work for nearby Condé Nast, it's sometimes referred to as Club Condé. The rooms are gorgeous, with sleek slate fireplaces and marvellous round Starck bathtubs.
**Hotel services** *Air-conditioning. Bar. Car park. Conference facilities. Currency exchange. Fax. Fitness centre. Laundry. Multi-lingual staff. Restaurant.* **Room services** *Cable TV. Mini-bar. Radio. Room service. VCR.*

### SoHo Grand Hotel

*310 West Broadway, NY 10013, between Grand & Canal (965 3000/1-800-637 7200/fax 965 3200). Subway A, C or E to Canal Street.* **Rates** *singles/doubles $349-$369; suite $949-$1,149.* **Credit** AmEx, DC, MC, V.

At last, a hotel in SoHo. This is the area's first since the 1800s, and though locals might have looked on it with some dismay, it's truly a gem for travellers. The unusual design pays homage to SoHo's contemporary artistic community and to its past, when many of today's lofts were working factories. Architecturally speaking, it's one of the city's most striking hotels, and of course it's terribly 'in'. A dramatic bottle-glass and cast-iron stairway leads up from street level to the elegant lobby and reception desk, presided over by a monumental clock. Rooms are decorated in soothing greys and beiges, with non-fat munchies in the mini bar and photos from local galleries on the walls. Both the Grand Bar and Canal House restaurant are worth a visit.
**Hotel Services** *Air-conditioning. Bar. Conference facilities. Fax. Fitness centre. Laundry. Restaurant.* **Room Services** *Cable TV. Mini-bar. PC port. Room service (24 hours). Voice mail.*

## First Class

### Doral Tuscany

*120 East 39th Street, NY 10016, between Lexington & Park Avenues (686 1600/1-800 223 6725/fax 779 7833/779 0148 for reservations). Subway 4, 5, 6 or 7 to Grand Central.* **Rates** *single $194-$279; double $195-$299; suite from $450.* **Credit** AmEx, DC, Disc, MC, V.

Hard to believe Grand Central Station is just around the corner: the Doral Tuscany is nestled among brownstones in the historic Murray Hill district. Standard rooms are absolutely enormous; there's an entrance hallway with separate dressing room, vanity mirror and Italian marble baths. Suites go one step further, with a tiny portable TV in the bathrooms.
**Hotel services** *Air-conditioning. Bar. Conference facilities. Disabled: rooms. Fax. Laundry. Multi-lingual staff. Restaurant.* **Room services** *Cable TV. Hair dryer. Mini-bar. Radio. Refrigerator. Room service. VCR on request.*

### Helmsley Windsor Hotel

*100 West 58th Street, NY 10019, at Sixth Avenue (265 2100/1-800 221 4982/fax 315 0371). Subway Q, N or R to 57th Street/Sixth Avenue.* **Rates** *single $160-$185; double $170-$195; suite from $250.* **Credit** AmEx, DC, Disc, MC, V.

The tiny rooms don't quite live up to the wonderfully old-fashioned panelled lobby, but Central Park is close by and the hotel is comfortable.
**Hotel services** *Air-conditioning. Babysitting. Fax. Laundry. Meeting room for 10 people. Multi-lingual staff.* **Room services** *Cable TV. Hair dryer on request. Radio. Refrigerator on request and in suites. VCR.*

### The Mark

*25 East 77th Street, NY 10021, between Fifth & Madison Avenues (472 5183/1-800 843 6275/fax 472 5714). Subway 6 to 77th Street.* **Rates** *single $315-$355; double $340-$380; suite $525-$2,400.* **Credit** AmEx, DC, MC, V.

Towering potted palms and arched mirrors line the entranceway to this cheerful European-style Upper East-Sider. The marble lobby, decorated with eighteenth-century Piranesi prints and magnums of Veuve-Cliquot, is usually bustling with dressy international guests and white-gloved bellmen. Especially popular are Mark's Bar, a clubby hideaway with lots of dark green and polished wood, and the more elegant Mark's restaurant.
**Hotel services** *Air-conditioning. Bar. Conference facilities. Fax. Fitness centre. Laundry. Multi-lingual staff. Restaurant.* **Room services** *Cable TV. Hair dryer. Room service.*

### New York Helmsley

*212 East 42nd Street, NY 10017, between Second & Third Avenues (490 8900/1-800 221 4982/fax 682 6299). Subway 4, 5, 6 or 7 to Grand Central.* **Rates** *single $230-$270; double $255-$295; suite from $500.* **Credit** AmEx, MC, V.

It may have the same owners as the Helmsley Windsor, but this is primarily a business hotel, complete with telephones by the bath. All rooms are the same size and facilities are sleek and modern.
**Hotel services** *Air-conditioning. Babysitting. Bar. Car park. Conference facilities. Fax. Laundry. Multi-lingual staff. Restaurant.* **Room services** *Hair dryer. Radio. Room service. TV. VCR on request.*

### Roger Smith

*501 Lexington Avenue, NY 10017, between 47th & 48th Streets (755 1400/1-800 445 0277/fax 319 9130). Subway 4, 5, 6 or 7 to Grand Central.* **Rates** *single from $195; double from $210; suite from $275.* **Credit** AmEx, DC, JCB, MC, V.

The hotel is owned by sculptor and painter James Knowles

and consequently some of his work can be found decorating the lobby. The large rooms are individually furnished, the staff are friendly and there's a well-stocked VCR library for those who want to spend the night in. It's popular with bands and there's often live jazz in the restaurant.
**Hotel services** *Air-conditioning. Babysitting. Bar. Conference facilities. Disabled: rooms. Fax. Laundry. Multi-lingual staff. Restaurant. Valet parking.* **Room services** *Cable TV. Hair dryer on request. Radio. Refrigerator. Room service. VCR.*

## Comfortable

### Algonquin

*59 West 44th Street, NY 10036, between Fifth & Sixth Avenues (840 6800/1-800 555 8000/fax 944 1419). Subway B, D, F or Q to 42nd Street.* **Rates** *single* from $255; *double* from $275; *suite* from $350. **Credit** AmEx, DC, Disc, JCB, MC, V.
Granted the lobby is slightly frayed, but who can resist New York's most famous literary landmark? This was the place where Dorothy Parker, James Thurber and other literary lights of the 1920s and 1930s gathered at the Oak Room's legendary Round Table to gossip and match wits. Much of that charming, flapper aura remains in the Edwardian lobby. It's still one of New York's best spots to meet for a cocktail. Rooms are on the small side, but charming with floral prints and striped wallpaper. Matilda, the house cat, has her own miniature suite and four-poster bed in a corner of the lobby.
**Hotel services** *Air-conditioning. Babysitting. Bar. Conference facilities. Currency exchange. Disabled: rooms. Fax. Laundry. Multi-lingual staff. Non-smoking floors. Restaurant.* **Room services** *Cable TV. Hair dryer. Radio. Refrigerator in suites and on request. Room service. Safe. VCR on request. Voice mail.*

### Ameritania

*1701 Broadway, NY 10019, at 54th Street (247 5000/1-800 922 0330/fax 247 3316). Subway E or F to 49th Street.* **Rates** *single/double* $165-$180; *suite* $245-$400. **Credit** AmEx, DC, Disc, JCB, MC, V.
The futuristic 'A' logo of the Ameritania resembles the *Star Trek Next Generation* emblem, which may explain why the lobby is so broodingly futuristic. Rooms are more traditionally decorated. The hotel is next door to the Ed Sullivan Theatre, home of the David Letterman Show, hence the occasional appearance of cameras – Dave likes to pop in unannounced. Location-wise, it's perfect for theatres but there are also numerous sex clubs nearby.
**Hotel services** *Air-conditioning. Bagel shop (24 hours). Bar. Fax. Fitness centre. Laundry. Multi-lingual staff. Restaurant. Theatre/excursion desk.* **Room services** *Cable TV. Hair dryer in suites, on request in rooms. Radio. Refrigerator on request. Room service.*

### Barbizon

*140 East 63rd Street, NY 10021, at Lexington Avenue (838 5700/1-800 223 1020/fax 888 4271). Subway B or Q to Lexington Avenue.* **Rates** *single* $170-$375; *double* $190-$375; *suite* from $375. **Credit** AmEx, DC, Disc, JCB, V.
The Barbizon was originally a hotel for emancipated women, whose parents could feel confidant that their daughters were safe in its care. During its years as a women-only residence, guests including Grace Kelly, Ali McGraw, and Candice Bergen abided by rules such as only entertaining men in the lounge. The hotel recently completed a $40 million renovation which included adding a branch of the local Equinox health club (free for guests) with an Olympic-size pool and full spa. Children under 12 stay free, if sharing with parents.
**Hotel services** *Air-conditioning. Currency exchange. Disabled: rooms. Fax. Laundry. Multi-lingual staff.* **Room services** *Cable TV. Hair dryer on request. Refrigerator.*

### Casablanca Hotel

*147 West 43rd Street, NY 10036, between Sixth Avenue & Broadway (869 1212/fax 944 6223). Subway 1, 2, 3, 7, 9, N, R or S to Times Square/42nd Street.* **Rates** *single* from $225; *double* from $245; *suite* from $325. **Credit** AmEx, MC, V.
The Casablanca has recently been completely refurbished in Moroccan style. Prices have risen, but the hotel's proximity to the theatre district is a bonus.
**Hotel services** *Air-conditioning. Conference facilities. Disabled: rooms. Fax. Laundry. Multi-lingual staff. Restaurant.* **Room services** *Cable TV. Radio.*

### Days Hotel

*790 Eighth Avenue, NY 10019, between 48th & 49th Streets (581 7000/1-800 572 6232/fax 974 0291). Subway C or E to 60th Street.* **Rates** *single* $130-$165; *double* $142-$177. **Credit** AmEx, DC, Disc, MC, V.
This is a dependable hotel, decorated as you'd expect from a chain, and reasonably priced. It's in a good midtown location and, 15 floors up, there's a rooftop swimming pool and cocktail lounge.
**Hotel services** *Air-conditioning. Babysitting on request. Bar. Car park. Conference facilities. Fax. Outdoor pool. Restaurant.* **Room services** *Cable TV. Hair dryer on request. Radio. Room service. Safe.*

### Elysée

*60 East 54th Street, NY 10022, between Park & Madison Avenues (753 1066/fax 980 9278). Subway E or F to Lexington Avenue.* **Rates** *single/double* $225-$245; *suite* $325-$775. **Credit** AmEx, DC, JCB, MC, V.
A charming and discreet hotel with friendly service, antique furniture and Italian marble bathrooms. Some of the rooms also have coloured glass conservatories and roof terraces. It's popular with publishers so don't be surprised if you see a famous author enjoying the complimentary afternoon tea in the club room. You can also eat in the famous Monkey Bar and restaurant. Room prices include continental breakfast and, in the evening, wine and hors d'oeuvres. The Elysée has been restored to its original 1930s décor and displays photographs showing the likes of Joan Crawford and Marlene Dietrich gathered around the piano.
**Hotel services** *Air-conditioning. Babysitting. Bar. Conference facilities. Disabled: rooms. Fax. Laundry. Library. Multi-lingual staff. Valet parking.* **Room services** *Cable TV. Hair dryer. Mini-bar. Radio. Refrigerator. Room service. TV. VCR. Voice mail.*

### Gorham

*136 West 55th Street, NY 10019, between Sixth & Seventh Avenues (245 1800/1-800 735 0710/fax 582 8332). Subway N or R to 57th Street; B or Q to 57th Street.* **Rates** *single/double* $180-$320; *suite* $190-$370. **Credit** AmEx, DC, JCB, MC, V.
The Gorham stands opposite the unusual domed City Center dance theatre. Unfortunately, the room furnishings look rather tacky after the stylish marble and maple in the lobby. However, there's a mini-bar in each room, and kitchen facilities in suites are particularly good. Espresso coffee machines are available on request.
**Hotel services** *Air-conditioning. Babysitting. Bar. Car park. Conference facilities. Fax. Disabled: rooms. Fitness centre. Laundry. Multi-lingual staff. Restaurant.* **Room services** *Cable TV. Hair dryer. Microwave. Mini-bar. Radio. Refrigerator. Room service. Safe. VCR on request.*

### Gramercy Park Hotel

*2 Lexington Avenue, NY 10010, at East 21st Street (475 4320/1-800 221 4083/fax 505 0535). Subway 6 to 23rd Street.* **Rates** *single* $135-$140; *double* $145-$180; *suite* from $180. **Credit** AmEx, DC, Disc, JCB, MC, V.
The hotel is in a surprisingly quiet location for midtown Manhattan, adjoining the small green oasis of Gramercy

Park. Guests vary from business travellers to rock stars. Unusually, there are no non-smoking rooms.
**Hotel services** *Air-conditioning. Bar. Beauty salon. Car park. Conference facilities. Disabled: rooms. Fax. Laundry. Multi-lingual staff. News-stand/theatre ticket office. Restaurant.* **Room services** *Cable TV. Fridge. Radio. Room service.*

### Lexington
*511 Lexington Avenue, NY 10017, at 48th Street (755 4400/fax 751 4091). Subway 6 to 51st Street.* **Rates** *single/double $160-$205; suite $185-$260.* **Credit** AmEx, Disc, DC, MC, V.
The Lexington is popular with business travellers and is close to both Grand Central Station and the United Nations. The lobby is marble-floored with rosewood pillars; 20 of the 27 floors have been renovated. There are two restaurants: Vuli, serving Italian dishes, and the Chinese J Sung Dynasty.
**Hotel services** *Air-conditioning. Babysitting on request. Bar. Coffee shop. Conference facilities. Currency exchange. Disabled: rooms. Exercise room. Fax. Laundry. Multi-lingual staff. Restaurants.* **Room services** *Cable TV. Hair dryer. Radio on request. Refrigerator. Room service. Safe.*

### Metro
*45 West 35th Street, NY 10001, between Fifth & Sixth Avenues (947 2500/1-800 356 3870/fax 279 1310). Subway B, D, F, Q or R to 34th Street.* **Rates** *single/double $145-$220; suite $185-$260.* **Credit** AmEx, DC, MC, V.
It's not posh by any stretch of the imagination, but Hotel Metro (*pictured above*) does good service in a good location near the Empire State. Halls are army-chic, with olive-drab doors and greenish-grey carpets. Rooms are small, but neat and clean, and the roof terrace offers splendid views.
**Hotel services** *Air-conditioning. Fax. Fitness centre. Laundry. Multi-lingual staff. Rooftop terrace.* **Room services** *Cable TV. Hair dryer. Radio.*

### Mayflower
*15 Central Park West, NY 10023, at 61st Street (265 0060/fax 265 5098). Subway 1, 9, A, B, C or D to Columbus Circle.* **Rates** *single $155-$195; double $170-$210; suite $205-$285.* **Credit** AmEx, DC, Disc, MC, V.
This haven for musicians faces Central Park and is just around the corner from Lincoln Centre. You can't argue with the spectacular park views from the front rooms, though the décor is getting a bit worn and faded and the hotel is bound to have stiff competition from its new neighbour – the Trump International down the street.
**Hotel services** *Air-conditioning. Babysitting. Bar. Car park. Conference facilities. Fax. Fitness centre. Laundry. Multi-lingual staff. Restaurant.* **Room services** *Cable TV. Hair dryer on request. PC ports. Radio. Refrigerator. Room service. VCR on request.*

### Quality Hotel Fifth Avenue
*3 East 40th Street, NY 10016, between Fifth & Madison Avenues (447 1500/1-800 228 5151/fax 213 0972). Subway B, D, F or Q to 42nd Street; 7 to Fifth Avenue.* **Rates** *single $154-$180; double $164-$195.* **Credit** AmEx, DC, Disc, JCB, MC, V.
Rooms are basic, but clean, neat and well-lit, with dark paisley furnishings and sizable bathrooms. Ask for numbers three to six – the higher the floor the better – for a street view with more light; back rooms are darker and look directly into office windows. The Quality offers good value a stone's throw from the New York Public Library, Bryant Park, and Lord & Taylor. Enquire about corporate and weekend rates.
**Hotel services** *Air-conditioning. Business services. Complimentary newspaper. Disabled: rooms. Fax. Restaurant.* **Room services** *Cable TV. Coffee maker. PC port. Radio. Room service.*

### Radisson Empire
*44 West 63rd Street, NY 10023, at Broadway (265 7400/1-800 333 3333/fax 245 3382). Subway 1, 9, A, B, C or D to Columbus Circle.* **Rates** *single/double $155-$175; suite $275-$600.* **Credit** AmEx, DC, Disc, JCB, MC, V.
This hotel is perfectly located: opposite the Lincoln Center and next door to the eccentrically stylish Iridium bar. The lobby is surprisingly baronial, with wood panelling and velvet drapes. The rooms are small but tasteful, with plenty of chintz and an adequate amount of closet space.
**Hotel services** *Air-conditioning. Bar. Conference facilities. Currency exchange. Disabled: rooms. Fax. Laundry (self-service). Multi-lingual staff. Restaurant. Theatre/tour ticket desk. Valet parking.* **Room services** *Cable TV. Hair dryer. Mini-bar. Radio. Refrigerator on request. Room service. VCR, CD & cassette player.*

### Shelburne Murray Hill
*303 Lexington Avenue, NY 10016, between 37th & 38th Streets (689 5200/fax 779 7068). Subway 4, 5, 6 or 7 to Grand Central.* **Rates** *suite from $189-$425.* **Credit** AmEx, MC, V.
An elegantly furnished all-suite hotel with an attractive lobby and pleasant rooms. Suites have a full kitchen with all the necessary appliances: microwave, iron, and filter coffee machine. The Shelburne's good value for New York, considering the facilities, which include a restaurant and health club with sauna.
**Hotel services** *Air-conditioning. Bar. Car park. Conference facilities. Disabled: rooms. Fax. Fitness club. Laundry. Multi-lingual staff. Restaurant. Safe.* **Room services** *Cable TV. Hair dryer on request. Iron. Microwave. Radio. Refrigerator. Room service. VCR on request.*

### Southgate Tower
*371 Seventh Avenue, NY 10001, at 31st Street (563 1800/1-800 637 8483/fax 643 8028). Subway A, C or E to Penn Station.* **Rates** *studio suite $134-$199; one-bedroom suite $164-$244.* **Credit** AmEx, DC, Disc, JCB, MC, V.
Popular with conference-goers headed for the Javits Convention Center nearby, the Southgate Tower has been completely renovated. It's an all-suite hotel so none of the rooms is boxy – in fact, some of the balcony suites are positively enormous. Kitchens contain toasters, filter coffee machines and microwaves, but there's also room service until midnight.
**Hotel services** *Air-conditioning. Bar. Car park. Conference facilities. Currency exchange. Disabled: rooms. Drug store. Fax. Fitness centre. Laundry. Multi-lingual staff. Restaurants.* **Room services** *Cable TV. Hair dryer on request. Microwave. Radio. Refrigerator. Room service. Toasters. VCR on request.*

## Warwick

*65 West 54th Street, NY 10019, at Sixth Avenue (247 2700/fax 957 8915). Subway B or Q to 57th Street/Sixth Avenue.* **Rates** *single* $220-$270; *double* $245-$295.
**Credit** AmEx, DC, JCB, MC, V.

Built by William Randolph Hearst and patronised by Elvis and the Beatles in the 1950s and 1960s, the Warwick is still polished and gleaming. It was once an apartment building, and the rooms are exceptionally large by midtown standards. Ask for a view of Sixth Avenue (double glazing keeps out the noise). The top floor suite, once the home of Cary Grant, is bookable for weddings.

**Hotel services** *Air-conditioning. Babysitting. Bar. Car park. Conference facilities. Currency exchange. Disabled: access, rooms. Drug store. Fax. Fitness centre. Laundry. Men's clothing store. Multi-lingual staff. Restaurant. Theatre desk.* **Room services** *Cable TV. Hair dryer. Mini-bar. Radio. Refrigerator. Room service. Safe. VCR.*

## Wyndham Hotel

*42 West 58th Street, NY 10019, between Fifth & Sixth Avenues (753 3500/1-800 257 1111/fax 754 5638). Subway N or R to Fifth Avenue; B or Q to Sixth Avenue/57th Street.* **Rates** *single* $120-$135; *double* $135-$150; *suite* $180-$220. **Credit** AmEx, CB, DC, MC, V.

Popular with actors and directors, the Wyndham contains generous rooms and beautiful spacious suites with walk-in closets. It's in a good location and keenly priced, so book well ahead.

**Hotel services** *Air-conditioning. Bar. Disabled: rooms. Fax. Multi-lingual staff. Restaurant.* **Room services** *Cable TV. Hair dryer on request. Radio.*

## Under $150

## Best Western Manhattan

*17 West 32rd Street, NY 10001, between Broadway & Fifth Avenue (736 1600/1-800 551 2303/fax 563 4007). Subway N to 23rd Street.* **Rates** *single* $149; *double* $199; *suites* from $130-$209. **Credit** AmEx, DC, Disc, JCB, MC, V.

A good-value hotel with a stylish black-and-grey marble lobby and rooms themed for different neighbourhoods; guests can choose between a floral Central Park look and a trendy SoHo motif. The hotel is a sophisticated little haven, but the block is a bit seedy. Intrepid travellers will enjoy exploring the eclectic Korean shops lining 32nd Street; first-timers might want to opt for a busier locale.

**Hotel services** *Air-conditioning. Beauty salon. Disabled: rooms. Fax. Multi-lingual staff. Restaurant. Valet parking.* **Room services** *Cable TV. Hair dryer & mini-bar in most rooms.*

## Comfort Inn Murray Hill

*42 West 35th Street, NY 10001, between Fifth & Sixth Avenues (947 0200/1-800 228 5150/fax 594 3047). Subway B, D, F, N, Q or R to 34th Street.* **Rates** *single* $99-$159; *double* $129-$199. **Credit** AmEx, CB, DC, Disc, MC, V.

A small, family-oriented hotel around the corner from Macy's and the Empire State Building, which underwent a $4.5 million renovation several years ago. Guests get a free continental breakfast complete with the *New York Times*. Alex at the front desk is a hoot. A hotel fixture for more than 13 years, he loves collecting bizarre English place names, so take along a Ramsbottom or a Puddletown.

**Hotel services** *Air-conditioning. Fax. Multi-lingual staff.* **Room services** *Cable TV. Hair dryer on request. Radio.*

## Edison

*228 West 47th Street, NY 10036, near Broadway (840 5000/1-800 637 7070/fax 596 6850). Subway N or R to 49th Street.* **Rates** *single* $105; *double* $115; *suite* $120-$150. **Credit** AmEx, DC, Disc, JCB, MC, V.

After its full renovation, the Edison looks decidedly spruced

up. The colourful art deco lobby is particularly lovely and even the green marble-lined corridors look good. Rooms are standard. As well as Sofia's Restaurant, there's a supper club, café and the Rum House bar.

**Hotel services** *Air-conditioning. Babysitting. Bar. Beauty salon. Car park. Currency exchange. Disabled: rooms. Dry cleaning. Fax (guest fax 596 6868). Laundry. Multi-lingual staff. Restaurants. Travel/tour desk.* **Room services** *Cable TV. Hair dryer on request. Radio.*

## Excelsior

*45 West 81st Street, NY 10024, between Columbus Avenue & Central Park West (362 9200/1-800 368 4575/fax 721 2994). Subway 1 or 9 to 79th Street; B or C to 81st Street.* **Rates** *single/double* $109-$129; *suite* $139-$159. **Credit** AmEx, MC, V.

A favourite with visiting lecturers at the American Museum of Natural History, the Excelsior is a comfortable Upper West Side hotel close to Central Park.

**Hotel services** *Air-conditioning. Coffee shop. Fax.* **Room services** *Radio. Room service from coffee shop. TV.*

## Hotel Beacon

*2130 Broadway, NY 10023, between 75th & 76th Streets (787 1100/1-800 572 4969/fax 724 0839). Subway 1 or 9 to 72nd Street.* **Rates** *single* $115-$125; *double* $135-$145; *suite* $175-$325. **Credit** AmEx, DC, MC, V.

If you're looking for a break from the throngs of tourists clogging Times Square, or want to see how Gothamites really live, consider the Beacon. It's in a desirable residential neighbourhood and only a short walk from Central Park, Lincoln Center for the Performing Arts and Zabar's food market. The hotel has a cheerful, black-and-white marble lobby and friendly staff. Halls are a bit drab and rooms vary in décor, but all are clean and spacious. Since the Beacon is the tallest building around, unlike many New York hotels its windows let in light and offer views of the neighbourhood.

**Hotel services** *Air-conditioning. Coffee shop. Fax. Laundry (self-service). No smoking rooms. Valet dry cleaning (24 hours).* **Room services** *Cable TV. Coffee maker. Hair dryer. Kitchenette. Radio. Refrigerator. Voice mail.*

## Howard Johnson

*429 Park Avenue South, NY 10016, between 29th & 30th Streets (532 4860/1-800 258 4290/fax 545 9727). Subway N or R to 28th Street; 6 to 28th Street/Park.* **Rates** *single* $105-$199; *double* $115-$249; *suite* $149-$449. **Credit** AmEx, DC, Disc, JCB, MC, V.

Popular with Europeans, this recently renovated hotel has particularly good value suites and friendly staff. There's a small breakfast bar that doubles as a cocktail lounge in the evenings. Enough to make you forget you're at the less fashionable end of Park Avenue.

**Hotel services** *Air-conditioning. Babysitting. Bar. Disabled: rooms. Fax. Laundry. Multi-lingual staff.* **Room services** *Cable TV. Hair dryer. Mini-bar. Radio. Room service for breakfast.*

## Iroquois

*49 West 44th Street, NY 10036, between Fifth & Sixth Avenues (840 3080/1-800 332 7220/fax 398 1754). Subway 4, 5, 6 or 7 to Grand Central.* **Rates** *single* from $99; *double* $125-$150; *suite* $150-$300. **Credit** AmEx, DC, JCB, MC, V.

It's hard to imagine James Dean kickin' back in any of the Iroquois' dusky pink and blue rooms but he was a guest here in 1951, staying in room 82. These days the hotel is favoured by hard-up tourists.

**Hotel services** *Air-conditioning. Barber's. Bars. Fax. Laundry. Multi-lingual staff. Restaurants.* **Room services** *Cable TV. Computer & fax on request. Hair dryer on request. Radio. Refrigerator. Room service.*

### Pickwick Arms

*230 East 51st Street, NY 10022, between Second &
Third Avenues (355 0300/fax 755 5029). Subway 6 to
51st Street.* **Rates** *single* $105; *suite* $125-
$155. **Credit** AmEx, DC, MC, V.
The Pickwick charges one of the best hotel rates for poorly
served single customers. Although rooms are small, it's clean
and in a reasonably quiet district. Handy for restaurants, cinemas, Radio City Music Hall and the United Nations. Most,
but not all, rooms have a private bathroom.
**Hotel services** *Air-conditioning. Coffee shop. Fax.
Multi-lingual staff.* **Room services** *Radio. Room service.
TV. Voice mail.*

### Ramada Milford Plaza

*270 West 45th Street, NY 10036, at Eighth Avenue (869
3600/1-800 221 2690/fax 944 8357). Subway 1, 7, 9, A or
C to 42nd Street/Port Authority.* **Rates** *single* $99-$225;
*double* $115-$250. **Credit** AmEx, Disc, JCB, MC, V.
This enormous hotel has a hideous shopping mall lobby with
lighting that makes guests resemble extras from *Night of the
Living Dead.* It was recently renovated but nothing can give
a place this big much in the way of character. Still, it's handy
for Broadway shows and there's 24-hour security.
**Hotel services** *Air-conditioning. Bar. Beauty salon. Car
park. Conference facilities. Disabled: access. Fax. Fitness
centre. Laundry. Multi-lingual staff. Restaurant.
Tour/transport desk.* **Room services** *Cable TV. Radio.*

### Remington

*129 West 46th Street, NY 10036, between Sixth Avenue
& Broadway (221 2600/fax 764 7481). Subway 1, 2, 3,
7, 9, N, R or S to Times Square/42nd Street.* **Rates**
*single* $119; *double* $129; *triple* $139; *quad* $149. **Credit**
AmEx, DC, JCB, MC, V.
Another hotel in the Times Square district, this is cheap,
clean and basic.
**Hotel services** *Air-conditioning. Fax. Lifts. Multi-
lingual staff. Restaurant.* **Room services** *Cable TV.
Hair dryer on request. Radio.*

### Wellington

*871 Seventh Avenue, NY 10019, at 55th Street (247
3900/fax 581 1719). Subway N or R to 57th Street/
Seventh Avenue.* **Rates** *single/double* $154; *suite* from
$155; *triple* $170. **Credit** AmEx, DC, Disc, JCB, MC, V.
Close to Central Park, Broadway and the Museum of Modern
Art, the Wellington also has a diner and steakhouse. Popular
with tour groups.
**Hotel services** *Air-conditioning. Bar. Beauty salon. Car
park. Conference facilities. Disabled: access. Fax.
Laundry. Multi-lingual staff. Restaurant. Ticket service.*
**Room services** *Cable TV. Refrigerator in some rooms.
Room service.*

### Wentworth Quality Hotel & Suites

*59 West 46th Street, NY 10036, between Fifth & Sixth
Avenues (719 2300/1-800 848 0020/fax 768 3477). Subway
B, D, F or Q to Rockefeller Center.* **Rates** *single* $149; *double*
$150-$160; *suite* $209-$239. **Credit** AmEx, CB, DC, MC, V.
Despite a recent renovation, the lobby is filled with tacky
murals of New York City and the rooms with equally taste-
less prints. Still, if you can cope with the décor, the
Wentworth is fairly priced and well located for the theatre.
**Hotel services** *Air-conditioning. Barber shop. Beauty
salon. Fax. Multi-lingual staff.* **Room services** *Cable
TV. Radio.*

## Dive Hotels

Some hotels simply transcend minor details such
as whether there's a hair dryer in the room or a
beauty salon on the premises. Atmosphere is all
that counts, even if the place is, to all intents and
purposes, a dive. The following are some of the
more famous – or notorious – steeped in history
and atmosphere.

### Carlton Arms

*160 East 25th Street, NY 10010, near Third Avenue
(679 0680/684 8337). Subway 6 to 23rd Street.*
**Rates** *single* $49-$57; *double* $62-$84. **Credit** MC, V.
A cheerful basic budget/dive hotel popular with Europeans.
The corridors are brightly decorated with murals of the city
and each room has been painted by a different artist. It's hit
and miss, but fun – we like the Astroturf in one of the bathrooms. Discounts for students and overseas guests.
**Hotel services** *Multi-lingual staff. Café. Telephone in
lobby.* **Room services** *Hair dryer on request.*

### Chelsea

*222 West 23rd Street, NY 10011, between Seventh &
Eighth Avenues (243 3700). Subway 1, 2, 3 or 9 to West
23rd Street.* **Rates** *single* $125; *double* $150-$385; *studio*
$150; *suite* from $275-$400. **Credit** AmEx, DC, JCB,
MC, V.
The Chelsea has a reputation to uphold. Plaques dedicated to
former residents Mark Twain, Thomas Wolfe and Brendan
Behan set standards for aspiring writers, while the lobby doubles as an art gallery, showing work by past and present
guests. No evidence remains of the hotel's infamous murder
in room 100 – where Sid Vicious killed Nancy Spungen – as
the room was immediately destroyed to make a larger apartment. Although there's an air of seediness, the Chelsea has
atmosphere. Stay if you want an adventure and can cope with
the occasional cockroach. Most, but not all, rooms have a
private bathroom.
**Hotel services** *Air-conditioning. Fax. Multi-lingual
staff. Valet parking.* **Room services** *Kitchenettes &
refrigerators in some rooms. Safe. TV.*

### Hotel 17

*225 East 17th Street, NY 10003, between Second &
Third Avenues (475 2845/fax 677 8178). Subway 4, 5,
6, L, N or R to Union Square.* **Rates** *single* $65; *double*
$75-$90; *weekly rates* from $303. **No credit cards.**
The magazine ads say it all: no room service, no bright lights,
no phony staff, no rip-off prices. Seventeen is the ultimate
dive hotel and one of the hippest places to stay if you're an
artist, clubber or drag queen. The rooms are basic beyond
belief, but that didn't stop Madonna showing her knickers
for the front cover of *Details* magazine in room 114. Manager
Billy Candis encourages his guests' talents and increases
their contacts. Makeovers on request. Leave anything of
value in the safe. Think of it as an experience.
**Hotel services** *Air-conditioning in some rooms. Fax.
Laundry. Roof terrace.* **Room services** *Cable TV in
some rooms. Hair dryer on request.*

## Budget

### Broadway American

*2178 Broadway, NY 10024, at 77th Street (362
1100/fax 787 9521). Subway 1 or 9 to 79th Street.*
**Rates** *single* $55, *double* $85, with shared bathroom;
*single* $80, *double* $110, with private bathroom. **Credit**
AmEx, DC, MC, V.
Lots of hotel for your money, as the rooms are huge and dec-
orated in a spruce, vaguely Art Deco style. The Natural
History Museum is a couple of blocks away, along with
Central Park and the New York Historical Society.
**Hotel services** *Air-conditioning. Fax. Lifts. Multi-
lingual staff.* **Room services** *Cable. Refrigerator. Safe.*

# Boutique hotels

*Bachelor style at the **Mansfield**.*

Tired of neon banners, football-field sized lobbies, and throngs of conventioneers charging the front desk? If so, consider one of Manhattan's growing number of boutique hotels. These small (roughly a dozen to 150 rooms), primarily independently owned hotels tend to offer more personalised service and European flavour than the mega-chains. Many are tucked away in renovated old buildings with unusual architectural details, and an ambience ranging from cosy Victorian to ultra-chic contemporary.

## Broadway Bed & Breakfast Inn

*264 West 46th Street, NY 10036, at Eighth Avenue (921 1824/1-800 826 6300/fax 768 2807). Subway A, C or E to 42nd Street.* **Rates** *single* $105; *suite* $165. **Credit** AmEx, DC, Disc, MC, V.
In contrast to Times Square's mega-hotels (many with prices to match), this cosy newcomer (a renovated SRO) feels small and personal: think off-Broadway rather than Broadway. The lobby, though small, has exposed brick walls, book cases, ceiling fans, and a front desk with hospitable staff. The 40 guest rooms are a bit spartan, but are new, clean, and fairly priced for the district. However, the stairs are steep, and the inn has no lift. Rates include continental breakfast.
**Hotel services** *Air-conditioning. Multi-lingual staff.* **Room services** *Cable TV.*

## The Fitzpatrick

*687 Lexington Avenue, NY 10022, between 55th & 56th Streets (355 0100/1-800 367 7701/fax 355 1371). Subway 6 to 59th Street.* **Rates** *single* $149-$245; *double* $149-$260; *suite* $245-$265. **Credit** AmEx, DC, Disc, MC, V.
Lest you miss the fact that this cheerful, family-run East-Sider is New York's only Irish-owned hotel, there's a kelly-green carpet with a Book of Kells pattern in the lobby and a mat spelling out the day of the week in Gaelic in the lift. The 92 rooms are decorated with matched floral bedspreads and curtains. Fitzer's, the hotel restaurant serves rashers, bangers, and soda bread (what else?) daily from 7am until 10.30pm, and high tea from 3pm to 5pm.
**Hotel services** *Air-conditioning. Bar. Fax. Laundry. Restaurant.* **Room services** *Cable TV. Room service (24 hours). Trouser press/ironing board.*

## Franklin

*164 East 87th Street, NY 10128, between Third & Lexington Avenues (369 1000/1-800 600 8787/fax 369 8000). Subway 6 to 86th Street.* **Rates** $169-$189. **Credit** AmEx, MC, V.
Though nowhere near Seventh Avenue's Garment District, the Franklin is favoured by the fashion industry. The minimalist-chic décor and sandblasted steel make for a sombre atmosphere and, aside from the sheer white 'canopies' over the beds, the rooms are small and plain. However, rates are reasonable, and you'll find such pleasing amenities as fresh roses in the rooms, free cappuccino/espresso, and cedar-lined closets. Rates also include continental breakfast, nightly dessert buffet, and free onsite parking.
**Hotel services** *Air-conditioning. Car park. CD & Video library. Multilingual staff.* **Room services** *Cable TV. CD player. Hair dryer. VCR.*

## The Inn at Irving Place

*56 Irving Place, NY 10003 (533 4600/1-800 685 1447/fax 533 4611). Subway L, N, R, 4, 5, 6 to 14th Street.* **Rates** $275-$350. **Credit** AmEx, DC, MC, V.
For a bit of Victorian charm, book a room at this nineteenth-century townhouse tucked away near Gramercy Park. With only a dozen rooms, it's one of Manhattan's smallest inns and, not surprisingly, has been voted the most romantic by more than one magazine. Instead of a front desk there's a parlour with a blazing hearth and an antique serving cart set up with punch and sherry. Some rooms are quite small, but each has a fireplace and four-poster bed. The Madame Wollenska suite has pocket doors opening onto a window seat. Rates include continental breakfast.
**Hotel services** *Air-conditioning. Room service. Safe.* **Room services** *Cable TV. CD player. Hair dryer. Mini-bar. VCR.*

## Larchmont

*27 West 11th Street, NY 10011, between Fifth & Sixth Avenues (989 9333/fax 989 9496). Subway 1 or 9 to Christopher Street/Sheridan Square.* **Rates** *single* $60-$70; *double* $85-$99. **Credit** AmEx, DC, Disc, MC, V.
This attractive, affordable newcomer is housed in a renovated 1910 Beaux Arts building on a quiet sidestreet in Greenwich Village. Guests enter through a hallway adjacent to the lobby, making the place feel more like a private apartment. Some rooms are small, but all are cheerful and clean with peach walls, floral accents, and ceiling fans. Each is equipped with a washbasin, robe, and slippers, though none has private baths. Rates include continental breakfast.
**Hotel services** *Air-conditioning. Fax.* **Room services** *Cable TV. Hair dryer.*

## Lowell Hotel

*28 East 63rd Street, NY 10021, between Park & Madison Avenues (838 1400/fax 319 4230). Subway 4, 5 or 6 to 59th Street.* **Rates** *single* $295; *double* from $385; *suite* from $485. **Credit** AmEx, DC, Disc, MC, V.
A small, charming hotel in a landmark Art Deco building. Its rooms are delightfully old fashioned, with Scandinavian comforters, Chinese porcelain and marble baths – there are even wood-burning fireplaces in the suites. It's popular with stars; the gym suite has, in the

*The assiduously arty* **Shoreham**.

past, suited Madonna, Arnold Schwarzenegger and Michelle Pfeiffer.
**Hotel services** *Air-conditioning. Babysitting. Bar. Cable TV. Currency exchange. Fax. Fitness centre. Laundry. Multi-lingual staff. Restaurant.* **Room services** *Fax. Hair dryer. Mini-bar. PC ports. Radio. Refrigerator. Room service. VCR.*

### Mansfield

*12 West 44th Street, NY 10036, between Fifth & Sixth Avenues (944 6050/1-800 255 5167/fax 764 4477). Subway B, D, F, Q or 7 to 42nd Street.* **Rates** *standard* $195; *deluxe* $225; *double* $245; *one-bedroom suite* $275. **Credit** AmEx, MC, V.
Once a fashionable bachelors' residence, the Mansfield fell upon hard times until a boutique hotel company redeemed it a few years ago, uncovering the lobby's original white marble and spectacular ceilings. Halls on guest floors are narrow, rooms are tiny, and there's enough silver mesh and ebony for a film noir. But many find the minimalist-chic ambiance intriguing and the suites are elegant, with neutral tones and etched-glass sitting room doors. A cosy first-floor library has nightly piano/harp recitals. Rates include continental breakfast and nightly dessert buffet. **Hotel services** *Car Park. CD & Video Library. Multilingual staff.* **Room services** *Cable TV. CD player. Hair dryer. VCR.*

### Shoreham

*33 West 55th Street, NY 10019, between Fifth & Sixth Avenues (247 6700/1-800 553 3347/fax 765 9741). Subway B or Q to 57th Street; E or F to Fifth Avenue.* **Rates** *standard* $245; *suite* $295. **Credit** AmEx, DC, MC, V.
The look is Deco moderne at this midtowner, with 1930s-retro décor, cream marble floors, curvilinear ceilings, aluminium furniture in the Frank Lloyd Wright vein, and alcoves of artfully arranged flowers. In fact, the whole place feels a bit like a wing of MoMA. Rooms are of a decent size, with neutral tones and illuminated steel-mesh headboards. Rates include continental breakfast and nightly dessert buffet.
**Hotel services** *Complimentary passes to nearby health club. Multi-lingual staff. Valet parking.*

**Room services** *Cable TV. CD player. Hair dryer. Refrigerator. VCR.*

### Wales

*1295 Madison Avenue, NY 10128, at East 92nd Street (876 6000/fax 860 7000). Subway 6 to 96th Street.* **Rates** *single/double* from $185; *suite* $245-$265. **Credit** AmEx, MC, V.
The Wales is a charming, turn-of-the-century hotel in the attractive Carnegie Hill district. Complimentary afternoon tea is served in the Pied Piper Room, a Victorian parlour with palm plants, red roses and, occasionally, a harp player or pianist. Some suites overlook the Central Park reservoir. Quite an oasis.
**Hotel services** *Air-conditioning. Car park. Disabled: access, rooms. Fax. Laundry. Multi-lingual staff. Restaurant. VCR library.* **Room services** *Cable TV. Hair dryer. Radio. Refrigerator in some rooms. Room service. Safe. VCR.*

### Washington Square Hotel

*103 Waverly Place, NY 10011, between Fifth & Sixth Avenues (777 9515/1-800 222 0418/fax 979 8373). Subway A, B, C, D, E, F, Q to West 4th Street.* **Rates** *single* $90, *double* $115, *quad* $144.
Location, not luxury, is the key here. Both Bob Dylan and Joan Baez lived in this Greenwich Village hotel (*below*) when they were street musicians singing for change just steps away in Washington Square Park. The lobby has a cheerful courtyard feel with marble floors, wrought-iron gates, and lots of plants, though the security glass at the front desk is a bit off-putting. Rooms are no-frills and hallways are so narrow that you practically open your door into the room opposite. Rates include breakfast at C3 (the bistro next door to hotel).
**Hotel services** *Air-conditioning. Babysitting. Bar. Coffee shop. Conference facilities. Fax. Fitness centre. Multi-lingual staff. Restaurant.* **Room services** *Hair dryer on request.*

## Gershwin Hotel

*7 East 27th Street, NY 10016, between Fifth & Madison Avenues (545 8000/fax 684 5546). Subway N or R to 28th Street; 6 to 28th Street.* **Rates** $22 per person in 4-8 bed dorms; $75-$120 for 1-3 people in private rooms. **Credit** MC, V.

The colourful Gershwin offers extremely good-value accommodation just off Fifth Avenue. It pays homage to pop art, with Roy Lichtenstein posters, a signed Andy Warhol Campbell's soup can and gigantic colourful sculptures on the walls. The rooms are spartan, but clean; the bathrooms are decorated with Mondrian-esque tiling. The ambiance is definitely no-frills, with lots of student-types slouching around or playing pool beneath the enormous carved 1908 fireplace in the TV room, but it's lively.

**Hotel services** *Bars. Fax. Lockers. Multi-lingual staff. Public telephones. Restaurant. Roof garden. Transport desk.* **Room services** *TV in private rooms.*

## Herald Square

*19 West 31st Street, NY 10001, between Fifth Avenue & Broadway (279 4017/1-800 727 1888/fax 643 9208). Subway 1, 2, 3 or 9 to 34th Street/Penn Station.* **Rates** *single* $55, *double* $85, with shared bath; *single* $75, *double* $105, with private bath; *triple* $115; *quad* $125. **Credit** AmEx, Disc, JCB, MC, V.

Herald Square was the original *Life* magazine building and retains its charming cherub-adorned entrance. All rooms were recently renovated and most have private bathrooms; corridors are filled with framed *Life* illustrations. Well located for Macy's and the Empire State Building at the edge of the garment district, it's a good deal, so book well in advance. There are discounts for ISIC members and holders of an International Youth Travel Card.

**Hotel services** *Air-conditioning. Fax. Multi-lingual staff.* **Room services** *Cable TV. Radio. Safe.*

## Off-Soho Suites

*11 Rivington Street, NY 10002, between Christie & the Bowery (979 9808/1-800 633 7646/fax 979 9801). Subway B, D or F to Grand Street.* **Rates** *single suite* $89; *suite for two* $149. **Credit** AmEx, MC, V.

Excellent value for suite accommodation, but the Lower East Side location might not suit everyone. If you're into clubbing, bars and the SoHo scene, it's perfectly placed – just off the Bowery near Little Italy. But take a cab back at night. All suites are well sized, spotlessly clean and bright, with a fully equipped kitchen and polished wooden floors. There's a new café on the ground floor by the lobby.

**Hotel services** *Air-conditioning. Car park. Café. Disabled: rooms. Fax. Fitness room. Laundry. Multi-lingual staff.* **Room services** *Hair dryer. Microwave. Refrigerator. Room service. TV.*

## Portland Square Hotel

*132 West 47th Street, NY 10036, between Sixth & Seventh Avenues (382 0600/1-800 388 8988/fax 382 0684). Subway 1, 2, 3, 7, 9, N, R or S to Times Square/42nd Street.* **Rates** *single* $50 with shared bathroom; *single* $80; *double* $94-$104; *triple* $109; *quad* $125, with private bathroom. **Credit** AmEx, JCB, MC, V.

Basic, recently renovated and good value, the Portland Square is one of the older hotels in the theatre district. James Cagney once stayed here but today it's popular with less theatrical Europeans. Discounts for ISIC card-carrying students. **Hotel services** *Air-conditioning. Conference facilities. Fax. Fitness room. Laundry. Multi-lingual staff.* **Room services** *Cable TV. Radio. Safe.*

## Riverside Towers Hotel

*80 Riverside Drive, NY 10024, at 80th Street (877 5200/1-800 724 3136/fax 873 1400). Subway 1 or 9 to 79th Street.* **Rates** *single* $75; *double* $80; *suite* $90-$115. **Credit** AmEx, MC, V.

A good price for the Upper West Side and the only hotel located on the Hudson River. The views are fine, but accommodation is basic: this is strictly a place to sleep. The wonderful Zabar's deli is around the corner on Broadway.
**Hotel Services** *Air-conditioning. Fax. Laundry. Multi-lingual staff.* **Room services** *Hair dryer on request. Refrigerator. TV.*

## Wolcott

*4 West 31st Street, NY 10001, between Broadway & Fifth Avenue (268 2900/fax 563 0096). Subway B, D, F, N or R to 34th Street.* **Rates** *single/double* $65 with shared bath; *single/double* $90 with private bath; *suite* $120. **Credit** AmEx, JCB, MC, V.

The ornate, gilded, mirror-lined lobby comes as a surprise in this garment-district hotel. Rooms are small but inexpensive and air-conditioned.
**Hotel services** *Air-conditioning. Bar. Fax. Laundry. Multi-lingual staff.* **Room services** *Cable TV.*

# Hostels

## Chelsea Center

*313 West 29th Street, NY 10001, between Eighth & Ninth Avenues (643 0214/fax 473 3945). Subway A, C or E to 34th Street.* **Rates** $20 per person in dorm, incl linen. **No credit cards.**

A small, friendly hostel with clean bathrooms and a patio/garden at the back. It has the feel of a shared student house. As there's a limited number of beds in each dorm, book at least a week in advance. No curfew. Price includes continental breakfast.

**Hotel services** *All rooms no smoking. Fax. Garden/patio. Kitchen facilities. Multi-lingual staff. TV room.*

## Hosteling International of New York

*891 Amsterdam Avenue, NY 10025, at 103rd Street (932 2300/fax 932 2574). Subway 1 or 9 to 103rd Street.* **Rates** $24 per person in dorm sleeping 10-12 people; $25 in dorm sleeping 6-8; $27 in room sleeping 4; $3 extra for non-members; en-suite rooms sleeping 1-4 $100. **Credit** MC, V.

The hostel, formerly a home for women, was designed by the man behind the Statue of Liberty. With 500 beds, it's large and was recently renovated to include a new coffee bar with CD juke box. Rooms are basic but clean. Staff are friendly and there's a garden at the back.

**Hotel services** *Air-conditioning. All rooms no smoking. Café. Conference facilities. Fax. Garden. Laundry. Lockers. Multi-lingual staff. Travel bureau. TV lounge & games room.*

## International House of New York

*500 Riverside Drive, NY 10027, at 125th Street (316 6300/fax 316 8415). Subway 1 or 9 to 125th Street.* **Rates** *single* $95; *double/suite* $115. **Credit** MC, V.

This student-only hostel is in a peaceful location surrounded by college buildings and overlooking the small but well-tended Sakura Park. There's a subsidised cafeteria with main dishes at around $3 and a delightful living room and terrace overlooking the park. Only the suites have a private bathroom.

**Hotel services** *Air-conditioning in suites. Bar. Cafeteria. Conference facilities. Fax. Games room. Gymnasium. Laundry. Multi-lingual staff. TV room.*

## YMHA (de Hirsch Residence at the 92nd St Y)

*1395 Lexington Avenue, NY 10128, at 92nd Street (415 5650/1-800 858 4692/fax 415 5578). Subway 6 to 96th Street.* **Rates** *for stays less than two months* $49 nightly, $343 per week, single occupancy; $35 nightly, $245 per week, double occupancy; *for stays greater than two months* $550 per person per month double occupancy, or $685 per month in private rooms. **Credit** AmEx, MC, V.

The Young Men's Hebrew Association is rather like its Christian counterpart, the YMCA, in that to stay there you don't have to be young, male or – in this case – Jewish. All rooms are spacious and clean, with two desks and plenty of closet space. There are kitchen and dining facilities on each floor. The YMHA is good for tours, lectures and classes – and the classy Upper East Side location is a bonus.

**Hotel services** *Air-conditioning (extra charge). Disabled: rooms. Fitness centre with pool, steam room & sauna. Laundry. Library. Multi-lingual staff. TV lounge.* **Room services** *Refrigerator on request.*

### YMCA (Vanderbilt)

*224 East 47th Street, NY 10017, between Second & Third Avenues (756 9600/fax 752 0210). Subway 4, 5, 6 or 7 to Grand Central.* **Rates** *single* $53; *double* $66; *suite* $100. **Credit** MC, V.

A cheerful, standard YMCA that was completely renovated in 1992. The more expensive rooms have sinks, but they're not very large; the beds can barely fit in some rooms. Book well in advance by writing to the Reservations Department and including a deposit for one night's rent. There are 377 rooms but only executive suites have a private bath.

**Hotel services** *Air-conditioning. Conference facilities. Fax. Disabled: rooms. Gift shop. Laundry. Left luggage room. Multi-lingual staff. Restaurant. Sport & fitness facilities.* **Room services** *All rooms no smoking. Cable TV. Radio. Refrigerator on request. Room service.*

### YMCA (West Side)

*5 West 63rd Street, NY 10023, between Central Park West & Broadway (787 4400/fax 875 1334). Subway 1, 9, A, B, C or D to Columbus Circle.* **Rates** *single* $53, $80 with bath; *double* $65, $90 with bath. **Credit** MC, V.

A large, echoing building close to Central Park and the Lincoln Center, whose rooms are simple and clean. Book well in advance. A deposit is required to hold a reservation. Most of the 540 rooms have shared bathrooms.

**Hotel services** *Air-conditioning. Cafeteria. Disabled: rooms. Fax. Laundry. Multi-lingual staff. Sport & fitness facilities.* **Room services** *Cable TV.*

## Bed & Breakfast

New York's bed and breakfast scene is deceptively large. There are thousands of beds available but as there isn't a central B&B organisation, rooms aren't well publicised. Many of the rooms are unhosted and breakfast is usually continental (if it exists at all). The main difference from a hotel is in the more personal ambiance. Prices are not necessarily low, but B&Bs are a good way to feel less like a tourist and more like a New Yorker. Sales tax of 8.25 per cent is payable on hosted rooms, but not on unhosted apartments if you're staying for more than seven days.

### At Home in New York Inc

*PO Box 407, NY 10185 (956 3125/1-800 692 4262/ fax 247 3294: private number, please call 10am-5pm Mon-Fri/e-mail athomeny@aol.com).* **Rates** *hosted single* from $60; *hosted double* from $75; *unhosted studio* from $100. **Credit** AmEx, MC, V.

Reasonably priced accommodation in more than 300 properties, most of them in Manhattan, with a few in Brooklyn. Minimum stay, two nights.

### Bed & Breakfast (& Books)

*35 West 92nd Street, Apt 2C, NY 10025 (865 8740: private number, please call 10am-5pm Mon-Fri).* **Rates** *hosted single* $60-$100; *hosted double* $85-$100; *unhosted studio* from $100. **No credit cards.**

Several of the hosts in this organisation are literary types, hence the bookish title. There are 40 hosted and unhosted rooms; two-bedroomed apartments cost about $200.

### Bed & Breakfast in Manhattan

*PO Box 533, NY 10150 (472 2528/fax 988 9818).* **Rates** *hosted* $80-$100; *unhosted* from $100. **No credit cards.**

Each of the 100 or so properties have been personally vetted by the owner, who also helps travellers select a B&B in the neighbourhood best suited to their interests.

### Bed & Breakfast Network

*134 West 32nd Street, Suite 602, NY 10001 (645 8134/1-800 900 8134).* **Rates** *hosted single* $60-$80; *hosted double* $90-$100; *unhosted apartments* $100-$300. **No credit cards.**

The B&B Network has more than 200 properties, mainly in Manhattan. The best deals are for stays of a week or more; monthly rates are generally three times the weekly rate. A 25% deposit is required in advance, with the balance payable on arrival to the host (by cash or travellers' cheque).

### City Lights Bed & Breakfast

*PO Box 20355, Cherokee Station, NY 10021 (737 7049/fax 535 2755).* **Rates** *hosted single* $75-$85 private bathroom, from $65 shared bath; *hosted double* $85-$110 private bathroom; *unhosted apartments* $115-$300. **Credit** DC, MC, V.

A helpful agency requiring a minimum two-night stay and a 25% deposit.

### Colby International

*139 Round Hey, Liverpool, L28 1RG, UK (0151 220 5848/fax 0151 228 5453).* **Open** 10am-5pm Mon-Fri. **Rates** *hosted single* $55-$75; *hosted double* $75-$85; *studio* from $100; *one-bedroom apartment* $120-$140; *two-bedroom apartments* from $225. **No credit cards.**

This British-based B&B organisation offers hundreds of places in Manhattan. Cheaper rates apply for stays longer than a month (unhosted only) and a small deposit is required. Minimum stay, three nights.

### New World Bed & Breakfast

*150 Fifth Avenue, Suite 711, NY 10011 (675 5600/ fax 675 6366).* **Rates** *hosted single* $60-$70; *hosted double* $80-$90; *unhosted studio* $70-$120; *unhosted one-bedroom apartment* $120-$135. **Credit** AmEx, DC, MC, V.

Accommodation can be arranged in most neighbourhoods of Manhattan. Hosted apartments include continental breakfast. There are reduced rates for monthly stays. Larger apartments also available.

## Apartments

### Apartments International

*67 Chiltern Street, London, W1M 1HS, UK (0171 935 3551/fax 0171 935 5351).* **Open** 7am-10pm Mon-Fri; *telephone enquiries only* 10am-5pm Sat, Sun. **Rates** £450-£980 per week. **No credit cards.**

A recent venture offering more than 150 unhosted apartments in Manhattan, mostly in the Upper East Side, Midtown and the Gramercy Park neighbourhoods. The one-bedroom apartments have twin beds and a king-size sofa bed in the sitting room. A 30% deposit is required, with the balance payable a full eight weeks before departure. There's a minimum three-night stay.

# New York by Season

**New York's yearly roster of carnivals, parades and festivals.**

Each new season, New York undergoes a personality change. The romance of the winter – when ice skaters whirl around the Rockefeller Center – is a sudden transformation from autumn's calming warmth, with its film festivals and the beginning of the opera, dance and music seasons. Spring is a flower-filled wake-up call from the wrappings of winter. And summertime is hot and sweaty and lived outdoors, at cafés, street festivals, concerts and theatres, in the parks and by the river.

The following parades and events are held regularly. For more information, including newer and smaller happenings that may not be included here, contact the **New York Convention & Visitors Bureau** (*see chapter* **Essential Information**). For other sources of entertainment information including websites, *see chapter* **Media**. Don't forget to confirm that an event is happening before you head off to it.

## Spring

### New York Flower Show
*(757 0915).* **Date** early Mar.
The Horticultural Society of New York always announces its annual show with a Peter Max poster. The usual location is the passenger-ship terminal at Pier 92, which is turned into a series of gardens for three to five days. Blooms and marrows are judged and lectures are held. Plants are for sale.

### Whitney Biennial
*Whitney Museum of American Art, 945 Madison Avenue, at 75th Street (570 3600). Subway 6 to 77th Street.* **Date** early Mar-early June.
Every two years, the Whitney showcases the most important American art, generating much controversy in the process. The next show is in 1999.

### St Patrick's Day Parade
*Fifth Avenue, from 44th to 86th Streets (397 8222).* **Date** 17 Mar.
New York becomes a mass of green for the annual American-Irish day of days, starting at 11am with the parade up Fifth Avenue and ending in bars all over the city late into the night. The Avenue is decorated with a green stripe to guide the marchers, requiring gallons of paint.

### Ringling Brothers and Barnum & Bailey Circus
*Madison Square Garden, Seventh Avenue, between 31st & 33rd Streets (465 6741). Subway 1, 2, 3, 9, A, C or E to Penn Station.* **Date** late Mar-early May.

One half of this famous three-ring circus – the Barnum & Bailey half – annexed the line 'The Greatest Show on Earth' back in its early days in New York City. There is usually a parade of animals through the streets to open the show.

### Baseball Season Begins
**Date** Apr-Oct. *See chapter* **Sport & Fitness**.

### Easter Promenade
*Fifth Avenue, from 44th to 57th Streets (397 8222).* **Date** Easter Sunday.
The annual Easter Sunday parade kicks off at 11am. Try to get a spot around St Patrick's Cathedral, which is the best viewing platform; but get there early.

### New York City Ballet Spring Season
*Lincoln Center, between Columbus & Amsterdam Avenues, 62nd to 65th Streets (875 5400). Subway 1 or 9 to 66th Street.* **Date** late Apr-June.
The NYCB's spring season usually features a new ballet by as well as at least one Balanchine classic.

### Bike New York: The Great Five Boro Bike Tour
*Starts at Battery Park; finishes at Staten Island (932 0778).* **Date** early May.
Every year, thousands of cyclists take over the city with a 42-mile (68km) bike ride through the five boroughs.

### You Gotta Have Park
*(360 3456).* **Date** May.
An annual celebration of New York's public spaces, with free events in all the city's major parks. This is the signal for the start of a busy schedule of concerts and other events in green places throughout the five boroughs.

### Ninth Avenue International Food Festival
*Ninth Avenue, between 37th & 57th Streets (581 7029). Subway A, C or E to Penn station.* **Date** mid May.
A glorious 20 blocks full of hundreds of stalls serving every type of food. Fabulously fattening.

### Fleet Week
*Sea, Air & Space Museum, USS Intrepid, Pier 86, West 46th Street & 12th Avenue, at the Hudson River (245 2533/recorded information 245 0072). Subway A, C, E or K to 42nd Street.* **Date** end May.
The US Navy visits New York in force with a sail past the Statue of Liberty, naval manoeuvres, parachute drops, air displays and various ceremonies. During the week, you can visit some of the ships at Pier 86.

### Martin Luther King Jr Day Parade
*Fifth Avenue, from 44th to 86th Streets (397 8222).* **Date** third Sun in May.
This annual event celebrates the life of the assassinated civil rights activist.

National Puerto Rican Day Parade.

## Toyota Comedy Festival
*(1-800 7986 9682).* **Date** early-mid June.
Some 150 of America's funniest men and women perform at 30 different venues around the city, from Carnegie Hall to local comedy clubs. The information line operates from May to mid June only.

## National Puerto Rican Day Parade
*Fifth Avenue, from 44th to 86th Streets (397 8222).*
**Date** first Sun in June.
A colourful display of floats and marching bands participate in what is now one of the city's busiest street celebrations.

## Advil Mini-Marathon
*Starts at Columbus Circle; finishes at Tavern on the Green, Central Park West at 67th Street (860 4455).*
**Date** early June.
Over 8,000 runners take part in the world's largest women-only road race. The course is 6.2 miles (10km).

## Buskers' Fare Festival
*Lower Manhattan (432 0900).* **Date** June.
A vast number of street entertainers appear at locations throughout lower Manhattan, including the Seaport and World Trade Center Plazas, in a free festival of busking. Ypu may decide now is the time to check out the Adirondacks.

## Central Park SummerStage
*Rumsey Playfield, Central Park, at 72nd Street (360 2777). Subway 6 to 77th Street.* **Date** June-Aug.
Free afternoon concerts featuring top international musicians and a wide variety of music. There are also dance and spoken word events and one or two paying gigs.

# Public holidays

New Year's Day 1 Jan
Martin Luther King Jnr Day third Mon in Jan
President's Day third Mon in Feb
Memorial Day last Mon in May
Independence Day 4 July
Labor Day first Mon in Sept
Columbus Day second Mon in Oct
Election Day first Tue in Nov
Veteran's Day 11 Nov
Thanksgiving fourth Thur in Nov
Christmas Day 25 Dec

## Metropolitan Opera Parks Concerts
*(362 6000).* **Date** June.
The Metropolitan Opera Company presents two different operas at evening open-air concerts in Central Park and other parks throughout the five boroughs. They are free – tickets are available on a first-come, first-served basis, and you need to arrive hours ahead to be sure of entry.

## Museum Mile Festival
*Fifth Avenue, between 82nd & 104th Streets (535 7710).*
**Date** second Tue in June.
Ten of New York's major museums hold an open-house festival. Crowds are attracted not only by the free admission (most of the museums are free on Tuesday evenings in any case) but by highbrow street entertainment.

## Lesbian & Gay Pride
*From Columbus Circle, along Fifth Avenue to Christopher Street (807 7433).* **Date** late June.
Every year, New York's gay community parades through the midtown streets to the Village, to commemorate the Stonewall Riots of 1968. The celebrations have expanded into a full week, and in addition to a packed clubs schedule, there is an open-air dance party on the West Side piers.

## New York Jazz Festival
*(219 3006/www.nyjazzfest.com).* **Date** late June.
More than 200 acts in ten different venues offer all kinds of jazz performances, from mainstream to acid, in this two-week festival.

## New York Shakespeare Festival
*Delacorte Theater, Central Park at 81st Street (539 8750/ 8500). Subway B or C to 81st Street; 6 to 77th Street.*
**Date** late June-Sept.
The Shakespeare Festival is one of the highlights of a Manhattan summer, with big-name stars pulling on their tights for a bite of the bard. There are two plays each year and tickets are free. *See chapter* **Theatre**.

## JVC Jazz Festival
*(501 1390).* **Date** late June-early July.
Saxophonists and percussionists thrill and trill all over New York City for two weeks, as some of the world's finest jazzeteers appear. Call the above number for information on programmes, venues and tickets.

## Bryant Park Free Festival
*Sixth Avenue, at 42nd Streets (983 4142). Subway 1, 2, 3, 7, 9, N or R to 42nd Street/Times Square.* **Date** June-Aug.
This reclaimed park, a lunching oasis for midtown's office population, is the site of a packed season of free dance, comedy, food festivals and music. Best of all are the evening open-air movies.

## Mermaid Parade
*From Steeplechase Park to Boardwalk, at 8th Street, Coney Island, Brooklyn (1-718 372 5159). Subway B, D or F to Stillwell Avenue.* **Date** third weekend in June.
Floats, people dressed up as seafood, kiddies' beauty contests and other kitsch celebrations at Coney Island.

## Washington Square Music Festival
*West 4th Street & LaGuardia Place (431 1088). Subway A, B, C, D, E, F or Q to West 4th Street.* **Date** Tue July, Aug, starts 8pm.
This open-air concert season, featuring mainly chamber music recitals, has been running in Greenwich Village for years.

*For lashings of Christmas spirit, head for the Rockefeller Center.*

## Macy's Fireworks Display

*East River (494 4495).* **Date** 4 July, starts 9.15pm.
The Independence Day highlight is the spectacular Fourth of July firework display. FDR Drive between 14th and 51st Streets is the best viewpoint; it's closed to traffic for a few hours as a million dollars of bangs and flashes light up the night. Another display is launched from the South Street Seaport.

## New York Philharmonic Concerts

*(875 5709).* **Date** late July-early Aug.
Go early and take a picnic to these evening treats. The Philharmonic presents a varied programme, from Mozart to Weber, at eight of New York's larger parks – including Central, Prospect and Van Cortlandt. The bugs are just part of the deal.

## Summerpier

*Pier 16, South Street Seaport, South Street at Fulton Street (732 7678). Subway 2, 3, 4, 5, J, M or R to Fulton Street.* **Date** July-Labor Day.
Free outdoor concerts – of all types of music – are held throughout the summer at the South Street Seaport. *See chapter* **Sightseeing** for more information on the seaport.

# Gotham goblins

New York only developed its version of a Mardi Gras-like parade in the wake of 1970s liberation. What started out in 1973 as a neighbourhood trick-or-treat walk for the children of a Greenwich Village puppeteer, has over the years expanded into a massive annual celebration that draws an estimated 20,000 participants and 1.5 million spectators to the Village streets. Commemorated in song by downtown's poet laureate, Lou Reed, the Hallowe'en Parade is a New York institution.

A flair for masks and costumes set the tone for the event. By its third year, it had been taken under the wing of the Theater for the New City's 'City in the Streets' programme. This alliance, and the parade's appeal to the deep theatricality

of the Village's sizeable gay community, produced exponential growth in the next few years. By 1982, a crowd of 100,000 was involved and the organising committee included a range of municipal, business and civic groups.

Within this structure, the parade remains a distinctively populist forum of grassroots personal expression – New York-style. Huge papier-mâché puppets, built to a scale equal to the brownstone terrain, dominate the march. New ones are created each year along themes that range, like the city itself, from the whimsical to the political, sometimes combining the two.

Several years devoted to the environment – endangered oceans, the rainforest, Antarctica – resulted in a giant ghost crab, spider monkey puppets and a 60ft (18m) whale skeleton. 'Great Snakes Alive' produced a Medusa so large that it had to limbo under the overhead cables – and she remains a perennial crowd favourite. Carried by teams of volunteers, a thousand people altogether, the puppets have rod-driven moveable parts that reach out into the crowds and filch the occasional hat.

Individual participants dress as the spirit moves them. Ghosts and goblins of the most imaginative sort are out in force, mixing with stiltwalkers, breakdancers and all manner of real and hybrid animals. Bizarre uniforms and blurred-gender eroticism are in the best of taste.

The parade has always been an example of New York cosmopolitanism at its finest. Bands, dancers and costumes from some 40 different cultures around the globe, each of whom have a presence in the city, join in the promenade. And, for one delirious night each year, Irish bagpipe bands playing the theme from the *Munsters* strut their stuff with 1940s screen-star drag queens. It's an ultimate New York moment.

### Hallowe'en Parade

*From Spring Street & Broadway up Sixth Avenue to Union Square Park (475 3333 ext 7323).* **Date** 31 Oct.

# Central Park SUMMERSTAGE '97

## New York City's favorite FREE music, dance, and spoken word festival. Every summer.

Pick up a copy of TIME OUT NEW YORK when you arrive this summer for a complete schedule of Central Park SummerStage events.
Call the CPSS hotline at 212-360-2777 or check out our website at www.SummerStage.org for calendar details.

   AMERICA WEST AIRLINES. Hard Rock CAFE

HMV RECORD STORES
serving music

Central Park SummerStage is a project of the City Parks Foundation in cooperation with the City of New York/Parks and Recreation

## Summergarden

*Museum of Modern Art, 11 West 53rd Street, between*
*Fifth & Sixth Avenues (708 9400/9480). Subway E or F*
*to Fifth Avenue/53rd Street.* **Date** July-Aug.
Free classical music concerts are organised with the Juillard
School, in MoMA's sculpture garden.

## Celebrate Brooklyn Festival

*Prospect Park, Flatbush Avenue, Brooklyn (1-718 875*
*4047). Subway 2 or 3 to Clark Street.* **Date** July-Aug.
Two months of free outdoor events – music, dance, theatre
and film – in celebration of Brooklyn.

## Football Season Starts

**Date** Aug-Dec. *See chapter* **Sport & Fitness**.

## Mostly Mozart

*Avery Fisher Hall, Lincoln Center, between Columbus and*
*Amsterdam Avenues, 62nd to 65th Streets (875 5135).*
*Subway 1 or 9 to 66th Street.* **Date** Aug.
For more than a quarter-century, the Mostly Mozart festival
has given New York an intensive four-week schedule of performances of Mozart's work. There are also lectures and
other side attractions.

## Harlem Week

*(427 7200).* **Date** early-mid Aug.
The largest black and Hispanic festival in the world features celebrations of music, film, dance, fashion, exhibitions and sport. The highlight is the street festival
between 125th and 135th Streets, which includes an international carnival of arts, jazz, gospel, R&B, entertainment
and great food.

## Dragon Boat Races

*(265 8888).* **Date** mid Aug.
Traditional Chinese dragon boats are ornately carved
masterpieces. They race each other, powered by highly competitive international teams, either on the Hudson River or
on the East River at Flushing Meadows, Queens.

## US Open

*USTA Tennis Center, Flushing, Queens (information*
*and tickets 1-718 760 6200). Subway 7 to Shea Stadium.*
**Dates** late Aug to early Sept.
One of the most entertaining tournaments on the international tennis circuit.

## Greenwich Village Jazz Festival

*(691 0045).* **Date** late Aug-early Sept.
This week-long festival brings together the Village jazz clubs
and includes lectures and films, culminating in a free concert in Washington Square Park.

## West Indian Day Carnival

*(1-718 625 1515).* **Date** Labor Day weekend.
A loud and energetic festival of Caribbean culture, with a
parade-ful of flamboyant costumes, that takes place in
Brooklyn, centred around the Museum.

## Richmond County Fair

*Historic Richmond Town, 441 Clarke Avenue, Staten Island*
*(1-718 351 1611).* **Date** Labor Day.
An authentic country fair, with crafts and produce and
strange agricultural competitions, just like in rural US.

## Wigstock

*(213 2438).* **Date** Sept.
A celebration of drag, glamour and artificial hair, when anyone who can muster some foundation and lipstick dresses
up as a woman. Real girls had better be extra fierce to cope
with the competition. The event has outgrown its origins in
the East Village's Tompkins Square Park and may well be
held in Central Park in future. Phone for information.

# Autumn

*See also page 37* **Gotham Goblins**.

## Feast of San Gennaro

*Mulberry Street to Worth Street, Little Italy (397 8222).*
*Subway 6, B, D, J, M, N or R to Canal Street.* **Date** third
week in Sept.
Celebrations for the feast of the patron saint of Naples last
a modest ten days, from noon to midnight daily, with fairground booths, stalls and plenty of Italian food and wine.

## Atlantic Avenue Street Festival

*(1-718 875 8993).* **Date** last Sun in Sept.
A huge multicultural street fair in Brooklyn.

## New York Film Festival

*Alice Tully Hall, Lincoln Center, between Columbus &*
*Amsterdam Avenues, 62nd to 65th Streets (875 5050).*
*Subway 1 or 9 to 66th Street.* **Date** late Sept-early Oct.
Premieres of a number of US movies, plus art films from around
the world. *See chapter* **Film**.

## New York City Opera Season

*New York State Theater, Lincoln Center,between*
*Columbus & Amsterdam Avenues, 62nd to 65th Streets*
*(870 5570). Subway 1 or 9 to 66th Street.* **Date** Sept-
Nov; Feb-Apr.
Popular and classical operas, more daring but lesser
known work and the occasional musical comedy. *See*
*chapter* **Music**.

## Ice Hockey Season Starts

**Date** Oct-Apr. *See chapter* **Sport & Fitness**.

## Columbus Day Parade

*Fifth Avenue, between 44th & 86th Streets (397 8222).*
**Date** Columbus Day.
To celebrate the first recorded sighting of America by
Europeans, the whole country gets a holiday with an Italian
flavour – and the inevitable parade up Fifth Avenue.

## Basketball Season Starts

**Date** Oct-July. *See chapter* **Sport & Fitness**.

## New York City Marathon

*Starts at the Staten Island side of the Verrazano Narrows*
*Bridge (860 4455).* **Date** last Sun in Oct, or first Sun in
Nov, starts 10.45am.
Over 32,000 runners cover all five boroughs over a 26.2 mile
(42km) course. The race finishes at the Tavern on the Green,
in Central Park at West 67th Street.

## Macy's Thanksgiving Day Parade

*Central Park West & 79th Street to Macy's, at Broadway*
*& 34th Street (494 4495).* **Date** Thanksgiving Day,
starts 9am.
This is the one to take the kids to: it features enormous
inflated cartoon characters, elaborate floats and Santa on
his way to sit out December in Santaland at Macy's department store.

# Winter

## The Nutcracker Suite

*New York State Theater, Lincoln Center, between*
*Columbus & Amsterdam Avenues, 62nd to 65th Streets*
*(870 5570). Subway 1 or 9 to 66th Street.* **Date** Nov-Dec.
The New York City Ballet performances of this famous
work, assisted by students from the School of American
Ballet, have become a much-loved Christmas tradition. *See*
*chapter* **Dance**.

## Christmas Tree Lighting Ceremony

*Rockefeller Center, Fifth Avenue between 49th & 50th Streets (397 8222). Subway B, D or F to Rockefeller Center.* **Date** early Dec.

The giant tree in front of the RCA Building is festooned with five miles (7.4km) of lights. The tree, the skaters on the rink in the sunken plaza and the shimmering statue of Prometheus make this the most enchanting Christmas spot in New York.

## Messiah Sing-in

*Avery Fisher Hall, Lincoln Center, Lincoln Center, between Columbus & Amsterdam Avenues, 62nd to 65th Streets (870 5570). Subway 1 or 9 to 66th Street.* **Date** mid Dec.

Usually one week before Christmas, 21 conductors lead the capacity audience of 3,000 in a rehearsal and then a performance of Handel's *Messiah*. You don't need any experience and can buy the score in the foyer.

## Christmas Spectacular

*Radio City Music Hall, 1260 Sixth Avenue, at 50th Street (632 4000). Subway B, D, F, or Q to Rockefeller Center.* **Date** Dec.

This is the long-running famous show in which the fabulous high-kicking Rockettes top off an evening of tableaux and musical numbers exhausting the thematic possibilities of Christmas, though its future is in doubt. *See chapter* **Music**.

## New Year's Eve Fireworks

*Central Park (360 3456).* **Date** 31 Dec.

The best viewing points for a night of flash-banging are the Bethsheda Fountain (Central Park at 72nd Street); Tavern on the Green (Central Park West at 67th Street); and Fifth Avenue at 90th Street. The fun and festivities start at 11.30pm and include hot cider and food.

## The Ball Drop

*Times Square (768 1560).* **Date** 31 Dec.

A traditional New York year begins and ends in Times Square, watching a light bulb-encrusted ball get hoisted above the crowd and dropped at midnight. A new glitz-driven ball overhaul means the sphere now sports 180 75-watt bulbs and some 12,000 rhinestones. There are plenty of other diversions, but the overall theme is drunken overcrowding. The surrounding streets fill up by 9pm.

## National Boat Show

*Jacob K Javits Convention Center, Eleventh Avenue between 34th & 39th Streets (216 2000). Subway A, C or E to Penn Station.* **Date** mid-Jan.

A great displays of boats, yachts and pleasure cruisers. Don't take your chequebook.

## Chinese New Year

*Around Mott Street, Chinatown (397 8222). Subway 6, J, M, N or R to Canal Street.* **Date** first day of the full moon between 21 Jan and 19 Feb.

The Chinese population of New York celebrates new year in style, with dragon parades, performers and delicious food on offer throughout Chinatown. Private fireworks have now been banned, so the celebrations no longer go with quite such a bang.

## Winter Antiques Show

*7th Regiment Armory, Park Avenue, at East 66th Street (1-718 665 5250). Subway 6 to 68th Street.* **Date** mid-Jan.

The most prestigious of New York's antique fairs, with items from most of the great antiques shops on the Upper East Side, as well as from all over the country.

## Black History Month

**Date** Feb.

Events to celebrate African American history. They change each year and take place at venues around the city. Watch the press for details.

## Empire State Building Run-Up

*350 Fifth Avenue, at 34th Street (860 4455). Subway B, D, F, N or R to 34th Street.* **Date** early Feb.

The race starts in the lobby; runners speed up the 1,575 steps to the 86th floor; the average winning time is an astonishing – or suicidal – 12 minutes.

# Sightseeing

**Feast your senses on New York, the gateway to a continent. It's a helluva town.**

*All that trouble, just to get to Brooklyn. An engineering feat of its time: the **Brooklyn Bridge**.*

New York has no shortage of sights to see. Most people's problem is finding time for all the celebrated places on their list. This is a guide to some of the essential and most famous ones. We also include recommendations for guided tours and hints about finding more unusual perspectives on the city. Many of the places listed here are also covered in other chapters, notably **New York by Neighbourhood**, **Architecture** *and* **History**.

## The Views

Flying in to New York on a clear day or night provides one of the world's most unforgettable views. It's impossible to be certain which landing route your plane will take, but the odds are best if you sit on the left side of the plane (for any of the three airports). Other jaw-dropping vistas can be seen at the Promenade in Brooklyn Heights (Subway 2 or 3 to Clarke Street); from Liberty Park, New Jersey, and the nearby length of the New Jersey Turnpike; from the elevated sections of the Brooklyn Queens Expressway; from the many bridges and tall buildings; and from the Staten Island Ferry.

## The Statue

### The Statue of Liberty & Ellis Island Museum

*Subway 4 or 5 to Bowling Green, then ferry from Battery Park (363 3200/ferry information 269 5755).*
**Ferries** every half hour 9.15am-3.30pm daily.
**Fare** $7; $3-$5 concessions, including admission.

**Ticket sales** Castle Clinton, Battery Park.
**Open** 8.30am-3.30pm daily. **No credit cards**.
'A big girl who is obviously going to have a baby. The Birth of a Nation, I suppose', wrote wartime wit James Agate about the Statue of Liberty. Get up close to this most symbolic New York structure by visiting the island it's on. A decades-long dispute between the states of New York and New Jersey over title to the island was recently settled in Solomonic fashion, with New York retaining the original acreage and the historic structures, and Jersey getting the 20-odd acres created over the years by landfill.

Frederic Auguste Bartholdi's statue was a gift from the people of France (the framework was designed by Gustav Eiffel), but it took the Americans years to collect enough money to give Liberty the pedestal she now stands on. There's an excruciating long wait to get to the top – we recommend you don't bother. It's claustrophobic, rarely takes less than two hours and, as you can no longer get out into the torch, not such a big deal anyway. Better to spend your time on Ellis Island, walking through the restored buildings dedicated to the millions of immigrants who passed through the quarantine station here, and pondering the ghostly personal belongings that hundreds of people left behind in their hurry to become part of a new nation. It's an arresting and moving museum. If you're on a tight budget, the way to see Liberty is to take a round trip on the Staten Island ferry, which passes close to the statue (*see p47* **Tours**). *See also chapter* **Museums**.

## The Places

*See chapter* **New York by Neighbourhood** for more information on the areas listed below, plus a round up of the city's other unmissable districts.

### Chinatown

*Subway 6, J, M, N, R or Z to Canal Street.*
New York's Chinatown is the closest you'll get to Hong Kong without actually going there. It's a colourful, noisy and smelly marketplace where traders will sell you anything from fresh fish to a fake Rolex. Tables and hand carts jam the sidewalks and the shops are filled to overflowing with Chinese treasures and kitsch *objets*. It has hundreds of excellent and inexpensive restaurants (everyone in New York has their favourite, the location of which it is impossible to describe to others). Additional attractions include the Mott Street Buddhist Temple (64B Mott Street) and the statue of Confucius in Confucius Plaza. You may be in America, but few locals speak English here.

### South Street Seaport

*Water Street to the East River, between John Street & Peck Slip (information 732 7678). Subway 2, 3, 4, 5, J, M or Z to Fulton Street.* **Admission** free. **Museum** *12 Fulton Street, at Front Street (748 8600).* **Open** 10am-6pm daily. **Admission** $6 adults; $3-$5 concessions. **Credit** AmEx, MC, V.
Despite being over-prettified, the seaport is well worth a visit to get a feel for the maritime history of the city. As well as the chance to dine on some of New York's finest seafood and to imbibe rum alongside the dubious fellows who work at the fishyard (often in the news for its alleged Mafia connections), you have the added pleasure of an all-American mall ambience. Admission to the Seaport Museum includes entry to the interesting galleries and tours around the historic vessels docked here. There are also several other boats on which you can take a quick cruise.

### Times Square

*Broadway & West 42nd Street. Subway 1, 2, 3, 7, N or R to Times Square.*
Visit Times Square at night and you'll find yourself among floods of people weaving between hotels, restaurants and big Broadway shows. This is New York's tourist mecca, full of bus-loads of Iowans gasping at the glittering acres of overhead neon. Have a look at the city-sponsored art projects which fill the dead movie theatres along 42nd Street towards Eighth Avenue: bizarre window displays and epigrams in place of movie titles. Soak up the (relatively safe) sleaziness of the place, soon to be a thing of the past as new zoning laws threaten the many sex shops and peep-shows. Even squeaky-clean Disney has put down roots here (*see p51*). Originally called Longacre Square, Times Square was renamed after the *New York Times* moved to the site in 1924, announcing its arrival with a spectacular New Year's Eve fireworks display. The *Times* erected the world's first moving sign, where it posted election returns in 1928. The paper has now moved a few blocks uptown, but the New Year's celebrations and moving signs remain.

## The Landmarks

*See also chapter* **Architecture**.

### Brooklyn Bridge

*Subway 4, 5 or 6 to Brooklyn Bridge (Manhattan side); A or C to Brooklyn Bridge (Brooklyn side).*
New York has many bridges but none as beautiful or famous as the Brooklyn Bridge. The twin Gothic arches of its towers offered a grand entrance for each city, though this symbolism was lessened somewhat when Brooklyn (thanks largely to the bridge) became part of New York in 1898. The walkway, with its overhead network of supporting cables, is great for an afternoon stroll (take the subway to Brooklyn and walk back into town for some incredible views). It took over 600 men some 16 years to build and when completed in 1883 was the world's largest suspension bridge – and the first to be constructed of steel. Engineer John A Roebling was one of 20 men who died on the project – before construction even started. His son continued the work until he was struck by caisson disease (the bends) and supervised construction, with the help of his wife, from the window of his Brooklyn apartment. 'All that trouble just to get to Brooklyn' was the Vaudevillian quip on the matter.

### Empire State Building

*350 Fifth Avenue, at 34th Street (736 3100). Subway B, D, F, N, Q or R to 34th Street.* **Open** 9.30am-midnight daily; last elevator up at 11.30pm. **Admission** $4.50 adults; $2.25 concessions; free under-5s. **No credit cards.**
As well as some amazing photos of the building's construction (and of the time a plane crashed into it), the lobby has occasional displays of bizarre artwork and a collection of useless facts about this Art Deco pinnacle. (Did you know that in theory it's structurally strong enough to build on 13 more storeys, adding enough height to regain the tallest-in-the-world title?) The best time to visit is when the sun sets over the New Jersey smog (angry reds and oranges merging into a green-black night), with the glittering lights of New York flickering on beneath you. After a shooting incident in February 1997, airport-style metal detectors have been installed, but the building is still impossibly romantic, so don't forget to pack a loved one for the ascent. The biggest queue is on the second stage at the 86th floor, where you wait for an elevator to take you to the giddy heights of floor 102.

### Rockefeller Center

*between Fifth & Seventh Avenues and 47th & 51st Streets (632 3975). Subway B, D, F or Q to Rockefeller Center.* **Admission** free.
Urban planners have been trying to emulate the Rockefeller Center ever since it was built in the 1930s, but no one has come near it. The scale is extraordinary – it originally covered three large city blocks and now stretches even further across Sixth Avenue. People crowd the pedestrian spaces

between the low-massed Maison Française and the British Empire Buildings, looking down on the ice-skating rink (a café in summer) and up at the slender apex of the RCA Building (now called the GE Building). If you go at sunset, the views accompanying the cocktails at the RCA's Rainbow Room can be spectacular. The famous Art Deco Radio City Music Hall is on the western side of the complex. An excellent finishing point for a Fifth Avenue shopping expedition.

## World Trade Center

*between Church, Vesey, West & Liberty Streets (435 4170). Subway 1, 2, 3, 9, C or E to World Trade Center.* **Open** *Oct-July* 9.30am-9.30pm daily; *Aug, Sept* 9.30am-11.30pm daily. **Admission** $10 adults; $5-$8 concessions; free under-6s. **Credit** MC, V.

With the stainless steel ribbing of these twin giants working to accentuate their size, the view, even from the bottom looking up, is enough to make your head spin. Ascend to the 110th floor, however, and you'll really feel the vertigo: the scariest thing is that there's another tower of equal size only a stone's throw away (first thing in the morning's the best time to avoid the queue, which can take up to an hour). Marvel at the city below and the view out to sea across the bay, and enjoy the slight swaying as the building bends in the wind. The observation deck on the 107th floor of Tower 1 has re-opened after extensive renovation and now features three theatres, two gift shops and an overpriced food court. Back on the ground, the lower concourse is a fast foodie's paradise and cheaper than the nastier offerings above.

# The Museums

*See also chapter* **Museums**.

## Metropolitan Museum of Art

*Fifth Avenue, at 82nd Street (535 7710). Subway 4, 5 or 6 to 86th Street.* **Open** 9.30am-5.15pm Tue-Thur, Sun; 9.30am-8.45pm Fri, Sat. **Admission** suggested donation $8; $4 concessions; free accompanied under-12s. **No credit cards**.

The city's attic, containing all manner of objects from modern art and sculpture to Native American antiquities. Don't even think about trying to 'do' all the Met: it has 1,400,000sq ft of floor space and 130,000sq ft of walls. Visit one of its excellent themed exhibitions, where a particular corner of the vast treasure trove is highlighted; or lose yourself wandering through the centuries until it's time for tea in the fabulous roof garden overlooking Central Park.

*Disabled: toilets. Foreign language tours (570 3711). Internet: http://www.metmuseum.org/*

## Museum of Modern Art

*11 West 53rd Street, between Fifth & Sixth Avenues (708 9400/9480). Subway E or F to Fifth Avenue/53rd Street.* **Open** 11am-6pm Mon, Tue, Sat, Sun; 10am-8.30pm. Thur, Fri. **Admission** $8.50; $5.50 concessions; free accompanied under-16s; voluntary donation 5.30-8.30pm Thur, Fri. **No credit cards**.

Even the most clueless of visitors will recognise almost every work here. With room after room of twentieth-century genius, arranged more or less chronologically, it's an unforgettable experience. The Museum is not physically that big, but the strength of the collection will soon have you aesthetically exhausted. Avoid the astronomical prices in the cafeteria but do have a look at the gift shop across the street selling classic design objects.

*Disabled: toilets.*

*The awesome sprawl of downtown Manhattan, overshadowed by the twin towers of the World Trade Center.*

## Solomon R Guggenheim Museum

*1071 Fifth Avenue, at 88th Street (423 3500). Subway 4, 5 or 6 to 86th Street.* **Open** 10am-6pm Mon-Wed, Sun; 10am-8pm Fri, Sat. **Admission** $8; $5 concessions; free accompanied under-12s; voluntary donation 6-8pm Fri. **Credit** AmEx, MC, V.

In 1943, when Frank Lloyd Wright drew a citrus press, labelled it Guggenheim and presented it to the New York building authorities, all hell broke loose. It was 16 years before the building, commissioned by Solomon R Guggenheim to house his remarkable collection of works by modern artists, was completed – six months after Wright had died. It was Wright's masterwork and his only New York building. There's a permanent collection of impressionist and post-impressionist works displayed in rotation; in the grand spiral walkway inside the shell are intriguing temporary exhibitions. The Guggenheim also has a downtown branch in SoHo that's well worth visiting and is open late.

*Disabled: toilets.*

**Branch: Guggenheim Museum, SoHo** 575 Broadway (423 3500).

# A Whole Day Out

## International Wildlife Conservation Park (Bronx Zoo)

*Bronx Park, corner of Fordham Road & Bronx River Parkway (1-718 367 1010). Subway 2 or 5 to East Tremont Avenue.* **Open** 10am-5pm Mon-Fri; 10am-5.30pm Sat, Sun. **Admission** $6.75 adults; $3 concessions; free under-2s; free Wed; under-16s must be accompanied by an adult. **No credit cards**.

The pythons crawl around a lush, indoor tropical rain forest not far beneath your feet. The ponds are brimming with crocodiles; the elusive snow leopard wanders around the mountain tops of the Himalayan Highlands; over 30 species of the Rodentia family co-exist in the Mouse House; birds, giraffes, lions and reptiles abound; and apes mercilessly mimic anyone who catches their eye. This is the largest urban zoo in America, home to over 4,000 creatures. Although it covers 265 acres (107 hectares), it's not too hard on the feet; there's a choice of trams, monorails, express trains or camels. Nearby are the New York Botanical Gardens, where you'll find a complex of grand glasshouses set among 250 acres (101 hectares) of lush greenery, including a large area of virgin forest along the Bronx River.

*Internet: http//:www.wcs.org*

## Coney Island

*Brooklyn. Subway B, D or F to Coney Island.*

In the 1920s and 1930s a series of apocalyptic fires destroyed the original wooden structures of the various competing funfairs here. Nowadays, despite a thriving collection of rides, sideshows and other spangly things, the greatest attraction is the air of decayed grandeur. Grab a Nathan's hot dog, take a look at the man-sized Vietnamese rats in the sideshows ('more feared than a sniper's bullet'), have a go on the new Cyclone at Astroland (*see chapter* **Children**: the old Cyclone rots scenically next to the famous parachute jump, now restored), walk out to the beach and stroll along the boardwalk, perhaps as far as the Aquarium with its famous Beluga whales.

## Corona Park, Flushing Meadows & Shea Stadium

*Queens. Subway 7 to Shea Stadium.*

If you've ever wondered what all those strange structures are, on the way into the city from JFK, this is the answer. Corona Park contains the remnants of the 1939 and 1964 World's Fair, a series of bizarre buildings, including the New York Hall of Science (*see chapter* **Children**) with its children's workshops and exhibitions, and dilapidated space junk (actual retrieved rocket bits) outside. Then there's the Unisphere,

*Get on board for some of the best views of the city (and Liberty).*

a 100ft (31m) diameter stainless-steel globe, backdrop for a hundred rap videos; and the Canadian Pavilion, a crown-of-thorns amphitheatre with a huge map of New York State inlaid in the floor. The park itself has a fierce local soccer league, where you can watch Puerto Rico take on Peru or Poland. It also contains barbecue pits, a boating lake and wide expanses of quiet space. Come here for a Mets baseball game at Shea Stadium or to the tennis centre (home of the US Open), and spend an afternoon wandering among the weirdness.

### Historic Richmondtown
*441 Clarke Avenue, Richmondtown, Staten Island (1-718 351 1611). Staten Island Ferry from Battery Park, then S74 bus.* **Open** *June-Sept* 10am-5pm Wed-Fri; 1-5pm Sat, Sun; *Oct-May* 1-5pm Wed-Fri, Sun. **Admission** $4 adults; $2.50 concessions. **No credit cards**.
This collection of 29 restored historic buildings is the best place to get an idea of the history of New York. Fourteen of them are open to the public, including Lake-Tysen House, a wooden farmhouse built in about 1740 in Dutch Colonial style for a French Huguenot; and Voorlezer's House, the oldest surviving elementary school in America. Many of the buildings, which include a courthouse, general store, baker's and butcher's as well as private homes, have been moved on site from elsewhere on the island. Actors in appropriate eighteenth-century garb lurk in the doorways; crafts workshops are never far away. It's as if you've left the city far behind for some historical excursion into upstate New York.

## Tours

### Big Apple Greeter
*20th Floor, 1 Center Street, at Chambers Street, NY 10007 (669 2896/fax 669 3685).* **Open** 9.30am-5pm Mon-Fri, recorded information at other times.
Go visit Vinny's mom in Bensonhurst, have Renata show you round the hidden treasures of Polish Greenpoint, or let Carmine take you to the parks in the South Bronx where hip-hop was invented. If you don't feel like letting one of the many tour companies herd you round the New-York-by-numbers trail, or if you would simply like to have a knowledgeable and enthusiastic friend to accompany you in discovering the city, put in a call to the Big Apple Greeter programme. This immensely successful scheme has been in operation since 1992, introducing visitors to one of 600 carefully chosen volunteer 'greeters' and giving them a chance to see New York beyond the well-trodden tourist traps. The service is completely free, though donations are welcome. Write, phone or fax the office to find yourself a New York friend. Just don't let Milton leave you in East Harlem after dark.

### New York Skyride
*Second Floor, Empire State Building, 350 Fifth Avenue, at 34th Street (279 9777). Subway B, D, F, N, Q or R to 34th Street.* **Open** 10am-10pm daily. **Admission** $11.50 adults; $9.50 concessions. **Credit** AmEx, JCB, MC, V.
If your intensive shopping schedule is cutting into your sightseeing, or if your three-clubs-a-day nightlife has destroyed your will to traipse, try the Skyride, a small slice of virtual reality designed especially for time-pressed New York visitors. Using the same technology as a military flight simulator, the Skyride takes you on a low-flying big-screen blast around all of the city's famous attractions in no more than 25 minutes.

## By Boat

### Circle Line
*Pier 83, West 42nd Street & Twelfth Avenue (563 3200). Subway A, C or E to 42nd Street.*
From April to November Circle Line operates a three-hour trip that circumnavigates Manhattan Island. From June to August there's also a two-hour harbour light cruise in the evening, one of the cheapest and best ways to see the city. *Internet: http//:www.scaportliberty.com*

# Central Park

New Yorkers like their relaxation to be as intensive as possible, and for this there is Central Park: the condensed NYC version of the great outdoors. This vast (840 acre/340 hectare) expanse of greenery, set in the centre of Manhattan Island, is home to a huge array of activities and has scores of distinct areas, each with its own atmosphere and purpose.

Though it was long believed that the land on which the park was built was nothing more than a swamp when construction began in 1840, it is now clear that a large settlement of free blacks, Irish and German immigrants occupied an area known as Seneca Village in what is now the west 80s. This enclave of nearly 600 people, complete with churches, schools and cemeteries, was gradually displaced through the 1850s. Journalist and landscaper Frederick Law Olmstead and architect Calvert Vaux worked for 20 years to create their masterpiece. Millions of tons of soil and rocks were moved, five million trees were planted, 58 miles (93km) of paths were laid, several lakes and a series of small ponds were dug (along with a reservoir), and four sunken transverse roads were excavated to allow traffic to pass discreetly through. Another road loops around the perimeter, time-shared by traffic and the park's joggers, cyclists and rollerbladers.

**Bethesda Fountain and Terrace**, at the centre of the 72nd Street Transverse Road, is a formal Byzantine ornament, a focal point for the park and the most heavily populated meeting place. Just south is the **Mall**, a romantic promenade, used for volleyball at the weekends and as a playground for countless careening rollerskaters and bladers. Pressure from rich, elderly Upper East Siders brought about the removal of their famous disco-funk sound system, so the skaters and bladers now synchronise radio stations on their Walkmans.

East of the Mall is a terrace, centred around the derelict **Naumberg Bandshell**. On the rise behind is an area used for the **Central Park SummerStage** and its impressive series of free performances (June to August). To the west is the **Sheep Meadow**, the Manhattan equivalent of the beach (sheep actually grazed here into the 1930s). You may see some kites flying around the edges, as well as Frisbee games and the odd small-scale soccer match, but the majority of people, at least in the summer months, are hard at work on their tans. You can buy cheap cold drinks here (illegally) from a costumed, bicycling superhero named Beerman. If the day's lounging leaves you peckish, repair to the sheepfold-turned-restaurant **Tavern on the Green**, to the west, where there's a choice of expensive food in a picturesque setting (*see chapter* **Restaurants**); or wolf down a hot dog from a nearby concession stand.

West of Bethesda Terrace, near the 72nd Street entrance, is **Strawberry Fields**, an area where games are outlawed in favour of contemplative quiet. This is where John Lennon, who lived and died nearby, is remembered.

Above Bethesda Terrace is the **lake**, crossed by the elegant **Bow Bridge**. You can hire a boat here, or even a gondola, and meander round the ornamental waters. East of the lake is the **Conservatory Water**, where model sailing boats are raced. North of the lake is the **Ramble**, a wild area known for birdwatching in the day and anonymous couplings in the night (Central Park after dark is not the safest place to be).

Above this is **Belvedere Castle**, with its children's centre, the **Delacorte Theater**, where the outdoor Shakespeare Festival is performed, and the Great Lawn, where classical concerts and large events are held.

North of this is the **Reservoir**, its perimeter a favourite jogging route, and then an area of sports fields and tennis courts. Above the Reservoir, the park is mostly wild and wooded, with the restored **Harlem Meer** at the top eastern corner and the beautiful formal **Conservatory Garden** just below this.

### Belvedere Castle

*Central Park, at West 79th Street (772 0210). Subway B or C to 81st Street.* **Open** *Oct-Feb* 11am-4pm Tue-Sun; *Feb-Oct* 11am-5pm Tue-Sun. **Admission** free.
At the Discovery Chamber here, kids can learn about the park through games and activities. Family workshops are held on Saturdays (1-2.30pm); children should be aged 5 to 11, should bring their parents and must book. Occasional dance concerts, magic shows and musicals are held.

## Central Wildlife Conservation Center

*Fifth Avenue, at 64th Street (861 6030). Subway N or R to Fifth Avenue.* **Open** *Apr-Oct* 10am-5pm Mon-Fri; 10.30am-5.30pm Sat, Sun; *Nov-Mar* 10am-4.30pm daily. **Admission** $2.50 adults; ¢50-$1.25 concessions. **No credit cards.**

This small zoo is one of the highlights of the park. Watch seals frolic both above and below the waterline, crocodiles snapping at monkeys swinging on branches of tropical forest, and huge polar bears swimming underwater.

## The Dairy

*Central Park, at 64th Street (794 6565).* **Open** *mid Apr-mid Oct* 11am-5pm Tue-Sun; *mid Oct-mid Apr* 11am-4pm Tue-Sun. **Admission** free.

This information centre for Central Park contains an interactive exhibition and a six-minute video on the history of the park. The Dairy was built in 1870 to show city kids where milk came from. Nearby is the beautiful antique carousel (90¢ a ride) and Heckscher Playground, which has handball courts, horseshoes, softball diamonds, a puppet theatre, a wading pool and a crèche.

## Department of Parks & Recreation

*(Recorded information 360 3456).*

Recorded information on activities in all city parks.

## Loeb Boathouse

*Central Park, near Fifth Avenue & East 74th Street (517 4723). Subway 6 to 77th Street.* **Open** *summer* 11.30am-6pm daily; *spring & autumn* 10.30am-6pm Sat, Sun. **Rates** $10 per hour plus $30 refundable deposit; $30 per hour for chauffeured gondola. **No credit cards.**

Rowing boats can be hired on the Fifth Avenue side of the lake at the boathouse, which incorporates an Italian restaurant and café; picnic lunches are also available.

## Urban Park Rangers

*(360 2774).* **Open** 9am-5pm daily.

The Rangers are a division of the Department of Parks and Recreation, and provide information and emergency services. Call for information about guided walks and other activities.

## Wollman Memorial Rink

*Central Park, 59th Street at Sixth Avenue (396 1010). Subway B, N, Q or R to 57th Street.* **Open** phone for details. **Rates** $7 adults; $3.50 concessions; skate and blade hire $3.50. **Credit** (group rentals only) MC, V.

Donald Trump scored major points when he took over the renovation of this long-derelict ice-rink. Quite the best open-air rink in Manhattan, and impossibly romantic at night, when the city lights tower over the park's leafy canopy. In summer months it's a roller disco. *Disabled: toilets.*

### Petrel

*Battery Park (825 1976). Subway 1 or 9 to South Ferry.*
A 70ft (21m) yawl designed by Sparkman & Stephens, *Petrel*
is built of teak and mahogany. It was launched in 1938 as a
racing yacht, and the owners still pride themselves on using
sail as much as possible. This is a New York favourite, so
you'll need to book two weeks in advance. Sailings run
between May and November.

### Seaport Liberty Cruises

*Pier 16 at the South Street Seaport (630 8888). Subway
2, 3, 4, 5, J, M or Z to Fulton Street.*
One-hour cruises and two-hour evening music cruises in a
large sightseeing boat.
*Internet: http//:www.seaportliberty.com*

### Staten Island Ferry

*Battery Park (806 6940). Subway 1 or 9 to South Ferry.*
A sightseeing bargain, since as we went to press, the mayor
announced his intention of making the Staten Island Ferry
free to foot passengers. Boats depart the South Ferry at
Battery Park every half hour, 24 hours a day, and provide
views of New York harbour and Manhattan.

## By Bus

### Gray Line

*900 Eighth Avenue, between 53rd & 54th Streets (397
2600). Subway C or E to 50th Street.* **Open** 7.45am-8pm
daily. **Tickets** $17-$49. **Credit** AmEx, Disc, JCB, MC, V.
Gray Line offers 20 bus tours around the city, from a basic
two-hour ride to the monster nine-hour all-day 'Manhattan
Comprehensive', which includes lunch. The firm also runs
Central Park trolley tours ($15) at 10.30am, 1pm and 3pm.

### New York Double-decker Tours

*Empire State Building, 350 Fifth Avenue, at 34th Street
(967 6008).* **Open** 9am-5pm daily. **Tickets** $15-$25.
**Credit** MC, V.
Take a two-hour guided tour either uptown or downtown, or
combine the two for a four-hour ride around Manhattan in
open-top, ex-London Transport double-deckers. Once you
have a ticket, you can get on and off at any point on the route
(on the combined tour you can spread this over two days).
Buses are frequent enough to make this practicable: they
leave the Empire State Building every hour to go uptown,
every half hour for downtown.

## By Helicopter

### Island Helicopters

*Heliport East River, at East 34th Street (564 9290/
recorded information 683 4575). Subway 6 to 33rd
Street.* **Open** 9am-9pm daily. **Tickets** $44-$139.
**Credit** AmEx, DC, JCB, MC, V.
Tours include the Statue of Liberty and a circuit of
Manhattan; reservations aren't necessary. The tours are best
on clear days with little wind. Long trips are better; get a seat
by the window.
*Internet: http//:www.natheli.rotor.com*

### Liberty Helicopter Tours

*Corner of Twelfth Avenue & West 30th Street (967 6464/
recorded information 465 8905). Subway A, C or E to
34th Street.* **Open** 9am-8.45pm daily. **Tickets** $45-$129.
**Credit** MC, V.
Several tours are offered. The Liberty 'copters are larger than
most, which apparently makes the ride smoother. There are
between 10 and 40 rides a day, depending on the weather.
Reservations are unnecessary. Even the shortest ride is long
enough to get a good close-up view of the Statue of Liberty,
Ellis Island and the Twin Towers.

## On Foot

For more information on various walking tours of
New York – from tours of historic neighbourhoods,
to Beatles or architectural tours – consult the
Around Town section of *Time Out New York*.

### Grand Central & 34th Street Partnerships

These neighbourhood organisations offer free tours of their
districts, including a monthly tour of the remnants of the
demolished Penn Station (868 0521 for information) and a
grand tour of midtown, including Grand Central Station itself
(818 1777 for information).

### Harlem Spirituals

*690 Eighth Avenue, between 43rd & 44th Streets
(391 0900/757 0425). Subway A, C or E to 42nd Street.*
**Open** 9am-6pm Mon-Sat. **Credit** AmEx, MC, V.
Sunday morning gospel tours take in Sugar Hill, Hamilton
Grange and Morris-Jumel Mansion as well as a service at
a Baptist church. Wednesday morning gospel tours
include a visit to the Schomburg Institute for Research into
Black Culture and a Baptist church choir. Visit cabarets
on the evening 'soul food and jazz' tours (Thur-Sat). The
historical tour includes lunch and runs on Thursdays.
Prices start at $33 and places must be booked at least 24
hours in advance.

### Heritage Trails New York

*Federal Hall National Memorial, 26 Wall Street, at Broad
Street (269 1500). Subway 4 or 5 to Wall Street.* **Open**
9am-5pm daily.
Your guides are a booklet and a trail of coloured markers set
in the sidewalk, along with panels of information and photographs at various sites. There are four trails, all taking you,
at your own pace, through an area of interest in downtown
Manhattan. The necessary guidebook costs $5 and is avail-
able from the office. Heritage Trails also offers paid tours of
the Federal Reserve and the Stock Exchange.

### Municipal Art Society Tours

*457 Madison Avenue, between East 50th & East 51st
Streets (935 3960). Subway 6 to 51st Street.* **Open**
11am-5pm Mon-Wed, Fri, Sat.
The Society organises some very informative tours, including hikes around Harlem, the Upper West Side, Greenwich
Village, Grand Central Station and Brooklyn Heights. All
tours cost $10.

### Talk-A-Walk

*Waterside Plaza, NY 10010 (phone/fax 686 0356).*
This service offers by mail-order a choice of five 85-minute
tour cassettes to slot into your Walkman, each containing
directions and commentary for a walk lasting two to four
hours. They're $9.95 each, and you can order by mail or
phone. If you've a fax that can be set to call and receive, dial
the above number for a three-page catalogue.

### Tours with the 92nd Street Y

*1395 Lexington Avenue, at East 92nd Street (996 1100).
Subway 4, 5 or 6 to 86th Street.*
Tours ($16-$80) include Park Avenue, Irish New York and
the Bowery and run from the end of May to early
September. Most are on Sunday. Some weekend trips out
of town are run.

### Urban Park Rangers

*1234 Fifth Avenue, at 104th Street (360 2774).* **Open**
9am-5pm daily.
A service of the Parks Department, the Rangers' central
office organises pleasant free walks and talks in all the city
parks. Subjects and activities covered include fishing,
wildlife, birdwatching and Native American history.

# A walk on the mild side

The sanitisation of Times Square is well under way. The emblematic 'Crossroads of the World' is still a centre of tourism, full of theatres, restaurants and souvenir shops. Acres of neon still blaze nightly and huge crowds still gather for the annual New Year's Eve Ball Drop (*see chapter* **New York by Season**). A certain piquancy however, is gone from the mix. Most notably, 'The Deuce' (42nd Street between Seventh & Eighth Avenues), the sleaze basket of all America, a magnet for hustlers, runaways and losers of every stripe, is now a ghost town, the peep shows shuttered and the three-card monte dealers swept from the block.

It has been a long decline from 42nd Street's glory days as the centre of vaudeville and legitimate theatre at the turn of the century, then as a mecca for movie palaces and burlesque in the 1930s. With the postwar flight of the middle class to the suburbs, the Deuce emerged as the city's sexual supermarket. By the 1970s it was a degraded bazaar enshrined in popular myth by movies like *Midnight Cowboy* and *Taxi Driver*. Its massage parlours, hard-core porn and streetwalkers of every sort both rankled and titillated the puritan strain in the American psyche and made it an irresistible target for civic-improvement types.

The current transformation has been in the works since 1984, but only gathered force when the State of New York condemned most of the property on the block in 1990. An official business improvement scheme has joined with City Hall to provide new lighting in the district and drive the homeless and the beggars to outlying areas. A squadron of private security guards now patrols the streets, while private street cleaners boast of their 100-pound daily haul of cigarette butts.

Most significantly, new zoning laws have been enacted, aimed at the regulation of 'adult entertainment' and intended, specifically, to drive the flesh peddlers from the Deuce. While the matter is still being fought out in the courts, the sleaze merchants have seen the writing on the (bathroom) wall, and several sex-related enterprises have moved around the corner to Eighth Avenue.

Devotees of the *demi-monde* find it especially foreboding that the ultimate purveyors of all that is ersatz, the Disney Corporation, has lately emerged as a major player on 'the new 42nd Street'. With a massive merchandising outlet already dispensing all manner of Disney trinkets at the west end of the street, Mickey & Co have completed the renovation of the historic New Amsterdam Theatre (once home to the *Ziegfeld Follies*) next door, and the presentation of its particular brand of wholesome middle-brow entertainment. It seems inevitable that what once offered a glimpse of New York's most secret desires will instead reflect its corporate mentality.

# Architecture

**When the expansion of a city is constricted by its island location, the only way to go is up...**

*The* **United Nations Headquarters***. See pages 56-57.*

O Henry said of New York: 'It'll be a great place if they finish it' – and it is the constant construction of the city, layer on Troy-like layer, that has made it such an architectural wonderland. Its influx of European immigrants brought with them a wide range of architectural styles to be adopted, adapted or ignored, and the city's riches and arrogance encouraged nothing but the very finest, most impressive buildings.

Like few other cities, New York is truly three-dimensional. A map is useless in conjuring it; better a model, or a helicopter ride. Space, rather than land, is what is valuable here, so a building plot is a mere footprint: its true worth can only be measured when multiplied by height. And apart from Inwood Hill Park at Manhattan's northernmost tip, hardly a square inch of the island has escaped the attention of planners, builders and architects. Even the seemingly haphazard geography of Central Park is a deliberate architectural feat.

These are some of the architectural highlights of New York, though there are hundreds of other notable buildings worth seeing. Most are accessible to the public in at least a limited way (especially the lobbies) and many of the more historic ones are now museums.

Anyone with a strong interest in the architecture of the city would do well to get themselves orientated with a visit to the **Urban Center** at 457 Madison Avenue, home to both the Municipal Art Society and the Architectural League, where you'll find gallery space, lecture series and a wonderful bookstore devoted to architecture and urban design issues. The Center's building is quite appealing in its own right, a Stanford White creation the bulk of which is now the Palace Hotel. Pick up some of the Center's literature and plan your foray through the city while dining at Le Cirque 2000, in the same building (if you can afford it), or at one of the tables in the charming courtyard.

### Urban Center
*457 Madison Avenue, between 50th & 51st Streets
(bookstore 935 3592/Architectural League 753 1722/
Municipal Art Society 935 3960). Subway E or F to Fifth
Avenue/4, 5, 6 to Lexington Avenue/51st Street.* **Open**
10am-7pm Mon-Thur; 10am-6pm Fri; 10am-5pm Sat.

## Dutch Beginnings

Under Dutch rule (1626-64) the city grew only as
far north as Wall Street (the site of a defensive wall)
and resembled a Dutch country town, even down
to the odd windmill. The earliest buildings were
built of fieldstone or were wooden-framed with
brick facing, and had quirks brought from the
Netherlands, such as tiled roofs, stepped gables,
decorative brickwork and stone stoops (from the
Dutch 'stoep' for step), originally designed to elevate the entrance from the wet Dutch landscape.

None of the buildings on Manhattan has sur-
vived, but in Brooklyn you can see the **Pieter
Claesen Wyckoff House**, built in 1652 and the
oldest home in New York City. In Queens there is
**Bowne House** (1661), built by John Bowne, a
Quaker who secured the rights of religious freedom for the colony, as well as the Friends' Meeting
House he built in 1694. **Dyckman Farmhouse
Museum**, the only remaining Dutch farmhouse in
Manhattan, wasn't built until 1785, though it
retains the high-shouldered gambrel roof and
flared eaves of the mature Dutch Colonial style.
**Historic Richmond Town** on Staten Island (*see
chapter* **Sightseeing**) contains several buildings
in the Dutch style.

### Bowne House
*37-01 Bowne Street, between 37th & 38th Avenues,
Flushing, Queens (1-718 359 0528). Train 7 to Main
Street, Flushing.* **Open** 2.30-4.30pm Tue, Sat, Sun.
**Admission** $2; $1 concessions. **No credit cards.**

### Dyckman Farmhouse Museum
*4881 Broadway, at West 204th Street (304 9422). Train
A to Dyckman Street.* **Open** 11am-4pm Tue-Sun.
**Admission** free.

### Pieter Claesen Wyckoff House Museum
*Clarendon Road, at Ralph Avenue, Brooklyn (1-718
629 5400). Bus B7, B8 or B78.* **Open** times vary;
phone for details. **Admission** $2; $1 concessions.
**No credit cards.**

## The British

The arrival of the British was a spur to growth,
and there was much building during the 100 years
of their rule. Landfill projects extended the island's
shoreline and commercial buildings were erected,
driving the wealthier residents northwards. New
York grew to become the second largest city in the
British Empire and expanded as far as the site of
City Hall. The British were eager to make their
mark, and many of the new structures were built
in the Georgian style of the new colonists.

The present **Trinity Church** is actually the
third to stand on this site. The first was consecrated in 1698 but was destroyed by fire soon after
the Revolution. The second was completed in 1790
but demolished due to structural problems and the
present structure, a square-towered Episcopal
church designed by Richard Upjohn, was built in
1846. Its elegant Gothic Revival spire was the
tallest structure in Manhattan until the 1860s.

In fact very few buildings remain from the century of British rule. One exception is St Paul's
Chapel (1766), on Broadway at Fulton Street, a
beautiful example of the style of church popularised in London by Christopher Wren. It is
modelled on St Martin-in-the-Fields, with an
elegant temple portico and a steeple rising from
the roof.

The **Fraunces Tavern** (*see chapter* **Museums**)
is actually a twentieth-century reconstruction, but
gives a good idea of how the original structure,
built in 1719 as a private residence, must have
looked. This was where George Washington celebrated victory against the British in 1783. The
**Van Cortlandt** mansion was built by Frederick
Van Cortlandt in 1748, as the homestead for his
wheat plantation in what is now the Bronx.
Though simply constructed, with rugged fieldstone walls and hand-carved keystones, its traditional Georgian proportions are evident. The
wooden **Morris-Jumel Mansion**, built in 1765,
has the elegant low-pitched roof and colossal portico of the grand Georgian style. Apart from these
selected buildings, the best place to see Colonial
New York is at Historic Richmond Town, where
many buildings of the period have been gathered
and restored (*see chapter* **Sightseeing**).

### Morris-Jumel Mansion
*Roger Morris Park, Edgecombe Avenue, at 160th Street
(923 8008). Subway A or B to 163rd Street.* **Open** 10am-
4pm Wed-Sun. **Admission** $3; $2 concessions.
**No credit cards.**

### Van Cortlandt House Museum
*Van Cortlandt Park, Broadway, north of West 242nd
Street, Riverdale, Bronx (1-718 543 3344). Subway 1 or
9 to 242nd Street/Van Cortlandt Park.* **Open** 10am-3pm
Tue-Fri; 11am-4pm Sat, Sun. **Admission** $2; $1.50
concessions; free under-12s. **No credit cards.**

### Trinity Church Museum
*Broadway, at Wall Street (602 0872). Subway 2 or 3 to
Wall Street.* **Open** 7am-6pm Mon-Fri; 7am-4pm Sat, Sun
(closed during concerts). **Admission** free.

## A Proud City

After the Revolution, architecture was used to
express the city's new independence and its brief
role as capital of the fledgling United States. The
favoured building style in the first half-century of
the new republic was Federal, an Americanised
version of English Georgian.

# What goes up...

All those skyscrapers New York is so well known for wouldn't be very much in demand from the fourth floor up if you had to take the stairs. There is a yearly contest to see who can race first up the 86 flights of the Empire State Building but, let's face it, fitness aside, who has the time? Tens of thousands of elevators are what make New York the great vertical city and make possible its quasar-like density.

Mechanical hoists have been traced back at least to ancient Greece and steam driven and hydraulic freight elevators were developed in the early years of the Industrial Revolution, but passenger elevators only came into wide use after one Elisha Otis devised a mechanism that would automatically stop a cab's fall in the event of a broken rope. Otis caught the public eye with a demonstration of his invention at New York's Crystal Palace exhibition of 1857 and, that same year, installed what is generally considered the first working passsenger elevator in the five-storey Haughwout Building at the corner of Broadway and Broome Streets (*see page 56*).

New construction techniques and advances in elevator technology blossomed in tandem through the Gilded Age. The opulent furnishings of the elevators of the day utilised fine chandeliers and richly upholstered benches. Marcel Duchamp was reportedly quite fond of those at the old Hotel Biltmore, spending the occasional afternoon riding them in peaceful meditation. While almost all of those grand dowagers are now gone, replaced by prosaic stainless steel boxes, one classic cab of that time can still be found in the lobby at 34 Gramercy Park, over 100 years old and still in use, its ornate woodwork and inlaid floors carefully maintained.

New York's great elevators for speed and height today are, naturally, at the tallest buildings: the Empire State and the World Trade Center, where riders grab an express to a choice of 'sky lobbies', then switch to a local for intermediary floors. While the world's fastest elevator is in Japan, these babies top out at 1,200 feet/366 metres per second.

New Yorkers undoubtedly had a different, more human experience in vertical transit before automatic and computerised controls displaced the ubiquitous elevator operator, and certain buildings around town still keep them on. Claustrophobes may never feel at home in them, though psychologists have developed 'virtual elevators' for desensitisation treatments. The ultimate acculturation of these beasts of burden may have been the late 1980s fad of riding on top of them up and down the shafts, a rite of passage that cost the lives of several housing project youths of the time. Don't try this at home.

Finally, two items of note, unsettling though they may be: two thirds of the city's official elevator safety inspectors were fired in April 1997 for bribery and extortion and, that autumn, the union representing most of New York's elevator repairmen went on strike. City spokesmen insist there is no problem. Have a nice day.

Pockets of Federal architecture can still be seen in lower Manhattan. The 1832 **Merchant's House Museum** is a lonely survivor of the period when this area was fashionable (*see chapter* **Museums**). A row of nine red-brick houses dating from 1828 in Harrison Street, TriBeCa, have recently been restored as private homes. The largest group of Federal-style houses in New York City is in the Charlton-King-Vandam Historic District (1820s) on the southern boundary of Greenwich Village.

Many grand civic buildings were also erected, in an area known as the Civic Center. The beautiful **City Hall** (1811) combined the Federal style with French Renaissance influences, with its delicate columns and domed rotunda.

The continuing vogue for neo-Classicism led to an American version of Greek Revival architecture, exemplified by the massive colonnaded **Federal Hall** (1842) on Wall Street, built in the form of a Greek temple. Another fine surviving example of this fashion is the 1832 Colonnade Row (Lafayette Street between 4th Street and Astor Place), which contained some of the most exclusive houses in the city. The less wealthy lived in brownstones: elegant middle-class row houses (terraces) which were built in their thousands through the nineteenth century. At the same time, vast overcrowded tenement buildings were built to house the poorest and most recent immigrants.

### Charlton-King-Vandam Historic District

*9-43 & 20-42 Charlton Street, 11-49 & 16-54 King Street, 9-29 Vandam Street, 43-51 MacDougal Street. Subway 1 or 9 to Houston Street.*
As well as the largest concentration of Federal-style houses in New York, the historic district includes fine examples of Greek Revival, Italianate and late nineteenth-century domestic architecture.

### City Hall

*City Hall Park, between Broadway & Park Row (Mayor's office 788 3000). Subway 4, 5 or 6 to City Hall; J, M or Z to Chambers Street.* **Open** 10am-4pm Mon-Fri. **Admission** free.

### Federal Hall National Monument

*26 Wall Street, at Nassau Street (825 6888). Subway 2, 3, 4 or 5 to Wall Street.* **Open** 9am-5pm daily. **Admission** free.
George Washington took the presidential oath in the Federal Hall that once stood on this site. The present building was erected from 1834-42 as a customs building. It is now a national monument and contains exhibits relating to the Constitution.

### Beaux Arts

Another period of proud expansion occurred around the turn of the century as the robber barons of the Gilded Age put their newfound wealth to work. The majority of the new landmarks employed the Beaux Arts style, a careful appropriation of European Renaissance forms. Richard Morris Hunt gave the city the **Metropolitan**

**Museum** (1895; Fifth Avenue at 82nd Street – *see chapter* **Museums**), and under Andrew Carnegie's patronage, **Carnegie Hall** (1891; Seventh Avenue & 57th Street – *see chapter* **Music**). Cass Gilbert, later to design the Woolworth Building (*see below*), created the **US Custom House** (1907; Bowling Green), a beautiful tribute to the city's role as a seaport (and now the National Museum of the American Indian – *see chapter* **Museums**).

The firm of Carrere & Hastings provided a home for the **New York Public Library** (1911; Fifth Avenue at 42nd Street – *see chapter* **Museums**), a building which epitomises the city's Beaux Arts architecture. Warren & Wetmore built the majestic soaring spaces of **Grand Central Terminal** (1913), still New York's grandest port of entry and recently restored to its full glory, as well as the Helmsley Building (1929; 46th Street at Park Avenue).

The city's most important architectural firm, and easily the most famous, was that of McKim, Mead and White, which propounded the classical idioms of the Italian Renaissance. Its Municipal Building (1914; Centre Street) echoes the City Hall it faces with a grand colonnaded tower. Charles McKim's University Club (1899; Fifth Avenue at 54th Street) is an elegant Renaissance-style palazzo, and White's grand Metropolitan Club (1894; Fifth Avenue at 60th Street) is more French than Italian, with an inventive colonnaded gateway.

McKim was also responsible for what is now the **Pierpont Morgan Library** (1917; Madison Avenue at 36th Street), one of New York's great buildings (*see chapter* **Museums**). It's a low classical temple, built of marble blocks carefully honed so they could be laid without mortar, in the Greek manner. His last work, Pennsylvania Station, is now, alas, destroyed, living on only in the firm's complementary design for the United States General Post Office (1913, Eighth Avenue at 34th Street), across the street. White is probably best remembered for his Washington Arch (1895), which enriches the southern end of Fifth Avenue.

### Grand Central Terminal

*42nd Street, at Park Avenue. Subway 4, 5, 6 or 7 to Grand Central.* **Open** 24 hours daily. Free tours (935 3960) 12.30pm Wed; meet on Chemical Bank Concourse.

### Cast Iron

Coinciding with the massive waves of immigration which did so much to define New York, new building techniques were also being imported. Based on the British factories of the Industrial Revolution, structures made of prefabricated cast iron parts could be built large, fast and cheap. In fact, you could bolt together your building by ordering numbered parts from a foundry catalogue. The resulting buildings were made of layers of columns, their gridded skeletons clearly visible in their façades, which were often painted to resemble stone. Architects made Classical, Renaissance and Baroque forms with the cast iron building blocks – you can see examples of the evolving styles throughout mid- and downtown Manhattan, especially around SoHo, which has the highest concentration of cast iron architecture anywhere in the world.

Since the medium lent itself to repetitive use of a single element, it was the Palazzo style, often with successive rows of slender columns, which dominated. The first cast iron building to use this defining style was the AT Stewart Dry Goods Store (1846; 280 Broadway between Chambers and Reade Streets).

One of the finest examples is the Haughwout Building (1856; Broome Street and Broadway), which has been called 'the Parthenon of cast iron architecture' for its elegant proportions and beautiful detail. It is notable, too, as the site of the first Otis safety elevator, another development of this time which allowed buildings to grow ever taller (see page 54).

Another early cast iron masterpiece is the Carey Building (1857; 105-107 Chambers Street), a five-storey Palazzo design of Corinthian columns topped with a triangular pediment. Other fine examples include 72-76 Greene Street, the 'King Of Greene Street', and 28-30 Greene Street, known as 'The Queen', as well as a great many larger buildings in the district known as Ladies' Mile (Broadway between Union and Madison Squares).

### Cast Iron Tours

*c/o The 92nd Street Y, 1395 Lexington Avenue, at 92nd Street (996 1100). Subway 6 to 96th Street.*
Joyce Mendelsohn, an expert on New York's cast iron buildings, offers guided tours of SoHo's Cast Iron Historical District and Ladies' Mile.

## Touching the Sky

The architecture that is most closely associated with New York is the assertive verticality of its skyscrapers. With the development of steel-framed construction – an advancement of the techniques used for cast iron buildings – the restrictions on height imposed by the need for load-bearing walls were eliminated. The first skyscrapers, such as the Flatiron Building (1902; Fifth Avenue and 23rd Street) and the Woolworth Building (1913; Broadway at Park Place), echoed traditional construction in their façades – the former a restrained Renaissance palazzo and the latter a gothic cathedral complete with gargoyles – but by the 1920s and 1930s the curtain wall had an expressive life of its own and was used as a palette for many Art Deco designs.

The famous **Empire State Building** (1931; Fifth Avenue at 34th Street – *see chapter* **Sightseeing**), a perfectly massed 102-storey

tower of limestone and granite with thin vertical strips of nickel that glint when they catch the sun, was the work of William F Lamb, who was given a brief to 'make it big'. It took only 18 months to build and quickly became the world's favourite building, as well as its tallest.

The Chrysler Building (1930; Lexington Avenue and 42nd Street) was William van Alen's homage to the automobile. Its glinting stainless steel spire with an illuminated 'sunrise' motif (an addition to the original plans to add prestigious height) is just one part of the design which conjures up the steel forms of its tenant's products. At the foot of the main tower are brickwork cars complete with chrome hubcaps, their radiator caps enlarged to vast proportions and projected out over the edge as gargoyles.

A lesser-known but equally striking example of the Art Deco skyscraper is across the street: the Chanin Building (1929; Lexington Avenue and 42nd Street). The Chanin housed a network of public passageways which connected it to the nearby subway station. This, along with its ground-level storefronts accessible from inside the complex, made it the first building to be a 'city-within-a-city'.

The **Rockefeller Center** (1931; *see chapter* **Sightseeing**) was a far grander expression of this idea. Occupying three city blocks and comprising 21 buildings connected by open plazas and an extensive subterranean world of shops, restaurants and subway connections, it provides all the services its daytime occupants could ever need. Built by John D Rockefeller and designed by a committee of architects led by Raymond Hood, it is an urban complex much admired for its masterful co-ordination of public space. The centre was extended in the 1970s with the addition of four powerful towers on the west side of Sixth Avenue.

Other important art deco works include the monochrome tower of the Fuller Building (1929; 45 East 57th Street); the twin copper crowns of the Waldorf Astoria Hotel (1931; Park Avenue at 50th Street); Raymond Hood's Daily News Building (1930; 42nd Street at Second Avenue), a soaring skyscraper of white brick piers with black and reddish-brown spandrels (as seen in the *Superman* films); and the McGraw Hill Building (1931; 42nd Street and Eighth Avenue), with shimmering blue-green bricks and ribbons of double-hung windows, once described as 'proto jukebox modern'.

## Monuments of Glass & Steel

The Depression and World War II slowed New York's architectural pace but by the 1950s designers were once again experimenting with the daring forms made possible by steel-framed construction. The main building of the **UN Secretariat** (1950), a perfectly proportioned single rectangle (its face is designed to the 'Golden

**Battery Park City** – *92 acres of planned community built on landfill.*

Ratio' of the Greeks), included New York's first entirely glass walls. It is attributed to Le Corbusier, but in fact he was just one of an international committee of architects and was said to be unhappy with the final result.

Lever House (1952; Park Avenue at 54th Street), took glass curtain walls to the staid respectability of Park Avenue. Mies van der Rohe's Seagram Building (1958; Park Avenue and 52nd Street) epitomised the new glass architecture, reflecting the world in its elegant bronze-framed surfaces.

It was notable, too, for its pioneering atrium, a public space in a private building. The building laws were changed to encourage this concept. Frank Lloyd Wright's only New York building, the **Guggenheim Museum** (1959; Fifth Avenue at 88th Street – *see chapters* **Sightseeing** *and* **Museums**) caused a stir for its daring form. The upturned shell of its striking exterior contains a single spiral walkway.

The Pan Am Building, now the Met Life Building (1963; 45th Street at Park Avenue), towers behind Grand Central Terminal. Park Avenue actually rises up and hugs the building's façade as it circles it. Designed by Walter Gropius, it was the largest commercial building in the world and, with its famous (now closed) heliport, symbolised the modern jet-set life of the 1960s in countless movies.

With a daytime population of around 50,000, the **World Trade Center** (1970; Church Street and Liberty Street – *see chapter* **Sightseeing**) carries the 'city-within-a-city' concept to its modernist limits. The famous twin towers are just one element of

a network of connected blocks, their colossal height further emphasised by the narrow stainless steel detailing rising vertically across their surface (actually a load-bearing structure rather than a decorative curtain wall). The Center's architecture has been widely criticised as banal but, especially since the 1993 bomb attack, it has come to be looked on with some affection – at least by New Yorkers.

Hugh Stubbins and Associates' Citicorp Building (1977; Lexington Avenue at 53rd Street) is instantly recognisable for its smooth aluminium skin and sloping 'sliced' roof. From street level you see the radical way the building's bulk is supported on huge stilts.

One of New York's most famous post modernist buildings is Philip Johnson's AT&T (now Sony) Building (1983; Madison Avenue at 55th Street), with its grand six-storey entrance arch and instantly recognisable 'Chippendale' top. Cesar Pelli's **World Financial Center** (1988) is the focal point of the landfill development of Battery Park City on the tip of Manhattan. Its quirky yet elegant towers are topped by domes and pyramids with stepped cut-backs and walls whose proportion of reflective glass increases with their height.

### United Nations Headquarters

*First Avenue, at 46th Street (recorded information 963 1234). Subway 4, 5, 6 or 7 to Grand Central.* **Open** 9.15am-4.45pm daily. **Admission** free. **Tours** every half-hour $7.50; $3.50-$5.50 concessions.
The Modernist headquarters of the United Nations is so very 1950s. You can visit the foyer and basement of the General Assembly Building, but to see any of the council rooms and the General Assembly itself, you must take a tour which lasts

*The glittering towers of the Financial District rise from the waters of New York Bay.*

about an hour and is rather dull. Free tickets are available to General Assembly and council sessions on a first-come, first-served basis from the Information Desk (754 7539).

### World Financial Center

*West Street, at Liberty Street (945 0505). Subway 1, 2, 3, 9, A, C or E to Chambers Street.*

The WFC is a sleek 1990s public space in the tradition of the Rockefeller Center, with restaurants and stores, great views of the Hudson River and a pretty new park. Its focal point is the Winter Garden, a frequent venue for concerts and recitals (*see chapter* **Music**).

## Towards 2000

The cost and complexity of real estate construction in New York entails a lengthy gestation for any project of real significance. Much of the interest in matters architectural now relates as much to preservation as to development. What major new action there is on the horizon currently centres on three prominent city locales that have suffered decline and look to innovative design for re-invigoration.

Downtown, the capstone for the renovation of Union Square has been selected, a building to be constructed at the square's southern end and featuring an 'artwall' 100 feet (30 metres) high and 60 feet (18 metres) wide. A competition for the site picked the installation art team of Jones and Ginzel's proposal for a Zen-like vertical rock garden of concentric circles and time pieces. With a steaming void at its center, the wall promises to be very millennial, contemplative and vaguely apocalyptic.

Midtown's architectural focus is Columbus Circle, a confusing intersection born of the City

Beautiful movement of the late nineteenth century. It houses the city's most prominent white elephant, the Coliseum, a large-scale exhibition hall whose architecture is undistinguished and whose function is now displaced by the Javits Convention Center. A design competition for the site is under way but is likely to drag on – a similar fever of interest in the Circle a dozen years ago died out in a flurry of lawsuits and financial dilemmas. Elsewhere in midtown, Times Square's renovation has sparked several new development plans and drawn the interest of architects such as Frank Gehry, whose plan for redesign of One Times Square (where the New Year's ball drops) features 25 storey-high billowing mesh movable walls. It seems appropriately fantastical for the milieu, but unlikely to be realised in that form.

Even long-neglected Harlem has re-entered the developers' spotlight. A huge retail complex called Harlem USA, with corporate investors including Disney and the Gap, is to be the lynchpin for a revived 125th Street, long the commercial heart of the neighbourhood. The high-profile participation of actor Robert De Niro and restaurateur Drew Nieporent has drawn a good deal of interest in the proposed renovation of jazz landmark Minton's Playhouse. Further south, an ambitious proposal for a 'Harlem Arts Corridor' of arts and music schools, clubs and artists' housing is under consideration. All this uptown work is too embryonic for actual design features to take shape as yet, but it will be interesting to see if and how planners respect Harlem's unique place in American society and culture.

# History

# Key Events

## The First New Yorkers

**1524** Giovanni da Verrazano is the first European to visit what is now Manhattan.
**1570** Hiawatha's Five Nations alliance brings together the Iroquois tribes. They declare war on the Algonquin.
**1600** The Algonquin are all but defeated.
**1609** Henry Hudson sails into the bay.
**1613** A trading post is established at Fort Nassau (now Albany).
**1624** The colony of New Amsterdam is founded and the first settlers arrive.
**1626** Peter Minuit, the first governor, arrives and 'buys' Manhattan from the Indians. New Amsterdam has a population of 300.
**1637** William Kieft, the governor, antagonises the native population until war breaks out between the Dutch and the Indians.
**1643** Peter Stuyvesant is made governor.
**1644** Manuel de Gerrit is the first free black man to settle in New York, farming an area of what is now SoHo.
**1661** The Dutch colony is nearly bankrupt.
**1662** John Bowne's struggle wins the people of New Amsterdam the right of religious freedom.

## British Rule

**1664** The British invasion. New Amsterdam becomes New York.
**1683** A 21-month rebellion is led by Jacob Leisler, in protest at British plans for the colony.
**1700** New York's population is around 20,000.
**1725** *The Gazette* is New York's first newspaper.
**1733** The *New York Weekly Journal*, a more independent paper, establishes the right to free speech.
**1754** King's College (now Columbia University) is founded.
**1774** Colonial delegates protest British rule with the Declaration of Independence, and urge revolution.
**1776** The War of Independence rages. The British send 200 ships and occupy New York.
**1789** George Washington is elected the United States' first President.
**1783** The defeated British army leaves New York.

## An American City

**1785-90** New York is made US capital.
**1811** The Randel Plan envisages the grid into which the city is to grow.
**1812-14** America fights a further war with Britain. New York is isolated from international trade.
**1837** Financial panic ruins all but three of the city's banks.
**1843** Waves of mass immigration flood into the city.
**1851** The *New York Times* first published.
**1858** Central Park laid out.
**1859** The Cooper Union, the city's foremost political forum, is established.
**1860** Abraham Lincoln elected president.
**1861** Civil war over the issue of slavery.
**1863** Conscription causes riots in New York.
**1865** The Union (the North) wins and slavery is ended.
**1870** Metropolitan Museum of Art founded.
**1872** Organised labour strikes for an eight-hour day.
**1883** Brooklyn Bridge completed.

**1886** Statue of Liberty unveiled.
**1895** Photo-journalist Jacob Riis publishes *How the Other Half Lives*, encouraging new housing regulations. New York Public Library founded.
**1898** Brooklyn ceases to be a separate city, making New York the world's second-largest.

## The Twentieth Century

**1902** The Flatiron, the world's first skyscraper, is built.
**1907** Metered taxicabs introduced.
**1911** The Triangle Shirtwaist fire encourages workplace safety regulations.
**1917** America enters WWI.
**1920** Women win the right to vote. Prohibition introduced.
**1929** Wall Street crash brings enormous hardship and unemployment.
**1930s** Roosevelt's New Deal funds massive public works schemes. Empire State Building, Chrysler Building and Rockefeller Center built.
**1939** Corona Park, Queens, hosts the World's Fair. America enters WWII.
**1946** United Nations established, based in New York.
**1947** Brooklyn Dodger Jackie Robinson breaks the colour bar in major league baseball.
**1959** Guggenheim Museum opens.
**1962** Lincoln Center opens.
**1964** Race riots in Harlem and Brooklyn. The Beatles play Shea Stadium.
**1968** Columbia University sit-in. Hippies camp in Central Park.
**1970** World Trade Center built.
**1975** The city is bankrupt.
**1977** 25-hour city-wide power blackout; the birth-rate soars nine months later.
**1978** Mayor Ed Koch presides over a shortlived economic turnaround.
**1986** The other Wall Street crash.
**1990** David Dinkins is the city's first black mayor.
**1991** The city's budget deficit hits a record high.
**1993** Terrorists attempt to blow up the World Trade Center. Rudolph Guiliani is the city's first Republican mayor for 28 years. Staten Islanders vote to secede from New York City.
**1995** New municipal zoning laws drive porn from Times Square.
**1997** New wave of immigration peaks; Dow Jones average tops 7000; federal welfare cuts made by Clinton and Gingrich in 1996 take effect; murder rate hits a 30-year low; Disney arrives on 42nd Street.

# The First New Yorkers

*The fate of New York's indigenous peoples is sealed as they are evicted first by the Dutch and then by the British.*

The story of New York as a settlement begins with the Algonquins and the Iroquois, two distinct groups of Native Americans – with different languages and cultures – who lived in the surrounding area. Their fate was decided swiftly by the genocidal attitudes and foreign diseases brought by European settlers and, apart from various Algonquin placenames – such as Weckquaesgeek, Canarsee and Mannahatta or Manhattan, their name for a certain 13 mile-long island – the white man left little trace of the original New Yorkers.

The Native Americans of the New York region lived in longhouses covered in bark. They cultivated fields of corn, squash, potatoes, beans and peas; grew tobacco; planted fruit orchards; and raised domesticated animals and livestock. In the winter, they supplemented their diet by hunting. Clothes were made of cured skins, often fringed and brilliantly decorated with complicated beadwork.

The women cooked and cleaned, grew crops and raised the children, while their men went out to fight and hunt. But the women were the centre of the community. The tribes were organised into matrilineal family units, called *owachira*, with the eldest woman at the head. Husbands lived with their wives' families, the women owned all the marriage property – land, house and chattels – and inheritance of name and property was through the female line.

Leisure time was spent playing games like lacrosse (played with a solid-headed curved bat, and balls made of deer hide), and a violent type of football, both played on large fields without boundaries and with any number of players. Teams would train hard before an important game, a considerable number of bets would be laid and the winners would be the heroes of the hour.

## HIAWATHA & THE FIVE NATIONS

The Iroquois enjoyed a powerful political structure based around the Five Nations alliance, a confederacy of the Mohawk, Seneca, Onondaga, Cayuga

and Oneida tribes. This was created in around 1570, when Hiawatha, the warrior-turned-pacifist immortalised in verse by Henry Longfellow, united these previously feuding Iroquois tribes. The resulting confederacy controlled a huge swathe of the northern USA from the Mississippi River to New England.

Not long before the coming of the Europeans, the Iroquois engaged the Algonquin in a series of bloody wars. When the Dutch began trading firearms for fur, the Five Nations ensured their victory by arming themselves with guns.

The war was long and bloody, bringing great losses to both sides. This tragic conflict lasted until the mid-1600s, when the Native Americans found themselves confronting a powerful new enemy – the colonising Europeans.

## MASSACRES AND LAND THEFT

The explorer Henry Hudson, in 1609, described how the Indians welcomed him and his crew in the waters off Manhattan: 'This day the people of the country came aboard of us, seeming very glad of our coming'. Little could the Native Americans have dreamed that these friendly intruders would ultimately bring about their destruction.

The treatment of the American Indian is a blot on American history. It's a story of the misappropriation of native land by treachery and gunpowder, and the introduction of European diseases and alcohol that wiped out whole tribes.

The nineteenth century was probably the darkest period for the country as a whole, with massacres, forced relocations and the wholesale theft of Indian land. In New York the destruction was completed much earlier and few Indians remained alive after the eighteenth century.

It is often noted that, ironically, the US Constitution mirrors the unique political structure that Hiawatha created for the Five Nations confederacy – with states, like the Iroquois tribes, being both independent and interdependent. It's tragic that the fundamental rights of liberty and property later enshrined in America's defining document were not accorded to the country's original inhabitants.

## THE 'DISCOVERERS'

Christopher Columbus never set eyes on what is now New York City. The first European to do so was Giovanni da Verrazano in 1524. A Florentine sailing under the French flag, searching for the fabled North-West Passage to China, Verrazano took refuge from a storm in what is

# So good they named it twice

'The Naked City', 'The City That Never Sleeps', 'Babylon on the Hudson' – New York, New York (for city and state) has been named many more times than twice.

The first name, **Mannahatta**, or Manhattan, was given to the sheltered island by its original tenants, the Algonquin Indians. Centuries later, Brooklyn-born poet Walt Whitman praised the name: "'Mannahatta, the place encircled by many swift tides and sparkling waters.' How fit a name for America's great democratic island city!".

When the Dutch moved in it became **New Amsterdam**, the name gaining currency after about 1624 when the first settlers began arriving. The settlement wasn't called **New York** until August 1664, when four British warships were welcomed into town and Captain Richard Nicolls signified British rule by honouring Charles II's brother, the Duke of York.

Besides its official appellations, New York, in fact, fiction and fantasy, has had many names. **Gotham**, its comic-book alter-ego – the city Batman inhabits – is a name taken from a village near Nottingham famous for its insane residents (Gotham actually means 'goat town'). It was coined in 1807 in a satirical story by Washington Irving, who felt, as many have noticed since, that New Yorkers work hard to preserve an appropriately impressive level of madness. The satire is subtle as the original Gothamites were only feigning insanity, in order to avoid King John's taxation.

The **Big Apple** was a phrase popularised around the 1920s meaning 'the pinnacle'. It was used by actors and musicians (especially jazz folk) to signify that performing in New York represented the height of success. In 1971, the nickname was given a boost when the city began using it to market itself to tourists, replacing the less successful 1960s campaign which had christened New York **Fun City** (the subject of much derision).

**Metropolis**, alluding to the city of the future, was the title of Fritz Lang's 1926 film in which a world of skyscrapers and flying cars is the background for a Fascistic society of exploited workers. The same name was used for Superman's home town, a thinly veiled version of New York.

In the real future, as satellite communities ooze over the naked countryside and the notion of a city centre dies – killed by the flight to the suburbs and an era of telecommuting – New Yorkers might find themselves living in a gigantic conurbation extending from Boston to Washington DC. William Gibson, who gave us the word 'cyberspace', has written about this scenario, giving New York surely the last name it will need – **The Sprawl**.

*New York in fact, fiction and fantasy, from its early years as 'New Amsterdam' (bottom), to futuristic cinematic visions of the city in Fritz Lang's 'Metropolis' (right) and Luc Besson's 'The Fifth Element'.*

now New York harbour, and later took a small boat into the Upper Bay, where he was greeted by the local Indians.

It was a full 85 years later – in 1609 – when the next European arrived. Henry Hudson was employed by the Dutch East India Company, a purely commercial concern involved in the romance of discovery only in so far as it furthered the company's economic gains.

Hudson, too, was searching for the North-West Passage. He sailed his ship, the *Half-Moon*, up the river that now bears his name, as far as Fort Nassau (today the state capital Albany). According to the ship's log book, they found 'friendly and polite people who had an abundance of provisions, skins, and furs of martens and foxes, and many other commodities, such as birds and fruit, even white and red grapes, and they traded amicably with the peoples'.

## DUTCH RULE

In 1611, Adriaen Block, an Amsterdam lawyer, heard of the riches of the newly discovered land, and tried his hand at trading with the Indians for fur. His first ship, the *Tiger*, was burned to the waterline with a full cargo, but using Indian labour, he built a new vessel, *Onrust* ('Restless'), with which he charted much of the local coastline. In 1613 a trading post was established at Fort Nassau, the beginnings of the eventual Dutch settlement of the area.

In 1624, the Dutch West India Company was granted a long-term trade and governing monopoly by the Dutch government. It was authorised to make alliances with native rulers, to establish colonies, to appoint and discharge governors and other officers and to administer justice.

Following this, the first settlers arrived – 30 families, most of whom were Protestants fleeing a

Belgian inquisition. Of these, eight families stayed on Nut Island (now Governor's Island), while the others sailed up the river to Fort Nassau.

The company imposed tough conditions on the colonists: they were to stay put for six years, worship only through the Reformed Protestant Church, buy all their supplies from Company stores and provide community labour on forts and public buildings. Trading outside the limits of the colony was forbidden, as was the sale of home-made goods for profit.

## BUYING MANHATTAN FOR BEADS

By 1626, when the first governor, Peter Minuit, had arrived, there were 300 Europeans living on the tip of Manhattan in a settlement named New Amsterdam. In the honourable tradition of European colonisers, Minuit negotiated a land deal with the locals – that is, he gave an Indian chief a few trinkets and blankets, got him to sign an incomprehensible document and assumed that the Dutch had bought themselves all of Manhattan Island.

In fact, the Indians had very different ideas about the possession of property, and could not conceive of individuals – rather than groups – owning land, let alone in perpetuity; the trading goods that Minuit gave to the chief were probably considered to be no more than the traditional gifts exchanged between visitors and their hosts.

Once the Europeans had moved in they refused to budge. Later governors exercised a deliberate policy of harassing Indian hunters, even though they were the main source of fur

*Peter Minuit, first governor of New Amsterdam.*

supplies and therefore crucial to the company's financial success. Attempts were made to tax them, they were forbidden firearms and harsh reprisals for petty crimes were enforced. As a result, a bloody war between the Dutch and the Indians broke out in the 1640s, which lasted for two and a half years.

## 'PEG-LEG' PETE

The war drastically reduced the Dutch West India Company's profits. After a massacre of more than 100 Indians in 1643, the company decided its best interests would be served by trying to calm things down. Their solution was Peter Stuyvesant, an experienced colonialist and staunch authoritarian. Stuyvesant's right leg had been shattered by a cannonball, hence his nickname, 'Peg-leg' Pete. He was sent out with express orders to restore the peace and consolidate the company's investment in New Amsterdam.

Stuyvesant saw how the strain of living under constant threat of attack had prevented the town's proper establishment. 'The people have grown very wild and loose in their morals,' he commented, and set about cleaning up the inhabitants, their town and their habits.

He ordered a fortified structure (a defensive ditch and wall) to be built along the northern end of New Amsterdam – today's Wall Street. The muddy streets were paved with cobblestones; houses were built in Dutch style, with gables, checkered brickwork and brass door knockers; gardens were planted. Most importantly, a commercial infrastructure was established – banks, brokers' offices, wharves – and the waterfront, experiencing a boom, was soon lined with chandlers and taverns.

Stuyvesant founded the first municipal assembly, where members represented New Amsterdam and towns in the outlying areas, and encouraged the education of the colony's children. In the 17 years that he was governor, trade prospered and the settlement doubled in size.

## STUYVESANT'S INTOLERANCE

As it grew, New Amsterdam attracted and accepted a number of religious refugees, a challenge to the dominance of the Dutch Reformed Church. When a group of Jews arrived in 1653, Stuyvesant wrote to the directors of the Dutch West India Company, complaining that such immigrants jeopardised the cohesion of the colony. He didn't want to see it, as he put it, 'populated by the scrapings of all sorts of nationalities'. However, Holland had a tradition of religious tolerance and, in any case, European Jews were important shareholders in the company. Stuyvesant was very firmly rebuked.

However, he persisted in his intolerance, sparking a rebellion by the people of Flushing, led by

'Peg-leg' Pete Stuyvesant.

John Bowne, a merchant and landowner. Bowne stood firm and invited members of the Religious Society of Friends, known as the Quakers, to hold meetings of worship in his kitchen.

Bowne was arrested and banished in 1662, only to be vindicated by the directors of the Dutch West India Company, who once again scolded Governor Stuyvesant and allowed Bowne to return two years later, thus giving the official nod of approval to religious freedom in the colony.

### THE BRITISH ARRIVE

In the end, Stuyvesant was a little too authoritarian for his own good. And the Dutch West India Company was a little too eager to exploit the colony. By 1661 New Amsterdam was bankrupt.

When four British warships sailed into the harbour one day in August 1664, the population abandoned the fortifications Stuyvesant had built and welcomed Captain Richard Nicolls and his crew. New Amsterdam was renamed after the British king's brother, the Duke of York. Apart from a brief period between 1673 and 1674 when the city fell into Dutch hands again, the British ruled uninterrupted until the American Revolution.

The British inherited a cosmopolitan settlement that was predominantly Dutch but included English, French, Portuguese, Scandinavians and the first African slaves among its inhabitants. Both English and Dutch were spoken. The administrative system that Stuyvesant had put in place was retained, and the Dutch were allowed to continue their way of life. The settlement continued growing.

Strategically, New York was important for the British. They had long claimed the entire east coast of America, from New England south to Virginia, and year by year their settlements crept towards New York. In English eyes, New York was first and foremost a port: the finest natural harbour in the eastern United States, well protected from the elements, and providing access along the Hudson to the agriculturally rich Midwest.

In 1683, while they squabbled with the Dutch in Europe, the British attempted to rationalise New York, New Jersey and New England into a single dominion to cut administrative costs. The colonies rebelled. Affluent German merchant Jacob Leisler led a militia to take control of New York City and Long Island for 21 turbulent months. The town was divided, and Leisler and his supporters – Dutch and German artisans, retailers and farmers who were known as 'the Black people', alienated the rich merchants and landowners, the 'Whites'. When the British regained New York, Leisler and nine supporters were hanged for treason.

### THE MELTING POT

By 1700, New York's population had reached about 20,000. It was, as it continues to be, a population of immigrants. Alongside the English and Dutch were sizeable groups from France and Germany; settlers from Ireland and Sweden and some from other American colonies. Perhaps as many as 15 per cent were Africans, almost all of them slaves.

The mix of religions was just as complex. In 1687 Governor Dongan reported that there were 'not many of the Church of England, few Roman Catholicks, but an abundance of Quakers, ranting Quakers, Sabbatarians, Anti-sabbatarians, some Anabaptists, some Independents, some Jews; in short, of all sorts of opinions there are some, and the most part of none at all'.

New York's first newspaper, the *New York Gazette*, was established in 1725, at which time it was not much more than a mouthpiece for the British. Eight years later John Peter Zenger founded a rival, the *New York Weekly Journal*. Zenger soon got himself into trouble when he attacked Governor Cosby and his corrupt administration. Zenger's trial on libel charges brought a landmark decision: the newspaper publisher was acquitted because, his lawyer argued, the truth cannot be libellous. The Zenger verdict sowed the seeds for the First Amendment to the Constitution, in which are enshrined the principles of freedom of the press and the public's right to know.

This was just the beginning of trouble for the British.

# Independence & Civil War

**Britain loses its American colony. Less than a century later the new nation fights a civil war over slavery.**

In eighteenth-century Europe, the Age of Reason had arrived and the concept of monarchy was hanging on by its coat-tails. The radical European social philosophies were studied by such Americans as Benjamin Franklin, Thomas Jefferson and John Adams, who in turn spread the ideals of fair and democratic government. Meanwhile, the British were imposing more and more taxes on their colonial possessions in order to pay off debts accumulated in colonial wars against France. Bostonians rebelled by dumping British tea into Boston Harbour.

In 1774 the Americans set up the Continental Congress, made up of delegates from each of the colonies. With their interests growing even further apart from those of the British government, the colonial delegates, meeting in Philadelphia in September 1774, urged the people to withold taxes and – importantly – to arm themselves. Revolution had become inevitable. The Congress's most far-reaching decision was to accept the Declaration of Independence, drawn up in 1776 principally by Thomas Jefferson. The Declaration, proclaimed John Adams, was 'the greatest single effort of national deliberation that the world has ever seen'.

## NEW YORK AT WAR

New York was in a key position during the revolutionary war because of its dominant position on the Hudson River, which divided the New England colonies from their southern counterparts. The British commander, Lord Howe, sailed 200 ships into New York Harbour in the summer of 1776 and

*The **Fraunces Tavern** – where George Washington declared his retirement from the army.*

occupied the town. New Yorkers vented their fury by tearing down a gilded equestrian statue of George III which stood on Bowling Green.

At the Battle of White Plains the American forces, led by George Washington, were initially defeated and forced to regroup away from New York, preparing for a long drawn-out war.

On 11 September 1776, there was a peace initiative. Three colonists, led by Benjamin Franklin, met Lord Howe in Staten Island's Billop-Manor House (now known as the Conference House) only to refuse his conciliatory offer of rights and treatment equal to all other British subjects. 'America cannot return to the domination of Great Britain', said Franklin, demanding independence.

Life in occupied New York was grim. The population swelled from 20,000 to 30,000 as the town was overrun with British soldiers and loyalists fleeing the American army. As war raged throughout the colonies, the besieged town succumbed to disease and lack of essential supplies. Fires destroyed much of the city and many of the inhabitants died slowly of starvation.

In 1783 the British surrendered; two years later they were driven out of the American colonies.

## THE NEW REPUBLIC

New York was relieved in November 1783. The last British act was to grease the flagpole in the hope of making it harder for the revolutionaries to raise the flag of the new Republic.

But the war was won. On 4th December, Washington joined his officers for an emotional farewell dinner held at the Fraunces Tavern in Pearl Street, where the Virginian farmer and victorious general declared his retirement. However, he was not to fade from public life, and on 23rd April 1789, in the Old Federal Hall (on the same site as the present one) he took the oath of office as the first President of the United States of America. New York was the new nation's first capital.

Though the capital for barely a year, in this time the city's business boomed, merchants grew richer and the port was busy. However, the city streets were narrow and dirty, and hygiene wasn't helped by the pigs, goats and horses that roamed free. Rents were high and demand was great. At the turn of the century, over 60,000 people lived in what is now downtown New York. The authorities decided the city was getting untidy and came up with the famous 'grid' plan as a solution.

In 1811, the commissioners presented their blueprint. It ignored all the existing roads – with the exception of Broadway, which ran the length of the island, following an old Indian trail – and organised New York into a rectangular grid with wide numbered avenues and streets river-to-river. Commenting on the vast area thus earmarked for the city, they observed: 'It may be a subject of merriment that the Commissioners have provided space for a greater population than is collected at any spot on this side of China'.

## FORTUNES & PHILANTHROPY

When the 362-mile (582-km) Erie Canal opened in 1825, New York was linked, via the Hudson and the Great Lakes, with the Midwest. Along with the new railroads this trade route facilitated the making of many fortunes, and New York's merchants and traders flourished. Summer estates and mansions were built and by 1830 new villas had sprung up along Fifth Avenue as far as Madison Square. When met with the democratic ideals of the Revolution, these new riches spawned a clutch of charitable organisations and philanthropic institutions.

Education was highly valued and the New York Society Library, which was established in 1754, rebuilt its collection, which had been vandalised during the British occupation. The Astor Library, a mid nineteenth-century building opposite Colonnade Row on Lafayette (now the Public Theater), was built as the city's first free library, and Peter Cooper made plans for his Cooper Union for the Advancement of Science and Art.

## POPULATION BOOM

Up until the 1830s, most families lived in row (terrace) houses. But the city was too successful, and growing too fast. By 1840, 300,000 people lived in it, and the flood of immigrants from Ireland and Europe had started. The first grim tenement buildings, where whole families rented a bare room or two and shared washing facilities, were built.

By 1850, the wealthy in their Fifth Avenue mansions were enjoying indoor plumbing and central heating, benefits of the reliable water supply that the city had secured with the building in 1842 of the Croton Reservoir system (where the 42nd Street New York Public Library now stands). In addition, more than 100 miles (161km) of sewer pipes had been installed in the city streets.

Middle-class neighbourhoods were also establishing themselves. In Brooklyn Heights and Park Slope, you can still see the rows of houses built in various styles – including Federal and Greek Revival – but all in brownstone, creating a unified, elegant whole.

## CIVIL WAR

Throughout the first half of the nineteenth century a bitter division was deepening between the northern and the southern states of America. The issue was slavery. For the South, there seemed no other way; its agricultural prosperity was based on the possession of slaves. But the urbanised and increasingly egalitarian northerners found it impossible to continue to accept this inhuman practice. The numbers involved

The Public Theater, once the Astor Library.

were staggering: in 1860, over four million black people were shackled to a white population numbering eight million.

Attempts by the northern states to legislate nationwide against slavery horrified the white southerners. They could not conceive of a peaceful end to slavery (as had happened in the north), believing that freed blacks would want revenge. And as new states were joining the Union, upsetting the balance of power in Congress, violent conflict between North and South grew inevitable.

## THE ABOLITIONISTS

'For revolting barbarity and shameless hypocrisy, America reigns without a rival', declared former slave Frederick Douglass, stoking the fires of the abolitionist cause.

In Boston William Lloyd Garrison had published an anti-slavery journal, *The Liberator*, since 1831. In New York, the cause was kept alive in the columns of Horace Greeley's *Tribune* newspaper and in the sermons of Henry Ward Beecher, pastor of the Plymouth Church of the Pilgrims in Orange Street, Brooklyn. The minister (brother of Harriet Beecher Stowe, who wrote *Uncle Tom's Cabin*) once shocked his congregation by auctioning a slave from his pulpit and using the proceeds to buy her freedom.

## LINCOLN & WAR

Abraham Lincoln was known in the country as a vehement opponent of slavery. But in an attempt to preserve the Union, he proposed the return of runaway slaves to their 'owners', and supported the idea of returning the black population to Africa. This prompted abolitionist orator Wendell Phillips to call him 'that slavehound from Illinois'.

Despite his complex position, Lincoln took a firm abolitionist stance addressing a meeting in the Great Hall of the Cooper Union in New York (the first American school open to any race, religion, or sex). Here he declared: 'Neither let us be slandered from our duty by false accusations against us, nor frightened from it by menaces of destruction to the government nor of dungeons to ourselves. Let us have faith that right makes might, and in that faith, let us to the end, dare to do our duty as we understand it.'

Following this famous speech, the newly formed Republican Party – a liberal alliance with little in common with the party of today – took Lincoln up as a serious contender for their presidential candidacy. In 1860, with the announcement of his victory, the southern states seceded from the Union.

## WARTIME NEW YORK

Although New York sided with the Union against the Southern Confederacy, there was considerable sympathy for the South, particularly among poor Irish and German immigrants, who feared that freed slaves would compete with them for work.

When Lincoln introduced conscription in 1863, the streets of New York erupted in rioting. The rioters protested conscription and the fact that since the wealthy could buy out of the army it was the poor who'd have to fight – in a battle for the freedom of people they felt would take their jobs.

For three days New York raged. Blacks were attacked in the streets, the homes and offices of the abolitionists were gutted. The violence came to an end only when Union troops returning from victory at Gettysburg subdued the city. There were 100 fatalities and over a thousand people injured. It was the worst riot in American history.

## VICTORY

The inevitable northern victory was achieved in 1865, engineered by General Ulysses S Grant, who had been made supreme commander of the Union armies two years earlier. It was helped by General Sherman's infamous 'scorched earth' march through the South, during which the Union army burned mansions, wrecked railroads, freed slaves and gorged themselves on the crops and livestock they found en route. Robert E Lee's southern troops surrendered in April 1865.

For his efforts, Lincoln was assassinated a week after victory. After the disastrous presidency of Andrew Johnson, the country elected General Grant, who had ended the Civil War.

# The Making of the Metropolis

**New York becomes a vast, sprawling city of fantastic wealth and grotesque poverty, defined by waves of immigration.**

New York emerged from the Civil War virtually unscathed. It had not seen any actual fighting (only rioting) and instead had prospered as the financial centre of the North and the most convenient port of entry from Europe. But as the city thrived, rich and poor grew further apart and there was desperate economic competition between the immigrant groups.

## IMMIGRATION

'Give me your tired, your poor, your huddled masses yearning to breathe free,' entreats Frederic Auguste Bartholdi's 1886 Statue of Liberty, one of the first sights of America that ocean-borne arrivals would have seen.

The first great waves of immigration to America's twin ports of welcome – Boston and New York – started well before the Civil War.

German liberals were fleeing their failed 1848 revolution and a huge influx of Irish had begun after the 1843 potato famine. In the 1880s large numbers of immigrants from the old Russian empire – Ukrainians, Poles, Romanians and Lithuanians, many of them Jews – arrived, along with southern Italians. Additionally, many of the Chinese labourers who had been brought to America to do the back-breaking work on the railroads in California moved east to New York.

From 1855 to 1890, the immigration centre at Castle Clinton in Battery Park processed eight million newcomers. The Ellis Island centre, built in 1892, served the same purpose for roughly the same length of time, and handled double that number. To the immigrants it was the 'Isle of Tears', where they were herded like cattle, separated from

loved ones, physically examined and sometimes – thoroughly isolated – sent back to their homelands. With the introduction of a quota system in 1921, the flood of newcomers slowed, and Ellis was closed in 1932.

The new arrivals stuck together in communities of common origin. While they preserved their religion, customs, cuisine and language, they also relentlessly pursued the dream of bettering themselves and their children. The Jews, in particular, opened schools and libraries, published newspapers and supported theatres and charitable institutions. By 1910, over 1.5 million Jews were living in New York City.

At the same time, a quarter of New York's population was Irish. Although they were stuck in poverty, the Irish experienced a freedom which they hadn't enjoyed in three centuries of British occupation: the right of political action. They entered city government wholeheartedly, and within a few decades controlled it.

## HOMES OF PAUPERS & KINGS

New immigrants usually ended up in the grim, crowded tenements of the Lower East Side, which in 1894 filled six blocks. Whole families lived in one or two dark rooms, with no hot water or heating, sharing toilets with neighbours.

When Jacob Riis published his *How the Other Half Lives*, an exposé of life in the ghetto, the city was horrified. The children working in the sweatshops of the Lower East Side, the squalid housing conditions and the struggle to retain human dignity were evident in Riis's harrowing story and in his photographs (now in the Museum of the City of New York).

Stirred into action, in 1879 the city passed the first of a series of housing laws which laid down minimum water and toilet requirements, allowed for airshafts between buildings to let in light and air and made fire escapes mandatory.

As the population of New York swelled, the established middle classes – the merchants and industrialists who were benefitting from the city's vigorous post-war economy – moved into brownstones like those on Park Slope in Brooklyn, or the row houses that sprang up in midtown.

The very wealthy were drawn further north by the magnet of Central Park, the construction of which had started in 1857. The Fifth Avenue side became the playground of the rich, with enormous mansions built for monied families such as the Vanderbilts, the Astors and the Whitneys.

On the Upper West Side street after street of row houses were built, attracting well-off European immigrants and intellectuals to the neighbourhood. Massive luxury apartment blocks, such as the stately Dakota on West 72nd Street and Central Park West, started to dominate the skyline and, after a slow start, the neighbourhood became very desirable.

## ESTABLISHING AN INFRASTRUCTURE

The city's infrastructure was gradually developed to sustain its crowded population. Supplies of clean water had been ensured by the Croton Reservoir, sewers built throughout the island, and electricity harnessed by New Yorker Thomas Edison (even today, New Yorkers' electricity is delivered by his company, Consolidated Edison).

Railroads already connected the city to the rest of the country: now elevated railways cast shadows over the avenues and subway lines were excavated under the streets. Trams, too, rattled their way through the city; the perilous, occasionally fatal, turn at Broadway and 14th Street was dubbed 'Dead Man's Curve' and drew crowds of morbidly curious onlookers.

All these great technological feats paled into insignificance beside the extraordinary achievement of the Brooklyn Bridge (1869-1883). At the time it was built, it was the longest suspension bridge in the world and the first to use steel cable. Designed by John A Roebling, who died in an accident on site before construction started, and completed by his son Washington, the bridge opened up the independent city of Brooklyn to Manhattan, and eventually led to its accession to New York in 1898.

## THE SAD LOT OF LABOUR

The frenetic growth of the city's industrial strength created appalling health and safety conditions. Combined with low wages – some women workers would average only $2 or $3 for a 60-hour week – the squalid conditions forced the labourforce into action. In 1872, 100,000 workers went on strike for three months until they won the eight-hour day. Doubts about their 'Americanism' were raised.

A year later, the country was plunged into a serious depression, and many of New York's workforce were forced on to the streets: 90,000 hungry and unemployed people went homeless.

Enormous crowds overflowed from labour and political meetings at the Cooper Union. The whole country was in disarray for nearly five years: the railroad strikes, in particular, turned very bloody, with the companies hiring private security forces and enlisting the sympathetic and often brutal support of the police.

The workers' resistance was eventually broken when the bosses took to employing newly arrived immigrants, whom they could pay even less. In addition child labour was common. 'Nearly any hour on the East Side of New York City you can see them – pallid boy or spindling girl – their faces dulled, their backs bent under a heavy load of garments piled on head and shoulders, the muscles of the whole frame in a long strain', wrote Edwin Markham in 1907.

It took the horror of the 1911 fire at the Triangle Shirtwaist factory, in Washington Place in Greenwich Village, which killed 146 workers, to

*The 'huddled masses' pass through Ellis Island, on their way to a new life in New York.*

stir politicians into action. Over 50 health and safety measures were passed by the state legislature within months of the fire. Today, an annual memorial gathering at the site on the northwestern corner of Washington and Greene Streets in Greenwich Village is sponsored by the needle trades union every 25th March.

## HIGH FINANCE

With the industrial revolution spurring the economy ever onwards, New York's financiers, dominated by the Dutch since the early days of European settlement, made sure to carve themselves a substantial piece of the pie.

Market activity was frenzied. Swindles, panics and collapses were frequent, but reached new heights in the late nineteenth century. Jay Gould made enormous profits during the Civil War by having the outcome of military engagements cabled to him secretly and trading on the results before they became public knowledge. Another master swindler was Jim Fisk, who, together with Gould, seduced Cornelius Vanderbilt into buying vast quantities of Erie Railroad bonds before the price dropped out of the market. Vanderbilt had the resources to sit out such a crisis, and the grace to call Gould 'the smartest man in America'. Vanderbilt, Andrew Carnegie and banker JP Morgan had consolidated their fortunes on the railroads. John D Rockefeller made his in oil, owning, by 1879, 95 per cent of the refineries in the United States. His company, Standard Oil, was finally broken up by an anti-monopoly case bought by Theodore Roosevelt, who insisted 'no amount of charities in spending such fortunes can compensate for the misconduct in acquiring them.'

## POLITICAL MACHINATIONS

Theodore Roosevelt became president in 1901 on the assassination of William McKinley, after having been Governor of New York State. He was an instinctive politician who was among the first world leaders to understand the importance of public image. Roosevelt was also an empire-builder. He took America into the Philippines, leased a coast-to-coast stretch of Panama and stationed US troops there, built up the navy fleet and increased the regulatory powers of his own federal government.

In New York, politics had become mired in corruption. William Marcy 'Boss' Tweed, the young leader of a Democratic Party faction called Tammany Hall (named after a famous Indian chief) had turned city government into a lucrative operation. As commissioner of public works he collected large payoffs from companies receiving city contracts. Tweed and his 'ring' are estimated to have misappropriated $160 million, enough of which they distributed in political bribes to keep a lot of influential mouths shut.

But by 1871 Boss Tweed's number was up. A disgusted City Hall clerk passed damaging documents to the *New York Times*, whose publisher was reputed to have refused a half-million dollar bribe. The crusade against Tammany Hall corruption continued in cartoonist Thomas Nast's *Harper's Weekly*. Tweed said he didn't care what the newspapers wrote, because most of his supporters couldn't read, but they could understand 'them damn pictures'.

The most spectacular monument to Tweed's graft is the New York County Courthouse, known as the Tweed Courthouse. The city paid $14 million for it, $10-$12 million more than its true cost. Consequently, some of the work was very fine indeed: 'if you pay a carpenter $360,747 for a month's work, they have to do something'. In recent years the Tweed Courthouse has been declared a landmark and restored to use as municipal offices.

## FURTHER PHILANTHROPY

As the wealth of the city grew, further gifts were made to the city as the millionaires of New York signalled their success in the form of concert halls, libraries and entire art collections complete with a building to put them in.

Steel baron Andrew Carnegie, who, they say, never forgot his penniless immigrant origins, gave New York Carnegie Hall. And when the New York Public Library was established in 1895 he offered $52 million to establish branch libraries. The nucleus of the library is the combined collections of John Jacob Astor, Samuel Jones Tilden and James Lenox.

The Metropolitan Museum of Art was founded in 1870 by members of the Union League Club and opened two years later with a modest collection of 174 Dutch and Flemish paintings and some antiquities donated by General di Cesnola, a former US consul to Cyprus. Now it is the largest art museum in the Western world.

## NEW YORK LITERATURE

The successful city developed further its own artistic and literary movements. Following on from the first figures of New York letters – people like satirist Washington Irving and gothic storyteller Edgar Allen Poe – were Brooklyn poet Walt Whitman and writers like Edith Wharton and Mark Twain. Wharton became one of the most astute critics of old New York society and her most memorable novels, among them *The Age of Innocence*, are detailed renderings of New York life at the turn of the century.

Mark Twain (whose real name was Samuel Clemens), one of the most widely read writers in nineteenth-century America, moved from the West Coast to New York in 1870. *The Adventures of Tom Sawyer* was published six years later, followed by *Huckleberry Finn* in 1884. In addition to his humorous and optimistic tales, Twain was a gifted satirist and a robust political commentator, publishing pithy columns about government corruption and social conditions of the time.

## THE SUBWAY

New York's subway system, an unceasing network of civic arteries pumping a human fluid of 3.5 million passengers a day (a billion and a quarter a year), was this century's largest single factor in the growth of the city. By offering a fast and inexpensive method of travelling between home and work, it finally allowed working people to leave the polluted congestion of lower Manhattan while retaining their stake in the life of New York. Only once the tracks had been laid would the city extend northwards.

The subways hold a unique place in the city's imagination, offering the perfect metaphor for New Yorkers' fast, crowded lives lived among strangers. Most famously, Duke Ellington's song implored its listeners to 'Take the A-train', noting 'that's the quickest way to get to Harlem'. Tin Pan Alley's songwriters penned such popular ditties as 'Rapid Transit Gallop' and 'The Subway Glide', and new words and phrases like 'rush hour' entered the language. The most lyrical homage to the subway was New York wit O Henry's observations on the opening of the first underground line. Capturing the city's delirious affection for its new way of getting around, he wrote: 'The rapid transit is poetry and art; the moon but a tedious, dry body moving by rote.'

The ancestor of the subway system was an elevated 1868 line, which ran along Greenwich Street, powered by a steam-driven cable. By the turn of the century it had been electrified and was part of an aerial network which extended into the Bronx, Queens and Brooklyn, darkening the streets above which it clattered and encouraging hookers to rent third-floor rooms level with the trains where they could sit in the window to lure the punters in. Outside Manhattan much of the elevated track remains in use to this day, but on the island it was gradually dismantled and the routes sunk underground.

In 1900 building started on the first of three subterranean systems which were eventually united to make up today's subway. The first was the IRT (Interborough Rapid Transit), running from City Hall to Grand Central, to Times Square, and then following Broadway to 145th Street. After digging a ceremonial hole to inaugurate construction, the mayor was so moved that he took away some soil in his hat.

New lines followed – the BMT, the IND – their names preserved in old signs, and in the confusing alternatives many New Yorkers still use to describe various routes. By the 1940s the system was very much as it is today.

There are now 714 miles (1142km) of subway routes, with 469 stations. The trains are new, the graffiti is gone, crime in the subway is beaten back to a minimum and apart from the occasional flooding and derailment, it is the most convenient daytime way to travel round the city.

# The Twentieth Century

**New York grows up and endures Prohibition, Depression, World War, Cold War and a still-increasing population.**

World War I thrust America onto centre stage as a world power. Its pivotal role in the defeat of Germany had strengthened the nation's confidence. New York, particularly, had benefited from wartime trade and commerce. When Wall Street prospered, the nation prospered. As President Calvin Coolidge said in 1925: 'the business of America is business'.

## THE JAZZ AGE

The Roaring Twenties, perhaps the nation's adolescence, were ushered in with two important legislative changes. Firstly the 19th Amendment gave women the vote, giving them an independence also evident in fashions for shorter hair, shorter skirts and supposedly provocative dances like the Charleston. The other law passed in 1920 was Prohibition, which may not have been the cause of the Jazz Age but which certainly added to its wildness. The bootleg liquor that flowed at the speakeasies made many a gangster's fortune.

In Harlem's Cotton Club such musicians as Lena Horne, Josephine Baker and Duke Ellington played for an exclusively white audience, as New Yorkers enjoyed 'that Negro vogue', as poet Langston Hughes called it. On Broadway, the Barrymore family – Ethel, John and Lionel (Drew's forebears) – were treading the boards between movies. Over at

*Crowds gather in Wall Street, as news of the 1929 crash breaks.*

the New Amsterdam Theater on West 42nd Street the high-kicking Ziegfeld Follies dancers were opening for such entertainers as WC Fields, Fanny Brice and Marion Davies. In 1926, hundreds of thousands of New Yorkers were on the streets mourning the death of matinee idol Rudolph Valentino. The same year the city elected Jimmy Walker, a party-loving ex-songwriter, as mayor.

## THE WALL STREET CRASH

On 29 October 1929 the party was over. New York was in panic as the stock market collapsed, destroying many small investors and leading to massive poverty and unemployment. Central Park filled with the shantytowns of the newly-homeless – known as Hoovervilles, after President Herbert Hoover. One in four New Yorkers were out of work by 1932. Banks were failing every day – 1,326 of them in 1930 alone – wiping out savings and making bankers one of the most hated groups in the country. The song of the day was Yip Harburg's 'Brother, Can You Spare a Dime?'

## LAGUARDIA AND THE NEW DEAL

With the country in turmoil, people searched for new political ideas. New York became a bastion of socialism, as Trotskyites, anarchists and communists gained influence. Against this background the city elected a young congressman, Fiorello LaGuardia, as mayor in 1932. LaGuardia, a stocky,

short-tempered man, took over the crisis-strewn city and, surprisingly, his austerity programmes won wide support.

He was boosted by Franklin D Roosevelt's election as president. Roosevelt's New Deal restored public confidence by re-employing the jobless on public works programmes and allocating federal funds to roads, housing and parks. The Works Progress Administration (WPA) also made money available to actors, writers, artists and musicians – the only time in American history that the arts have been adequately subsidised by federal government.

LaGuardia held mayoral office for 12 years, during which he reduced corruption within city government, waged war against organised crime and launched the most extensive public housing programme in the country. He is still regarded as the city's best-loved mayor.

## ART & ARCHITECTURE

Some of the great twentieth-century New York buildings went up in this period: the Chrysler Building, the Empire State, and the Rockefeller Center were all built in the 1930s. And as the Nazis terrorised the intelligentsia in Europe, New York became the favoured refuge for artists, architects and designers. Walter Gropius, the former director of the influential Bauhaus school of design, and architect Ludwig Mies van der Rohe moved to America from Germany.

When painters such as Arshile Gorky, Piet Mondrian, Hans Hofmann and Willem de Kooning shifted to New York, gradually the centre of the art world did too. The Museum of Modern Art was founded, the idea of three collectors – Abby Aldrich Rockefeller, Lillie P Bliss and Mrs Cornelius Sullivan – to document the Modern Movement and represent the most important contemporary artists, a daring concept in 1929.

## NEW YORK VOICES

The literary scene was dominated by Ernest Hemingway and his friend F Scott Fitzgerald, whose *Great Gatsby* turned a dark gaze on the 1920s. They worked with the editor Maxwell Perkins at Scribner's publishing house, along with Thomas Wolfe, who constructed enormous semi-autobiographical mosaics of small-town life, and Erskine Caldwell, author of *Tobacco Road*, the Depression novel set in the rural deep South.

Many of the city's other great chroniclers of the time gathered regularly at the famous Round Table at the Algonquin Hotel. These included such literary lights of the time as Dorothy Parker, Robert Benchley, George S Kaufman and Alexander Woolcott. It was also frequently graced by visiting royalty of stage and screen like Douglas Fairbanks, Tallulah Bankhead and various Marx brothers. Much of the modern concept of sophistcation and wit took shape in the alcoholic banter of this glamorous clan.

## WORLD WAR II

America's involvement in World War II jolted it out of the Depression. Government spending for war production revived the economy and New York Harbor bustled with ships carrying soldiers, sailors and supplies to the battlefields of Europe.

After the victory began a long period of paranoia and distrust as the Cold War raged between the United States and the Soviet Union. New York, a city with a long tradition of radicalism in its politics, saw bitter disputes between communists, anti-communists and civil libertarians. The crusading political spirit of the 1930s and 1940s gave way to the enforced conformity and conservativeness of the 1950s.

The United Nations established its headquarters overlooking the East River in Manhattan, seeing New York as very much a world city. Artists venturing into the new world of abstract expressionism also made the city their own, and a new generation of Le Corbusier-inspired architects, transformed its skyline with new buildings that took the form of glass and steel boxes.

## POPULATION GROWTH

With increasing affluence, many families moved out to the suburbs. Towns sprang up around the new highways and about one million children and grandchildren of European immigrants – mostly Irish, Italian and Jewish – moved to live in them. Their places were taken by a new wave of immigrants, as

*Star of the Round Table ('Groucho is not my real name. I'm just breaking it in for a friend.')*

one million Puerto Ricans and African-Americans from the South, moved to the city.

By the mid-1960s, New Yorkers could no longer ignore the large and growing non-white communities, largely excluded from the city's power structure and prosperity. Until then, the Democratic politicians who dominated the city had given little more than token recognition to the newcomers. Discrimination and the decline in the city's manufacturing base limited black and Latino prospects for economic success.

Despite some creative efforts to bring these newcomers into the city's mainstream – especially in the administration of Mayor John Lindsay – entrenched poverty and prejudice made for slow progress. Meanwhile, increases in street crime cast a shadow of fear across the entire city.

## 1960S COUNTER-CULTURE

New York remained a centre for radical politics and the avant-garde. The East Coast faction of the Beat movement of the 1950s was born in the meeting of Columbia University dropouts Allen Ginsberg and Jack Kerouac with Times Square denizens like William Burroughs and Herbert ('the Junkie') Huncke. The Beats evolved into the hippie counter-culture of the 1960s, and Manhattan provided the stage: from the folk music that floated from the coffee houses of Greenwich Village to the student protests against racism and the Vietnam war that boiled out of the campus of Columbia University.

Elsewhere in the city, in more conservative working- and middle-class neighbourhoods, many white New Yorkers grew disenchanted with liberalism, which seemed incapable of providing safe streets or effective schooling. To make matters worse, by 1975 the city was all but bankrupt. With a growing population on welfare and a declining tax base caused by middle-class flight to the suburbs it had resorted to heavy municipal borrowing.

## BOOM & BUST

To the rescue rode Mayor Edward I Koch, a one-time liberal from Greenwich Village, who steered the city back to fiscal solvency with austerity measures and state and federal help. By shrewdly, if cynically, playing the city's racial and ethnic politics and riding the 1980s boom in construction and finance, Koch won three successive four-year terms.

But there would not be a fourth. Amid the greed and conspicuous consumption of the 1980s Koch was finally undone by a combination of corruption scandals, growing black political strength and an inability to defuse the city's racial hostilities.

He was succeeded by David N Dinkins, the city's first African-American mayor. Dinkins, an old-fashioned clubhouse politician with liberal instincts, took office in 1990, inheriting a multitude of problems left over from the ugly underside of

*Italian-American lawyer, Rudolph Giuliani.*

the Koch years: racial conflicts, poverty and large numbers of homeless people. Soon afterwards, the city was battered by a deep economic recession. Dinkins excelled at grand symbolic gestures, such as handsomely welcoming Nelson Mandela to the city. He made important initiatives in the fight against crime by implementing new community policing strategies. But he could not overcome global economic trends that drew manufacturing jobs away from the city. And as a likeable, conciliatory man, many felt he lacked the sabre-toothed aggression necessary to run New York.

He was succeeded in 1994 by Rudolph Giuliani, a tough Italian-American lawyer, who had entered the political limelight as a fearless federal prosecutor. Though initially welcomed as the antidote to the equivocal, often bumbling Dinkins, Giuliani's dictatorial style and the social implications of his policies, quickly alienated him from many of his supporters.

## TOWARDS THE MILLENNIUM

The problems facing the mayor of New York are many, but they are simply those of any other city, magnified. Racial tension, a depleted tax base, increasingly polarised wealth and a concentration of AIDS, homelessness and crime are simply the sad signs of urban life in the 1990s. The city is a modern invention struggling to survive in these confused post-modern times. However, there are still plenty of people willing to stake their claim here. Recent arrivals – legal and otherwise – from Asia, Latin America, the Caribbean and the former Soviet Union make up a foreign-born population of more than two million.

As at any time throughout its history, New York remains a city of pioneers. It is the constant flow of humanity which gives the city its energy, and it is the hope of harnessing some of it which keeps people coming. After all, if you can make it here, you'll make it anywhere.

# New York Today

**The city of dreams suffers the strains of pre-millennial tension.**

For a city that finds itself the undisputed, one-and-only capital of the world as it leaves the second millennium, it's a very strange moment. To hear all the 'good' news in the air these days – crime is down, the Market is up, the Iron Curtain has fallen, Ellen is out – you'd think you'd find people dancing in the streets. You won't.

New Yorkers at the bottom keep grinding away to keep the wolf from the door. Those in the middle have to fight to hold on to the little they've gathered. Those at the top hoard it all or blow it away in an anxiety of affluence. This composite daily struggle for survival, at one extreme, and dominance, at the other, lends life in New York its intensity. At the same time, there's an air of – not optimism, exactly, but a determination and a focus that hasn't existed since before the racial conflicts of the 1960s. It may be grounded in exhaustion or desperation, but it exists.

## BOOM TOWN
In the upper reaches of the social strata, this energy rides the crest of the unprecedented Clinton bull market. With eight billion dollars in bonus money paid out on Wall Street last year, Brylcreemed thirtysomethings haunt the car showrooms of the East Side sizing up the latest models from Aston Martin and Lamborghini. All over town, buildings with 'condos' priced in six or even seven figures sell out within weeks of coming on the market. Limousines line the blocks outside the 'hot' eateries.

And it's not just Wall Street that's booming. The American economy has spent several decades enduring the transition to post-industrialism. New York, the largest of the Rust Belt cities, has had a particularly painful adjustment. As that process nears completion, however, New York's strong presence in high technology and the consciousness industry – the information/entertainment axis – has brought a huge pay-off. The city has also reaped a fortune by catering to the economic winners, offering luxury services like fashion, food, design and the fine arts.

## WORLD GUMBO
Globalisation of the market economy and the rise of new technology have only reinforced New

York's position as the universal city. That status works both ways, however. It has always been a city of immigrants (the great port of entry to the New World), and the immense energy in the air these days draws in large measure from a renewed surge of immigration. It's as if the city has come full circle, to realise the vision of its native poet, Walt Whitman, who saw New York as the great crucible of humanity.

It has been estimated that by the end of the century, half of New Yorkers will be immigrants or the children of immigrants. What's different now is the wider spectrum of cultures in the mix; New York today is a world gumbo like never before. Where most of the immigration of the post-war decades came from the Caribbean islands and Latin America, current trends show more arrivals from Asia and Europe. The city's Chinese population long ago spilled over the boundaries of its traditional enclave in lower Manhattan and now includes satellite Chinatowns in Brooklyn and Queens. Throughout the city, people from all the lands of the Indian subcontinent have a new visibility. With the collapse of Communism, immigration from Poland and, especially, the former Soviet Union, has exploded.

# The glitterati

Andy Warhol's prediction has come true only in the sense that anyone can become famous for 15 minutes. New York has a tremendous hunger for celebrity and a vast machinery devoted to its manufacture.

The city today is a seamless web of communications, an immense stage where the stars of show business, politics, business and the arts strut and fret. Fame is the worst drug of all.

The culture of celebrity first came into being in the nightclubs of New York between the two world wars, when high society began to socialise outside the home. Bluebloods mingled with figures from entertainment, sport and the *demi-monde*; café society was conceived, the birth assisted by the tabloids' gossip columnists. 'Cholly Knicker-bocker', at the *American*, named it; Walter Winchell, at the *Mirror* (and later on nationally syndicated radio) brought it to maturity.

The press remains the primary field for public relations. Not counting the weekly supermarket tabloids, which consist of little else but gossip, every major daily paper has a regular slot devoted to the doings of Madonna, Sly, Calvin and company. Even the august *New York Times* now deigns to join the fray with its sedate 'Chronicle' column.

In other media, local television uses celebrity journalism to fill the air between evening news and prime time programming. The cable television channel, E!, is nothing less than a 24-hour whisper mill. The new frontier for image-mongering is the Internet, where various on-line services now provide cyber gossip.

The perverse symbiosis of paparazzi and glitterati has spawned a breed of pilot fish: the pinstriped flack. Generally found escorting the celebs around a circuit that stretches from Elaine's, the Upper East Side media star eaterie, to downtown clubs like Pravda and Spy, the

flack's chief function is blowing air kisses to the worthy, feeding copy to the press and generally sculpting their clients' carefully constructed images. Some big-time publicists like Bobby Zarem and Howard Rubenstein come to be celebrities in their own right.

The usual boundaries between different categories of public life have all been burned away in the PR spotlight. Bill Clinton and Woody Allen both find their sexual proclivities fair game for debate and speculation. Princess Di and Liz Taylor contend in the 'triumph over adversity' sweepstakes. Does John-John Kennedy belong to publishing, politics or Hollywood? And how much OJ can a nation stomach?

You can sample the buzz at several of the clubs and bars around town on any night of the week. Just check the columns to see where's hot. You'll have to dress appropriately and expect to spend a small bankroll in the process.

If you're feeling really adventurous (and want to mind your budget), Earl Blackwell's Celebrity Bulletin (757 7979) is a good guide to the schedule of celebrity events, galas and receptions around town. Even if you can't slip past the velvet ropes, the excitement in the streets – cops, cameras and crowds – usually makes a great show.

Immigration has provided a shot in the arm to the economic life of the city, balanced the decades-long diaspora of older groups, and stabilised the housing stock of many areas of the city that were on the verge of serious decline.

It's not just from overseas that they come to the Big Table. The city of ambition continues to draw in a relentless stream of disaffected refugees from middle America: kids from the heartland blinded by the sheer excess and possibility of the place.

Lower Manhattan, especially, teems with young hopefuls and trendoids. The prototypical success story of the day is Beck Hanson hopping off a bus from sunny Southern California, making a bee-line for the dark, dank railroad flats of the Lower East Side and emerging some time later as *Rolling Stone*'s (and everyone else's) Artist of the Year. And all it took was two turntables and a microphone. More sophisticated technology lures other would-be superstars. Cybernetics has entered the

# Three Little Indias

'Hanging out on Second Avenue
Eating chicken vindaloo'
(The Ramones, *I Just Wanna Have Something To Do*)

The South Asian presence is prominent enough in New York for the stereotype of the Asian convenience store clerk to have entered the popular imagination. Halal hasn't yet replaced kosher in the common vocabulary, but signs in South Asian and English script advertise 'Indo-Pak-Bangla' groceries and delis throughout the city.

The earliest significant South Asian settlement came through California in the years before World War I, when Punjabi farm workers drifted east in the wake of crop failures on the West Coast. Any further growth was hobbled by American restrictions on immigration from Asia until a 1965 elimination of race and country-of-origin quotas prompted a 'brain drain' of underemployed professionals from the subcontinent. This group settled uptown near Columbia University, though the first 'Little India' in New York emerged along Lexington Avenue below 34th Street, where an Armenian merchant was the first in the city to carry the foods and spices of Indian cuisine.

A second enclave developed in the late 1960s along 6th Street in the East Village, where an enterprising clan of Bengalis established a string of restaurants serving inexpensive cuisine to a hippie clientele. Nearly 30 such restaurants jam the block today, virtually all of them still owned and staffed by Bangladeshis. City folklore has it that they share a single kitchen.

As they prospered, Indian families left Manhattan for Queens, particularly the Flushing neighbourhood. There are now an estimated 60,000 South Asian Americans in the borough. The most visible commercial activity centres along 74th Street in Jackson Heights, where crowds of women in saris come with their extended families from all over the Northeast United States to shop at weekends.

South Asian Americans (SAAs) are noticeable in the everyday life of the city because they have so thoroughly saturated a number of highly visible occupations. Two brothers named Kapoor obtained a municipal lease on city newsstands in the 1980s, leading to many Indians, Pakistanis and Bangladeshis eager for a foothold on the economic ladder entering this line of business. SAAs also make up nearly half of New York's cabbies, chiefly young men sharing apartments and co-ordinating shifts to utilise the cabs on a 24-hour basis.

While social life still centres around the various houses of worship in the community, SAA presence is also notable at mainstream venues like the China Club on upper Broadway. Nusrat Fateh Ali Khan's renditions of Pakistani quawwali are popular at downtown scenes like the Cooler, and S.O.B.s features a night of Bhangra on the first Thursday of every month. And Bollywood's Hindi hip-hop is just starting to make itself known in New York. Music may once again be the cutting edge of assimilation.

life of the city and vice versa and America's best and brightest come to New York to make their mark on the digital frontier.

## CAPITAL CRUSH

This youthful influx and the renewed surge of immigration give the city the feel of the Mad Hatter's Tea Party: 'No room! No room!' The pressure has emerged clearly in the battle over rent control, the state law that for generations has placed limits on what landlords can charge their tenants. It is residential housing at issue, in a city where apartments are handed down like family heirlooms, where mobs of apartment-hunters throng the early drop-off points for the *Village Voice* to get first peek at its rental adverts, and where the uptown *Observer* runs a weekly apartment market report that reads like a society gossip page. Waiting for those regulations to expire in June 1997 was like waiting for the Red Chinese to enter Hong Kong. As it turned out, the landlords had the money but the tenants had the votes. A last minute compromise effectively kept the laws intact until 2003, though the contest is sure to be joined again.

## UNDERDOGS

If it is the best of times for some, it is the worst of times for others. The city seems determined to test itself against F Scott Fitzgerald's definition of genius, 'the ability to hold two opposed ideas in the mind at the same time, and still retain the ability to function'. For all the gravy at the top, New York still has the highest unemployment rate of any American city, a rate of inflation among the highest and a rate of overall job creation among the lowest. A midtown hotel advertising some 700 jobs recently, had to cope with a queue of 4,000 applicants that stretched for blocks. In the midst of the 'boom', the income of middle-class New Yorkers who work outside banking and finance has barely kept pace with inflation.

For those at the bottom of the economic ladder, *plus ça change*. Cutbacks in welfare spending as a result of the Gingrich-ite congressional electoral coup of 1994 and the centrist *realpolitik* of 'New Democrat' Bill Clinton have shredded the social safety net. Time limits on eligibility for benefits are particularly stringent on immigrants and the young.

## HIZZONER

Problems with the municipal budget (aggravated by cuts in federal aid to cities) drove Mayor Giuliani to attempt some bizarre measures. Much as he has tried to distance himself from the right wing of his party (an absolute necessity for any Republican in this overwhelmingly Democratic town) he still takes their credo of downsizing government for his own. Only a series of lost court battles forced the mayor to back down on the proposed privatisation of what remains of the city's public hospitals and the sale to New York State of the municipal water and sewer systems.

The last mayor to be re-elected to the post made his watchword 'How'm I doing?'; the current mayor, in meticulous fashion, pre-empted the question with charts and graphs that blazoned his news conferences. All that paper certainly created the perception of achievement, but the reality was a little more complex.

If the homeless are rarely seen on the streets of Manhattan these days, the city's public shelters are still overcrowded. A campaign that began in 1991 with the demolition of a shanty town in the East Village's Tompkins Square Park, reached its climax in the spring of 1997 with the bulldozing of a major homeless encampment in a group of Upper West Side railway tunnels. Advocates place the current homeless population at 100,000 and estimate that 20 per cent of that number are nomadic, camping under bridges and boardwalks in the outer boroughs and, in at least one case, in a crevice in the cliff walls on the Jersey side of the Hudson River over the Lincoln Tunnel.

Other claims were just as muddied. While crime rates have fallen, police relations with minority communities have soured in the wake of several highly publicised incidents of excessive force. The city's brief flirtation with the idea of police use of hollow-point (dum-dum) bullets, that expand on impact, turned out to be a public relations disaster and was swiftly withdrawn.

In schools, maths scores are up, but so are class sizes, while reading scores and spending per pupil is down. The Sanitation Department's claim that the streets are cleaner is seriously disputed by a *New York Times* study. The city's own figures indicate that Fire Department response times are down. All studies agree that AIDS deaths are down but the number of new cases holds steady.

The Giuliani administration's unprecedented secretiveness clouded the debate even further. Requests from a variety of news organisations and public service groups for what had formerly been considered routine information on government activity have been regularly denied. While the city finds itself sued, and losing, on Freedom of Information Act grounds, the official stance remained that they are, as the mayor put it, 'actually working, rather than spending their time answering questions'.

## WHO RUNS NY?

New Yorkers would suffer plenty of heat and occasional light in the mayoral election campaign of 1997. One thing that was immediately apparent was the city's continuing divisions along ethnic lines, splitting the Democratic opposition and strengthening the incumbent's hand.

Extremely well-funded and with an immense public relations machine, the mayor was a heavy favourite for re-election. He may not be well-loved – he's often abrasive and positively seethes with rectitude – but New Yorkers have a deep vein of self-distrust. It will be no surprise if they once again vote to keep a disciplinarian in charge of their most unruly town.

**DREAM ON**

New York still palpitates with enormous energy but it is multi-faceted and multi-directional. In everything from art to politics, the centre has long since given way. A long period of social instability has ended in a new consolidation of tension. Neither the dream of a Great Society nor the individualistic ethos of Reaganism stirs the population. Whether this reflects moral fatigue or a new maturity is impossible to say. If the old idols lie shattered and no single vision dominates, at least the field is clear for something new. High rollers on Wall Street plan the next mega-merger; downtown artists push the aesthetic envelope; and everyone else hopes just to keep it together. As ever, the streets of New York are paved with dreams, great and small, but dreams nonetheless.

# The new order

The catchphrase of the day in New York's public discourse, one much bandied about in the 1997 mayoral campaign, is 'quality of life'. That quality is chiefly determined in New York by the activity of the streets and, until recently, the city's streets seemed to be coming apart at the seams. Night-time sidewalks were littered with portable shantytowns of cardboard. Insane outbursts of daylight theatre from wandering schizophrenics were a normal part of a trip to the market. Beggars roamed the subways and petty drug merchants openly worked the public squares.

It's probably fair to say that New Yorkers feel more secure these days, though the inconveniences, indignities and injustices still occur, if less commonly. These modest facts are the basis of an incessant barrage of self-promotion on the part of the city administration. The crown jewel of their case is a significant drop in the murder rate but they also claim credit for a sea-change in the public mood.

Quality of life as it is now understood, stems from the adoption by Mayor Giuliani's first commissioner of police, William Bratton, of the 'broken window' theory of crime. This holds that aggressive enforcement of laws concerning petty misdemeanors leads to the prevention of more serious crime – if one window in a building is broken and goes unrepaired, all the windows will be broken eventually.

More concretely, arrests for minor crimes like jumping turnstiles in the subways, the theory goes, instills a sense of public order, takes a criminally-inclined individual off the street and, often enough, results in the seizure and removal of an unlicensed handgun.

The effort to eliminate the signs of anarchy in everyday life can be traced back to Mayor Edward Koch's mid-1980s war on graffiti. In a

period when crack cocaine and AIDS spiralled out of control, the city did manage to suppress that most visible form of underclass expression – literally, the writing on the walls. The ill-fated Dinkins administration witnessed the two plagues at their peak, as well as a period of extreme racial and ethnic tension. In a time of governmental downsizing, Dinkins managed to significantly increase the size of the police force but was driven from office before any results were effected.

The Giuliani crackdown includes public alcohol consumption, public urination, panhandling, and assorted street hustles. It has also targeted a number of street artists (who plan a lawsuit on free speech grounds) and some of the city's more outrageous night clubs.

Unquestionably, New York's murder rate has dropped, though there may be other contributing factors. And certainly, those parts of the city frequented by tourists and the well-to-do are cleaner and safer. At the same time, no one can argue that poverty and homelessness have been eradicated. The suspicion endures that quality of life is for those who can afford it.

# New York by Neighbourhood

# Downtown

**From the vibrant Village to the stuffed wallets of Wall Street, downtown is where contrasts are concentrated.**

New York City grew upwards from its southern tip, leaving the richest and most diverse concentration of places and people in the area below 14th Street. Here the streets are crooked, made for walking, and have names, not numbers. This is the place most visitors concentrate on, wandering from the architectural wonderland of the Financial and Civic Center, through the pretensions of SoHo and the vivid ethnicities of the Lower East Side, to the 'punk's-not-dead' spirit of the East Village and the café society of Greenwich Village.

## The Seaport

Though it now wears many faces, New York was always a port, its fortune built by the salt water that crashes around its natural harbour. It was perfectly placed for trade with Europe – with goods from middle America reaching the city via the Erie Canal and Hudson River. And as New York was the point of entry for millions of immigrants, its character was formed primarily by the waves of humanity that arrived at its docks.

The **South Street Seaport**, an area of reclaimed and renovated buildings given over to shops, restaurants, bars and a museum, is where you'll best see this seafaring heritage. Though the shopping area of Pier 17 is not much more than a picturesque mall of gift shops by day and an after-office yuppie watering hole by night, the other piers are crowded with antique vessels. The **Seaport Museum** – detailing New York's maritime history – is fascinating and well presented. The Seaport's public spaces are a favourite with street performers; there's a season of outdoor concerts through the summer. The **Fulton Market** building (with gourmet food stalls and seafood restaurants that expand onto the cobbled streets in summer) is a great place for slurping oysters as you watch tourists scurry by.

There are fine views of the **Brooklyn Bridge** just to the north (*see chapter* **Sightseeing**) and plenty of restored nineteenth-century buildings, including Schermerhorn Row, constructed on landfill in 1812. **Fulton Fish Market**, America's largest, is here too, though the fish come in by road and the market lives under the constant

*Gotham Gothic: the ornate lobby of the* **Woolworth Building**. *See page 86.*

threat of relocation. Organised crime has always had a presence here and may have had something to do with the fire that damaged much of the area in 1996. Still, the district continues to thrive. If you wish to continue with a salt-water theme to your day, Pier 16 is where to find the tour boats of **Seaport Liberty Cruises** (*see chapter* **Sightseeing**).

### Fulton Fish Market

*South Street, at Fulton Street (669 9416 tour information).* **Open** midnight-9am daily. **Tours** *Apr-Oct* 6am first and third Thur of the month. **Tour tickets** $10; reservations required. **Credit** AmEx, MC, V.

### Seaport Museum

*See chapter* **Museums** *for listings.*

### South Street Seaport

*Water Street to the East River, between John Street & Peck Slip (for information about shops and special events call SEA PORT/732 7678). Subway 2, 3, 4, 5, J, M or Z to Fulton Street.*

## Battery Park

The southern tip of Manhattan is where you are most conscious of being on an island. The Atlantic breeze blows in from the bay, taking the route of the millions who arrived here by sea: past the golden torch of the **Statue of Liberty** (*see chapter* **Sightseeing**), over the immigration and quarantine centre of **Ellis Island** (now a splendid museum) and on to the promenade of **Battery Park**, with its ranks of coin-operated telescopes and numerous statues. It's not unusual to see marquees and circus big tops here, as the park often plays host to international touring events such as the Cirque du Soleil (*see chapter* **Children**). Free outdoor music is often a feature of summer evenings here as well.

**Castle Clinton**, inside the park, was originally built during the Napoleonic wars when New York felt threatened by the British it had just thrown

# Black leather Broadway

You could do worse for a slice of contemporary New York bohemia, youth division, than a Saturday night pub crawl along Avenue A. From Tompkins Square Park (scene of police/squatter street battles in the mid-1980s) south to Houston Street, this is Slackerville.

New boho hang-outs line the street, from **Nice Guy Eddie's** at No 5, with its retro-nuevo 'Greatest Hits of the 1970s' jukebox and **2A's** lit-crit pick-up scene (corner of 2nd Street), to **Wally's** lo-fi fusion vibe and **Brownie's** alterna- and grunge bands (No 112, at East 7th Street and No 169, between 10th & 11th Streets). You can make a detour around the park and find another string of cantinas along the way. Local cuisine tends to be either Polish or sushi, and while no one has yet concocted a hybrid form, **Doc Holliday's**, a redneck-themed eatery with 'nouveau Vietnamese' food, comes close (No 141).

On a busy night, the strip is a very white, vaguely post-modern collegiate and it's clear that gentrification has arrived. One block already sports a pan-Asian bistro next to an organic market, across the street from a multi-culti pizza and indie-style video complex. Some of the new or newly renovated housing offers on-line capability built in.

The emergence of Avenue A reflects the inexorable eastward creep of downtown gentrification. An immigrant enclave since the 1840s (and host at different times to such proto-bohemians as Edgar Allan Poe and Emma Goldman), the Lower East Side was home to a mixed population

of white immigrants and Puerto Ricans when the first wave of Beats, drawn to the lowest rents in the city, arrived in the 1950s. Their legacy of avant-gardism made the East Village the natural home of the New York counterculture of the 1960s, then the punk No Wave of the 1970s. Now a revived, post-Reaganite, art student/deviant culture has cut a further ethnic swathe in the area.

South of Houston Street and east of the Bowery, where the streets are grittiest and a Latino presence still predominates, is the current frontier of downtown bohemia. The anarchist arts collective at **ABC No Rio** has been fighting off eviction notices here since 1980 (156 Rivington Street, between Clinton and Suffolk Streets), and several cutting edge performance spaces (Surf Reality at 172 Allen, Collective Unconscious, Nada, and Expanded Arts on Ludlow) have lately taken root. Hipster bars, led by the venerable **Max Fish** (*see chapter* **Cafés & Bars**), now line Ludlow Street, and local journals already speak of the area as the next SoHo.

The Chinese blocks south of here, where Chinatown long ago spilled over its old boundaries, probably have the economic clout to stave off any such Anglicisation, but the Puerto Rican and Dominican enclave to the east is already starting to give way. Their presence may be reduced but, like the Italian-Americans of that older bohemian settlement, Greenwich Village, it will never be eradicated. It's nice to think there'll always be some salsa in the late night air of the Lower East Side.

*The graves of New York's founding fathers overlooked by skyscrapers in Trinity Churchyard.*

out. It has been a theatre and an aquarium, and now it's a National Parks visitors' centre with historical displays. This is where you buy your tickets for The Statue of Liberty and Ellis Island.

Round the shore to the east is where you catch the famous **Staten Island Ferry**, now free, and a great way to capture the wonder of arriving by sea (*see* **Tours** *in chapter* **Sightseeing**). The historic terminal was destroyed by fire, and a replacement is yet to be built, but next door is the beautiful Battery Maritime Building, terminal for the many ferry services that sailed between Manhattan and Brooklyn in the years before the Brooklyn Bridge was built.

North of Battery Park is the triangle of **Bowling Green**, the city's first park and home to the beautiful Beaux Arts **US Custom House**, now the fascinating **National Museum of the American Indian**. Near here is Arturo DiModica's dynamic bronze bull sculpture that represents the snorting power of Wall Street, as well as the **Shrine of Elizabeth Ann Seton** (7-8 State Street), a strange curved building in the Federal style (1793), dedicated to the first American-born saint. Also nearby is the **Fraunces Tavern Museum**, a restoration of the alehouse where Washington celebrated his victory against the British, now a museum of revolutionary New York and a restaurant (*see chapters* **Architecture** *and* **Museums**).

## Civic Center

The business of running New York takes place among the many grand buildings of the **Civic Center**. Originally this was the city's focal point, and when **City Hall** was built in 1812, its architects were so confident the city would grow no further north, they didn't bother to put any marble on its northern side (*see chapter* **Architecture**). The building, a beautiful blend of Georgian formality, Federal detailing and French Renaissance influences, sits in its own area of green: **City Hall Park**. In 1776, the park was where the Declaration of Independence was read to Washington's army. You're still likely to see city officials giving press interviews here, as well as political protests and rallies of every sort.

The much larger **Municipal Building**, which faces City Hall and reflects it architecturally, is home to the overspill of civic offices, including the marriage bureau which can churn out newly-weds at remarkable speed. **Park Row**, east of the park and now populated by an array of cafés and stereo shops, used to be known as 'Newspaper Row', and once held the offices of 19 daily papers. It was also the site of Phineas T Barnum's sensationalist American Museum, which burnt down in 1865.

Facing the park from the west is Cass Gilbert's famous **Woolworth Building** (1913; Broadway at Park Place), a vertically elongated Gothic cathedral of an office building that has been called 'the Mozart of Skyscrapers'. Its beautifully detailed lobby is open to the public during working hours. Two blocks down Broadway is **St Paul's Chapel**, an oasis of peace, modelled on London's St Martin-in-the-Fields in 1766, and one of the few buildings left from the century of British rule.

Civic Center is also the focus of crime and punishment. Here you'll find the **New York County Courthouse** (1926; 60 Centre Street), a hexagonal building with a beautiful interior rotunda, and the **United States Courthouse** (1933; 40 Centre Street), a golden pyramid-topped tower above a Corinthian temple, both overlooking Foley Square.

Back next to City Hall, the Old New York County Courthouse, more popularly known as the **Tweed Courthouse**, was a symbol of the runaway corruption of mid nineteenth-century city government, as Boss Tweed, leader of the political strong-arm faction Tammany Hall, pocketed $10 million of the building's soaring $14 million cost. But you can't spend that much and fail to get a beautiful building. Though symbolic of immense greed, its Italianate detailing is of the very best.

The **Criminal Courts Building** (1939; 100 Centre Street) is by far the most intimidating of them all. Great Babylonian slabs of granite give it an awesome presence, emphasised by the huge judgemental towers guarding the entrance. This Kafka-esque home of justice has been known since its creation as 'the Tombs', a reference not only to its architecture but to the deathly conditions of the city jail it once contained.

All of these courts are open to the public (9am-5pm Mon-Fri), though only some of the courtrooms will allow visitors. Your best bet for a little courtroom drama is the Criminal Courts, where if you can't slip into a trial you can at least observe the hallways full of seedy-looking lawyers and the criminals they are representing.

## Wall Street

From New York's earliest days as a fur trading post to its place today at the hub of international finance, commerce has always been the backbone of the city's prosperity. Wall Street is the thoroughfare synonymous with the world's greatest capitalist gambling den.

It took its name from a defensive wall the Dutch settlers built and which, for a long time, marked the city's northern limits. In the days before speedy telecommunications, financial institutions crowded their headquarters here to be near the action. This was where corporate America made its first architectural assertions – there are many great buildings built here by grand old banks and businesses. Some notable ones are the **Citibank Building** (1842; 55 Wall Street), a colonnaded lesson in the Greek orders;

the **Equitable Building** (1915; 120 Broadway), whose greedy use of vertical space inspired the zoning laws governing skyscrapers; and the **Cunard Building** (1921; 25 Broadway), the beautiful domed ticket office for the grand shipping company, now a post office.

At the western end of Wall Street is the Gothic spire of **Trinity Church**, once the island's tallest structure, but now dwarfed by skyscrapers. A block east is the **Federal Hall National Monument**, a Doric shrine to American constitutional history and the place where Washington became the country's first President.

Across the street is the **New York Stock Exchange**, though its grand frontage and public entrance are around the corner on Broad Street. The visitors' centre here is excellent for educating the clueless in the workings of financial trading, and lets you look out over the trading floor in action. It's all computerised these days, so except for crashes and panics, none too exciting as a spectator sport (for the buy! buy! buy! action you've seen in the movies, you want the far more frenzied **Commodities Exchange**; *see below*).

The **Federal Reserve Bank**, a block north on Liberty Street, is the world's largest gold depository (you saw Jeremy Irons clean it out in *Die Hard 3*), holding bullion for half the countries of the world. This Florentine palazzo-fort is where they print money; the origin of any banknote with a big B next to its president. Take an empty canvas bag for the guided tour...

As you'd expect, the Wall Street area is fairly deserted outside office hours, though the empty expanses of concrete and pavement make it a night-time magnet for young daredevils on skateboards. The time to see it is around midday when the suits emerge for their hurried lunches. Join them in stopping for a burger at the ultimate **McDonald's** (160 Broadway). By some quirk of individualism, it boasts liveried doormen, a special dessert menu and a Liberace-style pianist.

### Federal Reserve Bank

*33 Liberty Street, between William & Nassau Streets (720 6130)*. **Open** by appointment only. **Admission** free.
The free one-hour tours through the bank must be arranged at least one week in advance; tickets are sent by post.

### New York Stock Exchange

*20 Broad Street, at Wall Street (656 5168 )*. Subway 4 or 5 to Wall Street. **Open** 9am-4.30pm Mon-Fri. **Admission** free.
A gallery overlooks the trading floor, and there are lots of multimedia exhibits.

### Trinity Church Museum

*Broadway, at Wall Street (602 0872/0768)*. **Open** 9-11.45am, 1-3.45pm, Mon-Fri; 10am-3.45pm Sat; 1-3.45pm Sun (closed during concerts). **Admission** free.
The small museum inside features exhibits on the history of the church and its place in New York's history.

## World Trade Center & Battery Park City

The area to the west of Wall Street extends the city's financial district with grand developments that combine vast amounts of office space with new public plazas, restaurants and shopping areas. There have been concerted efforts to inject a little cultural life into these spaces, and plenty of street performers work the area in summer months, though the general atmosphere is defined by the schedule of the working day.

The **World Trade Center** is actually six buildings, though to most visitors it means the famous twin towers that dominate the downtown skyline (*see chapter* **Sightseeing**). Visit the observation deck – on good days you can walk outside – and spare a thought for the crazies who have suction-climbed the walls, parachuted off the top floor or walked a tightrope between the two towers. It's the city's tallest structure and, until Chicago's Sears Tower was completed, also held the world height record. Building number four contains the **Commodities Exchange**, a great free floorshow.

Across the highway of West Street is **Battery Park City**, built on landfill generated by the excavations for the World Trade Center's foundations. This is partly residential, housing, among others, wealthy Wall Streeters whose high rents go to subsidise public housing elsewhere in the city. The beautiful new park here links Battery Park with the piers to the north, which are slowly being claimed for public use, allowing you to spend a pleasant afternoon strolling along the riverside from Manhattan's southern tip right up to Christopher Street, in the company of rollerbladers and cuddling couples.

The **World Financial Center**, the development's centrepiece, is the ultimate expression of the city-within-a-city concept. Crowned by Cesar Pelli's four elegant postmodern office towers, it contains an upmarket retail area, a marina and a series of plazas with terraced restaurants. The stunning vaulted glass-roofed Winter Garden, with its indoor palm trees, has become a popular venue for concerts and other entertainment, most of which are free (for more information, *see chapter* **Music**).

### Commodities Exchange
*Ninth Floor, 4 World Trade Center (748 1006).* **Open** 10.30am-3pm Mon-Fri. **Admission** free.
The Stock Exchange can be a little undramatic in these days of computerised trading, but not the Commodities Exchange. This is where manic figures in colour-coded blazers scream and shout at each other as they buy and sell gold, pork bellies and orange juice. There are three tours a day, at 11am, 1pm and 3pm; book two weeks in advance.

### Lower Manhattan Cultural Council
*(432 0900).*
Information on all sorts of cultural events happening in and around this part of lower Manhattan.

*Snacking it in Chinatown.*

### World Financial Center
*West Street to the Hudson River (945 0505). Subway 1, 2, 3, 9, A, C or E to Chambers Street.* **Admission** free. Phone for information about the many free arts events.

## Lower East Side

The Lower East Side tells the story of New York's immigrants: the cycle of one generation making good and moving to the suburbs, leaving space for the next wave of hopefuls. It is busy and densely populated, a patchwork of strong ethnic identities; great for dining and exploration. Today, outside **Chinatown** and **Little Italy** (which, strictly speaking, are part of this area), Lower East Side residents are largely Asian or Hispanic – Puerto Rican and Dominican – though the area is more famous for its earlier settlers, most notably as a Jewish stronghold, full of people from Eastern Europe.

It was here that mass tenement housing was built to accommodate the nineteenth-century influx. The original insanitary, overcrowded buildings forced the introduction of building codes. To appreciate the conditions in which the mass of immigrants lived, take a look at the reconstructions at the **Tenement Museum**.

Between 1870 and 1920 hundreds of synagogues and religious schools were established here, Yiddish newspapers were published and associations for social reform and cultural studies flourished. Now only 10-15 per cent of the population is Jewish. **Congregation Anshe Slonim**

(172 Norfolk Street), the city's oldest synagogue, is now a condominium, and the **Eldridge Street Synagogue** finds it hard to round up the ten adult males required to conduct a service.

Instead, the area today is characterised by its large Hispanic population. *Bodegas* or corner groceries abound, with their brightly coloured awnings, and there are many restaurants serving Puerto Rican dishes of rice and beans with fried plantain, pork chops and chicken. In the summer, the streets ring with the sounds of salsa and merengue as the residents hang out drinking beer and playing dominoes.

But in turn these people are being nudged by what could be described as the latest immigrants: the growing population of young artists, musicians and other rebels, attracted by the area's high drama and low rents. **Ludlow Street** is the main drag for these folk – an East Village extension with an increasing number of interesting shops, small clubs and hip bars, including the intriguing **Max Fish** (*see page 85 and chapter* **Cafés & Bars**).

Some remnants of the neighbourhood's Jewish traditions remain. **Ratner's**, at 138 Delancey Street, is a kosher dairy restaurant that has become a New York institution. The shabby **Sammy's Roumanian** (157 Chrystie Street) is for those with strong stomachs. Hearty servings of East European food come with a jug of chicken fat on the side – but it's one of the most famous of the Lower East Side eateries. On a lighter note, **Katz's Deli**, on the corner of Ludlow and East Houston Streets, sells some of the best pastrami in New York, and the orgasms are pretty good, too, if Meg Ryan's performance in *When Harry Met Sally* is anything to go by – the scene was filmed in Katz's. For all three, *see chapter* **Restaurants**.

### Eldridge Street Synagogue
*12-14 Eldridge Street (219 0888). Subway F to East Broadway.* **Open** 11am-4pm Tue, Wed, Sun.
A beautifully decorated, and now restored, building, the pride of the Jewish congregation that once filled it. Tours are at 11.30am and 2.30pm on Tuesdays and Thursdays.

### First Shearith Israel Graveyard
*55-57 St James Place, between Oliver & James Streets. Subway B or D to Grand Street.*
The burial ground of the oldest Jewish community in the United States – Spanish and Portuguese Jews who escaped the Inquisition. The earliest gravestones are dated 1683.

### Israel Israelowitz Tours
*(1-718 951 7072).*
Phone for details of guided tours of the Lower East Side, boat tours of Jewish New York and lecture programmes.

### Lower East Side Tenement Museum
*See chapter* **Museums** *for listings.*

### Schapiro's Winery
*126 Rivington Street (674 4404).* **Tours** on the hour, 11am-4pm Sun. **Admission** $1.
Schapiro's has been making kosher wine since 1899 ('so thick you can cut it with a knife'). The wine tours include tastings.

## Chinatown

Chinatown spills out beyond Canal Street and the Bowery, but its focal point is Mott Street. The New York version is far removed from the sanitised ones in San Francisco or London. More than 150,000 Chinese live and work here in a few score city blocks, and the feeling is of a very self-sufficient community. The busy streets get even wilder during the Chinese New Year festivities in January or February, and around 4th July when it is the city's source of (illegal) fireworks.

Food is everywhere. The markets on **Canal Street** sell some of the best fish, fruit and vegetables in the city. There are countless restaurants – Mott Street, from Worth right up to Kenmare Street, is lined with Cantonese and Sichuan places – and you can buy wonderful snacks from street stalls, such as bags of little sweet egg pancakes. Canal Street is also famous as a source of cheap imported trinkets and counterfeit designer items. From fake Rolexes to the cheapest 'brand-name' running shoes, it's a bargain-hunter's paradise.

A statue of Confucius marks **Confucius Plaza**, near the approaches of the Manhattan Bridge. On Bayard Street is the **Wall of Democracy**, where political writings are posted discussing events in Beijing. Through the open doors of the **Eastern States Buddhist Temple of America** comes the glitter of hundreds of Buddhas and the smell of incense.

A noisier place altogether is the **Chinatown Fair**, at 8 Mott Street, which is really nothing more than an amusement arcade. However, doors at the back lead to the **Chinese Museum**, a place of such mystery that it is virtually impossible to gain entry – 'only groups of eight', they say – but it is supposed to contain the dragon used in the New Year festival.

### Eastern States Buddhist Temple of America
*64B Mott Street, between Canal & Bayard Streets (966 6229). Subway 4, 5, 6 or N to Canal Street.* **Open** 9am-7pm daily.

## Little Italy

In common with the other parts of the Lower East Side, Little Italy is a vivid pocket of ethnicity, with the sights and sounds of the mother country turned up full. It's getting smaller, though, as the neighbourhood is eaten away by the growth of Chinatown and by an Italian exodus to the suburbs. Really all that's left of the Italian community which has lived here since the mid-nineteenth century are the cafés and restaurants on Mulberry, between Canal and East Houston, and short sections of cross streets. There is, however, a strong ethnic pride, and limo-loads of Italians parade in from Queens and Brooklyn to show their love for the old neighbourhood during the **Feast of San Gennaro** each September (*see chapter* **New York by Season**).

The restaurants here are mostly pricey and ostentatious grill and pasta houses. Even if you choose to eat elsewhere, make your after-dinner destination one of the smaller cafés lining the streets serving rich desserts and coffee.

As you'd expect, there are great food stores (good strong cheeses, excellent wines, spicy meats, freshly made pasta and so on), and the iconic **Forzano Italian Imports**, at 128 Mulberry, best place in New York for papal souvenirs, espresso machines, ghastly Italian pop music and football memorabilia.

Two buildings of note here are **Old St Patrick's Cathedral** (1863; 264 Mulberry Street), which was once the premier Catholic church of New York but was demoted when the Fifth Avenue cathedral was consecrated, and the **Police Building** (1909; 240 Centre Street). Once the headquarters for the city's police, this has now been converted into much sought-after co-operative apartments.

## SoHo

SoHo is designer New York, in all senses of the word. Walk around its cobbled streets, among the elegant cast-iron architecture, the boutiques, art galleries and bistros, and you'll find yourself sharing the sidewalks with the beautiful people of young, monied, fashionable NYC. The chic bars and eateries are full of these trend-setters, while the shop windows display the work of the latest arrivals in the world of art and fashion.

SoHo (South of Houston Street) was earmarked for destruction during the 1960s, but the area was saved by the many artists who inhabited its (then) low-rent ex-industrial spaces. They protested against the demolition of these beautiful buildings, whose cast-iron frames prefigured the technology of the skyscraper (*see chapter* **Architecture**). As loft-living became fashionable and the buildings were renovated for residential use, the landlords were quick to sniff gentrification's increased profits.

Surprisingly, plenty of sweatshops remain here, especially down towards Canal Street, carrying on the manufacturing for which these buildings were originally made. Increasingly, however, they house such businesses as graphics studios, magazines and record labels and there has been a noticeable invasion over the last few years by a number of large chain stores: Starbucks, Staples, Pottery Barn, J Crew, Williams-Sonoma and Banana Republic have all put down roots, leading locals to mutter darkly about the 'malling of SoHo'.

For an increasing number of more singular shops, head for the newly emerging area that borders SoHo, Chinatown and Little Italy (dubbed BoHo by some, for Bowery, south of Houston). *See* **Lafayette Street** *in chapter* **Shopping & Services** for more information.

West Broadway is the main thoroughfare of SoHo, lined with the chains, pricey shops and art galleries – the famous **Leo Castelli**, at 420 West Broadway, has recently upped its artiness. The **Guggenheim Museum** has a branch here (575 Broadway, at Prince Street), exhibiting both temporary collections and selections from the museum's permanent collection. In addition, Broadway has a collection of other galleries specialising in lesser-known artists. The **New Museum of Contemporary Art**, at 583 Broadway, is the young cousin of MoMA, while the **Alternative Museum**, at 594, and **Museum of African Art** next door are both worth a look. Just off Broadway on Spring Street (at number 279) is the **Fire Museum**, a small building housing a collection of gleaming antique engines dating back to the 1700s (*see chapters* **Museums** *and* **Art Galleries** for more details of all these).

## TriBeCa

TriBeCa (for <u>Tri</u>angle <u>Be</u>low <u>Ca</u>nal Street) illustrates very nicely the process of gentrification in lower Manhattan. It's very much like SoHo was about 15 to 20 years ago, with some parts deserted and abandoned – the cobbles dusty and untrodden and the cast-iron architecture chipped and unpainted – and other pockets throbbing with *arriviste* energy. In particular this is the place for new restaurants, with the occasional bar and club also working hard to establish itself.

The buildings here are generally larger than in SoHo and, especially towards the river, mostly warehouses. However, there is some fine smaller-scale cast-iron architecture along White Street and the parallel thoroughfares (*see chapter* **Architecture**), and **Harrison Street** is home to a row of well-preserved Federal-style townhouses.

As in SoHo, art is the new industry here, and there are several galleries representing the more experimental (read 'hit or miss') side of things. The view from the balcony of **The Clocktower** – the gallery of the Institute for Art and Urban Resources in the tower-rooms of the old New York Life Insurance Building (108 Leonard Street, at Broadway) – is as inspiring as the art inside is experimental (*see chapter* **Art Galleries**).

One famous TriBeCa tenant is Robert De Niro, whose **TriBeCa Film Center** at 375 Greenwich Street, the old Martinson Coffee Building, houses screening rooms and production offices and is home base to several prominent New York and visiting film makers. They dine, of course, at De Niro's **TriBeCa Grill** on the ground floor.

## Greenwich Village

Greenwich Village (call it 'the Village') has been the scene of some serious hanging-out throughout its history. Stretching from 14th Street down to Houston Street, and from Broadway west to the river, these leafy streets with their townhouses, theatres, coffee houses and tiny bars and clubs have witnessed and inspired Bohemian lifestyles for almost a century.

It's a place for idle wandering; for people-watching from street-side cafés, for candle-lit dining in secret restaurants, or for hopping between bars and cabaret venues, smoothing the night away. The place is overcrowded in summer, and has lost some of its charm as the retail centre of lower Broadway has spread west, but much of what attracted New York's creative types is here still.

The jazz generation lives on in smoky clubs like **The Blue Note** and **The Village Vanguard** (*see chapter* **Music**). Sip a fresh roast in honour of the Beats – Kerouac, Ginsberg and their ilk – as you sit in the coffee shops they frequented. Jack Kerouac's favourite was **Le Figaro Café** on the corner of MacDougal and Bleecker.

The hippies, who tuned-out in **Washington Square**, are still there in spirit, and often in person, as the square hums with pot dealers, musicians and street artists. Chess hustlers and students from the surrounding **New York University** join in, along with today's new generation of hangers-out: the hip-hop kids who drive down in their booming jeeps and the Generation Y skaters/ravers who clatter around the fountain and the base of the arch (a miniature Arc de Triomphe built in 1892 in honour of George Washington).

The Village first became fashionable in the 1830s, when elegant townhouses were built around Washington Square. Literary figures including Henry James, Mark Twain and Edith Wharton lived on or near the square, and Herman Melville wrote *Moby Dick* in a house at the northern reaches of the Village. In 1870 this growing artistic community founded the **Salmagundi Club**, America's oldest artists' club, which is still extant, just above Washington Square on Fifth Avenue.

The area continued to attract writers, and through prohibition and beyond, people like John Steinbeck and John Dos Passos passed the time at **Chumley's**, a speakeasy, still unmarked at 86 Bedford Street (*see chapter* **Cafés & Bars**). And the **Cedar Tavern** on University Place was where the leading figures of abstract expressionism discussed how best to throw paint. Jackson Pollock, Franz Kline and Larry Rivers drank there back in the 1950s. Eighth Street, now a long procession of punky boutiques, shoe shops, piercing parlours and cheap jewellery vendors, was the closest New York got to San Francisco's

Haight Street. Jimi Hendrix's **Electric Lady Sound Studios** is still here at No 52.

In the triangle formed by West 10th Street, Sixth Avenue and Greenwich Avenue you'll see the **Jefferson Market Courthouse,** a neo-Gothic Victorian pile once voted America's fifth most beautiful building. It's now a library. Across the street is **Balducci's** (*see chapter* **Shopping & Services**), one of the finest food stores in the city, and down Sixth Avenue at 4th Street you stumble on the outdoor basketball courts where some of the hottest free sports action can be witnessed (*see chapter* **Sports & Fitness**).

The western reaches of the Village (the area beyond Seventh Avenue is known as the West Village) are quaint tree-lined streets of historic houses. This is also a famously gay area, centred on **Christopher Street**, the scene of the 1969 Stonewall riots marking the birth of the gay liberation movement. There are as many same-sex couples strolling along Christopher as straight ones, and plenty of shops, bars and restaurants that are out and proud (*see chapter* **Gay & Lesbian New York**).

### Salmagundi Club

*47 Fifth Avenue, near 12th Street (255 7740).* **Open** for exhibitions only; phone for details. **Admission** free. Now the home of a series of artistic and historical societies, the club's fine nineteenth-century interior is worth a look.

## East Village

The East Village is far scruffier than its western counterpart, housing today's young bohemians, rather than the grown-up variety. East of Broadway between 14th and Houston Streets, and until recently considered part of the Lower East Side, it's where you'll find an amiable population of punks, hippies, homeboys, homeless and unproductive trustafarians. This motley crew co-exists with older residents surviving from various waves of immigration, and provides the area with cheap but interesting clothes stores (check for quality before handing over any cash), record shops, bargain meals, grungey bars and punky clubs.

**St Mark's Place** (another name for East 8th Street), with bars squeezed into tiny basements and restaurants overflowing onto the sidewalks, is the centre of all this. It's packed until the early hours with crowds browsing in cheap boutiques, comic shops, bargain record stores and bookshops. The more interesting places are off to the east, and you'll find some great little shops and cafés along Avenue A and on or about 10th Street.

**Astor Place**, with its revolving cube sculpture, is where Peter Cooper built **Cooper Union** in 1859, the city's first free educational institute, and now a design school. This marked the boundary between the ghettos to the east and some of the city's most fashionable homes, such as **Colonnade Row**, on Lafayette Street. Facing

these was the distinguished Astor Public Library, now Joseph Papp's **Public Theater**, a haven for first-run American plays and home of the New York Shakespeare Festival (*see chapter* **Theatre**). Papp rescued the library from demolition and had it declared a landmark.

East of Lafayette on the Bowery is the famous **CBGB** club ('Country, Blue-Grass, Blues'), the birthplace of American punk, still packing in guitar bands new and used (*see chapter* **Music**). Many other local bars and clubs successfully apply the formula of cheap beer and loud music, including **The Continental**, **Brownies** and **Under Acme**.

East 7th Street is a Ukrainian stronghold, centred on the Byzantine-looking **St George's Ukrainian Catholic Church**, built in 1977 but looking at least a century older. Further along the street is **McSorley's Old Ale House**, the oldest drinking house in the city (or so it claims) and still serving just one kind of beer, a frothy brew made in the basement (*see chapter* **Cafés & Bars**).

On East 6th Street, between First and Second Avenues, is '**Little India**' (one of several in New York): there are about two dozen Indian restaurants side by side, the long-running rumour being that they all share a single kitchen. East 3rd Street between First and Second Avenues has more than its share of fat men on Harleys. The headquarters of the New York chapter of Hell's Angels is here.

Towards the East River are Avenues A to D, an area sometimes known as **Alphabet City**, for obvious reasons. Its largely Hispanic population is slowly being nudged eastward by the influx of young counterculture arrivals. The neighbourhood is famous for its heroin trade and, beyond Avenue B, can be dangerous at night. It's not without attractions, however: you can inflict your deathless verse on the audience at the **Nuyorican Poets' Café** (*see chapter* **Spoken Word**), a focus for the recent resurgence of espresso-drinking beatniks. It's famous for its 'slams', in which performance poets battle like rappers. **Tompkins Square Park** (7th to 10th Streets, between Avenues A and B), has long been a focus for political dissent and rioting. The latest uprising was in 1991, after the controversial decision to evict the park's squatters and renovate it to suit the taste of the area's increasingly affluent residents.

North of Tompkins Square, around First Avenue and 11th Street, are remnants of earlier communities: good Italian cheese shops, Polish restaurants, discount fabric shops, empty theatres and two great Italian pâtisseries. Visit **De Roberti's** (176 First Avenue) for delicious cakes and **Veniero's** (342 East 11th Street) for wonderful mini-pastries and butter biscuits.

### St Mark's-in-the Bowery

*131 East 10th Street, at Second Avenue (674 6377). Subway L to First Avenue.* **Open** 10am-6pm Mon-Fri.
St Mark's was built in 1799 on the site of a 1660 church on Peter Stuyvesant's farm. Stuyvesant, one of New York's first and most powerful governors, is buried here, along with most of his descendants. The church is now home to several arts groups and was the church in *The Group* where the wedding and funeral took place. Phone for details of the performances here.

# Midtown

**Where commuters and tourists crowd the streets by day, and the bright lights of Broadway beckon at night.**

Midtown, 14th to 59th Streets, is the city's engine room, powered by the hundreds of thousands of commuters who pour in each day. Most hotels are here and so are most of the 'tourist' tourists. By day it's a solid business district, with clothes manufacturing around Seventh Avenue and offices everywhere else. It's also where you'll find the department stores and classy retailers of Fifth Avenue and the Rockefeller Center. By night the area is all about big entertainment, with the neon of Times Square advertising all the Broadway shows, and restaurants of all kinds clamouring for the pre- and post-theatre crowds.

## Flatiron District

As diagonal Broadway meanders its way along Manhattan's length, it inspires a public square wherever it intersects with an avenue. Two such places, Union Square at 14th Street, and Madison Square at 23rd, used to mark the limits of a ritzy nineteenth-century shopping district known as **Ladies' Mile**. Extending along Broadway and west to Fifth Avenue, this was a collection of huge retail palaces attracting the 'carriage trade' of wealthy ladies buying the latest fashions and household goods from all over the world. The ground levels of most of these buildings have changed completely, making way for today's shops and restaurants, but the rest of their proud cast-iron façades still stand. The Fifth Avenue section has been rejuvenated over the past few years, and is where designers like Matsuda, Paul Smith and Armani showcase their wares.

The **Flatiron Building** – originally named the Fuller Building after its first owners – is famous for its triangular ground-plan and as the world's first steel-framed skyscraper (*see chapter* **Architecture**). It stands at the south of Madison Square, giving its name to the surrounding streets, an area also known as the photo district for its preponderance of studios, photo labs and wandering models.

**Madison Square** itself is rich in history. It was the site of PT Barnum's Hippodrome and the original Madison Square Garden, the scene of prize fights, society duels and lavish entertainment intertwined with celebrity scandal. Today, these are gone, leaving a scruffy park surrounded by imposing buildings such as the **Metropolitan Life Insurance Company** (1893; Madison Avenue at 23rd Street), the **New York Life Insurance Company** (1928; 51 Madison Avenue at 26th Street) and the **Appellate Court** (1900; 27 Madison Avenue at 25th Street).

**Union Square** is named not after the Union of the Civil War but simply for the union of Broadway and Bowery Lane (now Fourth Avenue). It is raised to accommodate the subway beneath, and from the 1920s until the early 1960s, had a reputation as a political hotspot, a favourite location for rabble-rousing oratory. These days the area has been gentrified. It's home to a regular farmers' market on Wednesdays and Saturdays. The square is a popular meeting point, with a chic hang-out clothes shop on its western edge and the bargain bonanza of 14th Street's downmarket retail centre extending west, offering cheap clothes and electronics (*see chapter* **Shopping & Services**).

### Union Square
*Junction of Broadway, 14th-17th Streets, and Park & Fourth Avenues. Subway 4, 5, 6, L, N or R to Union Square.*

## Gramercy Park

You need a key to enter **Gramercy Park**, something possessed only by those who live in the beautiful townhouses which surround it – or who stay at the **Gramercy Park Hotel** (*listed in chapter* **Accommodation**). Anyone, however, can enjoy the tranquillity of the surrounding district, squeezed in between Third and Park Avenues. It was developed in the 1830s, copying the concept of a London square. **The Players**, at No 16, housed actor Edwin Booth, brother of Lincoln's assassin, John Wilkes Booth, and the foremost actor of his day. Booth had it remodelled as a club for the theatrical profession (it also had Churchill and Mark Twain as members). No 15 is the **National Arts Club**, whose members have often donated impressive works in lieu of their subscriptions. The resulting collection is on view several times a year.

**Irving Place**, leading south from the park to 14th Street, is named after Washington Irving, who didn't actually live here (his nephew did). It does have a literary past, though: **Pete's Tavern**, which claims to be the oldest bar in town, was where the New York wit O Henry wrote *The Gift of the Magi*.

West of Gramercy Park is a small museum of **Theodore Roosevelt's Birthplace**. To the east is the **Police Academy Museum**, where you can see hundreds of guns, including Al Capone's, and exhibitions describing gruesome murders and famous cases. The low, fortress-like building of the **69th Regiment Armory** (Lexington Avenue at 25th Street), now used by the New York National Guard, was where the sensational Armory Show was held in 1913. This introduced modern art – in the form of cubism, fauvism, the precocious Marcel Duchamp and other outrages – to the New World.

### National Arts Club

*15 Gramercy Park (475 3424). Subway 6 to 23rd Street.* **Open** for exhibitions only.

### Police Academy Museum

*235 East 20th Street, between Second & Third Avenues (477 9753). Subway 6 to 23rd Street.* **Open** 9am-2pm Mon-Fri. **Admission** free.

### Theodore Roosevelt Birthplace

*28 East 20th Street, between Broadway & Park Avenue South (260 1616). Subway 6 to 23rd Street.* **Open** 9am-5pm Wed-Sun. **Admission** $2 adults; free concessions. **No credit cards.**
The popular president's birthplace was demolished in 1916, but has since been fully reconstructed, complete with period furniture and a trophy room.

## Chelsea

Chelsea is the region between 14th and around 30th Streets, west of about Sixth Avenue. It is populated mostly by young professionals, and given New York's homocentric creative life, this makes Chelsea an increasingly gay place to be. You'll find all the trappings of an urban residential neighbourhood on the upswing: good diners, (mostly) dull shops and a generous sprinkling of bars and fine restaurants. Its western warehouse district has a grouping of the city's dance clubs, and is now being developed for residential use. However, pioneer galleries like the **Dia Center for the Arts** at the very end of 22nd Street, have dragged the arts crowd westward, and the whole area (with lower rents than SoHo) has lately emerged as a new gallery district (*see* **West Chelsea** *in chapter* **Art Galleries**).

Cushman Row (1840; 406-418 West 20th Street) in the **Chelsea Historic District** gives a good idea of Chelsea's appearance when first developed in the mid-1800s: a grandeur that was destroyed 30 years later when the noisy elevated railways came to steal the sunlight and dominate the area. Just north is the **General Theological Seminary**, its garden a sublime retreat. Over on Tenth Avenue, the flashing lights of the **Empire Diner** (an art deco beauty in chrome, 1929) attract pre- and post-clubbers (*see chapter* **Restaurants**).

Sixth Avenue around 27th Street can seem like a tropical forest at times, as the pavements are filled to overflowing with the palm leaves,

decorative grasses and colourful blooms of Chelsea's **Flower District.**. The garment industry has a presence hereabouts as well, spilling down from its centre a little further north.

The swank **Barneys**, one of New York's livelier department stores, though under threat of bankruptcy, is here on Seventh Avenue. Round the corner on 23rd Street is the **Chelsea Hotel** where many famous people checked in, several of them – like Sid Vicious's girlfriend Nancy Spungen – only to check out again (permanently). It's worth a peek, having plenty of weird artwork and ghoulish guests (*see chapter* **Accommodation**). On Eighth Avenue you'll find the **Joyce**, a stunning renovated art moderne cinema that's a mecca for dance lovers, and the wonderful **Bessie Schonberg Theater**, where mime and poetry play. Way out towards the river is **The Kitchen**, the experimental arts centre with a particular bent for video (*see chapters* **Dance**, **Film** *and* **Theatre**).

When you reach the Hudson River, you'll see the piers; derelict fingers raking out into the water. These were originally the terminals for the world's grand ocean liners (this was where the *Titanic* was heading when she sank). Most are in a state of disrepair, though development has transformed the four between 17th and 23rd Streets into a dramatic sports centre and TV studio complex, **Chelsea Piers** (*see chapter* **Sport & Fitness**).

### Chelsea Historic District

*Between Ninth & Tenth Avenues and 20th & 21st Streets. Subway A, C or E to 14th Street.*

### General Theological Seminary

*175 Ninth Avenue, between 20th & 21st Streets (243 5150).* **Open** noon-3pm Mon-Fri; 11am-3pm Sat. **Admission** free.
You can walk through the grounds of the seminary (when open) or take a guided tour in summer (phone for details).

## Herald Square & the Garment District

Seventh Avenue around 34th Street has a second name: Fashion Avenue. Streets here are gridlocked permanently by delivery trucks. The surrounding area is the **Garment District**, where midtown office blocks mingle with the buzzing activity of a huge manufacturing industry. Shabby clothing and fabric stores line the streets (especially 38th and 39th), and there are intriguing shops selling only lace, or buttons, or Lycra swimsuits. Most are wholesale only, but some sell to the public.

**Macy's** will most definitely sell things to you, though its sales and bargains are no longer as dramatic as tourist legend might have it. A lot of

*Bumper-to-bumper on West 46th Street, otherwise known as Restaurant Row.*

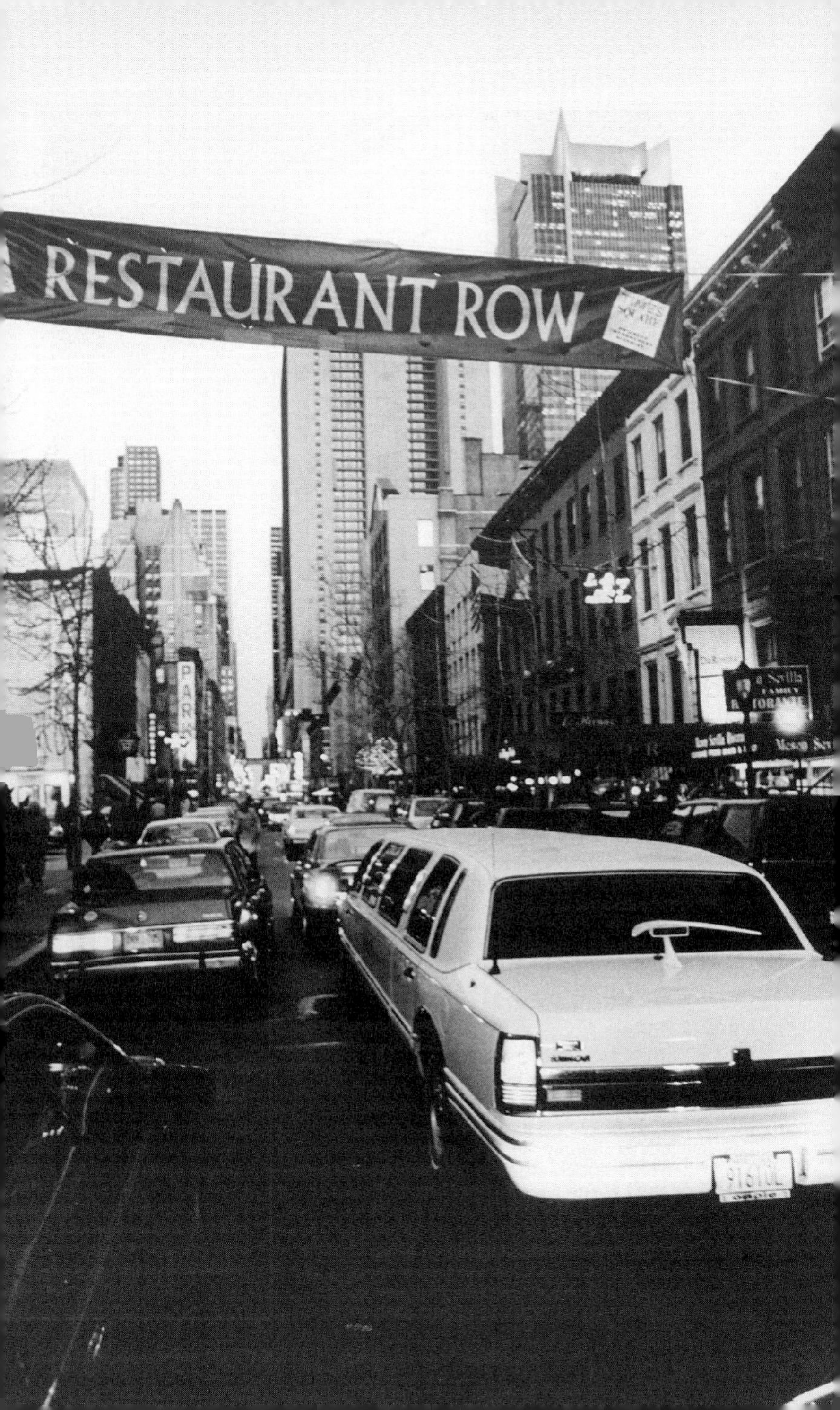
RESTAURANT ROW

what's on offer here is cheaper somewhere else, though Macy's will impress as the biggest department store in the world. **A&S Plaza** across the street is a phenomenally ugly building, resembling a neon and chrome jelly mould. However, this is good old American mall shopping at its best, and most of the big chains have an outlet here. This retail wonderland is **Herald Square**, named after a long-gone newspaper. The lower part is known as **Greeley Square** after the owner of the *Herald*'s rival, the *Tribune*, a paper in which Karl Marx wrote a regular column. *Life* magazine was based round the corner in 31st Street, and its cherubic mascot can still be seen over the entrance of what is now the **Herald Square Hotel**.

The famous sports and entertainment arena of **Madison Square Garden** is a block to the west, a giant doughnut of a building (*see chapter* **Sport & Fitness**). It occupies the site of the old **Pennsylvania Station**, McKim, Mead and White's architectural masterpiece which was destroyed by insane 1960s planners, an act which brought about the creation of the Landmarks Commission. The rail terminal is now underground, its name shortened to Penn Station, as if in shame. Thankfully, the **General Post Office** (1913), designed by the same prolific firm, still stands, an enormous colonnade occupying two city blocks.

**Herald Square**

*Junction of 34th Street, Broadway & Sixth Avenue. Subway B, D, F, N, Q or R to 34th Street.*

## Broadway & Times Square

The night is lit not by the moon and stars but by acres of moving neon. A monstrous television peers down, broadcasting its soundless message to the scurrying masses, making the place feel like a giant's brashly illuminated living room. Waves of people flood the streets as the blockbuster theatres disgorge their audiences. 'The centre of the world' is how it likes to describe itself, and there are few places that represent the collected power and noisy optimism of New York quite as well as **Times Square**.

It's really just an elongated intersection, but Broadway is here, the road and the idea – for this is the **Theater District**. It's home to 30 or so grand stages used for dramatic productions, plus probably 30 more that are now either peep shows, cinemas, nightclubs or just empty. The streets west of Seventh Avenue are where to find food. West 46th Street here is known as **Restaurant Row**, and has an almost unbroken string of them.

The cinematic lowlife of **42nd Street**, from Sixth Avenue west, has been increasingly neutralised. The sex industry is still here in force, but the video supermarkets and live peep shows share space with subsidised arts projects, and a giant Disney store – Mickey's squeaky-clean influence has gone a long (if perhaps regrettable) way towards sanitising the place. (*See* **A Walk on the Mild Side** *in chapter* **Sightseeing**).

As you'd expect, the offices here are full of entertainment companies: recording studios, theatrical management, record labels, screening rooms and so on. The **Brill Building**, 1619 Broadway, at 49th Street, has the richest history, having long been the headquarters of music publishers and arrangers. It's known as **Tin Pan Alley** (though the original Tin Pan Alley was West 28th Street). From here emerged the work of such names as Cole Porter, George Gershwin, Rodgers and Hart, Lieber and Stoller, and Phil Spector.

Close by is the **Hearst Magazine Building** at 959 Eighth Avenue, immortalised by inference as the newspaper headquarters of Orson Welles' Citizen Kane (Kane was, of course, based on print mogul William Randolph Hearst).

The great landmark on Broadway just south of Central Park is **Carnegie Hall** (*see chapter* **Music**). Nearby is the **Carnegie Deli**, the one of the city's most famous sandwich stops (*see chapter* **Restaurants**).

Moving west from Times Square, past the curious steel spiral of the Port Authority Bus Terminal's aerial bus park on Eighth Avenue, and the knotted entrance to the Lincoln Tunnel to New Jersey, is an area known as **Hell's Kitchen**. Formerly an impoverished Irish neighbourhood, it has now been given the more real-estate-friendly name of Clinton and attracts the forces of gentrification. There's also a little Cuban district, around Tenth Avenue and the mid-40s.

The main attraction here is the vast **Jacob K Javits Convention Center** on Twelfth Avenue between 34th and 38th Streets: an enormous four-block structure which hosts conventions and trade shows. Finally, there are the Hudson River piers. The **Circle Line** terminal is on Pier 83, level with 42nd Street, and at the end of 46th Street you'll find the aircraft carrier *Intrepid* and the **Sea, Air & Space Museum** it contains (*see chapter* **Museums**).

# Steam & the sidewalks

You've seen it in a hundred movies: a dramatic Manhattan street scene where strange vapours escape from manholes and billow around busy pedestrians and speeding yellow cabs. It's not a special effect. In fact, few things are more quintessentially New York than steam creeping upwards from the sidewalk.

Thomas Edison's company Consolidated Edison (Con Ed), the world's first electrical utility and still the name on New Yorkers' electricity bills, built the system in the 1890s. Even now it sells steam to more than 2,000 customers, mostly to heat large office blocks and apartment buildings. The company generates 10,400,000 pounds of steam per hour during winter, which hisses through a system of underground pipes at 500°F. Many of the original pipes are still in use and inevitable wear and tear means the steam occasionally bursts its way into the street. To preserve visibility and avoid injury the miasmic vapours are funnelled away from ground-level breaks by those striped Cat in the Hat-style plastic chimneys.

The New York steam system is the largest on the planet, and while it might seem like yet another example of New York lurching towards the Third World, since most of the steam is a by-product of Con Ed's electricity generation, it's more ecologically sound than most heating methods.

### Actors Studio

*432 West 44th Street, between Ninth & Tenth Avenues
(757 0870). Subway A, C or E to 42nd Street.* **Open**
9am-5pm Mon-Fri. **Admission** by appointment only.
Stars of the future perform at Lee Strasberg's famous acting
workshops. Obtain tickets from the International Theater
Institute (254 4141).

### Steinway Hall

*109 West 57th Street, between Sixth & Seventh Avenues
(246 1100). Subway N or R to 57th Street.*
**Open** 9am-6pm Mon-Fri; 9am-5pm Sat; noon-5pm Sun.
**Admission** free.
The showrooms of the famous piano company are fascinat-
ing, and there's a recital salon.

## The Glorious Fifth

There's a certain spot on Fifth Avenue where you
can look south and see the Flatiron Building, and
then turn to the north and still see the trees of
Central Park's bottom corner. This majestic
thoroughfare is New York's main street; the route
of the city's many parades and marches. With its
gentle slope, it passes through a region of chic
department stores and past some of the city's most
famous buildings and public spaces.

The **Empire State Building** (*see chapter*
**Sightseeing**) is at 34th Street. Though it's visible
over much of the city, only on this cross-street can
you see its height from top to bottom. At 39th
Street, **Lord & Taylor** is the first of the Avenue's
remaining grand department stores; and a block
north, impassive stone lions guard the steps of the
**New York Public Library**. This beautiful
Beaux Arts composition provides an astonishing
escape from the noise and traffic outside. Behind
the library is **Bryant Park**, once the site of New
York's own Crystal Palace (1853-58), now an
elegant formal lawn filled with lunching office

# A fine row

Mayor Giuliani, in an election-year outburst of
headline mongering, recently saw fit to engage
the UN in a very public row over diplomats'
unpaid parking fines, a subject dear to the
hearts of all automotive New Yorkers, to whom
parking space, especially in midtown, is a holy
grail. The mayor bowed to the higher authority of the State Department on the matter, grace-
lessly stating that his hands were tied but not
without speculation on the potential value of the
Secretariat for luxury housing, should the UN
feel compelled to pull up stakes. He failed to
mention that said diplomats pump an estimated
$1.5-$3.5 billion dollars into the local economy
annually. That's a lot of parking fines.

workers and with a busy schedule of free entertainment.

At 43rd Street there is the **Seth Thomas street
clock** for you to set your watch by. On the first
block of West 44th Street is the famous
**Algonquin Hotel**, where scathing wit Dorothy
Parker held court at Alexander Woollcott's Round
Table (*see chapter* **Accommodation**). The
**Iroquois** and the upstart **Royalton** hotels are also
here. 47th Street is known as **Diamond Row**. It's
here that the city's diamond trade is conducted, and
in front of glittering window displays you'll see the
many orthodox Jewish traders, precious gems in
their pockets, doing business in the street. Near
here (231 East 47th Street, but since demolished)
was where **Andy Warhol's Factory** enjoyed
most of its 15 minutes of fame.

Walk from Fifth Avenue into **Rockefeller
Center** (48th-51st Streets) and you will understand
the masterful use of public space for which this complex of buildings is so lavishly praised. You are
drawn down the Channel Gardens and gradually
the mass of the GE Building rises over you. At its
apex is the famous Rainbow Room restaurant and
bar; gathered round it are the lower blocks of the
International Building and its companions. Over on
the Sixth Avenue side is **Radio City Music Hall**,
built as the world's largest cinema, and the stark
towers of the much later Rockefeller Center Part II.

Across the street from Rockefeller's sweeping
lines is **St Patrick's Cathedral** (1878), a beautiful Gothic Revival structure and the largest
Catholic cathedral in the US.

In the 1920s, 52nd Street was 'Swing Street', a
row of speakeasies and jazz clubs. All that remains
is the 21 Club (at No 21), now a power lunching
spot. This street also contains the **Museum of
Television & Radio**. The **Museum of Modern
Art** is on 53rd Street, as is the **American Craft
Museum** (*see chapter* **Museums**).

The blocks of Fifth Avenue between
Rockefeller Center and Central Park contain
expensive retail palaces selling everything from
Rolex watches to gourmet chocolate. Here, in the
stretch between **Saks Fifth Avenue** (50th
Street) and **Bergdorf Goodman** (58th Street),
the rents are the highest in the world, and you'll
find such names as Cartier, Chanel, Gucci and
Tiffany's. Recently, however, some upstart neighbours have been joining them, including the
big themed outlets of the Warner Brothers and
Disney.

The pinnacle of this malling transformation has
to be the **Trump Tower**, Donald's soaring
chrome spire with its pink marble interior. Like an
episode of *Lifestyles of the Rich and Famous*, the
theme here is tasteless expenditure.

Fifth Avenue is crowned by **Grand Army
Plaza**, at 59th Street. A statue of General Sherman
presides over a public space with the sleek chateau

of the Plaza Hotel to the west and the General Motors building with the famous FAO Schwarz toy store at ground level.

### Grand Army Plaza
*Junction of Fifth Avenue & 59th Street. Subway N or R to Fifth Avenue.*

## Midtown East

Sometimes on New Year's Eve you can waltz in the great hall of **Grand Central Terminal** just as the enchanted commuters did in *The Fisher King*. This beautiful Beaux Arts station (an enormous $100 million renovation is due for completion some time in 1998), with the memories of muscular steam trains and lace-curtained carriages locked into its vaulted stone passageways, is surely the city's most spectacular point of arrival (though the constellations of the winter zodiac that adorn the ceiling on the main concourse were put on backwards). The station stands at the junction of 42nd Street and Park Avenue, the latter rising on a cast-iron bridge and literally running through the terminal.

Rising behind it, the **Met Life** (formerly Pan Am) building was once the world's largest office block. Its most celebrated tenants are the peregrine falcons that nest on the roof, living on a diet of pigeons which they kill in mid-air. On the other side of the Met Life tower is the **Helmsley Building**. Built by Warren and Whetmore, the architects responsible for Grand Central, its glittering gold detail presents a fitting punctuation to the vista south down Park Avenue.

On Park itself, amid the solid blocks of mansion-sized apartments, there's the Waldorf-Astoria Hotel (No 301), the sensation-causing glass Lever House (No 390), and the bronze and glass Seagram Building (No 375). On Madison is the IBM Building (at 56th Street), with one of the finest atrium lobbies. Across the street is the Sony (formerly the AT&T) Building, with its distinctive Chippendale crown. Inside are Sony's Public Arcade and Wonder Technology Lab, with hands-on displays of silicon stuff.

There's much of architectural interest on 42nd Street going east. Worth a look is the spectacular hall of the Bowery Savings Bank (at No 110); the Art Deco power and detail of the Chanin Building (No 122); the sparkling chromed Chrysler Building (at Lexington Avenue); and the Daily News Building (No 220), immortalised in the *Superman* films and still with a giant globe in its lobby.

The street ends with **Tudor City**, a pioneering 1925 residential development that looks like a sort of high-rise Hampton Court. North of here is an area known as **Turtle Bay**, though you won't see too many turtles in the East River today. This is dominated by the **United Nations**, and its famous glass-walled secretariat building. Though you don't need your passport, you are leaving US soil when you enter the UN complex – this is an international zone. Optimistic peacemongering sculptures are dotted around, and the **Peace Gardens** along the East River bloom with delicate avenues of rosebeds.

South of 42nd Street is a neighbourhood known as **Murray Hill**, still a fashionable address, but with only a few streets retaining the prettiness that made it so. Townhouses of the rich and powerful were clustered here around Park and Madison Avenues. **Sniffen Court**, at 150-158 East 36th Street, is an unspoilt row of carriage houses, within spitting distance of the ceaseless traffic of the Queens-Midtown Tunnel.

The charming, Italianate **Pierpont Morgan Library** is the reason most visitors come here. Two elegant buildings, linked by a glass cloister, house the silver and copper collections, manuscripts, books and prints owned by the famous banker, mostly gathered together during his travels in Europe (*see chapter* **Museums**).

### Grand Central Terminal
*42nd Street at Park Avenue. Subway 4, 5, 6 or 7 to Grand Central.*

# Uptown

**The Upper East Side has museums and glitzy shops; the Upper West Side has bookstores and a university. In common they have Central Park and immense wealth.**

At the end of the 1700s there wasn't much except farmland to be found this far north. Central Park is what made uptown desirable, turning country estates into Fifth Avenue mansions and seducing New York society into leaving the crowded streets downtown. The park's glorious green space, which is bigger than Monaco, will always dominate Manhattan life between 59th and 110th Streets. The neighbourhoods on either side are counterpoints: the east rich and respectable, full of 'establishment' fashion and museums; the west more intellectual, revolving around the academia of Columbia University to the north and the music and performance of Lincoln Center to the south.

## The Upper East Side

The Upper East Side is all about money. The greed and gold of New York high society resides in the mansions of Fifth and Park Avenues; old ladies and young trust-funders spend their spare change in Madison Avenue's plate-glassed boutiques; and rich businessmen use tax write-offs to fund the area's cultural institutions (which their families probably founded): the museums and societies of Museum Mile and beyond.

Once Frederick Law Olmstead and Calvert Vaux had wrenched the wondrous Central Park out of pestilential swampland (*see chapter* **Sightseeing**), fashionable New York felt ready to move north. In the mid-1800s the super-rich had built mansions along Fifth Avenue. By the beginning of this century, the merely rich had warmed to the – at first outrageous – idea of living in apartment buildings, provided they were near the park. Many grand examples of these were built along Park Avenue and the streets joining it to Fifth. Among the apartments sprang up the blossoms of tycoons' philanthropic gestures – the many art collections, museums and cultural institutes that attract most visitors to the area.

**Museum Mile** is actually a promotional organisation rather than a geographical description, but since most of the museums along Fifth Avenue are members, it is an apt name. The **Metropolitan Museum of Art**, set in Central Park, is the grandest of them all. Walking north from the steps of the Met, you reach the stunning spiral design of Frank Lloyd Wright's Guggenheim Museum at 88th Street; the National Academy of Design at 89th; the Cooper-Hewitt Museum – set in Andrew Carnegie's mansion – at 91st; the Jewish Museum at 92nd; and the International Center of Photography at 94 (see chapter Museums for all). The toy-town brick fortress façade at 94th and Madison is what's left of the old **Squadron A Armory**. Just off Fifth Avenue at 97th Street are the onion domes and rich ornamentation of the **Russian Orthodox Cathedral of St Nicholas** and a little further north are **El Museo del Barrio** (*see page 106*) and the **Museum of the City of New York**, at 104th and 105th Streets respectively.

There's another clump of museums near the south-east corner of Central Park. On Madison Avenue at 75th Street, the **Whitney Museum of American Art** occupies a brutal, looming cube by Marcel Breuer. The **Frick Collection**, an art-filled mansion, faces the park at 70th Street. A few blocks south is the **Society of Illustrators**.

The wealth concentrated in this area has also been used to found societies promoting interest in the language and culture of foreign lands. Rockefeller's **Asia Society** is on Park Avenue and 70th Street. Nearby are the **China Institute in America** and the **Americas Society**, dedicated to the nations of South and Central America. On Fifth Avenue is the **Ukrainian Institute** (at 79th), the **German Cultural Center** (at 83rd Street) and the **YIVO Institute for Jewish Research** (at 86th).

**Madison Avenue** used to be known as the home of the advertising industry. Now its reputation is more for ultra-expensive shops. Don't try shopping here unless you have some serious loot. This is the place to buy established designer labels – Yves Saint Laurent, Givenchy, Missoni, Geoffrey Beene. Rather than facing the cut and thrust of the Avenue, you could buy everything at **Bloomingdale's**, that frantic, glitzy supermarket of high fashion. There are also many commercial galleries hereabouts, including the Knoedler Gallery and Hirschl & Adler Modern. This is

*All that's left of the farm belonging to the president's daughter* **Abigail Adams Smith**, *now a museum. See page 102.*

where established artists such as Robert Rauschenberg and Frank Stella prefer to show, rather than down in the SoHo circus.

At 66th Street and Park Avenue is the **Seventh Regiment Armory**, whose interiors were designed and furnished by Louis Comfort Tiffany, assisted by a young Stanford White. It now houses the Winter Antiques show, among other events.

From Lexington to the East River, things become less grand. The **Abigail Adams Smith Museum**, at 421 East 61st Street near First Avenue, is a lovely old coach house dating from 1799, operated as a museum by the Colonial Dames of America. It was part of a farm owned by the daughter and son-in-law of John Adams, the second American President (*see chapter* **Museums**).

Kim Novak, Montgomery Clift, Tallulah Bankhead and Eleanor Roosevelt all lived a little bit further west in the tree-lined streets of three- and four-storey brownstones known as the **Treadwell Farm Historic District**, at 61st and 62nd Streets, between Second and Third Avenues.

The central building of **Rockefeller University** – from 64th to 68th Streets, on a bluff overlooking FDR Drive – is listed as a national historic landmark. The Founders' Hall dates from 1903, the year the university was established as a medical research centre. With the guard's permission, you may walk around the campus. Look out for the President's House and the domed Caspary Auditorium. Medical institutions, including the **New York Hospital/Cornell Medical Center**, into which the city's oldest hospital is incorporated, dominate the next few blocks of York Avenue.

### Seventh Regiment Armory

*643 Park Avenue, at 66th Street (452 3067). Subway 6 to 68th Street.* **Open** by appointment only.

### Society of Illustrators

*128 East 63rd Street, between Lexington & Park Avenues (838 2560). Subway B or Q to 63rd Street.*
**Open** 10am-8pm Tue; 10am-5pm Wed-Fri; noon-4pm Sat. **Admission** free.
Exhibitions featuring illustration are held regularly.

## Yorkville

The east and north-east parts of the Upper East Side are residential neighbourhoods inhabited by the young and professional (yes, yuppies). There are endless restaurants and bars here (including the super-swank **Elaine's** *see chapter* **Restaurants**), as well as gourmet food stores and, on streets like 86th, all the shops you could need.

Most of this area is known historically as **Yorkville**, extending from the 70s to 96th Street, east of Lexington Avenue. Once a pretty little hamlet on the banks of the river, Yorkville was predominantly a German stronghold. In the last decades of the nineteenth century, East 86th Street

became the Hauptstrasse, filled with German restaurants, beer gardens and pastry, grocery, butcher's and clothing shops. When World War II broke out, tensions naturally developed. Nazis and anti-Nazis clashed in the streets and a Nazi-American newspaper was published here. The European legacy includes the **Paprikas Weiss** shop (Second Avenue, betwen 81st and 82nd Streets) which sells 17 different varieties of coffee beans, among other things.

The famous comedy club Catch a Rising Star, where Robin Williams started out, has now moved to West 28th Street, but you can still have a good laugh at the **Comic Strip**, on Second Avenue near East 81st Street (*see chapter* **Cabaret**). This is where Eddie Murphy kicked off his career.

On East End Avenue at 86th Street is the **Henderson Place Historic District**, where 24 two-storey Queen Anne row (or terrace) houses – prettily decorated with turrets, double stoops and slate roofs – commissioned by fur dealer John C Henderson, still stand. Over the street is **Gracie Mansion**, New York's official mayoral residence and the only remaining Federal-style mansion in Manhattan still used as a home. The mansion is the focal point of the **Carl Schurz Park**, named in honour of the German immigrant, senator and newspaper editor. The park is remarkable for its tranquillity and offers spectacular views over the East River. Its long promenade, the John H Finley Walk, is one of the most beautiful in the city (especially in the early morning or at dusk).

### Gracie Mansion

*Carl Schurz Park, East 88th Street & East End Avenue (570 4751). Subway 4, 5 or 6 to 86th Street.* **Open** by appointment only.
This house became the official mayoral residence in 1942. The tour (phone for details) takes you through the mayor's living room, a guest suite and smaller bedrooms. One of the best things about it are the views down the river from this strategic site, where Washington built a battery during the war.

## Roosevelt Island

Roosevelt Island, the submarine-shaped island off the Upper East Side, was once called Welfare Island and housed a lunatic asylum, a smallpox hospital, prisons and workhouses. It now accommodates a largely residential community of 8,000 people, and is accessible by road from Queens. The red cable cars ('trams') that cross the East River from Manhattan to Roosevelt Island offer some of the very best views of Manhattan (embark at Second Avenue and 60th Street).

The Indians called the island Minnahanonck, or 'island place', then sold it to the Dutch, who made a vast creative leap and named it Hog's Island. The Dutch farmed it, as did Englishman Robert Blackwell, who moved here in 1686. His old clapboard farmhouse is in **Blackwell Park**, adjacent to Main Street (there's only one street – with several restaurants).

A new pier faces Manhattan, and there are numerous picturesque picnic spots. The recently opened **Octagon Park** includes tennis courts, hanging gardens and an ecological park. The riverfront promenades afford fabulous views of the skyline and East River, but the tram remains the biggest attraction: you've seen it in a host of films including, most recently, City Slickers. Wander down the **Meditation Steps** for river views, or take one of the riverside walks around the island. The latest addition to the island's attractions is the **Sculpture Center**, sited at Motorgate, the island's unusual transportation complex. Here, large outdoor work is displayed, many of the pieces inspired by features of the island.

On the southern tip are the weathered neo-Gothic ruins of **Smallpox Hospital** and the burned-out remains of **City Hospital**. The **Octagon Tower** is the remaining central core of the former New York City Lunatic Asylum.

Charles Dickens was a visitor and was disturbed by its 'lounging, listless, madhouse air'. In an early feat of investigative journalism, reporter Nellie Bly feigned insanity and had herself committed to the asylum for 10 days in 1887, and then wrote a shocking exposé of the conditions in the 'human rat trap'. The decaying buildings tend to crop up in rock videos.

### Roosevelt Island Operating Corporation

*591 Main Street (832 4540).* **Open** 9am-5pm Mon-Fri. Phone for details of events and free maps of the island.

## Upper West Side

The Upper West Side is a fairly affluent residential area, rich in cinemas, bars and restaurants, as well as bookstores and reclusive celebrities. Its reputation is serious, intellectual and politically liberal. European immigrants were attracted here in the late nineteenth century by the building boom sparked off by Central Park, as well as by Columbia University's new site to the north.

Because Americans can't deal with round-abouts, **Columbus Circle**, with its 700-ton statue of Columbus, is one of the most confused traffic junctions imaginable. The curved white marble slab on stilts here is New York City's **Department of Cultural Affairs**, location of the **New York Convention & Visitors Bureau**. West of the circle is The New York Coliseum. Apart from a few one-off events, it has been out of business since the Javits Convention Center was built in 1986. Donald Trump and other real estate moguls are in a heated contest to see who can grab the rights to new development in the area. On 68th Street there are 12 movies showing at Sony's new Lincoln Square theatre – with a huge 3D Imax screen as well, it's blockbuster heaven.

It's not unusual to see folk striding around here in evening dress. They've been to the **Lincoln Center**, a complex of concert halls and auditoriums that's the heart of classical music in the city. The different buildings are linked by sweeping public plazas and populated by sensitive musical types.

From the Lincoln Center Plaza you can see a small-scale replica of the **Statue of Liberty** on top of a building on West 64th Street. Round the corner, at 2 Lincoln Square, is the small but fascinating **Museum of American Folk Art**.

It took longer for the west side to become fashionable than it did for Fifth Avenue, but once the park was built, Central Park West soon filled up with luxury apartment blocks. Once well-off New Yorkers had re-adjusted themselves to living in 'French flats', as they called them, apartment living became almost desirable.

The art deco building at 55 Central Park West is best remembered for its role in Ghostbusters. On 72nd Street is the **Dakota**, most famous these days as the building outside which John Lennon was murdered. It's one of New York's first great apartment buildings, and the one that accelerated the drift to the west. Sceptical New Yorkers commented that it was so far away from the centre of town that it might as well be in Dakota. The developers defiantly took up the name and ordered decorative details straight out of the Wild West. Yoko Ono and other famous residents can be seen popping in and out. The massive twin-towered San Remo block at 74th Street dates from 1930 and is such prime real estate that even Madonna couldn't get an apartment here.

The **New York Historical Society**, the oldest museum in the country, is at 77th Street. Across the street, the **American Museum of Natural History** attracts visitors with its stuffed and mounted creatures, dinosaur skeletons, ethnological collections and the associated **Hayden Planetarium**, currently undergoing major renovation.

The avenues between Central Park West and Broadway – **Columbus** and **Amsterdam** – have long been gentrified and are full of restaurants,

shops, gourmet food outlets and fashion stores. The neighbourhood underwent a renaissance when the Lincoln Center was built, although a good few of the old inhabitants and shops remain.

On Broadway, the **72nd Street subway** is worth seeing for its Art Nouveau entrance. It's on Sherman Square, named after the general. The opposite triangle, at the intersection of 73rd and Broadway, is **Verdi Square**; a fitting name since – along with Arturo Toscanini and Igor Stravinsky – Enrico Caruso lived in the **Ansonia Hotel** and kept the other inhabitants entertained/awake with renditions of his favourite arias. The Ansonia, a vast Beaux Arts apartment building with exquisite detailing, was also the location for Single White Female. Bette Midler got her break at the **Continental Baths**, a gay spa and cabaret that occupied the bottom few floors in the 1970s. This was also where star DJs Frankie Knuckles and Larry Levan first honed their skills.

The **Beacon Theater** on Broadway was once a fabulous movie palace. It's now a concert venue with classy black music shows. The phenomenal interior is a designated landmark. A few blocks north are the **Children's Museum of Manhattan**, the famous **Zabar's**, supplier of delicious delicacies, and some of Manhattan's best bookshops.

Just off Broadway, a little way down the north side of 94th Street, is a quaint mews called **Pomander Walk**. Nearby is the **Claremont Riding Academy** where you can hire horses to ride in Central Park. Back on Broadway, the old movie theatre-turned-performance-centre **Symphony Space** (*see chapter* **Music**) features eclectic musical programmes, including the famous Wall-to-Wall concerts.

**Riverside Park** lies between Riverside Drive and the banks of the Hudson, from 72nd to 145th Streets. Once as fashionable an address as Fifth Avenue and similarly lined with opulent private houses, Riverside Drive was largely rebuilt in the 1930s with luxury apartment blocks. The park is a welcome stretch of undulating riverbank. You may see luxury yachts berthed at the little **79th Street Boat Basin**, along with a few houseboats. Further north, at 89th Street, the **Soldiers' and Sailors' Monument** is a memorial to the Civil War dead.

### New York Historical Society

*2 West 77th Street, at Central Park West (873 3400). Subway B or C to 81st Street.* **Open** noon-5pm Wed, Thur, Fri and by appointment. **Admission** $5 adults; $3 concessions. **No credit cards.**
The Society's library has an important architectural collection, including the archives of McKim, Mead & White, and Cass Gilbert and a magnificent collection of Tiffany lamps.

### Soldiers' & Sailors' Monument

*Riverside Drive, at West 89th Street. Subway 1 or 9 to 86th Street.*
The 1902 monument was designed by French sculptor Paul DuBoy and architects Charles and Arthur Stoughton.

# Northern Manhattan

*Head north of Central Park for the hubbub of Harlem, a venerable university and a whopping great cathedral.*

## Harlem

Harlem's reputation as a no-go area has been somewhat overstated. Certainly some parts are extremely depressed, and if you're white you should be prepared to stand out in the crowd, but a daytime visit to the main attractions should be wholly unproblematic.

Harlem is, in spirit, the blackest place there is. Its elegant stone buildings reverberate with the history of Black America's struggle for equality. The names of great liberators, teachers and orators christen its institutions and fill its street signs, and there are constant reminders of proud Afrocentric culture, from the Francophone Africans selling their trinkets, to the Jeeps booming out the latest hip-hop street politics.

When the subways arrived at the turn of the century, Harlem, previously composed of coun-

try estates, was developed for middle-class New Yorkers. When this group failed to fill the rows of grandiose townhouses, the speculators reluctantly rented them out to African Americans. The area's population doubled during the 1920s and 1930s, a growth which brought the cultural explosion of the Harlem Renaissance, when the district became a bohemian republic and its poets, writers, artists and musicians ushered in the Jazz Age.

Now Harlem's soundtrack is the rap and reggae of the younger generation and the salsa and merengue of the Cubans and Dominicans who have moved into the older black community, adding to the Hispanic populations of **Spanish Harlem**, or *El Barrio* ('the neighbourhood'). This is the section east of Fifth Avenue above 100th Street. Browse among the colourful fruit and veg, spice and meat at **La Marqueta** on Park Avenue, 110th-116th Streets.

# El Museo del Barrio

What had been a noticeable Hispanic population in New York City since the mid-nineteenth century became a massive presence in the postwar years. The first wave of new immigration was overwhelmingly Puerto Rican, but later included nationals from all of Latin America. Yet though one in four New Yorkers is now of Latino background, it is only recently that a major institution devoted to that culture has come into its own.

At the top of the Museum Mile, just blocks from the Hispanic quarter in East Harlem from which it takes its name, **El Museo del Barrio** is not what you'd expect. The museum is dedicated to the art of Latinos in the United States and that of Latin America generally. However, you won't find ethnographic kitsch and Mexican murals. Although the permanent collection includes everything from pre-Columbian vessels to contemporary folk art, the more typical exhibition is as contemporary, socially engaged and formally challenging as any you might see in a downtown exhibition space.

Recent shows have included a Cuban-born artist's AIDS-themed installation; a group exhibit from Mexico City of conceptual work on gender issues; and textile collages from Argentina on a feminist theme. The media are varied, with materials ranging from rusted shell casings to squares of taffy. The common threads are a heightened sense of drama and a vivid profusion of colour.

El Museo emerged as an adjunct to an East Harlem school district during the ferment of the late 1960s. It moved through a succession of spaces before settling, in 1977, at its present location at 104th Street and Fifth Avenue. Because it springs from a people who have been historically disadvantaged, El Museo is more socially radical than other city museums. Its AIDS-related 'Day Without Art' brings local school kids together with health care workers and AIDS survivors.

Visiting lecturers join community discussions on the relationship between domestic violence and the image of women in Latino culture.

On a lighter note, El Museo also sponsors the most festive events along the Museum Mile. An annual celebration of the Mexican Day of the Dead (1 November) centres on an elaborate community altar strewn with fruit, flowers, candy skulls and tissue-paper skeletons. A Three King's Day Parade (6 January), now in its twentieth year, features costumed school children, huge puppets and trains of camels, sheep and donkeys winding through the streets of Spanish Harlem. A summer evening music series is held in the museum's open courtyard and, when renovations are complete in the autumn of 1998, its little jewel box of a theatre will host the National Latino Film and Video Festival, soon to become a bi-annual event.

### El Museo del Barrio

*1230 Fifth Avenue, between 104 & 105th Streets (831 7272). Subway 6 to 103rd Street.* **Open** *June-Sept* 11am-5pm Wed, Fri-Sun; noon-7pm Thur; *Oct-May* 11am-5pm Wed-Sun. **Admission** suggested donation $4; $2 concessions; free under-12s. **Credit** AmEx, MC, V.

*The once grandiose town houses of Harlem date from the turn of the century.*

**Columbia University** *dominates Morningside Heights. See page 110.*

El Museo del Barrio (*see page 106*), Spanish Harlem's community museum, is on Fifth Avenue at 104th Street. It houses cultural artefacts of Hispanic New York.

The **Graffiti Hall of Fame** is at 106th Street between Park and Madison Avenues. It's actually just a schoolyard, but here you'll see the large-scale work of 'old-school' graffiti writers and may even bump into someone completing a piece. There are also several *casitas* – rough-and-ready Puerton Rican homes away from home, serving as a communal hang-out and creating a slice of island life among the high-rises – in the area. Two such 'little houses' can be found on the way from the 6 train subway station to the Museo del Barrio: one on a vacant lot on 103rd Street between Park and Lexington Avenues; the other around the corner on Lexington between 103rd and 104th Streets.

At 116th Street and Lenox Avenue is **Masjid Malcolm Shabazz**, the silver-domed mosque of Malcolm X's ministry. Opposite this is the market where the street vendors who once lined 125th Street now ply their trade in T-shirts, tapes and 'African' souvenirs. Just north of here the **Lenox Lounge** is the still-existing bar where Malcolm X's early career as a hustler began. Further up Lenox is **Sylvia's**, the most famous of Harlem's soulfood restaurants, and even further, at 138th Street, is the **Abyssinian Baptist Church**, containing a small museum dedicated to Adam Clayton Powell Jr, the first black man to be elected to Congress (in 1941) and Harlem's representative until 1970. Just below 125th Street, on Fifth

Avenue, **Marcus Garvey Park** (previously Mt Morris Park) is Harlem's only patch of green, the centre of an historic district of elegant brownstones. Some of the more beautiful are open to the public several times a year (call Mt Morris Park Community Association on 369 4241 for details).

The **Studio Museum in Harlem** has changing exhibitions about the area and its people, while the **Schomberg Center for Research in Black Culture** is the largest research collection for African-American culture (*see chapter* **Museums** for both).

Harlem's main drag is 125th Street and the **Apollo Theater** is its focus. In the 1920s, during Prohibition, this was one of the places – along with the Cotton Club, Connie's and Small's Paradise – where you could listen to Josephine Baker and Duke Ellington while sampling the bootleg liquor. Now it's used for television recordings along with hip-hop and R'n'B gigs (*see chapter* **Music**). The Theresa Towers office complex, at 125th and Seventh Avenue, was formerly the **Hotel Theresa**. Fidel Castro stayed here during a 1960 visit to the United Nations and his visitors included Nikita Khrushchev and Gamal Abdel Nasser.

The area between 125th and 155th Streets west of St Nicholas Avenue is known as **Hamilton Heights**, after Alexander Hamilton who had a

*The carefully reconstructed* **Cloisters** *in Fort Tryon Park. See page 110.*

farm here at Hamilton Grange (Convent Avenue at 142nd Street). This is the gentrified part of Harlem, where you'll find City College, the northern outpost of City University. It's also the location of Audubon Terrace, a double Beaux Arts row containing a group of museums: the **Hispanic Society of America**, the **American Numismatic Society** and the **American Academy of Arts and Letters** (*see chapter* **Museums**).

### Transport
*Subway 2, 3, A, B, C or D to 125th Street.*

### Harlem Spirituals
*690 Eighth Avenue, between 43rd & 44th Streets (757 0425). Subway A, C or E to 42nd Street.* **Open** 9am-6pm Mon-Sat. **Credit** AmEx, MC, V.
A wide range of tours are organised, including morning gospel tours, lunch-time historical tours and evening soul food and jazz tours. Prices range from $30 to $70.

## Morningside Heights

The area sandwiched between Morningside Park and the Hudson River, from 110th to 125th Streets, is **Morningside Heights**, a region dominated by **Columbia University**. One of the oldest universities in the USA, Columbia was chartered in 1754 as King's College (the name changed after Independence). Thanks to its large student presence, the surrounding area has an academic feel, with plenty of bookshops and cafés along Broadway and quiet leafy streets towards the west overlooking Riverside Park.

The neighbourhood has two immense houses of worship, the **Cathedral of St John the Divine** and the Baptist **Riverside Church**, speedily built with Rockefeller money and containing the world's largest carillon. You can ride to the top of the 21-storey steel-framed tower for views out across the Hudson and also of **Grant's Tomb** in Riverside Park (at 122nd Street), honouring victorious Civil War general, Ulysses S Grant.

The hammering and chiselling at St John's Cathedral will continue well into the next century. Construction began in 1892 in Romanesque style, was stopped for a redesign in Gothic Revival style in 1911 and wasn't restarted until 1941. There was another lapse to campaign for funds, but the last decade has seen work restart in earnest. When the towers and great crossing are completed, this will be one of the world's largest cathedrals. Services, concerts and tours take place inside. St John's is also where funerals of the rich and famous take place.

### Cathedral of St John the Divine
*Amsterdam Avenue, at 110th Street (662 2133). Subway 1 or 9 to 110th Street.* **Open** 7am-5pm daily.

### Columbia University
*Between Broadway & Amsterdam Avenue, 114th-120th Streets (854 1754). Subway 1 or 9 to 116th Street.*

### General Grant National Memorial
*Riverside Drive & West 122nd Street (666 1640). Subway 1 or 9 to 125th Street.* **Open** 9am-5pm daily. **Admission** free.
The classical temple that is more commonly known as Grant's Tomb dominates the upper reaches of Riverside Park. The architect of the Union victory, General Ulysses S Grant was elected President in 1868 and remained an immensely popular national hero, despite being a particularly inept president. He is buried here with his wife, Julia, in twin black marble sarcophagi underneath a small white dome. The surrounding mosaic benches were designed in the 1960s by local kids.

### Riverside Church
*Riverside Drive, at 122nd Street (870 6700). Subway 1 or 9 to 116th Street.* **Open** 9am-4pm daily.

## Washington Heights

The area from 155th Street to the northern tip of Manhattan is called Washington Heights. Here the island shrinks in width and the parks on either side culminate in the wilderness and forest of **Inwood Hill Park**, where, in 1626, a Dutchman called Peter Minuit 'bought' Manhattan Island from the Indians for a handful of beads.

**High Bridge** (Amsterdam Avenue at 177th Street) gives an idea of how old New York got its water supply. This aqueduct carried water across the Harlem River from the Croton Reservoir in Westchester County to Manhattan. The central piers were replaced in the 1920s to allow large ships to pass below.

The main building of **Yeshiva University** (186th Street at Amsterdam Avenue) is one of the strangest in New York, a Byzantine orange-brick structure decorated with turrets and minarets.

Equally unlikely is **The Cloisters** at the northern tip of the flower-filled Fort Tryon Park. It's a reconstructed monastery incorporating several original medieval cloisters shipped over from Europe, and might have been custom-designed for romantic picnics. The project, financed by the Rockefellers, is in fact the Metropolitan Museum's medieval outpost, and contains illuminated manuscripts and priceless tapestries, including the celebrated Unicorn tapestries (*see chapter* **Museums**).

The neighbourhood also has two significant historic sites. **Dyckman House**, a Dutch farmhouse built in 1748, is the oldest surviving home in Manhattan, and something of a lonely sight on busy Broadway (at 204th Street); inside it is filled with period and Dyckman family furniture.

**Morris-Jumel Mansion** (Edgecumb Avenue at 160th Street) was where George Washington planned some of his battles, and later where Governor Morris, a signatory of the Declaration of Independence, lived (*see chapter* **Architecture**). The handsome Federal-style house also has some fantastic views.

# The Outer Boroughs

**There's more to the metropolis than Manhattan – if you're after New Yorkers' New York, beat it to the boroughs and the 'burbs.**

If you're surprised at how compact New York is, that's because you probably haven't stepped off Manhattan yet. The city actually comprises five boroughs, each with its own character and all containing world-class museums, parks, restaurants and other attractions. Of course, Manhattan is the centre of it all, but if you want to see where the majority of New Yorkers live, find time to visit Brooklyn, Queens, the Bronx and Staten Island.

## Brooklyn

Brooklyn is no suburb. The grand spaces of its civic centre, the scale of its public buildings and the beauty of its private houses all hint at a proud and independent history. In the language of hip-hop it is a whole world: 'the Planet'. It has been part of New York for less than 100 years.

In the middle of the nineteenth century, Brooklyn was a rich and powerful city, the third largest in the United States (today it would still be the fourth largest). In 1861 Walt Whitman declared its destiny was 'to be among the most famed and choice of the half dozen cities of the world'. To join it to New York they had to build a bridge of unimaginable length.

More even than Manhattan, Brooklyn is a collection of vitally distinct ethnic neighbourhoods. There is Jamaican Flatbush, African-American Bedford-Stuyvesant, Jewish Crown Heights, Polish Greenpoint, Italian Bensonhurst and newly trendy Williamsburg with its tripartite population of Hispanics, Hasidim and art-rebel loft-loungers. This patchwork of communities has long made for a vivid cultural life. More famous Americans come from Brooklyn than anywhere else (*see page 115*).

**Spike's Joint**, Mr Lee's Brooklyn 'moviebilia' store. See page 112.

The **Civic Center**, a reminder of Brooklyn's earlier status, is dominated by the City Hall, now Borough Hall (1851; 209 Joralemon Street at Fulton Street), and the massive General Post Office (271-301 Fulton Street).

From here it's a short walk to **Brooklyn Heights**, with its well-preserved streets of Federal-style and Greek Revival brownstones. Middagh, Cranberry, Willow, Orange, Pineapple, Pierrepont and Montague are some of the prettiest streets. Pierrepont Street is also home to the **Brooklyn Historical Society** museum and library (*see chapter* **Museums**) and takes you to the Promenade overlooking the river for some breathtaking views of lower Manhattan. Also in the Heights is the imposing **Plymouth Church of the Pilgrims**, on Orange Street, founded by the famous abolitionist Henry Ward Beecher, who is remembered by a statue there.

Stroll through Cadman Plaza Park and you will reach the **Brooklyn Bridge** (*see chapter* **Sightseeing**). This much-loved 1883 construction astounded both cities, supplanted most of the 17 ferry companies that traversed the East River and made inevitable the marriage of Brooklyn with New York. Its anchorage space now houses the occasional rave.

The **Brooklyn Museum of Art** was designed to be the largest in the world. Though only a fifth of it was built, it is still imposing and enormous, housing 1.5 million artefacts, including one of the best Egyptian collections anywhere. Another museum worth visiting is the **New York Transit Museum**, which tells the intriguing story of New York's subways (for both *see chapter* **Museums**). Also nearby is the **Brooklyn Children's Museum** (*see chapter* **Children**).

The grand old opera house that is the **Brooklyn Academy of Music** is a further symbol of Brooklyn's independence. It puts on a fine range of musical and theatrical productions.

The surrounding neighbourhood of **Fort Greene** is Brooklyn's bohemian centre, with an increasingly multi-ethnic population of successful creative types. This is where Spike Lee calls home, and his 'moviebilia' store, **Spike's Joint**, is here (*see chapter* **Shopping & Services**).

At the **Concord Baptist Church of Christ** you can experience some old-time religion alongside the largest black congregation in the US. Let the fabulous gospel music prove that the devil doesn't have all the best tunes.

Like Manhattan, Brooklyn has a heart of green. Built by the same architects, **Prospect Park** is smaller than Central Park, but much calmer and more rural. At weekends it fills with families having barbecues and picnics, as well as active types who use its sports fields and closed road loop. On the eastern side the largely Caribbean community of Flatbush gathers; listen out for booming reggae

and huge drumming circles. The park's many attractions include a children's zoo, opened in 1993; a bandshell with a busy summer programme of jazz, hip-hop, soul, gospel, classical and opera concerts; and the restored Dutch-colonial style **Lefferts Homestead**, one of the city's first buildings, which now houses a children's museum and a visitors' centre.

At the park's main entrance is **Grand Army Plaza** with the **Brooklyn Public Library** to one side and the **Soldiers' and Sailors' Memorial Arch** in the centre. Designed, like the park itself, by Olmstead and Vaux (the architects of Central Park), it commemorates Brooklyn's dead from the Civil War. The plaza is also the site of New York's only monument to John F Kennedy.

Next door to the park and behind the museum is the peaceful **Brooklyn Botanic Garden**, famous for its Japanese cherry trees and the biggest bonsai collection in the US. Visit at the weekend and you're sure to see little Catholic girls being photographed in their communion dresses, and the occasional freshly wedded couple enjoying their reception among the blossoms.

**Park Slope**, the area west of the park, is another enclave of superbly elegant architecture: untouched nineteenth-century brownstone townhouses. This was the scene of Washington's 1776 retreat during the Revolutionary War.

Further afield, the rusted wonder of **Coney Island** (*see chapter* **Sightseeing**) is Brooklyn's answer to Blackpool. The beach itself is pretty dirty, but the amusement parks, boardwalk and piers which span its length are great fun. Walk along to the **Aquarium** (*see chapter* **Children**), where the collection of Beluga whales, sharks and other sea dwellers has recently been augmented by a huge (60,000sq ft/5,600sq m) recreation of the Pacific coastline. Neighbouring **Brighton Beach** is the place to buy caviar, vodka and smoked sausages. More East European than American, it's known as 'Little Odessa' because of its number by Russian immigrants.

### Brooklyn Botanic Garden

*1000 Washington Avenue, Brooklyn (1-718 622 4433). Subway 2 or 3 to Eastern Parkway.* **Open** 8am-6pm Tue-Fri; 10am-6pm Sat, Sun (with seasonal variations). **Admission** $3; $1 concessions.
Travel between jungle and desert in the extensive conservatories here. There's also a beautiful rose garden, an outdoor café, a perfume garden for the blind and an area set aside for meditation.

### Concord Baptist Church of Christ

*833 Marcy Avenue, near Fulton Street (1-718 622 1818). Subway A or C to Nostrand Avenue.*
Phone for times of concerts and services.

*A vision of eastern promise in multi-cultural Brooklyn: Greenpoint's Orthodox church.*

## Prospect Park

*Flatbush Avenue at Grand Army Plaza, Brooklyn (events hotline 1-718 965 8999/Leffert's Homestead 1-718 965 6505/zoo 1-718 399 7333). Subway 2 or 3 to Grand Army Plaza.*

## Queens

A visit to Queens is like a world tour using some kind of alternative geography. Here's Bombay, Athens, Columbia; there's Ecuador, Korea, Argentina; down the road is Kilkenny, Manila, Milan. Thanks to the efforts of New York's master builder, Robert Moses, and his taste for superhighways, this borough's postwar development had a patchwork quality. Originally a handful of towns, Queens has evolved as a collection of foreign cities: an urban suburbia. It is New York's new Lower East Side; today's destination for thousands of the immigrants (a third of Queens residents are foreign-born) who arrive in the US of A.

Queens County was named after Queen Catherine, Charles II's wife. It joined New York as a borough in 1898, the same year as Brooklyn and Staten Island. As communications improved – the Queensboro Bridge ('the 59th Street Bridge') was built in 1909 and the first train tunnels were cut under the East River in 1910 – it began to function as a residential satellite of Manhattan. Phenomenal building in the 1950s and 1960s merged the separate towns in a continuous sprawl, buffered only by several formal parks, highways and enormous cemeteries. Chances are that you started your visit

here: **LaGuardia** and **JFK** airports are both in Queens. Should you return here you'll find many attractions in the towns of Astoria, Long Island City, Jamaica, Flushing and Forest Hills.

**Long Island City**, closest to Manhattan, is home to the recently renovated **PS 1**, the Institute for Contemporary Art, housed in an old city school. A non-profit studio space attracting artists from around the world, it has open workshops, multimedia galleries, several large permanent works and controversial, censor-taunting exhibitions. Nearby, in a striking location at the riverside, the **Socrates Sculpture Garden** contains large-scale sculpture by well- and lesser-known artists, with occasional performances of music and video. A few doors down the road is the **Noguchi Museum** in Isamu Noguchi's great self-designed sculpture studios, where over 300 of his works are displayed in 12 galleries (*see chapter* **Museums**).

**Astoria**, a mainly Greek town, is home to the **American Museum of the Moving Image**, which occupies part of the Kaufmann-Astoria movie studios. These were opened in 1917; WC Fields, Rudolph Valentino, Gloria Swanson and the Marx Brothers all made films here. For more details, *see chapter* **Museums**.

Further east are **Flushing** and **Flushing Meadows-Corona Park**, a huge park that contains **Shea Stadium**, home to the New York Mets baseball team, and the **USTA National Tennis Center**, where the US Open championships are played every August. The 1939 and the 1964 World's Fairs were held in Corona Park, leaving

# Da People's Cherce

A cheerfully proletarian, resolutely egalitarian spirit makes up the classic myth of Brooklyn. Manhattan may have the glamour but Brooklyn is the soul of the city, the closest American equivalent to Cockney, in both language and character. Whatever Brooklynites may lack in refinement is more than made up for in their skilful skewering of the pretensions of the bourgeoisie. It is no coincidence that Brooklyn is the birthplace of much of America's great comic talent – Woody Allen, Mel Brooks, Jackie Gleason – or that the great American poet of democracy, Walt Whitman, was a longtime resident.

The borough's unique standing within the city stems from its long history as an independent entity. Brooklyn evolved out of 'Breukelen' and five other, chiefly Dutch, towns that bought or bullied out the indigenous Canarsee Indians through the course of the seventeenth century. It was an agricultural area until its transformation under the waves of European immigration in the nineteenth century. It remains a borough of immigrants to this day. In 1860 it was the third largest city in the US: it would be the fourth largest today but for its annexation by New York in 1898. With its extensive waterfront, and the immense complex of the Brooklyn Navy Yard, Brooklyn was the equal of any of America's great industrial cities.

While Brooklyn first gained world renown with the architectural and engineering triumph of the Brooklyn Bridge in 1883 (in its day, 'The Eighth Wonder of the World') other methods of transit shaped its character. The completion of a street railway system (whose drivers' recklessness spawned the legendary Brooklyn baseball club's original nickname, 'Trolley Dodgers') transformed the county. Its Atlantic beaches became a posh resort, and the district turned into America's horseracing capital in the Gay Nineties. The subway system, in its turn, opened the seaside to the masses in 1920 and gave birth to Coney Island's 'Nickel Empire' – a nickel to get there, a nickel for a hot dog, a nickel for a milkshake.

Another popular entertainment, the Brooklyn Dodgers ball club, was, in its day, the pre-eminent symbol of the borough. The first professional baseball team to break the colour line with Jackie Robinson, its glory years featured a colourful, often daft cast of players (originally 'the Bridegrooms' but later 'dem Bums') and devout and equally loony fans (a ragged group of instrumentalists on the bleachers styled themselves 'the Dodger Sym-Phony'). A heartbreaking history of second-place finishes to the Bronx aristocrats, the New York Yankees, gave the borough its near-official motto, 'Wait 'til next year'. There are many who claim that Brooklyn has never recovered from the team's departure for Los Angeles in 1957 and the recent news that the team was up for sale spurred a flurry of wistful speculation about luring the Dodgers back.

In the postwar era, many Brooklyn neighbourhoods had been marked by the general economic decline of the industrial north-east, a black and Hispanic influx, and the flight of the old white ethnics. Others have witnessed the renewed middle-class vigour of the brownstone revival movement, and the arrival of micro-breweries. No less a local hero than Spike Lee captured that ambivalent status with his semi-autobiographical *Crooklyn*. Warts and all, native pride endures.

some incredible half-derelict structures and the huge stainless steel **Unisphere** globe in their wake. Preservationists are working to make sure that the remaining structures are spared from the wrecker's ball. Outside the curved concrete structure of the **New York Hall of Science** are cast-off pieces of space rockets to marvel at. Have a look also at the ghostly amphitheatre overlooking the boating lake. A left-over 1939 World Fair pavilion is the home of the **Queens Museum**, where the main attraction is a 1:12,000 scale model of New York City made for the 1964 fair. **Corona Park** itself is the scene of weekend picnics and some hotly contested soccer matches between teams of European- and South American-born locals. You can rent bikes in the summer and there are plenty of good restaurants and coffee shops around.

Queens also has several noteworthy historical buildings. East of Flushing Meadows is the **Friends' Meeting House** (1694), built by religious protester John Bowne and still used as a Quaker meeting place, making it the oldest house of worship in the USA in continuous use. Next door is **Kingsland House**, a mid-eighteenth century farmhouse which is also the headquarters of the **Queens Historical Society**. You can also visit John Bowne's own house, which dates back to 1661 (*see chapter* **Architecture**).

On the edge of Queens is the **Queens County Farm Museum**, where a farm dating back to 1772 is managed as it was back then. In the south of the borough, near JFK Airport, are the tidal wetlands of **Jamaica Bay Wildlife Refuge**, home to a large population of birds, plants and animals.

Water-fowl flock here during the autumn. Bring your binoculars and spot both birds and planes.

### Friends' Meeting House
*137-16 Northern Boulevard, between Main & Union Streets, Flushing, Queens (1-718 358 9636). Subway 7 to Main Street.* **Open** by appointment only. **Admission** voluntary donation.

### Institute for Contemporary Art (PS 1)
*46-01 21st Street, Long Island City, Queens (1-718 784 2084). Subway E or F to 23rd Street/Ely Avenue.* **Open** noon-6pm Wed-Sun. **Admission** $2 suggested donation. *Disabled: toilets.*

### Jamaica Bay Wildlife Refuge
*Cross Bay Boulevard, at Broad Channel, Queens (1-718 318 4340). Subway A to Broad Channel.* **Open** 8.30am-5pm daily. **Admission** free.
Part of a local network of important ecological sites, administered through the National Parks Service. Guided walks, lectures and all sorts of nature-centred activities are held.

### Kingsland House/
### Queens Historical Society
*Weeping Beech Park, 143-35 37th Avenue, at Parson's Boulevard, Flushing, Queens (1-718 939 0647). Subway 7 to Main Street.* **Open** 2.30-4.30pm Tue, Sat, Sun. **Admission** $2; $1 concessions. **No credit cards.**
Built in 1785 by a wealthy Quaker, the house was moved to a site beside Bowne House. Queens Historical Society now uses it for local history exhibitions. Staff can give you further information about the borough's historical sites. *Disabled: toilets.*

### Queens Council on the Arts
*7901 Park Lane South, Woodhaven, Queens, NY 11421 (1-718 647 3377/information menu 1-718 291 ARTS).* **Open** 9am-4.30pm Mon-Fri.
Provides exhaustive details of all cultural events in the borough, updated daily.

### Queens County Farm Museum
*73-50 Little Neck Parkway in Floral Park, Queens (1-718 347 3276). Subway E or F to Kew Gardens, then Q46 bus to Little Neck Parkway.* **Open** 9am-5pm daily (farmhouse and museum galleries noon-5pm Sat, Sun). **Admission** voluntary donation. *Disabled: toilets.*

### Socrates Sculpture Park
*Broadway, at Vernon Boulevard, Long Island City, Queens (1-718 956 1819). Subway N to Broadway.* **Open** 10am-sunset daily. **Admission** free.
The setting, a vacant post-industrial lot by the river, is inspiring and appropriate. Some of the pieces crammed in, like the 'Sound Observatory', are engagingly interactive.

## The Bronx

The southern section of the Bronx is a depressing lesson in American apartheid, a forbidden zone where economic polarisation, running along clear racial lines, has left a whole community for dead. With run-down public housing looming from the smouldering rubble of what look like bomb sites, this urban hell is enough to frighten away even the hardiest visitor. However, this notorious corner is but an isolated part of the borough. The subway lines fly over the battle grounds, allowing you a

safe glimpse, and take you to the friendly territory of the northern parts.

The Bronx is so named because it once belonged to the family of Dutchman Jonas Bronck, who built his farm here in 1636. It is, therefore, "the Broncks'". As the rich folk of Manhattan were moving into baronial apartment blocks alongside Central Park and up Fifth Avenue, a similar process took place here, as **Grand Concourse**, a continuation of Madison Avenue, was built up in the 1920s into very grand Art Deco apartment buildings. This is the Bronx's main thoroughfare, well worth seeing for its sense of decaying architectural optimism.

Just west of Grand Concourse at 161st Street is the famous **Yankee Stadium**, home of New York's great baseball team. Halfway up Grand Concourse, just south of Fordham Road, is the rotunda of the **Hall of Fame of Great Americans**, a wonderful early twentieth-century institution honouring scholars, politicians and others worthy of the accolade 'great' (*see chapter* **Museums**). Several blocks north is the small clapboard house where Edgar Allan Poe lived out the last sad years of his life. Fordham Road itself leads past **Fordham University**, a Jesuit institution that was founded in 1841.

Watching a game of cricket in Van Cortlandt Park will do a lot to dispel the stereotyped impressions which the Bronx has so often had to fight. Amid this vast expanse of green is **Van Cortlandt Mansion**, a fine example of pre-revolutionary Georgian architecture, open to the public since 1897 (*see chapter* **Architecture**).

In the far north of the borough, in ritzy Beverly Hills-like Riverdale, is **Wave Hill**, a small, idyllic park overlooking the Hudson River. Originally a Victorian country estate where exotic plants were cultivated, it has been occupied by such illustrious tenants as William Thackeray, Theodore Roosevelt, Arturo Toscanini and Mark Twain.

The reason most visitors come to the Bronx is to visit the **Bronx Zoo** on the banks of the Bronx River. It's the largest urban zoo in the US and rare for the space and freedom given to its animals (*see chapter* **Sightseeing**).

Across from the zoo's main gate in **Bronx Park**, you'll find the **New York Botanical Gardens**, a wide-ranging botanical collection on the scale of Kew Gardens in London (*see chapter* **Children**). The area near the zoo is **Belmont**, Little Italy in the Bronx, and a far more expansive neighbourhood of restaurants, food markets and coffee shops than its tiny counterpart in Manhattan.

Much further to the north-east, facing Long Island Sound, is **Pelham Bay Park**, a large-scale park with all sorts of diversions, including the man-made shoreline of Orchard Beach (the city's favourite dumping ground for dead bodies). Inside the park is **Bartow Pell Mansion**, a

*Point of departure for a breakaway borough: the Staten Island ferry terminal.*

Federal manor sitting among romantic formal gardens.

Perhaps the most uncharacteristic part of the Bronx is **City Island** in Long Island Sound. The island, settled in 1685 and only a mile and a half long by half a mile wide, was originally a prosperous ship-building centre, with a busy fishing industry. In the days when New York was getting started, this tiny piece of real estate was a serious competitor for Manhattan's prestige. Nowadays it offers New Yorkers a doorstep slice of New England-style maritime recreation – it's packed with marinas, seafood restaurants and nautical bars.

And finally, though you may be forgiven for not wanting to go there, the wasteland of the **South Bronx** was the birthplace of one of the late twentieth century's most influential musical innovations – hip-hop. It was here, in parks and social clubs, that DJs like Kool Herc and Afrika Bambaata were the first to experiment with the boom-boom-bap of cut-up records and rhyming accompaniment. Today, even West Coast rappers like Ice Cube pay homage to the 'Boogie-Down' Bronx before they start their shows.

### Bartow-Pell Mansion

*895 Shore Road, Pelham Bay Park, Bronx (1-718 885 1461). Subway 6 to Pelham Bay Park, then one-mile walk or cab-ride.* **Open** noon-4pm Wed, Sat, Sun. **Admission** $2.50 adults; $1.25 concessions; free under-12s.

The International Garden Club has administered this 1836 mansion since 1914; the grounds include formal gardens, a fountain and a nineteenth-century carriage house and stable.

## Bronx County Historical Society Museum

*Valentine-Varion House, 3266 Bainbridge Avenue, between Van Cortlandt Avenue & 208th Street, Bronx (1-718 881 8900).* **Open** by appointment Mon-Fri; 10am-4pm Sat; 1-5pm Sun. **Admission** $2.

The 1758 fieldstone farmhouse is a fine example of the pre-Revolutionary Federal style which was popular in the colony.

## City Island

*Subway 6 to Pelham Bay Park, then BX21 bus to City Island.*

Phone the City Island Chamber of Commerce (1-718 885 9100) for information about events and activities.

## Edgar Allan Poe Cottage

*Grand Concourse, at East Kingsbridge Road, Bronx (1-718 881 8900). Subway 4, C or D to Kingsbridge Road.* **Open** 10am-4pm Sat; 1-5pm Sun. **Admission** $2.

Poe's cottage, in Fordham village (now part of the Bronx), has been moved across the street since he lived here and turned into a charming museum dedicated to his life.

## North Wind Undersea Institute

*610 City Island Avenue (1-718 885 0701). Subway 6 to Pelham Bay Park, then BX21 bus to City Island.* **Open** noon-4pm Mon-Fri; noon-5pm Sat. **Admission** $3; $2 concessions. **No credit cards.**

A charming old maritime folk museum, with whalebones, old diving gear and a 100 year-old tugboat.

## Pelham Bay Park

*(1-718 430 1890). Subway 6 to Pelham Bay Park.*

## Wave Hill

*675 West 52nd Street, at Independence Avenue, Bronx (1-718 549 2055). Metro North from Grand Central to Riverdale.* **Open** 9am-5.30pm Tue, Thur-Sun; 9.30am-dusk Wed (with seasonal variations). **Admission** $4; $2 concessions; free Tue. **No credit cards.**

Wave Hill, with its formal European gardens, is now the venue for concerts, educational programmes and exhibitions, including a permanent sculpture garden featuring works by Henry Moore, Alexander Calder and Willem de Kooning.

# Staten Island

Staten Island hates New York. The Islanders consistently vote to detach their community from the city, arguing that it takes their taxes to pay for its own problems and in return all it gives them is its garbage (the famous landfill at Fresh Kills is one of the world's largest man-made structures). Driving through its tree-lined suburban hills, admiring its open spaces and expansive parks, you can see why the generally well-to-do inhabitants are so keen on keeping themselves separate from the pressing inner-city concerns of the rest of NYC.

Thanks to its strategic location, Staten Island is one of the longest-settled places in America. Giovanni da Verrazano, whose name graces the bridge connecting the island to Brooklyn (at 4260ft/1311m the world's second-longest suspension bridge, after the Humber Bridge), christened it *Staaten* (States) *Eylandt* in 1524. In 1687 the Duke of York sponsored a sailing competition with Staten Island as the prize. The Manhattan representatives won the race and since that day it has been governed from New York.

You reach this tranquil island, of course, by the famous ferry. The ride from Battery Park in Lower Manhattan is free (*see chapter* **Downtown**). You pass close to the **Statue of Liberty** before sailing into St George, the island's main town.

On the waterfront facing Bayonne in New Jersey is **Snug Harbor Cultural Center**. Originally a maritime hospital and home for retired sailors, it comprises 28 buildings – grand examples of various periods of American architecture – in an 80-acre park. Sailors lived here until 1960, and the city took over the site in 1976, converting it into a cultural centre with exhibitions and arts events. Near the lighthouse at the island's tallest point is the **Jacques Marchais Center of Tibetan Art**, a collection of art and cultural treasures from the Far East, whose emphasis is on all aspects of Tibetan prayer, meditation and healing. Its Buddhist temple is one of New York's more tranquil places.

Visit **Historic Richmond Town**, a spacious collection of 29 restored historic buildings dating back to the seventeenth century, and it feels like you're in upstate New York. Many of the buildings have been moved on site from elsewhere on the island. There's a courthouse, general store, baker's and butcher's, as well as private homes. Actors and craftspeople in appropriate eighteenth-century clothing lurk with intent (*see chapter* **Sightseeing**). During the Revolutionary War, **Billop House** (now Conference House) was where an unsuccessful peace conference took place between the Americans, led by Benjamin Franklin and John Adams, and England's Lord Howe. The building has been turned into a museum. Combine your visit here with a trip to nearby Tottenville Beach.

For details of cultural events and travel directions on Staten Island, contact the Staten Island Chamber of Commerce, 130 Bay Street, Staten Island, NY 10301 (1-718 727 1900).

## Conference House (Billop House)

*7455 Hylan Boulevard, Tottenville, Staten Island (1-718 984 2086). Staten Island ferry, then S78 bus to Hylan Boulevard & Craig Avenue.* **Open** Mar-Dec 1-4pm Wed-Sun. **Admission** $2; $1 concessions.

John Adams, one of the US delegates, recalled that for the attempted peace conference at Billop House, Lord Howe had 'prepared a large handsome room… made [it] not only wholesome but romantically elegant'. The house is the earliest – circa 1680 – manor house in New York City, and has been restored to its eighteenth-century magnificence.

## Snug Harbor Cultural Center

*1000 Richmond Terrace (1-718 448 2500). Staten Island ferry, then Snug Harbor trolley or S40 bus.* **Open** 8am-5pm daily. **Tours** 2pm Sat, Sun. **Admission** $2 suggested donation.

Exhibitions of painting, sculpture and photography are held in the Newhouse Center; the Staten Island Botanical Garden is here, with tropical plants, orchids and a butterfly house; opera, chamber groups and jazz musicians play in the Veterans' Memorial Hall; the Art Lab offers art classes; and there's also a children's museum.

# Eating & Drinking

# Restaurants

*You've heard the legend: now it's time to savour New York, and taste the world.*

Listen to New Yorkers talk about the restaurants they love. You'll hear something more than just individual taste and habit, or civic pride. Like everything else in this city, dining out is part spectacle and sport, part protected solace. More than in most cities, restaurants are central to everyday life here. New Yorkers wear a good deal on their sleeves – mainly because they don't have room in their closets at home – and where you eat has a lot to do with how you like to, or can afford to, live. Everyone eats out, some all the time. To satisfy this voracity there is, famously, all manner of eating to be done in New York: the renowned hot-dog competes for attention with the rarefied talents of the best chefs on the planet. Gray's Papaya for lunch, Gramercy Tavern for dinner.

Newcomers immediately adopt restaurants as their own, and even born-and-bred New Yorkers are forever updating their lists as tastes and neighbourhoods change. The one rule to enjoyment is to embrace the vastness: the authentic Greek grill in Astoria; the intensely hip downtown ticket, whose light will burn out before you have time to tell friends about it; and the midtown joint that somehow escaped the wrecking ball and is still serving meat to old men who are there when young. New York is a city of unparalleled friction, and the best way to experience it is to eat out.

It can be as hard as ever to get a table in a place that's 'hot', but it's also a good idea to phone ahead and check if the place that was hot last week is still in business. Some places take reservations, but many prefer to operate on a first-come, first-served basis and you may have to wait at the bar. Book ahead, where possible, at all the restaurants listed in the **Celebrated Chefs**, **Landmark Restaurants** and **Contemporary American** sections and many of those in **Forever Chic**.

New Yorkers rely on the handy pocket *Zagat Survey* ($11.95) for a comprehensive annual overview of the better places and avidly peruse the Eat Out section of *Time Out New York*, and the food columns of the *New York Times* and *New York*, whose listings are more up to date than any annual guide to such a frenetic and constantly changing scene could hope to be.

During the first weeks of July the city holds a Restaurant Week, when some of its finest establishments offer a *prix fixe* lunch, which in 1998 will be $19.98. It's a great way to sample the talents of

chefs who are otherwise unaffordable. Needless to say, you should book well in advance. Check the press for details.

Few New York restaurants add a service charge to your bill, but it is the custom to double the 8.25 per cent local sales tax as a tip. Many small places accept cash only, and some credit cards – AmEx, Visa and Mastercard – are more welcome than others. Ask before you sit down. As with every other financial transaction in the Big Apple, restaurant customers complain vociferously if they feel that they're not getting a fair deal. Don't be afraid of offending your waiter by moaning, but never withhold a tip.

*The average prices quoted below are based on a three-course meal without alcohol.*

## Celebrated Chefs

### An American Place
2 Park Avenue, at East 32nd Street (684 2122). Subway 6 to 33rd Street. **Lunch** 11.45am-3pm Mon-Fri. **Dinner** 5.30-10pm Mon-Sat. **Average** $40. **Credit** AmEx, CB, DC, Disc, MC, V.
Larry Forgione has expanded his business into lines of jams and a new downtown restaurant, the Grill Room (945 9400), but the Place is still where to taste the talents of the godfather of new American cuisine. The patriotic premise at this grand, vaguely deco-ish Park Avenue institution, is that neither produce, wine nor inspiration need come from anywhere but home.

### Arcadia
21 East 62nd Street, between Madison & Fifth Avenues (223 2900). Subway 4 or 6 to 59th Street; N or R to Lexington Avenue. **Lunch** noon-2.30pm Mon-Sat. **Dinner** 6-10pm Mon-Thur; 6-10.30pm Fri, Sat. **Average** $55. **Credit** AmEx, DC, MC, V.
Founder of the International Association of Women Chefs and Restaurateurs, Anne Rozenzweig is at the forefront of a growing number of top-notch women chefs. Arcadia is a superb example of haute américaine cuisine served in a lovely townhouse setting.
*Disabled: toilets.*

### Aureole
34 East 61st Street, between Madison & Park Avenues (319 1660). Subway N or R to Lexington Avenue. **Lunch** noon-2.30pm Mon-Fri. **Dinner** 5.30-11pm Mon-Sat. **Average** $65. **Credit** AmEx, Disc, MC, V.
Charles Palmer, along with a select few New York chefs, has created a small but formidable gastronomic empire that includes three restaurants (Aureole, Lenox Room (772 0404) and Alva (228 4399) and a partnership in the rustic Egg Farm Deli. The smooth and sedate Aureole and Lenox Room feature elegant contemporary American cuisine, while the more affordable Alva specialises in sophisticated home-style American.

## Chanterelle

*2 Harrison Street, at Hudson Street (966 6960). Subway 1 or 9 to Franklin Street.* **Lunch** noon-2.30pm Tue-Sat. **Dinner** 5.30-11pm Mon-Sat. **Set lunch** $35. **Set dinners** $75, $89. **Credit** AmEx, Disc, MC, V.
Karen and David Waltuck's large and tasteful space in TriBeCa's landmark Mercantile Exchange Building is still a New York favourite. The casual atmosphere belies the seriousness with which food is treated. The menu changes every few weeks, but often includes contemporary French classics such as rack of lamb with savoury saffron.
*Disabled: toilets.*

## Felidia

*243 East 58th Street, between Second & Third Avenues (758 1479). Subway N or R to Lexington Avenue; 4 or 6 to 59th Street.* **Lunch** noon-3pm Mon-Fri. **Dinner** 5-11pm Mon-Thur; 5-11.30pm Fri, Sat. **Average** $52. **Credit** AmEx, Disc, MC, V.
Lidia Bastianich is considered the mother of authentic Italian restaurant cuisine in New York. At her flagship restaurant (and her other excellent projects, Becco and Frico Bar) the menu is predominantly northern Italian, handed down from her grandmother.
*Disabled: toilets.*

## Mesa Grill

*102 Fifth Avenue, between 15th & 16th Streets (807 7400). Subway F to 14th Street.* **Lunch** noon-2.30pm Mon-Fri; 11.30am-3pm Sat, Sun. **Dinner** 5.30-10.30pm daily. **Average** $40. **Credit** AmEx, Disc, MC, V.
Using traditional Southwestern ingredients (such as blue corn and jalapenos) with flair, chef Bobby Flay continues to keep Mesa Grill on the short list of perennially popular Manhattan restaurants. Large parties and couples alike will find this high-ceilinged, colourful restaurant inviting and memorable.
*Disabled: toilets.*

## Nobu

*105 Hudson Street, at Franklin Street (219 0500). Subway 1 or 9 to Franklin Street.* **Lunch** 11.45am-2.15pm Mon-Fri. **Dinner** 5.45-10.15pm daily. **Average** $58. **Credit** AmEx, DC, MC, V.
There may be Nobus on two coasts and now in London, but this one is still always booked up (lunch is the best bet). Welcome the chance to pay through the nose for one of Nobu Matsuhisa's masterful set pieces, and forget about being satisfied by any lesser sushi ever again.

## Oceana

*55 East 54th Street, between Madison & Park Avenues (758 5941). Subway E or F to Fifth Avenue.* **Lunch** noon-2.30pm Mon-Fri. **Dinner** 5-10pm Mon-Thur; 5.30pm Fri, Sat. **Average** $55. **Credit** AmEx, DC, Disc, V.
Rick Moonen has made a name for himself creating masterful seafood dishes with French and Asian influences. A veteran of Le Côte Basque and Le Cirque, he has come into his own with innovations such as the East Coast bouillabaisse and shrimp-and-pork potsticker dumplings.

## Patria

*250 Park Avenue South, at 20th Street (777 6211). Subway 6 to 23rd Street.* **Lunch** noon-2.45pm Mon-Fri. **Dinner** 6-11pm Mon-Thur; 5.30pm-midnight Fri, Sat; 5.30-10.30pm Sun. **Average** $45. **Credit** AmEx, DC, MC, V.
Lower Park Avenue's restaurant canyon keeps expanding, but the crowds haven't diminished at Patria. They come for the wild nuevo-Latin inventions of chef Douglas Rodriguez: fish and fruit fusion, assorted seafood ceviches, chocolate 'cigars' – all in colourful, swinging split-level and swank surroudings.

## Restaurant Daniel

*20 East 76th Street, between Fifth & Madison Avenues (288 0033). Subway 6 to 77th Street.* **Lunch** noon-2.30pm Tue-Sat. **Dinner** 5.45-11.15pm Mon-Sat. **Average** $70. **Credit** AmEx, DC, MC, V.
A native of Lyon, chef Daniel Boulud has won critical acclaim for his virtuoso ability to elevate classic peasant dishes to haute cuisine. When his restaurant opened in 1993 it shot to the upper strata of New York dining. It continues to be nearly impossible to get a reservation here, unless you book weeks in advance. Daniel is due to relocate soon, so phone to check its wherabouts.
*Disabled: toilets.*

## Vong

*200 East 54th Street, at Third Avenue (486 9592). Subway E or F to Lexington Avenue.* **Lunch** noon-2.15pm Mon-Fri. **Dinner** 6-10.45pm Mon-Thur; 5.30-11pm Fri; 5.30-11.45pm Sat; 5.30-10.45pm Sun. **Average** $40-$45. **Credit** AmEx, DC, MC, V.
An Alsatian with an Asian flair, Jean-Georges Vongerichten keeps dazzling at this original home of Thai-French fusion. The food – crab spring rolls, curried rabbit, Thai lobster – is even more interesting than the surroundings: a dreamily designed gold-leafed temple in cold midtown.
*Disabled: toilets.*

# Landmark Restaurants

## The 21 Club

*21 West 52nd Street, between Fifth & Sixth Avenues (582 7200). Subway B, D, F or Q to Rockefeller Center.* **Lunch** noon-2.30pm Mon-Fri. **Dinner** 5.30-10pm Mon-Thur; 5.30-11.15pm Fri, Sat. **Average** $70. **Credit** AmEx, MC, V.
The unofficial mess hall of capitalism has a new chef and a few nouveau infiltrators, like Hawaiian snapper tartare with papaya and mango. But toys still hang from the low ceiling and this hallowed haunt of old-boydom has retained the chicken hash and the famous burger the size and weight of a newborn. The other traditions of this former speakeasy – the money chatter, orchestrated swank and cheer – are still as present as the smell of well-prepared sirloin.
*Disabled: toilets.*

## Café des Artistes

*1 West 67th Street, between Columbus Avenue & Central Park West (877 3500). Subway 1 or 9 to 66th Street.* **Brunch** 11am-2.45pm Sat; 10am-2.45pm Sun. **Lunch** noon-3pm Mon-Fri. **Dinner** 5.30-11.45pm Mon-Sat; 5.30-10.45pm Sun. **Average** $55. **Set lunch** $19.50; **set dinner** $35. **Credit** AmEx, DC, MC, V.
Jackets are mandatory at this Upper West Side hold-out, where you'll eat amid murals of frolicking naked nymphs and couples who have come to dine at what's considered one of the most romantic restaurants in New York. Prices are high, but you'll find plenty of pleasant choices from the continental menu, including roast duckling and sturgeon schnitzel.

## Four Seasons

*99 East 52nd Street, between Park & Lexington Avenues (754 9494). Subway 6 to 51st Street.* **Lunch** noon-2.30pm Mon-Fri. **Dinner** 5-9.30pm Mon-Fri; 5-11pm Sat. **Average** $80-$100. **Credit** AmEx, DC, Disc, JCB, MC, V.
The two timeless and palatial dining rooms here are the lavish Pool Room, with a pool in the corner, and the Grill Room, aka the Bar Room, famous for its square bar. The latter is where tycoons have tables permanently reserved to do business over 'spa cuisine' (sophisticated food prepared with a healthy touch). Come here to witness the ultimate in power dining and don't forget to save room for the famous cakes.
*Disabled: toilets.*

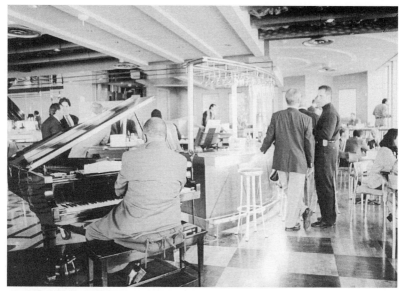

*Not even the pianist should distract from the panoramas at **Windows on the World**.*

### The Oyster Bar

*Lower Level, Grand Central Station, at 42nd Street &
Park Avenue (490 6650). Subway 4, 5, 6 to Grand
Central Station/42nd Street.* **Open** 11.30am-9.30pm Mon-
Fri. **Average** $38. **Credit** AmEx, Disc, DC, MC, V.
This beautiful station is currently getting some much needed rehabilitation, but luckily the Oyster Bar is open through
the long transition. Fine, straightforward seafood is served
under sloping vaulted ceilings and face to face with hard-
working chowdermen. The Oyster Bar can be noisy and
pricey (oysters Rockefeller, $14.95), but no experience is more
placid and dignified than stopping by here after the early
dinner rush to be alone with a plate of perfect oysters on ice.
*Disabled: toilets.*

### Rainbow Room

*30 Rockefeller Plaza, 49th Street, between Fifth & Sixth
Avenues (632 5000). Subway B, D, F or Q to Rockefeller
Center.* **Dinner** 5-11pm Tue-Thur; 6-11.30pm Fri, Sat; 6-
9pm Sun. **Average** $100. **Credit** AmEx, MC, V.
Chef Waldy Malouf has reinvigorated this timeless jewel at
the top of 30 Rock by adding contemporary dishes and bring-
ing back favourites such as lobster thermidor and oysters
Rockefeller. Dress to kill and dance to big bands and mambo
music while enjoying the restaurant's breathtaking view and
Art Deco trappings.

### Tavern on the Green

*West 67th Street, at Central Park West (873 3200).
Subway 1 or 9 to 66th Street.* **Brunch** 10.30am-3.30pm
Sat, Sun. **Lunch** 11.30am-3.30pm Mon-Fri. **Dinner** 5.30-
10.45pm daily. **Average** $45. **Credit** AmEx, Disc, MC, V.
Despite its enormous size (1,500 meals are served here a
night), Tavern on the Green is one of the prettiest places in
the city. The food is notoriously average, but the setting is
enchanting and romantic. To complete the effect, take a
horse-drawn carriage home through the park.
*Disabled: toilets.*

### Windows on the World

*107th Floor, 1 World Trade Center, West Street, between
Liberty & Vesey Streets (938 1111). Subway C or E to
World Trade Center.* **Lunch** (at bar) noon-2pm Mon-Sat;
11am-3pm Sun. **Dinner** 5-9pm Mon-Thur; 5-10.30pm Fri,
Sat. **Average** $45. **Credit** AmEx, DC, Disc, MC, V.
The $25 million renovation carried out in 1996 was no mere
Windows-dressing, but sited on the 107th floor this establishment is still all about the view. In the pale-coloured satellite party rooms, the mood is now muted, likeably-cheesey
and modern; it's jazzy in the Greatest Bar on Earth (the spiky
blown-glass lamps look like iridescent renderings of the skyscrapers below). Despite a little bill vertigo, the main dining
room is austere as a church – there's nothing to take the eye
off the heavenly panorama.
*Disabled: toilets.*

## Contemporary American

### Aja

*937 Broadway, at 22nd Street (473 8388). Subway N or
R to 23rd Street.* **Lunch** noon-3pm Mon-Fri. **Dinner** 6-
10pm Mon-Wed, Sun; 6-10.30pm Thur-Sat. **Average** $40.
**Credit** AmEx, Disc, MC, V.
A Flatiron favourite that serves quirky, eclectic Asian-influ-
enced food to a cool and good-looking crowd. One of the first
restaurants to produce tuna tartare and vertical food, Aja
continues to turn out very tasty exotic preparations.
*Disabled: toilets.*

### Arizona 206

*206 East 60th Street, between Second & Third Avenues
(838 0440). Subway 4, 5 or 6 to 59th Street; N or R to
Lexington Avenue.*
*Restaurant* **Lunch** noon-3pm Mon-Sat. **Dinner** 5.30-
10pm Mon-Thur; 5.30-11pm Fri, Sat; 6-10pm Sun.
**Average** $35.

*Café* **Open** noon-11pm Mon-Sat; noon-10pm Sun.
*Both* **Credit** AmEx, Disc, MC, V.
Although this Upper East Sider is moderately expensive, it's relatively relaxed and the food is exceptional. Customers can lounge beside the bar's fireplace before moving to the Southwestern-style dining room and ordering from the innovative menu that includes tortilla-crusted trout and Peking duck tamale.

### Gramercy Tavern

*42 East 20th Street, between Broadway & Park Avenue (477 0777). Subway 6, N or R to 23rd Street.*
*Restaurant* **Lunch** noon-2pm daily. **Dinner** 5-10pm Mon-Thur, Sun; 5.30-11pm Fri, Sat. **Average** *lunch* $32; *dinner* 3-course set menu $52.
*Tavern* **Open** noon-11pm Mon-Thur, Sun; noon-midnight Fri, Sat.
*Both* **Credit** AmEx, DC, MC, V.
Visitors have a number of equally inviting options at this Flatiron Mecca, a younger sibling of the ever-popular Union Square Café. The innovative *prix fixe* menu is offered only in the elegant dining room. Budget-minded guests, however, won't miss out on atmosphere or delightful dishes if occupying the couches and small tables in the front tavern area. Food can also be ordered from the cosiest section of the restaurant, Gramercy's beautiful bar.
*Disabled: toilets.*

### Indigo

*142 West 10th Street, between Greenwich Avenue & Waverly Place (691 7757).* **Dinner** 6-11pm Mon-Thur; 6-11.30pm Fri, Sat; 6-10.30pm Sun. **Average** $30.
**Credit** AmEx.
Delicious French-American cuisine from Scott Bryan, the chef at Luma. West Villagers love the bold-style dishes – like wild mushroom strudel and roast pork loin – and the affordable prices.

### JUdson Grill

*152 West 52nd Street, between Sixth & Seventh Avenues (582 5252). Subway 1 or 9 to 50th Street; N or R to 49th Street.* **Lunch** noon-2.30pm Mon-Fri. **Dinner** 5.30-11pm Mon-Thur; 5.30-11pm Fri, Sat. **Average** $40. **Credit** AmEx, DC, Disc, MC, V.
At night during the week, the bar can be clamorous with afterwork traffic, but the cathedral-sized dining room is all smooth and modern spaciousness. Knockout starters include a smoky sturgeon with sevruga caviar on little potato rösti ($12) and the pungent cured venison carpaccio. The first part of the name is the neighbourhood's old telephone prefix, recalling a lost Gotham glamour, while the second means a good selection of grilled fish and meats.
*Disabled: toilets.*

### Match Downtown

*160 Mercer Street, between Houston & Prince Streets (343 0020). Subway N or R to Prince Street.* **Open** 11.30am-2am Mon, Tue, Sun; 11.30am-4am Wed-Sat
**Credit** AmEx, MC, V.
A Soho hotspot that never gets too crowded thanks to its bars (one up and one down) and a large dining area. The food has a strong Asian influence which the customers (SoHo shoppers and off-duty models) can take in until 4am from Wednesday to Saturday.

### The River Café

*1 Water Street, at Cadman Plaza West, Brooklyn (1-718 522 5200). Subway A or C to High Street.* **Brunch** noon-2.30pm Sat; 11.30am-2.30pm Sun. **Lunch** noon-2.30pm Mon-Fri. **Dinner** 6-11pm daily. **Average** $58. **Credit** AmEx, DC, MC, V.
The irony of Manhattan's awe-inspiring skyline is that you have to leave it, in order to enjoy it. Hop across the Brooklyn Bridge to this romantic restaurant abutting the East River.

In winter, ask for a window table; in summer, enjoy American cuisine in the open air with the lights of the Brooklyn Bridge and the larger metropolis illuminating your table.

### Verbena

*54 Irving Place, between 17th & 18th Streets (260 5454). Subway L, N, R, 4 or 6 to Union Square/14th Street.* **Lunch** noon-2.45pm Sat, Sun. **Dinner** 5.30-10pm Mon; 5.30-10.30pm Tue-Thur; 5.30-11pm Fri, Sat; 5.30-9.30pm Sun. **Average** $45. **Credit** AmEx, DC, MC, V.
The theme here is flora, from the pressed flowers mounted in glass on the walls, to the back courtyard's herb garden. Chef Diane Forley's menu relies on the creative use of her home-grown herbs for such dishes as butternut squash ravioli flavoured with sage, and a rolled herb soufflé.

## Forever Chic

### 44

*Royalton Hotel, 44 West 44th Street, between Fifth & Sixth Avenues (944 8844). Subway B, D or F to 42nd Street.* **Lunch** noon-3pm daily. **Dinner** 5.45-11pm Mon-Thur, Sun; 5.45pm-midnight Fri, Sat. **Average** $40.
**Credit** AmEx, Disc, MC, V.
Ian Schrager, late of Studio 54, Palladium and more recently the Mondrian in LA, created this aggressively modern lair in the late 1980s. It still attracts major publishing honchos. Order a drink in the lounge or back in the dining area and keep your eyes peeled – especially at lunch.

### Elaine's

*1703 Second Avenue, between 88th & 89th Streets (534 8103). Subway 4 or 6 to 86th Street.* **Dinner** 6pm-2am daily. **Average** $35. **Credit** AmEx, Disc, MC, V.
Elaine's is the dinosaur of chic restaurants and even after all these years still pulls in an A-list crowd. The food, though respectable, isn't what counts. What does, is the outspoken proprietress, Elaine Kaufman, and a stellar cast of characters that on any given night might include Woody Allen, Barbra Streisand or George Plimpton.

### Lucky Strike

*59 Grand Street, between Wooster Street & West Broadway (941 0479). Subway A, C or E to Canal Street.* **Open** noon-4am daily. **Average** $22. **Credit** AmEx, DC, MC, V.
It has been years since Madonna anointed this laid-back bistro, but even though the swells have moved on, Lucky Strike still packs 'em in. Sit in the back for predictable bistro fare and a good wine selection, then hit the bar where the weekend DJ plays old soul and funk until last orders.

### Marion's

*354 The Bowery, between 3rd & 4th Streets (475 7621). Subway 6 to Bleecker Street.* **Dinner** 6pm-2am daily. **Average** $28. **Credit** MC, V.
Marion's is kitsch, but unimpeachably so. The Kennedy fetishism, the Hawaiian mementoes, the celebrity plates – it's all fun at this timewarp of 1950s glamour on The Bowery. The menu (excellent, darkly fried calamari, good salads) is best seen as a complement to margaritas on ice and other good drinks, stiff and sweet. If you really want to sweeten a lingering night, give yourself over to the ample, catch-all dessert sampler. On the first Sunday of each month (noon-3pm) there's brunch and a fashion show.
*Disabled: toilets.*

### Odéon

*145 West Broadway, between Thomas & Duane Streets (233 0507). Subway 1, 2, 3 or 9 to Chambers Street.* **Open** noon-2am Mon-Thur; noon-3am Fri; 11.30am-3am Sat; 11.30am-2am Sun. **Average** $35. **Credit** AmEx, DC, MC, V.

*The funky, late-night* **Restaurant Florent**.

It was big in the early 1980s and it continues to be full to this day. Trendy Odéon serves popular French bistro food including steak au poivre. Customers include youngish, downtown folk and Wall Street suits that have come to see and be seen. The lights are dim and the tables jammed together, obscuring the fact that they occupy a bare, cafeteria-like space.

### Raoul's

*180 Prince Street, between Sullivan & Thompson Streets (966 3518). Subway C or E to Spring Street.* **Dinner** 6pm-2am daily. **Average** $40. **Credit** AmEx, DC, MC, V.
The Elaine's of downtown, Raoul's is a time-tested favourite and is constantly packed for dinner. Quirky as only an older joint can be, it has a good bar scene for after-work gallery types and late night club crawlers, a romantic dining room that serves excellent French bistro food, and a tarot card reader upstairs.

### Restaurant Florent

*69 Gansevoort Street, between Greenwich & Washington Streets (989 5779). Subway A, C or E to 14th Street; L to Eighth Avenue.* **Open** 24 hours daily. **Average** $25. **No credit cards.**
After a night of club-hopping at lounges that line the cobble-stoned streets of the increasingly hip meatpacking district, stop by at Florent – established long before the recent rash of trendy night spots. It's open 24 hours, and the large portion of fries from its French-bistro menu will help absorb all that beer swishing around.

## Cheap Eats

### Ecco-La

*1660 Third Avenue, at 93rd Street (860 5609). Subway 6 to 96th Street.* **Lunch** 11.30am-3.45pm daily. **Dinner** 4-11.30pm Mon-Thur, Sun; 4pm-midnight Fri, Sat. **Average** $18. **Credit** AmEx.
The first room at Ecco-La is cheerful, noisy and boldly colourful, the second is quiet and a bit chintzy with gilt-framed pictures and upholstered chairs. Choose your room according to your mood and enjoy the simple menu that offers endless variations of pastas and sauces, most for under $10.

### Elvie's Turo-Turo

*214 First Avenue, between 12th & 13th Streets (473 7785). Subway L to First Avenue.* **Open** 11am-9pm Mon-Sat; 11am-8pm Sun. **Average** $7. **No credit cards.**
A Filipino buffet-style diner that caters to hungry New Yorkers from all walks of life. They come for Elvira Samora Cinco's stews, grills, barbecued pork and seafood – a choice of two served on a mountain of rice costs under $5. A New York delight.

### La Focacceria

*128 First Avenue, between St Marks & 7th Streets (254 4946). Subway 6 to Astor Place.* **Open** 10am-10pm Mon-Thur; 10am-11pm Fri, Sat. **Average** $20. **No credit cards.**
First, order a half carafe of the delicious house chianti, fill your tumbler and drink to the abolition of long-stemmed glasses and overpriced wine lists. Now, scan the food choices on the wall. (This brightly lit pasta factory has been here since 1914 and still hasn't got around to printing a menu.) Everything's so cheap you can probably afford to order appetisers, pasta and a main course, but portions are big enough that you don't have to.
*Disabled: toilets.*

### Mama's Food Shop

*200 East 3rd Street, between Avenues A & B (777 4425). Subway F to Second Avenue.* **Open** 11am-11pm Mon-Sat. **Average** $12. **No credit cards.**
An instant institution of the East Village, this pint-sized, casual eatery offers a taste of the South, cafeteria-style. Maybe it's the mother-sized portions of mashed potatoes, macaroni, fried chicken and meatloaf, or the portraits of various moms on the walls, that keep the regulars coming back for a dose of comfort.

### Margon

*136 West 46th Street, between Sixth & Seventh Avenues (354 5013). Subway N or R to 42nd Street; 1 or 9 to 5th Street.* **Open** 6am-4.45pm Mon-Fri; 7am-2.30pm Sat. **Average** $15. **No credit cards.**
A packed Cuban joint that offers a blessed deliverance from the usual midtown lunch hustle. Line up for Cuban sandwiches, octopus salad, tripe and pig's feet, or soft beef pot roast – all of it served with great amounts of beans (black or red) and rice. Sharing tables with strangers is encouraged, as long as you share the hot sauce.

### Panna II

*93 First Avenue, between 5th & 6th Streets (598 4610). Subway F to Second Avenue.* **Open** noon-midnight daily. **Average** $15. **No credit cards.**
An Indian restaurant American-style, with riotous paper decoration, loud, piped-in sitars and an East Village demographic mix of customers. Panna II serves North Indian specialities (most of which cost less than $5) at a rapid clip. You don't pay to linger, but fast food has its price.

### Plan-Eat Thailand

*184 Bedford Avenue, between North 6th & North 7th Streets, Brooklyn (1-718-599 5758). Subway L to Bedford Avenue.* **Open** 11.30am-11.30pm Mon-Sat; 1-11pm Sun. **Average** $ 12. **No credit cards.**
Sit at the bar and watch the cooks concoct extra-spicy peanut or coconut curries, or grab a table and take a gander at art created by some home-grown Williamsburg talent, while sampling the delicious vegetable pad Thai. Prices hover around $7, and the portions are big enough to warrant a doggie bag.

### Rush'n Express

*306 East 8th Street, between First & Second Avenues (982 8383). Subway 4, 5 or 6 to 86th Street.* **Open** 11am-10pm daily. **Average** $10. **Credit** AmEx, MC, V.
No express train to the 'Little Odessa' of Brighton Beach is faster than the quick fix of Rush'n Express. These insanely enthusiastic twin fast-foodies have a long menu of dishes such as hearty Siberian dumplings, all at Soviet-era prices. Where else can you get blini and caviar for $3.99?

### Taqueria de Mexico

*93 Greenwich Avenue, between 12th & Bank Streets (255 5212). Subway 1 or 9 to Christopher Street/Sheridan Square.* **Open** 11.30am-11pm Mon-Thur, Sun; 11.30am-midnight Fri, Sat. **Average** $12. **No credit cards.**

**Panna II:** *for cut-price North Indian specialities served at a clip. See page 125.*

Like its upmarket sister restaurant Mi Cocina, Taqueria serves traditional Mexican dishes with super-fresh ingredients. If the sombreros and other Mexican artefacts don't get you in the mood, the delicious enchiladas, chile rellenos and tacos (for nearly border-town prices) should do the trick. *Disabled: toilets.*

## American
### Cajun

**Acadia Parish**
*148 Atlantic Avenue, between Clinton & Henry Streets, Brooklyn (1-718 624 5154). Subway 2, 3, 4 or 6 to Court Street/Boro Hall.* **Dinner** 5-9.45pm Mon, Wed, Thur; 5-10.45pm Fri, Sat; 4-8.45pm Sun. **Average** $20. **Credit** AmEx, DC, Disc, MC, V.
In the best Southern style, the good folks at Acadia Parish will feed you, or try to, till there's hot sauce coming out of your ears. Dishes such as crawfish étouffée and blackened chicken breast are scrumptious, fortifying and served, as the menu puts it, 'with one starch and one vegetable'. *Disabled: toilets.*

**Cajun**
*129 Eighth Avenue, between 16th & 17th Streets (691 6174). Subway A, C or E to 14th Street/Eighth Avenue.* **Brunch** 11am-4pm Sun. **Lunch** noon-3pm Mon-Fri. **Dinner** 5-11pm Mon-Thur, Sun; 5pm-midnight Fri, Sat. **Average** *lunch* $10; *dinner* $20. **Credit** AmEx, DC, MC, V.
For the price of a main course, diners are treated to live jazz every night of the week, and a Big Easy aura of pleasant decadence. Enjoy specialities such as the gumbo, jambalaya or chicken creole, but be prepared to have the owner, a Louisiana native, admonish you if you don't clean your plate.

**Chantale's Cajun Kitchen**
*510 Ninth Avenue, between 38th & 39th Streets (967 2623). Subway A, C or E to 42nd Street.* **Open** 11.30am-7.30pm Mon-Thur; 11.30am-8.30pm Fri, Sat. **Average** $12. **No credit cards.**

Chantale's does thriving business at lunch-time, both eat-in and delivery, but it's also a great and inexpensive choice for a pre-theatre dinner. The menu includes meaty curries, gumbos and creolos, though also a good selection of vegetarian options.

**Great Jones Café**
*54 Great Jones Street, between The Bowery & Lafayette Street (674 9304). Subway 6 to Bleecker Street.* **Brunch** 11.30am-4pm Sat, Sun. **Dinner** 5pm-midnight Mon-Thur; 5pm-1am Fri, Sat. **Average** $20. **No credit cards.**
Minute, but easy to spot by its bright-orange exterior and a bust of Elvis in the front window, Great Jones is one of the best Cajun restaurants in the city. The basic menu is small and painted on the wall, but the changing specials almost always include some kind of catfish and a po'boy (French bread sandwich) or two.

**Orleans**
*1438 Third Avenue, between 81st & 82nd Streets (794 1509). Subway 4 or 6 to 86th Street.* **Open** noon-11pm Mon-Thur, Sun; noon-11.30pm Fri, Sat. **Average** $25. **Credit** AmEx, MC, V.
Cajun cooking served in a classy, rarified atmosphere. The standards such as jambalaya and po'boys are all here, as well as some twists like blackened lamb kebabs. There's no harm in eating expensive Cajun food if it's good (and it is), just don't expect to roll up your sleeves, drink a can of beer and chuck your crawfish husks on the floor. *Disabled: toilets.*

### Delis

**Carnegie Deli**
*854 Seventh Avenue, between 54th & 55th Streets (757 2245). Subway N or R to 57th Street.* **Open** 6.30am-4am daily. **Average** $15. **No credit cards.**
The décor is unprepossessing and the waiters are infamously rude at this deli in the theatre district, but the super-sized sandwiches, piled high with corned beef and other typical New York deli meat, are worth any visual or emotional distress you may suffer.

### Ess-a-Bagel

*831 Third Avenue, between 50th & 51st Streets*
*(980 1010). Subway 6 to 51st Street; E or F to Lexington*
*Avenue.* **Open** 6.30am-10pm Mon-Fri; 8am-5pm Sat, Sun.
**Average** $6. **Credit** AmEx, MC, V.
Let's talk about what a bagel should be: huge, with a crust that's
a little chewy but breaks. There should be no – or almost no –
space in the hole. At Ess-a-Bagel's original downtown location,
the ideal bagel is served by fat-fingered guys who touch everything and make dumb jokes. Perfection at 55¢ a pop.
**Branch**: 359 First Avenue (260 2252).

### Katz's Deli

*205 East Houston Street, at Ludlow Street (254 2246).*
*Subway F to Second Avenue.* **Open** 8am-11pm Mon-
Thur; 8am-midnight Fri-Sun. **Average** $10. **Credit**
AmEx, MC, V.
This venerable New York deli, famous for its old-style cafeteria décor and superb salamis and hot dogs, stands at the
invisible portals of the Lower East Side. Order a sandwich
piled high with thick slabs of pastrami or corned beef, a platter of salami and eggs, or an egg cream, an old-fashioned
drink with a misleading name.

### Pastrami King

*124-24 Queens Boulevard, Queens (1-718-263 1717).*
*Subway E or F to Union Turnpike/Kew Gardens.* **Open**
9am-10pm daily. **Average** $15. **Credit** AmEx, MC, V.
Although it's under new ownership which some claim has
changed Pastrami King for the worse, you can still head to
Queens for the ultimate pastrami sandwich at this famous
old Art Deco deli.

### Second Avenue Deli

*156 Second Avenue, at 10th Street (677 0606). Subway 6*
*to Astor Place.* **Open** 7am-midnight Mon-Thur, Sun;
7am-2am Fri, Sat. **Average** $14. **Credit** AmEx.
The dwindling number of authentic Jewish delicatessens in
town make this a mandatory East Village stop. Soothe your
soul with a matzo ball soup, and then embark on a trip down
heartburn lane with a hot corned beef sandwich, some knish-
es and a serving of chopped liver. Prices are a bit steep, but
most customers will find the large portions easy to share.

### Stage Deli

*834 Seventh Avenue, between 53rd & 54th Streets*
*(245 7850). Subway N or R to 57th Street.* **Open** 6am-
2am daily. **Average** $18. **Credit** AmEx, Disc, MC, V.
Famous for its monolithic sandwiches and top-quality deli
food, Stage Deli serves much the same food as nearby rival
Carnegie at the same high prices. Visit both and decide which
is better. Expect to see many tourists.

## Diners

### Cheyenne Diner

*411 Ninth Avenue, at 33rd Street (465 8750). Subway*
*A, C or E to 34th Street.* **Open** 24 hours daily. **Average**
$15. **Credit** AmEx, DC, MC, V.
Cheyenne is the kind of place that cigarette ad location scouts
would give a lung for; it's also the kind of authentic place
that locals feel lucky still to have on Manhattan soil: a silver-
sided, pink-neon-signed breadbox of a diner. Brunch specials
($6.95) include juice, fruit salad, coffee and mega-calorific
helpings of eggs and meat. Enjoy the indulgence, the gun-
metal grey housing and the delightfully crappy *mise en scène*
of Ninth Avenue.

### Comfort Diner

*214 East 45th Street, between Second & Third Avenues*
*(867 4555). Subway 4, 5, 6 or 7 to Grand Central/42nd*
*Street.* **Open** 7am-10pm daily. **Average** $15. **Credit**
AmEx, MC, V.

This retro diner is inspired by, rather than torn from, the
pages of history. The red lights along the wall look like they
were swiped from below a Cadillac's fin and the terrazo table-
tops are modelled on old diner floors. The only thing you
really need to know though, is that this is one of the friend-
liest spots in east midtown, perfect for a cup of joe and big
waffle breakfast, or a memory-jogging indulgence in grilled
s'mores ($3.75).
*Disabled: toilets.*

### Empire Diner

*210 Tenth Avenue, at West 22nd Street (243 2736).*
*Subway C or E to 23rd Street.* **Open** 24 hours Mon, Wed-
Sun; 9am-3am Tue. **Average** $18. **Credit** AmEx, Disc,
MC, V.
This west Chelsea all-nighter is the essence of preserved
Americana, with no signs of peeling chrome. Come on down
at night when the place glows, and sample some above-
average diner fare. At 3am everything tastes fine and a lit-
tle illicit. It's a shame the rest of the city isn't like this – shiny
and as edgily smooth as early Tom Waits.

### Jones Diner

*371 Lafayette Street, at Great Jones Street (673 3577).*
*Subway 6 to Astor Place.* **Open** 6am-6pm Mon-Sat; 8am-
6pm Sun. **Average** $16. **No credit cards**.
A brick and aluminium shanty that's been on this corner for
80 years and, fortunately, shows every bit of it. Though the
dingy façade keeps newcomers away, the craggy regulars
are devoted to the basic and ultra cheap sandwiches, breakfast specials and burgers.

### Tom's Restaurant

*2880 Broadway, at 112th Street (864 6137).*
*Subway 1 or 9 to 110th Street/Cathedral Parkway.*
**Open** 6am-1.30am Mon-Wed, Sun; 24-hours Thur-Sat.
**Average** $14. **No credit cards**.

*Elvis lives on at the* **Great Jones Café**. *P126.*

Columbia University students come to this diner on a weekly if not daily basis for the grilled cheese sandwiches, hamburgers, fries and milkshakes. Suzanne Vega sang about it, and the characters on the ever-popular *Seinfeld* use it as the seat for all their neurotic get-togethers (an exterior shot of Tom's precedes all diner scenes).

## Southern

### Café Beulah

*39 East 19th Street, between Park Avenue South & Broadway (777 9700). Subway N or R to 23rd Street.*
**Dinner** 5.30-11pm Mon-Wed; 5.30pm-midnight Thur-Sat; 4-10pm Sun. **Average** $30. **Credit** AmEx, DC, Disc, MC, V.
A popular Flatiron spot that features Alexander Small's contemporary versions of his mother's South Carolina specialties. The 'low country' menu includes succotash, biscuits, hams, yams and other comfort foods.
*Disabled: toilets.*

### Jezebel's

*630 Ninth Avenue, at 45th Street (582 1045). Subway A, C or E to 42nd Street.* **Open** 5.30-10pm Mon-Wed; 5.30-11.30pm Thur-Sat. **Average** $35. **Credit** AmEx.
In the brothel-inspired Southern Gothic dining room, patrons sit on porch swings beneath glittery chandeliers as a piano player tinkles away. The food – ham-hocks, pork chops, black-eyed peas – is delightful and religiously authentic. A New York jewel on gritty Ninth Avenue.
*Disabled: toilets.*

### Mekka

*14 Avenue A, between East Houston & 2nd Streets (475 8500). Subway F to Second Avenue.* **Brunch** 11.30am-3.30pm Sun. **Dinner** 6-11pm Mon-Wed, Sun; 6pm-midnight Thur; 6pm-2am Fri, Sat. **Average** $20. **Credit** AmEx, DC, MC, V.
Mekka's got a chic clientele, a nightclub vibe and a DJ who starts at 10pm at the weekend. The hip-hop and Caribbean music goes perfectly with the food – a combo of traditional soul food with Island references that includes rice and peas, barbecued pork and po'boys. Sit in the back garden and wash it all down with a Mambo beer.
*Disabled: toilets.*

### Pink Tea Cup

*42 Grove Street, between Bedford & Bleecker Streets (807 6755). Subway 1 or 9 to Christopher Street/ Sheridan Square.* **Open** 8am-midnight Mon-Thur, Sun; 8am-1am Fri, Sat. **Average** $15. **No credit cards**.
Within these pink West Village walls is a charmingly intimate restaurant that's a hot spot for brunch. There will most certainly be a queue at weekends; use it as an opportunity to decide whether you want grilled pork chops or fried chicken with your pancakes.

### Princess Pamela's

*78 East 1st Street, between First Avenue & Avenue A (477 4460). Subway F to Second Avenue.* **Open** 7pm-midnight daily. **Average** $15. **No credit cards**
Miss Pamela doesn't just host this six-table nook, she holds court. If you ask her nicely, she might even sing a song or two with the old-timer jazz combo after dinner. Her food is simple and homely: collard greens, macaroni, cornbread meatloaf and fried chicken. Bring your own booze and don't forget your manners.

### Sylvia's

*328 Lenox Avenue, between 126th & 127th Streets (996 0660). Subway 2 or 3 to 125th Street.* **Open** 7.30am-10.30pm Mon-Sat; 12.30-7pm Sun. **Average** $22. **Credit** AmEx, Disc, MC, V.
Harlem's most famous dining spot has become a bit touristy

(tour buses wait patiently outside the place). But no matter, the ribs are still tender, sweet and way ahead of any downtown contenders and the collard greens would sate any Southerner.
*Disabled: toilets.*

## Seafood

*See also page 141* **Aquagrill**.

### Blue Water Grill

*31 Union Square West, at 16th Street (675 9500). Subway L, N, R, 4 or 6 to 14th Street/Union Square.* **Open** 11.30am-12.30am Mon-Thur; 11.30am-1am Fri, Sat. **Average** $35. **Credit** AmEx, MC, V.
This cool, high-ceilinged Union Square building was once a bank, but if you listen closely you can hear the sea. The space of the old finely named Bank of the Metropolis is light and elegant, all marble and blue banquettes, the soft lights like beacons. The menu has an oyster lexicon, but it's not too fishcentric to be fun. Try the 'Coffee and Donuts' dessert: dewy cinnamon sweets with a mug of coffee-flavoured pot de crème.

### Crab House

*Chelsea Pier 61, between 23rd Street & West Side Highway (835 2722). Subway C or E to 23rd Street.* **Open** noon-11pm Mon-Thur, Sun; noon-midnight Fri, Sat. **Average** $20. **Credit** AmEx, CB, DC, MC, V.
Suburbanites the world over can now visit New York and eat in a friendly, sprawling chain restaurant that's just like the one at home. Secure a seat on the deck with its fine views down the Hudson. Softshell crab and all manner of unremarkable, overpriced seafood is available – but this is a themey suburban restaurant, so bet on dessert being the pearl in the dud oyster. With a slice of Key lime pie and a few frozen drink confections in you, you could be forgiven for going home with a 'I got hammered at the Crab House' T-shirt.
*Disabled: toilets.*

### Gage & Tollner

*372 Fulton Street, between Smith & Jay Streets, Brooklyn (1-718 875 5181). Subway A, C or F to Jay Street/Boro Hall.* **Lunch** 11am-3.30pm Mon-Fri. **Dinner** 5-10pm Mon-Thur; 5-11pm Fri; 3-11pm Sat. **Average** $35. **Credit** AmEx, Disc, MC, V.
This 117 year-old re-opened in 1996 after major renovations. Subtle Charleston she-crab soup, gigantic clams on the half-shell and absolutely anything that comes with tartar sauce are enough to lure even dredge-shy Manhattanites. The woody Pullman dining car-inspired room was the first restaurant interior to be awarded landmark status, but the real business here is in stuffing oneself exquisitely.

### Johnny's Reef

*2 City Island Avenue, at Belden's Point, City Island, Bronx (1-718-885-2086). Subway 6 to Pelham Bay Park, then Bx29 bus to City Island.* **Open** 11am-midnight daily. **Average** $10. **No credit cards**.
This cheapo fry-fest is one of the best ways to take part in a central ritual of city life – complaining about never leaving and then never going very far. City Island feels like a sleepy shoreside vacation spot, but is accessible by city bus. The main drag is lined with clam shacks, but go to the end, to Johnny's, for all manner of fried sea life to be eaten outside with the mob and low-circling seagulls.

### Lundy Bros

*1901 Emmons Avenue, between Ocean Avenue & Sheepshead Bay, Brooklyn (1-718-743 0022). Subway D or Q to Sheepshead Bay.* **Lunch** 10am-4pm Mon-Fri. **Dinner** 6-11pm Mon-Fri. **Open** 1pm-midnight Sat; 1-9pm Sun. **Average** $30. **Credit** AmEx, MC, V.
After a 17-year absence, more than just the Lundy name has been revived. This Sheepshead Bay waterfront institution is

alive – throbbing with families indulging in shore dinners, couples at the raw bar, and a good time being had by all. The combination dinners of chowder, lobster and chicken satisfy, as does the reconstructed spirit of a time when Brooklyn was the world.
*Disabled: toilets.*

## Steakhouses

### Gallagher's

*228 West 52nd Street, between Broadway & Eighth Avenue (245 5336). Subway C or E to 50th Street.* **Open** noon-midnight daily. **Average** $60. **Credit** AmEx, Disc, MC, V.
The attendant in candy-red uniform announces your departure back in time. Say to 1927, when this former speakeasy opened, selling steaks for $1.50 a go. The price has gone up (a 26oz steak for one is now $39.95), but the marbled shells still hang in view of the diners, and the photos on the wall honour horses and ball-players otherwise

forgotten. With its red-checked table-cloths, this not-quite-a-poor-man's '21' is an extremely likeable escape from modern midtown drudgery.
*Disabled: toilets.*

### Morton's of Chicago

*551 Fifth Avenue, on 45th Street, between Fifth & Madison Avenues (972 3315). Subway B, D or F to 42nd Street.* **Lunch** 11.30am-2.30pm Mon-Fri. **Dinner** 5pm-midnight Mon-Sat; 5-11pm Sun. **Average** $48. **Credit** AmEx, DC, Disc, MC, V.
Now with two Manhattan outlets, this businessman's chain is one you can sink your teeth into. The low-lit nouveau riche décor triggers a sense of *déjà vu*. The waiters are friendly, the wine list extensive and the steak is wet-aged and scarily moist and flavourful. The Midtown branch might do for a date, while the newer Wall Street branch caters to traders at lunch and bridge-and-tunnellers at night.
*Disabled: toilets.*
**Branch:** 90 West Street (732 5665).

# Best breakfasts

New Yorkers have an odd, manic relationship with breakfast. During the working week, the first meal of the day is given perfunctory attention; typical New Yorkers buy a doughnut or a muffin with a cup of coffee from a street vendor en route to work, the same way they remember to put petrol into the tank before embarking on a long road trip. Come Saturday, however, and Manhattanites are transformed into birds of prey, first stealthily choosing, then patiently circling their chosen breakfast nook – no matter how long the queue.

Yes, weekend brunch is serious business. On Saturdays and Sundays, the breakfast period often doesn't begin before ten in the morning and might end late in the afternoon. Some use the extended meal time to meet friends they've neglected during the week; others create a ritual around brunch during which they read the weekend edition of the *New York Times* from first page to last. Menus vary from down-home to refined, but typically involve eggs, omelettes, bacon, pancakes, oatmeal, bagels and lox (smoked salmon), or a serving of fresh fruit salad.

Certain eateries are as famous for their brunch crowds as they are for their food. Despite having three branches each, it's almost impossible not to end up queueing during the weekend at any of the following three establishments. **EJ's Luncheonette** (447 Amsterdam Avenue, between 81st & 82nd Streets, 873 3444; 432 Sixth Avenue, between 9th & 10th Streets, 473 5555; 1271 Third Avenue, at 73rd Street, 472 0600) serves diner-with-a-twist fare, such as French toast coated with cornflakes and almonds, to a twentysomething contingent. **Royal Canadian**

**Pancake House** offers mattress-sized pancakes and eggs that ultimately stump even the most voracious appetite (2286 Broadway, between 82nd & 83rd Streets, 873 6052; 1004 Second Avenue, at 53rd Street, 980 4131; 180 Third Avenue, at 17th Street, 777 9288). **Sarabeth's** (1295 Madison Avenue, between 92nd & 93rd Streets, 410 7335; Whitney Museum, 945 Madison Avenue, at 75th Street, 570 3670; 423 Amsterdam Avenue, between 80th & 81st Streets, 496 6280) is a slightly more upmarket brunch experience, where uptowners come for their 'Goldilocks' fix: scrambled eggs with lox and cream cheese.

Commoner still are restaurants with only one branch to satisfy the hordes of hungry weekenders. **Aggie's** has a wall-board menu that lists simple breakfast food in large portions (146 Houston Street, at MacDougal (673 8994). **Bubby's** serves brunch to the ever-growing population of trendsters who have decided to make TriBeCa their home (120 Hudson Street, at N Moore Street, 219 0666). **Le Gamin** in SoHo is a small café that gives a French spin on breakfast, with such offerings as tartines and croissants (50 MacDougal Street, between Prince & Houston Streets, 254 4678). Middle Eastern fare is mixed with American favourites at **Oznot's Dish** in Brooklyn (79 Berry Street, at North 9th Street, 1-718 599 6596). But for the most cosmopolitan of all breakfast experiences, head for **Fifty Seven Fifty Seven** (57 East 57th Street, between Madison & Park Avenues, 758 5757), where IM Pei's Four Seasons Hotel sets the tone for an impeccable morning repast.

## Old Homestead

*56 Ninth Avenue, between 14th & 15th Streets*
*(242 9040). Subway A, C or E to 14th Street; L to Eighth*
*Avenue.* **Lunch** noon-4pm Mon-Fri. **Dinner** noon-
10.45pm daily. **Open** 1-11.45pm Sat; 1-9.45pm Sun.
**Average** $60. **Credit** AmEx, CB, DC, MC, V.
There are plenty of pleasures at the oldest steakhouse in the
city (1868), but many come for the Kobe – that coddled, beer-
fed bovine of mythological softness. A Kobe steak is $100,
but this is the Grail for carnivores, so finely marbled and tender. Still, you'll be forgiven if you opt instead for a more classic porterhouse for two ($58) and soak in the meaty history
of the room.
*Disabled: toilets.*

## Palm

*837 Second Avenue, between 44th & 45th Streets*
*(687 2953). Subway S, 4, 5, 6, 7 to 42nd Street.*
**Open** noon-11.30pm Mon-Fri; 5-11.30pm Sat.
**Average** $48. **Credit** AmEx, MC, V.
A total of 15 other Palms have appeared around the USA,
but the East Side 70 year-old speakeasy is the original. Palm
Too opened across the street in 1973 and the two are basi-
cally identical: no frills, stern Italian waiters in flesh-coloured
jackets, yellowed walls bearing the cartoons and caricature
marks of such past regulars as Jackie Gleason and J Edgar
Hoover. Palm Too is, however, open on Sundays (2-10pm).
Go supple (filet mignon, $29) or savoury (New York strip,
$29), but either way have the cheesecake.
*Disabled: toilets.*
**Branch: Palm Too** 840 Second Avenue (697 5198).

## Peter Luger

*178 Broadway, between Driggs & Bedford Avenues,*
*Williamsburg, Brooklyn (1-718-387 7400). Subway J to*
*Marcy Avenue.* **Open** 11.45am-10pm Mon-Thur;
11.45am-11pm Fri, Sat; 1-10pm Sun. **Average** $50.
**No credit cards.**
Since 1887, anyone who has ever drooled as a Luger ancient
served them a piece of Porterhouse has dreamt of a heaven
that begins at the end of the Williamsburg Bridge. Here, eter-
nity would be spent under harsh lights in an austere beer
hall, in the presence of those sublime cuts of dry-aged beef
Hitchcock called the greatest in the universe (porterhouse for
two is $57.50). Skip the menu, order the hashbrowns, the
silky creamed spinach and pray you never wake up.

## Sparks

*210 East 46th Street, between Second & Third Avenues*
*(687 4855). Subway 4, 5 or 6 to 42nd Street.*
**Lunch** noon-3pm Mon-Fri. **Dinner** 5-11pm Mon-Thur;
5-11.45pm Fri, Sat. **Average** $49. **Credit** AmEx, CB,
DC, MC, V.
So maybe Big Paul Castellano did digest his last saturated
fats here before being unceremoniously gunned down. But
there's really no dark mystery at Sparks, with its big jer-
oboams, big family dinners and big queues. What's here is
a 30-year history of good steaks in a setting of comfortably
familiar swank. Waiters are happy to improvise lavish, off-
the-menu chopped salad – and what better warm-up for a
black and blue (charred outside, cold inside) sirloin than a
salad thick with bacon and blue cheese?

## Chinese

## 20 Mott Street

*20 Mott Street, between Pell Street & The Bowery*
*(964 0380). Subway 6, J, N or R to Canal Street.*
**Open** 9am-11pm Mon-Fri; 8.30am-11pm Sat, Sun.
**Average** $18. **Credit** AmEx, Disc, MC, V.
Come early to this three-storey dim sum emporium – one of
the most popular in Chinatown. The mouthwatering
appetiser-like dumplings, rolls and buns are served from

carts that stop periodically at each table. The menus are in
Chinese, the waiters can be unhelpful, but the dim sum selection, including duck feet and jelly fish, is extensive, guaran-
teeing a full stomach and a good time.

## House of Vegetarian

*68 Mott Street, between Canal & Bayard Streets (226*
*6572). Subway J, N, R or 6 to Canal Street.* **Open** 11am-
11pm daily. **Average** $9-$15. **No credit cards.**
There are only vegetables on the menu here, which means
that the roast duck appetiser is really wheat gluten in a clever
disguise. If faux-meat scares you, there are plenty of more
conventional veggie dishes.

## Jade Palace Seafood Restaurant

*136-14 38th Avenue, at Main Street, Brooklyn (1-718-*
*353 3366). Subway 7 to Main Street.* **Open** 8am-
midnight daily. **Average** $30. **Credit** AmEx, MC, V.
A neighbourhood favourite in Queens, Jade Palace has waiters, uniformed in black and white, who will promptly bring
pickled turnip, a finger-food standard, to your table. Skip the
usual Chinese menu choices and order a seafood dish such
as the seafood deluxe, a bowl of jumbo shrimp, scallops,
conch, octopus and sea-cucumber intestines. Expect clean,
warm hand towels at the end of the meal.

## Joe's Shanghai

*9 Pell Street, between Mott Street & The Bowery (233*
*8888). Subway J, N, R or 6 to Canal Street.* **Open** 11am-
11pm daily. **Average** $18. **No credit cards.**
Although you'll find dishes such as fried pork dumplings
and cold chicken in wine, the main attraction at Joe's are the
steamed buns, which hold inside them a mouthful of hot soup
and morsels of pork or crabmeat. For the uninitiated, don't
shove the whole dumpling into your mouth, but place it on
a spoon, gently take a bite and drink the liquid that collects
in the utensil's well.

## New Chao Chow Restaurant

*111 Mott Street, between Canal & Hester Streets*
*(226 2590/8222). Subway 6, J, N or R to Canal Street.*
**Open** 8.30am-10pm daily. **Average** $12.
**No credit cards.**
Ignore the unimpressive décor at this cheap noodle shop
where no dish tops $9, and focus instead on the soups, which
are the true draw. Try the Chao Chow fishball, a combo of
noodles in chicken broth, topped with more than enough fish-
balls to satiate any seafood lover's craving.

## Ollie's Noodle Shop

*2315 Broadway, between 84th & 85th Streets (362*
*3111). Subway 1 or 9 to 86th Street.* **Open** 8am-11.30pm
Mon-Thur, Sun; 8am-1am Fri, Sat. **Average** $15.
**Credit** AmEx, MC, V.
Acting as energy-supply stations for New Yorkers on the go,
Ollie's Noodle Shops crop up every 40 blocks on the Upper
West Side (there's a total of three). Choose one and fill your
belly with a tangle of noodles served in a gargantuan bowl
of soup. Even if you opt for a more traditional item off the
Chinese food menu, don't forget to order the slightly greasy
but unbeatable scallion (spring onion) pancakes.
**Branches:** 1991 Broadway (595 8181); 190 West 44th
Street (921 5988).

## Shun Lee Palace

*155 East 55th Street, between Lexington & Third*
*Avenues (371 8844). Subway 4, 5 or 6 to 59th Street;*
*N or R to Lexington Avenue.* **Open** noon-11.30pm daily.
**Average** $35. **Credit** AmEx, DC, MC, V.
In this city of a thousand cheap, accessible Chinese food
joints it might seem silly to venture to this place on the posh
Upper East Side, where main courses can cost as much as
$20. But the food at Shun Lee, such as the rare tuna in spicy
Hunan sauce, will rid you of any reverse snobbery you might

be feeling. And if the elegance of this atypical Chinese restaurant doesn't surprise you, maybe the courteous and friendly service will.

# Eastern European

*See also page 141* **Firebird***.*

### Rasputin
*2670 Coney Island Avenue, at Avenue X (1-718-332 8333). Subway F to Avenue X; D to Neck Road.* **Open** noon-3pm daily. **Average** $45. **Credit** AmEx, MC, V.
Come to this restaurant in Brooklyn's 'Little Odessa' for an authentic Russian version of evening entertainment – some dining and dancing and much smoking and drinking. Order typical Russian menu offerings such as boiled tongue, radish salad and caviar before heading to the crowded dance floor. Arrive early if you want to catch the Vegas-style floor show.

### Russian Samovar
*256 West 52nd Street, between Broadway & Eighth Avenue (757 0168). Subway C or E to 50th Street.* **Lunch** noon-3pm Tue-Sat. **Dinner** 5pm-midnight daily. **Average** $30. **Credit** AmEx, MC, V.
You may not recognise them, but this mid-priced, theatre-district restaurant is where Russia's beautiful people go when they are in town. Baryshnikov and Joseph Brodsky took shares in the late 1980s.

### Ukrainian East Village Restaurant
*140 Second Avenue, between 8th & 9th Streets (529 5024). Subway 6 to Astor Place.* **Open** noon-11pm daily. **Average** $15. **No credit cards.**
Experience true Ukrainian dining and service at this plain-looking restaurant tucked away behind the Ukrainian National Home. Try the Ukrainian combo platter and stuff yourself with stuffed cabbage, kielbasa, four types of pierogi and a choice of potatoes or kasha (buckwheat). And if you're full, don't let the grandmother-like waitresses convince you otherwise.

### Veselka
*144 Second Avenue, at 9th Street (228 9682). Subway 6 to Astor Place.* **Open** 24 hours daily. **Average** $13. **Credit** AmEx, MC, V.
This bohemian Ukrainian coffee shop that's open around the clock was recently renovated, so it might not seem like the old East Village hang-out that it actually is. After a tour of the small shops in the vicinity, stop here for a cheap bowl of chicken soup and a slab of challah bread.

# French

### Alison on Dominick
*38 Dominick Street, between Varick & Hudson Streets (727 1188). Subway 1 or 9 to Canal Street.* **Dinner** 5.15-10pm Mon-Thur; 5.15-11pm Fri; 5.15-9.30pm Sun. **Average** $45. **Credit** AmEx, DC, M C, V.
A French country restaurant that's one of the most romantic hideaways in the city, with light – almost healthy – versions of southwestern French cuisine and a quiet, jazz-tinged atmosphere.

### Les Deux Gamins
*170 Waverly Place, at Grove Street (807 7047). Subway 1 or 9 to Christopher Street/Sheridan Square.* **Open** 8am-midnight daily. **Average** $20. **Credit** AmEx.
Watch the village go by as you soak up an atmosphere that's very Parisian and bistro food that's almost as authentic.

**Alison on Dominick** *– for candle-lit dinners.*

### Félix
*340 West Broadway, at Grand Street (431 0021). Subway A, C or E to Canal Street.* **Lunch** 12.30-4pm, **dinner** 6pm-midnight, daily. **Average** $36. **Credit** AmEx.
A solid SoHo bistro with an accent and an attitude that makes it a home from home for countless Parisian expats. It's particularly fun on late summer nights when diners on the sidewalk get front-row seats for the chic parade on this hip stretch of West Broadway.

### Le Grenouille
*3 East 52nd Street, between Fifth & Madison Avenues (752 1495). Subway E or F to Fifth Avenue.* **Lunch** noon-2.30pm, **dinner** 5.45-11.15pm, Tue-Sat. **Set lunch** $42. **Set dinner** $75. **Credit** AmEx.
An eternally romantic restaurant, bedecked in flowers. The menu is classic ancien cuisine at pretty steep prices, and the guest list regularly includes Ines de la Fressange and Elizabeth Tilberis. There are, of course, frogs' legs alongside pike quenelles, amazing choucroute with foie gras, and dessert soufflés.

### Jean Claude
*137 Sullivan Street, between Houston & Prince Streets (475 9232). Subway G or E to Prince Street; 1 or 9 to Houston Street.* **Dinner** 6.30-11pm Mon-Thur; 6.30pm-midnight Fri, Sat; 6.30-10pm Sun. **Average** $32. **No credit cards.**
Perpetually mobbed, Jean Claude Iacovelli's second restaurant has fast become a SoHo favourite, with its imaginative mix of continental and nouvelle cuisine offered at bistro prices.
*Disabled: toilets.*

### Jules
*65 St Mark's Place, between First & Second Avenues (477 5560). Subway 6 to Astor Place.* **Open** 11am-1am Mon-Thur, Sun; 11am-2am Fri, Sat. **Average** $30. **Credit** AmEx.
Jules may be at its best at Sunday brunch-time, when the sun shines through the lace curtains and an accordionist wanders around the room. Regulars favour the omelette made with goat's cheese, steak frites and the salad frisée aux lardons.
*Disabled: toilets.*

### Lespinasse
*2 East 55th Street, between Fifth & Madison Avenues (339 6719). Subway 4, 5 or 6 to 51st Street/Lexington* **Open** 7am-10pm Mon-Sat; 7am-noon Sun. **Average** $70. **Credit** AmEx, DC, MC, V.
Award-winning food and a sophisticated, palatial setting have proved successful at Lespinasse. Devotees relish the

French food with Far Eastern influences and think nothing of shedding a few hundred dollars for the privilege. *Disabled: toilets.*

### Provence

*38 MacDougal Street, between Houston & Prince Streets (475 7500). Subway C or E to Spring Street.* **Lunch** noon-3pm daily. **Dinner** 6-11pm Mon-Sat; 6-10pm Sun. **Average** $45. **Credit** AmEx.
A SoHo institution since 1986 thanks to its informal and flirtatious staff and superb Provençal food. During the warm months, the back garden is a perfect setting for specials such as the langoustines and classic rabbit stew.

### Savann

*414 Amsterdam Avenue, between 79th & 80th Streets (580 0202). Subway 1 or 9 to 79th Street.*
**Dinner** 6-11pm Mon-Thur, Sun; 6pm-midnight Fri, Sat. **Average** $30. **Credit** DC, MC, V.
An Upper West Side bistro with an inexpensive and innovative menu that mixes French basics and Asian flavourings,

putting an emphasis on the light and the fresh. Its new sister restaurant on the Upper East Side is also a delight. *Disabled: toilets.*
**Branch**: Savann Est 181 East 78th Street (396 9300).

## Greek

### S'Agapo

*3421 34th Avenue, at 35th Street, Astoria, Queens (1-718-626 0303). Subway N to Broadway; R to Steinway.* **Open** 3pm-midnight Tue-Fri; noon-midnight Sat, Sun. **Average** $25. **Credit** AmEx, DC, Disc, MC, V.
Servicing Astoria's Greek population, S'Agapo produces the real stuff in its undiluted form. The grilled octopus is among the tenderest on earth, while pastitsio is a satisfying rendition of 'Greek lasagne'. At weekends, a singer and accordionist add to the fun; the owner has been known to dim the lights and dance a little. *Disabled: toilets.*

# Snacking it

Food that is quintessentially New York is grub that can be eaten anywhere: standing up, sitting down or (best of all) running. The classics are pizza, falafel, hot dogs, bagels, grilled sandwiches, soup; but the list also includes anything that is cooked up quickly and requires one utensil at most. You'll never need to search hard for a cart, a shallow storefront or a kiosk where cheap but delicious food is sold. In fact, follow that appetising smell wafting your way down the street and you'll be sure to find a tasty lunch at its source.

Each vendor has his or her own set of local groupies, but there are also some universal favourites. **Soup Kitchen International** (259A West 55th Street, between Eighth & Ninth Avenues, 757 7730) offers deliciously thick soups with innovative ingredients, and operates from a small midtown kiosk. The notorious owner is commonly known as the 'Soup Nazi', a reference to his cantankerous personality made famous by the *Seinfeld* show.

There are as many pizza parlours in this city as nutcases and cabs, but if you're passing through Greenwich Village, **Joe's Pizza** has a thin, chewy crust topped with a tangy sauce and fresh mozzarella (233 Bleecker Street, at Carmine, 366 1182).

No one agrees on who makes the best bagels, but it's hard to argue with **Columbia Bagels** (2836 Broadway, between 110th & 111th Streets, 222 3200), which has an unforgettable, and very oniony, tuna fish salad; **H&H Bagels** (2239 Broadway, at 80th, 595 8003 or 639 West 46th Street, at Twelfth Avenue, 595 8000) serves

bagels that are large, chewy and always fresh.

In SoHo, massive sandwiches with Italian standards such as prosciutto and roasted peppers can be ordered from **Melampo** (105 Sullivan Street, between Prince & Spring, 334 9530) and can be eaten on a nearby bench, weather permitting. Just know what you want – the owner is known for his quick temper.

Falafel, a staple food of the Middle East, has made New York its second home. Try the chickpea and houmous balls at **Rainbow Falafel** (26 East 17th Street, between Broadway & Fifth Avenue, 691 8641) or from **Moshe's Falafel**, a stand with an enormous lunch-time following – just look for the crowds (south-east corner of 46th Street & Sixth Avenue).

While in midtown, walk over to 45th Street, between Vanderbilt and Lexington Avenues, in the shadow of the Met Life building. You'll find as many as six food carts lining this small street. Choose from baked potatoes, a nice (and very popular) soup guy, hot dogs, Middle Eastern chicken and rice, Philly cheese steak sandwiches, and even an entire cart devoted to nuts.

When in Chinatown, stop by and visit the egg-cake lady, a middle-aged Chinese woman in a small shack who makes slightly sweet, waffle-like treats and offers a small but satisfying serving for only $1 (Mosco Street, between Mott & Mulberry).

Finally, don't forget to stop by at **Gray's Papaya** for a couple of cheap and tasty hot dogs (2090 Broadway, at 72nd Street, 799 9243 or 402 Sixth Avenue, at 8th Street, 260 3532). With a perfect dog in hand, you're ready to start hunting your next snack.

## Agrotikon

*322 East 14th Street, between First & Second Avenues*
*(473 2602). Subway L to First Avenue.* **Dinner** 5pm-
midnight Tue-Sun. **Average** $25. **Credit** AmEx, MC, V.
Cheaper and more adventurous than an *haute* Greek like
Peryiali (*see below*), Agrotikon is a happy and relatively
recent addition to 14th. Dolmades are wonderful here, as is
the sheep's milk cheese Saganaki. For fish, choose grilled
over baked. Or try the fisherman's pie – a stew with chunks
of fish and squid baked under garlic-cod mashed potatoes.
The chocolate baklava is a true original.

## Elias Corner for Fish

*2402 31st Street, at 24th Avenue, Astoria, Queens*
*(1-718 932 1510). Subway N to Astoria Boulevard.*
**Open** 4pm-midnight daily. **Average** $25. **No credit cards.**
This newly expanded, but still simple Greek seafood restaurant doesn't take reservations, so there may be queues.
Which is fine, since you can take advantage of the time in
the lobby selecting the right fish from the glass case. There's
no menu, but no matter: everything comes in extremely fresh
and leaves the grill perfectly charred and full of flavour. The
crowds come for swordfish kebabs and whole red mullet,
snapper and striped bass. Treat the waitresses nicely and
perhaps they'll bring a platter of fried dough with honey, a
free dessert that's as sweet as the mood here.
*Disabled: toilets.*

## Meltemi

*905 First Avenue, at 51st Street (355 4040). Subway 6*
*to 51st Street; E or F to Lexington/Third Avenues.* **Open**
noon-11pm daily. **Average** $30. **Credit** AmEx, MC, V.
The look – airy room, open kitchen, horseshoe bar – fits the
Sutton Place location, but Meltemi gets its atmosphere from
its Greek customers. Food is authentic. The chef takes exact-
ing care with ingredients and knows his way around a grill.
The squid are perfect: cooked over charcoal until just moist,
they're sweet and tender to the point of indecency.
*Disabled: toilets.*

## Peryiali

*35 West 20th Street, between Fifth & Sixth Avenues*
*(463 7890). Subway N or R to 23rd Street.* **Lunch** noon-
3pm Mon-Fri. **Dinner** 5.30-11pm Mon-Fri; 5.30pm-
midnight Sat. **Average** $42. **Credit** AmEx, DC, MC, V.
Peryiali was one of the first restaurants in Manhattan to elevate Greek cuisine above the level of coffee-shop spanikopi-
ta. And though the best Greek cooking is now available more
cheaply in Astoria, this traditional coal-grill place is still a
good upmarket venue for moussaka, taramasalata, grilled
meat and vegetable appetisers.

# Indian

## Dawat

*210 East 58th Street, between Second & Third Avenues*
*(355 7555). Subway 4 or 6 to 59th Street; N or R to*
*Lexington Avenue.* **Lunch** 11.30am-2.45pm daily.
**Dinner** 5.30-10.45pm Mon-Thur, Sun; 5.30-11.15pm Fri,
Sat. **Average** *lunch* $12.95, $13.95; *dinner* $35. **Credit**
AmEx, DC, MC, V.
Perhaps the best Indian in the city, Dawat has pretty peach
walls and a long, diverse, pricey menu. East Midtown is an
unlikely place for midday finds, so Dawat's *prix fixe* lunches
are a bargain ($12.95-$13.95). Standbys such as chicken
keema masala are transformed here into subtle dishes that
float on the tongue.
*Disabled: toilets.*

## Haveli

*100 Second Avenue, between 5th & 6th Streets (982*
*0533). Subway 6 to Astor Place.* **Open** noon-midnight
daily. **Average** $25. **Credit** AmEx, MC, V.
The best thing about 6th Street's Little Delhi isn't even on
6th. Just around the corner, Haveli is better than the neighbourhood deserves. Behind the shattered-on-purpose wall of
glass, all the standards are served a notch above average
with only a moderate price jump. The rogan josh may top

*Pick your piscine fancy at* **Elias Corner for Fish.**

**Haveli:** *better than Little Delhi deserves. P134.*

ten bucks, but the lamb is cooked in a good onion sauce with yoghurt and spices and a sweet touch of pineapple.
*Disabled: toilets.*

### Jackson Diner
*37-03 74th Street, at Thirty-seventh Avenue, Jackson Heights, Queens (1-718 672 1232). Subway E or F to 74th Street/Broadway.* **Open** 11am-10pm daily. **Average** $17. **No credit cards.**
Word has got out about this Queens diner; people now queue for its huge portions of Indian food. There's also the added attraction of leaving the East Village to dine in a place that services a large Indian community. The murg lajawab (chicken in a ginger and chilli sauce) has kick. Jackson also has a small choice of mostly-vegetarian, South Indian food.
*Disabled: toilets.*

### Nirvana
*30 West 59th Street, between Fifth & Sixth Avenues (486 5700). Subway N or R to Fifth Avenue.* **Open** noon-1am daily. **Average** $38. **Credit** AmEx, DC, Disc, MC, V.
The high-rent views of Central Park are the real attraction here. The menu is virtually identical to every place on 6th Street – despite the elephantine prices. Those determined to have their curry with a view should go for the 'theatre dinner', which is served all day. For $5 more than a main course you'll also receive an appetiser sampler, dessert and coffee.
*Disabled: toilets.*

## Italian

### Il Bagatto
*192 East 2nd Street, between Avenues A & B (228 0977). Subway F to Second Avenue.* **Open** 7pm-midnight Tue-Thur; 7pm-1am Fri, Sat; 6-11pm Sun. **Average** $20. **No credit cards.**
There are few convincing reasons to send anyone unfamiliar with Alphabet City into its bowels. Count the spinach gnocchi at the dark and cosy Il Bagatto as one of them. These plump morsels are made fresh at least four times a week and are served in a ripe, creamy Gorgonzola sauce. Other dishes worth the inconvenience of dodging prone junkies: the antipasto Il Bagatto, a sampler of the house antipasti; and the stracceti al rosmarino, a round of beef sliced paper-thin.

### Barolo
*398 West Broadway, between Spring & Broome Streets (226 1102). Subway C or E to Spring Street.*
**Open** 10am-midnight Mon-Fri; 10am-1am Sat, Sun. **Average** $40. **Credit** AmEx, Disc, MC, V.
A SoHo attraction, drawing an upmarket crowd that's heavily into money and looks. Barolo's a place where you can comfortably chat on your mobile phone while digging into penne with lamb and artichokes. It's also a perfect summer

choice due to the enormous garden in the back, complete with lush trees lit with tiny lights.
*Disabled: toilets.*

### Bona Fides
*60 Second Avenue, between 3rd & 4th Streets (777 2840). Subway 6 to Astor Place.* **Dinner** 5-11pm Mon-Thur, Sun; 5pm-midnight Fri, Sat. **Average** $15. **Credit** AmEx, DC, MC, V.
A mellow and unremarkably pretty place with a long dining room and a partially tented garden area, this East Village Italian restaurant serves meals that never exceed the $10 mark and include bruschetta for free. Even regular diners still regard Bona Fides as a place they have just stumbled upon, wondering at their luck.

### Carmine's
*2450 Broadway, between 90th & 91st Streets (362 2200). Subway 1, 2, 3 or 9 to 96th Street.* **Open** 5-11pm Mon-Thur; 5pm-midnight Fri; 5pm-1am Sat; 2-10pm Sun. **Average** $25. **Credit** AmEx, MC, V.
Plenty of pasta and garlic are the hallmarks of Manhattan's two Carmine's, both southern Italian eateries that serve gargantuan portions of noodles in a warm, raucous setting. The more people you come with, the better, since Carmine's only accepts reservations for parties of six or more – and that's only at weekends and early evening during the week. Otherwise, get ready to wait.

### John's Pizzeria
*278 Bleecker Street, between Sixth & Seventh Avenues (243 1680). Subway A, B, C, D, E or F to West 4th Street; 1 or 9 to Christopher Street.* **Open** 11.30am-midnight Mon-Sat; noon-midnight Sun. **Average** $15. **No credit cards.**
The brick-oven pizza at John's has long been a contender for annual best pizza awards. Although there are two newer uptown branches, head to the original in the Village (which has also expanded). Find the oldest part of the restaurant and sit in a scratched wooden booth – someone will inevitably push Sinatra on the jukebox. Your thin-crusted pizza, which can easily be shared by two, will arrive within minutes. **Branches:** 408 East 64th Street (935 2895); 48 West 65th Streeet (721 7001).

### Lombardi's
*32 Spring Street, between Mott & Mulberry Streets (941 7994). Subway 6 to Spring Street.* **Open** 11.30am-11pm Mon-Thur; 11am-midnight Fri, Sat; 11.30am-10pm Sun. **Average** $15. **No credit cards.**
This pizzeria in Little Italy first opened at the turn of the century as a restaurant that mostly served pasta. The narrow space closed for business in the late 1980s and re-opened just two years ago to sell only pizza, quickly becoming a favourite. The pizza, made with fresh ingredients, is baked in a coal oven and has a thin but chewy crust.
*Disabled: toilets.*

### Le Madri
*168 West 18th Street, between Sixth & Seventh Avenues (727 8022). Subway 1 or 9 to 18th Street.* **Lunch** noon-3pm, **dinner** 5.30-11pm, daily. **Average** $45. **Credit** AmEx, DC, MC, V.
You'll be hungry after an arduous day of shopping at the original, downtown Barney's, but by then your threshold for anything made poorly or cheaply will be quite low. Just a step away is this spotless, classy Tuscan restaurant serving exciting pastas, pizzas, bread salads and grilled vegetables. The garden patio opens with the arrival of warm weather.

### La Mela
*137 Mulberry Street, between Grand & Broome Streets (431 9493). Subway B or D to Grand Street.* **Open** noon-11pm daily. **Average** $26. **Credit** AmEx, DC, MC, V.

Located on the main strip in Little Italy, La Mela looks a bit touristy, but you'll still find many old-timers ordering wine by the colour (white or red), mounds of traditional Italian antipasti, heaps of pasta (lasagne, tortellini, ravioli and spaghetti) and large plates of desserts.

### Orologio
*162 Avenue A, between 10th & 11th Streets (228 6900). Subway 6 to Astor Place; L to First Avenue.* **Dinner** 5.30pm-midnight Mon-Thur, Sun; 5.30pm-1am Fri, Sat. **Average** $20. **No credit cards**.
Orologio is one of the many restaurants that have sprouted in the past five years on the formerly desolate and newly hip Avenue A. There's little elbow room at this trattoria, which offers cheap pasta that's always properly al dente and never swimming in sauce. Make a selection from the modestly priced wine list and you'll soon forget the geographical inconvenience.

### Pó
*31 Cornelia Street, between Bleecker & West 4th Streets (645 2189). Subway A, B, C, D, E or F to West 4th Street.* **Lunch** 11.30am-2pm Wed-Sun. **Dinner** 5.30-11pm Tue-Thur; 5.30-11.30pm Fri, Sat; 5-10pm Sun. **Average** $35. **Credit** AmEx.
Chef Mario Battali, who has his own show on cable's TV Food Network, makes this tiny West Village restaurant an unforgettable treat. The complimentary rosemary-laced white bean bruschetta that's brought to the table as you're seated is a harbinger of the simple masterpieces to come.
*Disabled: toilets.*

### Trattoria del Arte
*900 Seventh Avenue, between 56th & 57 Streets (245 9800). Subway N or R to 57th Street.* **Brunch** 11.45am-3.30pm Sat, Sun. **Lunch** 11.30am-2.30pm Mon-Fri. **Dinner** 5-11.30pm Mon-Sat. **Average** $38. **Credit** AmEx, Disc, MC, V.
Decorated with artwork of large body parts, including a huge nose near the entrance, this midtown pre-theatre spot has three floors and is popular with celebrities and office workers. Hope to get seated downstairs, though the contemporary Italian food will taste great no matter where you are.
*Disabled: toilets.*

## Japanese

*See also page 121* **Nobu**.

### Honmura An
*170 Mercer Street, between Prince & Houston Streets (334 5253). Subway N or R to Prince Street.* **Lunch** noon-2.30pm Wed-Sat. **Dinner** 6.30-10pm Tue-Thur; 6-10.30pm Fri, Sat; 6-9.30pm Sun. **Average** $38. **Credit** AmEx, DC, MC, V.
There's quiet, Zen-like harmony just off Houston – for a price. Start with edamame pea pods, then get into elevated noodles like you've never tasted, including hearty nabeyaki udon with chicken and shrimp.

### Oikawa
*805 Third Avenue, at 50th Street (980 1400). Subway 6 to 51st Street; E or F to Lexington/Third Avenues.* **Lunch** 11.30am-2.30pm Mon-Fri. **Dinner** 5.30pm-12.30am Mon-Fri; 5.30-11pm Sun. **Average** $40. **Credit** AmEx, DC, MC, V.
Located in a glassy, mall-like midtown building, Oikawa may look sterile, but the food is thrilling. Returning to your local, standard sushi hole will be a let-down after you've dabbled with the likes of shredded jelly fish, chopped shark's fin with plum sauce, or squid with spicy cod's roe. Even the sushi is pretty creative; try the salmon and eel roll gently fried tempura-style.
*Disabled: toilets.*

### Omen
*113 Thompson Street, between Prince & Spring Streets (925 8923). Subway C or E to Spring Street.* **Dinner** 5.30-10.30pm daily. **Average** $36. **Credit** AmEx.
Not even the salads are bad omens at this calm SoHo sushiteria. The house salad is enlivened with seaweed and baby scallops, a perfect accompaniment to an assortment of sashimi. Order the herby chiso rice on the side.

### Takahachi
*85 Avenue A, between 5th & 6th Streets (505 6524). Subway 6 to Bleecker Street.* **Dinner** 5.30pm-12.45am daily. **Average** $22. **Credit** AmEx, MC, V.
Fresh slivers of fish, and waiters in matching T-shirts are about the only consistent elements here; everything else is Avenue A eclectic. Early bird specials (5-7pm) are a good bet for beating the rush as well as the high-price of healthy living.
*Disabled: toilets.*

### Tomoe Sushi
*172 Thompson Street, between Houston & Bleecker Streets (777 9346). Subway A, C, D, E or F to West 4th Street; 1 or 9 to Houston Street.* **Lunch** 1-3pm Wed-Sat. **Dinner** 5-11pm Mon, Wed-Sat. **Average** $30. **Credit** AmEx.
The fussy folks here only take American Express and expect you to wait outside in the cold for a table. Everyone puts up with it though, because the bargain sushi is always big as your fist and, sometimes, it's among the silkiest, tastiest in the city.

### Yama
*122 East 17th Street, at Irving Place (475 0969). Subway L, N, R, 4 or 6 to 14th Street/Union Square.* **Lunch** noon-2.20pm Mon-Fri. **Dinner** 5.30-10.20pm Mon-Thur; 5.30-11.20pm Fri, Sat. **Average** $28. **Credit** AmEx, MC, V.
Good, fresh sushi and big bento-box dinner deals keep this Gramercy former home of Washington Irving packed. If you have to queue outside, you couldn't pick a prettier block.

## Kosher

### Kosher Tea Room
*193 Second Avenue, at East 12th Street (677 2947). Subway L to Third Avenue; N, R, 4 or 6 to 14th Street.* **Lunch** 11.45am-3.30pm Mon-Thur, Sun. **Dinner** 5-10.30pm Mon-Thur, Sun; two hours after sunset-1am Sat. **Average** $40. **Credit** AmEx, Disc, MC, V.
Situated among the hang-outs of the East Village's young and pierced, this formal kosher dining spot features Russian dishes such as borscht, blinis and chicken Kiev. The décor is a tad sparse, but the roses on every table and the pianist lend a certain, albeit slightly clichéd, elegance.
*Disabled: toilets.*

### Le Marais
*150 West 46th Street, between Sixth & Seventh Avenues (869 0900). Subway N, R, 1, 2, 3 or 9 to Times Square/42nd Street.* **Lunch** noon-3pm Mon-Fri. **Dinner** 5.30-11pm Sat. **Open** noon-midnight Mon-Thur, Sun. **Average** $38. **Credit** AmEx, DC, MC, V.
A kosher French bistro might seem like an oxymoron (margarine on a baguette, anyone?), but the pre-theatre crowds are testament to Le Marais' strengths. Bistro staples such as steak, lamb and chicken are as good as those at the non-kosher bistro Les Halles, owned by the same people.

### Ratner's
*138 Delancey Street, between Norfolk & Suffolk Streets (677 5588). Subway F, J, M or Z to Delancey Street.* **Open** 6am-11pm Mon-Thur, Sun; 6am-3pm Fri; 7pm-1am Sat. **Average** $20. **Credit** AmEx, Disc, MC, V.
One of the few reminders that the Lower East Side once held

Vegans should hot-foot it to **Angelica's Kitchen**. See page 138.

one of the world's largest Jewish communities. Come to Ratner's for the plain or fruit-filled cheese blintzes or the pierogi dumplings. Don't expect any meat specialities however, since only dairy products or fish are used.

### Sammy's Roumanian
*157 Chrystie Street, at Delancey Street (673 0330). Subway F to Delancey Street; J to Essex Street.* **Open** 3-11pm Mon-Thur, Sun; 3pm-midnight Fri, Sat. **Average** $40. **Credit** AmEx, MC, V.
Your arteries will immediately begin to thicken after a meal at Sammy's, which includes obscenely long steaks, chopped liver that's mixed at the table with schmalz (yellow, rendered chicken fat) and a bottle of vodka served in an ice block. The sour pickles and peppers will help cut the massive quantities of fat you're ingesting, and the loud band playing Yiddish favourites will keep you from thinking about that impending heart attack.

## Mexican

### Rosa Mexicana
*1063 First Avenue, at East 58th Street (753 7407). Subway 4 or 6 to 59th Street; N or R to Lexington Avenue.* **Dinner** 5pm-midnight daily. **Average** $36. **Credit** AmEx, DC, MC, V.
Although Rosa Mexicana is pricey, at no other restaurán will you have the pleasure of watching your guacamole be prepared at the table in a molcajete, a mortar made from a wedge of volcanic rock. Über-American homemaker and taste arbiter Martha Stewart has called this Mexican establishment her favourite.

### Taqueria de Mexico
*93 Greenwich Avenue, between 12th & Bank Streets (255 5212). Subway 1, 2, 3 or 9 to 14th Street.* **Open** 11.30am-11pm Mon-Thur, Sun; 11.30am-midnight Fri, Sat. **Average** $15. **No credit cards**.
It opened in 1994 mainly as a takeaway, but this attractive taqueria has since expanded, making more room for the eager beavers who come for its Mexican standards made

with ultra-fresh ingredients. Remember to breathe while you gulp down the chicken enchilada or chile relleno (a roasted chilli pepper filled with cheese, coated in egg, and cooked in tomato sauce).
*Disabled: toilets.*

### Zarela
*953 Second Avenue, between 50th & 51st Streets (644 6740). Subway E or F to Lexington Avenue.* **Lunch** noon-3pm Mon-Fri. **Dinner** 5-11pm Mon-Thur; 5-11.30pm Fri, Sat; 5-10pm Sun. **Average** $35. **Credit** AmEx, DC.
Distinguished by its authentic menu, this upmarket but still festive Mexican restaurant has two floors, the upper being quieter. Owner Zarela Martinez is serious about the food she offers and has even penned a cookbook, *Food From My Heart*.

### Zócalo
*174 East 82nd Street, between Lexington & Third Avenues (717 7772). Subway 4 or 6 to 86th Street.* **Dinner** 6pm-midnight daily. **Average** $35. **Credit** AmEx, MC, V.
At this candlelit spot with orange-coloured walls and a green ceiling, you can expect the kind of food that Mexicans eat in their homes. Empanadas are filled with such ingredients as oysters or zucchini, and the pozole (pork and hominy stew) is a great choice after too many margaritas.
*Disabled: toilets.*

## South American/Caribbean

### Ipanema
*13 West 46th Street, between Fifth & Sixth Avenues (730 5848). Subway B, D, F or Q to 42nd Street.* **Open** noon-10pm daily. **Average** $26. **Credit** AmEx, DC, Disc, MC, V.
One of the best places on 46th Street's 'Little Brazil' and an ideal pre-theatre or mid-shopping pitstop. Try shrimp in its many incarnations (garlicky and grilled as an appetiser, or served in a coconut with olives and mashed potatoes). It's

odd for a midtown block to hold as much distinct flair as this bit of Brazil, but Ipanema lives up to its name and promise.

## Victor's Café

*236 West 52nd Street, between Broadway and Eighth Avenue (586 7714). Subway C or E to 50th Street.* **Open** noon-midnight Mon-Thur, Sun; noon-1am Fri, Sat. **Average** $30. **Credit** AmEx, DC, MC, V.
Nearly 30 years old, this estimable Theater District restaurant is the father of all Manhattan Cubans. Get into the mood with a mojito, Hemingway's favourite pre-Castro cocktail, and then let yourself go with a helping of regional flavours, from porky and spicy to sweet and, well, porky.

## South-east Asian

### Dok Suni

*119 First Avenue, between 7th Street & St Mark's Place (477 9506). Subway 6 to Astor Place.* **Open** 4.30-11.30pm daily. **Average** $20. **No credit cards**.
Korean 'home cooking' might not resemble anything you've ever cooked at home. But this woody East Villager is downtown-homey, featuring an ample menu of stir-fried kimchi with rice, braised short ribs, grilled squid and other straightforward alternatives to Chinese takeaway fodder.

### Kelley & Ping

*127 Greene Street, between Houston & Prince Streets (228 1212). Subway N or R to Prince Street.* **Lunch** 11.30am-5pm, **dinner** 6-11.30pm, daily. **Average** $20. **Credit** AmEx, MC, V.
This hip spot is part Saigon corner deli, part pan-Asian noodle bar. Nothing beats the cold weather like an oversize bowl of steaming soup with chow fun noodles and shredded pork. K&P is narrow and packed at lunch, but you and your credit card will feel far away from the area's shopping traps.

### Penang

*109 Spring Street, between Greene & Mercer Streets (274 8883). Subway N or R to Prince Street.* **Open** 11.30am-midnight Mon-Thur; 11.30am-1am Fri, Sat; 1pm-midnight Sun. **Average** $26. **Credit** AmEx, MC, V.
The Penangs are variously owned but share a transporting, slightly silly décor and menu of serious Malaysian intrigue. Ask for traditional fish head soup, or stick to more approachable fare such as spring rolls with jimca, or a whole striped bass in banana leaves.
**Branches:** 3804 Prince Street (1-718-321 2078); 240 Columbus Avenue (769 3988); 64 Third Avenue (228 7888).

### Pho Bang

*117 Mott Street, at Hester Street (966 3797). Subway J, N, R or 6 to Canal Street.* **Open** 10am-10pm daily. **Average** $15. **No credit cards**.
The AOR background music and the dapper waiting staff in vests and bowties add to the charm of this Vietnamese diner. The Bang family has six restaurants in the metropolitan area, but this is where to get the greatest Bang for your buck: for $5.95 you get logs of beef stuffed with onions, to roll with squares of vermicelli rice noodles and crisp greens, and then dunk in a sweet fish sauce. But think twice before ordering the salty lemonade.

## Spanish

### El Faro

*823 Greenwich Street, at Horatio Street (929 8210). Subway A, C or L to 14th Street/Eighth Avenue.* **Open** 11.30am-midnight Mon-Thur; 11.30am-1am Fri, Sat. **Average** $26. **Credit** AmEx, Disc, MC, V.
Ancient and constant, this West Villager is widely regarded as having some of the best Spanish food in Manhattan.

## Ñ

*33 Crosby Street, between Broome & Grand Streets (219 8856). Subway 6 to Spring Street.* **Dinner** 5pm-midnight daily. **Average** $20. **No credit cards**.
Straight out of an Almodóvar movie, Ñ (pronounced en-yay) has yellow and red polka-dotted walls and copper penny sculptures. It's a narrow, cool, dark spot, great for beating the heat of a SoHo summer with a pitcher of sangria, or cosying up in cooler seasons with multitudes of tapas. Tuck yourself into a table and try the pan con tomate, and marinated anchovies called boquerones.

### El Quixote

*226 West 23rd Street, between Seventh & Eighth Avenues (929 1855). Subway 1 or 9 to 23rd Street.* **Open** noon-midnight Mon-Thur, Sun; noon-1am Fri, Sat. **Average** $26. **Credit** AmEx, DC, Disc, MC, V.
It's in the eternally quirky Chelsea Hotel, but El Quixote is straight-faced, old-school Spanish. With its endearingly serious uniformed waiters, murals and ubiquitous presence of Mr La Mancha, as well as its huge platters of paella and cut-rate lobster specials, El Quixote proves it's hip to be square.

### Rio Mar

*7 Ninth Avenue, at Little West 12th Street (243 9015). Subway A, C or E to 14th Street.* **Open** noon-3am daily. **Average** $25. **Credit** AmEx.
On a desolate, ragged piece of the Meat Packing district sits Rio Mar, partying all by itself. It's an unexpected home of sangria by the pitcher, fantastically oily and garlicky tapas, a nearly all-Spanish jukebox, and a hell of a lot of up-late fun.

### Tapas Lounge

*1078 First Avenue, between 58th & 59th Streets (421 8282). Subway N or R to Lexington Avenue; 4 or 6 to 59th Street.* **Dinner** 5.30pm-midnight Mon, Tue, Sun; 5.30pm-3am Wed-Sat. **Average** $25. **Credit** AmEx.
Little Spanish snacks are the familiar premise around which the guys at Tapas Lounge have built an on-going party. Music, chatter, low lighting, low seating, and a higher than expected pretty people ration for this residential Siberia all add to the good time. The look is midway between a fetishist's dark chamber and a theme park exotic lounge, but the paella is moist and huge. Where else in the neighbourhood can you stay up all night smoking Turkish tobacco in a hookah?

## Vegetarian

### Angelica Kitchen

*300 East 12th Street, between First & Second Avenues (228 2909). Subway L to First Avenue; 4, 6, N or R to Union Square/14th Street.* **Open** 11.30am-10.30pm daily. **Average** $17. **No credit cards**.
The best vegan restaurant in the city, this soothing oblong fishbowl serves up tasty dishes such as the velvety sesame-noodle dish soba sensation, the (huge) wee dragon and an array of cheesy cheeseless specials.

### B&H Dairy

*127 Second Avenue, between 7th Street & St Mark's Place (505 8065). Subway 6 to Astor Place.* **Open** 6.30am-10pm Mon-Sat; 7am-10pm Sun. **Average** $15. **No credit cards**.
B&H looks just like a standard ham'n'eggs American diner, but serves an astonishing range of hearty vegetarian soups, juices, great homemade challah bread and veggie burgers. It's the antidote to prissy, self-righteous vegetarian dining.

*Two culinary landmarks:* **Katz's** *East Side deli, above (see page 127) and* **Gage & Tollner** *in Brooklyn (page 128).*

### Kate's Joint

*58 Avenue B, between 4th & 5th Streets (777 7059).*
*Subway F to Second Avenue.* **Open** 8.30am-11pm Mon-
Wed; 8.30am-midnight Thur-Sun. **Average** $23. **Credit**
AmEx, DC, MC, V.

A lazy, laid-back Alphabet City family business, with a comfy
living room area at the front. Kate, the chef, is a master at *faux*
meat. Try her mock popcorn shrimp with Abijah's Secret
Sauce and *faux* grilled barbecue chicken. Watch out for her
kids.

### Strictly Roots

*2058 Adam Clayton Powell Boulevard, between 122nd &
123rd Streets (864 8699). Subway 2 or 3 to 125th Street.*
**Open** 11am-11pm Mon-Sat; noon-7pm Sun. **Average**
$15. **No credit cards.**

A Harlem diner that serves 'nothing that crawls, swims,
walks or flies'. Delicious food such as the mock-beef stew
make it worth a visit, but don't miss the frothy shakes with
names like Bad Man, served by friendly Rasta dudes.

### Zen Palate

*34 East Union Square, at 16th Street (614 9291).*
*Subway 4, 6, N or R to 14th Street/Union Square.* **Lunch**
11.30am-3pm Mon-Sat. **Dinner** 5.30-11pm Mon-Sat; 5-
10.30pm Sun. **Average** $25. **Credit** AmEx, DC, MC, V.

Decorated like delicate Japanese bistros, these restaurants
have quickly become favourites among many New Yorkers,
vegetarian or not. Despite names such as Shredded Melody,
the food is good and each branch is perennially packed.
**Branches:** 663 Ninth Avenue (582 1669); 2170 Broadway
(501 7768).

---

# Fresh pastures

Restaurants come and go in New York faster
than you can say contemporary American
bistro. To really make it in this city, a fresh venture needs that something extra, be it a scene to
sustain it or exceptional food. Below are some
new restaurants that trade in both.

### Aquagrill

*210 Spring Street, at Sixth Avenue (274 0505).*

A newcomer to SoHo's world of the raw and the booked,
Aquagrill is distinguished by location and extremely
fresh aquatic fare. A briny to creamy range of oysters is
FedExed in every day, from locations veering from north-
eastern Malestina to Japanese Kumamoto. Average spend
is $35.

### Balthazar

*80 Spring Street, between Broadway & Crosby Street
(965 1414).*

If you wished you'd taken your vacation in Paris not New
York, let Balthazar, Keith McNally's newest coup, transport you (at least for a meal). The food in this grand bistro
send-up is good, not excellent, with lots of seafood and
brasserie choices. The tastiest part is the crowd, which in
its first frenetic months looked like a casting call for an
Altman movie with regulars Uma Thurman, Calvin Klein,
Ed Koch and various Baldwin brothers. Expect to pay $60
for three courses.

### Le Cirque 2000

*New York Palace Hotel, 455 Madison Avenue, between
50th & 51st Streets (794 9292).*

The Sirio Maccioni machine has returned, a few blocks
north with a new, brash, post-modern design and all the
manic energy of the old somewhat stodgier restaurant.
Just like old times, expect the crowds, the surroundings
and the food to be over the top. Dinner will set you back
around $70 a head.

### Firebird

*365 West 46th Street, between 8th & 9th Avenues
(586 0244).*

Seeking to fill the void left by the closing of the Russian
Tea Room, Firebird (*pictured*) dedicates itself to old-
Russian extravagance. if you're not up to trying some of
the grander main courses such as marinated lamb, order
from the daily zakuska menu (a sort of Russian tapas) that
changes daily. Expect to pay from $35 for dinner.

### Jean-Georges

*Trump International Hotel & Tower, 1 Central Park
West, at Columbus Circle (299 3900).*

One of New York's most famous chefs joins forces with one
its most infamous entrepreneurs to create an exciting new
venue. Jean-Georges Vongerichten's latest coup in the
Trump International Hotel focuses on locally available wild
plants for food that is ethereal, earthy and lush (and cost
up to $95 a head for dinner). The room is beautiful

### The Independent

*179 West Broadway, between Leonard & Worth
Streets (219 2010).*

From the chef of the social centre that is the Odéon (*see
p123*) comes this venture which has gathered enough
fanfare and supermodels to rival its predecessor. Oh,
and the food consists of perfectly delicious American
standards with a bistro twist. Entrées cost between $14
and $24.

### Mesa City

*1059 Third Avenue, between 62nd and 63rd Streets (207
1919).*

Quesadillas get the royal treatment at Bobby Flay's (Mesa
Grill and Bolo) newest restaurant, stuffed with ingredients such as grilled shrimp and coriander pesto, or the
lamb and rocket quesadilla (entrées cost between $12 and
$23). The South western-inspired menu has quickly
become a favourite of stylish Upper East Siders.

### Quilty's

*177 French Street, between Thompson & Sullivan
Streets (254 1260).*

A sweet and enjoyable restaurant, where Chef Katy
Sparks has a seductive way with stodgy standbys, using
such ingredients as steak and halibut. Expect to pay
around $45 for dinner.

Where do you find out what's happening in London?

http://www.timeout.co.uk

**TimeOut** Your weekly guide to the most exciting city in the world

# Cafés & Bars

***Where to drink your fill, and quaff a heady slug of New York life to boot.***

## Cafés

A number of hybrid cafés have recently sprouted from the ever-burgeoning coffee scene. The most obvious are ubiquitous chains such as Starbuck's and New World Coffee, where coffee is meant to be perfunctorily imbibed and gets trussed to the point of silliness (raspberry flavoured coffee?). Here, customers order an espresso or latte from a bar and then sit on stools that face a short ledge or window.

The other offshoot is the coffee lounge, often decorated with large lounge furniture and sometimes even computers, where the goal is to stretch your legs, relax and stay as long as possible. Of course, there are still many more traditional cafés in New York, the kind with a few small tables and chairs, an ashtray and a view of the sidewalk. Whatever your choice, find a seat (or a sofa), pick a brew and get caffeinated.

### Barnes & Noble

*2289 Broadway, at 82nd Street (362 8835). Subway 1 or 9 to 86th Street.* **Open** 9am-11pm Mon-Thur, Sun; 9am-midnight Fri, Sat. **Credit** AmEx, MC, V.

New Yorkers everywhere mourned the closing of local bookstores when the Barnes & Noble chain began expanding a few years ago. The storm passed as they quickly discovered the advantage of going to a bookstore where they could lounge for hours in soft chairs, or even relax in the in-house cafés with a cappuccino and a brownie.
*Disabled: toilets.*
**Branches**: 675 Sixth Avenue (727 1227); 4 Astor Place (420 1323).

### Big Cup

*228 Eighth Avenue, between 21st & 22nd Streets (206 0059). Subway C or E to 23rd Street.* **Open** 7am-2am Mon-Thur, Sun; 7am-3am Fri, Sat. **No credit cards**.
Although this Chelsea coffee shop is a popular morning hang-out for local gays, the café has a comfortable mix of living room furniture that makes it an ideal place to grab a muffin and some coffee while reading the newspaper.
*Disabled: toilets.*

### Café Lalo

*201 West 83rd Street, between Amsterdam Avenue & Broadway (496 6031). Subway 1 or 9 to 86th Street.* **Open** 9am-2am Mon-Thur, Sun; 9am-4pm Fri, Sat. **No credit cards**.
This perennially popular Upper West Side café has one of the city's largest choices of dessert, including all sorts of chocolate and fruit cakes, plus American classics such as

**BB's**, *formerly the Bowery Bar and still a poseurs' paradise. See page 147.*

pecan and apple pie. In summer, the long windows are opened on to the tree-lined street, adding a European feel to the space. Classical melodies are the music of choice here.

### Caffe Reggio

*119 MacDougal Street, between West 3rd & Bleecker Streets (475 9557). Subway A, B, C, D, E, F or Q to West 4th Street.* **Open** 10am-2am Mon-Thur, Sun; 9.30am-4am Fri, Sat. **No credit cards**.

A favourite spot with tourists and New Yorkers who don't live downtown (if they did, they'd know of more chic and less crowded places to go), Caffe Reggio is a great spot for people watching and coffee drinking, European-style.

### Ceci-Cela

*55 Spring Street, between Lafayette & Mulberry Streets (274 9179). Subway 6 to Spring Street.* **Open** 7am-7pm Mon-Fri; 9am-7pm Sat, Sun. **Credit** MC, V.

Tucked in a narrow space away from the weekend throngs of SoHo, Ceci-Cela offers its own French pastries and crispy croissants in a cosy and relaxed setting. Get some dessert on the go, or walk to the back room where there are a few rattan tables and waitress service.

### Cupcake Café

*522 Ninth Avenue, at 39th Street (465 1530). Subway A, C or E to 42nd Street.* **Open** 7am-7.30pm Mon-Fri; 8am-6pm Sat; 9am-5pm Sun. **No credit cards**.

There's little room for loungers at this off-the-beaten-track bakery in Hell's Kitchen: it only has a few shabby tables. Cupcakes and cakes are exquisitely decorated with rich, buttery frosting swirled into colourful flowers. If you can't stomach so much fat, try an own-made doughnut or muffin.

### Cyber Café

*273A Lafayette Street, at Prince Street (334 5140). Subway N, R to Prince Street.* **Open** 11am-10pm Mon-Thur, Sun; 11am-1am Fri, Sat. **Credit** AmEx, MC, V.

It may look more like a bohemian office than a café, but coffee and food is served in this computer-filled corner of SoHo. Sit at one of the multimedia workstations and play with software from the café's library, or surf the net while sipping coffee and relaxing in the comfortable chairs.
*Disabled: toilets.*

### DeRoberti's

*176 First Avenue, at East 11th Street (674 7137). Subway L to First Avenue.* **Open** 9.30am-11pm Mon-Thur, Sun; 9.30am-midnight Fri, Sat. **Credit** MC, V.

Located in a pocket of the East Village that closely resembles Little Italy, DeRoberti's is a decades-old pâtisserie where espresso, cappuccino and Italian desserts such as cannolis and hazelnut meringues are served in a beautiful old-fashioned setting *(pictured on pages 146-147)*.

### Drip

*489 Amsterdam Avenue, between 83rd & 84th Streets (875 1032). Subway 1 or 9 to 86th Street.* **Open** 7am-1am Mon-Thur; 7am-3pm Fri; 9am-3am Sat; 9am-midnight Sun.* **Credit** MC, V.

Brightly coloured mock-leather couches fill this coffee lounge and bar. Its walls display junk food props such as Cap'n Crunch cereal and Orangina soda. The list of coffees – espresso, cappuccino, au lait, mochaccino – is short, but sufficient. At the back is a 'love life' noticeboard, where you can fill out a questionnaire for a date.
*Disabled: toilets.*

### DT/UT

*1626 Second Avenue, at 84th Street (327 1327). Subway 4, 5 or 6 to 86th Street.* **Open** 7.30am-midnight Mon-Thur, Sun; 7.30am-2am Fri, Sat. **No credit cards**.

Located between sleek Third Avenue and ragged First Avenue, this abbreviation for downtown/uptown is about couches, easy chairs, brick walls, Gothic candles and

**Max Fish**: *a Lower East Side institution. See page 148.*

# Cigar bars

Let's go over this one more time, since it's such a curious irony. Just as New York restaurants got *extremely* puritanical about the smoking of cigarettes – see the main course cleared, see your friends head for the exit – places began popping up on every other block to embrace the bigger, more invasively smoky cigar. Aside from the fact that this is a bit like outlawing public kissing while legalising whorehouses, the ascension of 'stogie joints' poses a problem for visitor and local alike: do you really want to go to a place just to smoke?

These are stereotypically masculine (cough, cough) places, full of forced sophistication, hushed reverence for all manner of liquid pleasures and the rare and fetish-inspiring foreign smoke. It would take a page just to list the new restaurants with cigar-friendly environments, not to mention the dedicated cigar outlets with cutting-edge filtration systems and obscenely pricey cigar menus. Still, they're as good a place as any to see how a certain segment of the city population disposes of its income and, occasionally, its senses. So smoke 'em, if you've got 'em, here.

### Carnegie Bar & Books

*156 West 56th Street, between Fifth & Sixth Avenues (957 9676). Subway N or R to Fifth Avenue.* **Open** 4.30pm-2am Mon-Thur, Sun; 4.30pm-4am Fri, Sat. **Credit** AmEx, DC, MC, V.

The city's first cigar lounge is now a full-blown chain, with four outlets of varying sizes and styles. The most charming is the newest. Close to Carnegie Hall, it's a pleasant nouveau-Gothic retreat from midtown. The book-lined cases are strictly decorative, but the attractive women servers know how to light your fire.
*Disabled: toilets.*
**Branches: Lexington** 1020 Lexington (717 3902); **Hudson** 636 Hudson Street (229 2642); **Beekman** 889 First Avenue (980 9314).

### City Wine & Cigar Co

*62 Laight Street, at Greenwich Street (334 2274). Subway 1, 2, 3, 9 to Franklin Street.* **Open** 4.30pm-2am Mon-Wed; 4.30pm-3.30am Thur-Sat. **Credit** AmEx, Disc, JCB, MC, V.

Smoking goes downtown at the hippest of this swinging group. It's in the middle of dark nowhere, but should draw crowds as it's designed with a sense of style and humour. *Disabled: toilets.*

### Club Macanudo

*26 East 63rd Street, between Park & Madison Avenues (752 8200). Subway N, R, 5 or 6 to Lexington Avenue/ 59th Street.* **Open** noon-1am Mon, Tue; noon-2am Wed-Fri; 5pm-2am Sat. **Credit** AmEx, DC, MC, V.

This is the theme park of cigar bars, decorated with the boxes and labels of rare cigars. It's overdone and garish, but the golden lounge will swallow you up and satisfy your every single-malt and combustible need.

### Havana Tea Room-Cigar House

*265 East 78th Street, between Second & Third Avenues (327 2012). Subway 6 to 77th Street.* **Open** 3pm-1am Tue-Thur, Sun; 3pm-2am Fri, Sat. **Credit** AmEx, MC, V.

The best cigar bar in the city has only recently gained a liquor licence; it now serves beer, champagne, wine and port, as well as tea. Pray that the introduction of the booze doesn't spoil the calm of this Upper East Side room with its slowly moving fans and pre-Castro style. The cigar menu can't be beaten in terms of selection or description.

### Patroon

*160 East 46th Street, between Lexington & Third Avenues (883 7373). Subway 4, 5 or 6 to 42nd Street.* **Open** noon-10.45pm Mon-Fri; 5.30-10.45pm Sat. **Credit** AmEx, MC, V.

Upstairs at this new favourite of the power-dining set, is an extremely masculine cosy smoking room. The feel is mid-century New York meets cruise ship, with wooden shutters and pictures of men pummelling men in war and sport. Sink into a beautifully battered club chair, and ignore the bozos tormenting the waitresses with their connoisseurship of vintage ports.
*Disabled: toilets.*

---

primitive art. A counter displays a tantalising array of baked goods – which make a perfect accompaniment to one of the many different types of coffee listed on the blackboard.

### Fellisimo

*10 West 56th Street, between Fifth & Sixth Avenues (247 5656). Subway N or R to Fifth Avenue.* **Open** 10.30am-5.30pm Mon-Fri; 10.30am-6.30pm Sat. **Credit** AmEx, DC, Disc, MC, V.

Fellisimo is a chic bazaar occupying a narrow townhouse off the deluxe shopping extravaganza that is Fifth Avenue. Climb to the top floor where you'll find a tranquil café serving sandwiches, cakes and tea. The simplified Japanese-style décor offers an extremely welcome oasis for tired feet and souls. Sometimes a tarot card reader takes up residence in one corner, selling a glimpse of the future to the forever hopeful.
*Disabled: toilets.*

### Hungarian Pastry Shop

*1030 Amsterdam Avenue, at 111th Street (866 4230). Subway 1, 9, B or C to 110th Street.* **Open** 8am-11.30pm Mon-Sat; 9am-10.30pm Sun. **No credit cards.**

A Morningside Heights original, this plain looking coffee shop offers coffee, tea and many pastries (made in-house) to Columbia University students and teachers. Ignore the pretentious students around you reading Kant and pull out that Jackie Collins novel you've been meaning to read.

### Limbo

*47 Avenue A, between 3rd & 4th Streets (477 5271). Subway F to Second Avenue.* **Open** 7am-midnight daily. **No credit cards.**

To get a real sense of what the East Village is now about, come to this stylish self-service coffee hang-out. Freelance writers, actors and artists sit for hours drinking large cups

of tea or coffee, reading scripts and typing manuscripts on their portable computers. A continuous stream of book, poetry and tarot card readings attract crowds in the evenings. *Disabled: toilets.*

### Newsbar Inc
*2 West 19th Street (255 3996). Subway 1 or 9 to 18th Street.* **Open** 7.30am-8pm Mon-Fri; 8am-8pm Sat, Sun. **Credit** MC, V.
Each branch of this chain of newspaper kiosks-cum-cafés has an industrial chic look that leaves little space for lounging. The walls are devoted to racks of magazines from around the world. Quiche and fresh sandwiches are served to the young and media-obsessed folk who use Newsbar as a pitstop.

### Rumpelmayer's
*St Moritz Hotel, 50 Central Park South, between Fifth & Sixth Avenues (755 5800). Subway N or R to Fifth Avenue.* **Open** 7am-4pm Mon, Sun; 7am-11pm Tue-Sat. **Credit** AmEx, DC, MC, V.
Treat the kids with a visit to this old-fashioned ice-cream parlour, decorated with toys and stuffed animals. Dig into a banana split or one of the many other ice-cream concoctions, and if you're really hungry, a dish from the continental menu. *Disabled: toilets.*

### Tea & Sympathy
*108 Greenwich Avenue, at 13th Street (807 8329). Subway 1, 2, 3, 9 or L to 14th Street/Sixth Avenue.* **Open** 11.30am-10.30pm Mon-Fri; 10am-10.30pm Sat, Sun. **No credit cards.**
Visit this cramped English nook during the week – at weekends the wait is annoyingly long – and order delights from

Blighty, including beans on toast and cucumber sandwiches. Afternoon tea consists of an assortment of finger sandwiches, two cakes, two scones, clotted cream, jam and a pot of tea. Here, Britannia rules.

## Bars

The city's recent crackdown on nightclubs and the subsequent closing of several New York hot spots (*see chapter* **Clubs**) has led to the proliferation of a new breed of bar: the lounge, a sort of bar/club hybrid where patrons can perch on overstuffed couches, drink trendy Cosmopolitans, preen and check each other out, usually without a cover charge. Lounges have all the trappings of nightclubs (velvet ropes, doormen and booming music) with one hitch – the law won't allow dancing and any booty shaking is strictly forbidden. But if all you want is a bar, a stool and a good draught, there are plenty of good old watering holes.

### 288
*288 Elizabeth Street, between Houston & Bleecker Streets (260 5045). Subway 6 to Bleecker Street.* **Open** noon-4am daily. **No credit cards.**
A cavernous drinking hall that gets smoky and loud, but also serves a great Guinness to an arty, slightly slackerish crowd.

## BB's (Bowery Bar)

*40 East 4th Street, at The Bowery (475 2220). Subway 6 to Bleecker Street.* **Open** *11.30am-4am daily.* **Credit** AmEx, DC, MC, V.

Formerly the Bowery Bar, before someone else claimed prior rights to the name and the owners were forced to abbreviate. You've probably already seen BB's in paparazzi shots – it's a favourite downtown haunt of the rich and famous (or 'sick and shameless' as a nearby handmade sign proclaims). The outside dining area is great for summer socialising.

## Beauty Bar

*231 East 14th Street, between Second & Third Avenues (539 1389). Subway L, N, R, 4 or 6 to 14th Street/Union Square.* **Open** *5pm-4am daily.*

Formerly a hairdresser's, the Beauty Bar is bedecked in high kitsch, having a 1950s beauty salon theme. The décor includes a bank of overhead dryers and there's an 86 year-old in-house manicurist to groom your nails as you drink.

## Botanica

*47 East Houston, between Mott & Mulberry Streets (343 7251). Subway F to Houston; B, D or F to Broadway/Lafayette.* **Open** *5pm-4am daily.* **No credit cards.**

It's easy to choke on the bohemian atmosphere here, but besides a few modern beatniks and a lot of Gitanes smoke, Botanica is a fine neighbourhood gin mill with excellent DJs throughout the week.

## Bubble Lounge

*228 West Broadway, between Franklin & White Streets (431 3433). Subway 1 or 9 to Franklin Street; A, C or E to Canal Street.* **Open** *5.30pm-4am Mon-Thur; 4.30pm-4am Fri, Sat; 4.30pm-1am Sun.* **Credit** AmEx, DC, MC, V.

TriBeCa's very own cigar and champagne bar, with the requisite sofas, wing-back chairs and chandeliers made bearable only by the live jazz.

## Buddha Bar

*150 Varick Street, at Vandam Street (255 4433). Subway 1 or 9 to Houston Street.* **Open** *10pm-4am daily.* **No credit cards.**

Glossy red walls, dim lighting and golden Buddha statuettes create in Buddha Bar an exotic and sinful atmosphere. There's a bright red pool table at the back, and room to boogie should you come on one of the bar's regular club nights.

## Chumley's

*86 Bedford Street, between Barrow & Grove Streets (675 4449). Subway E to West 4th Street.* **Open** *5pm-midnight Mon-Fri; 5pm-2am Sat, Sun.* **No credit cards.**

Someone needs to tell Chumley's that the days of prohibition are over. This ex-speakeasy still doesn't have a sign over the door, so it's easy to walk straight past. Inside is a pub/restaurant with book-lined walls and a cosy atmosphere. The food is passable and of medium price.

## P J Clarke's

*915 Third Avenue, at East 55th Street (355 8857). Subway 6 to 51st Street; E or F to Lexington Avenue.* **Open** *10am-4am daily.* **Credit** AmEx, DC, MC, V.

A classic mahogany and cut-glass saloon from the days when Third Avenue was darkened by an elevated train and every corner had a watering-hole. It survived prohibition as well as notoriety as the location for *The Lost Weekend*. The whisky's still good, and even the urinals should be a landmark.

### Fanelli's

*94 Prince Street, at Mercer Street (226 9412). Subway 6 to Bleecker Street; B, D or F to Broadway/Lafayette Street; N or R to Prince Street.* **Open** 10am-2am Mon-Thur, Sun; 11am-3am Sat. **Credit** AmEx, DC, Disc, MC, V.

The oldest and one of the best bars in SoHo. It has a great wooden bar, wonderful barmen, tiled floors, framed pictures of boxers on the walls, and local beers. Fanelli's is decidedly unpretentious and a favourite with gallery owners. The food is good but many use it as ballast for the shots of Jack.

### Fez

*at Time Café, 380 Lafayette Street, at Great Jones Street (533 7000). Subway 6 to Astor Place.* **Open** 6pm-2am Mon-Thur, Sun; 6pm-4am Fri, Sat. **Credit** AmEx, MC, V.

Downstairs you'll find music and readings, but the bar itself is right for lounging inaction. Deep sofas, low tables, good low lighting and a slight Moroccan theme (just copper tables and paintings of Magreb mamas) all conspire to keep you reclining long into the night.

### Global 33

*93 Second Avenue, between 5th & 6th Streets (477 8427). Subway 6 to Astor Place.* **Open** 6pm-1am Mon-Thur; 6pm-2am Fri, Sat. **Credit** AmEx.

Global 33's big modernist clocks in its back room tell you the time in Monte Carlo, Shanghai, Tangier, Istanbul and Havana – helpful if you're on an international espionage mission. But even if you're not, the sleek 1960s design practically forces you to drink something sophisticated, and the bar staff won't disappoint.

### The Greatest Bar on Earth

*Windows on the World, One World Trade Center, at Church Street (524 7011). Subway C or E to World Trade Center; 1 or 9 to Cortland Street.* **Open** 4pm-midnight Mon-Thur; 4pm-2am Fri; noon-2am Sat; 11am-11pm Sun. **Credit** AmEx, DC, Disc, MC, V.

No, this postmodern saloon in the sky certainly doesn't live up to the hyperbolic name, but it is nicely un-earthy. Get high among the odd spiky sculpture in the sky, and the whole city below appears festive.

### Jet Lounge

*286 Spring Street, between Hudson & Varick Streets (675 2277). Subway 1, 9, A, C or E to Canal Street.* **Open** 8pm-4am daily. **Credit** AmEx, MC, V.

A hyper-hip bar at the eastern reaches of SoHo, Jet Lounge has South Beach roots (where its owners have the popular Groove Jet). The décor includes zebra stripes and an overabundance of mirrors; the waiting staff are struggling models.

### Joe's

*520 East 6th Street, between Avenues A & B (473 9093). Subway F to Second Avenue.* **Open** noon-4am daily. **No credit cards.**

Joe's is an East Village refuge for barflies young and old, with Hank Williams and Dolly Parton on the jukebox and a pool table in the back.

### Kettle of Fish

*130 West 3rd Street, between MacDougal Street & Sixth Avenue (533 4790). Subway A, B, C, D, E or F to West 4th Street.* **Open** noon-4am daily. **Credit** AmEx, DC, MC, V.

This is one NYU-area bar that hasn't been ruined by idiot pretension or a goony theme. Its back area swells with darts players on league nights. A good place to go for beers and black and white TV while making your way further downtown.

### Landmark Tavern

*626 Eleventh Avenue at 40th Street (757 8595). Subway A, C or E to 42nd Street.* **Open** noon-11pm Mon-Thur, Sun; noon-midnight Fri, Sat. **No credit cards.**

One of the most beautiful and tranquil of the town's old saloons, with tin ceilings, wood-burning potbelly stoves and about five dozen single-malt Scotches on hand.

### McSorely's Old Ale House

*15 East 7th Street, between Second & Third Avenues (473 9148). Subway 6 to Astor Place; N or R to 8th Street.* **Open** 11am-1am Mon-Sat; 1pm-1am Sun. **No credit cards.**

The oldest pub in Manhattan now admits women – and to judge by the night-time custom, it's mainly women who like their men in baseball caps and slobbery stages of inebriation. Still a classic place for a mug of warm ale and a whiff of a time when all New York was filled with drinkers' bars.

### Max Fish

*178 Ludlow Street, between Houston & Stanton Streets (529 3959). Subway F to Second Avenue.* **Open** 5.30pm-4am daily. **No credit cards.**

Ludlow Street has become the Lower East Side's main street, thanks, mostly to this seven year-old institution. Though new bars keep popping up nearby, Max Fish continues to entertain a cool bunch of musicians and artists who have remained loyal regulars.

### Milano's

*51 East Houston Street (226 8632). Subway B, D, F or Q to Broadway/Lafayette Street.* **Open** 8am-4am Mon-Sat; noon-4pm Sun. **No credit cards.**

Have yourself a New York moment and a great pint of Guinness at this Irish/Italian dive bar on the cusp of Little Italy. Frank Sinatra's on the walls and on the jukebox and the die-hard barflies are always ready for boozy conversation should you be in the mood.

### North Star Pub

*93 South Street, corner of Fulton Street (509 6757). Subway A or C to Broadway/Nassau Street; 2, 3, 4, 5, J, M or Z to Fulton Street.* **Open** 11.30am-midnight daily. **Credit** AmEx, CB, DC, MC, V.

Much frequented by homesick Brits and New York Anglophiles, the North Star Pub bar and restaurant is refreshingly pubby and normal by this city's standards. Plenty of imported Brit beers and HP sauce to drench your pub grub with.

### Oak Room/Blue Bar

*Algonquin Hotel, 59 West 44th Street, between Fifth & Sixth Avenues (840 6800). Subway 4, 5, 6 or 7 to Grand Central.* **Open** 11.30am-1am daily. **Credit** AmEx, CB, DC, Disc, MC, V.

The home of the legendary round table wears its heritage well. The Oak Room bar has the sedate atmosphere of a gentlemen's bar, while the adjoining, dimly lit Blue Room is the place to raise a midday glass to Dorothy Parker.

### Old Town Bar

*45 East 18th Street, near Broadway (529 6732). Subway 4, 5, 6, N, R or L to Union Square.* **Open** 11.30am-midnight Mon-Fri; noon-midnight Sat; 3-10pm Sun. **Credit** AmEx, MC, V.

Old Town Bar has been here for over a century, but unlike New York's other historic bars, it serves great food. Stop by for a quintessential burger and fries at this wood-panelled bar with a genuine old New York feel. The two floors fill up with regulars and after-work mobs, but make your way to the long bar, order some stiff drinks and you'll feel welcome.

### Rudy's

*44 Ninth Avenue, between 43rd & 44th Streets (974 9169). Subway A, C or E to 42nd Street.* **Open** 10am-4am daily. **No credit cards.**

Ninth Avenue may finally be getting its share of hip lounges, but the real place to be is still parked at the bar at this unchanging institution. The red banquettes are full of customers because the beer is cheap, the hot dogs are free and the juke box is full of great jazz. Plus there's the human jazz of Rudy's dedicated regulars, young and old.

### Sophie's
*East 5th Street, between Avenues A & B (385 0909). Subway F to Second Avenue.* **Open** 11am-4am daily. **No credit cards**.
Expect to find a young crowd here at weekends, when the bar gets packed with co-eds looking for cheap draught beer and a turn on the pool table.

### Spy
*101 Greene Street, between Prince & Spring Streets (343 9000). Subway N or R to Prince Street; 6 to Spring Street.* **Open** 5pm-4am daily. **Credit** AmEx, DC, MC, V.
Overtaking Bowery as the downtown bar to see and be seen at. It's appropriately decadent, with dripping chandeliers and over-stuffed seating. Even with the proliferation of sofas this is no place for relaxing – you've got too much posing to do.

### Temple Bar
*332 Lafayette Street, between Bleecker & Houston Streets (925 4242). Subway 6 to Bleecker Street.* **Open** 5pm-1am Mon-Thur; 5pm-2am Fri, Sat. **Credit** AmEx, DC, MC, V.

Temple's bartenders are dedicated masters of their trade and the décor is sophisticated and opulent, lending an other-worldly air to what could become a long dark night of expensive drinking.

### Vasac
*108 Avenue B, at 7th Street (473 8840). Subway L to First Avenue.* **Open** noon-4am daily. **Credit** AmEx, DC, Disc, MC, V.
Also called 7B and the Horseshoe Bar, Vasac, with its spit and sawdust atmosphere, has been featured in countless films. The formerly edgy crowd has been replaced by a younger, bridge-and-tunnel set that likes to rock out to the Smashing Pumpkins.

### White Horse
*567 Hudson Street, at 11th Street (243 9260). Subway A, C, E or L to 14th Street/Eighth Avenue.* **Open** 11am-2am Mon-Thur, Sun; 11am-4am Fri, Sat. **No credit cards**.
The White Horse is best visited on weekdays – in the evenings and at weekends the crowd becomes cheesy and noisy. It is one of New York's oldest pubs and is famous for being the site where Dylan Thomas had his final whisky before he collapsed and died from an excess of alcohol back in 1953. Don't expect anything special from the food.

# Brew pubs

The life expectancy of the brew pub/restaurant trend may be in doubt, since New York's oldest, Zip City, has just emptied its tanks and shut its doors. For the time being, though, there are enough brew pubs in town to satisfy any lover of hand-crafted, made-on-the-premises, pumpkin-infused ale. These places are of a similar mould – the design distinguished by the presence of massive shiny tanks and elaborate, glassed off systems; the clientele made up of hop-heads in baseball caps. At many brew pubs, 'flights' of four or five beers are available, a good way to test what's on tap. For the most part, food is of secondary concern.

### Carnegie Hill Brewing Company
*1600 Third Avenue, at 90th Street (369 0808). Subway 4 or 6 to 86th Street.* **Open** 4pm-2am Mon-Thur; 4pm-4am Fri; noon-4am Sat; noon-2pm Sun. **Credit** AmEx, MC, V.
The walls are green, the menu is of basic pub grub, but there are many agreeable beers, five on tap at a time. Fruit and wheat beers are highlights.
*Disabled: toilets.*

### Chelsea Brewing Company
*Pier 59, West Side Highway, at 18th Street (336 6440). Subway A, C, E or L to 14th Street.* **Open** noon-2am Mon-Sat; noon-11pm Sun. **Credit** AmEx, CB, DC, Disc.
A big, fun brew-bar inside the republic-sized sports facility known as Chelsea Piers (*see chapter* **Sport & Fitness**). The golfer and Wall Streeter customers tend to skip the food and focus their attention on porters and lemon wheats.
*Disabled: toilets.*

### Commonwealth Brewing Company
*35 West 48th Street, between Fifth & Sixth Avenues (977 2269). Subway B, D or F to Rockefeller Center.* **Open** 11.30am-11pm Mon-Thur; 11.30am-12.30am Fri; 11.30am-10.30pm Sat; noon-7pm Sun. **Credit** AmEx, DC, Disc, MC, V.
A Rockefeller Center after-work madhouse, with an unusual modernist-industrial look. The beer finds its way into almost every dish on the menu, with inventive play.

### Hansens Times Square Brewery
*160 West 42nd Street, between Broadway & Seventh Avenue (398 1234). Subway N, R or S to 42nd Street/Times Square.* **Open** 11am-2am daily. **Credit** AmEx, DC, MC, V.
Notable mainly for its size and grand views of blazingly neon Broadway Babylon. The German owners (from Flensburg) make sure the bocks and pilsners here are produced according to the strict regulations of their fatherland.

### Heartland Brewery
*35 Union Square West, at 17th Street (645 3400). Subway N, R, L, 6 or 4 to Union Square/14th Street.* **Open** noon-1am Mon-Thur; noon-2am Fri, Sat; noon-midnight Sun. **Credit** AmEx, DC, MC, V.
The beer is always changing at this popular old-world Union Square restaurant. Look for rye beer and ciders to complement a solid menu of above-average burgers and chicken.
*Disabled: toilets.*

### Typhoon Brewery
*22 East 54th Street, between Fifth & Madison Avenues (754 9006). Subway E or F to Lexington/Third Avenue.* **Open** noon-11.30pm Mon-Sat. **Credit** AmEx, DC, Disc, MC, V.
The original chef has departed, but Typhoon continues to pair an unlikely Thai-influenced menu with its own beers. The modern, split-level, midtown space is also atypical – dark bar downstairs, upstairs a hopping dining room.

# Shopping & Services

**DIESEL HISTORICAL MOMENTS:**

# BIRTH OF THE MODERN CONFERENCE, YALTA, 1945

We are pleased to offer you the perfect environment for a modern and successful conference.

We provide you with all the equipment you need. You may rest assured that everything here is top of the line; not only beautifully designed and elegant, but also function

Furthermore: our service is famous for its persona touch - guaranteed to make your participants feel co fortable and relaxed.

# The DIESEL Superstore · 60th Street and Lexington Avenu

# Shopping
# & Services

*If you can't find it here, they probably don't make it any more.*

The impeccably elegant **Henri Bendel**. *P155*.

A substantial part of the American experience involves spending money. It's really not hard once you get started. Whether you have bushels of it or hardly any at all, there are endless opportunities to test your buying skills in New York.

## TACTICAL SPENDING

It's best to arrange your shopping trips by neighbourhood. Starting at the southern tip of Manhattan, the **World Financial Center** features enormous skyscrapers crammed with restaurants and shops. The Winter Garden, located in the central courtyard, is full of high palm trees and flanked by a wide variety of boutiques and cafés.

Shopping becomes more serious as you head uptown, into **SoHo**. During the 1960s and 1970s, this was an artists' neighbourhood, but since the 1980s, the area has become too fashionable for its own good. Look here for bookshops, art galleries, good quality vintage clothes, modern furniture and new designers, as well as flagship stores for the likes of Comme des Garçons and Agnès B. **Lower Broadway below Houston**, bordering on SoHo, is starting to resemble a pedestrian mall, with chain stores galore – Banana Republic, J Crew and Victoria's Secret are all represented here. **Canal Street** is where to find fake Rolexes and Prada bags, as well as the best DJ mix tapes, from market stalls selling endless piles of counterfeit designer wares to electronics, sports shoes and T-shirts.

The **Lower East Side** is bargain-hunting territory. Many of the shops close early on Fridays and all day on Saturdays for the Jewish Sabbath. Don't miss **Orchard Street** from Houston to Delancey Streets, where you'll find leather goods, luggage, designer clothes, belts, shoes and yards of fabric. Another strip on **Ludlow Street** showcases a different side of the neighbourhood: here there are plenty of hip bars and boutiques filled with clothes by up-and-coming designers. The **East Village** has plenty of the latter, along with an abundance of second-hand shops. Check **Ninth Street** for clothes and furnishings, and **Seventh Street** for young designers.

As you wander west through **Greenwich Village**, the streets become progressively more deserted and winding. As in the East Village, shops

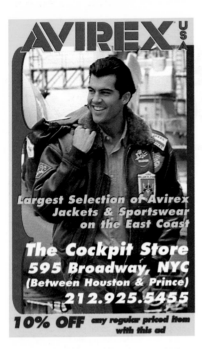

here stay open late and are especially good for jazz records, rare books and vintage clothing, not forgetting the unmissable food shop, Balducci's.

**Fifth Avenue**, between 14th and 23rd Streets, shelters quite a few designer outlets, with the famous department stores – with fantastic window displays – ranged along the upper stretch. **Madison Avenue** is the place for expensive top designers: Prada, Valentino, Versace et al. It's also great for window shopping and celebrity spotting, especially at weekends. On the **Upper West Side**, Columbus Avenue boasts another mall-like stretch of stores. It's much more interesting to proceed north to **125th Street in Harlem** where you can eat delicious food at Mart 125 and shop for hip-hop clothing along 125th Street.

## EVERYTHING MUST GO!

Don't be fooled by shops that give the impression that their owners are preparing to flee the country: permanent closing-down sales and bazaar-like floor plans are the norm (except, of course, for the grand environs of upper Fifth Avenue and the SoHo designer stores). Department stores usually host sales at the end of the season, in August and March. The post-Christmas reductions now seem to occur earlier in December, but most shopkeepers think all holidays are a good enough reason for a sale. For the latest information, see *Time Out New York*'s Check Out section, the weekly Sales & Bargains column in *New York* magazine and the ads in the *New York Times*.

Designers' sample sales are good sources of low-priced clothes: for information about what's on where, either pick up a copy of the *S&B Report* (available from 108 East 38th Street, suite 2000, NY 10016, telephone 683 7612); or call the Bargain Hotline (540 0123). These are also sources for details of appliance, furniture and other sales.

The beauty of New York is that many shops are open late, especially downtown (they tend to open later in the morning, too). At some of the larger and more tourist-orientated places you can avoid paying the 8.25 per cent city sales tax if you arrange to have your purchase shipped outside New York State. Although the governor of New York is considering a law that would drop sales tax entirely in the city, the tax is otherwise added on at the time of purchase.

## The Stores

### Barneys

*154 West 17th Street, near Seventh Avenue (593 7800). Subway 1, 2, 3 or 9 to 14th Street; L to Sixth Avenue.* **Open** 10am-9pm Mon-Thur; 10am-8pm Fri; 10am-7pm Sat; noon-6pm Sun. **Credit** AmEx, MC, V.

All the top designers are represented at this haven for New York style, as well as a decent selection of lesser-known labels. There are also a selection of hip home furnishings and unusual children's clothes, and the Christmas windows are usually the best in town. Take a shopping break at the airy atrium and elegant café on the lower floor. Every August

and March, the store hosts the Barneys Warehouse Sale, worth exploring if you're in town. Alterations are free. **Branch**: 660 Madison Avenue, at 61st Street (826 8900).

### Bergdorf Goodman

*754 Fifth Avenue, at 58th Street (753 7300). Subway E or F to 53rd Street.* **Open** 10am-6pm Mon-Wed, Fri, Sat; 10am-8pm Thur. **Credit** AmEx, JCB, MC, V.

While Barneys is the younger, flashier crowd, Bergdorf's is for the elegant one – just check out the hat department. It is one of the best of the department stores for clothes and accessory shopping, being neither too big nor too cavernous. As well as selling all the major American and European designers, Bergdorf's has a number of exclusive lines. Be warned, though: clothes are expensive. The men's store is across the street.

### Bloomingdale's

*1000 Third Avenue, at East 59th Street (355 5900). Subway 4, 5, 6, N or R to 59th Street.* **Open** 10am-8.30pm Mon-Fri; 10am-7pm Sat; 11am-7pm Sun. **Credit** AmEx, MC, V.

A gigantic department store that has everything you could want to buy, if you can bear to search for it. During the weekends, the store is filled with Long Island girls. The ground floor features handbags, scarves, hosiery, make-up and jewellery, and upstairs you'll find linens, two different floors of shoes, designer names and a variety of cheaper goods. The sale racks are always worth a glance.

### Henri Bendel

*715 Fifth Avenue, at 56th Street (247 1100). Subway 4, 5, 6, N or R to 59th Street/Lexington Avenue.* **Open** 10am-7pm Mon-Wed, Fri, Sat; 10am-8pm Thur; noon to 6pm Sun. **Credit** AmEx, DC, JCB, MC, V.

Bendel is a sweet-smelling sliver of heaven. Its lavish quarters resemble a plush townhouse – there are elevators, but it's nicer to mount the elegant, winding staircase, created by Marie-Paulle Pelle. Designer James Mansour kept the original boutiques and has added several eye-grabbing extras. There are Claude Montana and Todd Oldman boutiques as well as a Susan Bennis/Warren Edwards Shoe Salon on the fourth floor. Prices are comparable with those in other upmarket stores, but somehow things look more desirable here. It must be the darling brown-and-white striped bags.

### Lord & Taylor

*424 Fifth Avenue, between 38th & 39th Streets (391 3344). Subway B, D, F or Q to 42nd Street.* **Open** 10am-7pm Mon, Tue; 10am-8.30pm Wed-Fri; 9am-7pm Sat; 11am-6pm Sun. **Credit** AmEx, Disc, MC, V.

Lord & Taylor's is a conservative, rather old-fashioned department store, the only one left that stocks Germaine Monteil cosmetics. American designers are well represented, and the furniture and shoe departments are traditionally its strengths. Service is decent and there are often good sales. It was here that the Fifth Avenue tradition of dramatic Christmas window displays began.

### Macy's

*Herald Square, 151 West 34th Street, between Broadway & Seventh Avenue (695 4400/494 5151 customer service). Subway B, D, F, N, Q, R, 1, 2, 3, 9 to 34th Street.* **Open** 10am-8.30pm Mon-Sat; 11am-7pm Sun. **Credit** AmEx, MC, V.

It's worth the trip for nostalgia alone. Macy's still calls itself the biggest department store in the world; it occupies an entire city block. Since the parent company went into bankruptcy protection in 1991, the excesses of its famous sales have been considerably reduced, and most things are cheaper somewhere else. But you'll still find everything from designer labels to cheap colourful casuals, plus a pet shop, fish market, Metropolitan Museum gift shop and bar. Beware the aggressive perfume sprayers and resign yourself to getting hopelessly lost. The store has its own concierge service (560 3827) to help you maximise your shopping potential.

## Saks Fifth Avenue
*611 Fifth Avenue, between 49th & 50th Streets (753 4000). Subway B, D, F or Q to Rockefeller Center; E or F to 53rd Street.* **Open** 10am-6.30pm Mon-Wed, Fri, Sat; 10am-8pm Thur; noon-6pm Sun. **Credit** AmEx, CB, DC, Disc, JCB, MC, V.
A classic department store that features all the big names, an excellent menswear department, fine household linens, a newly expanded kids' section and good service. The ground floor is packed with accessories and has a stylish beauty area where personal consultations and makeovers are available. Upstairs, you'll find a well-chosen selection of designer labels.

## Takashimaya
*693 Fifth Avenue, between 54th & 55th Streets (350 0100). Subway E or F to 53rd Street.* **Open** 10am-6pm Mon-Wed, Fri, Sat; 10am-8pm Thur. **Credit** AmEx, DC, Disc, JCB, MC, V.
The first New York branch of this Japanese department store opened in April 1993 and has been giving Bergdorf's a run for its money ever since. The five-storey forum mixes Eastern and Western aesthetics. The first two floors offer 4,500sq ft (419 sq m) of art gallery space and a men's and women's signature collection, as well as Japanese make-up and exotic plants; the top floor is dedicated to designer accessories.

## Beauty Shops

Most drugstores stock a range of good, cheap make-up and general beauty products (*see below* **Pharmacists**). Department stores are a good source for the major names, but you will probably pay more than you would at some of the discount stores. *See also page 171* **Green**.

## Aveda
*509 Madison Avenue, between 52nd & 53rd Streets (832 2416). Subway 6 to 51st Street.* **Open** 10am-7pm Mon-Fri; noon-6pm Sat; noon-5pm Sun. **Credit** AmEx, JCB, MC, V.
A small but tranquil boutique filled with an exclusive line of hair- and skincare products, make-up, massage oils and cleansers, all made from flower and plant extracts.
**Branches:** 233 Spring Street (807 1492); 456 West Broadway (473 0280); 140 Fifth Ave (645 4797).

## Face Stockholm
*110 Prince Street at Greene Street (334-3900). Subway N, R to Prince Street.* **Open** 11am-7pm Mon-Wed, 11am-8pm Thur-Sat; noon-7pm Sun. **Credit** AmEx, MC, V.
Along with a full line of shadows, lipsticks, tools and blushes (at very reasonable prices), Face offers two services: make-up applications cost $40 and lessons $75. Phone for an appointment.
**Branch:** 224 Columbus Avenue (769 1420).

## I Natural
*430 West Broadway, between Prince & Spring Streeets (965 1002). Subway N or R to Prince Street.* **Open** 11am-7pm Mon-Sat; noon-6pm Sun. **Credit** AmEx, MC, V.
This self-proclaimed 'beauty sanctuary' features make-up that ranges from $6-$32.50. Customers are encouraged to experiment with any of the make-up, which is displayed on the Great Wall of Color.

## MAC
*14 Christopher Street, between Sixth & Seventh Avenues (243 4150). Subway 1 or 9 to Christopher Street.* **Open** 11am-7pm Mon-Sat; noon-6pm Sun. **Credit** AmEx, MC, V.

Make-up Art Cosmetics, a Canadian company, is committed to cruelty-free products and famed for its matte lipsticks and otherwise unattainable colours. The Queen of New York, drag star Lady Bunny, used to give consultations here; current spokespersons are RuPaul and kd lang. The SoHo branch is enormous: there are nine makeover counters, and best of all, four are private.
**Branch: MAC SoHo,** 113 Spring Street, between Greene and Mercer Streets (334 4641).

## Manic Panic
*64 White Street, at Broadway & Church Streets (254 5517). Subway 1 or 9 to Franklin Street; A, C, E to Canal Street.* **Open** 9am-5pm Mon-Fri; noon-8pm Sat Sun. **Credit** MC, V.
It's all about glamour at Manic Panic. Choose from semi-permanent hair colour in Electric Sunshine, Hot Hot Pink or Infra Red, nail polish and lipsticks, false eyelashes and, of course, hair pieces. Not for the meek at heart.

## L'Occitane
*1046 Madison Avenue, at 80th Street (396 9097). Subway 6 to 77th Street.* **Open** 10am-7pm Mon-Sat; noon-6pm Sun. **Credit** AmEx, MC, V.
It used to be that fans of L'Occitane, a 20-year-old line of bath and beauty products made in Provence, had to pick up their fix of brick-sized soaps, massage balm and hand cream at Barneys, AdHoc Softwares and Portico Bed and Bath. That's changed since this store opened last year.

## Books

New York is not short of bookshops. Most will post books overseas for you (if the books are shipped out of state, you don't pay sales tax, which usually works out about the same as mailing charges). The chain, Barnes & Noble, has expanded considerably in the past few years and its new 'complete and unabridged' outlets offer massive discounts on recent hardbacks and bestsellers. It's uncertain what effect this will have on smaller landmark stores, which continue to provide meticulous service. For **A Different Light Bookstore & Café** and the **Oscar Wilde Memorial Bookshop**, *see chapter* **Gay & Lesbian New York**.

## General

## Barnes & Noble
*105 Fifth Street, at 18th Street (675 5500). Subway 4, 5, 6, L, N or R to Union Square.* **Open** 9.30am-7.45pm Mon-Fri; 9.30am-6.15pm Sat; 11am-5.45pm Sun. **Credit** AmEx, DC, Disc, MC, V.
The world's largest bookstore and the flagship of this bustling chain is a good source of recent hardbacks and discount prices. The record, tape and CD department has one of the largest classical music selections in the city, as well as videos, and there are also children's books and toys and an enormous number of second-hand paperbacks, including play scripts. Of B&N's many branches, the new megastore at 2289 Broadway (at 82nd Street) carries over 1500 magazines and newspapers and features a children's theatre, reading area, gift-wrapping service and more.

## Blackout Books
*50 Avenue B, between 3rd & 4th Streets (777 1967). Subway 2 to Second Avenue.* **Open** 11am-10pm daily. **Credit** A, MC, V.
The spirit of '68 lives. Anarchist, enviro-feminist, situationist

*Fishing for rare tomes at the* **Gotham Book Mart**.

and leftwing texts of every description; information central for local pinks and greens.

### Gotham Book Mart

*41 West 47th Street, near Sixth Avenue (719 4448). Subway B, D, F or Q to Rockefeller Center.* **Open** 9.30am-6.30pm Mon-Fri; 9.30am-6pm Sat. **Credit** AmEx, MC, V.
'Wise men fish here' (Gotham's motto) for the fine selection of out-of-print titles, first editions and rare books. Started by Frances Steloff in the 1920s, Gotham was one of the leaders in the fight against censorship, stocking banned books by James Joyce, DH Lawrence and Henry Miller. Upstairs is a gallery showing work on literary themes. It's dusty and wonderful.

### Gryphon Book Shop

*2246 Broadway, between 80th & 81st Streets (362 0706). Subway 1 or 9 to 79th Street.* **Open** 10am-midnight daily. **Credit** MC, V.
Gryphon specialises in poetry and fiction, and also stocks rock 'n' roll records. A good source for second-hand and rare books on theatre, film, music and drama.

### Shakespeare & Co

*716 Broadway, at Washington Place (529 1330). Subway 6 to Astor Place; N, R to 8th Street.* **Open** 10am-11pm Mon-Thur, Sun; 10am-midnight Fri, Sat. **Credit** AmEx, MC, V.
This bookshop has no real connection to the famous Hemingway haunt in Paris, except in spirit. Real service is the *raison d'être* here; the major qualification for staff is that they must be readers. They'll order anything you covet, and probably have heard of it, too.
**Branches**: 2259 Broadway (580 7800); 939 Lexington Avenue (570 5148).

### St Mark's Bookshop

*31 Third Avenue, between Eighth & Ninth Avenues (260 7853). Subway 6 to Astor Place.* **Open** 10am-midnight Mon-Sat; 11am-midnight Sun. **Credit** AmEx, Disc, MC, V.

This late-night East Village literary and political bookshop stocks works on cultural criticism and feminism, and university and small press publications. Newspapers and over 800 periodicals are also sold, and it's the place to find the most obscure underground newspapers, magazines and imports.

### Strand Book Store

*828 Broadway, at East 12th Street (473 1489). Subway 4, 5, 6, L, N or R to 14th Street/Union Square.* **Open** 9.30am-9.30pm Mon-Sat; 11am-9.30pm Sun. **Credit** AmEx, Disc, MC, V.
As recently as the 1950s there were 40 or 50 antiquarian booksellers ranged along Broadway between Astor Place and 14th Street. The Strand is the only one left and is reputedly the largest second-hand bookshop in the US: over two million books on all subjects are stocked. Most are sold at half the published price or less and the Strand is a great source of remainders.

### Tompkins Square Books & Records

*111 East 7th Street, between Avenue A and First Avenue (979 8956). Subway 6 to Astor Place; F to Second Avenue; L to First Avenue.* **Open** noon-11pm daily. **No credit cards.**
It's hard to leave this cosy second-hand book and record shop. There's also a vintage record collection of writers reading from their work.

### Tower Books

*383 Lafayette Street, at 4th Street (288 5100). Subway 6 to Bleecker Street.* **Open** 11am-11pm daily. **Credit** AmEx, Disc, MC, V.
Tower isn't just about movies and CDs; Tower Books is a decent stop for literature, travel books, photography titles and paperbacks. There's also a vast selection of fanzines and domestic and international magazines on the ground floor.
*For* **Tower Records,** *see p180.*

# Specialist

## A Photographers Place

*133 Mercer Street, between Prince & Spring Streets (431 9358). Subway C or E to Spring Street; N or R to Prince Street.* **Open** 11am-8pm Mon-Sat; noon-6pm Sun. **Credit** AmEx, Disc, MC, V.

Books on all subjects by the world's best photographers.

## Biography

*400 Bleecker Street, at West 11th Street (807 8655). Subway A, C, E to 14th Street; L to Eighth Avenue.* **Open** noon-8pm Mon-Thur; noon-10pm Fri; 11am-11pm Sat; 11am-7pm Sun. **Credit** AmEx, MC, V.

Proof, if proof were needed, that biography is of wide interest: this whole store is devoted to it. New titles only.

## Complete Traveler Bookstore

*199 Madison Avenue, at East 35th Street (685 9007). Subway 6 to 33rd Street.* **Open** 9am-7pm Mon-Fri; 10am-6pm Sat; 11am-5pm Sun. **Credit** AmEx, DC, Disc, MC, V.

Travel books and maps of all descriptions, covering New York City, the US and the world.

## Drama Bookshop

*723 Seventh Avenue, at West 48th Street (944 0595). Subway C or E to 50th Street.* **Open** 9.30am-7pm Mon, Tue, Thur, Fri; 9.30am-8pm Wed; 10.30am-5.30pm Sat; noon-5pm Sun. **Credit** AmEx, MC, V.

In the middle of the Theatre District: play scripts, biographies, everything for the actor and theatre-goer.

## Forbidden Planet

*840 Broadway, corner of East 13th Street (473 1576). Subway 4, 5, 6, L, N or R to 14th Street.* **Open** 10am-8.30pm daily. **Credit** AmEx, Disc, MC, V.

If you're a devotee of science fiction and fantasy, you won't be able to resist Forbidden Planet's vast selection of comics – vintage and new titles from around the world. It also has stacks of classic sf, as well as fantasy, horror and thriller books and magazines. There's a pricey toy section.

## Murder Ink

*2486 Broadway between 92nd & 93rd Streets (362 8905). Subway 1, 2, 3 or 9 to 96th Street.* **Open** 10am-7.30pm Mon-Sat; 11am-6pm Sun. **Credit** AmEx, MC, V.

If you're in need of a killer title, this is your best bet. Murder Ink's enormous stock ranges from William Faulkner's *The Unvanquished* to the entire Jim Thompson series, along with books on how to write mysteries and *The Mystery Reader's Walking Tour of New York*.

**Branch**: 1465 Second Avenue (517 3222).

## Mysterious Book Shop

*129 West 56th Street, between Sixth & Seventh Avenues (765 0900). Subway B, D or E to Seventh Avenue; N or R to 57th Street.* **Open** 11am-7pm Mon-Sat. **Credit** AmEx, DC, MC, V.

Over 20,000 new and second-hand mystery and murder titles. There's a free rare book-finding service.

## New York Bound

*Associated Press Building, lobby of 50 Rockefeller Plaza, between Fifth & Sixth Avenues, 49th & 50th Streets (245 8503). Subway B, D, F or Q to Rockefeller Center.* **Open** 10am-5pm Mon-Fri; noon-4pm Sat. **Credit** AmEx, MC, V.

This is a gem: nothing but books on New York, both current and out-of-print titles. You can pick up a 1930s restaurant guide, a novel from 1885, children's titles or photographic essays.

## See Hear

*33 St Mark's Place, between Second & Third Avenues (505 9781). Subway 6 to Astor Place.* **Open** 11am-11pm daily. **Credit** AmEx, MC, V.

A haven for fanzines, music books, comics and assorted subcultural text; an ideal place to lose an afternoon.

## Village Comics

*214 Sullivan Street, between West Third and Bleecker Streets (777 2770). Subway A, B, C, D, E, F or Q to West 4th Street.* **Open** 9.30am-8.30pm Mon-Wed; 10am-9.30pm Thur-Sat; 11.30am-7.30pm Sun. **Credit** AmEx, Disc, MC, V.

Comics are big business: shop here for complete sets, missing back-numbers of Marvel or underground comics and new issues. There's a free mail order service. The Science Fiction Shop is run by the same company (940 Third Avenue, at 56th Street, 759 6255).

# Cameras & Electronics

The midtown electronics area (14th-23rd Streets, between Broadway and Sixth Avenue) offers some great bargains. Rapid turnover allows shopkeepers to price items such as Walkmans, CD players and computers at low prices. Know exactly what you want before venturing inside: if you look lost, staff will certainly give you a hard sell. If buying a major item, check newspaper ads for price guidelines (the Science section in Tuesday's *New York Times* is good). If you're brave, you can get small things such as Walkmans even cheaper in the questionable establishments along Canal Street, but don't expect a warranty. Another reason to go to a more reputable place is to get reliable (and essential) advice about compatibility with whatever country you want to use the equipment in. For video and TV rental, *see page 186* **Television & Video**.

## J & R Music World

*33 Park Row, near Centre Street (732 8600). Subway 4, 5 or 6 to City Hall; J or M to Chambers Street.* **Open** 9am-6.30pm Mon-Sat; 11am-6pm Sun. **Credit** AmEx, Disc, MC, V.

Everything for home entertainment is here at discount prices: CD players, hi-fi, Walkmans and tapes. See the weekly ads in the *Village Voice* for the latest deals.

## Nobody Beats the Wiz

*726 Broadway, at 7th Street (677 4111). Subway N or R to 8th Street.* **Open** 10am-10pm Mon-Sat; 10am-7pm Sun. **Credit** AmEx, Disc, MC, V.

With Wiz's claim to match or beat any advertised price on electronic equipment, even the illegal importers on Canal Street have a hard time keeping up. Check the ads in the *Voice* and load up on gear and gadgets at unbelievable prices. Phone for details of your nearest branch.

## Willoughby's

*136 West 32nd Street, between Sixth & Seventh Avenues (564 1600). Subway B, D, F, N, R or Q to 34th Street.* **Open** 8.30am-8pm Mon-Fri; 10am-7pm Sat, Sun. **Credit** AmEx, DC, Disc, MC, V.

Willoughby's claims to be the world's largest camera and audio store – and it does seem to stock everything. Know what you are looking for and expect long queues, slow service and heavy security.

# Photo Processing

Pharmacies and most department stores have photo developing services. You get better results from those that develop on the premises and the best results from professional places, most numerous in the midtown electronics district.

### Harvey's One Hour Photo
*698 Third Avenue, between 43rd & 44th Streets (682 5045). Subway 4, 5, 6 or 7 to Grand Central.* **Open** 8am-6pm Mon-Fri. **Credit** AmEx, MC, V.
Colour films can be developed in 60 minutes; slides and black and white need an overnight stay.

### Showbran Photo
*1347 Broadway, at 36th Street (947 9151). Subway B, D, F, Q, N or R to 34th Street.* **Open** 7am-6pm Mon-Fri. Credit AmEx, Disc, MC, V.
Passport and visa photos are taken and developed while you wait. Showbran also offers other developing and printing services as well as photocopying.
**Branches:** 512 Seventh Avenue (575 9580); lobby of the Empire State Building, 33rd Street and Fifth Avenue entrances (868 5888).

## Clothes Hire

### Just Once
*292 Fifth Avenue, between 30th & 31st Streets (465 0960). Subway 6 to 28th Street.* **Open** by appointment only. **Credit** AmEx, MC, V.
This bridal service stocks a wide selection of expensive gowns (Vera Wang and Carolina Herrera are among labels) for sale or hire. Rentals range from $300 to $800.

### Zeller Tuxedos
*Second floor, 201 East 56th Street, at Third Avenue, (355 0707). Subway 4, 5, or 6 to 59th Street; N or R to Lexington Avenue.* **Open** 9am-6.30pm Mon-Fri; 10am-5pm Sat. **Credit** AmEx, MC, V.
Travellers not wishing to tote their tuxes around with them can take their pick from a large selection here, bearing labels such as Armani, Ungaro and Valentino.

## Cross-dressing

### Miss Vera's Finishing School For Boys Who Want to Be Girls
*(242 6449).* **No credit cards.**
Feeling feminine? Private classes begin at $550 and are taught by Veronica Vera and her faculty. Day sessions begin at $1,125 and a weekend on the town with Vera and the girls can cost anything from $3,250. Consult the back pages of the *Village Voice* and the *New York Press* for similar services.

## Dry Cleaners

### Midnight Express Cleaners
*(921 0111/1-800 999 8985).* **Open** 8am-10pm Mon-Fri; 9am-3pm Sat. **Credit** AmEx, MC, V.
Phone Midnight Express and your laundry will be picked up anywhere below 96th Street within ten to 15 minutes. It costs $7.25 for a man's suit to be cleaned, including pick-up and delivery. There are various minimum charges, depending on your location. If you're in a hotel you may have to play sneaky to avoid upsetting the concierge.

### Sutton Cleaners
*1060 First Avenue, between East 57th & East 58th Streets (755 1617). Subway 4, 5 or 6 to 59th Street; N or R to Lexington Avenue.* **Open** 7am-6.30pm Mon-Fri; 8am-4pm Sat. **Credit** AmEx, MC, V.
Offers one-hour jobs as well as a normal, non-urgent service.

Same-day alterations on garments brought in before 10am. Collection and delivery is free up to 10 blocks from the store.

## Fashion
### The Designers

### Agnès B
*116 Prince Street, between Wooster & Greene Streets (925 4649). Subway N or R to Prince Street.* **Open** 11am-7pm Mon-Sat; noon-6pm Sun. **Credit** AmEx, MC, V.
Simple designs for women, men and children – though the men's lines are available only at the new flagship branch in Greene Street. If only the timeless styles could withstand wear-and-tear a bit longer.
**Branches:** 1063 Madison Avenue (570 9333); 79 Green Street (431 4339).

### Anna Sui
*113 Greene Street, between Spring & Prince Streets (941 8406). Subway C or E to Spring Street.* **Open** noon-7pm Mon-Sat; noon-6pm Sun. **Credit** AmEx, MC, V.
Judging from her frequent sweeps of thrift stores in the East Village, Anna Sui's ideas come directly from the past. Her clothes, displayed in a lilac- and black-decorated boutique, are popular with wealthy poseurs – models, movie stars and trust-fund kids.

### Betsey Johnson
*130 Thompson Street, between Prince & Houston Streets (420 0169). Subway N or R to Prince Street.* **Open** 11am-7pm Mon-Sat; noon-7pm Sun. **Credit** AmEx, MC, V.
Johnson's bright and flamboyant clothes have been on the market since the 1970s, but never look out of date. And the prices are relatively reasonable, too.
**Branches:** 248 Columbus Avenue (362 3364); 251 East 60th Street (319 7699); 1060 Madison Avenue (734 1257).

### Calvin Klein
*654 Madison Avenue, at 60th Street (292 9000). Subway 4, 5 or 6 to 59th Street.* **Open** 10am-6pm Mon-Wed, Fri, Sat; 10am-8pm Thur; noon-6pm Sun. **Credit** AmEx, Disc, MC, V.
Here's where to come if you want to look like Gwenyth Paltrow. This flagship store opened in 1995 and is *tout* CK, from the couture lines to footwear and housewares.

### Chanel
*15 East 57th Street, between Fifth & Madison Avenues (355 5050). Subway 4, 5, 6, N or R to 59th Street/ Lexington Avenue.* **Open** 10am-6.30pm Mon-Wed, Fri; 10am-7pm Thur; 10am-6pm Sat. **Credit** AmEx, DC, MC, JCB, V.
The spirit of Mademoiselle Chanel lives on at this opulent flagship store. There's even the Chanel Suite, a Baroque salon modelled after Coco's private apartment on the rue Cambon in Paris.

### Christian Dior
*703 Fifth Avenue, at 55th Street (223 4646). Subway E or F to Fifth Avenue.* **Open** 10am-6pm Mon-Wed, Fri, Sat; 10am-7pm Thur; 11am-5pm Sun. **Credit** AmEx, JCB, MC, V.
Like Alexander McQueen at Givenchy, John Galliano has breathed new life into predictable designs. This elegant boutique carries the famous French line.

### Comme des Garçons
*116 Wooster Street, between Spring & Prince Streets (219 0660). Subway N or R to Prince Street; C, E or K to Spring Street.* **Open** 11am-7pm Mon-Sat; noon-6.30pm Sun. **Credit** AmEx, DC, MC, V.
This minimalist store is devoted to Rei Kawakubo's

architecturally constructed, quintessentially Japanese designs for men and women, with clothes exhibited like the art in the surrounding SoHo galleries.

## Les Copains

*807 Madison Avenue, between 67th & 68th Streets (327 3014). Subway 6 to 68th Street.* **Open** 10am-6pm Mon-Sat. **Credit** AmEx, DC, JCB, MC, V.

This clothier specialises in Italian knits. It's very expensive, though; check out the more aggressive Trend line for better prices and the jeans collection.

## Emporio Armani

*601 Madison Avenue, between 67th & 68th Streets (317 0800). Subway 6 to 68th Street Hunter College.* **Open** 10am-8pm Mon-Fri; 10am-6pm Sat; noon-6pm Sun. **Credit** AmEx, DC, JCB, MC, V.

The main store, a recent addition to Madison Avenue, is purely postmodern and features top Armani designs as well as an Armani Café. Gorgeous but casual suits and separates for men and women from the diffusion line can be found at the downtown store, which is a renovated Stanford White building. Cheaper but not cheap.
**Branch**: 110 Fifth Avenue (727 3240).

## Gianni Versace

*647 Fifth Avenue, between 51st & 52nd Streets (759 3822). Subway E or F to Fifth Avenue.* **Open** 10am-6pm Mon-Wed, Fri, Sat; 10am-7pm Thur. **Credit** AmEx, DC, MC, V.

Housed in the former Vanderbilt mansion, at 28,000 sq ft (2,600 sq m), this is one of the largest boutiques in the city. Go and stare longingly at the mosaics.

## Giorgio Armani

*760 Madison Avenue, at 65th Street (988 9191). Subway 6 to 68th Street Hunter College.* **Open** 10am-6pm Mon-Wed, Fri, Sat; 10am-7pm Thur. **Credit** AmEx, MC, V.

This enormous boutique features all three Armani collections, including the signature Borgonuovo – tailored suits, eveningwear and a bridal line – the Classico and Le Collezioni. Keep an eye out for Jodie Foster.

## Givenchy

*954 Madison Avenue, at 75th Street (772 1040). Subway 6 to 77th Street.* **Open** 10am-6pm Mon-Sat. **Credit** AmEx, DC, MC, V.

With the talented English designer Alexander McQueen behind the scissors, the styles are no longer quite as discreet as when Hubert de Givenchy created Audrey Hepburn's elegant ensembles. McQueen may be wildly imaginative, but his clothes aren't unwearable.

## Gucci

*685 Fifth Avenue, at 54th Street (826 2600). Subway E or F to Fifth Avenue.* **Open** 9.30am-6pm Mon-Wed, Fri, Sat; 9.30am-7.30pm Thur; noon-6pm Sun. **Credit** AmEx, DC, JCB, MC, V.

People are still talking about the Gucci revitalisation that transformed old lady's clothes into the hippest creations around. Tunics inspired by the 1960s and 1970s, blouses and pants start at $400, and there are always plenty of logo belts, key chains and sunglasses to choose from.

## Issey Miyake

*992 Madison Avenue, at 77th & 78th Streets (439 7822). Subway 6 to 77th Street.* **Open** 10am-6pm Mon-Fri; 11am-6pm Sat. **Credit** AmEx, MC, V.

This minimalist store houses Issey Miyake's timeless women's and men's collections and accessories.

## Luca Luca

*690 Madison Avenue, at 62nd Street (755 2444). Subway 4, 5, 6, N or R to 59th Street/Lexington Avenue.*

**Open** 10am-6.30pm Mon-Wed, Fri, Sat; 10am-8pm Thur; noon-5pm Sun. **Credit** AmEx, MC, V.

The young Italian designer Luca Orlandi can't stand black; as long as you're expecting some colour, you'll do just fine here.

## Missoni

*836 Madison Avenue, at 69th Street (517 9339). Subway 6 to 68th Street.* **Open** 10am-6pm Mon-Sat. **Credit** AmEx, MC, V.

Italian polychromatic fine knits made of wildly beautiful fabric; the designs sometimes don't quite match up.

## Miu Miu

*100 Prince Street, between Mercer & Greene Streets (334 5156). Subway N or R to Prince Street.* **Open** 11am-7pm Mon-Sat; noon-6pm Sun. **Credit** AmEx, MC, V.

The first home for Prada's secondary line, Miu Miu. It's still expensive though – you won't find much for less than $100.

## Moschino

*803 Madison Avenue, between 67th & 68th Streets (639 9600). Subway 6 to 68th Street.* **Open** 9am-6pm Mon-Wed, Fri, Sat; 10am-7pm Thur. **Credit** AmEx, MC, V.

Expensive and irreverent clothes for men and women. Oh well, you can always pick up a pencil kit for $5. Really.

## Omo Norma Kamali

*11 West 56th Street, between Fifth & Sixth Avenues (957 9797). Subway B or Q to 57th Street.* **Open** 10am-6pm Mon-Sat. **Credit** AmEx, MC, V.

Classic-cut clothes with a slightly offbeat touch. Suits and dresses are shapely, with perhaps an oddly pleated skirt, a strangely shaped collar or an unusual cut-out. Relatively inexpensive knits are sold alongside great daywear, provocative swimsuits and some spectacular evening designs.

## Paul Smith

*108 Fifth Avenue, between 15th & 16th Streets (627 9770). Subway L, N, R, 4, 5 or 6 to 14th Street.* **Open** 11am-7pm Mon-Wed, Fri, Sat; 11am-8pm Thur; noon-6pm Sun. **Credit** AmEx, Disc, MC, V.

For the relaxed English gentleman look. These designs are exemplary in their combination of wit, style and quality. Accessories available too.

## Polo/Ralph Lauren

*867 Madison Avenue, at 72nd Street (606 2100). Subway 6 to 68th Street.* **Open** 10am-6pm Mon-Wed, Fri, Sat; 10am-8pm Thur. **Credit** AmEx, DC, Disc, JCB, MC, V.

Ralph Lauren spent $14 million turning the old Rhinelander mansion into an Ivy League superstore, filled with oriental rugs, English paintings, riding whips, leather chairs, old mahogany and fresh flowers. The homeboys, skaters and other young blades who've adopted Ralphie's togs for a season or two head straight to Polo Sport across the street at number 888 (434 8000).

## Prada

*841 Madison Avenue, at 70th Street (327 4200). Subway 6 to 68th Street Hunter College.* **Open** 10am-6pm Mon-Wed, Fri, Sat; 10am-7pm Thur. **Credit** AmEx, MC, V.

Miuccia Prada has created quite a sensation with her suits (for men and women), coats and dresses, and for good reason. The clothes are just dreamy. The Madison Avenue location is the largest Prada shop in the world and features high-tech computer-sensored windows with polarised glass that changes according to the light.
**Branch**: 45 East 57th Street (308 2332).

## Romeo Gigli & Spazio

*21 East 69th Street, between Madison & Park Avenues. (744 9121). Subway 6 to 68th Street.* **Open** 10.30am-6.30pm Mon-Sat. **Credit** AmEx, MC, V.

This three-storey former townhouse is worth visiting for the

*Something old, something new, something borrowed and something from **Blue**.*

interior alone, with its Fornasetti screens and Murano light fittings. And then of course there's Romeo Gigli.

### Todd Oldham
*123 Wooster Street, between Spring & Prince Streets (219 3531). Subway C or E to Spring Street; N or R to Prince Street.* **Open** *11am-7pm Mon-Sat; noon-6pm Sun.* **Credit** AmEx, MC, V.
This popular boutique, which houses Todd Oldham's imaginative and attractive fashions, has been open for three years.

### Valentino
*747 Madison Avenue, at 65th Street (772 6969). Subway B or Q to Lexington Avenue.* **Open** *10am-6pm Mon-Sat.* **Credit** AmEx, MC, V.
Celebrities and New York ladies who lunch just adore Valentino. Can you be as elegant as Sharon Stone? Only if you have enough money, honey.

### Yohji Yamamoto
*103 Grand Street, near Broadway (966 9066). Subway 6, J, M, N or R to Canal Street.* **Open** *11am-7pm Mon-Sat; noon-6pm Sun.* **Credit** AmEx, DC, MC, V.
The designer's flagship store is a huge, lofty space filled with well-cut designs.

### Yves Saint Laurent
*855-59 Madison Avenue, between East 70th & East 71st Streets (988 3821). Subway 6 to 68th Street.* **Open** *10am-6pm Mon-Sat.* **Credit** AmEx, DC, JCB, MC, V.
Saint Laurent is tired chic, but his clothes are still sought-after and expensive.

## The Stores

### APC
*131 Mercer Street, between Prince & Spring Streets (966 9685). Subway N or R to Prince Street.* **Open** *11am-7pm Mon-Sat; noon-6pm Sun.* **Credit** AmEx, JCB, MC, V.
France's answer to Gap: basic essentials in muted colours

and minimal styling in a stunning store designed by Julian Schnabel.

### Banana Republic
*552 Broadway, between Spring & Prince Streets (925 0308). Subway N or R to Prince Street.* **Open** *10am-8pm Mon-Sat; noon-6pm Sun.* **Credit** AmEx, Disc, JCB, MC, V.
The most superior chain of them all, which means it doesn't mass produce everything hysterically. Try walking by a window and not becoming a little turned on. Prices are often slashed during sales, but original prices are higher than that of Gap. Kind of classy. Phone to find out the location of your nearest branch.

### Blue
*125 St Mark's Place, between First Avenue & Avenue A (228 7744). Subway 6 to Astor Place; F to Second Avenue.* **Open** *noon-8pm Mon-Sat; noon-6pm Sun.* **Credit** AmEx, MC, V.
A must-stop if you're in the market for a cocktail dress, a fancy suit or just a pick-me-up. The uptown store caters to brides and those in the need for party gowns.
**Branch**: 310 Columbus Avenue (579 2089).

### Brooks Bros
*346 Madison Avenue, at East 44th Street (682 8800). Subway 4, 5, 6 or 7 to Grand Central.* **Open** *9am-7pm Mon-Wed, Fri, Sat; 9am-8pm Thur; noon-6pm Sun.* **Credit** AmEx, DC, JCB, MC, V.
The classic men's store, now owned by Marks & Spencer, is still the place for high-quality preppy clothing – button-down shirts, madras jackets, chinos and wonderful striped dressing gowns.
**Branch**: 1 Liberty Plaza (267 2400).

### Canal Jeans
*504 Broadway, between Spring & Broome Streets (226 1130). Subway N or R to Prince Street; 6 to Spring Street.* **Open** *10am-8pm Mon-Thur, Sun; 10.30am-9pm Fri, Sat; 11am-9pm Sun.* **Credit** AmEx, DC, JCB, MC, V.
Browse among a vast acreage of jeans, T-shirts and other

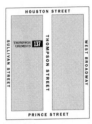

basics, plus new (like French Connection) and vintage clothing and accessories, socks, T-shirts, bags and fun jewellery. Canal's prices are definitely worth the trip.

## Charivari 57

*18 West 57th Street, between Fifth & Sixth Avenues (333 4040). Subway E or F to Fifth Avenue.* **Open** 10.30am-7pm Mon-Wed, Fri; 10.30am-8pm Thur; 10.30am-6.30pm Sat; 12.30-6pm Sun. **Credit** AmEx, MC, V.
The good, stylish working clothes for men and women are carefully selected from a variety of designers: Gaultier, Ghost, Yamamoto… Pricey.

## Club Monaco

*160 Fifth Avenue, at 21st Street (352 0936). Subway N or R to 23rd Street.* **Open** 10am-8pm Mon-Fri; 10am-7pm Sat; noon-6pm Sun. **Credit** AmEx, DC, JCB, MC, V.
This Canadian-owned chain has acquired quite a following (there are 38 stores in Korea alone). In this one you'll find an impressive array of men's and women's sportswear, cosmetics and jewellery.
**Branch:** 2376 Broadway (579 2587).

## Daryl K

*21 Bond Street, between The Bowery & Lafayette Street (777 0713). Subway N or R to Prince Street.* **Open** noon-7pm daily. **Credit** AmEx, MC, V.
Daryl Kerrigan's clothing attracts rock 'n' rollers for her vinyl pants, coloured cords, hip-hugger bootlegs and Latin-inspired dresses.

## Gap

*133 Second Avenue, at St Mark's Place (353 2090). Subway 6 to Astor Place.* **Open** 11am-9pm Mon-Thur; 11am-10pm Fri, Sat; noon-8pm Sun. **Credit** AmEx, Disc, JCB, MC, V.
You can't fight Gap – it's everywhere. Cheap staples like T-shirts, jackets, blue jeans and dresses abound. Phone for details of your nearest branch.

## Hotel Venus

*382 West Broadway, between Broome & Spring Streets (966 4066). Subway A or C to Spring Street.* **Open** noon-8pm daily. **Credit** AmEx, JCB, MC, V.
Patricia Field's new store features a Jap-animation influence; the décor is more mod, and the staff more serious and dressed up than at her 8th Street boutique (*see below*). Along with clothing, Hotel Venus stocks platforms, stationery, barettes, wallets, blow-up furniture and lots of bags.

## J Crew

*99 Prince Street, between Mercer & Greene Streets (966 2739). Subway N or R to Prince Street; B, D, F or Q to Broadway/Lafayette Street.* **Open** 10am-8pm Mon-Sat, 11am-6pm Sun. **Credit** AmEx, MC, V.
J Crew's new giant store carries all of its men's and women's lines, including shoes, accessories and the women's 'Collection'. The clothes are far from middle-American cheesy and there's plenty of SoHo black.

## Mary Adams The Dress

*159 Ludlow Street, at Stanton Street (473 0237). Subway F to Second Avenue.* **Open** 1-6pm Thur-Sun and by appointment. **No credit cards**.
For frocks' sake: Mary Adams makes beautifully girly new versions of the old-fashioned party dress, favouring silks, satins, velvets and cottons.

## Mark Montano

*434 East 9th Street, between First Avenue & Avenue A (505 0325). Subway 6 to Astor Place; L to First Avenue; F to Second Avenue.* **Open** 1-8pm Tue-Fri; noon-8pm Sat; 1-6pm Sun. **Credit** MC, V.
A mixture of classic movie-style suits and siren satin dresses

from an emerging designer. If you have to go to a wedding and want to look better than the bride, look no further.

## Old Navy

*610 Sixth Avenue, at 18th Street (645 0663). Subway F, N or R to 23rd Street.* **Open** 9.30am-9pm Mon-Sat; 11am-6pm Sun. **Credit** AmEx, Disc, JCB, MC, V.
Owned by Gap, this chain features own-brand clothing at inexpensive prices. If you phone the store, a recorded message let's you know what's on sale. You can also phone for the location of your nearest branch.

## Patricia Field

*10 East 8th Street, at Fifth Avenue (254 1699). Subway N or R to 8th Street.* **Open** noon-8pm Mon-Sat; 1-7pm Sun. **Credit** AmEx, Disc, MC, V.
Field is New York's Vivienne Westwood: brilliant at working club and street fashion. Her store, with its ambisexual staff, has an eclectic mix of original jewellery, make-up, on-the-edge club gear and East Village design. There's always something new, the clothing is gorgeous and durable, and the wigs are the best in town. *See also above* **Hotel Venus**.

## Phat Farm

*129 Prince Street, between West Broadway & Wooster (533 7428). Subway C or E to Spring Street.* **Open** 11am-7pm Mon-Sat; noon-6pm Sun. **Credit** AmEx, MC, V.
Russell Simmons's classy and conservative take on hip-hop couture. Phunky-phresh oversized and baggy clothing.

## Product

*71 Mercer Street, between Broome & Spring Streets (274 1494). Subway N or R to Prince Street; C or E to Spring Street.* **Open** 11am-7pm Mon-Sat; noon-6pm Sun. **Credit** AmEx, MC, V.
A hip clothier for women that features the finest of stretchy fabrics. Very good-looking clothes, and not as expensive as APC (*see p161*), which is just up the block.

## Steven Alan

*330 East 11th Street, between First & Second Avenues (982 2881). Subway 6 to Astor Place; L to First Avenue.* **Open** 1-8pm daily. **Credit** AmEx, MC, V.
Steven Alan's stock is coveted by hip girls in all neighbourhoods. This East Village branch is filled with clothing by names like Built by Wendy, Pixie Yates and Rebecca Dannenberg.
**Branch:** 60 Wooster Street (334 6354).

## Stüssy Store

*104 Prince Street, between Mercer & Greene Streets (274 8855). Subway N or R to Prince Street.* **Open** noon-7pm Mon-Thur; 11am-7pm Fri, Sat; noon-6pm Sun. **Credit** AmEx, MC, V.
All the fine hats, T-shirts and other skatesome/surfy West Coast gear that Mr Stüssy is famous for.

## Trash & Vaudeville

*4 St Mark's Place, between Second & Third Avenues (982 3590). Subway 6 to Astor Place.* **Open** noon-8pm Mon-Fri; 11.30am-9pm Sat; 1-7.30pm Sun. **Credit** AmEx, MC, V.
This original punk store has two floors of fashion, accessories and shoes: stretchy tube-dresses, leathers, snakeskin boots, collar tips and jewellery.

## Urban Outfitters

*628 Broadway, between Houston & Bleecker Streets (475 0009). Subway B, D, F or Q to Broadway/Lafayette Street.* **Open** 10am-10pm Mon-Sat; noon-8pm Sun. **Credit** AmEx, MC, V.
Clothes for urban survival. Basics include jeans and T-shirts for men and women, but this is also a good source for trendy and inexpensive clothing. Labels include Girbaud, Antho-

# Flea markets

Once you've explored a New York flea market, you'll wonder why you bother with retail. There's no better way to walk off a hearty weekend brunch than by wandering through aisles of records, 8-tracks, clothes, books and furniture.

Although, mayor Giuliani has clamped down on the number of illegal street vendors working in the city, you might still get lucky: East Village vendors are persistent. Try along **Second Avenue** and **Avenue A** in the East Village at night for vintage clothes, records and magazines. And when the weather's nice, there are **sidewalk sales**. Although not so common in Manhattan, Saturdays are reserved for stoop sales in parts of Brooklyn (Park Slope especially) and Queens. If you have a car, you'll quickly spot the signs attached to trees; if not, local papers provide the hours, dates and addresses. Sidewalk shopping is popular with the natives and they're serious, so head out early. Happy hunting!

**Annex Antiques & Flea Market** *Sixth Avenue, between 25th & 27th Streets (243 5343). Subway F to 23rd Street.* **Open** 9am-5pm Sat, Sun. The largest of them all. Todd Oldham hunts regularly here, as do plenty of models and questionable 'celebrities'. The market is broken up into two sections, but go into the free one first. The other side pompously charges $1 entry. There's anything and everything in both sections: second-hand clothing, old-fashioned bicycles, shoes, birdcages, tools, accessories. And don't miss the incredible glasses frame stand.

**Antique Flea & Farmer's Market** *PS 183, East 67th Street, between First & York Avenues (721 0900/1-718 897 5992). Subway 6 to 68th Street.* **Open** 6am-6pm Sat. Small but good for antique lace, silverware and tapestries. Fresh eggs, fish and vegetables are also often available.

**IS 44 Flea Market** *Columbus Avenue, between 76th & 77th Streets (721 0900). Subway B or C to 72nd Street.* **Open** 10am-6pm Sun. One of Andy Warhol's

favourite haunts, this features more than 300 stalls of antiques, jewellery, linens and records, as well as T-shirts and the like.

**Park Slope Flea Market** *Seventh Avenue, between 1st & 2nd Streets, Brooklyn (1-718 330 9395). Subway 2, 3, to Grand Army Plaza.* **Open** 9am-6pm Sat. If you don't mind braving Brooklyn, this is quite a good market; items tend to be cheaper than in Manhattan.

**SoHo Antique Fair & Collectibles Market** *Grand Street, at Broadway (682 2000). Subway 4, 5, 6, N, R to Canal Street.* **Open** 9am-5pm Sat, Sun. This opened in 1992, and is also wonderful for vintagewear, old radios, linens and all manner of kitsch. There isn't a huge selection (when the weather's bad, the choice is hit or miss), but prices are fair. Sunday is always best.

---

pologie, Free People and Esprit. It also stocks vintage 'urban renewal' clothing, gifts and postcards.
**Branches**: 374 Sixth Avenue (677 9350); 127 East 59th Street (688 1200).

## Discount Fashion

### Century 21 Department Store
*22 Cortlandt Street, off Broadway (227 9092). Subway 1, 9, N or R to Cortlandt Street.* **Open** 7.45am-7pm Mon-Thur; 11am-9pm Fri, Sat. **Credit** AmEx, Disc, MC, V.
Some discerning shoppers report finding clothes by Romeo Gigli and Donna Karan here, but you have to visit every ten days or so to get these kinds of bargains. Rack upon rack is heavy with discounted designer and name-brand fashions. Housewares and appliances are also sold at good discounts,

plus underwear, accessories, cosmetics and fragrances, and women's shoes. Service is good, but there are no fitting rooms (except for in the designer section). Regulars use the toilets in McDonald's nearby.

### Daffy's
*111 Fifth Avenue, at 18th Street (529 4477). Subway 4, 5, 6, L, N or R to 14th Street/Union Square.* **Open** 10am-9pm Mon-Sat; noon-7pm Sun. **Credit** MC, Disc, V.
An out-of-town favourite for years, Daffy's has now opened in Manhattan. There are three floors of current mainstream fashions: silk blouses, leather jackets and bags, Calvin Klein and French lingerie, and affordable men's suits and shirts. Prices are much lower than retail stores and there are often remarkable bargains. The kids' clothes are fabulous.
**Branch**: 335 Madison Avenue (557 4422).

### Dollarbills
*32 East 42nd Street, between Madison and Fifth
Avenues (867 0212). Subway 4, 5, 6, 7 or S to Grand
Central.* **Open** 10am-8pm Mon-Fri; 10am-6pm Sat; noon-
5pm Sun. **Credit** AmEx, DC, MC, V.
Two floors of designer heaven – Versace, Montana, Byblos,
Gigli and many more labels for men and women. Also dis-
counted accessories and underwear, belts and ties.

### Loehmann's
*101 Seventh Avenue, between 16th & 17th Streets
(352 0856). Subway 1 or 9 to 18th Street.* **Open** 9am-
9pm Mon-Sat; 11am-7pm Sun. **Credit** MC, Disc, V.
After 75 years of waiting, bargain-happy Manhattanites
finally got a branch of the Bronx original in the city. The fantastic prices and designer merchandise are the same as ever,
as is the enormous turnover of stock.
**Branch:** 60-66 99th Street, Rego Park, Bronx
(1-718 271 4000).

### TJ Maxx
*620 Sixth Avenue, at 18th Street (229 0875). Subway F
or L to 14th Street/Sixth Avenue.* **Open** 9.30am-9pm
Mon-Sat; 10am-6pm Sun. **Credit** AmEx, DC, MC, V.
This new discount designer clothes store, with its brightly
lit Woolworths-like appearance, is less of an obvious treasure trove than Century 21 (*see above*), but if you're prepared to put up with the rather high rubbish-to-discovery
ratio, you will undoubtedly find some fabulous purchases. Maxx also stocks household goods, luggage and shoes,
among other things.

### Syms
*42 Trinity Street, near Rector Street (797 1199).
Subway R to Rector Street.* **Open** 9am-6.30pm Mon-Wed;
9am-8pm Thur, Fri; 10am-6.30pm Sat; noon-5.30pm Sun.
**Credit** AmEx, Disc, MC, V.
Seven storeys of designer discount fashions for men, women
and children, with labels still intact. Also shoes and luggage.

## Vintage & Second-hand Clothes

The pyramid rule of second-hand clothes means the
less you browse, the more you have to pay. Although
we've included them in our listings, the shops along
lower Broadway tend to ask inflated prices for anything except the most mundane items. The alternatives, too numerous and fast-changing to list here,
are the many small outlets between Avenue A, and
Second Avenue and about 6th-10th Streets. These (-
together with the now-famous Domsey's) are where
real bargains are to be found. Salvation Army and
Goodwill stores are also worth checking out.

### Alice Underground
*481 Broadway, at Broome Street (431 9067). Subway B,
D, F or Q to Broadway/Lafayette Street.* **Open** 11am-
7.30pm daily. **Credit** AmEx, MC, V.
A good selection of 1940s-1960s gear in all sorts of fabrics
and in varied condition. Prices are high, but the bins at the
front are always worth rummaging through.

### Allan & Suzi
*416 Amsterdam Avenue, at 80th Street (724 7445).
Subway 1 or 9 to 79th Street.* **Open** noon-7pm Mon, Tue,
Sat; noon-8pm Wed-Fri; noon-6pm Sun. **Credit** AmEx,
JCB, MC, V.
Models drop off their once-worn Comme des Garçons,
Muglers and Gaultiers here. The platform shoe collection is
unmatched. Great store, but not cheap.

### Andy's Chee-Pees
*691 Broadway, between East 3rd & East 4th Streets
(420 5980). Subway B, D, F or Q to Broadway/Lafayette
Street.* **Open** 11am-9pm Mon-Sat; noon-8pm Sun. **Credit**
AmEx, MC, V.
Pricey, but good for jeans and shirts.
**Branch:** 16 West 8th Street (460 8488).

*A bit of the Bronx in Manhattan:* **Loehmann's** *bargain joint.*

## Antique Boutique

*712-714 Broadway, at Washington Place (460 8830).
Subway 6 to Astor Place; N or R to 8th Street.*
**Open** 11am-10pm Mon-Sat; noon-8pm Sun. **Credit**
AmEx, DC, Disc, JCB, MC, V.
This used to be one of the largest shops for vintage gear; now
the collection has been banished to the basement. The good
news is that most of it (generally in the 1960s-1970s frame)
is sold by the pound.
**Branch**: 227 East 59th Street (752 1680).

## Cheap Jack's

*841 Broadway, between West 13th & West 14th Streets
(777 9564). Subway 4, 5, 6, L, N or R to 14th
Street/Union Square.* **Open** 11am-8pm Mon-Sat; noon-
7pm Sun. **Credit** AmEx, MC, V.
A great vintage selection, but exorbitant prices for anything
nice. With army surplus gear that runs into the high hundreds, cheap is the last thing Jack's is.

## Domsey's Warehouse

*431 Kent Avenue, Williamsburg, Brooklyn (1-718 384
6000). Subway J, M or Z to Marcy Avenue.* **Open** 8am-
5.30pm Mon-Fri; 8am-6.30pm Sat; 11am-5.30 Sun.
**No credit cards.**
It seems almost a crime to alert more people to the presence
of this fabulous source of second-hand clothes. Choose from
a huge selection of used jeans, jackets, military and industrial wear, ballgowns, shoes and hats. Especially notable are the
Hawaiian shirts at around $5, the sports gear bearing high-
school team names and the unreal prices on cowboy boots.

## FAB208

*77 East 7th Street, between First & Second Avenues
(673 7581). Subway 6 to Astor Place; F to Second
Avenue.* **Open** noon-8pm Mon, Wed-Sun. **Credit** JCB,
MC, V.
This East Village staple attracts club kids, and it's so much

cheaper than Patricia Field! The branch features funky accessories, shoes and men's T-shirts.
**Branch**: 117 East 7th Street (260 6495).

## Resurrection

*123 East 7th Street, between First Avenue & Avenue A
(228 0063). Subway L to First Avenue; F to Second
Avenue; 6 to Astor Place.* **Open** 1-9pm Mon-Sat; 1-8pm
Sun. **Credit** AmEx, MC, V.
This vintage boutique is a Pucci wonderland – Kate Moss
and Anna Sui are regulars. Owner Katy Rodriguez rents the
space from the Theodore Wolinnin Funeral Home next door.
Two dressing rooms take the place of the altar, and as you
walk along the racks of leopard coats, 1940s dresses and
beaded cardigans, you'll find yourself stepping on the metal
outline of a coffin lifter. But Rodriguez's shop looks more like
a jewel box than a haunted house.

## Screaming Mimi's

*382 Lafayette Street, at 4th Street (677 6464). Subway 6
to Astor Place; N or R to 8th Street.* **Open** 11am-8pm
Mon-Fri; noon-8pm Sat; 1-7pm Sun. **Credit** AmEx, DC,
Disc, MC, V.
During the 1980s, this is where Cyndi Lauper shopped. The
prices are more reasonable and the selection more carefully
chosen than the Broadway stores around the block, and the
window displays are always worth viewing.

## Transfer International

*Suite 1002, 220 East 60th Street, between Prince &
Houston Streets (355 4230). Subway 6 to Spring Street;
R or N to Prince Street.* **Open** 1-7pm Tue-Sun.
**Credit** AmEx.
Well-connected Manhattanites Roberto Mitrotti and Linda
Stein have collected celebrity cast-offs from Ivana Trump,
Christie Brinkley, Trudie Styler and a host of others. This is
now the best place to buy designer clothes by everyone from
Azzedine Alaia to Zang Toi.

*Old frocks get a new lease of life at* **Resurrection**.

# Children's Clothes

## Baby Gap & Gap Kids
*Baby Gap, 1037 Lexington Avenue at 74th Street (327 2614). Subway 6 to 68th Street.* **Open** 10am-7.30pm Mon-Sat; 11am-6pm Sun. **Credit** AmEx, Disc, MC, V.
Gap sure knows how to hit a nerve. Even those repulsed by the mass-produced Gapwear swoon at the sight of a pair of tiny blue jeans or a miniature V-neck sweater. Gap Kids also features adult clothing. *See also* **Gap** *p163*.
**Branch: Gap Kids** 1056 Lexington Avenue (988 4460).

## Julian & Sara
*103 Mercer Street, between Spring & Prince Streets (226 1989). Subway N or R to Prince Street.* **Open** 11.30am-7pm Tue-Fri; noon-6pm Sat, Sun. **Credit** AmEx, MC, V.
Choose from ingenious hats, dresses, and dressy outfits for boys. It's all quite swank.

## Lilliput
*265 Lafayette Street, between Prince & Spring Streets (965 9567). Subway N, R to Prince & Spring Streets Broadway/Lafayette Street.* **Open** noon-6pm Mon, Sun; 11am-7pm Tue-Sat. **Credit** AmEx, DC, MC, V.
This hip staple for kids and babies sells second-hand as well as new clothing.

## Me-Ki Kids
*149 Avenue A, between 9th & 10th Streets (995 2884). Train 6 to Astor Place.* **Open** 1-7pm Mon-Fri; 1-6pm Sat, Sun. **Credit** MC, V.
Seriously trendy clothes for kids. Some accessories, too.

## Oh Baby
*153 Ludlow Street, between Stanton & Rivington Streets (673 5524). Subway F to Second Avenue.* **Open** 1-6pm Wed-Sun. **No credit cards.**
A baby haven, smack on the ever-cool Ludlow Street. Funky velvet hats, pantsuits and hilarious aprons.

## Shoofly Q
*465 Amsterdam Avenue, near West 83rd Street (580 4390). Train 1, 9, B or C to 86th Street.* **Open** 11am-7pm Mon-Sat; noon-6pm Sun. **Credit** AmEx, MC, V.
Boaters, caps, fleece-lined boots, braces, gloves and shoes are to be found among the Flintstones-furniture, tree-trunk and animal-footprint décor.
**Branch:** 42 Hudson Street (406 3270).

## Space Kiddets
*46 East 21st Street, between Park Avenue & Broadway (420 9878). Subway 6 to 23rd Street.* **Open** 10.30am-6pm Mon, Tue, Fri; 10.30am-7pm Wed, Thur; 10.30am-5.30pm Sat. **Credit** AmEx, MC, V. Map
A shop which specialises in that unique combination: hip practical, comfortable, fun-for-kids clothing. There's always a range of one-off items (including some furniture and toys) created by tiny, artsy companies, as well as second-hand clothes (it's *the* place for 1950s cowboy outfits).

# Florists

For Interflora deliveries worldwide, phone City Floral on 410 0303/1-800 248 4692.

## Elizabeth Ryan Floral Designs
*411 East 9th Street, between Avenue A & First Avenue (995 1111). Subway 6 to Astor Place; L to First Avenue.* **Open** 9.30am-7pm Mon-Fri; 10am-6pm Sat. **Credit** AmEx, MC, V.
Elizabeth Ryan has arranged her shop like one of her gorgeous bouquets – it's magical. Fork out $20 for an original bouquet or request whatever you're interested in.

## Renny
*505 Park Avenue, at 59th Street (288 7000). Subway 4, 6 to 59th Street; N or R to Lexington Avenue.* **Open** 9am-6pm Mon-Fri. **Credit** AmEx, DC, MC, V.
'Exquisite flowers for the discriminating,' goes the slogan. Customers include David Letterman, Calvin Klein and myriad party-givers. Renny also arranges over-the-top parties.

## Very Special Flowers
*204 West 10th Street, between Bleecker & West 4th Street (206 7236). Subway A, C, E, F or Q to West 4th Street.* **Open** 10am-5pm Mon, 10am-7pm Tue-Fri; 11am-5pm Sat. **Credit** AmEx, MC, V.
And very special they are, indeed. Dried flower arrangements, exotic bonsai, miniature topiary and extravagant bouquets are the specialities.

# Food & Drink

## Balducci's
*424 Sixth Avenue, at 9th Street (673 2600). Subway A, B, C, D, E, F or Q to West 4th Street.* **Open** 7am-8.30pm daily. **Credit** AmEx, MC, V.
Over three generations the Balducci family's grocery store has grown into a gourmet emporium that can provide every luxurious foodstuff imaginable, from exotic fruit and freshly picked funghi to edible flowers and properly hung game. It also sells own-brand pasta and sauces, preserves and salamis.

## Dean & DeLuca
*560 Broadway, at Prince Street (431 1691). Subway N or R to Prince Street.* **Open** 10am-8pm Mon-Sat; 10am-7pm Sun. **Credit** AmEx, MC, V.
Dean & DeLuca is consolidating its position as *the* designer deli. The uninitiated will be amazed by the range and quality of the stock. The cheese counter is almost legendary, but this is the place to come for every kind of gourmet delicacy from raspberry vinegar to pâté de foie gras.

## Erotic Baker
*Telephone orders only (721 3217).* **Open** 10am-6pm Tue-Fri. **Credit** AmEx, MC, V.
They get through a lot of flesh-toned icing sugar here. Need we say more? At least you can practice safe sex.

## Gourmet Garage
*453 Broome Street, at Mercer Street (941 5850). Subway N, R to Prince Street.* **Open** 7.30am-8.30pm daily. **Credit** AmEx, Disc, MC, V.
A converted garage full of gourmet goodies, this was the first store in Manhattan to sell fresh gourmet food at wholesale prices and in retail quantities. The Starving Artist sandwiches are delish, as is the vast assortment of olives. Try a few.
**Branch:** 301 East 64th Street (535 6271).

## Grace's Marketplace
*1237 Third Avenue, at 71st Street (737 0600). Subway 4, 5 or 6 to 68th Street.* **Open** 7am-8.30pm Mon-Sat; 8am-7pm Sun. **Credit** AmEx, DC, MC, V.
A schism in the Balducci family (*see above*) caused Grace to move to the Upper East Side, where she has established an admirable food store with a similarly overpowering selection of all sorts of fabulous foods. Her Marketplace is the best bet for one-stop gourmet shopping in the neighbourhood, but expensive.

## Greenmarket
*(Information 477 3220, 9am-5pm Mon-Fri.)*
There are more than 20 open-air markets, sponsored by the City authorities, in various locations and on different days. The most famous is the one in Union Square at 14th Street (8am-6pm Mon, Wed, Fri), where small producers of organic

cheeses, honey, vegetables, herbs and flowers sell their wares from the back of their flat-bed trucks; arrive early, before they sell out.

## Guss Pickles

*35 Essex Street, between Grand & Hester Streets (254 4477). Subway F to East Broadway.* **Open** 9am-6pm Mon-Thur, Sun; 9am-3pm Fri. **Credit** MC, V.

Once upon a time there was a notorious rivalry between two pickle merchants, Guss and Hollander, but eventually the thing was settled and Guss put his name over the door of the old Hollander store and became the undisputed Pickle King, selling them sour or half-sour and in several sizes. Also excellent are the sauerkraut, pickled peppers and watermelon rinds.

## Kam Man Food Products

*200 Canal Street, at Mott Street (571 0330). Subway J, M, N, R or Z to Canal Street.* **Open** 9am-9pm daily. **Credit** MC, V.

A selection of fresh and preserved Chinese, Thai and other oriental foods, as well as utensils and kitchenware.

## Li-Lac

*120 Christopher Street (242 7374). Subway 1 or 9 to Christopher Street.* **Open** *summer* noon-8pm Tue-Sat; noon-5pm Sun; *winter* 10am-8pm Mon-Sat; noon-5pm Sun. **Credit** AmEx, Disc, MC, V.

Handmade chocolates *par excellence*.

## Lung Fong Bakery

*41 Mott Street, at Pell Street (233 7447). Subway J, M, N, R or Z to Canal Street.* **Open** 7.30am-9pm daily. **No credit cards**.

Fortune cookies, plus delicious breads and biscuits.

## Meyer & Thompson Fish Co

*146 Beekman Street (233 5427). Subway J, M or Z to Fulton Street.* **Open** *fishmongers* 3-11am Mon-Fri; *art gallery* noon-6pm Fri-Sun and by appointment. **Credit** *art gallery only* AmEx.

In the afternoons the fish shop, famous for its smoked cod, turns into a gallery displaying paintings by Naima Rauam.

## Myers of Keswick

*634 Hudson Street, between Horatio & Jane Streets (691 4194). Subway A, C, E or L to Eighth Avenue-14th Street.* **Open** 10am-7pm Mon-Fri; 10am-6pm Sat; noon-5pm Sun. **Credit** AmEx, V.

Can't live without Heinz beans, treacle sponge or rice pudding? Hungry for Bovril, Bird's custard or Ribena? You don't have to be if you head for Myers of Keswick, popularly known as the English Shop, a little corner of Coronation Street in the Big Apple.

## Once Upon a Tart...

*135 Sullivan Street, between Prince & Houston Streets (387 8869). Subway C or E to Spring Street; N or R to Prince Street.* **Open** 8am-8pm Mon-Fri; 9am-8pm Sat; 9am-6pm Sun. **Credit** AmEx, MC, V.

**Elizabeth Ryan Floral Designs**: *magic. Page 167.*

Along with fresh sandwiches, vegetable tarts and soup, this delectable bakery carries brownies, biscotti, a range of madeleines and fresh bread.

### Raffeto's Corporation

*144 West Houston Street, at MacDougal Street (777 1261). Subway A, B, C, D, E, F or Q to West 4th Street.* **Open** 9am-6.30pm Tue-Fri; 8am-6pm Sat. **No credit cards.**
In business since 1906, Raffeto's is the source of much of the designer pasta that is sold in gourmet shops all over town. But the staff will serve special raviolis, tortellini, fettucine, gnocchi and manicotti in any quantity to anyone who calls in, with no minimum order.

### Russ & Daughters

*179 East Houston Street, between Allen & Orchard Streets (475 4880). Subway F to Second Avenue.* **Open** 9am-6pm Mon-Wed; 9am-7pm Thur-Sat; 8am-6pm Sun. **Credit** MC, V.
A New York institution. Founded in 1914, this shop still boasts Sunday morning queues of loyal customers waiting patiently for the most delicious smoked fish, gefilte fish, herring and whitefish salad in the city. A treasure.

### Zabar's

*2245 Broadway, at 80th Street (787 2000). Subway 1 or 9 to 79th Street.* **Open** 8am-7.30pm Mon-Fri; 8am-8pm Sat; 9am-6pm Sun. **Credit** AmEx, MC, V.
By common consent the best food store in the city and, naturally therefore, the world. Zabar's is not only an excellent delicatessen but a great grocer and a first-class fish shop. The variety and quality of the coffee and cookies, cheeses and croissants is breathtaking: sniff the air and you'll understand why Zabar's is Heaven. Expect to queue (you won't begrudge the wait).

### A Zito & Sons Bakery

*259 Bleecker Street, at Seventh Avenue (929 6139). Subway A, B, C, D, E, F or Q to West 4th Street.* **Open** 6am-6pm Mon-Sat; 6am-3pm Sun. **No credit cards**.
The customers of this Bleecker Street bakery have included Frank Sinatra, who stopped by for a Sicilian loaf, and Bob Dylan, whose preference is for wholewheat. Tony Zito makes the best Italian bread in the Village, so if you're planning a picnic this is the place to begin.

## Liquor Stores

Most supermarkets and corner delis sell beer and aren't too fussed about ID – but may ask for proof that you are over 21. To buy wine and spirits in New York you need a liquor store. And, just to confuse you, most liquor stores don't sell beer, nor are they open on Sundays.

### Astor Wines & Spirits

*12 Astor Place, at Lafayette Street (674 7500). Subway 6 to Astor Place; N or R to 8th Street.* **Open** 9am-9pm Mon-Sat. **Credit** AmEx, JCB, MC, V.
A modern wine supermarket that would serve as the perfect blueprint, were it not for a law preventing liquor stores from branching out. There's a wide range of wines and spirits.

### Best Cellars

*1291 Lexington Avenue, between 86th & 87th Streets (426 4200). Subway 4, 5, 6 to 86th Street.* **Open** 10am-9pm Mon-Thur; 10am-10pm Fri, Sat. **Credit** AmEx, MC, V.
This wine shop stocks only 100 delicious selections, each one tasted by the owners (who tested more than 1,500 bottles). The best part is that they're all under $10.

**Russ & Daughters**: *for lox around the clock.*

### Maxwell Wine & Spirits

*1657 First Avenue, at 86th Street (289 9595). Subway 4, 5 or 6 to 86th Street.* **Open** 9am-11pm Mon-Wed; 10am-midnight Thur-Sat. **Credit** AmEx, MC, V.
Maxwell stocks popularly priced French, Italian and Californian wines, as well as vodka, gin and the usual run of rums, scotch and bourbons.

### Park Avenue Liquor Shop

*292 Madison Avenue, between East 40th & East 41st Street (685 2442). Subway 4, 5, 6 or 7 to Grand Central.* **Open** 8am-7pm Mon-Fri; 8am-5pm Sat. **Credit** AmEx, MC, V.
An unparalleled range of over 400 Californian wines is complemented by an excellent selection of spirits and fine European bottles. Buy by the case to qualify for a 16 per cent discount.

### Schumer's Wine & Liquor

*59 East 54th Street, between Park & Madison Avenues (355 0940). Subway 6, E or F to 51st Street/Lexington Avenue.* **Open** 9am-midnight Mon-Sat. **Credit** AmEx, DC, MC, V.
Schumer's has a large selection of French, Californian and Italian wines as well as champagnes and spirits, including cognacs, armagnacs and single-malt scotches. They deliver.

### Sherry-Lehmann Inc

*679 Madison Avenue, at East 61st Street (838 7500). Subway 4, 5 or 6 to 59th Street; N or R to Lexington Avenue.* **Open** 9am-7pm Mon-Sat. **Credit** AmEx, MC, V.
Perhaps the most famous of New York's numerous liquor stores, Sherry-Lehmann has a vast selection of scotches, brandies and ports, as well as a superb range of French, American and Italian wines.

### Warehouse Wines & Spirits

*735 Broadway, between 8th Street & Waverly Place (982 7770). Subway 6 to Astor Place; N or R to 8th Street.* **Open** 9am-8.50pm Mon-Thur; 9am-9.50pm Fri, Sat. **Credit** AmEx, MC, V.

For the best prices in town for wine and liquor, look no further. Grab a cart, because you'll need it.

## Gifts

### Alphabets

*115 Avenue A, between St Mark's Place & 7th Street (475 7250). Subway L to First Avenue.* **Open** noon-10pm Mon-Thur; noon-midnight Fri, Sat; noon-8pm Sun. **Credit** AmEx, MC, V.

Hilarious postcards, wrapping paper and tiny treasures fill the packed shelves here, together with a range of Josie and the Pussy Cat T-shirts and offbeat souvenirs of New York. The Sanrio line is extensive – new items come in weekly. **Branches:** 47 Greenwich Avenue (229 2966); 2284 Broadway (579 5702).

### Cobblestones

*314 East 9th Street, between First & Second Avenues (673 5372). Subway 6 to Astor Place; L to First Avenue.* **Open** noon-7pm Tue-Sat; noon-6pm Sun. **Credit** AmEx, MC, V.

A thrift store of sorts, this wonderful place stocks everything from elegant cigarette holders to antique dresses and shoes. Gazing into the glass cases filled with bejewelled chokers can take the good part of a day.

### Eclectiques

*55 Wooster Street, at Broome (966 0650). Subway C or E to Spring Street.* **Open** 1-5.30pm daily. **Credit** AmEx, MC, V.

A peculiar mix of old Vuitton luggage, Lalique and other beautiful, covetable objects.

### Hammacher Schlemmer

*147 East 57th Street, between Third & Lexington Avenues (421 9000). Subway 4, 5 or 6 to 59th Street; E or F to Lexington Avenue.* **Open** 10am-6pm Mon-Sat. **Credit** AmEx, JCB, DC, Disc, MC, V.

Six floors of bizarre toys for home, car, sports and leisure, each one supposedly the best of its kind. The perfect place to buy a gift that will permanently attach a smile on anyone's face. Especially the electric nose hair remover.

### Little Rickie

*49½ First Avenue, at East 3rd Street (505 6467). Subway F to Second Avenue.* **Open** 11am-8pm Mon-Sat; noon-7pm Sun. **Credit** AmEx, DC, MC, V.

A bizarre collection of ludicrous, eye-popping, mirth-making toys, cards and trinkets gathered from around the world. Visit the photo booth and have your face added to the window display.

### Love Saves the Day

*119 Second Avenue, at East 7th Street (228 3802). Subway 6 to Astor Place.* **Open** noon-8pm Mon-Thur; 11am-11pm Fri-Sun. **Credit** AmEx, MC, V.

More kitsch toys and tacky novelties than you can shake an Elvis doll at. There are Elvis lamps with pink shades, Elvis statuettes, ant farms, lurid machine-made tapestries of Madonna, glow-in-the-dark crucifixes and Mexican day-of-the-dead statues.

### Mxyplyzyk

*125 Greenwich Avenue, at 13th Street (989 4300). Subway 1, 9 to Christopher Street/Sheridan Square.* **Open** 11am-7pm Mon-Sat; noon-5pm Sun. **Credit** AmEx, MC, V.

It's a hotchpotch of fun at this West Village store (the name doesn't mean anything). Choose from lighting, furniture, toys, stationery, housewares and gardening items. **Branch**: 123 Greenwich Avenue (647 0777).

### Serendipity

*225 East 60th Street, between Second & Third Avenues (838 3531). Subway 4, 5, 6, N or R to 59th Street/Lexington Avenue.* **Open** 11.30am-12.30am Mon-Thur; 11.30am-1am Fri; 11.30am-2am Sat; 11.30am-midnight Sun. **Credit** AmEx, DC, MC, V.

Serendipity has been in business for over 35 years as a restaurant and general store selling clothing and gifts. The restaurant is famous for its frozen hot chocolate.

### Warner Bros Studio Store

*1 East 57th Street, at Fifth Avenue (754 0300). Subway 4, 5, 6 to 59th Street.* **Open** 10am-8pm Mon-Sat; 11am-6pm Sun. **Credit** AmEx, DC, JCB, MC, V.

The outlet for anything and everything that has a Warner Bros character slapped on it features baseball hats, T-shirts and a few surprises.

## Gift Deliveries

### Baskets by Wire

*(724 6900/1-718 746 1200). **Open** 8am-7pm Mon-Sat; 8am-3pm Sun. **Credit** AmEx, DC, Disc, MC, V.

Fruit, gourmet food, flowers and mylar or helium balloon bouquets delivered nationwide.

### Select-a-Gram

*(1-800 292 1562/874 4464). **Open** 9am-6pm Mon-Sat. **Credit** AmEx, DC, MC, V.

Create your own gift basket with anything from champagne to caviar or jelly beans, T-shirts and stuffed animals. Nationwide delivery.

## Children's Toys

### Enchanted Forest

*85 Mercer Street, between Spring & Broome Streets (925 6677). Train 6 to Prince Street.* **Open** 11am-7pm Mon-Sat; noon-6pm Sun. **Credit** AmEx, DC, Disc, JCB, MC, V.

A gallery of beasts, books and handmade toys in a magical forest setting.

### FAO Schwarz

*767 Fifth Avenue, at 58th Street (644 9400). Train 4, 5 or 6 to 59th Street; E or F to Lexington Avenue.* **Open** 10am-6pm Mon-Wed; 10am-7pm Thur-Sat; 11am-6pm Sun. **Credit** AmEx, DC, Disc, JCB, MC, V.

The famous toy store has been supplying New York kids with toys and games since 1862 and stocks more stuffed animals than you could imagine in your worst nightmares, as well as kites, dolls, games, miniature cars, toy soldiers, bath toys and so on. The closest you can come to Disneyland in New York.

### B Shackman & Co

*85 Fifth Avenue, at 16th Street (989 5162). Train 4, 5, 6, B, D, L, N, Q or R to 14th Street-Union Square.* **Open** 9am-5pm Mon-Fri; 10am-4pm Sat. **Credit** AmEx, MC, V.

Old-fashioned toys, miniatures, doll's house furniture, wind-up toys, china dolls and flick books make this nostalgic for adults and fascinating for kids.

### Tiny Doll House

*1146 Lexington Avenue, between 79th & 80th Streets (744 3719). Train 6 to 77th Street.* **Open** 11am-5.30pm Mon-Fri; 11am-5pm Sat. **Credit** AmEx, MC, V.

Everything in the shop is tiny: miniature furniture and furnishings for doll's houses, including chests, beds, kitchen fittings and cutlery. Adults love it.

# Green

## Body Shop
*773 Lexington Avenue, near East 61st Street
(755 7851). Subway 4, 5 or 6 to 59th Street; N or R to
Lexington Avenue.* **Open** 10am-7pm Mon-Wed, Fri;
9.30am-7.30pm Thur; 10am-6pm Sun. **Credit** AmEx,
Disc, MC, V.
Body Shop junkies can relax – it has crossed the pond. For
the uninitiated (where have you been?) here's where to come
for natural beauty products in no-nonsense, bio-degradable
plastic bottles – at slightly higher prices here than in the UK.
**Branches:** 2159 Broadway (721 2947); 485 Madison
Avenue (832 0812).

## Felissimo
*10 West 56th Street, at Fifth Avenue (956 4438).
Subway N, R, B or Q to 57th Street.* **Open** 10am-6pm
Mon-Wed, Fri, Sat; 10am-8pm Thur. **Credit** AmEx, JCB,
MC, V.
This five-storey townhouse is a Japanese-owned, eco-hip
speciality store that stocks a collection of covetable items for
the heart and home. Choose from jewellery, furnishings,
clothing and collectibles. Assistance is available in nine
different languages.

## Planet Hemp
*423 Broome Street, between Crosby & Lafayette Streets
(965 0500/1-800 681 HEMP). Subway 6 to Spring Street.*
**Open** noon-6pm daily. **Credit** AmEx, Disc, MC, V.
The hemp rage lives on at this eco-friendly shop that sells
men's and women's sportswear, bed linens, paper goods and
body products. There are even shoes made from hemp and
'Terra-gard', a leather substitute.

## Terra Verde
*120 Wooster Street, between Prince & Spring Streets
(925 4533). Subway R to Prince Street.* **Open** 11am-7pm
Mon-Sat; noon-6pm Sun. **Credit** AmEx, MC, V.
Manhattan's first eco-market, combining art and activism.
Architect William McDonough renovated the SoHo space
using non-toxic building materials and formaldehyde-free
paint. Get your chemical-free linens, natural soaps and solar
radios here.

# Hats

## Kelly Christy
*235 Elizabeth Street, between Houston & Prince Streets
(965 0686). Subway N or R to Prince Street.* **Open** noon-
7pm Tue-Sat; noon-6pm Sun. **Credit** AmEx, MC, V.
The selection, for both men and women, is lovely, and the
atmosphere relaxed. Try on anything you like – Christy is
more than happy to help and give the honest truth.

## Amy Downs Hats
*103 Stanton Street, at Ludlow Street (598 4189).
Subway F to Second Avenue.* **Open** 1-6pm Wed-Sun.
**No credit cards.**
Downs's hats are of the soft wool and felt variety. You can
crumple them up and shove them in your bag, and still they
won't die. Check out her trademark Twister: cone-shaped
with tassels.

## The Hat Shop
*120 Thompson Street, between Prince & Spring Streets
(219 1445). Subway N, R to Prince Street; C, E to Spring
Street.* **Open** noon-7pm Tue-Sat; 1-5pm Sun. **Credit**
AmEx, JCB, MC, V.
Linda Pagan isn't a hat designer herself – she's a hat nut.
Her delightful boutique is a cross between a millinery shop
and a department store – not only are customers able to

choose among 40 different designers, they receive scads of
personal attention too.

## Lola Millinery
*2 East 17th Street, between Fifth Avenue & Broadway
(366 5708). Subway 4, 5, 6, L, N or R to 14th Street.*
**Open** 11am-7pm Mon-Fri; 11am-6pm Sat. **Credit** AmEx,
MC, V.
Probably the best-known hat designer in the city, Lola
designs classical and modern shapes for men and women.
Prices range from $175 for feather clips and fancy combs to
$275 for an animal-print fedora. Hats can be bought off the
rack, customised or made to order.

## van der Linde Designs
*Second Floor, Lombardy Hotel, 111 East 56th Street,
between Park & Lexington Avenues (758 1686). Subway
4, 5, 6, N or R to 59th Street.* **Open** by appointment
only. **Credit** AmEx, MC, V.
Susan van der Linde is the protégée of designer Don
Marshall (whose creations graced the heads of Joan Crawford
and Grace Kelly, among others). Her small boutique is akin
to an elegant 1930s parlour. There are stunning cocktail hats,
rain wear as well as polarfleece wrap hats – very diva – or
ski bunny versions.

## Worth & Worth
*331 Madison Avenue, at 43rd Street (867 6058). Subway
4, 5, 6, 7 or S to 42nd Street-Grand Central.* **Open** 9am-
6pm Mon-Fri; 10am-5pm Sat. **Credit** AmEx, DC, MC, V.
This is the grandest men's hat shop in the city, where you'll
find the finest panama hats under the sun and a vast assortment of fedoras.

# Hairdressers

## Model Nights

Swank salons free up their $200 chairs one night
a week for those willing to be a guinea pig for
trainees. The results are wonderful and cost a frac-
tion of the usual price. All of the following have
model nights, with prices ranging between $25 and
$45 (often payable in cash only). Phone for details
of their next model night: you may well have to get
yourself on a waiting list.

**Peter Coppola Salon** (988 9404)
**Frederic Fekai at Bergdorf Goodman** (753 7300)
**Louis Licari** (517 8084/327 0639)
**Pierre Michel Salon** (759 3000)
**Vidal Sassoon** (223 9177)

## Cheap Cuts

### Astor Place Hair Designers
*2 Astor Place, near Broadway (475 9854). Subway 6 to
Astor Place; N or R to 8th Street.* **Open** 8am-8pm Mon-
Sat; 9am-6pm Sun. **No credit cards.**
A classic New York experience, and cheap. An army of bar-
bers do anything from neat trims to shaved designs, all to a
loud rock or hip-hop accompaniment. No appointments are
taken; you just take a number and wait with the crowd outside. Sunday mornings are quiet. Cuts cost from $11.

### Ginger Rose 2
*37 East 8th Street, between University Place & Greene
Street (677 6511). Subway N, R to 8th Street.*
**Open** 9.30am-8pm Mon-Wed; 9.30am-10pm Thur-Sat;
noon-7pm Sun.
Similar to the Astor. Haircuts cost from $10.

### Heads & Tales Haircutting
*22 St Mark's Place, between Second & Third Avenues (677 9125). Subway 6 to Astor Place.* **Open** 1pm-midnight Tue-Fri; 11.30am-7pm Sat. **No credit cards**.
A basic hairdressing service – wash and cut, styling and blow-drying. Just walk in: no appointment is necessary.

## Stylists

### Robert Stuart Salon
*510 Amsterdam Avenue, between 84th & 85th Streets (496 1530). Subway 1, 9 to 86th Street.* **Open** 10.30am-6.30pm Tue-Fri; 9am-5pm Sat. **Credit** AmEx, MC, V.
The ever friendly Stuart, who worked at Henri Bendel and Vidal Sassoon, has been cutting hair in his own salon for the past 15 years; haircuts $70, colour from $55.

### Studio 303
*Chelsea Hotel, 222 West 23rd Street between Seventh & Eighth Avenues (633 1011). Subway C, E, 1, 9 to 23rd Street.* **Open** 11am-8pm Tue-Fri; 10am-6pm Sat.
**No credit cards**.
Owned by three ex-Racine stylists, Studio 303 is located in the wonderfully spooky Chelsea Hotel. Haircuts start at $65.

### Wardwell Salon
*200 West 80th Street, between Amsterdam Avenue & Broadway (362 7617). Subway 1, 9 to 79th Street.*
**Open** 11am-8pm Tue-Sat. **No credit cards**.
Deborah Wardwell, who gave up a career in magazine work to open her own salon, reserves an hour for each haircut and does colour as well; the results are breathtaking. Haircuts from $60; highlights start at $125.

## Home Furnishings

### Bed, Bath & Beyond
*620 Sixth Avenue, at 18th Street (255 3550). Subway F or L to Sixth Avenue/14th Street.* **Open** 9.30am-9pm Mon-Fri; 9.30am-8pm Sat; 10am-8pm Sun. **Credit** AmEx, Disc, MC, V.
As the name says: everything you need for your house, with particular emphasis on the sheets and towels which go in those two rooms. Inexpensive and generally good quality.

### Bennison Fabrics
*76 Greene Street, between Spring & Broome Streets (941 1212). Subway C or E to Spring Street.* **Open** 10am-6pm Mon-Fri. **Credit** MC, V.
A favourite downtown shop, with a classic but innovative range of fabrics that are silkscreened in the UK. Prices are steep but the fabrics – usually 70 per cent linen, 30 per cent cotton – end up in some of the best-dressed homes in town.

### Crate & Barrel
*650 Madison Avenue, at 59th Street (308 0011). Subway 4, 5 or 6 to 59th Street.* **Open** 10am-8pm Mon-Fri; 10am-7pm Sat; noon-6pm Sun. **Credit** AmEx, Disc, MC, V.
Crate and Barrel combines mid-range antique furniture and *objets* with the very best and latest in household goods.

### Design Find
*(1-516 365 4321).* **Open** by appointment only.
Interior designer Lauren Rosenberg-Moffit claims to know Manhattan like the back of her hand and will escort you on a memorable shopping tour of the city's showrooms, antique markets and back-alley stores, bringing you discounts of up to 20 per cent. Her fee varies according to your needs.

## Gracious Home

*1217 & 1220 Third Avenue, between 70th & 71st Streets (988 8990). Subway 6 to 68th Street.* **Open** 8am-7pm Mon-Fri; 9am-7pm Sat; 10am-6pm Sun. **Credit** AmEx, DC, MC, V.
If you need a new curtain rod, place mat or drawer pull, give them a call. They deliver all over Manhattan, and there's no minimum charge.

## Pottery Barn

*117 East 59th Street, between Lexington & Park Avenues (753 5424). Subway 4, 5 or 6 to 59th Street; N or R to Lexington Avenue.* **Open** 10.30am-7pm Mon-Wed, Fri; 10am-8pm Thur, Sat; noon-6pm Sun. **Credit** AmEx, Disc, MC, V.
Candlesticks, candlesticks, candlesticks! The 1990s answer to every decoration decision is melting wax, and Pottery Barn helps out in that department. You'll find plain ceramics, glassware and furniture (as in lamps and tables), tortoiseshell glass bowls, rattan chairs and picture frames. The designs are stripped down, stark and very appealing.

## Rhubarb Home

*26 Bond Street, between Lafayette Street & The Bowery (533 1817). Subway 6 to Bleecker Street.* **Open** noon-7pm daily. **Credit** AmEx, DC, MC, V.
Stacy Sindlinger scouts flea markets and yard sales in Ohio for impeccably battered furniture – chipped work tables, French deco mirrors, even a baker's table have all been in her comfortable store at one time or another.

## White Trash

*304 East 5th Street, between First & Second Avenues (598 5956). Subway F to Second Avenue; 6 to Astor Place.* **Open** 2-9pm Wed-Sat; 1-8pm Sun. **Credit** MC, V.
Formerly a monthly yard-sale event at First Avenue and 4th Street, white trash connoisseurs Kim Wurster and Stuart Zamksy opened this popular thrifty store to the delight of those in dire need of Jesus night lights, Noguchi lamps and 1950s kitchen tables. Great prices.

## Williams-Sonoma

*20 East 60th Street, near Madison Avenue (980 5155). Subway 4, 5 or 6 to 59th Street; N or R to Lexington Avenue.* **Open** 10am-7pm Mon-Fri; 10am-6pm Sat; noon-5pm Sun. **Credit** AmEx, Disc, MC, V.
A branch of the famous San Francisco kitchen store, Williams-Sonoma stocks all the best kinds of kitchen equipment: KitchenAid food mixers, Gaggia ice-cream machines, professional slicers, great copper and stainless steel pots, grills, fine glassware, maple salad-bowls, Sabatier knives... The outlet store sells end-of-line and sale items.
**Branch**: 580 Broadway (343 7330); **Williams-Sonoma Outlet** 231 10th Avenue (206 8118).

# Jewellery

## Cartier

*653 Fifth Avenue, at 52nd Street (753 0111). Subway 6 to 51st Street.* **Open** 10am-5.30pm Mon-Sat. **Credit** AmEx, DC, JCB, MC, V.
Cartier bought its Italianate building – one of few survivors of Fifth Avenue's previous life as a classy residential street – for two strands of Oriental pearls. All the usual Cartier items – jewellery, silver, porcelain – are sold within.

## Clear Metals

*72 Thompson Street, between Spring & Broome Streets (941 1800). Subway 6 to Spring Street.* **Open** 12.30-6pm Mon; 12.30-7pm Tue-Sat; 1-6pm Sun. **Credit** AmEx, MC, V.
Metalsmith Barbara Klar creates modernist silver forms that are engraved with signs and symbols. Her wedding rings are contemporary, and lovely.

## David Webb

*445 Park Avenue, at 57th Street (421 3030). Subway 4, 5 or 6 to 59th Street; N or R to Lexington Avenue.* **Open** 10am-5.15pm Mon-Fri; 10am-5pm Sat. **Credit** AmEx, DC, Disc, JCB, MC, V.
David Webb is best known for distinctive, and much imitated, gem-studded 18-carat gold jewellery. The pieces are

**Clear Metals**: *for the latest in contemporary designs.*

expansive, often figurative, the quality impeccable and the prices appropriately high.

## Ilias Lalaounis

*733 Madison Avenue, at 64th Street (439 9400). Subway 4, 5, 6, N or R to 59th Street.* **Open** 10am-5.30pm Mon-Sat. **Credit** AmEx, DC, Disc, JCB, MC, V.

This Greek jewellery designer's work is inspired by his native country's ancient symbols as well as American Indian and Arab designs. Expensive.

## Manny Winick & Son

*19 West 47th Street, near Fifth Avenue (302 9555). Subway B, D, F or Q to 47th Street/Rockefeller Center.* **Open** 10am-5pm Mon-Fri; 10am-4.30pm Sat. **Credit** AmEx, Disc, MC, V.

Fine jewellery in precious metals are sold alongside more sculptural contemporary pieces.

## Piaget

*730 Fifth Avenue, at 57th Street (246 5555). Subway 4, 5, or 6 to 59th Street; N or R to Lexington Avenue.* **Open** 10am-6pm Mon-Sat. **Credit** AmEx, MC, V.

This giant boutique full of glittering jewels would surely make Holly Golightly swoon. Piaget has a diamond (or an emerald) for every girl.

## Robert Lee Morris

*400 West Broadway, between Spring & Broome Streets (431 9405). Subway R to Prince Street; C or E to Spring Street.* **Open** 11am-6pm Mon-Fri; 11am-7pm Sat; noon-6pm Sun. **Credit** AmEx, MC, V.

Robert Lee Morris is the foremost contemporary designer; his brilliant SoHo gallery is filled with strong, striking pieces.

## Ted Muehling

*47 Greene Street, between Broome & Grand Streets (431 3825). Subway N or R to Prince Street.* **Open** noon-6pm Tue-Fri, Sat. **Credit** AmEx, MC, V.

Ted Muehling creates beautiful organic shapes in the studio behind the store, which sells the work of other artists, too.

## Tiffany & Co

*727 Fifth Avenue, between 56th & 57th Streets (755 8000). Subway 4, 5 or 6 to 59th Street; N or R to Lexington Avenue.* **Open** 10am-6pm Mon-Wed, Fri, Sat.; 10am-7pm Thur. **Credit** AmEx, DC, JCB, MC, V.

Tiffany's heyday was around the turn of the century, when Louis Comfort Tiffany was designing his famous lamps and sensational Art Nouveau jewellery. Today, the big star is Paloma Picasso, who designs big pieces at bigger prices. Three storeys are stacked with precious jewels, silver accessories, chic watches and porcelain. Don't forget your credit cards.

## Laundry

Most neighbourhoods have coin-operated laundries, but in New York it costs much the same if you drop off your washing and let someone else do the work. On the Upper West Side we recommend **Ecomat** (362 2300) on 72nd Street. It's one of the city's only laundries to use ecologically sound detergents.

## Leather Goods & Luggage

### Il Bisonte

*72 Thompson Street, between Spring & Broome Streets (966 8773). Subway C or E to Spring Street.* **Open** noon-6.30pm Tue-Sat; noon-6pm Mon, Sun. **Credit** AmEx, MC, V.

Good tough basics with style: bags, belts and saddlebags, from the famous Florentine company.

## Bag House

*797 Broadway, at 11th Street (260 0940). Subway 4, 5, 6, L, N or R to Union Square.* **Open** 11am-6.45pm Mon-Sat; 1-5.45pm Sun. **Credit** AmEx, MC, V.

All manner of bags from the tiniest tote to something you could stow a small family away in.

## Coach Menswear

*710 Madison Avenue, at 63rd Street (319 1772). Subway 4, 5 or 6 to 59th Street; N or R to Lexington Avenue.* **Open** 10am-7pm Mon-Wed; 10am-8pm Thur, Fri; 10am-7pm Sat; noon-6pm Sun. **Credit** AmEx, MC, V.

The buttery-soft leather briefcases, wallets and handbags found here are exceptional. It's the only Coach store in Manhattan to stock the complete clothing collection for men.

## Jutta Neumann

*317 East 9th Street, between First & Second Avenues (982 7048). Subway 6 to Astor Place; L to First Avenue.* **Open** noon-8pm Tue-Sat and by appointment. **Credit** AmEx, MC, V.

Neumann designs leather sandles ($130-$325) and bags ($100-$500) as well as belts and jewellery. Haven't you always wanted a leather choker?

## Louis Vuitton

*49 East 57th Street, between Park & Madison Avenues (371 6111). Subway 4, 5 or 6 to 59th Street; N or R to Lexington Avenue.* **Open** 10am-6pm Mon-Fri; 10am-5pm Sat; noon-5pm Sun. **Credit** AmEx, DC, Disc, JCB, MC, V.

The luggage and handbags are expensive, but beautiful.

## Lingerie

### Between the Sheets

*241 East 10th Street, between First & Second Avenues (677 7586). Subway 6 to Astor Place; L to First Avenue.* **Open** noon-8pm Mon-Sat; noon-6pm Sun. **Credit** AmEx, MC, V.

Sylvia Shum stocks American and European brands of bras and pants, along with silk slips, lacy cotton camisoles and teddies. Everything's extra pretty – she knows that many of her clients wear their underthings on the outside.

### Enelra

*485 East 7th Street, between First & Second Avenues (473 2454). Subway 6 to Astor Place; F to Second Avenue.* **Open** noon-9pm Mon-Sat; noon-8pm Sun. **Credit** AmEx, MC, V.

During the 1980s Madonna was a regular. Plenty of corsets, bras and slinky slips, as well as fluffy marabou mules.

### Lingerie & Co

*1217 Third Avenue, between 70th & 71st Streets (737 7700/1-800 737 1217). Subway 6 to 68th Street/Hunter College.* **Open** 9.30am-7pm Mon-Sat; noon-5pm Sun. **Credit** AmEx, Disc, MC, V.

Owners Mark Peress and Tamara Watkins take a look at your body (and ask a few questions) before they announce their lingerie recommendations.

### La Petite Coquette

*51 University Place, between 9th & 10th Streets (473 2478). Subway N or R to 8th Street; 6 to Astor Place.* **Open** 11am-7pm Mon-Sat, noon-6pm Sun. **Credit** AmEx, MC, V.

There are too many goodies for the eye to take in at Rebecca Apsan's tiny lingerie boudoir. Customers can flip through panels of pinned-up bras and underpants before making a selection. Once you know what you like, she'll order it for you.

*Lingerie heaven at* **La Petit Coquette***.*

# Lafayette Street

No one disputes the charm of the neighbourhood that borders SoHo, Chinatown and Little Italy. The battle is over what to call it. Esso (for East SoHo), Little Chitaly, East SoHo (the M&R bar serves East SoHo fries) and BoHo (meaning 'Bowery, south of Houston') have all been mooted. Disaster! Once a neighbourhood has a name, it's ruined. Don't call it anything. Just go. Over the past year and a half, a number of shops have opened in the streets south of Houston from Prince Street, along Lafayette, Mulberry, Mott and Elizabeth Streets. It's not a replica of the crammed East Village, nor does it contain copies of stark SoHo stores. The area is friendly and quiet – an oasis only a block away from noisy Broadway. Along with clothing shops, there are outlets for shoes, glasswear, stationery, hats and records.

At 280 **Mott Street**, Christiane Celle's **Calypso** (965 0990) sells gorgeous slip dresses, suits, sweaters and scarves, many of which are from small designers who work in France. **Sigerson Morrison** – owned by Kylie Sigerson and Miranda Morrison – specialises in shoes that come in the prettiest of colours: ruby-red, shiny

pearl, olive crocodile and burnt orange among them (No 242, between Houston and Prince Streets; 219 3893). **Wang** (No 219; 941 6134), a boutique owned by sisters Sally and Jennifer Wang, features the perfect complements for the shoes – simple, chic clothes.

On **Prince Street**, you'll come across **Dö Kham**, a shop that specialises in treasures from Tibet and the Himalayas (No 51, between Lafayette and Mulberry; 996 2404). Practically next door is the **Dressing Room**, a violet-painted boutique with a small but stylish selection of new and second-hand clothing. Labels include Jill Stuart, Katharine Hamnett, Claudie Pierlot and designers like Tripp and Savage (No 49, between Mulberry and Lafayette; 431 6658). **Ina** (334 9048, at No 21) is in the recycling fashion business: here you'll find worn Chanel, Ann Demeulemeester, John Galliano and tons of Manolo Blahnik shoes. On the corner of Prince and Elizabeth Streets is **About Time** (941 0966), another shop for antique couture and vintagewear. Owner Beverly Wilburn, who worked at Barneys and Bergdorf's before opening her beautiful boutique, stocks

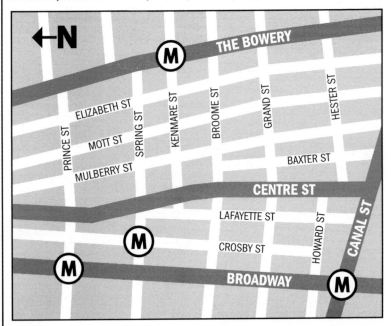

only the best – early Geoffrey Beene, Courrèges, Dries Van Noten, Yohji Yamamoto and Commes des Garçons. Also on Prince Street is **Scarlet and Sage** cluttered with artefacts from all over the world – including India, Turkey, Spain and Portugal (No 7, between Elizabeth and The Bowery; 219 1290).

**Elizabeth Street** is really booming: for fantasy hats, try **Kelly Christy** (*see page 171*). At **Daily 2-3-5** (at No 235; 334 9728) a general store of sorts, you'll find a variety of necessary and not-so-necessary objects like soap, the daily papers, magazines, condoms, rubber bugs, cigarettes and voodoo dolls. **Shi**, which means 'is' in Chinese, sells hanging glass vases and gorgeous lamps (No 233; 334 4330), while **orio/trio** (No 248; 219 1501) stocks objets – nineteenth-century spice jars, glass serving dishes, vases from the 1950s and 1960s and a line of button-down shirts and skirts. Eclectic furniture is up for grabs at **Claudia Bogan**'s shop, where the merchandise is 'a step below antiques and a step above junk' (No 269; 226 5123). Lamps, lamps and more lamps (owner Ignez Whitaker claims you can never have enough) are crowded into **Elizabeth 260** (941 6158).

On **Mulberry Street**, check out Karen Karch's shop **Push**, which specialises in handmade jewellery – gorgeous engagement rings, necklaces and bracelets for men and women, made from sterling silver, 14k gold and platinum.

**Lafayette Street** is by far the busiest street of them all, but not to be missed. Here, you'll find ravewear galore at **Liquid Sky** (No 241, at Prince; 343 0532) from fresh originals to cavernous bag-gies, dopey hats and backpacks. While you're there, walk down the stairs to **Temple Records**, a haven for US and imported techno, trance and jungle (343 3595). **Supreme** is a skaters' dream, stocking the latest decks, trucks and wheels, and the fashions to go with them (No 274, at Prince Street; 966 7799). At No 222B (between Spring and Broome Streets; 431 0342) **Smylonyon** ('smile on nylon') stocks the greatest, sometimes strangest, 1960s and 1970s styles, usually made out of nylon. **X-Girl** at No 248 (226 0151) – owned by Sonic Youth rocker Kim Gordon and Daisy von Firth – features inexpensive skirts, jeans, T-shirts and dresses, while **X-Large** (No 267, between Spring and Prince Streets; 334 4480), which is part-owned by Beastie Boy Mike D, is a trendy LA label that includes heavy cotton work jackets, cords and polo shirts. **Pop Shop** sells all the posters, badges, bath pillows, inflatable babies, groovy fridge magnets and T-shirts designed by the late Keith Haring (No 292, near Prince Street; 219 2784).

The **Urban Archaeology Co** is one of the largest stores in this area, specialising in the discarded everyday items of the past. Here you'll find architectural and household items, from a bookshelf to a pair of wrought-iron gates complete with stone pillars (No 285, between Prince & Houston Streets; 431 6969). And for fashion, don't forget to poke your head in **Label** (No 265, between Prince and Spring; 966 7736), for clothes inspired by female revolutionaries (think Patty Hearst) and **555 Soul** (No 290; 431 2404), Camelia Ehike's line of sportswear for men and women, coveted by rap acts including De La Soul and LL Cool J.

### Victoria's Secret

*565 Broadway, corner of Prince Street (274 9519).*
*Subway N or R to Prince Street.* **Open** 10am-8pm Mon-
Sat; noon-7pm Sun. **Credit** AmEx, Disc, MC, V.
There's lots of coloured satin and plenty of sales at this lin-
gerie chain. Surprisingly well-made.

## Magic

### Altar Egos

*110 West Houston Street, between Sullivan & Thompson*
*Streets (677 9588). Subway C, E to Spring Street; 1, 9 to*
*Christopher Street/Sheridan Square.* **Open** 1-8pm Tue-
Sun. **Credit** AmEx, MC, V.
Roger Pratt and Billy Barbanes, co-owners of this pagan
shop, stock statues, candles, books, and of course, good
advice. Custom work is done on the premises.

### Prophecy

*213 West 80th Street, between Broadway & Amsterdam*
*Avenue (799 3000). Subway 1 or 9 to 79th Street.* **Open**
noon-8pm Tue-Sun. **Credit** AmEx, MC, V.
Phoebe Ungerer has been quoted as saying she wants to be
to the witchcraft business what Ben & Jerry's is to ice-cream.
Her giant candles ($20) conquer whatever it is you want.

### Other Worldly Waxes

*131 East 7th Street, between Avenue A & First Avenue*
*(260 9188). Subway L to First Avenue; 6 to Astor Place;*
*F to Second Avenue.* **Open** 2-10pm Mon-Fri; 1-10pm Sat,
Sun. **Credit** AmEx, MC, V.
Witchery by a psychologist? Dr Catherine Riggs-Bergesen
blends both crafts and will do her damnedest to straighten
out your life. Her book Candle Therapy is sold at her shop
and is a must for amateurs.

**Kiehl's**: *almost an institution. See p180.*

## Mail Order

It isn't instant gratification, but shopping from the
comfort of your hotel room or apartment beats
fighting the crowds in the mean stores of
Manhattan. Simply pick up your phone, and
boom! You're the proud owner of a power drill,
contact lenses, a personal computer or a string of
pearls. Most services are open 24 hours a day and
deliver within 48 hours All you need is a phone
and a credit card. Most of the major stores –
Tiffany's, Saks, Barnes & Noble – produce catalogues (see above for their listings); some of the
major catalogues companies – Victoria's Secret,
Sharper Image – also have stores. If you have a
favourite shop, try the toll free directory (1-800
555 1212) to see if it has a listing. Otherwise, try
one of the following:

**Austads** *(1-800 759 4653)*. Essential for golfers,
Austad's novelty items are dead funny.

**LL Bean** *(1-800 221 4221)*. One of the top ten catalogue
companies: country clothing (denim, khaki etc) and home
accessories.

**Lillian Vernon** *(1-800 285 5555)*. Great gifts and nifty
little items.

**Mac Warehouse** *(1-800 255 6227)*. One of the most
affordable ways of laying your hands on any software
you need for your Apple Macintosh.

**Nature's Bounty** *(1-800 645 5412)*. A hypochondriac's
dream – page after page of every dietary supplement you
could possibly ingest.

**Orvis** *(1-800 815 5900)*. An established and reliable
source of sporting goods and clothing.

**Pottery Barn** *(1-800 922 5507)*. Cheap and fashionable
home furnishings with a vaguely ethnic or country
flavour.

## Opticians

### Alain Mikli Optique

*880 Madison Avenue, at 71st Street (472 6085). Subway*
*6 to 68th Street.* **Open** 10am-6pm Mon-Fri; 9.30am-7pm
Thur; 10.30am-6pm Sat. **Credit** AmEx, Disc, MC, V.
French frames and eyeglasses for the bold and beautiful are
available from this Madison Avenue outlet.

### Cohen's Optical

*117 Orchard Street, at Delancey Street (674 1986).*
*Subway F to Delancey Street; J to Essex Street.*
**Open** 9am-6pm daily. **Credit** AmEx, DC, MC, V.
The main branch of a large Manhattan firm (phone for the
location of their other branches). There are thousands of
frames in stock and most prescriptions (glasses or contact
lenses) can be dealt within the hour.

### MYOPTICS

*42 St Mark's Place, at Second Avenue (533 1577).*
*Subway 6 to Astor Place.* **Open** 11am-7pm Mon-Fri;
11am-6pm Sat; noon-5pm Sun. **Credit** AmEx, Disc, MC,
V.
A full optician's service, and frames by Matsuda, Oliver
Peoples, LA Eyeworks and Paul Smith.
**Branches:** 82 Christopher Street (741 9550); 96 Seventh
Avenue (633 6014).

# Spas & salons

As everyone knows, sightseeing is arduous work – the queues, the traffic, the crowds, oy vey! What better use of time, between the Met and MoMA, than to pamper yourself with a slimy seaweed wrap or a shiatsu pounding? Too expensive? But most spa treatments only cost the same as a nice sweater – say $60 or so. It's just a matter of choosing what treatment your body is most in need of.

The perfect Californian New Age experience can be had at the **Aveda Salon and Spa**, where everything is earth-friendly and even the air is scented with plant and flower essences. **Bliss Spa** is a bit more expensive than others (body wraps and scrubs cost $55-$175), but you'll have plenty of opportunities to mellow out in the relaxation area, where there are pitchers of chilled water with slices of lemon, soda, wine and snacks. **Carapan**, which is Pueblo Indian for 'a beautiful place of tranquillity where one comes to restore one's spirit', offers reiki ($80), Craniosacral therapy ($85) and manual lymph drainage (90 minutes for $125). **La Casa de Vida Natural New York Day Spa** (*above*) specialises in flotation, which costs $40, or $20 with another treatment. It's a nice cross between a paediatrician office and a tropical bordello – you can't miss the mini-waterfall.

**Frédéric Fekkai Beauté de Provence** is modelled after Fekkai's hometown of Aix-en-Provence. The hair services are especially good and range from a shea butter mask at $35 to an actual appointment with the hair god himself for $290. Both the **Elizabeth Arden Red Door Salon** and **Georgette Klinger** pride themselves on skin care. In other words, if you go in for a facial, you're probably walk out with $200 in products. At the much more crusty, though popular **Russian & Turkish Baths**, facilities include a Russian and Turkish steam room, sauna, Jacuzzi, ice-cold pool, Swedish shower, health bar and lounge with cable TV. And finally, find some Zen peace at **Kozué Aesthetic Spa**, where massages cost $50-$72, and there are seven kinds of body treatments to wrap yourself in. However spaced-out you feel at the end of your treatment, don't forget to leave a tip (15 to 20 per cent).

**Aveda Salon and Spa** *The Aveda Institute, 233 Spring Street, between Sixth Avenue & Varick Street (807 1492). Subway 1 or 9 to Houston Street; C or E to Spring Street.* **Open** *10am-7pm Mon-Fri; 10am-6pm Sat; noon-6pm Sun.* **Credit** *AmEx, MC, V.* **Branch:** *456 West Broadway (473 0280).*

**Bliss Spa** *Second Floor, 568 Broadway at Prince Street, (219 8970). Subway N or R to Prince Street.* **Open** *12.30-10pm Mon, Wed; 11am-8pm Tue, Thur, Fri.* **Credit** *AmEx, MC, V.*

**Carapan** *5 West 16th Street, between Fifth & Sixth Avenues (633 6220). Subway F to 14th Street.* **Open** *10am-9.30pm daily.* **Credit** *AmEx, MC, V.*

**Elizabeth Arden Red Door Salon** *691 Fifth Avenue, between 54th & 55th Streets (546 200). Subway E or F to Fifth Avenue.* **Open** *8am-6pm Mon, Tue, Fri, Sat; 8am-7.30pm Wed; 8am-8pm Thur; 9am-5pm Sun.* **Credit** *AmEx, MC, V.*

**Frédéric Fekkai Beauté de Provence** *Chanel, 15 East 57th Street, between Fifth & Madison Avenues (753 9500). Subway 4, 5, 6, N or R to 59th Street/Lexington Avenue.* **Open** *9am-6pm Mon-Wed, Fri, Sat; 9am-8pm Thur.* **Credit** *AmEx, MC, V.*

**Georgette Klinger** *501 Madison Avenue, at 53rd Street (838 3200). Subway E or F to Fifth Avenue.* **Open** *9am-8pm, Mon, Wed; 9am-6pm Tue, Thur, Fri; 9am-4pm Sat; 9am-3pm Sun.* **Credit** *AmEx, MC, V.* **Branch:** *978 Madison Avenue (744 6900).*

**Kozué Aesthetic Spa** *Second Floor, 795 Madison Avenue, between 67th & 68th Streets (734 8600). Subway 6 to 68th Street.* **Open** *11am-9pm Mon-Fri; 10am-6pm Sat, Sun.* **Credit** *AmEx, MC, V.*

**La Casa de Vida Natural New York Day Spa** *41 East 20th Street, between Park Avenue South & Broadway (673 2272). Subway 6 to 23rd Street.* **Open** *10.30am-4.30pm Mon; noon-6-8pm Tue Tue-Fri; 10am-8pm Wed-Fri; 10am-6pm Sat, Sun.* **Credit** *AmEx, MC, V.*

**Russian & Turkish Baths** *268 East 10th Street, between First Avenue & Avenue A (473 8806). Subway 6 to Astor Place.* **Open** *7.30am-10pm daily; women only Wed; men only Thur, Sun.* **Credit** *AmEx, Disc, MC, V.*

*Track that rare Broadway musical recording down at **Footlight Records**. See page 181.*

## Pharmacists

### Boyd's Chemists
*655 Madison Avenue, between 60th & 61st Streets (838 6558). Subway 4, 5, 6, N or R to 59th Street.* **Open** 8.30am-7.30pm Mon-Fri; 9.30am-7pm Sat; noon-6pm Sun. **Credit** AmEx, DC, Disc, JCB, MC, V.
This 50-year-old pharmacy, boutique and salon stocks the largest selection of hair accessories and eyeshadow ever assembled under one roof. It also offers facials, makeovers, manicures and so on. Boyd's has its own cosmetics line, Renoir, which includes all the hot matte shades from the 1960s that are so hard to find.

### Caswell-Massey
*518 Lexington Avenue, at East 48th Street (755 2254). Subway 6 to 51st Street.* **Open** 9am-7pm Mon-Fri; 10am-6pm Sat. **Credit** AmEx, Disc, MC, V.
America's oldest chemist was established back in 1752, and still supplies the types of product that are much appreciated: soaps made of almond cream, seaweed, lettuce or coconut oil; extracts of roses; fragrant oils; cucumber creams; huge sponges and loofahs.

### Duane Reade Drug Stores
*Empire State Building, 350 Fifth Avenue, at 34th Street (736 3100). Subway 1, 9, N or R to 42nd Street.* **Open** 7.30am-9pm Mon-Fri. **Credit** AmEx, Disc, MC, V.
This chain of stores offers good discounts on cosmetics, vitamins, soaps, shampoos and other essentials. There are branches everywhere; phone for the location of your nearest.

### Kiehl's
*109 Third Avenue, between 13th & 14th Streets (677 3171). Subway 4, 5, 6, L, N or R to 14th Street/Union Square.* **Open** 10am-6.30pm Mon-Fri; 10am-6pm Sat. **Credit** AmEx, DC, MC, V.
Kiehl's is practically a New York institution; once you stop by for a sample of the company's luxurious face cream, body lotion or silk groom for hair, you'll be hooked for life. Staff are knowledgeable and friendly.

### Kaufman Pharmacy
*Beverly Hotel, 557 Lexington Avenue, at 50th Street (755 2266). Subway E, F or 6 to 51st Street/Lexington Avenue.* **Open** 24 hours daily. **Credit** AmEx, MC, V.
New York's only all-night full-service pharmacy. You can take prescriptions here.

## Records, Tapes & CDs

### HMV
*1280 Lexington Avenue, at 86th Street (348 0800). Subway 4, 5 or 6 to 86th Street.* **Open** 9am-11pm Mon-Sat; 10am-10pm Sun. **Credit** AmEx, Disc, MC, V.
The biggest record shop in North America, with a jaw-dropping selection of vinyl, cassettes, CDs and videos (note that US videos won't play on UK VCRs).
**Branches**: 2081 Broadway (721 5900); 57 West 34th Street (629 0900).

### J&R Music World
*23 Park Row, between Beeckman & Ann Streets (238 9000). Subway 4, 5, 6 to Brooklyn Bridge/City Hall; J, M, Z to Chambers Street.* **Open** 9am-6.30pm Mon-Sat; 11am-6pm Sun. **Credit** AmEx, Disc, MC, V.
J&R is a block long. You'll find box sets, jazz, Latin and popular titles by such luminaries as Madonna and Prince.

### Tower Records
*692 Broadway, at 4th Street (505 1500). Subway N or R to 8th Street.* **Open** 9am-midnight daily. **Credit** AmEx, Disc, MC, V.
All the current sounds on CD and tape. Visit the clearance store round the block at Lafayette for knockdown stuff in all formats, including vinyl of all kinds, especially classical.
**Branch**: 1961 Broadway (799 2500).

## Virgin Megastore

*1540 Broadway, between 45th & 46th Streets (921 1020). Subway 1, 2, 3, 7, 9, N, R or S to Times Square/ 42nd Street.* **Open** 9am-1am Mon-Thur, Sun; 9am-2am Fri, Sat. **Credit** AmEx, Disc, MC, V.

As far as enormous record stores go, this one is pretty good. Check out the Virgin soda machine and keep an eye out for dates of in-store performances. Vinyl is available.

# Dance

## 8-Ball Records

*105 East 9th Street, between Third & Fourth Avenues (473 6343). Subway 6 to Astor Place.* **Open** noon-9pm Mon-Sat; 1-7pm Sun. **Credit** AmEx, MC, V.

Since the label owns the store, this is where you'll get those 8-Ball faves first. It's also a great house resource, with a broad range of imports and a fruitful bargain bin.

## Dance Tracks

*91 East 3rd Street, at First Avenue (260 8729). Subway F to Second Avenue.* **Open** noon-9pm Mon-Thur; noon-10pm Fri; noon-8pm Sat; 1-6.30pm Sun. **Credit** AmEx, Disc, MC, V.

Hot off the plane with those Euro imports (nearly as cheap to buy here) and with fast-flowing racks of domestic house, dangerously enticing bins of Loft/Paradise Garage classics and private decks to listen on, Dance Tracks is a must.

## Fat Beats

*Second Floor, 406 Sixth Avenue, between 8th & 9th Streets (673 3883). Subway A, B, C, D, E, F to West 4th Street.* **Open** noon-9pm Mon-Thur; noon-10pm Fri, Sat; noon-8pm Sun. **Credit** MC, V.

This is hip-hop central. A small store with a large selection of the latest in hip-hop, acid jazz and reggae.

# Specialist

## Adult Crash

*66 Avenue A, between 4th & 5th Streets (387 0558). Subway F to Second Avenue.* **Open** noon-11pm Mon-Thur, Sun; noon-11pm Fri, Sat. **Credit** AmEx, Disc, MC, V.

This small shop stocks the finest variety of post-punk punk and pop from America, New Zealand, Australia, Japan and the UK. There are new and used CDs, vinyl, 'zines, books and clothes.

## Bleecker Bob's Golden Oldies

*118 West 3rd Street, between Sixth Avenue & MacDougal Street (475 9677). Subway A, B, C, D, E, F or Q to West 4th Street.* **Open** noon-1am Mon-Thur, Sun; noon-3am Fri, Sat. **Credit** AmEx, MC, V.

Imports, independents, deleted records, tapes and CDs and all sorts of rarities are sold here. It's the place to go when you really can't find what you want anywhere else.

## Footlight Records

*113 East 12th Street, between Third & Fourth Avenues (533 1572). Subway 4, 5, 6, N, R to 14th Street/Union Square.* **Open** 11am-7pm Mon-Fri; 10am-6pm Sat; noon-5pm Sun. **Credit** AmEx, DC, MC, V.

Ron Saja and Richard Brezner own this spectacular store which specialises in vocalists, cast recordings and film soundtracks.

## Gryphon Record Shop

*251 West 72nd Street, between Broadway & West End Avenue (874 1588). Subway 1, 2, 3 or 9 to 72nd Street.* **Open** 11am-7pm Mon-Sat; noon-6pm Sun. **Credit** MC, V.

A solidly classical store, with a sprinkling of jazz and show music. Vinyl only.

## Jazz Record Center

*Eighth floor, 236 West 26th Street, between Seventh & Eighth Avenues (675 4480). Subway C, E or L to 23rd Street.* **Open** 10am-6pm Tue-Sat. **Credit** AmEx, MC, V.

The best jazz shop in the city, selling current and out-of-print records. You can have your purchases shipped worldwide.

## Kim's Underground

*6 St Mark's Place, between Second & Third Avenues (598 9985). Subway 6 to Astor Place.* **Open** 9am-midnight daily. **Credit** AmEx, MC, V.

Located in the old St Mark's Baths, this gigantic music store carries more vinyl and CDs than you'd think possible. **Branches:** 144 Bleecker Street (387 8250); 350 Bleecker Street (675 8996).

## Midnight Records

*263 West 23rd Street, between Seventh & Eighth Avenues (675 2768). Subway C or E to 23rd Street.* **Open** 10am-6pm Tue-Sat. **Credit** ($15 minimum) AmEx, MC, V.

A great place for rarities and hard-to-find rock records. The 1960s and 1970s are the years Midnight does best.

## Other Music

*15 East 4th Street, between Broadway & Lafayette Streets (477 8150). Subway 6 to Astor Place.* **Open** noon-9pm Mon-Sat; noon-7pm Sun. **Credit** AmEx, MC, V.

This music store is a gem; owned by three former Kim's slaves (*above*), it stocks a full selection of indie, ambient, kraut rock, psychedelia, noise and French pop. The luscious François Hardy is practically everywhere you turn.

## Record Mart

*Times Square subway station, near the N & R platform (840 0580). Subway 1, 2, 3, 9, N, R, S to 42nd Street.* **Open** 9am-9pm Mon-Thur; 9am-11pm Fri; 10am-10pm Sat; noon-8pm Sun. **Credit** MC, V.

It costs the price of a subway token to get in, but Record Mart stocks the largest selection of Caribbean and Latin American music in the city with much of it still on vinyl.

## Rocks in Your Head

*157 Prince Street, between Thompson & West Broadway (475 6729). Subway A, B, C, D, E, F to W 4th Street; C, E to Spring Street.* **Open** noon-9pm daily. **Credit** MC, V.

Good for vinyl browsing. You'll find plenty of indie and alt-rock LPs as well as singles and ten-inches.

## St Mark's Sounds

*16 & 20 St Mark's Place, between Second & Third Avenues (677 3444). Subway N or R to 8th Street; 6 to Astor Place.* **Open** noon-10.30pm Mon-Thur; noon-11.30pm Fri, Sat. **No credit cards.**

Two stores situated side by side: one is smaller and features new releases, the other focuses more on budget vinyl.

## Subterranean Records

*5 Cornelia Street, between West 4th & Bleecker Streets (463 8900). Subway A, B, C, D, E, F or Q to West 4th Street.* **Open** noon-7pm Mon-Thur, Sun; noon-8pm Fri, Sat. **Credit** AmEx, MC, V.

It's an indie world at Subterranean, which focuses attention on that genre as well as alt rock and its predecessors.

## Venus Records

*13 St Mark's Place, between Second & Third Avenues (598 4459). Subway N or R to 8th Street; 6 to Astor Place.* **Open** noon-8pm Mon-Thur, Sun; noon-11pm Fri, Sat. **Credit** AmEx, Disc, MC, V.

The basement is filled with excellent vinyl – hardcore, country, rock, jazz – and the main floor stocks second-hand CDs. Prices are usually good. Gets crowded at the weekend.

# Cameras & Camcorders

## B&S Camera Repair
*110 West 30th Street, between Sixth & Seventh Avenues (563 1651). Subway N or R to 28th Street.* **Open** 9am-6.30pm Mon-Fri; 11am-4pm Sat. **Credit** AmEx, MC, V.
All kinds of camera and camcorder problems can be solved here, with an eye to speed if necessary.

# Computers

## Emergency Computer Repairs
*250 West 57th Street, between Eighth & Ninth Avenues (586 9319/1-800 586 9319). Subway N or R to 57th Street.* **Open** noon-midnight daily. **Credit** AmEx, Disc, MC, V.
Specialists in Apples, IBMs and all related peripherals. Staff can recover your lost data and soothe you through all manner of computer disasters. On-site repairs.

# Leather

## R&S Cleaners
*176 Second Avenue, near 11th Street (674 6651). Subway 4, 5, 6, L, N or R to 14th Street/Union Square.* **Open** *Sept-July* 7.30am-6.30pm Mon-Fri, 7.30am-5pm Sat; *Aug* 7.30am-6.30pm Mon-Fri; 7.30am-noon Sat. **No credit cards**.
Specialists in cleaning, repairing and tailoring leather jackets; prices start at $30 and cleaning generally takes three to five business days (24-hour service available).

# Clothes

## Raymond's Tailor Shop
*306 Mott Street, between Houston & Bleecker Streets (226 0747). Subway 6 to Bleecker Street; B, D or F to Broadway/Lafayette Street.* **Open** 7.30am-7.30pm Mon-Fri; 9am-6.30pm Sat. **No credit cards**.
Raymond's can do alterations and repairs to 'anything that can be worn on the body'. There's also an emergency service; delivery and collection is free over much of Manhattan.

# Shoes

## European Shoe Repair
*124 Fulton Street, at Nassau Street (227 5818). Subway 2, 3 or 4 to Fulton Street.* **Open** 7.30am-6.30pm Mon-Fri. **No credit cards**.
All leather repairs undertaken, from shoes to jackets, with the advantage of a pick-up and delivery service.
**Branch**: 113 East 31st Street (889 7258).

# Watches

## Falt Watch Company
*Third floor, Grand Central Station, 42nd Street, at Park Avenue (697 6380). Subway 4, 5, 6 or 7 to Grand Central.* **Open** 10am-5pm Tue-Fri. **No credit cards**.
Staff will repair just about any watch.

West 8th Street has a large number of shoe shops full of sneakers, boots and designer seconds. For shoe repairs, *see above*.

## Aldo
*700 Broadway, at 4th Street (982 0958). Subway 6 to Astor Place.* **Open** 10am-8pm Mon-Sat; noon-7pm Sun. **Credit** AmEx, MC, V.
This Montreal-based company sells trademark shoes, boots and handbags.

## Anbar Shoes
*60 Reade Street, between Church Street & Broadway (227 0253). Subway 1, 2, 3 or 9 to Chambers Street.* **Open** 9am-6.30pm Mon-Fri; 11am-6pm Sat. **Credit** AmEx, Disc, MC, V.
You can save up to 70 per cent on Jourdan, Ferragamo and other high-priced footwear at this two-floor emporium.

## Athlete's Foot
*390 Fifth Avenue, at 36th Street (947 6972). Subway 6 to 33rd Street.* **Open** 10am-8pm Mon-Sat; noon-7pm Sun. **Credit** AmEx, Disc, MC, V.
Best of all the sneaker-led chainstores, with the widest selections and the newest models, plus minimal amounts of casual sports gear. Phone for the location of your nearest branch.

## Billy Martin's
*810 Madison Avenue, at 68th Street (861 3100). Subway 4, 5, 6 to 68th Street/Hunter College.* **Open** 10am-7pm Mon-Fri; 10am-6pm Sat; noon-5pm Sun. **Credit** AmEx, MC, V.
Founded in 1978 by ex-Yankee manager Billy Martin and ex-Yankee slugger Mickey Mantle, this western superstore features heaps of cowboy boots in all colours and sizes.

## John Fluevog
*104 Prince Street, between Mercer & Greene Streets (431 4484). Subway N or R to Prince Street.* **Open** 11am-7pm Mon-Sat; noon-6pm Sun. **Credit** AmEx, JCB, MC, V.
Unique, stylish, often outrageous and definitely unmissable.

## McCreedy & Schreiber
*37 West 46th Street, between Fifth & Sixth Avenues (719 1552). Subway 1, 2, 3, 7, N or R to Times Square.* **Open** 9am-7pm Mon-Sat. **Credit** AmEx, DC, Disc, MC, V.
This well-known quality men's shoe shop is good for all traditional American styles: Bass Weejuns, Sperry Topsiders, Frye boots and the famous Lucchese boots in everything from goatskin to crocodile.
**Branch**: 213 East 59th Street (759 9241).

## Manolo Blahnik
*15 West 55th Street, between Fifth & Sixth Avenues (582 3007). Subway B, D, F or Q to Rockefeller Center.* **Open** 10.30am-6pm Mon-Fri; 10.30am-5.30pm Sat. **Credit** AmEx, MC, V.
From the high priest of style, timeless shoes in innovative designs and maximum taste.

## Martinez Valero
*1029 Third Avenue, at East 61st Street (753 1822). Subway 4, 5 or 6 to 59th Street; B, N or R to Lexington Avenue.* **Open** 10am-8pm Mon-Fri; 11am-7pm Sat; noon-6pm Sun. **Credit** AmEx, DC, MC, V.
These beautiful Spanish shoes are made in combinations of coloured suede and leather. Styles range from elegant but practical flats to sleek heels. The men's shoes are just as well made, although a bit less vibrant.

## Steve Madden
*540 Broadway, between Prince & Spring Streets (343 1800). Subway N, R to Prince Street; 6 to Spring Street.* **Open** 10.45am-8.30pm Mon-Sat; 11.30am-7.30pm Sun. **Credit** AmEx, MC, V.
Funky styles for all seasons at deeply reasonable prices. There's almost always a decent sale.

## Timberland

*709 Madison Avenue, on the corner of 63rd Street (754 0434). Subway 4, 5 or 6 to 59th Street; N or R to Lexington Avenue.* **Open** 10am-6.30pm Mon-Fri; 10am-6pm Sat; noon-5pm Sun. **Credit** AmEx, MC, V.
The complete American line of Timberland shoes and boots for men and women is sold here, marginally cheaper than in Europe. The ruggedly elegant apparel is also available.

## Tootsi Plohound

*413 West Broadway, between Prince & Spring Streets (925 8931). Subway N or R to Prince Street.* **Open** 11.30am-7.30pm Mon-Fri; 11am-8pm Sat; noon-7pm Sun. **Credit** AmEx, MC, V.
One of the best places for shoes, Tootsi carries a good range of stylish imports, especially flats and lace-ups, at tolerable prices. Note the wide and witty selection of socks for women. **Branch:** 137 Fifth Avenue (460 8650).

## V.I.M.

*686 Broadway, between 3rd & 4th Streets (677 8364). Subway B, D, F, Q or 6 to Bleecker Street or Broadway/Lafayette Street.* **Open** 10am-8pm Mon-Sat; 11am-7pm Sun. **Credit** AmEx, MC, V.
They treat sneakers like hit singles, with a 'latest release' display. One of the largest selections of athletic footwear in the city, complete with overhead monorail delivery system. **Branches:** 15 West 34th Street (736 4989); 16 West 14th Street (255 2262).

## JM Weston

*812 Madison Avenue, at 68th Street (535 2100). Subway 6 to 68th Street.* **Open** 10am-6pm Mon-Wed, Fri, Sat; 10am-7pm Thur. **Credit** AmEx, MC, V.
JM Weston shoes appeal to such diverse men as Woody Allen, Yves Saint Laurent and the King of Morocco. The beautiful, handmade shoes are available in 34 styles: 'Weston's don't fit you; you fit them', said Robert Deslauriers, the man who established the Manhattan store. The shop also stocks women's shoes – and they're also expensive.

# Speciality Shops & Services

## Arthur Brown & Bros

*2 West 46th Street, between Fifth & Sixth Avenues (575 5555). Subway B, D, F or Q to Rockefeller Center.* **Open** 9am-6.30pm Mon-Fri, 10am-6pm Sat. **Credit** AmEx, DC, Disc, MC, V.
Pens of the world unite at Arthur Brown's, which has one of the largest selections anywhere, including Mont Blanc, Cartier, Dupont, Porsche and Schaeffer.

## Big City Kite Company

*1210 Lexington Avenue, at 82nd Street (472 2623). Subway 4, 5 or 6 to 86th Street.* **Open** 11am-6.30pm Mon-Wed, Fri; 10am-6pm Sat; 11am-7.30pm Thur; noon-5pm Sun. **Credit** AmEx, Disc, JCB, MC, V.
Go fly a kite – there are over 150 to chose from here, with all kinds of visual and acrobatic properties.

## Collectors' Stadium

*17 Warren Street, between Church Street & Broadway (353 1531). Subway 1, 2, 3 or 9 to Chambers Street.* **Open** 10am-6pm Mon-Fri; 10am-5pm Sat. **Credit** AmEx, MC, V.
This is where you may be able to find that elusive card to complete your 1938 set of Yankees baseball cards – or just ponder a US obsession.

## Condomania

*351 Bleecker Street, at 10th Street (691 9442). Subway 1 or 9 to Christopher Street.* **Open** 11am-10.45pm Sun-Thur; 11am-11.45pm Fri, Sat. **Credit** AmEx, DC, Disc, JCB, MC, V.
Condoms in all shapes, sizes, flavours and colours. The biggest selection anywhere.

## Evolution

*120 Spring Street, between Greene & Mercer Streets (343 1114). Subway C or E to Spring Street.* **Open** 11am-7pm daily. **Credit** AmEx, Disc, JCB, MC, V.
If you are into natural history and would like to take some home, this is the store for you. Insects in plexiglass, giraffe skulls, sea shells and wild boar tusks are among the items for sale in this relatively politically correct store – the animals died of natural causes or were culled.

## Game Show

*1240 Lexington Avenue, at 83rd Street (472 8011). Subway 4, 5 or 6 to 86th Street.* **Open** 11am-6pm Mon-Wed, Fri, Sat; 11am-7pm Thur; noon-5pm Sun. **Credit** AmEx, MC, V.
Every board game imaginable, and plenty that you'll be quite surprised/intrigued/offended to discover.

## Goldberg's Marine Distributors

*12 West 37th Street, between Fifth & Sixth Avenues (594 6065). Subway B, D, F or Q to 34th Street.* **Open** 9am-6pm Mon-Sat; 10am-6pm Sun. **Credit** AmEx, Disc, MC, V.
'Where thousands of boaters save millions of dollars,' is Goldberg's intriguing slogan: get your marine supplies, fishing gear, nautical fashion and deck shoes here.

## Jerry Ohlinger's Movie Material Store

*242 West 14th Street, between Seventh & Eighth Avenues (989 0869). Subway 1, 2, 3, 9, A, C, E, L to 14th Street.* **Open** 1-7.45pm daily. **Credit** AmEx, Disc, MC, V.
Ohlinger has an extensive stock of 'paper material' from movies past and present – includes photos, programmes, posters and lists of information on the stars.

## Karen's for People & Pets

*1195 Lexington Avenue, between 81st & 82nd Streets (628 2312). Subway 4, 5 or 6 to 86th Street.* **Open** 8am-6pm Mon-Fri; 9am-6pm Sat. **Credit** AmEx, MC, V.
Karen designs and manufactures witty clothing, accessories and even fitted sheets for the dog, cat or canary in your life.

## Kate Spade

*59 Thompson Street, between Broome & Spring Streets (965 0301). Subway C or E to Spring Street.* **Open** 11am-7pm Mon-Sat; noon-6pm Sun. **Credit** AmEx, MC, V.
Cult handbag designer Kate Spade sells affordable, chic bags ($80-$400) from her stylish store.

## Metropolitan Opera Shop

*331 West 65th Street, at Broadway (580 4090). Subway 6 to 68th Street.* **Open** 10am-9.30pm Mon-Sat. **Credit** AmEx, Disc, MC, V.
This Upper East Side outlet of the Metropolitan Opera sells CDs, cassettes and laser discs of every opera imaginable. There's also a wealth of opera memorabilia.

## Nat Sherman

*500 Fifth Avenue, at 42nd Street (246 5500). Subway 4, 5, 6, 7 or S to 42nd Street/Grand Central.* **Open** 9am-7pm Mon-Fri; 10am-5.30pm Sat; 11am-5pm Sun. **Credit** AmEx, DC, MC, V.
Just across the street from the glorious New York Public Library, Nat Sherman specialises in 'slow burning' cigarettes, cigars and smoking accoutrements from a cigar hostler to a smoking chair. Upstairs is the famous smoking room where you can test out your tobacco.

# Time Out

# Film
## Guide

## Edited by John Pym

**Annually updated, the *Time Out* Film Guide is a comprehensive A-Z of films from every area of world cinema and has stronger international coverage than any other film guide.**

Each entry includes full details of director, cast, running time, release date and reviews from the *Time Out* magazine critics. There are also indexes covering films by country, genre, subject, director and actor. So if you want to get the lowdown on a film, pick up the latest edition of the *Time Out* Film Guide - available in a bookshop near you.

**'Without doubt, the "bible" for film buffs.'**
*British Film and TV Academy News*

## Paramount Vending

*1158 Second Avenue, at 61st Street (279 1095). Subway 4 or 6 to 59th Street.* **Open** 10am-6pm Mon-Fri. **Credit** AmEx, Disc, MC, V.
An excellent source of second-hand jukeboxes, pinball machines and bowling machines.

## Pearl Paint Co

*308 Canal Street, between Church Street & Broadway (431 7932). Subway 6, A, C, E, J, N, M, R or Z to Canal Street.* **Open** 9am-6pm Mon-Wed, Fri; 9am-7pm Thur; 9am-5.30pm Sun. **Credit** AmEx, Disc, MC, V.
Pearl Paint is as big as a supermarket, and supplies everything you could possibly need to be artistic.

## Pearl River Chinese Products Emporium

*277 Canal Street, corner of Broadway (431 4770). Subway 6, B, D, J, M, N, R or Z to Canal Street.* **Open** 10am-7.30pm daily. **Credit** AmEx, MC, V.
In this downtown emporium you can find all things Chinese, from clothing to pots, woks, teapots, groceries, bonsai, medicinal herbs and traditional stationery. Cheap.

## Poster America Gallery

*138 West 18th Street, between Sixth & Seventh Avenues (206 0499). Subway 1 or 9 to 18th Street.* **Open** 11am-6pm Tue-Sat. **Credit** AmEx, MC, V.
The gallery has extensive stocks of original advertising posters from 1880 onwards from both sides of the Atlantic.

## Quark Spy Center

*537 Third Avenue, at 35th Street (889 1808). Subway 6 to 33rd Street.* **Open** 9am-6pm Mon-Fri; by appointment only Sat. **Credit** AmEx, MC, V.
A little creepy, but worth a visit if you're curious or interested in donning some body armour, or hooking your flat up with all the bug detectors James Bond could ever wish for.

## Rand McNally Map & Travel Center

*150 East 52nd Street, between Lexington & Third Avenues (758 7488). Subway 6 to 51st Street; E or F to Lexington Avenue.* **Open** 9am-6pm Mon-Fri; 11am-5pm Sat; noon-5pm Sun. **Credit** AmEx, Disc, JCB, MC, V.
Rand McNally stocks maps, atlases and globes, published by rival publishers as well as their own products.

## Spike's Joint

*1 South Elliott Place, Brooklyn (1-718 802 1000). Subway D, M, N, Q or R to DeKalb Avenue.* **Open** noon-7pm Mon-Fri; 10am-7pm Sat; noon-6pm Sun. **Credit** AmEx, MC, V.
A gang of funky memorabilia from Mr Lee's movies, plus an exclusive line of jeans and jackets with the 40 Acres & a Mule label. Spike lives around the corner.

## Stack's Coin Company

*123 West 57th Street, between Sixth & Seventh Avenues (582 2580). Subway B, N, Q or R to 57th Street.* **Open** 10am-5pm Mon-Fri. **No credit cards**.
The largest and longest-established coin dealer in the USA, dealing in rare and ancient coins from all over the world.

# Sports

## Blades Downtown

*659 Broadway, between Bleecker & Bond Streets (477 7350). Subway B, D, F or Q to Broadway/Lafayette Street.* **Open** 11am-9pm Mon-Sat; noon-7pm Sun. **Credit** AmEx, MC, V.
This is where to come for those rollerblades, as well as a wide range of skateboard and snowboard equipment and clothing. Phone for the location of other branches.

## Gerry Cosby

*3 Pennsylvania Plaza, inside Madison Square Garden (563 6464). Subway 1, 2, 3 or 9 to 34th Street.* **Open** 9.30am-6.30pm Mon-Fri; 9.30am-6pm Sat; noon-5pm Sun. **Credit** AmEx, Disc, MC, V.
A huge selection of official team-wear and other sporting necessaries.

## Modell's

*51 East 42nd Street, at Madison Avenue (661 4242). Subway 4, 5, 6 or 7 to Grand Central.* **Open** 8am-8pm Mon-Fri; 9am-6pm Sat; 11am-6pm Sun. **Credit** AmEx, DC, MC. V.
A comprehensive range of sporting equipment and clothing at competitive prices.
**Branches:** 901 Sixth Avenue (594 1830); 200 Broadway (964 4007); 280 Broadway (962 6200).

## Niketown

*6 East 57th Street, between Fifth & Madison Avenues (891 6453). Subway 4, 5, 6, N, R to 59th Street/Lexington Avenue.* **Open** 10am-8pm Mon-Fri; 10am-7pm Sat, 11am-6pm Sun. **Credit** AmEx, Disc, JCB, MC, V.
Every 20 minutes a huge screen drops down and plays a Nike ad and there are interactive CD-ROMs to help you make your choice. Don't scoff – you may need some help: there are 1,200 kinds of footwear to choose from.

## Paragon Sporting Goods Co

*867 Broadway, near East 18th Street (255 8036). Subway 4, 5, 6, L, N or R to 14th Street/Union Square.* **Open** 10am-8pm Mon-Sat; 11am-6.30pm Sun. **Credit** AmEx, Disc, MC, V.
A full line of sports equipment and sportswear is available at this old-fashioned store. There's a good range of swimwear, surfwear, tennis rackets, climbing gear and shoes.

# Tattoos & Piercing

Tattooing is only legal in New York by private arrangement – you can't drop in off the street. Check the advertisements on the back page of the *Village Voice* for more information. Piercing is completely unregulated, so be discriminating.

## Cicada Body Adornments

*130 East 7th Street, between Avenue A & First Avenue (353 0726). Subway 6 to Astor Place; F to Second Avenue.* **Open** noon-10pm daily. **Credit** AmEx, MC, V.
It's a self-mutilator's dream at Cicada, where body adornment is taken to a new level. Discs of stainless steel, hand-made coloured glass and imported wood from Burma and Laos are used to stretch earlobes; custom barbell navel rings are available, as are exotic stones. Piercing is done on the very sterile premises.

## Gauntlet

*144 Fifth Avenue, at 19th Street (229 0180). Subway N or R to 23rd Street.* **Open** 12.30-7.30pm Mon-Sat. **Credit** AmEx, MC, V.
A place with unrivalled experience, Gauntlet is where to go if you aren't satisfied with the holes you were born with. A Prince Albert costs $35, though navels, nipples and noses remain the more popular perforations.

## Temptu

*Fifth Floor, 26 West 17th Street, between Fifth & Sixth Avenues (675 4000). Subway 4, 5, 6, N, R or L to Union Square; F to 14th Street.* **Open** 9am-5pm Mon-Fri. **Credit** MC, V.
For those who can't take the needle, this is the home of the temporary tattoo. It has every design imaginable in paint-

on, water-based and rubbing alcohol formats. Prices start at $1.25 a sheet. Temptu gave Robert DeNiro those nasty tats for Cape Fear.

## Television & Video

Current ID (such as a passport) plus a credit card, and sometimes proof of address, are needed if you want to rent a video from any of the following outlets. US videos are NTSC format and don't work in UK or Australian VCR machines, which are PAL.

### Columbus TV & Video Center
*552 Columbus Avenue, at 86th Street (496 2626). Subway 1, 9, B or C to 86th Street.* **Open** 9am-7pm Mon-Fri; 9am-6pm Sat. **Credit** AmEx, Disc, MC, V.
VCRs and TVs of all types available for hire.

### Couch Potato Video
*9 East 8th Street, at University Place (260 4260). Subway N or R to 8th Street.* **Open** 10am-10pm Mon-Sat; noon-10pm Sun. **Credit** AmEx, MC, V.
No membership is required at this video store, which delivers within a ten-mile radius of the shop.

### Evergreen Video
*37 Carmine Street, between Bleecker & Bedford Streets (691 7362). Subway A, B, C, D, E, F, Q to West 4th Street/Washington Square.* **Open** 10am-10pm Mon-Thur; noon-10pm Fri-Sun. **Credit** AmEx, MC, V.
Steve Feltes launched Evergreen as a mail-order company, renting and selling videos of independent and foreign films. It grew into a rental business, due to the popularity of its owner and local demand for offbeat titles. Evergreen remains the best place to purchase hard-to-find laser discs and videos, and the staff can order whatever you can't find.

### Kim's Video
*6 St Mark's Place, between Second & Third Avenues (505 0311). Subway 6 to Astor Place.* **Open** 8am-midnight daily. **Credit** ($20 minimum) AmEx, MC, V.
If Kim's doesn't have it, no one else will. Kim's stocks over 7,000 titles and specialises in cult, classic and foreign films. **Branches**: 85 Avenue A (529 3410); 144 Bleecker Street (260 1010); 350 Bleecker Street (675 8996).

### Tower Video
*1961 Broadway, at 66th Street (496 2500). Subway 1 or 9 to 66th Street.* **Open** 9am-midnight daily. **Credit** AmEx, MC, V.
Tower sells and rents out every type of video – culture, exercise, theatrical, special interest, music, the lot.
**Branches**: 1721 Fifth Avenue (838 8110); 383 Lafayette Street (505 1500).

## Visas

### Visa Express Inc
*421 Seventh Avenue, at 33rd Street (629 4541). Subway A, C or E to 34th Street.* **Open** 10.30am-6pm Mon-Fri. **Credit** MC, V.
Visas for all countries can be obtained here, for individual or business use, though not extensions to tourist visas.

## Weddings

So you want to get hitched in Manhattan? Whether it's a complicated affair or just a laid-back trip to City Hall, look no further. For rings, *see page 173* **Jewellery**; most bridal shops stock veils, but if you're in the mood for something different, *see page 171* **Hats**.

## Bridal Wear

*See also page 161* **Blue**, *page 163* **Mary Adams**, *page 159* **ZellerTuxedos** *and* **Just Once**.

### Ghost Tailor
*80 Fifth Avenue, at 14th Street (645 1930). Subway F to Sixth Avenue.* **Open** by appointment only. **Credit** AmEx, MC, V.
Gorgeous custom-made dresses for brides who are anything but conventional.

### Kleinfeld
*82nd Street & Fifth Avenue, Bay Ridge, Brooklyn (1-718 833 1100). Subway R to 86th Street.* **Open** 11am-9pm Tue, Thur; 10am-6pm Wed, Fri; 9am-6pm Sat, Sun. **Credit** AmEx, MC, V.
Kleinfeld, which opened in 1940 as a fur store, is one of the biggest names in the wedding business. Everything from veils to pumps to gowns.

### Legacy
*109 Thompson Street, between Spring & Prince Streets (966 4827). Subway N, R to Prince Street; C, E to Spring Street.* **Open** noon-7pm daily. **Credit** AmEx, MC, V.
Rita Brookoff carries a number of low-priced dresses by little-known designers, including Heather Scott and Colleen MacCallum.

### Vera Wang Bridal House
*991 Madison Avenue, at 77th Street (628 3400). Subway 6 to 77th Street.* **Open** by appointment only. **Credit** AmEx, MC, V.
Bridal creations at Wang's famous wedding boutique.

## Groom Wear

### D/L Cerney
*13 East 7th Street, between Second & Third Avenues (673 7033). Subway 6 to Astor Place.* **Open** noon-8pm daily.
A vintage shop specialising in menswear from the 1930s to the 1960s. For the swanky groom.

## Ceremonies

### Civil Marriage Ceremony
*City Hall (669 2400).*
To get married in NYC, find your nearest City Hall by calling the number above. You'll need a $30 money order to cover the marriage licence. After 24 hours, you can get married. The ceremony costs $25; and you don't need a blood test.

### Local Judges
You can reach the Hon Howard Goldfluss, who's appeared on Gordon Elliot and Geraldo Rivera, on 421 5300. If the waiting list is too long, phone 417 4911 for a list of former judges willing to perform wedding ceremonies.

### Marcy Blum & Associates
*(688 3057)*
An international wedding consultancy that will arrange every last detail for people who want a romantic experience without the traditional complications.

# Museums & Galleries

# Museums

**From the vast treasure houses of the Museum Mile to the dozens of specialist collections, New York is a museum-addict's paradise.**

New York's museums are superb. More than 60 institutions hold collections of everything from art, antiquities and hands-on science to Ukrainian folk costumes and doll collections. The buildings themselves are equally impressive and eclectic. Nearly everyone stops dead when they see the spiral **Guggenheim** for the first time, and the seemingly incongruous granite-cube of the **Whitney Museum**, with its cyclops-eye window and concrete moat, is nothing if not striking.

It's hard not to exhaust yourself trying to cram too many museums into one day or, worse still, take in all the collections at a major museum such as the **Metropolitan Museum of Art** or the **American Museum of Natural History**. Pace yourself: some museums have excellent cafés or restaurants so you can break for coffee or a full-blown meal. Sarabeth's at the Whitney, Dean & DeLuca at the Guggenheim, MoMA at the Museum of Modern Art, the Museum Café in the Pierpont Morgan Library and the Jewish Museum's Café Weissman all provide an excellent excuse to take a break from the displays.

Museum admission prices may come as a shock, but entry really costs no more than the price of a movie ticket. This is because most New York museums are funded privately and not by government money, and is partly why the **New York Historical Society** – the city's oldest museum – had to close for two years (it has now re-opened). However, most of the city's major museums, including the Metropolitan, the Whitney and the **Museum of Modern Art**, offer the public at least one evening a week when admission is free or by voluntary donation.

Many of New York's famous, more established museums – such as the **Frick Collection**, the **Pierpont Morgan Library**, the Whitney and the Guggenheim – started out as private collections. **The Cloisters**, at the northern tip of Manhattan in Fort Tryon Park, was John D Rockefeller's gift. It's a reconstructed Gothic monastery housing the Met's medieval collection. When the sun's shining and the sky's a deep blue, take a picnic, admire the red tiled roof and inhale the delicate scents from the garden. Unmissable.

Also try not to miss the audio tour at the thought-provoking **Ellis Island Museum**, or the tour at the **Lower East Side Tenement Museum**. Both give visitors an insight into the multi-cultural 'melting pot' that makes up the city, and goes a long way towards explaining why many New Yorkers are driven, ambitious and 'in your face'. The **Liberty Science Center**, with its hands-on exhibits and rooftop terrace overlooking Manhattan and the Statue of Liberty, is an unexpected pleasure. If you go at the weekend when the ferry service is operating, it doubles as a sightseeing trip.

The prize for most neglected museum has to go to the **Brooklyn Museum of Art**. Its size and grandeur come as a shock as you emerge from the subway station, but there's an even greater surprise inside: the excellent exhibits. Even though it's the second largest museum in New York, it rarely draws the huge crowds that head for museums in Manhattan. And that's a shame, for its Egyptian collection rivals the Met's.

It might be traditional to save museums for a rainy day, but since most are air-conditioned they also offer a glorious respite from summer heat.

*Most of New York's museums are closed on New Year's Day, Washington's Birthday, Memorial Day, Independence Day, Labor Day, Columbus Day, Thanksgiving and Christmas Day. Some change their opening hours in summer, so it's wise to check before setting out.*

## Major Museums

### American Museum of Natural History

*Central Park West, at 79th Street (769 5000/recorded information 769 5100). Subway B or C to 86th Street.* **Open** 10am-5.45pm Mon-Thur, Sun; 10am-8.45pm Fri, Sat. **Admission** suggested donation $7; $4-$5 concessions. **Credit** (gift shop only) AmEx, MC, V.
The fun begins immediately, as a towering Barosaur, rearing high on hind legs, protects its young from an attacking Allosaurus in the main rotunda. It's an impressive welcome from the largest museum of its kind in the world, and signals its most recent achievement: the re-opening of the fourth-floor dinosaur halls after a four-year, $12-million renovation. The resulting gallery banishes memories of the dark dusty halls, whose low ceilings have been removed to reveal the original vaults and panoramic views of Central Park. The new exhibits, designed by the firm responsible for much of the excellent Ellis Island Museum, have been a great success, with several specimens being remodelled in the light of

*Sixteenth century unicorn, trapped at the* **Metropolitan Museum of Art**. *See p191.*

When it came to his library, **JP Morgan** wanted more than a few shelves from IKEA. See p194.

recent discoveries. The Tyrannosaurus Rex, for instance, was once believed to walk upright, Godzilla-style: now it stalks, head down, with tail parallel to the ground and is altogether more menacing. The rest of the museum is equally impressive. There's a particularly good Native American section and a stunning collection of gems, including the obscenely large Star of India blue sapphire. There's also an Imax theatre showing nature programmes and innovative temporary exhibitions, such as the recent CD-ROM audio guide around the museum's permanent collection.
*Disabled: toilets.*

## Brooklyn Museum of Art

*200 Eastern Parkway, at Washington Avenue, Brooklyn (1-718 638 5000). Subway 2 or 3 to Eastern Parkway.* **Open** 10am-5pm Wed-Fri, Sun; 10am-9pm Sat.
**Admission** suggested donation $4; $1.50-$2 concessions. **No credit cards.**

The Brooklyn Museum recently appended the word 'art' to its name as part of a concerted campaign to draw wider attention to its copious world-class collections. In past years, attendance has suffered purely from its off-Manhattan location, despite its strong holdings and gorgeous nineteenth-century Beaux Arts building. Among the museum's permanent collections, the African art and pre-Columbian textile galleries are particularly good; the Native American collection is outstanding and works from the ancient Middle East are extensive, as are watercolours by American masters Winslow Homer and John Singer Sargent. The Egyptian galleries, however, are exceptional all the time: the Rubin Gallery's gold and silver gilded Ibis coffin, for instance, is sublime. Two floors up, the Rodin sculpture court is surrounded by paintings from French contemporaries such as Monet and Degas. The 1997-98 season includes two related presentations of special significance: one shows more than 50 sculptures made by the hand of Auguste Rodin; the other assembles, for the first time, 60 of Monet's most important paintings – those of his travels through France and Italy from 1884-1908, many of which have never been shown to the public before. There's an art reference library on the second floor and, on the third, the renowned Wilbour Library of Egyptology. Both are open to the public by appointment only. There's also a handy café.
*Disabled: toilets.*

## The Cloisters

*Fort Tyron Park (923 3700). Subway A to 190th Street.* **Open** *Mar-Oct* 9.30am-5.15pm, *Nov-Feb* 9.30am-4.45pm, Tue-Sun. **Admission** suggested donation $8; $4 concessions (includes admission to the Metropolitan Museum of Art on the same day); free accompanied under-12s. **No credit cards.**

Few people venture this far north in Manhattan, and that's a pity, for the Cloisters houses the Met's medieval art collections in an unexpectedly rural setting. This tranquil twentieth-century museum was constructed, as its name suggests, with monastic cloisters and Gothic chapel, in authentic Middle Ages style. The result is a convincing red-tiled Romanesque museum on a hill overlooking the Hudson River, providing an oasis from the high-rises further south. Don't miss the famous Unicorn tapestries or the *Annunciation Triptych* by Robert Campin. There are also flower and herb gardens stocked with more than 250 species of plants grown in the Middle Ages.
*Disabled: toilets.*

## Cooper-Hewitt National Design Museum

*2 East 91st Street, at Fifth Avenue (860 6868). Subway 4, 5 or 6 to 86th Street.* **Open** 10am-9pm Tue; 10am-5pm Wed-Sat; noon-5pm Sun. **Admission** $3; $1.50 concessions; free under-12s; free 5-9pm Tue. **No credit cards.**

The Smithsonian's National Design Museum is well worth a visit for both its content and architecture – the turn-of-the-

century building belonged to Andrew Carnegie, then one of the wealthiest men in America. Architects responded to his request for 'the most modest, plainest, and the most roomy house in New York' by designing a 64-room mansion in the style of an English Georgian country house. Look out for the carved bagpipes in the ceiling of the music room, now the museum shop (Carnegie was born in Scotland). This is the only museum in the US devoted exclusively to historical and contemporary design and its changing exhibitions are always interesting.
*Disabled: sign language interpretation on request (860 6977); toilets.*

## Frick Collection

*1 East 70th Street, at Fifth Avenue (288 0700). Subway 6 to 68th Street.* **Open** 10am-6pm Tue-Sat; 1-6pm Sun. **Admission** $5; $3 concessions; no under 10s; under-16s must be accompanied by an adult. **No credit cards.**

This private, predominantly Renaissance collection, housed in an opulent residence once owned by industrialist Henry Clay Frick, is still more like a stately home than a museum. American architect Thomas Hastings designed the 1914 building in eighteenth-century European style. The paintings, sculptures and furniture on display are consistently world class, among them works by Gainsborough, Rembrandt, Renoir, Vermeer and Whistler and French cabinet maker Jean-Henri Riesener. The indoor garden court is particularly lovely.
*Disabled: toilets.*

## Solomon R Guggenheim Museum

*1071 Fifth Avenue, at 88th Street (423 3500). Subway 4, 5 or 6 to 86th Street.* **Open** 10am-6pm Mon-Wed, Sun; 10am-8pm Fri, Sat. **Admission** $8; $5 concessions; free accompanied under-12s; voluntary donation 6-8pm Fri. **Credit** AmEx, MC, V.

The museum itself is a work of art. Designed by Frank Lloyd Wright and completed six months after his death in 1959, the Guggenheim is the youngest building to be designated a New York City Landmark. With works by Kandinsky, Picasso, Van Gogh, Degas and Manet, the museum also contains Peggy Guggenheim's cubist, surrealist and abstract expressionist works of art and the Panza di Biumo collection of American minimalist and conceptual art from the 1960s and 1970s. The photography collection began after a donation of more than 200 works by the Robert Mapplethorpe Foundation in 1992, when the museum re-opened after its two-year renovation. The addition of a ten-storey tower, based on an early Wright design, has increased the museum's exhibition space to include a sculpture gallery with great views over Central Park. Even if you don't want to see the collection inside, visit the museum to admire the stunning white building coiled amongst the turn-of-the-century mansions on Fifth Avenue.

The **SoHo Guggenheim**, housed in a nineteenth-century building, opened in 1992 to showcase selections from the Fifth Avenue museum's permanent collection as well as a number of multimedia-enriched or otherwise fashionable temporary exhibitions of both a contemporary and historical nature. There's a terrific museum shop here too.
*See also chapter* **Sightseeing**.
*Disabled: toilets*
**Branch: Guggenheim Museum, SoHo** 575 Broadway (423 3500).

## Metropolitan Museum of Art

*Fifth Avenue, at 82nd Street (535 7710). Subway 4, 5 or 6 to 86th Street.* **Open** 9.30am-5.15pm Tue-Thur, Sun; 9.30am-8.45pm Fri, Sat. **Admission** suggested donation $8; $4 concessions; free accompanied under-12s. **No credit cards.**

It could take several days, even weeks, to cover the Met's one and a half million square feet of exhibition space, so try to be selective. Egyptology fans should head straight for the

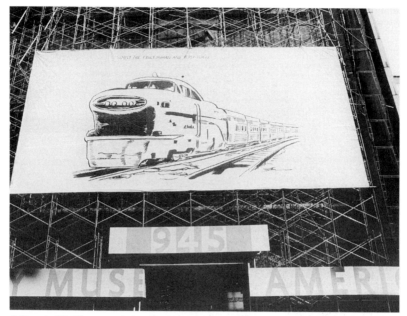

*A Raymond Pettibon mural sheathes the grim-grey concrete of the* **Whitney**. *See p194.*

Temple of Dendur, stopping on the way to peruse the finest collection outside Cairo. There's also an excellent Islamic art collection and more than 3,000 European paintings, including major works by Rembrandt, Raphael and Vermeer. Try not to miss the galleries of south and south-east Asian art or the recently re-opened English Decorative Arts collections. If you have time, see the Tiepolo gallery as well. The Greek and Roman halls have had a face-lift, and the museum has also been adding to its galleries of twentieth-century painting; a number of its sculptures from the same period have been installed in the open-air roof garden (open between May and October), where you can have a drink or a sandwich while taking in the panorama of Central Park and the surrounding city skyline. On view from autumn 1997 is Edgar Degas' private collection of paintings and prints, and the drawings of Jackson Pollock. To gather your wits, take a table by the reflecting pool in the Museum Restaurant or have a snack in the Museum Bar and Café. On weekend evenings, enjoy the classical quintet performing on the mezzanine overlooking the Great Hall. And don't forget the Costume Institute – always a big draw – or, opening in spring 1998, the Man Ray photographs from his Dada/Surrealist period. Whew!
*Disabled: toilets. Foreign language tours (570 3711).*
*Internet: http://www.metmuseum.org/*

### Museum of Modern Art

*11 West 53rd Street, between Fifth & Sixth Avenues (708 9400/9480). Subway E or F to Fifth Avenue/53rd Street.* **Open** *11am-6pm Mon, Tue, Sat, Sun; 10am-8.30pm. Thur, Fri.* **Admission** *$8.50; $5.50 concessions; free accompanied under-16s; voluntary donation 5.30-8.30pm Thur, Fri.* **No credit cards.**
The Museum of Modern Art, or MoMA, holds perhaps the most comprehensive and cutting-edge collection of twentieth-century art in the world. It encompasses painting, design, photography, film and sculpture with recent major exhibitions devoted to Jasper Johns, Willem de Kooning and Chuck Close. The permanent collection is particularly strong on works by Matisse, Picasso and Miró, while the film and video department contains more than 13,000 films and four million film stills. The Abby Aldrich Rockefeller Sculpture Garden is lovely, overlooked by the elegant Italian Sette restaurant upstairs. There are free gallery talks at 1pm and 3pm daily (except Wednesday) and on Thursday and Friday evenings at 6pm and 7pm. A sculpture touch-tour is available to visually impaired visitors by advance appointment. The museum recently acquired the neighbouring Dorset Hotel, and expansion plans are afoot.
*Disabled: toilets.*

### National Museum of the American Indian

*George Gustav Heye Centre, US Custom House, 1 Bowling Green, near Battery Park (668 6624). Subway 1 or 9 to South Ferry.* **Open** *10am-5pm Mon-Wed, Fri-Sun; 10am-8pm Thur.* **Admission** *free.*
The galleries, resource centre and two workshop rooms of this branch of the Smithsonian's sprawling organisation of museums and research institutes, occupies two floors of the grand rotunda in the old US Customs House. Located just around the corner from Battery Park and the Ellis Island Ferry, its displays are based on a permanent collection of documents and artifacts that offer valuable insights into the realities of Native American history. Exhibitions are thoughtfully explained, usually by Native Americans. Particularly interesting is All Roads Are Good, which explains the personal choices of storytellers, weavers, anthropologists and tribal leaders. Only 500 of the collection's million objects are on display: one reason, apart from the building's lofty proportions, why the museum seems surprisingly small. A main branch, on the Mall in Washington, DC, will open in 2002.

## Pierpont Morgan Library

*29 East 36th Street, between Park & Madison Avenues (685 0008). Subway 6 to 33rd Street.* **Open** 10.30am-5pm Tue-Fri; 10.30am-6pm Sat; noon-6pm Sun. **Admission** $5; $1-$3 concessions. **No credit cards.**
This charming Italianate museum was once the home of financier JP Morgan. The collection, mostly gathered during Morgan's trips to Europe, includes Rembrandts, original Mahler manuscripts and the gorgeous silver, copper and cloisonné twelfth-century Stavelot triptych. Ask about guided tours to get the most out of the numerous treasures. A subtly colourful marble rotunda, with carved sixteenth-century Italian ceiling, separates the three-tiered library from the rich red study. There's a modern conservatory attached to the museum containing a tranquil courtyard café.
*Disabled: toilets.*

## Whitney Museum of American Art

*945 Madison Avenue, at East 75th Street (570 3600). Subway 6 to 77th Street.* **Open** 11am-6pm Wed, Fri-Sun; 1-8pm Thur. **Admission** $8; $6 concessions; free under-12s; free 6-8pm Thur. **No credit cards.**
Some may think this great grey granite cube unprepossessing but it is an entirely appropriate setting for the similarly uncompromising modern American art that it houses. Founded by the sculptor Gertrude Vanderbilt Whitney in 1930, the museum counts among its 10,000 works noted pieces by Edward Hopper, Georgia O'Keeffe, Jackson Pollock, Willem de Kooning, Alexander Calder, Louise Nevelson, Jasper Johns, Robert Rauschenberg, Andy Warhol and Jean-Michel Basquiat. Themed exhibitions change every three or four months and a biennial of contemporary American art is held in every odd-numbered year – except the next one, which is set for the year 2000. Meanwhile, look out for the Andy Warhol exhibition starting in late 1997; a career survey of renowned video artist Bill Viola follows in spring 1998, with a major look at the work of Mark Rothko scheduled soon after. Sarabeth's, the lovely museum café, is flooded with daylight and allows an interesting up-from-under view of the street.
*Disabled: toilets.*

## Whitney Museum of American Art at Philip Morris

*120 Park Avenue, at East 42nd Street (878 2550). Subway 4, 5, 6, 7 or S to Grand Central Station.* **Open** *gallery* 11am-6pm Mon-Fri; 11am-7.30pm Thur; *sculpture court* 7.30am-9.30pm Mon-Sat; 11am-7pm Sun. **Admission** free.
A branch of the Whitney uptown, this lobby gallery gives itself over to special projects by contemporary artists. There is a new one every few months, so phone for details, or check the Art pages of *Time Out New York.*

## Art & Design

### American Academy & Institute of Arts & Letters

*Audubon Terrace, Broadway, between 156th & 155th Streets (368 5900). Subway 1 to 157th Street.* **Open** 10am-6pm Mon, Fri-Sun; 10am-8pm Thur. **Admission** free.
This organisation honours a fixed 250 American writers, composers, painters, sculptors and architects. Edith Wharton, Mark Twain and Henry James were once members and today's list includes Terrence McNally, Kurt Vonnegut and Alison Lurie. It's not strictly a museum but there are annual exhibitions open to the public and a magnificent library of original manuscripts and first editions open to researchers by appointment only.
*Disabled: toilets.*

### American Craft Museum

*40 West 53rd Street, between Fifth & Sixth Avenues (956 3535). Subway B, D or F to Rockefeller Center.* **Open** 10am-8pm Tue; 10am-5pm Wed-Sun. **Admission** $5; $2.50 concessions. **No credit cards.**
The country's leading art museum for twentieth-century crafts in clay, fibre, glass, metal and wood. There are temporary shows on the four bright and spacious floors and one or two exhibitions from the permanent collection each year

*The **ICP** specialises in conscience-prodding photography, but is happy to lighten the mood.*

*Find out which way the cultural winds are blowing at the* **Museum of American Folk Art**.

concentrating on a specific medium. The shop, though small, sells some unusually stylish jewellery and ceramics. *Disabled: toilets.*

### Dahesh Museum

*601 Fifth Avenue, at 48th Street (759 0606). Subway F to 47th Street and Avenue of Americas.* **Open** 11am-6pm Tue-Sat. **Admission** free.

This jewel-box museum houses the private collection of a Lebanese-born eccentric with a consuming passion for European Academic art. It focuses on worthy but minor examples of Orientalism, landscapes, scenes of rural life, and historical or mythical images painted by nineteenth- and early twentieth-century artists whose work you won't see in public collections anywhere else.

### Forbes Magazine Galleries

*62 Fifth Avenue, at West 12th Street (206 5548). Subway 4, 5, 6, N, R or L to Union Square.* **Open** 10am-4pm Tue, Wed, Fri, Sat. **Admission** free; under-16s must be accompanied by an adult.

A wonderful private collection of treasures belonging to the late magazine publisher Malcolm Forbes. Toy boats and soldiers aside, galleries display historic presidential letters and – the highlight of the museum – superbly intricate pieces by the famous Russian jeweller and goldsmith Peter Carl Fabergé. The selection of more than 300 *objets de luxe* includes diamond-encrusted bonbonnières; gold and nephrite carriage clocks decorated with emeralds and pearls; and, of course, the trademark Fabergé eggs. Twelve Imperial Easter eggs are on show, made for the last two czars of Russia. Gallery hours are subject to change without warning, so phone to check before visiting.

### International Center of Photography (ICP)

*1130 Fifth Avenue, at 94th Street (860 1778). Subway 6 to 96th Street.* **Open** 11am-8pm Tue; 11am-6pm Wed-Sun. **Admission** $4; $1-$2.50 concessions. **No credit cards**.

The collection began in the 1960s as the International Fund for Concerned Photography, containing work by Robert Capa, Werner Bischof, David Seymour and Dan Weiner, who were all killed on assignment. Their photographs were preserved and exhibited by Cornell Capa, brother of Robert, who went on to found the ICP in 1974. Given this heritage, it's no surprise that exhibitions are particularly strong on photojournalism and documentary. Photographic images, Cornell said, 'are both works of art and moments in history; they sharpen human awareness and awaken conscience'. There's an extensive bookshop, space for video installations and a small screening room.

The smaller **midtown ICP** has two floors of gallery space and a museum shop. Exhibitions change throughout the year. *Disabled: toilets.*
**Branch:** ICP Midtown 1133 Sixth Avenue (768 4680).

### Museum of American Folk Art

*2 Lincoln Square, Columbus Avenue & 66th Street (977 7298). Subway 1 or 9 to 66th Street.* **Open** 11.30am-7.30pm Tue-Sun. **Admission** suggested donation $3. **No credit cards**.

Here's proof that beautiful things can come in small packages. The exhibits are exquisite. Decorative, practical and ceremonial folk art encompasses pottery, trade signs, delicately stitched log cabin quilts and even wind toys. The craftsmanship is often breathtaking. There are occasional lectures, demonstrations and performances, and a museum shop next door. *Disabled: toilets.*

### National Academy of Design

*1083 Fifth Avenue, at 89th Street (369 4880). Subway 4, 5 or 6 to 86th Street.* **Open** noon-5pm Wed, Thur, Sat, Sun; noon-8pm Fri. **Admission** $5; $3.50 concessions; free under-5s; free 5-8pm Fri. **No credit cards**.

The Academy comprises the School of Fine Arts and a museum containing the world's foremost collections of nineteenth- and twentieth-century American art. The arts of design are painting, sculpture, architecture and engraving with the permanent collection represented by artists and architects such as Mary Cassatt, John Singer Sargent and Frank Lloyd Wright. Temporary exhibitions in this elegant Fifth Avenue townhouse are always impressive.

## Isamu Noguchi Garden Museum

*32-37 Vernon Boulevard, at 33rd Road, Long Island City, Queens (recorded information 1-718 204 7088). Subway N to Astoria Broadway/shuttle bus from Asia Society, 725 Park Avenue, at West 70th Street, every hour on the half hour 11.30am-3.30pm.* **Open** *Apr-Oct* 10am-5pm Wed-Fri; 11am-6pm Sat, Sun. **Admission** suggested donation $4; $2 concessions. **No credit cards.**

Sculptor Isamu Noguchi designed stage sets for the late Martha Graham and George Balanchine as well as sculpture parks and immense works of great simplicity. Noguchi's studios are now a showcase for his pieces, with 12 small galleries and a sculpture garden. There's a guided tour at 2pm (call 1-718 721 1932) and films are shown throughout the day.

## Queens Museum of Art

*New York City Building, Flushing Meadows-Corona Park, Queens (1-718 592 9700). Subway 7 to Willets Point/Shea Stadium.* **Open** 10am-5pm Wed-Fri; noon-5pm Sat, Sun. **Admission** suggested donation $3; $1.50 concessions. **No credit cards.**

The wide boardwalk from the subway station, away from the Mets' Shea Stadium and past the US Open tennis stadium, introduces visitors to the scale of what was once the site of the 1964-65 World Fair. The museum, in the park itself, is next to the towering steel globe of the Unisphere. It re-opened recently after a $15 million renovation; in addition to the art collections, it still offers an insight into the visionary nature of the World Fair. There's a sleek 'Futurama' model car from General Motors and posters showing Billy Graham promoting his pavilion's 'Man in the Fifth Dimension' film, whose showings had counsellors on stand-by in case anyone wanted to accept Christ afterwards. For many people, the highlight is a permanent miniature model of New York City. It's fun to try to find where you're staying – binoculars are on hire for $1. Dusk falls every 15 minutes, revealing tiny illuminated buildings and a fluorescent Central Park. The model is constantly updated – 60,000 changes at the last count. *See also chapter* **New York by Neighbourhood: The Outer Boroughs.**
*Disabled: toilets.*

## Nicholas Roerich Museum

*319 West 107th Street, at Riverside (864 7752). Subway 1 to 110th Street.* **Open** 2-5pm Tue-Sun. **Admission** free.

Russian-born Roerich was a philosopher, artist, architect, explorer, pacifist and scenery painter who collaborated with Nijinsky, Stravinsky and Diaghilev. The Roerich Peace Pact of 1935, an international agreement on the protection of cultural treasures, earned him a Nobel Peace Prize nomination. Roerich's wife bought this charming townhouse specifically as a museum to house her late husband's possessions. Paintings are mostly from his Tibetan travels and display his interest in mysticism. It's a fascinating place but Roerich's intriguing life story tends to overshadow the museum.

## Studio Museum in Harlem

*144 West 125th Street, between Seventh & Lenox Avenues (864 4500). Subway 2 or 3 to 125th Street.* **Open** 10am-5pm Wed-Fri; 1-6pm Sat, Sun. **Admission** $5; $1-$3 concessions; free 1st Sat of each month. **No credit cards.**

The Studio Museum started out as rented loft space in 1967.

Within 20 years it had expanded on to two floors of a 60,000sq ft (5,500 sq m) building – a gift from a New York bank – and became the first accredited black fine arts museum in the country. Today it shows changing exhibitions by African-American, African and Caribbean artists and continues its prestigious artists-in-residence programme.
*Disabled: toilets.*

## Urban Center

*457 Madison Avenue, between 50th & 51st Streets (935 3960/439 1049 tour information). Subway 6 to 51st Street; E or F to Fifth Avenue/53rd Street.* **Open** 11am-5pm Mon-Wed, Fri, Sat. **Admission** voluntary donation.

The Municipal Art Society founded this centre for the urban design arts in 1980. It functions as a gallery, bookshop, lecture forum and campaign office, with exhibitions leaning towards architecture, public art and community-based projects. The Center also acts as headquarters for the Architectural League and the Parks Council, but its greatest attraction must be its location: inside the historic Villard Houses opposite St Patrick's Cathedral.
*Disabled: toilets.*

# Arts & Culture

For **El Museo del Barrio,** *see chapter* **By Neighbourhood: Northern Manhattan.**

# African

## Museum for African Art

*593 Broadway, between Houston & Prince Streets (966 1313). Subway 6 to Spring or Bleecker Street; N or R to Prince Street; B, D, Q or F subway to Broadway/Lafayette.* **Open** 10.30am-5.30pm Tue-Fri; noon-6pm Sat, Sun. **Admission** $5; $2.50 concessions; free under-2s. **Credit** (over $10 ) MC, V.

This tranquil museum was designed by Maya Lin – creator of the stunningly simple Vietnam Veterans' Memorial in Washington DC. Exhibits change about twice a year and the quality of works shown is high. There's a particularly good bookshop with a children's section.
*Disabled: toilets.*

# Asian

## Asia Society

*725 Park Avenue, at East 70th Street (288 6400). Subway 6 to 68th Street.* **Open** 11am-6pm Tue, Wed, Fri, Sat; 11am-8pm Thur; noon-5pm Sun. **Admission** $3; $1 concessions; free accompanied under-12s; free 6-8pm Thur. **No credit cards.**

The substantial eight-storey headquarters of the Asia Society reflects its importance in promoting Asian-American relations. The Society's activities include sponsoring study missions, conferences and public programmes in both continents. Galleries show major art exhibitions from public and private collections, including the permanent Mr and Mrs John D Rockefeller III collection of Asian art. Asian musicians and performers often play here so it's well worth picking up a programme.
*Disabled: toilets.*

## China Institute in America

*125 East 65th Street, between Lexington & Park Avenues (744 8181). Subway 6 to 68th Street.* **Open** 10am to 5pm Mon-Sat; 1-5pm Sun. **Admission** suggested donation $5; $3 concessions; free children. **Credit** AmEx, MC, V.

With only two small gallery rooms, the China Institute is rather overshadowed by the Asia Society, but its exhibitions

# The dream factory

'The greatest toy any boy ever dreamed of', as Orson Welles put it, is available to anyone who makes the short trek out to the **American Museum of the Moving Image** (AMMI), in the Astoria section of Queens, where a freshly minted, intensely interactive exhibition, 'Behind the Screen', offers two floors of hands-on experimentation with the machinery of movies and television.

AMMI covers the whole range of moving image manufacture. The entrance to the show is graced with a wall of the superb turn-of-the-century motion study photographs of Edward Muybridge. There are demonstrations of early animation toys such as the zoetrope. You can make a computerised stop-motion study of yourself (and buy a copy of it in the gift shop on the way out) or make a short film at a digital animation stand.

The bulk of the exhibit concerns motion picture sound and image editing. You get to mix and match sound effects for *Duck Soup* or *Terminator II* or dub your own 'You talkin' to me?' over De Niro's image. Museum personnel provide regularly scheduled demonstrations of more sophisticated machinery, including a digital video editing system or a Silicon Graphics 3-D morphing workstation.

A particularly illuminating section on directing provides a detailed examination of film development – of a two-sentence concept into a ten-minute scene in *Dressed to Kill*. You can see how the still photo sequences, or storyboards, are used, or leaf through the script supervisor's log, the loose-leaf paper trail that tracks and co-ordinates all the elements – costumes, props, personnel, sets, locations – of the film.

AMMI is, inevitably, a storehouse of nostalgia. A great wall of black and white glossies of stars from Dietrich to Brando, and barely lesser lights such as Dorothy Lamour or Tyrone Power, is hopelessly captivating. There's a briefer but no less compelling display of director's portraits – a long-haired young Scorsese standing on a mean downtown corner, an eye-patched Nicholas Ray with his life-affirming leer, a stogied Sam Fuller with a 1,000-yard stare. A section on merchandising and promotion is just as rich: a huge display case of classic fan magazines from the 1940s, artefacts ranging from Betty Boop socks and Valentino cigars to *Welcome Back, Kotter* and *Charlie's Angels* lunch boxes. The Archie Bunker card game with the 'dingbat tally' spinnaker is a gem.

AMMI also offers wonderful film and video series and an ongoing programme of visits from industry pros. A dynamic and entertaining day out, just 15 minutes by subway from midtown.

### American Museum of the Moving Image

*35th Avenue at 36th Street, Astoria, Queens (1-718 784 0077). Subway G or R to Steinway Street.* **Open** noon-5pm Tue-Fri; 11am-6pm Sat, Sun. **Admission** $8; $4-$5 concessions. **No credit cards.** *Disabled: toilets.*

are impressive and range from Chinese women artists and bronze vessels to selections from the Beijing Palace Museum. The Society is particularly strong on lectures and courses, on subjects like cooking, calligraphy and Confucianism.

### Japan Society
*333 East 47th Street, near First Avenue (832 1155). Subway 6 to 51st Street; E or F to 53rd Street.* **Open** (during exhibitions only) 11am-5pm Tue-Sun. **Admission** suggested donation $3. **No credit cards.**
The Japan Society promotes a number of cultural exchange programmes, special events and studies, with exhibitions taking place three or four times a year. The gallery shows both traditional and contemporary Japanese art from decorative art from the Meiji period to Buddhist prints and the use of umbrellas in Japanese art. The Society's film centre is a major showcase for Japanese cinema in the United States and there's a library and language centre in the lower lobby wing. *Disabled: toilets.*

### Tibetan Museum
*338 Lighthouse Avenue, off Richmond Road, Staten Island (recorded information 1-718 987 3500). Ferry to Staten Island, then 78 bus.* **Open** *Apr-Nov* 1-5pm Wed-Sun; *Dec-Mar* by appointment only. **Admission** $3; $1-$2.50 concessions. **No credit cards.**
This mock Tibetan temple stands on the highest hilltop on the eastern seaboard. It contains a fascinating Buddhist altar and the largest collection of Tibetan art in the West, including religious objects, bronzes and paintings. There's a comprehensive (English-language) library containing books on Buddhism, Tibet and Asian art. The landscaped gardens house a zoo of stone animals, with birdhouses and wishing well, and offer good views.

## European

### Goethe House/German Cultural Center
*1014 Fifth Avenue at 82nd Street (439 8700). Subway 4, 5 or 6 to 86th Street.* **Open** *library* 10am-7pm Tue, Thur; 10am-5pm Wed, Fri; noon-6pm Sat. **Admission** free.
Goethe House is the New York branch of the Goethe Institute, a German cultural organisation founded in 1951. Located across the street from the Metropolitan Museum in a landmark Fifth Avenue mansion, it mounts four solo or group shows annually, featuring German-born contemporary artists. Phone for details of current programmes, which include well-attended concerts, film screenings and lectures. An extensive library offers books in German or English translation as well as current German periodicals, videos, and audio cassettes.

### Hispanic Society of America
*Audubon Terrace, between West 155 & 156th Streets (926 2234). Subway 1 to 157th Street.* **Open** 10am-4.30pm Tue-Sat; 1-4pm Sun; *library* 1-4.30pm Tue-Fri; 10am-4.30pm Sat. **Admission** free.
Two limestone lions flank the entrance to this majestic building in Hamilton Heights, the gentrified area of Harlem. Outside, an equestrian statue of El Cid, Spain's medieval hero, stands on the Beaux Arts terrace between the Society's two buildings. Inside, there's an ornate Spanish Renaissance court and an upper gallery lined with paintings by El Greco, Goya and Velázquez. The collection is dominated by religious artefacts – including a number of sixteenth-century tombs from the monastery of San Francisco in Cuellar in Spain.

### Ukrainian Museum
*203 Second Avenue, between East 12th & 13th Streets (228 0110). Subway 4, 5, 6, L, N or R to Union Square.* **Open** 1-5pm Wed-Sun. **Admission** $1; 50¢ concessions. **No credit cards.**
The Ukrainian National Women's League of America provided most of the folk art here. It's a small, rather sorry-looking museum on two tiny floors, showing woven and embroidered textiles plus assorted crafts and objects from the nineteenth and early twentieth centuries. Fund-raising is underway for a relocation project and cultural centre.

## Fashion

### The Museum at FIT
*Seventh Avenue, at West 27th Street (760 7970). Subway 1 or 9 to 28th Street.* **Open** noon-8pm Tue-Fri; 10am-5pm Sat. **Admission** free.
The Museum at the Fashion Institute of Technology has the world's largest collection of costumes and textiles, yet it contains only two public galleries. Exhibitions are tailored towards the 25 courses at the FIT and have covered everything from sportswear, Balenciaga and East Village fashions to a history of lingerie. *Disabled: toilets.*

## Historical

### The Statue of Liberty & Ellis Island Museum
*Subway 4 or 5 to Bowling Green, then ferry from Battery Park to Liberty Island and Ellis Island (363 3200/269 5755 ferry information).* **Ferries** every half hour 9.15am-3.30pm daily. **Fare** $7; $3-$5 concessions, including admission. **Ticket sales** Castle Clinton, Battery Park. **Open** 8.30am-3.30pm daily.
**No credit cards.**
There's an interesting museum about the statue's history contained in the pedestal itself but, whatever you do, don't miss the Immigration Museum on Ellis Island, where the tour boat takes you on the way back to Manhattan. More than 12 million people passed through this immigrant station and the exhibitions are an evocative and moving tribute to anyone who ever packed their bags and headed for America with dreams of a better life. The audio tour, available in five languages, is highly recommended ($3.50, $2.50-$3 concessions). Look out for a photograph of Fiorello LaGuardia, one of Ellis Island's interpreters, who went on to become one of New York's most popular mayors and now lends his name to one of the city's airports. *See also chapter* **Sightseeing.**

### Brooklyn Historical Society
*128 Pierrepont Street, near Clinton Street, Brooklyn (1-718 624 0890). Subway 2, 3, 4, 5 to Borough Hall; N or R to Court Street.* **Open** noon-5pm Tue-Sat. **Admission** $2.50; $1 concessions. **No credit cards.**
What do Woody Allen, Mae West, Isaac Asimov, Mel Brooks and Walt Whitman have in common? Answer: they were all – along with Al Capone, Barry Manilow and Gypsy Rose Lee – born in Brooklyn. Consequently they merit tributes in this tiny museum dedicated to Brooklyn's former glories. There are displays on its firefighters, the Navy Yard and local baseball team the Brooklyn Dodgers, which won the World Series in 1955 before being sold, en masse, to Los Angeles two years later. As we went to press, the museum was closed for renovation, due to open sometime in 1998. *Disabled: toilets.*

### Fraunces Tavern Museum
*Second & Third Floors, 54 Pearl Street, corner of Broad Street (425 1778). Subway 1 or 9 to South Ferry.* **Open** 10am-4.45pm Mon-Fri; noon-4pm Sat, Sun. **Admission** $2.50; $1 concessions; free under-6s. **No credit cards.**
This tavern used to be George Washington's drinking hole and was a prominent meeting place for anti-British groups before the Revolution. The eighteenth-century building (which has been partly reconstructed) is an unexpectedly quaint site on the fringes of the financial district and displays

most of its artefacts in period room settings. The changing exhibitions are often interesting.

## Hall of Fame for Great Americans

*Hall of Fame Terrace, West 181st Street & University Avenue, Bronx (1-718 289 5161). Subway 4 to Burnside Avenue.* **Open** 10am-5pm daily. **Admission** free.

The Hall of Fame is a covered walkway lined with bronze busts of pre-eminent Americans, with sections such as scientists, authors, soldiers and statesmen. As the last two suggest, the tributees are mostly male, such as the Wright Brothers, Thomas Mann and Franklin D Roosevelt. If this was in Central Park it would be a popular attraction – but it's not. Instead you have to take a long subway ride and then walk through the Bronx for 20 minutes, so it hardly seems worth it. The neglected Hall is at the back of the Bronx Community College and is built on the highest natural summit of New York City.

## Merchant's House Museum

*29 East 4th Street, between Lafayette Street & The Bowery (777 1089). Subway 6 to Astor Place.* **Open** 1-4pm Mon-Thur, Sun. **Admission** $3; $2 concessions; free accompanied under-12s. **No credit cards**.

Seabury Tredwell was the merchant in question. He made his fortune selling hardware and bought this elegant Greek Revival house three years after it was built in 1832. The house has been virtually untouched since the 1860s; decoration is spare (bar the lavish canopied four-poster beds) and ornamentation tasteful. Guided tours are conducted on Sundays; phone for details.

## Museum of the City of New York

*1220 Fifth Avenue, at 103rd Street (534 1672). Subway 6 to 103rd Street.* **Open** 10am-5pm Wed-Sat; 1-5pm Sun. **Admission** suggested donation $5; $4 concessions. **No credit cards**.

This is one of those charming little village museums brimming with photographs, mementos and curious objects – except for the fact that the village whose life it records is the metropolis of New York. A vast archive of objects, prints and photographs tells the story of the city, with displays about its people and examples of the artefacts produced along the way. As well as 300,000 photos and prints and 2,000 paintings and sculptures there's an unparalleled collection of Broadway memorabilia, and impressive historical collections of clothing, costumes and decorative household objects. Much of this vast treasure trove is displayed only selectively, in themed exhibitions. The museum is at its informative best when a visit is combined with one of the many frequent lectures or walking tours.
*Disabled: toilets.*

## New York Historical Society

*2 West 77th Street, between Central Park West & Columbus Avenue (873 3400). Subway B or C to 81st Street.* **Open** noon-5pm Wed-Sun. **Admission** suggested donation $3; $1 concessions. **No credit cards**.

The Society has now re-opened after being closed for several years due to lack of funding. It was one of the first cultural educational institutions in the United States and New York's oldest museum, founded in 1804. Exhibitions are constantly changing – there's even a section on the real Pocahontas following the Disney film – while the permanent collection ranges from Tiffany lamps and lithographs to a lock of George Washington's hair.
*Disabled: toilets.*

## South Street Seaport Museum

*12 Fulton Street, at Front Street (669 9400). Subway 2, 3, 4 or 5 to Fulton Street; A or C to Broadway Nassau.* **Open** *1 Oct- 31 Mar* 10am-5pm Mon-Wed; *1 Apr-30 Sept* 10am-6pm Mon-Wed, Fri; 10am-8pm Thur. **Admission** $3-$6 concessions. **Credit** AmEx, MC, V.

The museum spreads out over 11 blocks alongside the harbour as a collection of galleries, historic ships, nineteenth-century buildings and a visitor's centre. The staff (mostly volunteers) are particularly friendly and it's fun to wander around the streets, popping in to see an exhibition on tattooing before climbing on board the four-masted 1911 *Peking*. The Seaport itself is pretty touristy but is still a charming place to spend an afternoon and there are plenty of cafés to choose from near the Fulton Market building. *See also chapter* **Sightseeing**.

# Jewish

## Jewish Museum

*1109 Fifth Avenue, at 92nd Street (423 3230). Subway 6 to 96th Street.* **Open** 11am-5.45pm Mon, Wed, Thur, Sun; 11am-8pm Tue. **Admission** $7; $5 concessions; free under-12s; free 5-8pm Tue. **No credit cards**.

The Jewish Museum is a fascinating collection of art, artefacts and media installations housed in the 1908 Warburg Mansion. The museum commissions a contemporary artist or group of artists to install a new show each year, and the results are always stellar. The permanent exhibition tracks the Jewish cultural experience through exhibits ranging from a Statue of Liberty Hanukkah lamp and filigree silver circumcision set to a sixteenth-century mosaic wall from a Persian synagogue and an interactive Talmud. This eclectic collection – the largest of its kind in America – is also historic: most of it was rescued from European synagogues before World War II. Look out for 'Assignment Rescue: the Story of Varian Fry', which runs from late 1997 to early 1998. The tranquil Weissman Café dates from the 1993 renovation.
*Disabled: toilets (information 423 3271).*

## Yeshiva University Museum

*2520 Amsterdam Avenue, near West 185th Street (960 5390). Subway 1 to 181st Street.* **Open** 10.30am-5pm Tue-Thur; noon-6pm Sun. **Admission** $3; $2 concessions. **No credit cards**.

The museum usually holds one major exhibition a year and a number of changing shows, mainly on Jewish themes.

# Media

*See also page 197* **The Dream Factory**.

## Museum of Television & Radio

*25 West 52nd Street, between Fifth & Sixth Avenues (621 6600). Subway E or F to Fifth Avenue & 53rd Street; N or R to 49th Street; 1 or 9 to 50th Street; B, D, F or Q to Rockefeller Center.* **Open** noon-6pm Tue, Wed, Sat, Sun; noon-8pm Thur; noon-9pm Fri. **Admission** $6; $3-$4 concessions. **No credit cards**.

A living, working archive of over 60,000 radio and TV programmes. Just head to the fourth-floor library and use the computerised system to access a favourite *Star Trek* or *I Love Lucy* episode. Minutes later, the assigned console downstairs will play up to four of your choices within two hours. The radio listening room works the same way. Cinemas provide major screenings and there are numerous galleries and changing exhibits. A must for TV and radio addicts.
*Disabled: toilets.*

## Military

### Sea, Air & Space Museum

*USS Intrepid, Pier 86, West 46th Street & 12th Avenue, at the Hudson River (245 2533/recorded information 245 0072). Subway A, C, E or K to 42nd Street.* **Open** *Memorial Day-Labor Day* 10am-5pm Mon-Sat; 10am-6pm Sun; *Labor Day-Memorial Day* 10am-5pm

The **New York Public Library** reading room, just about the quietest spot in the city.

Mon-Wed, Sun. **Admission** $10; $5-$7.50 concessions. **Credit** AmEx, MC, V.

The museum is based on the World War II aircraft carrier *Intrepid*, whose decks are crammed with space capsules and various aircraft. There are plenty of audio-visual shows and hands-on exhibits to appeal to children.

## Neighbourhood

### Lower East Side Tenement Museum

*90 Orchard Street, at Broome Street (431 0233). Subway F to Delancey Street; B, D or Q to Grand; J, M or Z to Delancey & Essex.* **Open** *Visitor Center* 11am-5pm Tue-Sun. **Admission** $7; $6 concessions. **Credit** AmEx, MC, V.

A fascinating look at the history of immigration by guided tour of a nineteenth-century tenement. The building, in the heart of what was once Little Germany, contains two reconstructed apartments belonging to a German Jewish dressmaker and a Sicilian Catholic family. Tours are obligatory if you want to see the tenement itself, and it's worth booking ahead since they sell out. They run at 1pm, 2pm and 3pm Tue-Fri and every 45 minutes at the weekend. The museum also has a gallery, shop and video room and organises local heritage walking tours.

## Science & Technology

The **Hayden Planetarium** is currently closed for major renovations and will re-open in 2000.

### Liberty Science Center

*Liberty State Park, 251 Phillip Street, Jersey City, New Jersey (recorded information 1-201 200 1000). PATH subway to Grove Street, then connecting park bus; weekend ferry service (call 1-800 533 3779).* **Open** 9.30am-5.30pm Tue-Sun. **Admission** *exhibition halls* $9.50; $6.50-$8.50 concessions; *halls & Omnimax cinema* $13.50; $9.50-$11.50 concessions. **Credit** AmEx, Disc, MC, V.

An excellent museum with innovative exhibitions and America's largest and most spectacular Imax cinema. It also has an observation tower providing great views over Manhattan and an unusual sideways look at the Statue of Liberty. The Center's emphasis is on hands-on science so it's elbows out if you want to get a look in among the over-excited kids. A great day out if travelling by ferry at the weekend. *Disabled: toilets.*

### New York Hall of Science

*4701 111th Street, Flushing Meadows-Corona Park (1-718 699 0005). Subway 7 to 111th Street.* **Open** group bookings Mon, Tue 9am-2pm; 10am-5pm Wed-Sun. **Admission** $4.50; $3 concessions; free 2-5pm Wed, Thur. **Credit** AmEx, MC, V.

Since its opening during the 1964-65 World's Fair, the New York Hall of Science has built the largest collection of hands-on science exhibits in the city and is now one of the top ten science museums in the US. The emphasis here is on education and the place is usually filled with young schoolchildren, for whom it successfully demystifies science with bright, interactive exhibits. A new expansion includes a 48-foot tall entrance rotunda, a new dining pavilion, and a 300-seat auditorium. *Disabled: toilets. Internet http://www.nyhallsci.org*

## Transport

### Fire Museum

*278 Spring Street, at Varick Street (691 1303). Subway 1 or 9 to Houston Street.* **Open** 10am-4pm Tue-Sun; 10am-9pm Thur. **Admission** suggested donation $4; $1-$2 concessions. **Credit** AmEx, MC, V.

A bright and cheerful three-storey museum strictly for enthusiasts. There are two tours a day for groups of up to 30. *Disabled: toilets.*

### New York Transit Museum

*Corner of Boerum Place & Schermerhorn Street, Brooklyn (1-718 243 3060). Subway 2, 3, 4 or 5 to Borough Hall; M, N, or R to Court Street; G to Hoyt/Schermerhorn.* **Open** 10am-4pm Tue, Thur, Fri; 10am-6pm Wed; noon-5pm Sat, Sun. **Admission** $3; $1.50 concessions. **No credit cards.**

Don't look for a building – the Transit Museum is housed underground in an old 1930s subway station. Its entrance, down a flight of stairs, is beneath the Board of Education building, opposite the black and white striped New York City Transit Authority Building. Vintage carriage subways with wicker seats and canvas hand straps line up alongside a selection of antique turnstiles and plenty of adverts – including one explaining how spitting 'is a violation of the sanitary code'. So there!

## And the Rest...

### Abigail Adams Smith Museum

*421 East 61st Street, at First Avenue (838 6878). Subway 4, 5, 6, N or R to 59th Street.* **Open** 11am-4pm Tue-Sun. **Admission** $3; $2 concessions; free under-13s. **No credit cards.**

An eighteenth-century coach house once belonging to the daughter of John Adams, the second American president. The house is filled with period articles and furniture (Abigail died in 1813) and there's an adjoining formal garden.

### American Numismatic Society

*Audubon Terrace, between West 155th & 156th Streets (234 3130). Subway 1 to 157th Street.* **Open** 9am-4.30pm Tue-Sat; 1-4pm Sun. **Admission** free.

A collection covering 26 centuries. For enthusiasts.

### Garibaldi Meucci Museum

*420 Tomkins Avenue, Staten Island (1-718 442 1608). Transport Subway 1 or 9 to South Ferry, then Staten Island Ferry and bus S52.* **Open** 1-5pm Tue-Sun. **Admission** suggested donation $3.

The 1840s Gothic revival home of Italian inventor Antonio Meucci and former refuge of Italian patriot Garibaldi.

## Libraries

# New York Public Library

The multi-tentacled New York Public Library comprises four major research libraries and 82 local and specialist branches, making it the largest and most comprehensive library system in the world. The library grew out of the combined collections of John Jacob Astor, Samuel Jones Tilden and James Lenox at the end of the nineteenth century. Today it holds a total of 50 million items, including nearly 18 million books, with around a million items added to the collection each year. Unless you are interested in a specific subject, you are most likely to visit the system's flagship building, officially called the Center for Humanities. Founded in 1895, the Library recently celebrated its centennial and the newest branch, the Science, Industry and Business Library, opened in 1996.

### Center for the Humanities

*Fifth Avenue, at 42nd Street (recorded information 869 8089). Subway 7 to Fifth Avenue; B, D or F to 42nd Street.* **Open** 10am-6pm Mon, Thur-Sat; 11am-6pm Tue, Wed. **Admission** free.

This landmark Beaux Arts building on Fifth Avenue, flanked by lions and limestone columns, is what most people call the New York Public Library. The famous lions are crowned with holly at Christmas and during summer people sit on the steps or sip iced drinks at the outdoor tables beneath the arches. There are free guided tours of the building at 11am and 2pm, which include the beautiful public reading room, the first Gutenburg Bible brought to America and a hand-written copy of Washington's Farewell Address. The Bill Blass Public Catalog room was recently restored and renovated and now contains computers where visitors can surf the Internet. Special exhibitions are frequent. *Disabled: toilets.*

### Donnell Library Center

*20 West 53rd Street, between Fifth & Sixth Avenues (621 0618). Subway B, D or F to Rockefeller Center.* **Open** noon-6pm Mon, Wed, Fri; 9.30am-8pm Tue, Thur; 10am-5.30pm Sat. **Admission** free.

This branch of the NYPL has an extensive collection of records, films and videotapes with appropriate screening facilities. The Donnell also specialises in foreign-language books – over 80 languages – and there's a children's section of more than 100,000 books, films, records and cassettes. *Disabled: toilets.*

### Library for the Performing Arts

*Lincoln Center, 111 Amsterdam Avenue, at West 65th Street (870 1630). Subway 1 or 9 to 66th Street.* **Open** noon-8pm Mon, Thur; noon-6pm Tue, Wed, Fri, Sat. **Admission** free.

Outstanding research and circulating collections on music, drama, theatre and dance.

### Science, Industry and Business Library

*Madison Avenue, between 34th & 35th Streets (930 0747). Subway 6 to 53rd Street.* **Open** 10am-6pm Mon, Fri, Sat; 11am-7pm Tue-Thur. **Admission** free.

The largest public information centre in the world devoted to science, technology, economics, and business occupies the first floor and lower level of the old B Altman department store. Opened in May 1996, after a $100 million renovation, the new Gwathmey/Siegel-designed branch of the New York Public Library has a circulating collection of 50,000 books, an open-shelf reference collection of 60,000 volumes, and a mission to help people in small businesses. It also places special emphasis on digital technologies and provides ultra-sophisticated access to information on the Internet. *Disabled: toilets. Internet: http://www.nypl.org/research/sibl/index.html*

### Schomburg Center for Research in Black Culture

*515 Malcolm X Boulevard, at 135th Street (491 2200). Subway 2 or 3 to 135th Street.* **Open** noon-8pm Mon-Wed; 10am-6pm Thur-Sat. **Admission** free.

A collection relating to black and African culture founded by the Puerto Rican Arthur Schomburg in 1926. It includes photographs, maps, paintings, exhibitions and artefacts of significance to American culture and collecting. *Disabled: toilets.*

# Art Galleries

**In the face of encroaching commercialism, SoHo galleries continue to seek fresh pastures in the wilds of West Chelsea.**

At the moment, the art market owes its health and personality as much to speculation in commercial real estate as to resident artists and dealers. Galleries are clustered in neighbourhoods that range from the scruffy melting pot of the Lower East Side and the almost Dickensian sidewalks of SoHo, to the staid environs of 57th Street and the more rarefied air of upper Madison Avenue.

Over the last few years, a concentrated new district dedicated to the exhibition and sale of contemporary art has sprung up among the warehouses of **West Chelsea** (*see page 204*), while the young artist-led **Williamsburg** area of Brooklyn continues to offer homegrown delights among its burgeoning community of non-profit spaces. Although retail stores and new hotels threaten to overwhelm **SoHo**, it has maintained its cutting-edge profile and gained renewed vitality from diversity. In **TriBeCa**, fine, artist-friendly restaurants are more bountiful than ever, while the art hinterlands now lie in a **West Village** triangle just below 14th Street that previously belonged solely to meat packers. The whole makes for a scene as entertaining as it is edifying.

In fact, the art world's current structure has begun to resemble the film industry: uptown corporate studios bearing the names **Gagosian**, **PaceWildenstein** and **Marlborough**; major independents spread over both SoHo and Chelsea, surrounded by smaller, art-house upstarts, and satellite fringe productions. Local wags have even dubbed one gallery complex in Chelsea 'the MGM building'.

There has also been an intelligible curatorial shift in many galleries from object-orientated exhibitions to theatrical project-orientated installations that incorporate work in all media and add an 'anything-goes' atmosphere to viewing and collecting. You might find it all a horrifying muddle – or a welcome challenge.

Dedicated gallery-goers should check the reviews in Friday's *New York Times*, the weekly reviews in *Time Out New York*, and the monthly notices in such glossies as *Artforum* ($7) and *Art in America* ($4.95). The *Art Now Gallery Guide*, free for the asking at most galleries (or $1.50 at museum bookstores), dependably lists exhibitions and gallery hours each month, and includes helpful neighbourhood maps. For an overview of the market itself, look to the monthlies *Art and Antiques*

($3.95), *Art & Auction* ($6), or *Art News* ($6).

*Opening times listed are for the 'season' – September to May or June. Summer hours tend to be more erratic, and many galleries close during August. Phone before visiting.*

## Upper East Side

Many of the galleries on the Upper East Side sell masterworks at prices marked for millionaires, but anyone can look for free, and much of what you'll see are treasures that could swiftly vanish into somebody's private collection.

### DC Moore Gallery
*724 Fifth Avenue between 55th & 56th Streets (247 2111). Subway N or R to Fifth Avenue.* **Open** 10am-5.30pm Tue-Sat.
This airy gallery, once the bastion of dealer Grace Borgenicht, shows prominent twentieth-century and contemporary artists such as Milton Avery, Paul Cadmus, Robert Kushner, Jacob Lawrence and George Platt Lynes.

### Dintenfass/Salander-O'Reilly
*20 East 79th Street (581 2268). Subway 6 to 77th Street/Lexington Avenue.* **Open** *winter* 10am-5.30pm Tue-Sat.
A merger between two notable galleries has expanded their artist-base to include important European and American realists.

### Gagosian
*980 Madison Avenue, at 76th Street (744 2313). Subway 6 to 77th Street.* **Open** *Sept-June* 10am-6pm Tue-Sat.
The prince of 1980s success – Larry Gagosian is still one of New York's major players in contemporary art, showing new work by such artists as Francesco Clemente and David Salle; he has also been hugely successful in secondary-market sales.

### M Knoedler & Co Inc
*19 East 70th Street, between Madison & Fifth Avenues (794 0550). Subway 6 to 68th Street.* **Open** *Sept-May* 9.30am-5.30pm Tue-Fri; 10am-5.30pm Sat.
Knoedler shows famous abstract expressionists and other greats: Frank Stella, Nancy Graves, Robert Rauschenberg, Howard Hodgkin and David Smith among others.

### Michael Werner
*21 East 67th Street, between Madison & Fifth Avenues (988 1623). Subway 6 to 68th Street.* **Open** *Sept-May* 10am-6pm Mon-Sat.
The genteel Werner's Manhattan addition to his successful operation in Germany is a small but elegant space with finely curated exhibitions of work by such protean European art stars as Marcel Broodthaers, Sigmar Polke, and Per Kirkeby.

## 57th Street

The home of Carnegie Hall, exclusive boutiques and numerous art galleries, 57th Street is an old-style slice of elegant, moneyed New York – ostentatious and expensive but fun to explore. Most of the galleries here are established names, and therefore more conservative than their SoHo counterparts. Lately, though, there has been greater commerce between the two areas, as some uptown galleries have expanded downtown.

## ACA Galleries
*41 East 57th Street, at Madison Avenue (644 8300). Subway 4, 5 or 6 to 59th Street; N or R to Lexington Avenue.* **Open** *Sept-June* 10am-5.30pm Tue-Sat.
Major nineteenth- and twentieth-century American artists, such as Georgia O'Keeffe, Milton Avery and Reginald Marsh.

## André Emmerich
*41 East 57th Street, between Madison & Fifth Avenues (752 0124). Subway 4, 5 or 6 to Lexington Avenue; N or R to Fifth Avenue/59th Street.* **Open** *Sept-May* 10am-5.30pm Tue-Sat.
Now a division of Sotheby's, this establishment gallery's interest is divided between important modern painting, particularly from the colour-field school, and antiquities from major civilisations. Various works by David Hockney are on show as well as pieces by Anthony Caro, Sam Francis and Morris Louis, among others.

## Marian Goodman
*24 West 57th Street, between Fifth & Sixth Avenues (977 7160). Subway B, N or R to 57th Street.* **Open** 10am-6pm Mon-Sat.
Work by acclaimed European contemporary painters, sculptors and conceptualists predominates here, usually in striking installations. The impressive roster of gallery artists includes Anselm Kiefer, Christian Boltanski, and Rebecca Horn, as well as Jeff Wall, Juan Munoz and Gabriel Orozco.

## Marlborough
*Second Floor, 40 West 57th Street, between Fifth & Sixth Avenues (541 4900). Subway B, N or R to 57th Street.* **Open** *Sept-May* 10am-5.30pm Mon-Sat.
This monolithic gallery shows work by modernist bigwigs Larry Rivers, Red Grooms, Marisol, Alex Katz, Francis Bacon, RB Kitaj, Kurt Schwitters, Magdalena Abakanowicz and more... and more. Marlborough Graphics is just as splendiferous.

## Mary Boone
*Fourth Floor, 745 Fifth Avenue, between 57th & 58th Streets (752 2929). Subway E, F, N or R to Fifth Avenue.* **Open** 10am-6pm Tue-Fri; 10am-5pm Sat.
This former SoHo celeb's current location on Fifth Avenue is smaller than her downtown digs were, but the art she presents has lost none of its lustre. Boone's list of contemporaries continues to grow, and currently includes Eric Fischl, Ross Bleckner, Barbara Kruger and Sean Scully, with young 'uns Ellen Gallagher and Leonardo Drew.

## PaceWildenstein
*32 East 57th Street, between Park & Madison Avenues (421 3292). Subway 4, 5 or 6 to 59th Street; N or R to 59th Street/Fifth Avenue.* **Open** *Sept-May* 9.30am-6pm Tue-Fri; 10am-6pm Sat.
The heavyweight in dealerships, this corporate giant offers work by some of the most significant artists of the century: Picasso, Mark Rothko, Alexander Calder, Lucas Samaras, Sol Lewitt and Chuck Close, along with Julian Schnabel, Kiki Smith, and Elizabeth Murray. Pace Prints and Primitives, at the same address, publishes prints from Old Masters to big-name contemporaries, and has a fine collection of African art. *See also p207 and p210.*
*Internet: http://www.pacewildenstein.com*

## Robert Miller
*Second Floor, 41 East 57th Street, at Madison Avenue (980 5454). Subway 4, 5 or 6 to 59th Street; N or R to 59th Street/Fifth Avenue.* **Open** *Sept-May* 10am-6pm Tue-Sat.
Robert Miller shows work by artists as familiar to museums as to private collections: Lee Krasner, Louise Fishman, Alice Neel and the late Jean-Michel Basquiat and Robert Mapplethorpe. For contemporary art enthusiasts, no trip to 57th Street would be complete without a visit.

## Yoshii
*20 West 57th Street, between Sixth & Seventh Avenues (265 8876). Subway B, N or R to 57th Street.* **Open** 10am-6pm Tue-Sat.
This relatively young gallery consistently presents lively shows by both contemporaries in painting, photography, sculpture and installation, as well as terrific historical surveys.

# SoHo

Though a number of mature SoHo galleries have decamped for Chelsea (*see page 204*), the area remains home to several mainstream dealers, with over 200 other galleries surrounding them. What follows is a selection of the most consistently rewarding galleries in the community, though you can certainly find something of interest and import on every street.

## Broadway

There are a number of gallery-rich buildings along Broadway, with the largest concentrations near Prince Street, at Numbers 560 and 578.

## Anton Kern
*558 Broadway, between Prince & Spring Streets (965 1706). Subway N or R to Prince Street.* **Open** *Sept-June* 10am-6pm Tue-Sat.
The son of artist Georg Baselitz, this Gladstone gallery protégé presents installations by young American and European artists who shun object-art to render futuristic site-specific installations.

## Curt Marcus Gallery
*578 Broadway, between Houston & Prince Streets (226 3200). Subway 6 to Bleecker Street; B, D or F to Broadway/Lafayette Street; N or R to Prince Street.* **Open** *Sept-May* 10am-6pm Tue-Sat.
This is a place for the peculiar but appealing, from Richard Pettibone's Shakerish objects to the mysterious and resonant pinhole photography of Barbara Ess.

## John Gibson
*568 Broadway, between Prince & Houston Streets (925 1192). Subway N or R to Prince Street.* **Open** 11am-6pm Tue-Sat.
Long resident in SoHo, Gibson presents cutting-edge conceptual work from a bevy of international artists.

## Nolan/Eckman
*Sixth Floor, 560 Broadway, at Prince Street (925 6190). Subway 6 to Spring Street; N or R to Prince Street.* **Open** *Sept-May* 10am-6pm Tue-Sat.
This small but high-level gallery primarily shows work on paper by established contemporary artists from the US and Europe, which sells at mid-range prices.

# West Chelsea

Four years ago, West Chelsea was all broken sidewalks, windowless brick warehouses and cavernous garages for trucks. Today, it's about art.

The district lies near the Hudson River, stretching north from West 20th to West 26th Streets. All the galleries are between Tenth and Eleventh Avenues, beneath the remains of the old West Side Highway – one of New York's haunting civic ruins. Galleries tend to be large, architecturally distinct spaces, most of whose owners first established themselves in SoHo. More seem to open each month. No longer lost among the shoppers and film location crews that now fill the old neighbourhood, the galleries are as much the stars as the artists, whose work tends to be high-end and ground-breaking. There are a number of newer galleries devoted to lower-priced emerging artists, a number of them from Europe and California.

*Take the C or E subway to 23rd Street and Eighth Avenue (although a taxi or the 23rd Street crosstown bus will bring you closer – the blocks between avenues are long).*

**Metro Pictures.** *See page 205.*

## West 20th Street

### Bill Maynes
*Eighth Floor, 529 West 20th Street (741 3318).*
**Open** 11am-6pm Wed-Sun.
Maynes is a bright, energetic fellow whose beautiful gallery also offers a great downtown view. He shows youngish American painters and sculptors who take traditional media to quirky, emotionally affecting, new heights.

### Stefan Stux
*Sixth Floor, 535 West 20th Street (352 1600).*
**Open** 11am-6pm Wed-Sun.
European and American contemporary painters and sculptors show throughout a warren of rooms in this SoHo emigré's new space. The building was formerly a cold storage facility and will eventually house nothing but galleries and artists' studios.

## West 21st Street

### Paula Cooper Gallery
*534 West 21st Street (255 1105).*
**Open** 11am-6pm Tue-Sat.
Cooper opened the first art gallery in SoHo and, as an early settler in West Chelsea, built one of the grander palaces for exhibiting the predominately minimalist, largely conceptual work of artists whose careers flourished under her administration. They include Donald Judd, Carl Andre and Robert Gober, as well as photographers Andres Serrano and Zoe Leonard.

## West 22nd Street

### Annina Nosei
*Second Floor, 530 West 22nd Street (741 8695).*
**Open** 11am-6pm Tue-Sat.
This SoHo pioneer rented her primarily painters' gallery to Prada's Miu Miu boutique and opened in Chelsea with an ambient sound installation by Paul Miller (aka DJ Spooky). Other shows have included work by photographer Shirin Neshat and painters Manuael Ocampo and Theresa Serano.

### D'Amelio-Terras
*525 West 22nd Street (352 9460).*
**Open** 11am-6pm Tue-Sat.
Christopher D'Amelio and Lucien Terras cut their dealer-teeth at Paula Cooper, then opened this space to emerging Americans as well as artists established in Europe and Japan but little known in New York. In addition to mounting engaging group shows, they are also working with Tony Feher and the art of former Cooper upstart Cady Noland.

### Dia Center for the Arts
*548 West 22nd Street (989 5912).* **Open** noon to 6pm Thur-Sun. **Admission** $4; $2 concessions.
Chelsea first became an art-specific destination in 1987, when the non-profit Dia Center opened its doors in this former warehouse on West 22nd between Tenth and Eleventh Avenues – the block some refer to as 'the Park Avenue of Chelsea'. Dia presents commissioned work by major contemporaries that remain on view throughout the season. The 1997-98 programme includes installations by

that wizard of perception Robert Irwin and by film-maker/photographer Tracey Moffatt.
*Internet: http://www.diacenter.org*

### Jessica Fredericks
*504 West 22nd Street (633 6555).*
**Open** 11am-6pm Tue-Sat.
Fredericks and partner Andrew Freiser live and work out of this small gallery on the ground floor of an art-dedicated townhouse. They have been effective in developing a new generation of collectors for work by both mid-career and emerging artists from New York and Los Angeles, with a roster that includes Brenda Zlamany and John Wesley.

### Linda Kirkland
*504 West 22nd Street (627 3930).*
**Open** 11-6pm Wed-Sun.
The brains behind the conversion of this 1860 townhouse, Kirkland runs a nifty operation on the third floor, which she gives over to the work of 'the most emerging artists on the street' as well as to a number of joyous group shows.

### Matthew Marks
*522 West 22nd Street (243 1650).*
**Open** noon-6pm Mon-Sat.
The second of the precocious Marks's three Manhattan galleries, this beautifully lit converted garage is devoted to large-scale work by blue-chip modernist heroes Willem de Kooning, Elsworth Kelly, Brice Marden and Richard Serra.

### Max Protetch Gallery
*511 West 22nd Street (633 6999).*
**Open** by appointment only.
As well as showing important contemporary painting, sculpture and ceramics, Max Protetch Gallery is one of the few places that finds space for architects' drawings and models.

### Morris-Healy
*530 West 22nd Street (243 3753).*
**Open** 11am-6pm Tue-Sat.
With Matthew Marks and Pat Hearn, partners Paul Morris and Tom Healy have not only done wonders for the Chelsea art community, they've been very successful on their own with a programme that has revived the reputations of mid-career artists, while bringing into the limelight young New York talent as well as the work of artists living abroad. Particular favourites have been Americans Tom Sachs, George Stoll and Meg Webster, and Finnish photographer Esko Manniko.

### Pat Hearn Gallery
*530 West 22nd Street (727 7366).*
**Open** 11am-6pm Wed-Sun.
This vanguard gallerist helped establish the East Village and SoHo art scenes before moving up to Chelsea to continue presenting her roster of rigorous abstractionists and conceptualists. Hearn represents Mary Heilmann, Jutta Koetker, Renee Green and Lincoln Tobier, among others. Never a dull moment.

### 303 Gallery
*525 West 22nd Street (255 1121).*
**Open** 11am-6pm Tue-Sat.
A recent transplant from SoHo, Lisa Spellman's cutting-edge gallery features American artists working in several media who have all garnered critical acclaim. They include Rikrit Tiravanija, photographers Thomas Ruff and Collier Schorr, sculptor Daniel Oates and painter Sue Williams.

## West 24th Street

### Barbara Gladstone
*515 West 24th Street (206 9300).*
**Open** *Sept-June* 10am-6pm Tue-Sat.
Gladstone is strictly blue-chip and presents often spectacular shows of high-quality painting, sculpture, photography and video by established artists including Richard Prince, Matthew Barney, Rosemarie Trockel, Anish Kapoor, Matt Mullican and Vito Acconci.

### Matthew Marks
*523 West 24th Street (243 0200).*
**Open** 10am-6pm Tue-Sat.
Ambitious Marks, the driving force in Chelsea's rebirth as an art centre, divides this 10,000 sq ft two-storey space into two separate galleries where he features new work by contemporary painters, photographers and sculptors including Nan Goldin, David Armstrong and the late Peter Cain.

### Metro Pictures
*519 West 24th Street (206 7100).*
**Open** *Sept-May* 10am-6pm Tue-Sat.
This great playground for artists features hip, keenly critical, cutting edge work. Projects include Cindy Sherman's unnerving cibachromes, Louise Lawler's cool photographic critiques, Mike Kelley's conflations of viciousness and pathos and Tony Oursler's eerie, psychologically searing video projections.

## West 23rd Street

### Cheim & Read
*521 West 23rd Street (242 7727).*
**Open** 10am-6pm Tue-Sat.
Louise Bourgeois, Alice Neel, and Jenny Holzer are examples of the high-profile artists these expatriates from West 57th Street's Robert Miller Gallery have put on view. Look for a high concentration of photographers such as Adam Fuss and Robert Mapplethorpe along with contemporary sculptors and painters.

## West 26th Street

### Greene/Naftali
*Eighth Floor, 526 West 26th Street (463 7770).*
**Open** 10am-6pm Wed-Sat; noon-6pm Sun.
Carol Greene's airy eyrie has wonderful light, a spectacular view, and a history of stellar group shows as well as fine solo work by American painters and installation specialists.

### Team
*527 West 26th Street (279 9219).* **Open** 11am-7pm Thur-Sun, and by appointment.
This non-profit gallery, directed by former SoHo dealer Jose Freire, is dedicated to long-term exhibitions of project-orientated work by a group of multimedia artists as entertaining as they can be provocative.

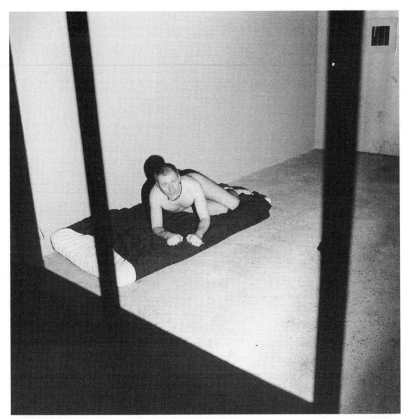

*Oleg Kulik courting controversy at the **Deitch Projects**.*

## Grand Street

### Boesky & Callery Fine Art

*51 Greene Street, between Broome & Grand Streets
(941 9888). Subway A, C or E to Canal Street.*
**Open** *Sept-May* 10am-6pm Tue-Sat.
Among SoHo's newer galleries, this one often gets it exactly
right, with a bright constellation of young, mostly female
artists whose shows tend to sell out quickly.

### CRG Art

*93 Grand Street, between Mercer & Greene Streets
(966 4360). Subway 6, N or R to Canal Street.*
**Open** *Sept-May* 11am-6pm Tue-Sat.
Carla Chammas, Richard Desroche and Glenn McMillan's
newish downtown premises represent such eminent risk-tak-
ers as Cathleen Lewis, Mona Hatoum and Sam Reveles.

### Deitch Projects

*76 Grand Street, between Wooster & Greene Streets
(343 7300). Subway 6, N or R to Canal Street.*
**Open** noon-6pm Tue-Sat.
Former Saatchi Gallery curator Deitch opened this solo-
project space to wide acclaim. Openings tend to be huge

affairs that attract the brightest lights in the art world. The
focus is on emerging artists who create elaborate, usually
quite provocative, multimedia installations.

### Paul Kasmin

*74 Grand Street, between Wooster & Greene Streets
(219 3219). Subway A, C, E, N or R to Canal Street.*
**Open** *Sept-May* 10am-6pm Tue-Fri; 11am-6pm Sat.
In amongst well-chosen group shows of gallery artists are
painters such as Alesandro Twombly, Suzanne McClelland,
Donald Baechler, Donald Sultan and sculptor Nancy
Rubins.

## Greene Street

### Casey M Kaplan

*Fourth Floor, 48 Greene Street, between Broome &
Grand Streets (226 6131) Subway C or E to Spring
Street; 6, N or R to Canal Street.*
**Open** *Sept-June* 10am-6pm Tue-Sat.
Twenty-something Kaplan's transfer from a micro gallery
has allowed him to exhibit paintings, photographs and large
installations by an energetic crew of young artists who are
based primarily in California and the UK.

## David Zwirner

*43 Greene Street, between Broome & Grand Streets (966 9074). Subway A, C or E to Canal Street; 6, N or R to Canal Street.* **Open** *Sept-May* 10am-6pm Tue-Sat.
This maverick German ex-pat's shop has been the hot spot on Greene Street since it opened four years ago, offering shows that easily serve as a barometer of what's important in art, not just in New York but internationally. The stable of cutting-edge talent includes Raymond Pettibon, Jason Rhoades, Toba Khedoori and Stan Douglas.

## Jack Tilton

*49 Greene Street, between Broome & Grand Streets (941 1775). Subway 6, C or E to Spring Street.* **Open** *Sept-June* 10am-6pm Tue-Sat.
Tilton's often provocative shows and his focus on painting make this a must on a SoHo gallery tour.

## Jay Gorney Modern Art

*100 Greene Street, between Prince & Spring Streets (966 4480). Subway N or R to Prince Street; C or E to Spring Street.* **Open** *Sept-June* 10am-6pm Tue-Sat.
Now one of SoHo's senior gallerists, Gorney represents artists of superior intelligence and accomplishment including Alexis Rockman, Sarah Charlesworth and James Welling.

## John Weber

*Third Floor, 142 Greene Street, between Houston & Prince Streets (966 6115). Subway B, D, F or Q to Broadway/Lafayette Street; N or R to Prince Street.* **Open** *Sept-May* 10am-6pm Tue-Sat; 10am-8pm Wed.
Weber shows strong conceptual and minimal work, with the emphasis on sculpture. Artists include Sol LeWitt, Hans Haacke, Daniel Buren, Alice Aycock, Hamish Fulton and Allan McCollum.

## PaceWildenstein

*142 Greene Street, between Prince & Houston Streets (431 9224). Subway 6 or F to Broadway/Lafayett Street; N or R to Prince Street.* **Open** *Sept-May* 10am-6pm Mon-Sat.
This luxurious downtown branch of the 57th Street gallery is where you'll find grand-scale installations by such big-time contemporaries as Robert Irwin, Sol Lewitt, Joel Shapiro, Julian Schnabel and Robert Whitman.

## Postmasters

*Second Floor, 80 Greene Street, between Spring & Broome Streets (941 5711). Subway 6, C or E to Spring Street.* **Open** *Sept-July* 11am-6pm Tue-Sat.
Drawings, photographs, videos, paintings and sculpture, all with strong conceptual leanings, are presented at this intriguing international gallery.

## Sperone-Westwater

*142 Greene Street, between Houston & Prince Streets (431 3685). Subway B, D, F or Q to Broadway/Lafayette Street; N or R to Prince Street.* **Open** *Sept-mid June* 10am-6pm Tue-Sat.
A stronghold of painting, and one of the best places to see work by the Italian neo-Expressionists Francesco Clemente, Sandro Chia, Luigi Ontani and Mimmo Paladino. Among the gallery's other illustrious contemporaries are Frank Moore, Jonathan Lasker, and McDermot and McGough.

# Mercer Street

## Holly Solomon Gallery

*172 Mercer Street, at Houston Street (941 5777). Subway B, D, F or Q to Broadway/Lafayette Street; N or R to Prince Street.* **Open** *Sept-May* 10am-5pm Tue-Fri.
Solomon's dramatic space shouldn't be missed. She shows distinctive work in all media, especially that of the Pattern

*Cutting-edge talent at* **David Zwirner**.

& Decoration school, by a quirky selection of artists including Nam June Paik, Izhar Patkin, Kim McConnel, Suzan Etkin and Thomas Lanigan-Schmidt.

## Ronald Feldman Fine Arts

*31 Mercer Street, between Grand & Canal Streets (226 3232). Subway 6, N or R to Canal Street.* **Open** *Sept-June* 10am-6pm Tue-Sat.
Feldman's history in SoHo is marked by landmark shows by such artists as Ilya Kabakov, Komar and Melamid, Ida Applebroog, Leon Golub and Hannah Wilke, but also includes more avant-garde installations by Eleanor Antin, Roxy Paine and Nancy Chunn.

## Sean Kelly

*43 Mercer Street, between Broome & Grand Streets (343 2405). Subway 6, N or R to Canal Street.* **Open** *Sept-June* 10am-6pm Tue-Sat.
This ex-Brit's project-orientated gallery offers exhibitions by established conceptualists including Ann Hamilton, Lorna Simpson and Marina Abramovic and also showcases emerging talents such as Cathy de Monchaux.

# Prince Street

## Andrea Rosen Gallery

*Third Floor, 130 Prince Street, between Wooster Street & West Broadway (941 0203). Subway C or E to Spring Street.* **Open** *Sept-May* 10am-6pm Tue-Sat.
Count on this place to show you the young heroes of the decade, when Rita Ackermann's endearing but unsettling waifs, John Currin's equally unsettling young babes and Wolfgang Tillmans' punky but intimate fashion photos all found their way into the limelight. With the emphasis on the experimental and the confrontational, work can inevitably be uneven but it is always fresh, reasonably priced and completely of-the-moment.

## Luhring Augustine

*Second Floor, 130 Prince Street, between Wooster & West Broadway (219 9600). Subway C or E to Spring Street.* **Open** *Sept-May* 10am-6pm Tue-Sat.
Luhring Augustine's gracious gallery features work from an impressive stable of artists that includes the Germans Albert Oehlen, Gerhard Richter and Günther Förg, Britain's Rachel Whiteread and Richard Billingham, and Americans Jack Pierson, Christopher Wool, Larry Clark and Paul McCarthy.

## Tanya Bonakdar

*Third Floor, 130 Prince Street, between Wooster & West Broadway (925 8035). Subway C or E to Spring Street; N or R to Prince Street.* **Open** *Sept-June* 10am-6pm Tue-Sat.
British-born Bonakdar presents quirky, often rather disturbing installations by such vanguard artists as Damien Hirst, Charles Long, Uta Barth and Mat Collishaw.

# West Broadway

## Charles Cowles
*420 West Broadway, between Prince & Spring Streets (925 3500). Subway C or E to Spring Street.*
**Open** *Sept-June* 10am-6pm Tue-Sat.
This gallery shows modern and contemporary paintings, sculpture and installations, including the formalist fugues of Caio Fonseca and fantabulous blown-glass works by Dale Chihuly.

## Leo Castelli
*420 West Broadway, between Spring & Prince Streets (431 5160). Subway C or E to Spring Street.*
**Open** *Sept-June* 10am-6pm Tue-Sat.
As one of the most revered personalities on New York's art scene, Castelli's decisions are followed with interest by collectors and dealers worldwide, and as he reaches his ninetieth year, much thought is given to the shake-up that will occur after his passing. He is known for representing such seminal Pop figures as Jasper Johns, Roy Lichtenstein and James Rosenquist, as well as the rigorous conceptions of Lawrence Weiner and Hanne Darboven. He also shows artists such as the Starn twins and Sophie Calle.
**Branch**: 578 Broadway (431 6279).

## Sonnabend Gallery
*420 West Broadway, between Spring & Prince Streets (966 6160). Subway C or E to Spring Street.*
**Open** *Sept-June* 10am-6pm Tue-Sat.
Make sure you visit this elegant venue for strong work from artists such as Haim Steinbach, Ashley Bickerton, Gilbert & George, Jeff Koons and Anne and Patrick Poirier.

# Wooster Street

## American Fine Arts
*22 Wooster Street, at Grand Street (941 0401). Subway A, C or E to Canal Street.* **Open** 11am-6pm Tue-Sat.
Colin de Land began his gallery business in the East Village but moved to the southern fringe of SoHo a few years ago. His shows retain a refreshingly ad hoc feeling which belies the consistently strong quality of the work.

## Basilico Fine Arts
*26 Wooster Street, at Grand Street (966 1831). Subway A, C or E to Canal Street.* **Open** *Sept-June* 11am-6pm Tue-Sat.
Formerly gallery director at Sonnabend, Stefano Basilico has a group of strong contenders for future art stardom in his stable, most of them artists working in various media who turn 1960s conceptualism into a fractured 1990s visual pleasure.

## Friedrich Petzel
*26 Wooster Street, between Grand & Canal (334 9466). Subway A, C, or E to Canal Street.* **Open** *Sept-June* 11am-6pm Tue-Sat.
Locals have nicknamed this 'the morphing gallery' for its emphasis on the conceptually-based art of mutating forms seen in work by Victor Estrada, Jorge Pardo, Karl Blossfeldt and Hirsch Perlman.

## Gagosian
*136 Wooster Street, between Houston & Prince Streets (228 2828). Subway C or E to Spring Street; N or R to Prince Street.* **Open** *Sept-June* 10am-6pm Tue-Sat.
A branch of Larry Gagosian's blue-chip uptown gallery, this dazzling space provides a perfect setting for the imposing, at times mammoth, pieces it houses – by such names as Damien Hirst, Richard Serra and Andy Warhol.

## Peter Blum
*99 Wooster Street, at Spring Street (343 0441). Subway C or E to Spring Street.* **Open** 10am-6pm Tue-Fri; 11am-6pm Sat, and by appointment.

Eclectic, elegant survey shows are *de rigueur* in this serene space, where you might see anything from African Boliw shrines to breathtaking work by Mondrian.

# Downtown Beyond SoHo
## West SoHo & TriBeCa

## Ace Gallery New York
*275 Hudson Street, at Spring Street (219 8275). Subway C or E to Spring Street.* **Open** 10am-6pm Tue-Sat.
A beautiful, cavernous poured-concrete bunker given to career retrospectives and special projects by living contemporaries from East and West coasts. Sol Lewit constructed a cinderblock extravaganza here a couple of years ago and LA installation artist Tim Hawkinson also took a star turn here, while Carl Andre enjoyed a memorable look back on some of his more significant sculptures.

## AC Project Room
*Second Floor, 15 Renwick Street, near Spring & Hudson Streets (219 8275). Subway A or C to Spring Street.* **Open** 11am-6pm Tue-Sat.
A consistently innovative artist-run space whose somewhat remote location doesn't keep it from connecting to a cross-generational mix of New York-based artists working in diverse forms.

## Apex Art
*291 Church Street, at Walker Street (431 5270). Subway 1 or 9 to Franklin Street.* **Open** 11am-6pm Wed-Sat.
An interesting gallery, where the impulse comes from independent curators, not artists, allowing this erudite and well-connected bunch to experiment with cleverly themed shows.

## Gavin Brown's Enterprise
*558 Broome Street, at Varick Street (431 1512). Subway C or E to Spring Street.* **Open** 11am-6pm Wed-Sat.
Londoner Gavin Brown champions young hopefuls in an admirably anti-establishment gallery that has managed to establish such artists as Rikrit Trivanija and Elizabeth Peyton, while showcasing talents including Stephen Pippin and Peter Doig.

# Non-Profit Spaces

## Alternative Museum
*Suite 402, 594 Broadway, near Prince Street (966 4444). Subway 6 to Spring Street; N or R to Prince Street.* **Open** 11am-6pm Tue-Sat.
The Alternative Museum has a reputation for exhibitions with humanitarian and socio-political concerns, especially from artists who are well beyond the mainstream.

## Art in General
*79 Walker Street, between Broadway & Lafayette Streets (219 0473). Subway 6, N or R to Canal Street.* **Open** *Sept-June* noon-6pm Tue-Sat.
On its fourth and sixth floors, this venerable TriBeCa institution holds exhibitions of contemporary work in development by emerging and under-recognised artists, with an emphasis on cultural diversity. It also sponsors eye-catching window installations at street-level all year round.
*Internet: http://www.artingeneral.org*

## Artists Space
*38 Greene Street, between Grand & Broome Streets (226 3970). Subway A, C or E to Canal Street.* **Open** *Sept-June* 10am-6pm Tue-Sat.
Laurie Anderson, Jonathan Borofsky, Cindy Sherman, Robert Longo and David Salle all had exhibitions here early in their careers. The emphasis is on innovative work in all

forms, so expect performance art, installations and video art and some terrific curatorial adventures.

### The Clocktower
*108 Leonard Street, at Broadway (233 1096). Subway 6, J, M, N, R or Z to Canal Street.*
**Open** noon-6pm Wed-Sun.
Run by the Institute for Art and Urban Resources, the Clocktower is primarily a subsidised studio space. Though not always open to the public, the gallery (located in the clocktower McKim, Mead & White added to the New York Life Insurance Building) stages entertaining exhibitions.

### Drawing Center
*35 Wooster Street, between Broome & Grand Streets (219 2166). Subway N or R to Prince Street.* **Open** 10am-6pm Tue, Thur, Fri; 10am-8pm Wed; 11am-6pm Sat.
Over the last few years, the Drawing Center has emerged as the most high-spirited, non-profit space downtown. Shows here are devoted to work on paper by emerging international talent which the Center promotes in its 'Selections' group shows; the young art stars of today often made their first New York gallery appearance here. Each spring, the Center runs important historical exhibitions, and from September to June hosts the monthly NightLight Readings (for adults and children). The Center recently opened The Drawing Room, a project space across the street at 40 Wooster Street, where visitors will find site-specific solo shows that serve as an extension to the 'Selections' installations.

### Exit Art: The First World
*Second Floor, 548 Broadway, between Prince & Spring Streets (966 7745). Subway B, D, F or Q to Broadway/ Lafayette.* **Open** 10am-6pm Tue-Thur; 10am-8pm Fri; 11am-8pm Sat.
Expect the best in multimedia cross-pollenations and culture clashes at this vibrant alternative space. There's also a charming tapas bar and shop that sells artists' work.

### New Museum of Contemporary Art
*583 Broadway, between Houston & Prince Streets (219 1355). Subway 6 to Spring or Bleecker Streets; B, D, F or Q to Broadway/Lafayette Street; N or R to Prince Street.* **Open** noon-6pm Tue-Fri, Sun; noon-8pm Sat.
**Admission** $4; $3 concessions; free under-12s; free 6-8pm Sat. **Credit** AmEx, DC, Disc, MC, V.
A major venue for experimental and multi-media work centring on recent pieces by living artists. Each year it mounts retrospectives by significant contemporaries such as Carolee Schneeman and Andres Serrano. Window displays always draw a crowd.

### Sculpture Center
*167 East 69th Street, between Third & Lexington Avenues (879 3500). Subway 6 to 68th Street.* **Open** 11am-5pm Tue-Sat.
One of the best places to see contemporary work by emerging and mid-career sculptors. The Sculpture Center also runs an ongoing project on Roosevelt Island.

### Thread Waxing Space
*Second Floor, 476 Broadway, between Grand & Broome Streets (966 9520). Subway 6 to Spring Street.* **Open** 10am-6pm Tue-Sat.
A block-through, truly dynamic multimedia space for contemporary art that also hosts video, performance, poetry and lecture series as well as the occasional musical evening.

### White Columns
*Second Floor, 154 Christopher Street, between Greenwich & Washington Streets (924 4212). Subway 1 or 9 to Christopher Street.* **Open** Sept-June noon-6pm Wed-Sun.
Events at this venerable alternative space have helped launch the careers of a number of today's important artists.

# Art fairs

Each year, New York plays host to several art fairs – sprawling commercial exhibitions where dealers of every sort showcase a broad spectrum of artists who command an equally wide range of prices. These shows require stamina but are worth at least an energetic browse. For exact dates and times, check *Time Out New York* or flyers at the participating galleries.

### The Art Show
*Seventh Regiment Armory, Park Avenue, at East 67th Street (715 1685). Subway 6 to 68th Street/Lexington Avenue.* **Date** late February. **Admission** $10.
Begun in 1988 and sponsored by the Art Dealers Association of America, this is the Big Daddy of New York art fairs. Exhibitors offer paintings, prints and sculpture from the seventeenth century to the present. Revenue goes to a Lower East Side social service agency.

### Crest Hardware Show
*558 Metropolitan Avenue, Brooklyn (1-718 388 9521). Subway L to Lorimer Street.* **Date** mid-May. **Admission** free.
A highlight of the annual art calendar, this inspired spring show, organised over the last few years by performance artist Gene Poole (1-718 486 8386), invites independent Brooklyn-based artists to contribute objects they can exhibit amid the wonderfully appointed old store's usual displays. Prices are low and it's great fun to root out the art from the tools.

### Gramercy International
*Gramercy Park Hotel, 2 Lexington Avenue, at East 21st Street (979 7591). Subway 6 to 18th Street & Park Avenue.* **Date** early May. **Admission** $5.
Organised by a group of young Chelsea dealers, this hip, five year-old downtown annual has proved among the most popular events in the contemporary art world: a weekend-long party at the nexus of culture and commerce, where the crowds are as much fun as the show. Dealers who take rooms on three floors here, exercise their own creative strategies by inventively showcasing work they can sell from a suitcase.

### Photography Show
*New York Hilton Hotel, West 53rd Street, at Avenue of the Americas. Subway E or B to Seventh Avenue. Information from the Association of International Photography Art Dealers (1-202 986 0105).* **Date** second weekend in March. **Admission** $10.
Dealers from the US, Europe and Japan exhibit vintage and traditional contemporary work at the biggest international fair devoted to fine art photography.

### Works on Paper
*Seventh Regiment Armory, Park Avenue, at East 67th Street (777 5218). Subway 6 to 68th Street/Lexington Avenue.* **Open** second weekend in March. **Admission** $10.
A something-for-everyone atmosphere attends this enormous three-day sale of visual material presented by dealers from the US and Europe. Collectors will find work in all styles from Old Master to contemporary, at prices that range from rock-bottom to top-drawer.

New talent is given space in the gallery's 'white room', and shows are often guest-curated by up-and-coming critics. The gallery is scheduled to move to 535 West 20th Street in Chelsea, so phone before visiting.

## Photography

For an overview of photography exhibitions in the city, buy the bi-monthly directory *Photography in New York International* ($2.95). *See also chapter* **Museums** for more collections.

### Bonni Benrhubi
*52 East 76th Street, at Madison Avenue (517 3766). Subway 6 to 77th Street/Lexington Avenue.* **Open** *Sept-June* 11am-6pm Tue-Sat.
Survey work by Walker Evans, Andreas Feininger, Robert Frank, Weegee, and Joel Meyerowitz.

### Houk Friedman
*851 Madison Avenue, between 70th & 71st Streets (628 5300). Subway 6 to 68th Street/Lexington Avenue.* **Open** 11am-6pm Tue-Sat.
These highly respected specialists in twentieth-century vintage and contemporary photography have an elegant space in which to show superb artists such as Sally Mann, Dorothea Lange, Man Ray, Alfred Stieglitz and Laszlo Moholy-Nagy, all of whom command top dollars.

### Howard Greenberg & 292 Gallery
*Second Floor, 120 Wooster Street, between Prince & Spring Streets (334 0010). Subway N or R to Prince Street; C or E to Spring Street.* **Open** 11am-6pm Tue-Sat.
These connecting galleries exhibit one enticing show after another of name twentieth-century photographers including Berenice Abbot, William Klein, Robert Frank and Imogen Cunningham.

### James Danziger
*130 Prince Street at Wooster Street (226 0056). Subway N or R to Prince Street.* **Open** 11am-6pm Wed-Sat, and by appointment.
With a collection of photographs that belong as comfortably to the classic as to the trendy, this serious downtown gallery shows work by artists including Peter Lindberg, Annie Liebovitz and Ansel Adams.

### Janet Borden
*560 Broadway, between Prince & Spring Streets (431 0166). Subway 6 to Spring Street; N or R to Prince Street.* **Open** *Sept-May* 11am-5pm Tue-Sat.
This SoHo stalwart's many contemporary artists include Oliver Wassow, Jan Groover, Tina Barney, David Levinthal and Lewis Baltz.

### Laurence Miller Gallery
*138 Spring Street, between Wooster & Greene Streets (226 1220). Subway 6 to Spring Street.* **Open** *Sept-June* 10am-6pm Tue-Fri; 11am-6pm Sat.
Laurence Miller shows interesting contemporary work. Recent shows have included work by Cartier-Bresson, Helen Levitt and David Levinthal.

### PaceWildensteinMacGill
*32 East 57th Street, between Park & Madison Avenues (759 7999). Subway 4, 5 or 6 to 59th Street; N or R to Lexington Avenue.* **Open** *Sept-May* 9.30am-5.30pm Tue-Fri; 10am-6pm Sat.
Look out for such well-known names as Weegee, Elliot Erwitt, Lisette Model, Joel-Peter Witkin and Walker Evans in addition to important other contemporaries, Harry Callahan, PL DeCorcia and William Christenberry.

### Staley-Wise Gallery
*560 Broadway, near Prince Street (966 6223). Subway R to Prince Street; B, D or F to Broadway/Lafayette Street.* **Open** *Sept-June* 11am-6pm Tue-Sat.
Strong themed group shows, with an historical emphasis on fashion and Hollywood glamour by masters including Horst and Arnold Newman, and Helmut Newton.

### Witkin Gallery
*415 West Broadway, at Spring Street (925 5510). Subway C or E to Spring Street.* **Open** 11am-6pm Tue-Sat.
Witkin shows major photographers, from contemporary works by Fay Godwin, Ruth Orkin and Willy Ronis, to classic prints by Robert Doisneau and Edward Weston.

### Zabriskie Gallery
*41 East 57th Street, at Madison Avenue (307 7430). Subway E or F to 53rd Street; N or R to Fifth Avenue.* **Open** *Sept-May* 10am-5.30pm Tue-Sat.
Zabriskie specialises in photography, showing works by Brassai, Steiglitz, Atget, William Klein and Scott Richter, but also deals in modern painting and sculpture.

## Williamsburg

Now that Manhattan rents have gone through the roof, the population of artists living and/or working in this post-industrial, blue-collar Polish/Italian neighbourhood has generated several non-profit galleries as well as art-friendly bars and restaurants. The most popular place for draught beer is the beautifully preserved **Teddy's** (96 Berry Street, at North 8th Street). There are pierogis and apple sauce at neighbourhood stand-by **Kasia's** (146 Bedford Avenue, at North 9th Street), and there's always a free pint of fresh lager for visitors to the landmark **Brooklyn Brewery** (79 North 11th Street), which occasionally mounts art exhibitions.

Some weekends, area artists hold group exhibitions in their studios or big, almost carnival-style art fairs such as the **Crest Hardware Show** (*see page 209*). Check the neighbourhood newsletter *Waterfront Week* for details. You might also want to seek out **Arena** (1-718 624 1307), an art salon in Cobble Hill.

### Momenta
*72 Berry Street, between North 9th & 10th Streets (1-718 218 8058). Subway L to Bedford Avenue.* **Open** noon-6pm Mon, Fri-Sun.
The most professional and imaginative organisation in the area, Momenta presents strong solo and group exhibitions by an exhilarating mix of emerging artists. Catch their work here, before it's snapped up by Manhattan dealers.

### Pierogi 2000
*167 North 9th Street, between Bedford & Driggs Avenues (1-718 599 2144). Subway L to Bedford Avenue.* **Open** *Sept-June* noon-6pm Mon, Sat, Sun, and by appointment.
Monthly openings at this artist-run gallery feature work by emerging and mid-career Brooklyn artists and tend to attract the whole neighbourhood, which shows up as much for the free drinks and pierogis as for the art. The big draw is the Flatfile, where you can peruse an impressive collection of drawings, prints and photos by a local artists that sell for under $200.

# Arts & Entertainment

# Media

**All the latest scoops for news junkies, couch potatoes and web surfers.**

New York is awash in so many streams of information that you can get into town, check into your room and keep yourself entertained for a good week without wandering further than the local newsstand. The city is saturated by mass communications: New Yorkers either listen to 'drive-time' news or talk radio on the ride in to work or read the papers on the train; the network television news is an evening ritual on returning to the nest; and the real sabbath of the city's intellectuals is the Sunday morning reading of the *New York Times*, generally to the accompaniment of bagels and lox.

## Newspapers & Magazines

### The Dailies

The **New York Times**, 'the grey lady of 43rd Street', Olympian as ever after nearly 150 years, remains the city's (and the nation's) paper of record. It has the broadest and deepest coverage of world, national and local events – as the masthead proclaims: 'All the news that's fit to print'. The mammoth Sunday edition checks in at a full five pounds of newsprint, including magazine, book review, sports, arts, finance, real estate and other sections.

Change comes slowly to this institution; a slightly hipper use of language in recent years was greeted in some quarters with an outcry comparable to that surrounding the début of vernacular mass in the Roman Catholic Church. The appearance of something like a gossip column, however sedate, set tongues wagging. And now New Yorkers will have to adjust to the Times' use of colour printing.

Two tabloids soldier on in the Times' wake, running much that may be less fit to print but closer to the city's heart, stomach or, often enough, groin. The **Daily News**' long tradition of sensational coverage of crime, scandal and disaster has produced classic headlines like 'Ford To City: Drop Dead' (of then president Gerald Ford's refusal of federal aid in a municipal fiscal crisis) and 'Two Slugs End Joey's Party' (of the slaying of mobster 'Crazy' Joe Gallo). The News has drifted politically from the Neanderthal right in the 1950s and 1960s to slightly left-of-centre under the ownership of real estate mogul Mort Zuckerman. The columnists Stanley Crouch and Juan Gonzalez from, respectively, the African-American and Latino communities, have great street sense and the paper's new editor, local legendary journalist Pete

Hammill has promised to connect with the city's new immigrant population.

Competing tabloid the **New York Post** is the city's oldest surviving newspaper, founded in 1801 by Alexander Hamilton. After a lengthy period as a standard-bearer for political liberalism, the Post swerved sharply to the right under current owner

## Read all about it

There are newsstands throughout the city. The ones below are open 24 hours daily. Unless one is listed, they have no phones. There are also huge selections at **Eastern News** (687 1198) at the base of the Met-Life building (above Grand Central Station), **Hudson News**, 753 Broadway at 8th Street (674 6655), and **Tower Books**, 383 Lafayette Street (228 5100), which has a large collection of fanzines, as does **Nicos**, Sixth Avenue at 11th Street (255 9175). All carry a full range of foreign newspapers.

### Downtown

**Delancey Street**, *at Essex Street. Subway F, J, M or Z to Essex/Delancey Street.*
**Gem Spa**, *131 Second Avenue, at St Mark's Place (529 1146). Subway 6 to Astor Place.*
**Sheridan Square**. *Subway 1 or 9 to Christopher Street.*
*Sixth Avenue, at 8th Street. Subway A, B, C, D, E, F or Q to West 4th Street.*

### Midtown

**Broadway**, *at 50th Street. Subway 1, C or E to 50th Street.*
**162 East 23rd Street**, *between Madison & Park Avenue. Subway 6 to 23rd Street.*
**Eighth Avenue**, *at 42nd Street. Subway A, C or E to 42nd Street.*
**Grand Hyatt**, *East 42nd Street, at Park Avenue. Subway 4, 5, 6 or 7 to Grand Central.*

### Uptown

**First Avenue**, *at 63rd Street. Subway 4, 5, 6, N or R to 59th Street/Lexington Avenue.*
**Broadway**, *at 72nd Street. Subway 1, 2, 3 or 9 to 72nd Street.*
**Leighton's Newsstand**, *Columbus Avenue, at 81st Street. Subway B or C to 81st Street.*
**Sajjadzheer Newsstand**, *Amsterdam Avenue, at 79th Street. Subway B or C to 81st Street.*

Rupert Murdoch. The Post has more column-inches of gossip that any other local paper. The ardent and extensive coverage of local sports teams in the back of both tabloids reflects the deep partisanship of their readers. Many New Yorkers read the News and the Post from back to front.

**New York Newsday** is a Long Island-based daily with a tabloid format but a more sober news style. It made a major effort to crack the New York market for several years but has lately receded to coverage of Brooklyn and Queens. **USA Today**, often referred to as McPaper, specialises in skin-deep capsules of news and a heavy overlay of computer graphics. The **Amsterdam News** is one of the oldest black newspapers, offering a left-of-centre Afrocentric view. New York also supports two Spanish language dailies, **El Diario** and **Noticias del Mundo**, and daily or weekly papers in every foreign tongue you can think of.

## Weeklies

The **New Yorker** has served up fine wit, elegant prose and sophisticated cartoon art since the 1920s. In the postwar era it established itself as a venue for serious journalism. Recently, under Tina Brown's editorship, it entered a serious flirtation with post-modern thought and multi-culturalism, which some have greeted as new vigour and others

*Towering journo: CBS headquarters.*

dismissed as mere trendiness. It usually makes for a lively, intelligent read.

The **New York Observer**, published on the Upper East Side, is a full-size weekly newpaper on salmon-coloured paper. It focuses on the doings of 'the overclass', its term for the upper echelons of business, finance, media and politics, and it contains some of the most knowing observations to be had on New York's power élite. It would certainly be F. Scott Fitzgerald's paper of choice. **New York** magazine straddles a newsweekly approach, a lifestyle/celebrity focus and a sizable listings section. The approach has never really jelled, but much of it is well-written.

Downtown journalism is a battlefield where the punk neo-cons of the **New York Press** and the unreconstructed hippies of the **Village Voice** contend. The Press uses an all-column format and has both youth's energy and irreverence and its cynicism and self-absorption. The Voice is sometimes passionate and ironic; just as often strident and predictable.

Just as predictably, we think the best place to find out what's going on in town is **Time Out New York**, launched in 1995 – based on the tried and trusted format of its London parent – and already an indispensable guide to the life of the city.

## Monthlies

Andy Warhol's magazine, **Interview**, is still firmly New York-based, covering the world of fashion and entertainment with maximum style over content. **Paper** covers the city's trend-conscious set with plenty of insider buzz on bars, clubs, downtown boutiques and the people you'll find in them.

## Television

American TV, in all its vulgarity, is a sure source of culture shock and a visit to New York would be woefully incomplete without at least a small dose of cathode radiation. TV is unrelentingly advertising-led and each moment of broadcasting is constructed to instill fatal curiosity for the next, with commercial breaks coming thick and fast.

The TV day is rigidly scheduled, beginning with news and gossipy breakfast magazine programmes, leading into a lobotomised cycle of soap operas, vintage re-runs and game shows, which remains unbroken until around 3pm. Then the talk shows like *Oprah* and *Ricki Lake* take over, broadcasting peoples' not-so-private problems, with subjects in the range of 'I married my mother's lesbian lover' or 'I still love my serial killer boyfriend'.

At 5pm the showbiz chat of the pre-news warm-up begins along with local news, followed by national and international news from 6.30pm. Early evening is the domain of the highest-rated shows – syndicated quizzes such as *Jeopardy* and

*Wheel of Fortune* – leaving huge audiences for prime time, when action series, sports, movies, sitcoms and fly-on-the-wall 'cop-umentaries' fight it out for ratings. New episodes of shows are shown once a week, but re-runs are scheduled daily, so, for example, you can see *The Simpsons* six times a week. Finally, as things begin to wind down, out come the unsubtle plugs and overblown personalities of the various late-night chat shows.

The only broadcast alternative to this ultra-consumerist programming is the sluggish élitism of public television. These stations receive little money from the government and rely heavily on 'membership' donations garnered during embarrassing on-air funding drives. But it does have superior nightly news, twice the length of the networks' versions and many times the depth. Its Frontline and POV documentaries are also incisive.

And then there is cable, 50 or so channels of basic cable, plus 'Premium' channels offering uninterrupted movies and sports coverage. 'Pay-perview' channels have a menu of recent films, exclusive concerts and sports events to choose from. Cable is also where you'll find the paid programming and public access channels with their complement of weirdos and soft-core porn.

For TV schedules, including broadcast and cable television, save the Sunday *New York Times* TV section or get the indispensable *TV Guide* (99¢). Daily papers have comprehensive 24-hour listings.

## The Networks

There are four major networks which broadcast nationwide. All offer ratings-led variations on a theme. **CBS** (on channel 2 in NYC) has the best network news daily at 6.30pm and the top investigative show, *60 Minutes*, on Sundays. **NBC** (channel 4) is the home of the ailing *Saturday Night Live* and the *Tonight Show*. **ABC** (channel 7) is king of the daytime soaps and **Fox TV** (channel 5), a smaller network, is popular with younger audiences for shows like *Melrose Place*, *The Simpsons* and the *X-Files*.

**WWOR** (UPN 9) offers baseball and popular re-runs (*Baywatch*, *Married With Children*, *Cosby*); **WPIX** (channel 11) is 'New York's Movie Station'. There are also two Spanish channels, **WXTV** (channel 41) and **WNJU** (channel 47). As well as Mexican dramas and titillating gameshows, these are your best bet for soccer.

## Public TV

You'll find underfunded and pretentious public TV on channels 13, 21, 31 and 50. Hidden among schedules of classical music, wildlife shorts, cookery and DIY shows are British dramas (in the Masterpiece Theater slot) and re-runs of

# Sitcom city

Commercial television was born and bred in New York City. The first great public demonstrations of the new technology were at the city's 1939 World's Fair. The networks that dominate cathode ray mythmaking have always been headquartered in here and their news divisions anchored here. The live drama that was a staple of the medium's golden age drew on the resources of Broadway, and the late-night talk shows that most of America goes to bed with originated in New York.

It is however, the great staple of broadcast programming, the situation comedy, that has drawn most often on the peculiar dilemmas of big city life and middle America's fascination with the exotic fauna of the five boroughs.

A fictional middle-class Jewish family *The Goldbergs*, living at Apartment 3B, 1030 East Tremont Avenue in the Bronx, was the first of this breed and managed several years of success on three different networks in the early 1950s. Even the most whitebread American of the time knew that mama Molly's 'Yoo-hoo, Mrs Bloom' was the preface to a round of rear window gossip with a neighbour in the adjoining apartment building.

The great classic series of the time, *The Honeymooners*, took place in a threadbare flat in the Bensonhurst area of Brooklyn, where lived a foolishly self-important driver for the Gotham

*Inspector Morse, Poirot* and *Miss Marple* (in Mystery). *Fawlty Towers, The Young Ones* and long-forgotten episodes of *EastEnders* are shown at the weekend. Channel 21 broadcasts *ITN World News* daily at 7pm and 11.30pm.

### Cable

For music, there is **MTV**, its more conservative sibling **VH-1** and **The Box**, a 24-hour video juke-box channel. Sports fans have **ESPN**, **Sportschannel** and **MSG** (Madison Square Garden). **CNN**, **Headline News** and **NY-1** offer news all day, the last with a local bias. **C-SPAN** – one of the few channels worth watching – broadcasts the floor proceedings of the US House of Representatives and an array of public affairs seminars.

**Comedy Central** is 24-hour comedy, with British hits like *Absolutely Fabulous*, a glut of stand-up and nightly re-runs of classic *Saturday Night Live* shows starring such young guns as John Belushi and Eddie Murphy. **E!** is 'Entertainment Television', a pop-culture mix of celebrities and movie news. This is where you'll find New York icon Howard Stern (*see p216*) conducting hilariously intrusive interviews and such tabloid TV as *The Gossip Show* and the unmissable *Talk Soup* where you can watch daily highlights from the best of America's talk shows.

**Bravo** shows the kind of arts programmes which public TV would air if it could afford them, including *The South Bank Show* and a good ratio of quality movies. Its sister station, the **Independent Film Channel**, shows uninterrupted art-house movies. **BET** stands for Black Entertainment Television, a rap and soul-filled reminder of America's tendency to cultural separatism. The **Discovery Channel** and the **Learning Channel** offer the best of science and nature programmes, and show gruesome surgical operations, often around mealtimes. **Court TV** scores big ratings with hot trials like OJ. The **Country Channel** (musically speaking), the **Prayer Channel**, the **Home Shopping Network** and the **Weather Channel** are all self-explanatory. Watch out also for MTV's **The Goods**, its version of credit-card couch-potato consumer heaven.

**Public Access TV** is on channels 16, 17, 34 and 69 (only in Manhattan), which are surefire sources of bizarre camcorder amusement. Late night **Channel 35** is where you'll find the *Robin Byrd Show*, a kind of chat forum for Times Square porn stars, riddled with ads for escort services and sex lines. Premium channels, often available for a fee in hotels, include **HBO** (Home Box Office), **Showtime**, **Cinemax**, **Movie Channel** and **Disney**, all of which show uninterrupted feature films and exclusive 'specials'.

## Be the Audience

Tickets are available for all sorts of TV shows that are recorded in New York studios. Try the New York Convention & Visitors Bureau for more information.

### Ricki Lake Show

*(889 6767 ext 758)*
One of the more outrageous daytime talk shows. You must be over 18. Try for a standby one hour before taping (3.30pm and 5.30pm Wednesday to Friday).

---

Bus Company, Ralph Kramden (Jackie Gleason), and his upstairs neighbour Ed Norton (Art Carney), a transcendentally counter-logical sewer worker. Together with their endlessly tolerant wives Alice (Audrey Meadows) and Trixie (Joyce Randolph) they managed one brief season on air, but struck a chord so true it reverberates to this day in eternal syndication. This is a world so thoroughly imagined that just the core 39 shows reveal a treasure of detail: Ralph's bus route includes Madison and Fifth Avenue, Alice worked for a time as a riveter at the Brooklyn Navy Yard, top job at the sewer is foreman of the 42nd Street outlet to the East River. Aficionados can name the bars, delis and Chinese restaurants of the Kramden neighbourhood.

*I Love Lucy* provided the most widely viewed locale of the time, the Ricardo apartment at 623 East 68th Street (in reality, it would be somewhere in the East River) where Lucille Ball's hare-brained character (*left*) was constantly causing chaos for her Cuban-born bandleader husband and their neighbours and landlords, the Mertzes.

The Corona section of Queens held the spotlight through most of the 1970s with *All in the Family*, as the ultimate Joe Sixpack, Archie Bunker, ruled the roost at 704 Houser Street, spewing invective on the various ethnic groups of the neighbourhood. That his equal in bluster, next-door neighbour and African-American George Jefferson, succeeded in business and moved to Lucy's exclusive East Side neighbourhood (on a spinoff show of his own) may have been Archie's ultimate indignity.

Brooklyn was represented in the 1970s with *Welcome Back, Kotter* (with a young John Travolta) and, briefly, in the 1990s with *Brooklyn Bridge*. Manhattan is the locale of choice currently, with the bumptious yuppies of *Friends* (*pictured*), the media worker couple of *Mad About You* and the goofy entourage of *Seinfeld*, whose riffs on real life local restaurateur 'The Soup Nazi' have made him a celebrity in his own right. And that the real-life model for the show's Kramer now gives 'reality tours' in midtown only shows how blurred are art and life in New York today.

## The Late Show with David Letterman

*(975 5853)*
The foolish uncle of late night. Tapings are on Monday to Friday at 5.30pm. You have to be over 16. Queue for a stand-by ticket at noon on the day.

## Geraldo

*(265 8520 information; 265 1283 tickets)*
The talk show most likely to incite violence in its guests. Tapings are on Tuesday to Thursday at 1pm and 4pm. You must be over 18. Standby tickets are sometimes available 45 minutes before taping.

## Saturday Night Live

*(664 3056)*
An institution, but one always in danger of being cancelled for its increasing failure to amuse. Broadcasts and tapings are on Saturday at 11.30pm. Standby tickets are distributed at 9.15am at NBC (mezzanine level of the 49th Street side of Rockefeller Plaza). And you have to be over 16.

# Radio

There are nearly 100 stations in the New York area, offering a huge range of sounds and styles. On the AM dial you can find some intriguing talk radio, from phone-in shows that attract the city's nutcase population to fervently religious stations. There's plenty of news and sports as well. Radio highlights are printed weekly in the Sunday *New York Times* and *New York* magazine.

## News & Talk

WINS 1010 AM, WABC 770 AM and WCBS 880 AM offer news throughout the day, coupled with traffic reports. Ad-free public radio stations WNYC 93.9 FM/820 AM and WBAI 99.5 FM both provide excellent news, including the *All Things Considered* current affairs slot and guest-driven talk shows, notably WNYC AM's *New York and Company*. WBAI is one of the very few electronic media platforms for left-wing politics anywhere in the States.

The AM phone-in shows will take you from one extreme to the other. WLIB 1190 AM provides the voice of militant black New York, with news and talk from an Afrocentric perspective, interspersed with Caribbean music. Neo-fascist Rush Limbaugh airs his socially popular views on WABC, where you can also get a 45-minute late-morning dose of the barely-suppressed self-righteousness of former mayor Edward Koch and, in the evening, the heavily street-accented demagoguery of Guardian Angels founder Curtis Sliwa. Two classical stations, WQXR 96.3 FM and WNYC 93.9 FM, serve a varied diet of music and opera.

## Jazz

WBGO 88.3 FM 'Jazz 88' plays its records in phenomenal day-long chunks of a single artist, focusing on the birth-days and anniversaries of jazz greats. Less obsessive jazz buffs will find more variety on WCWP 88.1 FM and WQCD 101.9 FM.

## Dance & Pop

American commercial radio is rigidly formatted, which makes most pop stations extremely tedious and repetitive during daylight hours. However, in the evenings and at weekends, you'll find more interesting programmes. WQHT 97.1 FM 'Hot 97' is New York's commercial hip-hop station, with former Yo! MTV Raps hosts Dr Dre and Ed Lover cooking up a breakfast show for the homies, then rap and R'n'B through-out the day. The station also has some of the city's best house shows, with Tony Humphries very late on Fridays and Hex Hector and Johnny Vicious together late on Saturdays.

WBLS 107.5 FM is now an 'urban (meaning black) adult' station, playing classic and contemporary funk, soul and R'n'B. Grandmaster Flash has a splendid mix show (week-days at noon, Friday evening, Saturday night) and there's Chuck Chillout's house and R'n'B mix overnight on Saturday, plus Hal Jackson's Sunday (blues and soul) Classics. WRKS 98.7 FM 'Kiss' changed last year to 'adult' con-temporary format, which translates as unremarkable American pop. The only legacy of its more soulful days is the Sunday morning gospel show (6-9am). WCBS 101.1 FM is strictly oldies, while WDBZ 105.1 FM 'The Buzz' plays mainstream alt rock. WPLJ 95.5 FM is a top 40 station. WLTW 106.7 FM 'Lite FM' plays background music popular in elevators.

## Rock

WBAB 102.3 FM, WRCN 103.9 FM, WNEW 102.7 FM and WXRK 92.3 FM 'K-Rock' offer a digest of hard, classic and alternative rock. 'K Rock' also attracts the city's largest group of morning listeners with Howard Stern's 7-11am weekday show. WLIR 92.7 FM offers 'alternative' (indie and gothic) sounds with a British bias. WSOU 89.5 FM is a college station devoted to heavy metal. A similar diet can be found on the WAXQ 104.3. WFMU 91.1 FM is where the term 'free form radio' still has some meaning: an eclectic mix of avant-garde music and oddities like Joe Frank's eerie stream-of-consciousness monologues (7pm Thursdays).

## Other Music

WWRL 1600 AM plays gospel, WEVD 1050 AM talk, sports and music and WYNY 103.5 FM pop and disco.

## College Radio

College radio is innovative and free of ads. However, smaller transmitters mean that reception is often compromised by Manhattan's high-rise geography. Try WNYU 89.1 FM from New York University and WKCR 89.9 FM from Columbia for varied programming right across the musical spectrum.

# Gotham City Cyberspace

Web sites come and go with unpredictable frequency; check Time Out Net (*below*) for the latest.

**http://www.allianceforarts.org**
The New York City Culture Guide & Calendar, offering the latest news on major cultural events.

**http://www.avsi.com**
Lots of artsy New York stuff, including underground film directories and the website of trendy downtown guide, *Paper*.

**http://www.ci.nyc.ny.us/**
The 'Official New York Web Site' produced by the folks at City Hall.

**http://www.citysearch.com**
Up-to-the minute information on events and venues and a link to *Time Out New York*.

**http://www.clubnyc.com**
The latest news and grooves on the city's nocturnal scene.

**http://www.echonyc.com**
Arts reviews, events listings and a city guide.

**http://www.nynetwork.com**
Useful list of New York web sites.

**http://www.timeout.co.uk**
The Time Out website includes a guide to New York (among other cities) with listings, features and free classified ads.

**http://www.vilagevoice.com**
Listings and features from the *Village Voice*.

**http://www.whitehouse.gov**
Your connection to the high and mighty of US government.

# Spoken Word

**Poets, storytellers and rappers compete for attention in one of the best-value entertainments in the city.**

From a New York perspective, it's hard to believe that most Americans rank public speaking near the top of their lists of worst fears. The spoken word is a burgeoning part of the city's cultural life, and has long been an art form in its everyday life (just spend an afternoon in Washington Square Park, or riding the subway to hear for yourself). New Yorkers flock to authors' readings of their latest novels, poets try out their work on the public ear, speakers dazzle audiences with intellectual pyrotechnics – and often for free. It's one of the best-value entertainments in the city.

The big news in the spoken-word scene is performance poetry – a world in itself. Not since the beats re-invented the American aural tradition have poets attracted this kind of media attention, been so fashionable and pulled in so large an audience as in New York today. Walk into the **Nuyorican Poet's Café** on a Friday night and there's standing room only. Poetry cafés and bars keep popping up; and some of the city's hottest music venues host occasional poetry events and series. You'll even find poetry in clubland.

Despite all this, performance poetry is still an evolving, grassroots form – and proud of it. Its mainstays are the slam (a raucous sporting event in which selected audience members award points to competing poets) and the open mike (in which readers sign up for five minutes before the crowd). But the real innovations in the form are happening in the ongoing reading series and festivals, where poets have the opportunity to explore cross-pollination with performance art, theatre, dance

and music, particularly rap and jazz. Sometimes it works, sometimes it doesn't.

Dead poets (and novelists) are getting an airing too, in the form of marathon readings: a truly New York event. Some readings are held annually and star a stream of big-name literary personalities as readers. You can celebrate Good Friday with Dante's *Inferno* at the Cathedral of St John the Divine, complete with devils' food cake and red hots; Bloomsday with *Ulysses* at Symphony Space; or see in the New Year with *Finnegan's Wake* at the Paula Cooper Gallery. Also watch out for one-off marathons, usually in celebration of a literary anniversary.

For the most comprehensive listings of poetry and literary events, get the monthly *Poetry Calendar* free at poetry venues and in many book shops. For more selective listings, check the 'Books' and 'Around Town' sections of *Time Out New York* and 'Spoken Word' in the *New York Times*. Branches of the New York Public Library host poetry and author readings, listed in 'Events for Adults' available free at all branches. Some reading series take a long summer break, so phone to check events before setting out.

## Poetry

### 92nd Street Y Unterberg Poetry Center

*1385 Lexington Avenue, at 92nd Street (996 1100). Subway 6 to 96th Street.*
The Academy of American Poets and the 'Y' co-sponsor weekly readings featuring such luminaries as Saul Bellow, Adrienne Rich and John Irving. Panel discussions and lectures by high profile academics are also held. Readings usually start at 8pm on Mondays.

*An essential stop on the Spoken Word circuit – the **Nuyorican Poet's Café**. See page 218.*

### Biblio's

*317 Church Street, between Lispenard & White Streets (334 6990). Subway 6, J, N or R to Canal Street.*
This intimate poetry café/bookstore stages events at least twice a week, including regular Thursday night poetry and prose readings – 'Mad Alex Presents' and 'Devotional: Retrospectives' – in which one or two poets get a whole evening to present their *oeuvre*.

### Detour

*349 East 13th Street, at First Avenue (533 6212). Subway L to First Avenue.*
One of the most relaxed open mikes in town is held weekly (from 8pm on Sundays) at this jazz bar. Admission is free.

### A Different Light Bookstore & Café

*151 West 19th Street, between Sixth & Seventh Avenues (989 4850). Subway 1 or 9 to 18th Street.*
Saturday night open mike in a gay and lesbian bookstore (from 9.30pm on). Poets sign up for a ten-minute stint. *See also chapter* **Gay & Lesbian New York**.

### Dixon Place

*258 the Bowery, between Houston & Prince Streets (219 3088). Subway 6 to Spring Street.*
Ellie Covan hosts a performance salon in her loft, with open-performance night on the first Tuesday of each month. Poets mix with storytellers, fiction writers and performance artists... but not stand-up comics.

### Drawing Center

*35 Wooster Street, between Broome & Grand Streets (219 2166). Subway N or R to Prince Street.*
Nightlight is a dynamic series on alternate Wednesday nights in a pristine gallery, in which guest curator Linda Yablonsky blends spoken-word with a visual element. Phone for dates. *See also chapter* **Art Galleries**.

### Internet Café

*82 East 3rd Street, between First & Second Avenues (614 0747). Subway F to Second Avenue.*
Readings are simul-cast on alternate Wednesdays over the Net. *Internet: http//:www.bigmagic.com*

### KGB

*85 East 4th Street, between Second & Third Avenues (505 3360). Subway 6 to Bleecker Street; B, D or F to Broadway/Lafayette Street.*
A weekly reading series (on Sundays) in a funky East Village bar featuring luminaries of the downtown poetry scene. Admission is free.

### Knitting Factory/AlterKnit Theater

*74 Leonard Street, between Broadway & Church Street (219 3055). Subway A, C or E to Canal Street; 1 or 9 to Franklin Street.*
A weekly open mike session (Fridays in the bar) and monthly 'girlSpeak' (Sundays in AlterKnit), plus occasional poetry specials, are held in one of downtown's most happening music venues. *See also chapters* **Music** *and* **Dance**.

### Mo' Better

*570 Amsterdam Avenue, between 87th & 88th Streets (580 7755). Subway 1 or 9 to 86th Street.*
'Poetic Battles' is a regular open-mike/hip-hop contest spiced up with soul-food and drinks from the bar. Readings start at 7pm on Tuesdays.

### Mother

*432 West 14th Street, at Washington Street (366 5680). Subway A, C, E or L to 14th Street.* **Readings** 11.30pm first Tue of the month. **Admission** $10.
Performance poetry and nightlife blend at the monthly 'Verbal Abuse' series in this hip but unintimidating club

*Café-cum-bookstore:* **Biblio's**.

(Tuesdays from 11.30pm). The abuse is short, sweet and late-night (and often excellent); be prepared to chill to the beat when it's over. *See also chapter* **Clubs**.

### New School

*66 West 12th Street, between Fifth & Sixth Avenues (274 0343). Subway F to 14th Street.*
The Academy of American Poets occasionally schedules readings here (at the Tishman Auditorium) by some of the country's best-known poets. The New School itself runs the occasional fiction and poetry series, featuring contemporary writers, as well as performance-poetry festivals and esoteric lectures by visiting savants.

### Nuyorican Poet's Café

*236 East 3rd Street, between Avenues B & C (505 8183). Subway F to Second Avenue.*
The now-famous Nuyorican goes beyond open mikes and slams (open slam Wednesdays, 'slam invitational' Fridays) with multi-media events, staged readings and more. Elbow your way past slumming media execs on the hunt for new talent.

### Poetry Project

*St Mark's-in-the-Bowery, 131 East 10th Street, at Second Avenue (674 0910). Subway 6 to Astor Place.*
The legendary Poetry Project, whose hallowed walls first heard the likes of Ginsberg and Anne Waldman, is still a thriving centre for whatever's new and worth hearing. Living legends like Jim Carroll and Patti Smith still read here.

# Etiquette

As with any social event, attending a poetry performance has its do's and don'ts. Ignore the following at your own risk:

● At readings, don't clap until the program's over. At open mikes, clap after each poem.

● At slams, it's considered good manners to express your enthusiasm or disgust whenever you feel the urge, preferably mid-poem and at full volume.

● Don't forget to wear black.

# Cabaret

*Where to discover those kings of comedy, cabaret, and all that jazz.*

New York is the cabaret capital of the US, and quite possibly the world. No other city supports a cabaret industry where you can take your pick from a dozen different shows on any given night.

In the strict New York sense, the term 'cabaret' covers both a venue and an art form. It's an intimate club where songs are sung, usually by one person but sometimes by a small ensemble of performers. The songs are usually drawn from what's known as the Great American Songbook – the vast repertoire of the American musical theatre – and are supplemented with the occasional new number by a contemporary composer. More than anything, cabaret is an act of intimacy: the best singers are able to draw the audience in until each member feels that he or she is being sung to directly in the most private of concerts.

Cabaret's Golden Age in New York was the 1950s and early 1960s (see James Gavin's excellent book *Intimate Nights* for a lively history of that era). The advent of rock music and changing tastes eventually made cabaret an art form for the connoisseur, but today there are still plenty of fans and performers who keep it alive. Today's rooms basically fall into two groups: the classic, elegant, expensive *boîtes* like Rainbow & Stars, Cafe Carlyle, the Oak Room and Maxim's, where you'll spend $30-$50 just to get in and hear the likes of Barbara Cook, Bobby Short, Rosemary Clooney and Vic Damone; and the less formal neighbourhood clubs like Don't Tell Mama, Eighty Eight's and Danny's Skylight Room, where up-and-coming singers – many of them enormously talented – perform for enthusiastic fans who pay much lower cover charges.

Whether you choose to spend big bucks on a big singer at one of the major spots, or decide to check out the stars-of-tomorrow in one of the cosier clubs, you'll be guaranteed a true New York experience. After all, you're in the one city on earth that really is the heart and soul of cabaret.

## Putting on the Ritz

### Arcimboldo
*220 East 46th Street, between Second & Third Avenues (972 4646). Subway 4, 5, or 6 to 42nd Street/Grand Central.* **Shows** times vary. **Cover** $15, two-drink minimum. **Credit** AmEx, DC, MC, V.
One of the best and most opulent Italian restaurants in the city offers occasional cabaret performances. The décor of the restaurant is inspired by the Italian painter of the same name, who specialised in fanciful portraits concocted from fruit and vegetables. This is an elegant, somewhat pricey night on the town, but well worth it.

### Cafe Carlyle
*Hotel Carlyle, 35 East 76th Street, between Park & Madison Avenues (744 1600/1-800 227 5737). Subway 6 to 77th Street.* **Shows** 8.45pm, 10.45pm, Tue-Sat (closed July-mid Sept). **Cover** $50. **Credit** AmEx, DC, MC, V.
The epitome of chic New York, especially when Bobby Short or Eartha Kitt do their thing (and Woody Allen, who's become a regular on the early show on Monday nights). Don't dress down; this is about laying down some cash and remembering it's the Naughty Nineties. If you want to rub up against some atmosphere more cheaply, **Bemelmans Bar** across the hall always has a fine pianist like Barbara Carroll or Peter Mintun, from 9.30pm to 1.30am nightly with a $10 cover. *See also chapter* **Accommodation**.

### Maxim's
*680 Madison Avenue, between 61st & 62nd Streets (751 5111). Subway N, R, 4, 5, 6 to 59th Street.* **Shows** times vary. **Cover** $25-$50, plus dinner at early show, two-drink minimum at late show. **Credit** AmEx, DC, MC, V.
This super-elegant Upper East Side eatery is virtually a carbon copy of the original Maxim's in Paris. Award-winning chef David Ruggiero has taken the place over and instituted a cabaret programme that attracts some of the biggest names in the business, including Betty Buckley, Ann Hampton Callaway and Morgana King.

### The Oak Room
*Algonquin Hotel, 59 West 44th Street, between Fifth & Sixth Avenues (840 6800/1-800 555 8000). Subway B, D, F or Q to 42nd Street.* **Shows** 9.30pm Tue-Thur; 9.30pm, 11.30pm Fri, Sat. **Cover** $35, $15 drinks minimum. **Credit** AmEx, DC, Disc, MC, V.
This resonant banquette-lined room is the place to savour the cream of cabaret performers, including names like Julie Wilson, Andrea Marcovicci and Steve Ross. *See also chapter* **Accommodation**.

### Rainbow & Stars
*GE Building, Rockefeller Center, 30 Rockefeller Plaza, 49th Street, between Fifth & Sixth Avenues, 65th floor (632 5000). Subway B, D, F or Q to 47th Street/ Rockefeller Center.* **Shows** 8.30pm, 11.30pm Tue-Sat. **Cover** $40, dinner compulsory at first show. **Credit** AmEx, DC, MC, V.
Just off the famous Rainbow Room, in the GE (formerly the RCA) Building, Rainbow & Stars is suffused with elegance, giving it exactly the kind of Manhattan glamour you've seen in the movies. From the 65th floor you get a delirious view. The singers are big names like Rosemary Clooney and Vic Damone, who work with the theatre of the place.

### Supper Club
*240 West 47th Street, between Eighth Avenue & Broadway (921 1940). Subway 1 or 9 to 50th Street; N or R to 49th Street.* **Shows** times vary. **Cover** $15. **Credit** AmEx, DC, Disc, MC, V.
This beautifully restored ballroom is the setting for dinner and dancing to a 12-piece big band. The décor and better-

*Lay down some cash and catch Eartha Kitt when she plays the **Cafe Carlyle**. See page 219.*

than-average food attract a glamorous crowd of pre-theatre dahlings. It's also an occasional concert venue, hosting such intimacy-requiring performers as Michael Feinstein, Ute Lemper and Marianne Faithfull.
*Disabled: toilets.*

### Tatou
*151 East 50th Street, between Lexington & Third Avenues (753 1144). Subway 6 to 51st Street.* **Shows** times vary. **Cover** $15-$20, $20 drink minimum. **Credit** AmEx, MC, V.
Owned by a former Studio 54 proprietor Mark Fleishman, this opulently decorated supper club is swathed in heavy velvet curtains and pink brocade banquettes to look like a miniature opera house. The food's pretty good (try the $25 pre-theatre menu), but the evening hots up when the bass joins the jazz piano. There's dancing to contemporary club sounds every night from 11.30pm.

## Give My Regards to Broadway

### Danny's Skylight Room
*346 West 46th Street, between Eighth & Ninth Avenues (265 8133). Subway A, C or E to 42nd Street.* **Shows** times vary. **Cover** $8-$15. **Credit** AmEx, DC, MC, V.

A pastel nook of the Grand Sea Palace restaurant, 'where Bangkok meets Broadway' on touristy Restaurant Row. There's pop-jazz, pop and cabaret, with the accent on the smooth. This is a good place to catch up-and-comers, plus a few mature cabaret standbys like Blossom Dearie and Barbara Lea.

### Don't Tell Mama
*343 West 46th Street, between Eighth & Ninth Avenues (757 0788). Subway A, C or E to 42nd Street.* **Shows** times vary. **Cover** $6-$15 in cabaret room, free in piano bar, two-drink minimum at tables (no food served). **Credit** AmEx, V.
Showbiz pros like to visit this Theater District venue. The acts range from strictly amateurish to potential stars of tomorrow.

### Eighty Eights
*228 West 10th Street, between Bleecker & Hudson Streets (924 0088). Subway 1 or 9 to Christopher Street/Sheridan Square.* **Shows** 8pm, 10.30pm Mon-Thur; 8.30pm, 11pm Fri, Sat; 3pm, 5.30pm, 8pm, 10.30pm Sun. **Cover** $10-$15, plus two-drink minimum (no food except Sunday brunch). **No credit cards.**
Downtown's classy high-tech venue. Local favourites like Baby Jane Dexter and Charles Cermele perform upstairs,

while downstairs in the piano bar owner Karen Miller tickles a cultish crowd until closing time. Sunday brunch ($22.50) draws a crowd too. One of the most convivial spots in the West Village, where chorus boys and cabaret singers make up much of the clientele.

## 55 Grove Street
## Upstairs at Rose's Turn

*55 Grove Street, between Seventh Avenue & Bleecker Street (366 5438). Subway 1 or 9 to Christopher Street/Sheridan Square.* **Cover** $6-$15, two-drink minimum. **No credit cards.**
The oldest cabaret showroom in Greenwich Village where The Duplex started 40 years ago, before it moved to newer quarters across Seventh Avenue (*see below*). A rather dark, charmless room, it's got zero atmosphere. The emphasis tends toward comedy, as well-as pocket-sized one-act musicals, with only the occasional vocalist.

## Judy's

*49 West 44th Street, between Fifth & Sixth Avenues (764 8930). Subway 4, 5, 6, or 7 to 42nd Street.* **Shows** 9pm Mon-Thur; 9pm, 11pm Fri, Sat. **Cover** $8-$15, $10 minimum. **Credit** AmEx, MC, V.
The cosy, mirrored cabaret feels like a music lover's living room. There's also a separate piano bar where singer Judy Kreston (just one of the many Judys after whom the place is named) and pianist David Lahm perform on Saturday nights. Judy's is popular with tourists and theatre-goers.

# Roll Out the Barrel

## Bar d'O

*29 Bedford Street, at Carmine Street (627 2580). Subway 1 or 9 to Houston Street.* **Shows** times vary. **Cover** varies. **No credit cards.**
Bar d'O is a busy little mixed/gay bar packed with a bubbly crowd who come here to catch the very best acts on the drag circuit. A regular performer here is scene stalwart Joey Arias, who is guaranteed to astound with his breathtaking recreations of Billie Holiday numbers. *See also chapter* **Clubs.**

## Brandy's

*235 East 84th Street, between Second & Third Avenues (650 1944). Subway 4, 5, or 6 to 86th Street.* **Shows** times vary. **Cover** none, two-drink minimum. **No credit cards.**
An old, local good-time piano bar where singing bartenders meet shower singers. On weekends it draws a yuppie crowd, but after 2am evolves into a people's bar for a few hours.

## The Duplex

*61 Christopher Street, at Seventh Avenue South (255 5438). Subway 1 or 9 to Christopher Street/Sheridan Square.* **Shows** times vary. **Cover** $6-$12 ,plus two-drink minimum. **No credit cards.**
**Piano bar** 9pm-4am daily. **No credit cards.**
New York's oldest cabaret has been going for over 40 years, and sets the pace for camp, good-natured fun. It attracts a relaxed blend of regulars and tourists, laughing and singing along with classy drag performances, comedians and rising stars.

# All That Jazz

Almost all the established jazz clubs work to a cabaret format. For some of the larger venues, including Birdland, Fez, Iridium and others, *see chapter* **Music.**

## Arthur's Tavern

*57 Grove Street, between Bleecker Street & Seventh Avenue South (675 6879). Subway 1 or 9 to Christopher Street/Sheridan Square.* **Shows** 9.30pm daily. **Cover** none, two-drink minimum at tables. **No credit cards.**
A funky, divey-looking joint in the Village, where the schedule includes Dixieland bands and pianists Johnny Parker and Al Bundy.

## Five and Ten No Exaggeration

*77 Greene Street, between Spring & Broome Streets (925 7414). Subway N or R to Prince Street.* **Shows** 8pm Tue-Sun. **Cover** $5, $10 food or drinks minimum. **Credit** AmEx, DC, MC, V.
A warm, 1940s-style supper club where even the lamps wear beaded fringes and the jiving Swing survivors share their pink-draped stage with an old Esso gas pump. Various artefacts in the club are for sale, including rhinestone earrings, vintage radios and Coke signs.

## Tavern on the Green

*West 67th Street, at Central Park West (873 3200). Subway B or C to 72nd Street; 1 or 9 to 66th Street.* **Shows** 8pm, 9.30pm Tue, Thur, Sun; 8.30pm, 10pm Fri, Sat. **Cover** varies. **Credit** AmEx, Disc, MC, V.
You can dance in the oh-so-romantic garden throughout the week, preceded most nights by jazz performances in the Chestnut Room, ranging from trad to pop. The expensive dinner menu is the same as in the main restaurant (*see chapter* **Restaurants**).

# Comedy

American comedy is a vast desert of traditionalists, dotted with the occasional glinting diamond of an innovative genius. The underlying aim, therefore, of going to a comedy club, is of catching that sparky young nobody fresh out of the box. In New York, you will also catch the top names: while the very biggest will be filling Broadway theatres, smaller clubs welcome such famous folk as Saturday Night Live cast members, lesser sitcom regulars and comics who have made it to the cable TV showcases of HBO, VH-1 or Comedy Central.

Venues vary in size from the intimate and club-like to those with full-sized stages. What gives the event its excitement is the presence of the unexpected. The next Eddie Murphy or Bette Midler could well be working out a schtick; Rosanne Barr, Jim Carrey or, who knows, Homer Simpson, might stroll in. In New York, expect the unexpected.

Showtimes vary at the stand-up clubs listed below: it's always best to phone them in advance and check.

## Boston Comedy Club

*82 West 3rd Street, between Thompson & Sullivan Streets (477 1000). Subway A, B, C, D, E, F or Q to West 4th Street/Washington Square.* **Cover** $5 Mon-Thur, Sun; $10 Fri, Sat; two-drink minimum. **Credit** AmEx, MC, V.
This raucous Village favourite is a late-night option where the bill can include as many as 10 different acts. The first show on Saturdays is a new talent showcase.

*The place to catch up-and-coming talent:* **Caroline's Comedy Club**.

### Caroline's Comedy Club

*1626 Broadway, at 49th Street (757 4100). Subway C, E, 1 or 9 to 50th Street.* **Cover** $12.50-$17.50, two-drink minimum. **Credit** AmEx, DC, MC, V.

Squeezed in between porno theatres in Times Square, Caroline's harlequinned lounge is the place for up-and-coming TV faces and broad-appeal comics. Billy Crystal and Jay Leno honed their craft at the original Caroline's in Chelsea.

### Catch a Rising Star

*253 West 28th Street, between Seventh & Eighth Avenues (244 3005). Subway 1 or 9th 28th Street.* **Cover** $8-$15, two-drink minimum. **Credit** AmEx, V.

Newly re-opened, this 200-seater club and restaurant was the place that launched the careers of Jerry Seinfeld and Pat Benator, among others. Now jazz and rock bands share the bill with stand-up and cabaret shows, or sketch improv groups.

### Comedy Cellar

*117 MacDougal Street, between West 3rd & Bleecker Streets (254 3480). Subway A, B, C, D, E, F or Q to West 4th Street/Washington Square.* **Cover** $5 Mon-Thur, Sun; $10 Fri, Sat; two-drink minimum. **Credit** AmEx, MC, V.

Amid the coffee houses of MacDougal Street, this well-worn underground lair conjures up the counter-cultural vibe the Village is famous for, making the Comedy Cellar one of the city's best venues, with a roster to match.

### Comic Strip

*1568 Second Avenue, between East 81st & 82nd Streets (861 9386). Subway 6 to 77th Street.* **Cover** $8 Mon-Thur, Sun; $12 Fri, Sat; $9 drinks minimum. **Credit** AmEx, DC, Disc, MC, V.

With New York comedy occasionally suffering from over-dilution, this pub-like stand-up club is known for separating the wheat from the chaff. Monday is amateur night – wannabes should sign up the Friday before.

### Dangerfield's

*1118 First Avenue, between 61st & 62nd Streets (593 1650). Subway 4, 5 or 6 to 59th Street.* **Cover** $12.50 Mon-Thur, Sun; $15 Fri, Sat. **Credit** AmEx, DC, MC, V.

Opened by comedian and actor Rodney Dangerfield over 20 years ago, this glitzy lounge is now one of New York's oldest and most formidable clubs.

### Gotham Comedy Club

*34 West 22nd Street, between Fifth & Sixth Avenues (367 9000). Subway F, N, R, 1 or 9 to 23rd Street.* **Cover** $8, two-drink minimum. **Credit** AmEx, V.

The Gotham Comedy Club – located in Chelsea – books a country-wide line-up of top comedians.

### The Original Improv

*422 West 34th, between Ninth & Tenth Avenues (279 3446). Subway A, C or E to 34th Street.* **Cover** $10, $9 minimum. **Credit** AmEx, DC, Disc, MC, V.

Now 25 years old, this Theater District comedy club books big names and up-and-comers, avoiding the potentially embarrassing entry-level types. As you'd expect, most of the performances are of the improvisational variety.

### New York Comedy Club

*241 East 24th Street, between Second & Third Avenues (696 5233). Subway 6 to 23rd Street.* **Cover** $5 Mon-Thur, Sun; $10 Fri, Sat; two-drink minimum. **Credit** AmEx, D, MC, V.

A relative newcomer, the New York Comedy Club combines a democratic approach with a busy schedule and a bargain cover price.

### Stand Up NY

*236 West 78th Street, at Broadway (595 0850). Subway 1 or 9 to 79th Street.* **Cover** $7 Mon-Thur, Sun; $12 Fri, Sat; two-drink minimum. **Credit** AmEx, MC, V.

A clinically decorated but small and intimate place, with a growing reputation for booking the very best on the circuit. Catch the untested talent in their amateur pre-shows here.

# Clubs

**Despite gory goings-on and Giuliani's quality of life crackdown, New York's clublife still presents plenty of nocturnal options.**

New York's club culture is experiencing some challenging times. Although the scene is as creative and unique as ever, it has suffered from Mayor Giuliani's campaign against 'quality of life offenders' (*see chapter* **New York Today**). Outrageous scandals involving two of the scene's top movers and shakers haven't helped the club community's public image, either (*see page 229*). Don't worry, though: there are still plenty of nocturnal options to investigate, ranging from small bars to gargantuan megadiscos, from chic playgrounds of the rich and famous to scummy, illegal after-hours dives.

Those used to UK club culture may find the locals here not as 'up for it' as clubbers back home. New Yorkers are a cynical bunch and hard to impress. For some disco citizens, the most enjoyable part of clubbing is just coolly taking in the entire spectacle with a raised eyebrow. But despite the 'been there, done that' attitude, New York's club scene has a real sense of history and tradition. Whatever music you enjoy, you'll hear a good amount of club classics in the mix.

New York DJs tend to be more eclectic than their UK counterparts. Many, especially in smaller places, will spin everything from hip-hop, reggae and soul to house, disco, jungle and Latin over the course of a night. The crowds, too, tend to be varied; though recent years have seen a trend toward homogenisation, most clubs attract outlandishly dressed club kids as well as homeboys, yuppies in suits, club babe types and the near-ubiquitous drag queens. With the exception of the hip-hop scene, a gay presence and sensibility is common at most clubs: in the majority of cases, a 'straight' night at a club means 'mixed'.

The famously strict New York door policies pioneered by Studio 54 aren't as tough as they used to be. Although newly opened or more glamour-orientated clubs do discriminate (any restrictions are mentioned below), economic and fashion trends have forced most establishments to accept the money of the sartorially-challenged. You may want to come prepared, though. Certain venues (hip-hop clubs, and others that are particularly straight) refuse entry to groups of men in order to maintain a desirable gender balance and to prevent testosterone overload.

Clubs are very security-conscious, and door searches are common. Until Giuliani's crackdown, weapons were the only items *verboten*, but the current political climate has forced some clubs to monitor drug use as well. In several instances, undercover police have arrested users and dealers in and outside clubs. If getting high is your cup of E, be careful. And leave the guns and knives at home.

A positive note on overzealous law enforcement: crime, it must be said, has dropped dramatically, and New York isn't nearly as dangerous as it's reputed to be. However, this is a city where anything can happen, and since many clubs are in remote, industrial neighbourhoods, you may want to travel by taxi. They are easy to find – the most popular clubs even have lines of cabs waiting outside.

Clubbing here is a late-night sport. Alcohol is sold until 4am, and some after-hours clubs are open late enough that they re-open their bars at 8am, the earliest allowed by law (noon on Sunday). Wherever you go, most people won't arrive before midnight, and some after-hours clubs don't fill up (or even open their doors) until well past 4am. Rest assured that no matter how late you arrive, there will always be somewhere else to go after.

Though Friday and Saturday are of course the biggest nights to go out, many hipsters and locals stick to midweek clubbing in order to avoid the throngs of suburbanites (the 'bridge and tunnel' crowd) that overwhelm Manhattan every weekend. Because of this, many of the most interesting and unusual events happen during the week.

The club scene here is mercurial: parties move weekly, DJs are hired and fired and, given the current political climate, you can't take it for granted that your intended destination will be open for business. Phoning ahead is always a good idea, as is consulting the *Village Voice* or *Time Out New York*, or the monthly style magazine *Paper*. The gay listings magazine, *HX,* is also good for club reviews. Happy hunting.

*Admission prices for the clubs listed below vary according to the night, but usually range from $5-$20. The term 'club' is also used to describe live music venues, discos and DJ bars. Not all the venues below have cabaret licences (difficult to obtain in Manhattan), without which dancing is illegal; however some are prepared to turn a blind eye if you do want to shake a leg.*

## The Clubs

### Bar d'O
*See chapter* **Cabaret** *for listings.*
A cosy little lounge in the West Village, Bar d'O hosts

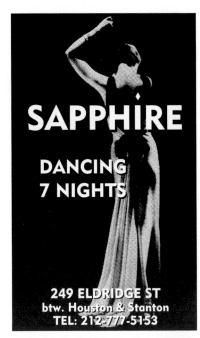

everything from drag shows and a lesbian night on Monday to offbeat DJ nights. For the loungecore fan, Wednesdays and Thursdays are recommended for a double dose of strip-hop, exotica and Moog music.

### Beige

*Bowery Bar, 40 East 4th Street, at the Bowery (475 2220). Subway 6 to Bleecker Street.* **Open** from 11pm Tue.
Erich Conrad's festival of fabulosity is totally frivolous fun. DJ and face-about-downtown Billy Beyond serves up a groovy, tongue-in-cheek-but-just-this-side-of-camp sound-track that can include anything from gay 1940s standards to cool 1980s electro disco classics. All the while, the gar-mentos gab, clubbies club, trendies talk, out-of-drag queens drink and the bathroom line lengthens. Hilarious, very visual and usually quite entertaining.

### Berlin

*1 West 125th Street, at Fifth Avenue (1-718 617 4783). Subway 2 or 3 to 125th Street.* **Open** midnight Fri-8am Sat.
In the heart of Harlem you'll find the unique phenomenon of a gay hip-hop club. House, R 'n' B and disco classics are thrown into the musical mix, and there's a rather more party-minded atmosphere than the surly vibes you can get at most rap spots. It's a solidly black crowd, but there's a genuine welcome for any new faces, regardless of their complexion.

### bOb

*235 Eldridge Street, between Houston and Stanton Streets (777 0588). Subway F to Second Avenue.* **Open** 7pm-4am daily.
More a pick-up bar than a club, but – as is the case with most similar places in the neighbourhood – there's a DJ tucked in the corner spinning classic funk, disco, Latin, hip-hop, reggae and a touch of house. You're not supposed to dance, but the staff usually look the other way, risking a stiff fine from the City in the process. Very crowded at weekends.

### Bowling Club

*Bowlmor Lanes, 110 University Place, between 12th & 13th Streets (255 8158). Subway L, N, R, 4, 5, 6 to 14th Street/Union Square.* **Open** from 10pm Mon.
Downtown scenesters exchange their platforms for bowling shoes, while DJ Kazimir spins a killer, import-heavy selec-tion of underground house. There's something humanising and downright democratic about a crowd of full-time night-crawlers and club employees on their night off letting their hair down and hanging out the classic American white-trash way: drinking, bowling and shootin' the shit.

### Broadway II

*2700 Queens Plaza, Long Island City, Queens (1-718 937 7111). Subway N to Queens Plaza; R to Queensboro Plaza.* **Open** 9pm-4.30am Thur-Sat. .
One of the city's premier Latin clubs, Broadway II is worth the trek. The dancers are first-rate, but you shouldn't encounter any attitude if you're not as skilled. Most nights fea-ture both a band and a DJ (spinning everything from New York and Colombian salsa to tribal house). Jackets are required for men.

### Chameleon Lounge

*81 Avenue A, between 5th & 6th Streets (473 7464). Subway F to Second Avenue.* **Open** times vary.
Chameleon's not particularly pretty, but it's a comfy, con-veniently located duplex, with a big bar and lots of couches upstairs and a stark, dark dancefloor in the basement. Different parties occur almost every night of the week, most-ly on the hip-hop/reggae/Latin/funk/classics tip. Saturday night's True New York party is recommended: it draws a friendly, unpretentious young crowd, racially mixed and mostly straight (looking to mate).

### Chaos

*23 Watts Street, between West Broadway & Thompson Street (925 8966). Subway C or E to Spring Street.* **Open** 5pm-4am daily.
The scene at Chaos is anything but, attracting, as it does, fairly affluent, mainstream straight folks. The music is an eclectic, hit-driven mixture designed to cause swaying and networking, not dancing.

### Coney Island High

*15 St Mark's Place, between Second & Third Avenues (674 7959). Subway 6 to Astor Place; N or R to 8th Street.* **Open** 11pm-4am alternate Sats.
Most of the week, Coney Island High is a vortex of punky rock posing in the Max's Kansas City/New York Dolls/CBGB vein (the club even has a Wednesday night party devoted to Max's, the late, legendary 1970s rock venue). You'll see lots of guys with eyeliner, bondage trousers, and hair like Rod Stewart – don't worry, they're probably the owners. Coney Island High hosts a variety of innovative club nights, though, such as Shindig, a Sunday night explosion of rockabilly, mambo and 1960s soul, where all the guys have Butch Wax in their hair, all the gals wear fishnets, and everyone's tat-tooed everywhere. It's an energetic, fun night, even if the

# Dial-a-club

Since many club events are movable parties that hop from space to space, it can be chal-lenging to keep up with their whereabouts. Though the late 1980s and early 1990s hey-day of floating parties seems to have yielded to a trend toward staying put, many clubs can move at the drop of a hat. Calling the var-ious club information hotlines should keep you up-to-date. These hotlines cover a wide range of events. Rave clothing and record store **Liquid Sky** has a popular phone line (226 0657), with details of rave-orientated par-ties. **Mello's** line (631 1023) is also rave-orientated but is geared more toward clubs and is less artsy.

Other rave lines include **Satellite Prod-uctions** (465 3299), **Digital Domain** (592 3676) and **Solar Luv** (629 2078). **Urban Works** (629 1786) is involved with a variety of events from hip-hop and rave to gay par-ties. **E-Man's** line (330 8101) covers a selec-tion of underground house clubs, mostly – but by no means exclusively – of the mixed-to-gay variety. **Giant Step's** line (714 8001) offers information on events such as acid jazz-related concerts and various parties run by friends of the club's owners. **Mixed Bag Productions** (604 4224) is involved with many events: in addition to running Konkrete Jungle, it helps promote various jungle, acid jazz and trip-hop parties, including larger-scale rave-like events. Mixed Bag co-owner Mac is also the doorman at Giant Step.

obsessive retro aspect of it is a little freaky. On Monday nights, Konkrete Jungle, the granddaddy of the New York jungle scene, continues its long run. The emphasis here is on hardstep – jazzier, deeper drum 'n' bass is either frowned on or relegated to the basement lounge.

## Copacabana
*617 West 57th Street, between Eleventh & Twelfth Avenues (582 2672). Subway 1, 9, A, B, C or D to Columbus Circle.* **Open** *June-Aug 6pm-3am Tue; 6pm-4am Thur-Sat; Sept-May 6pm-3am Tue; 6pm-5am Fri; 10am-5pm Sat.*
The famous Copa is a classy club catering to a 25-plus, mainly black and Hispanic clientele. Though this isn't the same place Barry Manilow sang about – the club moved from its original location a few years ago – the look and feel has been remarkably preserved. A live band plays salsa and merengue every night and a DJ fills in the gaps with hip-hop, R 'n' B and Latin sounds. Swank, in a costume party kind of way, with plenty of rugged caballeros and sultry senoritas. You saw it looking its best in Martin Scorsese's Goodfellas. The dress code requires customers to look 'casual but nice'; no jeans, sneakers, or work boots, and gents must have a collar on their shirt.

## Den of Thieves
*145 East Houston Street, between Eldridge & Forsyth Streets (477 5005). Subway F to Second Avenue.*
**Open** *9pm-3am Mon-Thur, Sun; 9pm-4am Fri, Sat.*
Den of Thieves is one of the bigger of the Lower East Side club-style bars – almost, but not quite, a dance club. They were forced by the authorities to ban dancing; though this isn't always enforced (wink, wink). The crowd is a youngish mix of homies and new trendies, and the weekend sees the same kind of slummers as most of its neighbouring establishments. Music is along the usual R&B/soul/hip-hop continuum, though Amoeba on Sundays features ambient and trip-hop, plus lots of chill-ful visuals and a sort of muso-raver crowd. There are also jungle and jazz nights, as well as various one-offs (record release parties and the like).

## Don Hill's
*511 Greenwich Street, at Spring Street (334 1390). Subway 1 or 9 to Houston Street.* **Open** *10pm-4am Tue-Sun.*
One of those clubs that functions equally well as a dance club or live music venue. Its best night, Squeezebox, combines both: it's a gay rock party, with live bands and a drag queen DJ spinning glammy, punky, scummy rock for a mixed (but queer in appearance and sensibility) crowd. Lots of celebrities from the fashion and music worlds drop by, and the atmosphere is a festive alternative to house music all night long. The long-running Soul Sunday Lounge attracts an easy -on-the-eyes, interracial straight crowd with its mix of hip-hop, classics and reggae. BeavHer on Thursdays is recommended for people with either insatiable appetites for cheese or poor musical taste. The menu essentially consists of Top 40 hits from the mid-1970s to the mid-1980s – roughly the childhood years of most of the crowd.

## Expo
*124 West 43rd Street, between Sixth Avenue & Broadway (819 0377). Subway B, D, F, Q to 42nd Street.* **Open** *10pm-4am Fri-Sun.*
The place is a dump, granted, and the crowd is mostly a suburban straight bunch with pretensions to glamour (Expo was once Xenon, the proless Studio 54). But there's something charming about the chaos and decrepitude. This is especially true of Sunday's Café Con Leche party, an excellent and long-running night with Hispanic flavour for the gay, straight and undecided. Café is about as New York as you can get.

*The morning after at* **Don Hill's**.

## King
*579 Sixth Avenue, between 16th & 17th Streets (366 5464). Subway B, D, F or Q to 14th Street.* **Open** *5pm-4am daily.*
A compact Chelsea hangout, with a sweaty little dancefloor upstairs and a relaxed, casual chill-out bar at ground level. A preponderance of gay nights, and some great mixed occasions too. Good music, mostly solid New York house.

## Krystal's
*8925 Merrick Boulevard, Jamaica, Queens (1-718 523 3662). Subway E, J or Z to Jamaica Center.* **Open** *10pm-4am Mon, Tue, Fri, Sat.*
If you fancy a trip out to the boroughs, you can get a slightly grittier taste of the city's musical life. Krystals, in the Caribbean locale of Jamaica, is where you'll hear regular hip-hop and reggae, played for a boisterous local audience.

## Latin Quarter
*2551 Broadway, between 95th & 96th Streets (864 7600). Subway 1, 2, 3 or 9 to 96th Street.* **Open** *9.30pm-4am Thur-Sat.*
The newest Latin nightclub in the city, where there's a constant roster of big salsa orchestras, linked by DJs playing a varied slice of hip-hop, house and Latin sounds.

## Life/the Ki Club
*158 Bleecker Street, at Thompson Street (420 1999). Subway A, B, C, D, E, F, Q to West 4th Street/ Washington Square.* **Open** *10pm-4am Thur-Sun.*
The newest disco in town at press time, Life opened in Greenwich Village on the former site of the almost legendary jazz club The Village Gate. In a neighbourhood already teeming with bars (and, at the weekends, drunken suburbanites), Life is playing it safe and attempting to keep the community happy by targeting an older, affluent, mostly straight white crowd and programming what it calls an 'eclectic' (i.e. heavy on the oldies) music mix. But Thursdays is the hip night to go, with promoter Erich Conrad drawing a beautiful, jaded but decadent downtown crowd, heavy on gay and fashion types. The music is a quite good blend of underground vocal and instrumental house, while the VIP lounge (and on Thursdays, pretty much everyone is a VIP) features a variety of cool classics – Paradise Garage disco one week, vintage new wave and punk (played by transsexual punk singer and DJ Jayne County) the next. Sundays cater to a white, gym-loving gay crowd. You may not get in unless you're dressed up or are looking particularly fashionable.

## Ludlow Bar

*165 Ludlow Street, between Houston & Rivington Streets
(353 0536). Subway F to Second Avenue.* **Open** 6pm-
4am daily.
Yet another Lower East Side DJ bar, Ludlow is simply and
tastefully appointed, and it features some of the most progressive music you'll hear in the neighbourhood. DJs spin
every week, usually playing a wide range that spans jazz,
trip-hop, hip-hop, drum 'n' bass, house, samba, salsa, bossa
nova and pretty much anything else that's groovy. The
crowd tends to be more mainstream at the weekends, but it
draws locals during the week.

## Mother

*432 West 14th Street, at Washington Street (366 5680).
Subway A, C, E or L to 14th Street/Eighth Avenue.*
**Open** times vary.
Run by longtime club faces Chi Chi Valenti (a writer) and
Johnny Dynell (a popular DJ), Mother is home to a variety of
highly imaginative events, ranging from gay techno parties
to modern dance recitals and spoken word evenings.
Whatever's going on, you can expect a reliably twisted,
artsy, fun sensibility. Tuesdays' Jackie 60 night (the club's
long-running flagship) is a fascinating mix of gay, straight
and everything in between. Lots of artists, celebrities, freaks
and club royalty are regulars, though the club's longevity
and many press clippings bring in the tourist crowd, too. As
for the rest of the week, the long-running Clit Club is a Friday
night lesbian institution and Saturday's Click and Drag is a
brilliant crossbreeding of technological and sexual fetishism
(featuring Internet chat and dominatrices alike). A vague
dress code exists on Tuesdays and Saturdays – according
to that week's theme – but is selectively enforced. Try sort
of bohemian or clubby for Tuesday and some sort of fetish
outfit (of the cyber or sexual school) for Saturday.

## Nell's

*246 West 14th Street, between Seventh & Eighth
Avenues (675 1567). Subway A, C, E or L to Eighth
Avenue/14th Street.* **Open** 10pm-4am daily.
Nells preserves its famous civility with a busy programme
of different nights and an attractive and happily multi-racial
clientele with money in their pockets. The usual formula is
laid-back jazz and funky soul (often with live bands)
upstairs, where there's a limited dining menu, and hip-hop
or house dance pressure below decks. The crowd is dressy,
and on crowded nights the dressed-up folks are given pre-
ferred treatment at the door.

## The 999999s

*Flamingo East, 219 Second Avenue, between 13th & 14th
Streets (533 2860). Subway L to Third Avenue; N, R, 4,
5, 6 to 14th Street/Union Square.* **Open** from 10pm Sun.
Though occasional incursions by voyeuristic yuppies can
dilute the crowd quality while overcrowding the smallish
room, most of the regulars at this over-the-top loungecore
event are fabulous indeed. The music is a fairly standard
mix of space-age bachelor pad, Moog, exotica and Latin
lounge tunes, but the floorshows are what puts the 999999s
head and shoulders above other lounge nights. Often featuring 1990s flapper Penelope Tuesdae running around topless or drag king Murray Hill impersonating everyone from
Hugh Hefner to Olympic coach Bela Karoli, the shows – and
the club itself – are a brilliantly silly take on loungecore.
Dressing up will get you in cheaper, and on particularly
crowded nights may make all the difference.

## Organic Grooves

*Various locations; phone 439 1147 for details.*
**Open** from 10.30pm Fri.
The roving Go Global folks throw their parties at any old
space, ranging from funky Lower East Side café-cum-
antique-shops to elegant places such as Flamingo East. DJ
Sasha spins soupy, trippy, decidedly nonstandard dub funk

and trip-hop. It's a bit hippyish in feel but funky nonetheless. Often enough, he's joined by an array of live musicians
as well. The crowd tends toward the sexually straight but
racially mixed (and it's not at all a bad-looking bunch, either).

## Palladium

*126 East 14th Street, between Third & Fourth Avenues
(473 7171). Subway 4, 5, 6, L, N or R to 14th Street/
Union Square.* **Open** 10pm-5am Fri, Sat (plus occasional
other nights for live shows).
The cavernous Palladium has been through more popularity
swings than a politician, going from ultra-trendy to synonymous with suburban unhipness. Right now, the cavernous old opera house hosts a mainstream straight Friday
night of commercial house and hip-hop, in association with
pop-dance radio station WKTU. Saturdays belong to ex-
Sound Factory DJ Junior Vasquez, who spins an increasingly
unfunky style of house music that's closer to HiNRG and
hardbag than the very black style of hardhouse he once was
famous for. The crowd is similarly white: Junior's fame and
musical shift have turned his following rather mainstream.
Things start off rather mixed to straight, but the place gets
progressively gayer as night turns into morning and morning turns into afternoon (some weeks, Junior goes until 4pm).

## Plush

*431 West 14th Street, between Ninth Avenue &
Washington Street (367 7035). Subway A, C, E to West
14th Street.* **Open** times vary.
A small-to-mid-sized club, Plush is partly owned by one of
the Scotsmen responsible for Lower East Side DJ bar
Sapphire. The music policy here, presumably aiming for an
ultra-New York flavour, is actually very UK: some of house
music's top DJ/remixers play here (Roger S, Angel Moraes,
Deep Dish), all of whom are big on the UK circuit but not on
the New York one. Perhaps for this reason, Plush hasn't
made a huge splash. However, it's a nice little place, and fans
of the above-mentioned jocks will want to check it out on
Thursday, Friday and Saturday, respectively. Also recommended is the Monday night mixed/gay party Sugar Babies.

## Pyramid Club

*101 Avenue A, between 6th & 7th Streets (473 7184).
Subway L to First Avenue.* **Open** times vary.
A small, dark, ground-level cocoon in the heart of East
Village bohemia, the Pyramid is something of a shrine to
modern drag and downtown culture; RuPaul and Deee-Lite
got their start here. The club is often given over to rock
shows but at other times hosts dancing events ranging from
jungle to drag, so it's worth checking out.

## Robots

*25 Avenue B, at 3rd Street (995 0968). Subway F to
Second Avenue.* **Open** 10pm-7am Wed, Thur; 10pm-noon
Fri, Sat.
Once a near-legendary, illegal after-hours club, Robots is now
mostly legal and has devolved from an ultra-hip speakeasy
with lots of downtowners and a sprinkling of yuppies on coke
to… a less hip speakeasy with a sprinkling of downtowners
and lots of yuppies on coke. Hard house and techno is usually
available on the small basement dancefloor, while the trippy,
comfortable lounge upstairs features a variety of DJs playing
everything from house and jungle to ambient and loungecore
(Thursdays' Killer party is a respected night of intelligent
techno). Robots generally stays open as late as attendance
dictates, and resumes selling liquor at 8am.

## Roxy

*515 West 18th Street, between Tenth and Eleventh
Avenues (645 5156). Subway A, C, E or L to Eighth
Avenue/14th Street.* **Open** times vary.
This warhorse of a club was originally a roller-disco, then
a seminal hip-hop/electro club (Afrika Bambaataa and
thousands of breakdancers), then a cheesy Latin hip-hop,

and for the last eight years or so, the unbeatable front-runner in the Saturday night gay disco sweepstakes. Lately, though, time and competition have forced some changes, and Roxy is now home to rather mainstream straight folks on both Friday and Saturday. Still, the room is immense and impressive and the sound system kicks ass. Worth a trip for first-timers.

### Sapphire

*249 Eldridge Street, between Houston & Stanton Streets (777 5153). Subway F to Second Avenue.* **Open** 7pm-4am daily.

Past its sell-by date, but still popular, Sapphire was one of the first trendy Lower East Side DJ bars. As with anything trendy, the crowd has since gone from downtown hipsters to uptown slummers to outer-borough weekend warriors. The music is fairly typical of these sorts of places: hip-hop, reggae, acid jazz, R&B, disco classics and the odd house tune.

### XVI

*16 First Avenue, between 1st & 2nd Streets (260 1549). Subway F to Second Avenue.* **Open** times vary.

The story goes that the incredibly funky basement used to be some sort of Middle Eastern coke den and was accidentally discovered during renovation of the ground-floor storefront space. The lower level really is from a different time: all mirrored tiles, stone floors and gaudy brick arches – XVI is a sight to behold. DJs play on both levels, and music tends

to be considerably more typical than the club's décor. Thursday nights feature members of Josh Wink's posse and a continual influx of trip-hop and dance music industry types, chilling and playing a wide variety of groovy records for each other.

### Sound Factory

*618 West 46th Street, between Eleventh & Twelfth Avenues (643 0728). Subway A, C, E to 50th Street.* **Open** times vary.

After more than a year of delays, hype and aborted openings, the long-awaited new incarnation of the Sound Factory finally opened in January 1997. The space is different, but the sound system is allegedly the very same one. However, the club does not have DJ Junior Vasquez, and for many, that means it will never be the Sound Factory. So far, though, the music hasn't been anything extraordinary. The Factory crowd is mixed genderwise and racially, and enthusiastic. The club is also keeping alive the long New York after-hours tradition of free munchies, offering a generous spread of fruit, cookies, potato chips, coffee and more. And it now has a full bar. Fridays are straight to mixed, and generally trendier than Saturdays.

### Studio 84

*3534 Broadway, at 145th Street (234 8484). Subway 1 or 9 to 145th Street.* **Open** 9pm-4am Wed-Sun.

The frenzied brass of salsa and merengue can be heard

---

# Rumours rock clubland

Two recent scandals have badly damaged the club scene's public image and have added fuel to the City's nightlife crackdown. Peter Gatien, who owns three of New York's (and, indeed, the nation's) largest clubs – Palladium, the Limelight and the Tunnel – is currently under indictment for profiting from an alleged Ecstasy distribution operation, run from the latter two establishments. After a series of police raids in the summer of 1996, the Tunnel and Limelight were both padlocked. The Tunnel re-opened after a month, but the Limelight is still awaiting approval to resume business (the club has more lives than a cat, so it's worth asking about). Palladium, where superstar DJ Junior Vasquez (*pictured*) makes his home on Saturday nights, is in the clear legally, but many wonder whether Gatien's empire will be able to withstand the financial pressure the indictment and closure have created, to say nothing of the pending trial.

Another sordid tale that's had tongues wagging is the murder of club kid Angel Melendez. Melendez, a fixture at both the Limelight and the Tunnel, was an alleged drugs dealer. He usually wore extremely tall platform boots,

white vinyl outfits and big angel's wings on his back. He disappeared in March 1996 and was rumoured to have been killed by Michael Alig, one of Gatien's former employees and, by all accounts, one of the most successful, innovative club promoters the city has ever seen. For many months, the grisly rumours circulating seemed too outrageous to believe: Alig and an accomplice were said to have bludgeoned Melendez with a hammer in a fight over drugs money, injected him with a drain-unclogging agent to finish him off, dismemembered him and dumped the body in the Hudson River. Alig, a seemingly gentle, almost childlike gay man, hardly fitted the stereotype of a vicious killer. But when a body finally washed up on Staten Island and was positively identified, Alig and his accomplice were arrested. They are currently in jail awaiting trial and are rumoured to have confessed. The episode has given the club scene a rather unsavoury reputation, and the city's tabloids have, not surprisingly, jumped on the moralistic bandwagon, publishing numerous 'exposés' of wrongdoings in clubs.

*Helping the police with their enquiries at the **Tunnel**.*

throughout the city's many Spanish-speaking neighbourhoods. Indulge in some Latin flavour at this energetic Dominican dance hall. DJs and live bands every night.

### System

*76 East 13th Street, between Broadway & Fourth Avenue (388 1060). Subway 4, 5, 6, L, N or R to 14th Street/ Union Square.* **Open** 10pm-4am Thur-Sat.
System has a phenomenal sound system created by the company that kitted out London's Ministry of Sound, and was originally going to have an equally incredible line-up of regular DJs. But the Upper East Side crowd (read: rich, white, straight, boring) wanted to hear hits, and so what you'll hear most nights is as close to wedding music as a club can get. Still, Wednesdays are 'messy night', as one promoter put it, featuring a young, working-class mixed crowd getting down to hard house, acid and techno.

### Tatou

*151 East 50th Street, between Third & Lexington Avenues (753 1144). Subway 4, 5, 6 to 59th Street; N, R to Lexington Avenue.* **Open** 5pm-4am Mon-Sat.
A midtown supper club cum disco, Tatou is chiefly the domain of businessmen, Upper East Side twentysomethings, Eurotrash and old-money types. Which isn't to say it's bad. Though we're obviously not talking underground here, the joint is pleasant enough in its own way. The upstairs lounge is comfy, and the DJs – who spin mostly well-known dance hits – are good at what they do. Downstairs, the dining room is turned over to dancing once the last table is cleared. There's no door policy, but dressing up, or casually but neatly, is advised.

### Tunnel

*220 Twelfth Avenue, at 27th Street (695 4682). Subway A, C or E to 23rd Street.* **Open** 10pm-6am Fri; 11pm-noon Sat; 10pm-4qm Sun.
A stunningly massive place with equally impressive décor – there's a unisex bathroom complete with a bar and banquettes, a coffee house, and the mind-blowingly psychedelic Cosmic Cavern, designed by pop artist Kenny Scharf (floor-to-ceiling fake fur, lava lamps, Internet terminals, blacklight paintings and a fountain). Unfortunately, the police raid in

August 1996 seems to have dealt a blow to its spirit (not to mention its trendy cachet) from which the Tunnel hasn't recovered. The crowd is generally mainstream, but the number of promoters and events required to fill the mammoth space ensures that there's always something hip going on somewhere inside. Music on Fridays tends toward the ravier side of house, with commercial hard house and a rather gayer crowd on Saturdays. Head for one of the many smaller rooms, which usually feature more interesting music, décor and people.

### Twilo

*530 West 27th Street, between Tenth & Eleventh Avenues. Subway C or E to 23rd Street/Eighth Avenue.* **Open** times vary.
Twilo, occupying the former Sound Factory, was the most talked-about club of 1996. With an immense sound system and dancefloor, the place is geared for music. Twilo wants to be both underground and trendy, a difficult feat indeed. The result, sadly, is generally excellent music and lame crowds. Friday is straight night and features lots of suburban ex-ravers who have graduated to disco shirts and club babe outfits. The music on Fridays, by a largely impressive series of international guest DJs, tends toward hard house, though the recently opened upstairs room has hosted everything from drum 'n' bass to loungecore. The crowd – 90% gay white muscle clones zonked on Ketamine – is more concerned with pecs and sex, and the energy level in the room is low. Recent developments may bring Junior Vasquez back to his old home – if he and Twilo owner (and former Factory partner) can get along, that is.

### Webster Hall

*125 East 11th Street, between Third & Fourth Avenues (353 1600). Subway 4, 5, 6, L, N or R to 14th Street/ Union Square.* **Open** 10pm-4am Thur-Sat.
Webster Hall is an out-and-out commercial nightclub worth visiting in a fun-night-out-with-your-mates sort of way. There are always four or five different musical zones running the gamut from commercial to mainstream, and though the crowd is essentially a suburban influx of bridge and tunnellers, there are a few New York freaks and rampant hetero hormones to amuse newcomers.

# Film

*Welcome to the most vibrant movie set in the world: New York City.*

**The Ziegfeld**: *for romantic movies, blockbusters or just a slice of history. See page 232.*

Visitors often feel as if they're in the middle of a movie as soon as they set foot on the mean streets of New York. It's not just the heightened intensity and quick-change pace of Manhattan life, it's the fact that many of the city's street corners have been the site of something cinematic, whether it's Lorraine Bracco taunting Ray Liotta in *Goodfellas* or Spike Lee tossing a trash can through a window in *Do the Right Thing*.

And the prospect of running into a movie being shot, whether a Hollywood thriller or an angst-filled indie, is increasingly likely. With its recent rise in film projects, New York could be renamed Cin City: more movies were made in 1996 than ever before – 201, a full 47 more than the year before. With better relations between production companies and local labour unions, and a mayor determined to boost film and TV production, the film business is booming. Hollywood projects – especially thrillers like *Ransom* that need Manhattan's sense of menace – are back in force, while the indie community, buoyed by local boy Ed Burns (*The Brothers McMullen*) can often be found on the Lower East Side, making use of the area's low-life atmosphere.

There are hundreds of screens throughout the metropolis, from the deluxe 12-plex blockbuster mecca, **Sony Lincoln Square** to one of the nation's premier homes for experimental film, the **Anthology Film Archives**. New Yorkers are famously knowledgeable about film; on opening nights of the latest blockbuster (or Scorsese picture) queues often wind around the corner and 'Sold Out' signs are pasted on to ticket-sellers' windows. To guarantee seats for the latest *Twister* or *Casino* on

## Screen test

These New York cinemas gain our top marks.
**Best for a blockbuster**: The Ziegfeld; Sony Lincoln Square; Cineplex Odeon Chelsea.
**Best for a foreign film**: Sony Paris; Angelika Film Center.
**Best for popcorn**: Cineplex Odeon Waverly Twin.
**Best for a midnight movie**: Cinema Village.
**Best for a romantic movie**: The Ziegfeld.

# Film on-line

New York has an excellent phone service for screening details. Simply dial 777-FILM and for the cost of a normal call you can touch-tone your way around an updated, automated system that gives the times and locations of screenings across the Tri-State area. It's often helpful if you know your area's zip code (postcode). The system is foolproof and you can even pre-book your seats using a credit card to avoid queues. The only drawbacks are that it doesn't include all the independent theatres, and you have to listen to the announcer's obnoxiously upbeat voice.

their first weekend, it's best to call the automated 777-FILM ticket system well in advance.

New York is often used as a test market, so you can catch first-run films here long before they open in the rest of the country, and months or years before they get distributed in the UK. It's also possible to be in at the birth of the film-making process; screenplay readings held at the **Nuyorican Poet's Café** (*see chapter* **Spoken Word**) have led to several production deals for local writers.

For the latest listings, including the where-abouts of your nearest first-run cinema, pick up the weekly *Time Out New York* or consult the film sections of the *Village Voice*, *New York* or the *New York Times*. And, if you stumble across a film set, remember that when they yell 'action!', it's time to hush up and watch.

For video rental stores, *see chapter* **Shopping & Services**.

## First-run Cinemas

There are scores of first-run cinemas throughout the city. New releases come and go relatively quickly; if a film does badly it might only show for a couple of weeks. Tickets usually cost $9, with discounts sometimes available for senior citizens (these are usually restricted to weekday performances start-ing before 5pm). Friday is the opening night for most films, and the queues then can be murderous-ly long. If you are queuing, check whether you're in the 'ticket buyers' line' or the 'ticket holders' line'. The first showings on Saturday or Sunday (around noon or 1pm) are relatively free of crowds, even for brand new releases.

### Cineplex Odeon Encore Worldwide
*340 West 50th Street, at Eighth Avenue (246 1583). Subway C, E, 1 or 9 to 50th Street.* **Tickets** $3. **Credit** AmEx, V.

Popular with the empty-of-pocket, this six-screen theatre shows Hollywood movies, recent but not new, at the bargain price of $3 a film.
**Branches include: Cineplex Odeon Chelsea**, 333 West 23rd Street (989 0060); **Cineplex Odeon Waverly Twin** 323 Sixth Avenue (929 8037).

### Sony Lincoln Square
*1998 Broadway, at 68th Street (336 5000/credit card bookings 228 7669). Subway 1 or 9 to 66th Street.* **Tickets** $9; $6-$7.50 concessions. **Credit** AmEx, MC, V.
Across Broadway from the high culture of the Lincoln Center, Sony has constructed a cinematic entertainment cen-tre that's more a theme park than a dull old movie multiplex. There's fibreglass decorations that conjure up classic movie sets; enough popcorn vendors to bloat entire armies; a gift shop selling movie memorabilia; and 12 decent-sized screens of first-run blockbusters. The added attraction is the centre's huge Imax screen, which apart from being truly enormous (eight storeys high), is seen through 3D headsets. Films screened here are the usual show-off-the-technology stuff (cities of the future and ultra-vivid underwater adventures) which last 35-45 minutes each.
*Disabled: hearing aids.*

### The Ziegfeld
*141 West 54th Street, between Sixth & Seventh Avenues (765 7600). Subway B, D or E to 53rd Street/Seventh Avenue.* **Tickets** $8.50; $5 concessions. **Credit** AmEx, MC, V.
A place rich in history, once home to the Ziegfeld Follies, and still the grandest picture palace in town. It is often the venue for glitzy New York premières, and has the biggest screen on which to see new releases.

## Revival & Art Houses

The following cinemas specialise in showing art movies or old films.

### Angelika 57
*225 West 57th Street, between Broadway & Seventh Avenue (586 1900). Subway B, D or E to Seventh Avenue.* **Tickets** $8; $4 concessions. **No credit cards.**
This large old 556-seater single-screen theatre was renova-ted in 1993; it shows an eclectic mix of films similar to its downtown sibling (*see below*).

### Angelika Film Center
*Corner of Houston & Mercer Streets (995 2000/box office 995 1081). Subway 6 to Bleecker Street; B, D, F or Q to Broadway/Lafayette Street; N or R to Prince Street.* **Tickets** $8; $4 concessions. **No credit cards.**
A six-screen cinema with very diverse programming, fea-turing new and foreign films, double features of old movies, retrospectives and science fiction films. There's an espresso bar to hang out in before or after the show.
*Disabled: toilets.*

### Carnegie Hall Cinema & Carnegie Screening Room
*887 Seventh Avenue, at 56th Street (265 2536). Subway 1, 9, A, B, C or D to Columbus Circle.* **Tickets** $8.50; $5 concessions. **Credit** AmEx, MC, V.
Carnegie Hall houses two cinemas, which show slightly off-beat American and European movies such as *Sting Blade* and *Unhook the Stars*, although you won't find anything too experimental.

### Cinema Village
*22 East 12th Street, between Fifth Avenue & University Place (924 3363/box office 929 3364). Subway 4, 5, 6, L,*

N, or R to Union Square. **Tickets** $8; $4 concessions. **No credit cards**.
A true revival house, Cinema Village usually changes its double bill daily, mixing Hollywood and European classics like *Breakfast at Tiffany's* and *Jules et Jim* with newer art movies and mini festivals. It shows midnight horror shows at the weekends.

### Film Forum

*209 West Houston Street, between Sixth Avenue & Varick Street (727 8110/box office 727 8112). Subway 1 or 9 to Houston Street.* **Tickets** $8; $4.50 concessions. **No credit cards**.
In an attractive home in SoHo, the three-screen Film Forum offers some of the best new films, documentaries and art movies around, as well as brilliantly-curated series of revivals.

### The Kitchen

*See chapter* **Dance** *for listings.*
New York's oldest experimental arts centre, the Kitchen presents innovative and alternative work by avant-garde video- and film-makers.

### Lincoln Plaza Cinemas

*30 Lincoln Plaza, entrance on Broadway, between 62nd & 63rd Streets (757 2280). Subway 1, 9, A, B, C or D to 59th Street/Columbus Circle.* **Tickets** $8.50; $5 concessions. **No credit cards**.
Commercially successful and worthy European art-house movies, such as *Kolya* or *La Ceremonie* can be seen here, alongside biggish American independent productions like *Suburbia*.

### Quad Cinema

*34 West 13th Street, between Fifth & Sixth Avenues (255 8800/box office 255 2243). Subway 4, 5, 6, L, N or R to Union Square; F to 14th Street.* **Tickets** $8; $4 concessions. **No credit cards**.
Four screens showing a broad selection of foreign films, American independents and documentaries, with a preponderance of those dealing with sexual and political issues. Often shows movies you can't see anywhere else.

### Sony Paris

*4 West 58th Street, between Fifth & Sixth Avenues (980 5656). Subway N or R to Fifth Avenue.* **Tickets** $8.50; $5 concessions. **No credit cards**.
Situated beside Bergdorf Goodman and opposite the Plaza Hotel, the Paris has a stylish programme of European art-house movies, alongside such eminently revivable films as Buñuel's *Belle De Jour*.

## Museums & Societies

Special film series and experimental films are often shown by museums and galleries other than those mentioned here. Check the press for details. *See also chapter* **Museums**.

### American Museum of the Moving Image

*See chapter* **Museums** *for listings.*
The first museum in the US devoted to moving pictures is to be found in Queens. Over 700 films and videos are on show each year, covering everything from Hollywood classics and series devoted to a single actor or director, to industrial safety films. An inspired and entertaining schedule.

### Anthology Film Archives

*32 Second Avenue, at Second Street (505 5181). Subway 6 to Bleecker Street; F to Second Avenue.* **Tickets** $7; $1-$5 concessions. **No credit cards**.
One of New York's treasures, housing the world's largest collection of written material documenting the history of independent film- and video-making. The Archives are sponsored by some of the biggest names in film and have a full programme of films, talks and lectures.

### Film Society of Lincoln Center

*Lincoln Center, 65th Street, between Broadway & Amsterdam Avenue (875 5610). Subway 1 or 9 to 66th Street.* **Tickets** $8; $4-$5 concessions. **No credit cards**.
The Society was founded in 1969 to promote film and support film-makers. It operates the Walter Reade Theater (built in 1991), equipped with state-of-the-art equipment for

*An ace café with a pretty good cinema attached: the* **Angelika Film Center.**

howcasing contemporary film and video. The programme is usually organised in long themed series, with a decisively international perspective. It culminates every autumn in the **NY Film Festival** (*see page 235*).
*Disabled: toilets.*

## Imax Theater
*American Museum of Natural History. See chapter* **Museums** *for listings.* **Screenings** every hour on the half-hour, 10.30am-4.30pm Mon-Thur, Sun; 10.30am-7.30pm Fri, Sat. **Admission** museum admission plus from $12 (varies). **Credit** A, AmEx, DC, V.
The Imax screen is four storeys high and the daily programmes concentrate on the natural world. At the weekend it's usually crowded with children and their parents. *See also chapter* **Museums**.

# You saw it here first

### Do the Right Thing
Brooklyn – once a city unto itself – had its edgy portrait sketched by Spike Lee in 1989. *Thing* is both a warning that the American mosaic is tearing itself apart, and a celebration of the anarchic energy of New York's most vibrant borough. No other film catches summer in New York with the same intensity, rhythm or raucous humour. Lee's film is an invitation to cross the Brooklyn Bridge to a world as fascinating as Manhattan.

### Manhattan
Woody Allen explores the Gotham of the mind: the neuroses, the restlessness, the black humour and hidden tenderness of the true New Yorker. The endless Manhattan conversation meets Gershwin in this, the greatest New York comedy ever. Coming to New York without watching Woody is like going to New Orleans without ever having listened to jazz.

### Taxi Driver
With this dark masterpiece, Scorsese perfectly caught the obsessiveness – and the jazzy undertone of danger – of modern New York. The steam rising from the sewers, the lonely young men striding down the street, the feeling of anonymity and the insane dreams – are still to be found in today's Manhattan. Catch Travis's 42nd Street while it's still a den of iniquity and not the Disney theme strip of the near future.

## International Center of Photography
*See chapter* **Museums** *for listings.*
The ICP holds regular screenings, mostly on the history and technique of photography.

## Metropolitan Museum of Art
*See chapter* **Museums** *for listings.*
The Met shows a full programme of documentary films on art (many of which relate to exhibitions on display) in the Uris Center Auditorium (near the 81st Street entrance). There are usually one or two screenings a day. In addition there are occasional themed film series, with weekend showings.

## Millennium Film Workshop
*66 East 4th Street (673 0090). Subway F to Second Avenue.* **Tickets** $6 non-members; $4 members.
**No credit cards.**
This media/arts centre holds film-making classes and workshops, and has several screenings a week of avant-garde works, sometimes introduced and discussed by the directors.

## Museum of Modern Art
*See chapter* **Museums** *for listings.*
MoMA was one of the first institutions to recognise film as an art form. Its first director, Alfred H Barr, believed that film was 'the only great art peculiar to the twentieth century'. The museum has massive archives of films, to which accredited film students and researchers have access (appointments must be made in writing). MoMA holds about 25 screenings a week, often part of seasons based on the work of a particular director, or on some other theme.

## Museum of Television & Radio
*See chapter* **Museums** *for listings.*
Television and radio works, rather than film, are archived here. There are some 30,000 programmes, which can be viewed at private consoles. In addition, there are two small screening rooms and a 63-seat video theatre where a number of programmes are shown daily. Screening theatres are open until 9pm on Fridays.

## Whitney Museum of American Art
*See chapter* **Museums** *for listings.*
In keeping with its brief of showing the best in contemporary American art, the Whitney has a busy and varied schedule of film and video works. Many of its exhibitions have a strong moving-image component, including the famous Biennial showcase of contemporary art works; entry is free with museum admission.

## Foreign Language Films

Most or all of the above institutions will screen films in languages other than English, but the following show only foreign films.

## Asia Society
*See chapter* **Museums** *for listings.*
Shows films from India, China and many other Asian countries, as well as Asian-American films.

## French Institute
*55 East 59th Street, between Park & Madison Avenues (355 6160). Subway 4, 5, 6, N or R to 59th Street.* **Open** 11am-7pm Tue-Fri; 11am-3pm Sat, Sun.
**Admission** $7 non-members; $5.50 concessions.
**Membership** $60 per year. **Credit** AmEx, MC, V.
The Institute – the overseas cultural development mission of the French Government – shows movies from back home. They're usually subtitled (and never dubbed).
*Disabled: toilets.*

### Goethe House/German Cultural Center

*See chapter* **Museums** *for listings.*
This German-language teaching institute shows regular German films in various locations round the city.

### Japan Society

*333 East 47th Street, between First & Second Avenues (832 1155/752 0824 recorded information). Subway 4, 5, 6 or 7 to Grand Central.* **Open** *phone to confirm film schedule and special exhibition times.* **Tickets** *prices vary.* **Credit** *AmEx, MC, V.*
The Japan Society organises a busy schedule of Japanese films, including two or three big series annually.

## Libraries

### Donnell Library Center

*See chapter* **Museums** *for listings.*
A branch of the New York Public Library, the Donnell shows and circulates films (phone to check screening times).

### Library for the Performing Arts

*See chapter* **Museums** *for listings.*
The library has an extensive research collection of books, periodicals, clippings and posters on film, as well as a vast catalogue of film memorabilia.

## Film Festivals

Every September and October, for more than a quarter of a century, the Lincoln Center film society has been running the prestigious **New York Film Festival**. More than 25 American and for-eign films are given New York, US or world pre-mières and the festival usually features several rarely seen classics as well as the New Directors series. Opening- and closing-night screenings are held in the grand Avery Fisher Hall. Tickets for new films by known directors are often hard to come by; booking opens several weeks in advance. The society, in collaboration with the Museum of Modern Art, is also responsible for the **New Directors, New Films** festival held in April.

An annual NY **Gay and Lesbian Film Festival** is held each July (phone 254 7228 for details). In August there's a month-long **Black Film Festival** (749 5298) as one of the attractions of the annual Harlem Week, with a blend of mili-tant documentaries and features involving Black music and culture. Screenings ($5) are at the Adam Clayton Powell Jr State Office Building, 163 West 125th Street (873 5040). Car-less New Yorkers have their very own 'drive-in' film festival in **Bryant Park** each year between June and September. The park (on Sixth Avenue, between 40th and 42nd Streets) has a series of free summer Monday night (8.30pm) screenings of classics like *Strangers on a Train* or *Casablanca* on a giant screen. *See chapter* **New York by Season** for details.

In addition, many of the art-house cinemas arrange their own, smaller festivals and series, often in conjunction with other institutions.

# On location

### Axis

*136 Duane Street, between Church Street & West Broadway (929 5285). Subway A or C to Chambers.* **Open** from 8pm 1st & 3rd Mon of month. **Admission** free.
This non-profit-making company has become a major nerve centre for the indie movement. Screenings might include shorts by Carl Franklin (*Devil in a Blue Dress*), work from the latest NYU film grads, and much besides. You can also meet the up-and-coming film generation before anyone's heard of them.

### Fifth Night

*Nuyorican Poets Café. See chapter* **Spoken Word** *for listings.* **Open** *Jan-May, Sept-Dec* from 8pm Tue.
Watch some of New York's best actors read the most promising new screenplays in front of an audience of stu-dio execs, aspiring writers and film-lovers at this hot new event.

### Screening Room

*54 Varick Street, at Canal Street (334 2100). Subway A, C, E, !, 9 to Canal Street.* **Lunch** noon-3pm Mon-Fri. **Dinner** 8pm-late Mon-Sat. **Brunch** 11.30am-3.30pm Sun **Credit** (restaurant only) AmEx, MC, V.
This place combines New Yorkers' three favouite activi-ties in one – eating, drinking and watching movies. The restaurant serves classic American cuisine and there's an adjoining screening room that shows a selection of inde-pendent and foreign releases.
*Disabled: toilets.*

### Spike's Joint

*See chapter* **Shopping & Services** *for listings.*
Buy hard-to-find jackets and shirts from Spike Lee's films and schmooze with the Mookies and the other Brooklyn types that congregate at this Lee-owned mecca. Lee's pro-duction offices are on the opposite corner.

### TriBeCa Grill

*375 Greenwich Avenue, at Franklin Street (941 3900). Subway 1 or 9 to Franklin Street.* **Open** 11.30am-10.45pm Mon-Fri; 5.30-10.45pm Sat; 11.30am-2.45pm, 5.30-10.45pm, Sun. **Credit** AmEx, DC, MC, V.
With Bobby's production offices upstairs and his late father's brilliantly-hued paintings on the wall, this elegant bistro is the first stop for the De Niro fan. The food is excellent, if a little pricey.
*Disabled: toilets.*

### Warner Bros Studio Store

*See chapter* **Shopping & Services** *for listings.*
If you can't get to Hollywood, this is your next-best bet. Tacky, overblown and shamelessly American, the Warner Brothers store is a lynchpin of newly touristy 57th Street. Road Runner T-shirts and Porky Pig keyrings are among the vast collection of merchandise.

# Music

*New York's vibrant music scene hits all the right notes, whether they're written by Schubert or Soundgarden.*

## TICKETS

You can buy tickets directly from most venues (though many of those listed under Rock, Roots & Jazz will only take cash). If you want to book by credit card, you can use the telephone services of **Ticketmaster**, which sells tickets for the New York City Opera, performances at BAM, Broadway musicals and most big-time rock concerts, but be prepared to pay a hefty booking fee. **CarnegieCharge** handles credit card bookings for Carnegie Hall events, and **Centercharge** does the same for the Alice Tully Hall and Avery Fisher Hall. The Ticket Buyers Club of the **New York Phlharmonic** provides orchestral tickets at considerable discounts, and the **Theater Development Fund** (*see page 260* **Dance**) offers good deals on Off-Off Broadway music, theatre or dance events. **TKTS** offers 25 to 50 per cent discounts (with a $2 service charge) for same-day tickets for most Lincoln Center events, including the New York Philharmonic, the Chamber Music Society, the Juilliard School and the New York City Opera (though not the Met).

### CarnegieCharge
*(247 7800).* **Open** 8am-8pm daily. **Credit** AmEx, MC, V.

### Centercharge
*(721 6500).* **Open** 10am-8pm Mon-Sat; noon-8pm Sun. **Credit** AmEx, Disc. MC, V.

### New York Philharmonic
### Audience Services
*(875 5656).* **Open** 10am-5pm Mon-Fri. **Credit** AmEx, DC, MC, V.

### Ticketmaster
*(307 4100).* **Open** 9am-10pm Mon-Sat; 9am-9pm Sun. **Credit** AmEx, MC, V.

### TKTS
*Duffy Square,·West 47th Street & Broadway (221 0013). Subway 1, 2, 3, 7, 9, N, R or S to Times Square.* **Open** 3-8pm Mon-Sat; noon-8pm Sun. **No credit cards.** **Branch**: Mezzanine, 2 World Trade Center (221 0013).

## Classical

A glance through the listings of a typical week can reveal more than a dozen classical music events going on in a single evening, more than in any other western capital except London. Carnegie Hall is still the place to play for visiting orchestras and soloists, and the Lincoln Center on a busy night

can have two operas, an orchestral concert and a piano recital going on simultaneously. The number of performances given at the city's churches, schools, cultural centres and other venues is still quite staggering.

Classical music is nonetheless in a state of flux. Two axioms that held sway for generations – that the grand, old institutions err on the side of stuffiness, while adventurous programmes can be found on the side streets, and that new music is the kiss of death for ticket sales – are being turned on their heads. The venerable Carnegie Hall has employed a resident composer, and instituted a series devoted to living composers. The formerly nomadic, post-minimalist Bang on a Can Festival has a new home at the Lincoln Center. The Brooklyn Academy of Music, long a champion of the avant garde, has seen the best of its programming equalled by the increasingly adventurous 92nd Street Y, and even the ultra-staid Metropolitan Opera has staged a successful return production of Philip Glass's *The Voyage*. All in all, it's a good time to be a new music lover in New York, and an even better time to be a composer.

Classical radio, on the other hand, seems to be on the downturn. New York now has only two classical stations, WQXR (96.3 FM), which has always been rather stodgy, and WNYC (93.9 FM), once a refuge for more adventurous listeners, now more conservative (and still looking for an audience). For information on concerts, times and venues, see *Time Out New York*'s 'Classical Music' listings or the *New York Times* on Sunday. The Theater Development Fund (*see page 260* **Dance**) also provides information on all music events via its NYC/On Stage service.

### Behind the Scenes

It's possible to go behind the scenes at several of the city's major concert venues. Lincoln Center's Guided Tours (875 5350) escort you inside all three of the centre's major halls; Backstage at the Met (769 7000) takes you around the famous opera house; Carnegie Hall (903 9790) runs several tours, including some connected with exhibitions at the Hall's Rose Museum. It's also possible to sit in on rehearsals of the New York Philharmonic, usually held on the Thursday before a concert.

## Concert Halls

For the New York State Theater, Avery Fisher Hall, Metropolitan Opera House and Alice Tully Hall, *see page 238* **Lincoln Center**.

## Brooklyn Academy of Music

*30 Lafayette Street, Brooklyn (1-718 636 4100). Subway 2, 3, 4, 5, B, D or Q to Atlantic Avenue.* **Tickets** *$25-$75.* **Credit** *AmEx, MC, V.*
BAM stages music and dance in a beautiful house that's America's oldest academy for the performing arts. The programming is more East Village than Upper West Side: BAM helped launch the likes of Philip Glass and John Zorn. Its resident Brooklyn Philharmonic Orchestra became a haven for American composers under conductor Dennis Russell Davies and remains so under current music director Robert Spano. Every winter, the Next Wave Festival of theatre and music provides an overview of the more established avant-garde. *See also chapters* **Dance** *and* **Theatre**.
*Disabled: toilets. Internet: http://www.bam.org*

## Carnegie Hall

*154 West 57th Street (247 7800). Subway 1, 9, A, B, C or D to 59th Street/Columbus Circle; N or R to 57th Street.* **Tickets** *$20-$70.* **Credit** *AmEx, MC, V.*
Tchaikovsky conducted the opening concert in 1891, and despite being earmarked for demolition in the 1960s, Carnegie Hall is still alive and well. A varied programme of American and international stars is presented, as well as a jazz series. There are two auditoriums, Carnegie Hall itself and the smaller Weill Recital Hall. The heavy hitters are well represented: from the Dresden Staatskapelle to the St Petersburg Philharmonic.
*Disabled: toilets.*

## Florence Gould Hall
## at the Alliance Française

*55 East 59th Street, between Park & Madison Avenues (355 6160). Subway B or Q to 57th Street; 4, 5 or 6 to 59th Street; N or R to Fifth Avenue.* **Tickets** *$15-$35.* **Credit** *AmEx, MC, V.*
Recitals and chamber works are performed in a small, intimate space. Programming has a decidedly French accent, in terms of both artists and repertoire.
*Disabled: toilets.*

## Kaufmann Concert Hall
## at the 92nd Street Y

*1395 Lexington Avenue, at 92nd Street (415 5440). Subway 4, 5 or 6 to 86th Street.* **Tickets** *$20-$40.* **Credit** *AmEx, MC, V.*
Back in the 1970s, the Y began to exercise the ears as well as the body by developing an extensive and imaginative series for its acoustically excellent Kaufmann Concert Hall. Originally it focused on orchestral, solo and chamber masterworks, but in the past couple of seasons the programme has taken off in a new direction with a year-long exploration of American musical roots and a new series on living composers.
*Disabled: toilets.*

## Merkin Concert Hall

*Abraham Goodman House, 129 West 67th Street, between Broadway & Amsterdam Avenue (509 3330). Subway 1 or 9 to 66th Street.* **Tickets** *$10-$25.* **Credit** *AmEx, MC, V.*
This unattractive theatre with rather dry acoustics is shamefacedly tucked away on a side street in the shadow of Lincoln Center, but its adventurous programming, heavy on recitals and chamber concerts, can make it a rewarding stop.
*Disabled: toilets.*

## Town Hall

*123 West 43rd Street, at Sixth Avenue (840 2824). Subway N or R to 42nd Street/Times Square.* **Tickets** *prices vary.* **No credit cards.**
The hall has a wonderful, intimate stage and excellent acoustics, but the classical music programme is still limited.
*Disabled: toilets.*

# Other Venues

Below are listed some of the more notable spaces. In addition, many other museums, libraries and galleries stage chamber music.

## Bargemusic

*Fulton Ferry Landing, Brooklyn (1-718 624 4061). Subway A to High Street.* **Tickets** *$15-$23.* **No credit cards.**
Two concerts a week (Thur, Sun) are held all year round on this barge moored by the Brooklyn Naval Yard. It's a magical experience, with gorgeous views of the Manhattan skyline, but dress warmly in winter.

## CAMI Hall

*165 West 57th Street, between Sixth & Seventh Avenues (397 6900). Subway A, B, C, D, 1 or 9 to 59th Street/Columbus Circle.* **Tickets** *prices vary.* **No credit cards.**
Opposite Carnegie Hall, this 200-seat recital hall is rented out for individual events, mostly by classical artists.

## The Kitchen

*512 West 19th Street, between Tenth & Eleventh Avenues (255 5793). Subway A, C or L to 14th Street.* **Tickets** *$10-$20.* **Credit** *AmEx, MC, V.*
Occupying a nineteenth-century building that was once an ice house, The Kitchen has just celebrated its twenty-fifth anniversary (Philip Glass played a benefit) as the meeting place of the avant-garde in music, dance and theatre.

## Kosciuszko Foundation House

*15 East 65th Street, at Fifth Avenue (734 2130). Subway 6 to 68th Street; N or R to Fifth Avenue.* **Tickets** *$10-$15.* **Credit** *MC, V.*
This renovated East Side townhouse accommodates a fine chamber music series with a twist: each programme must feature at least one work by a Polish composer.

## Metropolitan Museum of Art

*See chapter* **Museums** *for listings.*
Concerts are held in the Grace Rainey Rogers Auditorium, near the Egyptian galleries, or occasionally around the Temple of Dendur. This is one of the city's best chamber music venues; tickets sell out quickly.

## New York Public Library
## for the Performing Arts

*40 Lincoln Center Plaza (870 1630). Subway 1 or 9 to 66th Street.* **Tickets** *free.*
Recitals, solo performances and lectures are held in the Bruno Walter Auditorium. On the library's ground floor you can listen to recordings from the collection at private turntables; on the third floor is a wonderful archive, including programmes, cuttings, pressbooks and photographs.
*Disabled: toilets.*

## Roulette

*228 West Broadway, at Franklin Street (219 8242). Subway 1 or 9 to Franklin Street; A, C or E to Canal Street.* **Tickets** *$8.* **No credit cards.**
The place to go for a range of experimental music, from classical to jazz and rock, in a TriBeCa loft. Very downtown.

## Symphony Space

*2537 Broadway, at 95th Street (864 5400). Subway 1 or 9 to 96th Street.* **Tickets** *$10-$20.* **Credit** *AmEx, MC, V.*
The neighbourhood is a funky, ungentrified strip of upper Broadway. Symphony Space's programming is eclectic to a fault. Best bets are the annual Wall to Wall marathons, which offer a full day of music around a given theme.

# Lincoln Center

In the 1950s, the tenements and playgrounds that were the setting for Leonard Bernstein's *West Side Story* were demolished. The land, an area at the south-west corner of Central Park, was developed into the Lincoln Center, a four-block complex of buildings and public spaces that would house many of the city's most important musical institutions. The striking concrete-pillared 1960s architecture of Avery Fisher Hall, the New York State Theater and the Metropolitan Opera House surrounds a black marble fountain by Philip Johnson. There's also the Lincoln Center Theater building, containing the Vivian Beaumont and Mitzi E Newhouse theatres; the Guggenheim bandshell, set in Damrosch Park, and the New York Public Library for the Performing Arts (*see page 237*). Restaurants at the Center include Café Vienna and the Panevino Ristorante in Avery Fisher Hall (874 7000) and the Grand Tier at the Met (799 3400).

The Lincoln Center has tended to rely on the tried and true; the 'Great Performers' series (Oct-June) attracts the likes of Jessye Norman, Yo-Yo Ma and Daniel Barenboim. But recent additions like the Bang on a Can Festival and the Bard Music Festival, are a welcome change. More adventurous still is the Lincoln Center festival (*see page 241*): the polar opposite of the Center's long-running 'Mostly Mozart' festival. Clearly, the definition of 'classical' seems to be stretching.

**Lincoln Center** *between Columbus and Amsterdam Avenues, 62nd to 65th Streets (875 5400/programmes & information LIN COLN). Subway 1 or 9 to 66th Street.* **Credit** AmEx, MC, V.

### Alice Tully Hall
*(875 5050).* **Tickets** $25-$40.
Built to house the Chamber Music Society of Lincoln Center (875 5788), Alice Tully Hall somehow makes its 1,000 seats feel intimate. It has no central aisle, the rows having extra legroom to compensate. The hall accommodates both music and spoken text well, and as such its vocal recital series is one of the most extensive in town. *Disabled: toilets.*

### Avery Fisher Hall
*(875 5030).* **Tickets** $10-$65.
Originally called Philharmonic Hall, this 2,700-seat auditorium used to have unbearable acoustics. It took the largess of electronics millionaire Avery Fisher, and several major internal constructions, to improve the sound quality. The venue is now both handsome and comfortable. The New York Philharmonic (875 5656) moved here when it left Carnegie Hall. Now under the direction of Kurt Masur, it's the country's oldest orchestra (founded 1842), and one of the world's finest. Its evangelical philosophy has given rise to free concerts and regular open rehearsals. The hall also hosts performances by top international ensembles. Every summer, the famous 'Mostly Mozart' series is held here.

### Metropolitan Opera House
*(362 6000).* **Tickets** $43-$175.
With enormous murals painted by Marc Chagall hanging inside its five geometric arches, the Met is the grandest of the Lincoln Center buildings and a spectacular place in which to see opera. It's home to the Metropolitan Opera and is also where major visiting companies are most likely to appear. Met productions are as lavish (though not necessarily tasteful); casts are an international who's who of current stars. Under the baton of the artistic director, James Levine, the orchestra has become a true symphonic force. Audiences at the Met are knowledgeable and fiercely partisan – subscriptions stay in families for generations. Tickets are expensive, and unless you can afford good seats, the view won't be great. English-language translations, appearing on the backs of seats, are now available on request. Some Czech rarities have recently been programmed, as well as returning productions of Philip Glass's *The Voyage* and John Corigliano's *Ghosts of Versailles*, both Met commissions. Two acclaimed productions of 1996/97 were Britten's *Midsummer Night's Dream* and Berg's *Wozzeck*. *Disabled: toilets.*

### New York State Theater
*(870 5570).* **Tickets** $17-$78.
Philip Johnson's 'jewel box' of chandeliers and glass is home to the New York City Opera, which has tried to upgrade its second-best reputation first by being defiantly popular, then by being defiantly ambitious. This meant hiring only American singers, performing many works in English, bringing American musicals into opera houses, giving a more theatrical spin to old favourites, and developing supertitles for foreign-language productions. City Opera has championed modern opera, mixing *Moses und Aron* with *Madam Butterfly*, with a few great successes and other noble failures. It has recently embarked on a middle course between its early populism and later ambition. Tickets are about half the price of the Met and the theatre is a gem. *Disabled: toilets.*

## Walter Reade Theater

*(875 5601).* **Tickets** $15-$30.
The Lincoln Center's newest concert hall is a glorified movie house. It's home to the Film Society of Lincoln Center, and its acoustics are the driest in the complex. Yet the uniformly perfect sightlines make up for it. The Chamber Music Society uses the space for its 'Music of Our Time' series, and the post-minimalist Bang on a Can festival houses its resident ensemble here. A Sunday morning concert series usually features pastries and coffee in the lobby.
*Disabled: toilets.*

*Britten's 'A Midsummer Night's Dream' at the Met.*

### World Financial Center

*West Street to the Hudson River (945 0505). Subway 1, 2, 3, 9, A, C or E to Chambers Street.*
The glassed-in Winter Garden with its palm trees springing straight from the marble floor is fabulous. The free concerts (timed to fit the schedule of the working day, and usually amplified) range from chamber music to Eno-esque compositions for public spaces.

## Churches

An enticing variety of music, both sacred and secular, is performed in New York's churches. Many of the resident choirs are very fine indeed, while excellent acoustics and serene surroundings make the churches particularly attractive venues. And as a bonus, some concerts are free or very cheap.

### Cathedral of St John the Divine

*Amsterdam Avenue & 112th Street (662 2133). Subway 1 or 9 to 110th Street.*
The 3,000-seat interior is an acoustical cavern, but the stunning Gothic interior provides a comfortable home to such groups as the Ensemble for Early Music and its own fine choir.

### Christ & St Stephen's Church

*120 West 69th Street (787 2755). Subway 1, 9 or C to 72nd Street.*
A West Side church offering one of the most diverse roster of concerts in the city.

# Summer in the city

The **Washington Square Music Festival**, *celebrating its 39th season in July 1997.*

Summer has not traditionally been a time for adventurous classical programming. Most of the city's musical institutions move out into its parks and open spaces, and those that stay indoors, like Lincoln Center's popular 'Mostly Mozart' festival, become air-conditioning for the soul. The new **Lincoln Center Festival** is attempting to change all that. Combining music, opera, dance and theatre, the festival aspires to rival the festivals at Edinburgh and Spoleto, and so far has got off to a good start. Its first year in 1996 offered Virgil Thomson's opera *Four Saints in Three Acts*, John Eliot Gardiner and Kurt Masur conducting two versions of Beethoven's only opera, an overview of Asian music and a retrospective of the composer Morton Feldman. The second season will include a rare New York appearance by the Royal Opera and Ballet of Covent Garden, a tribute to Ornette Coleman, and a look at the state of the arts in South Africa. Other open-air events around town include:

### Bryant Park

*Sixth Avenue, at 42nd Street (983 4142). Subway 1, 2, 3, 7, 9, N or R to 42nd Street/Times Square.*

### Church of the Heavenly Rest
*Fifth Avenue & 90th Street (289 3400). Subway 4, 5 or 6 to 96th Street.*
This lovely church is home to the Canterbury Choral Society and the New York Pro Arte Chamber Orchestra.

### Church of St Ignatius Loyola
*980 Park Avenue, at 84th Street (288 2520). Subway 4, 5 or 6 to 86th Street.*
The 'Sacred Music in a Sacred Space', is a high point of East Side musical life.

### Corpus Christi Church
*529 West 121st Street, at Broadway (666 9350). Subway 1 or 9 to 125th Street.*
New York's early music fans get their fix from Music Before

Directly behind the 42nd Street branch of the New York Public Library, Bryant Park is a serene, attractive and distinctly European park with a substantial free concert series.

### Central Park
*See chapter* **Sightseeing** *for listings.*
This vast oasis takes on a magical air on summer nights when the New York Philharmonic and the Metropolitan Opera stage concerts (some with fireworks).

### Lincoln Center Out of Doors
*Lincoln Plaza & Damrosch Park, Lincoln Center (875 5108).*
Phone for details about the series of free summer concerts.

### Museum of Modern Art Summergarden
*See chapter* **Museums** *for listings.*
Twentieth-century works are performed in the MoMA sculpture garden. You'll think you're in a Woody Allen movie. Bring your own neuroses.

### Washington Square Music Festival
*West 4th Street & LaGuardia Place (431 1088). Subway A, B, C, D, E, F or Q to West 4th Street.*
**Dates** 8pm Tue July, Aug.
The summer concert series, held in the heart of Greenwich Village, features chamber orchestra and ensemble works.

1800, a resident ensemble that has also been in the forefront of presenting the US débuts of prominent European groups.

### Riverside Church
*Riverside Drive & 122nd Street (870 6700). Subway 1 or 9 to 125th Street.*
With its active internal musical life (fine choir, fine organ) and visiting guests (the Orpheus Chamber Orchestra, among others), Riverside plays a large part in local musical life.

### St Bartholomew's Church
*109 East 50th Street, between Park & Lexington Avenues (378 0248). Subway E or F to Fifth Avenue; 6 to 51st Street.*
Large-scale choral music and occasional chapel recitals fill the magnificent dome behind the church's Stanford White-designed façade.

### St Paul's Chapel
*Broadway, at Fulton Street (602 0747). Subway 2, 3, 4, 5, J, M or Z to Fulton Street.*
This historic church in the financial district hosts a Noonday Concerts series with nearby Trinity Church.

### St Thomas's Church Fifth Avenue
*1 West 53rd Street, at Fifth Avenue (757 7013). Subway E or F to Fifth Avenue.*
Some of the finest choral music in the city, with the only fully accredited choir school for boys in the country, can be heard here. The church's annual *Messiah* is a must.

## Schools

Juilliard, Mannes and the Manhattan School of Music are all renowned for their students, their faculty and their artists in residence, all of whom regularly perform for free or for minimal admission. But fine music and innovative programming goes on at several other colleges and schools in the city.

### Brooklyn Center for the Performing Arts at Brooklyn College
*Campus Road & Hillel Place, off Nostrand Avenue, Brooklyn (1-718 951 4543). Subway 2 or 5 to Flatbush Avenue.* **Tickets** $25-$40. **Credit** AmEx, MC, V.
Recent attractions have included the Bolshoi Symphony, the San Francisco Western Opera Theater and soloists Leontyne Price and Andre Watts.
*Disabled: toilets.*

### Greenwich House Music School
*46 Barrow Street, between Bedford Street & Seventh Avenue South (242 4770). Subway 1 or 9 to Christopher Street.* **Tickets** prices vary. **Credit** MC, V.
Greenwich House's Renee Wieler Concert Hall puts on a wide variety of chamber concerts by students, faculty and visiting guests. Student recitals are free.

### John L Tischman Auditorium
*at the New School, 66 West 12th Street, at Sixth Avenue (229 5689). Subway 1, 2, 3 or 9 to 14th Street.* **Tickets** $8. **Credit** AmEx, MC, V.
The New School offers a modestly priced chamber music series that runs from April to October, featuring up-and-coming young musicians as well as more established artists.

### Juilliard School of Music
*Paul Recital Hall, 60 Lincoln Center Plaza (769 7406). Subway 1 or 9 to 66th Street.* **Tickets** mostly free.
The students can be frighteningly good.
*Disabled: toilets.*

### Manhattan School of Music

*120 Claremont Avenue, at 122nd Street (749 3300).*
*Subway 1 or 9 to 125th Street.* **Tickets** mostly free.
Now directed by Marta Istomen, once of Washington's
Kennedy Center, the school offers masterclasses, recitals and
off-site concerts by its students, faculty and visiting pros.
The opera program is one of the most adventurous in town.

### Mannes College of Music

*150 West 85th Street, between Columbus & Amsterdam*
*Avenues (580 0210 ext 228). Subway 1 or 9 to 86th*
*Street; B or C to 86th Street.* **Tickets** free.
Long considered a distant third in the city's conservatory
triumvirate, Mannes' profile has recently been on the
upswing. Concerts are by a mix of student, faculty and pro-
fessional ensembles-in-residence. See the Orion String
Quartet at Lincoln Center for big bucks, or here for free.

### Sylvia & Danny Kaye Playhouse

*Hunter College, East 68th Street, at Lexington Avenue*
*(772 4448). Subway 6 to 68th Street.* **Tickets** $20-$45.
**Credit** MC, V.
Across town from Lincoln Center, this refurbished theatre
has an eclectic programme of professional music and dance.
*Disabled: toilets.*

## Opera

The Metropolitan Opera and New York City Opera
may be the big guys (*see page 238*), but they're not
the only ones in town. The following companies
perform a varied repertory, both warhorses and

works in progress, from Verdi's *Aida* to Puccini's
one-act *Gianni Schicchi*. Phone the individual
organisations for ticket prices, schedules and
venue details.

### Amato Opera Theater

*319 Bowery, at 2nd Street (228 8200).*
With a theatre only 20ft wide, Anthony and Sally Amato's
charming, fully-staged productions are like watching opera
in someone's living room. Lots of well-known singers have
sung here but multiple casting breeds inconsistency.

### American Chamber Opera Company

*6 East 87th Street, at Fifth Avenue (781 0857).*
This nomadic troupe presents mostly twentieth-century
opera sung in English in venues around town.

### American Opera Projects

*463 Broome Street, near Greene Street (431 8102).*
Not so much an opera company as a living, breathing workshop for the art form. Productions are often a way to follow
a work in progress.

### DiCapo Opera Theater

*DiCapo Theater, 184 East 76th Street, between Second &*
*Third Avenues (228 9438).*
This top-notch chamber opera troupe benefits from City
Opera-quality singers performing in intelligently designed
small-scale sets. A real treat.

### New York Gilbert & Sullivan Players

*251 West 91st Street (769 1000).*
NYGASP runs its season at Symphony Space each January,

# Rock sites

'Up to Lexington 'n' one, two, five/feel sick and
dirty, more dead than alive,' wrote Lou Reed in
'I'm Waiting for the Man', thus immortalising
the corner of Lexington Avenue and 125th
Street, a New York junction with not much else
to recommend it.

New York's rock roots go back to the late
1950s, when two distinct musical streams
emerged – one from mass culture and commercially oriented and the other rooted in tradition.
The first showed itself in the work of **Brill**
**Building** (1619 Broadway) songwriters like the
teams of Lieber and Stoller, Goffin and King and
Mort Shuman and Doc Pomus.

Out on the streets, the collateral phenomenon
of doo-wop took shape as teenagers of all races
gathered to harmonise on street corners. Groups
like Dion and the Belmonts (named for their
Bronx-Italian neighborhood) were promoted by
early DJs like Alan Freed, whose radio work and
legendary shows at Brooklyn's **Paramount**
**Theater** were critical in first bringing artists
like Chuck Berry, Little Richard and Fats
Domino to a white audience.

The other wing of what became rock grew out

of the folk revival of the late 1950s. What was
initially the preserve of leftists, bohemians and
academics gathered enough popular interest that
by 1961 clubs were flourishing throughout
Greenwich Village, particularly around the
Bleecker and MacDougal axis, although the first,
**Gerde's Folk City** (11 West 4th Street), was
further east. Gerde's was followed by the
**Gaslight** (116 MacDougal) and the still operating **Bitter End**. These and a host of other coffee houses and bars became the centre of a new
movement, spearheaded by the likes of Phil
Ochs, Judy Collins, Fred Neil and Bob Dylan.

By 1965 the folkies were going electric and
several clubs embraced amplification, notably
the **Nite Owl** (118 West 3rd Street) and the **Cafe**
**au Go Go** (152 Bleecker Street), which became
home base for the Lovin' Spoonful and the Blues
Project respectively. And in the summer of 1966,
you could see an unknown Jimi Hendrix and his
band (known as Jimmy James and the Blue
Flames) at the **Cafe Wha?**. By 1967, the real
scene had shifted to the East Village, especially
St Marks Place, where an old Polish social centre, **The Dom** (23 St Marks Place), was turned

presenting one of the Big Three (*HMS Pinafore*, *The Mikado* or *The Pirates of Penzance*) alongside another G&S work.

## Regina Opera Company

*Regina Hall, 65th Street & Twelfth Avenue (1-718 232 3555).*
The only year-round opera company in Brooklyn, Regina offers full orchestras and fully staged productions.

# Rock, Roots & Jazz

It was touring musicians who christened New York 'The Big Apple', deciding that of all their destinations this was the one that brought most reward. NYC is home of the jazz diaspora and the birthplace of hip-hop: it's the East Coast referred to in the 'East Coast/West Coast' rap rivalry. Lest you forget, the first modern rock 'scene' emerged here at CBGB almost a quarter of a century ago, emphasising a 'DIY' ethic nationwide at a time when corporate monoliths seemed to have squelched the possibilities for homegrown rock for ever. More recently, there's been a resurgence in live funk and soul driven by the breakbeat tastes of rap. And *everybody* comes from *everywhere* to play here.

The city attracts a constant flow of big names, and a barrage of bright young things, all eager to put New York in the list on the back of their tour T-shirts. The East Village is teeming with aspiring artistes, providing the local scene with all types of postpunk rock 'n' roll. Live hip-hop, apart from the big shows at places like the **Palladium** (*see chapter* **Clubs**) and the **Apollo**, is underpublicised, though live performances and openmike shows often crop up at club nights. Jazz tends to be expensive, and happens mostly in venues where the food and drink minimums add plenty more to your bill. Latin music is also booming in New York. Many clubs host Latin nights, including the **Copacabana** (*see chapter* **Clubs**) and **S.O.B.s**.

For more information, check the 'Upcoming Shows' box in *Time Out New York*. *The Aquarian* ($1.50) is good for rock information, as are the *Village Voice*, *New York Press* and *Downtown* (all free, *see chapter* **Media**). Keep an eye out for flypostings and 'invitations' (flyers), too. For more live music venues, *see chapters* **Clubs**, **Cabaret**, *and* **Gay & Lesbian New York**.

*If you want to drink at any of these venues, take photo ID that proves you're over 21. At concerts you are very likely to be 'carded', even if you are obviously old enough. This is done at the door, where drinkers are issued with a plastic wristband.*

into a mixed-media venue by Andy Warhol to promote his protégés the Velvet Underground. By the end of the year, the place had become the more commercial Balloon Farm and subsequently the Electric Circus. The Circus endured until the end of the decade and is now a community center.

The real rock centre of the era was round the corner: the **Fillmore East** (105 Second Avenue) was the rock theatre par excellence, where all the best-known acts played. It closed in 1971, reopened in 1980 as The Saint, a gay disco, and was demolished in 1995.

In 1972, the New York Dolls ushered in a new era at the **Mercer Arts Center** (Broadway at Mercer Street) with their celebration of all things glam and trash. The Mercer remained the centre of the scene until it collapsed (literally – the building fell down) in August 1973. By then punk was starting to happen, and the scene shifted to that legendary bar with the worst toilets in the world, **CBGB**, home to the likes of Television and Patti Smith.

Outside of the downtown area, few venues have passed into legend, though exceptions include two infamous late-night (and sadly defunct) hang-outs: **The Scene** (301 West 46th Street), where a seriously drunk Jim Morrison tried to proposition Hendrix (the latter was playing, only to be thwarted by Janis Joplin, and **Max's Kansas City** (213 Park Avenue South, at 17th Street), where the final Lou Reed-led line-up of the Velvets were resident for part of 1970.

The serious rock historian should visit the **Chelsea Hotel** (*see chapter* **Accommodation**), the site of a Warhol movie, a Lou Reed song, where Janis entertained all and sundry, and where Nancy Spungen checked out for the last time. In the 1960s, the **Albert Hotel** (University Place at 9th Street), was the last word in tolerance. It was the only place that accepted unmarried interracial couples and allowed the Spoonful and the Blues Project to rehearse in its roach-infested and waterlogged basement. Like the Chelsea it still exists, but is now an apartment complex. And finally, lest we forget, no rock visit to New York is complete without a moment of silence outside the Dakota (1 West 72nd Street), where Mark Chapman met John Lennon, and John Lennon met his maker.

## Major Venues

*See also chapter* **Cabaret.**

### Apollo Theater

*253 West 125th Street, between Malcolm X & Adam Clayton Powell Jr Blvds (Lenox & Seventh Avenues) (749 5838). Subway 2, 3, A, B, C, D to 125th Street.* **Tickets** $9-$30. **Credit** AmEx, MC, V.
There is no more atmospheric place to see a hip-hop gig, and with a steady schedule of soul and R&B stars, the world-famous Apollo Theater has regained its status as the Mecca of black entertainment. Wednesday is Amateur Night – once a launching pad for stars such as Ella Fitzgerald and Michael Jackson, and now full of militant black comedians and soul singers hitting as many notes as they can before they reach the right one. Taped for NBC's Showtime at the Apollo, this is a fun way to see the Apollo audience in all its glory. An obvious police presence, especially for the rap gigs, means there's no need to worry about venturing into Harlem at night, although if you're white, you'll feel conspicuous.

### Beacon Theatre

*2124 Broadway, at West 74th Street (496 7070). Subway 1, 2, 3, 9 to 72nd Street.* **Tickets** $30-$80. **No credit cards.**
Worth a visit just to see its astonishing décor, the all-seater Beacon hosts an eclectic program of big acts and is the stage of choice for established soul and R&B performers. Past stars have included Bob Dylan, Ani DiFranco, Bryan Ferry, Ruben Blades and Garbage.

### Central Park SummerStage

*830 Fifth Avenue, at 72nd Street (360 2777). Subway 4, 5, 6 to 72nd Street.* **Tickets** free; benefit gigs $15-$25. **No credit cards.**

During a humid summer weekend, SummerStage is one of the great treasures available to New Yorkers. Although there are always two or three shows during the season with a substantial ticket price, the majority of concerts are free at this amphitheatre. Think of it: Solomon Burke, or Stereolab, or Junior Brown, under crystal-blue skies, for no charge, with beer!

### Irving Plaza

*17 Irving Place, at 15th Street (777 6800). Subway 4, 5, 6, L, N, R to Union Square.* **Tickets** $10-$30. **No credit cards.**
Irving Plaza excels because it has virtually no competition. A mid-level venue with a balcony and lovely décor, it's the only suitable venue for acts on the verge of bigger things (Tricky, Kula Shaker), longtime artists with substantial cults (Paul Westerberg, Laibach) or huge acts craving more intimacy (Slayer, Erasure).

### Jones Beach

*Long Island (1-516 221 1000). LIRR from Penn Station to Freeport, then bus to the beach.* **Tickets** $18-$45. **No credit cards.**
From July to September, the 'shed' that services the New York area offers an eclectic programme of performances: Diana Ross, Oasis, Barry White and PJ Harvey have all performed under the setting sun at this beachside amphitheatre.

### Manhattan Center

*311 West 34th Street, between Eighth & Ninth Avenues (564 4882). Subway A, C, E to 34th Street.* **Tickets** $10-$20. **No credit cards.**
The Hammerstein Ballroom here, still under construction as we went to press, should be roughly equivalent to Roseland. Opening in May 1997, the venue will host shows by Luscious Jackson, the Offspring and the Orb.

# Vinyl heaven

The world's greatest record collection – the one you always dreamed about as a teenager – can be found in New York on a quiet TriBeCa street near the ghost of the Mudd Club. Having clocked up more than half a million discs as it passes its tenth anniversary, the **ARChive of Contemporary Music** (54 White Street; 226 6967) has a mission to preserve copies of everything that's been done in popular music on planet Earth since 1950.

The ARChive is the work of musicologist and author B George and librarian David Wheeler, who realised some time in 1986 that 'the Rodgers and Hammerstein Archives [at the Lincoln Center] doesn't collect the Butthole Surfers'. To remedy this, they started out to chronicle rock 'n' roll, realised it was only part of a broader phenomenon and decided to tackle the whole of global pop.

A core library of 20,000 of the founders' records quickly grew on infusions from the collections of DJ Jellybean Benitez, producer Nile Rodgers and

directors Martin Scorsese and Jonathan Demme. Key additional support came from record exec Jerry Wexler, songwriters Jerry Leiber and Mike Stoller, and artists Lou Reed, Keith Richard, Fred Schneider, Paul Simon and Todd Rundgren, all of whom sit on the board of advisors.

Books, video, film, photos, press kits, clippings and all sorts of pop music ephemera are also part of the collection. Some of the more bizarre items include revolve-and-sniff aroma discs, celebrity one-offs like the Cartwright family's 'Bonanza Christmas on the Prairie' and over 700 picture discs.

The ARChive's dream future would include a movie theatre, reading room, art gallery and free public listening rooms. For now, however, it functions chiefly as a research and consultation service to the music industry. It is open to the public for summer and pre-Christmas sales of whatever they hold more than two of, many of them sealed classics with prices consistently far below the usual collector's premiums.

## Madison Square Garden

*Seventh Avenue, between 31st & 33rd Streets (465 6741). Subway 1, 2, 3, 9 to 34th Street.* **Tickets** from $22.50. **No credit cards.**

'Awright, Noo Yawk!! Are you ready to rock and roll??!!' The acoustics of this arena may be more suited to the crunch of ice hockey and the slap of basketball, but MSG is the most famous rock 'n' roll venue the world over. It packs in the punters for massive events by folks such as Kiss and Celine Dion.

## Meadowlands

*East Rutherford, New Jersey (1-201 935 3900). Bus from Port Authority Bus Terminal (564 8484).* **Tickets** from $22.50. **No credit cards.**

New Jersey's answer to Madison Square Garden comes complete with racetrack and football stadium. Its Continental Airlines Arena (or the Giants Stadium next door) is the place to see Jersey natives Bon Jovi or Bruce Springsteen, or perhaps a visiting R Kelly.

## Nassau Coliseum

*1255 Hempstead Turnpike, Uniondale, NY (1-516 794 9303). LIRR to Hempstead, N70, N71, N72 bus to coliseum.* **Tickets** from $22.50. **No credit cards.**

Nassau Coliseum is Long Island's answer to Madison Square Garden. As such, Nassau doesn't have a lot of character, but that quality isn't usually required for enormodomes, is it?

## Radio City Music Hall

*1260 Sixth Avenue, at 50th Street (247 4777). Subway B, D, F, Q to Rockefeller Center.* **Tickets** from $25. **No credit cards.**

The grandest Art Deco concert hall in the city, Radio City only books huge acts such as Tina Turner and Barry Manilow, when the stage isn't the setting for *Riverdance* or the spring of Christmas Rockette extravaganzas. Ownership of the hall may change hands and the future of the Rockettes is unclear. Catch their kitsch masterwork now, before you have to track them down in some future road company version in Dubuque.

## Roseland

*239 West 52nd Street, between Broadway & Eighth Avenue (245 5761/concert hotline 249 8870). Subway B, D, E to Seventh Avenue.* **Tickets** from $15. **No credit cards.**

If an act isn't big enough for the Garden but too big for Irving Plaza, this Broadway ballroom does the trick. Soundgarden, Rage Against the Machine, the Cardigans, Beck and 'the Artist' have all packed them in here in the last year.

## Roxy

*515 West 18th Street, between Tenth & Eleventh Avenues (645 5156). Subway A, C, E to 14th Street; L to Eighth Avenue.* **Tickets** $12-$20. **No credit cards.**

Mainly a dance club with a history stretching back to when it was the epicentre of roller disco. Live performances don't happen regularly, but the Chemical Brothers, Everything But the Girl and Sick of It All have taken a bow at this cavernous space recently.

## Theater at Madison Square Garden

*Seventh Avenue, between 31st & 33rd Streets (465 6741). Subway 1, 2, 3, 9 to 34th Street.* **Tickets** price varies. **No credit cards.**

Underneath Madison Square Garden is this comfortable but sanitised modern venue hosting a broad selection of big-name pop artists (Sting, John Mellencamp) craving more intimacy than the Garden.

## Town Hall

*See page 237 for listings.*

A venerable old theatre that hosts occasional medium to large concerts by such folks as Cesaria Evora and Paul Weller.

## Webster Hall

*125 East 11th Street, between Third & Fourth Avenues (353 1600). Subway 4, 5, 6, L, N, R to Union Square.* **Tickets** $15-$20. **No credit cards.**

Downtown's biggest room for live music has drawn the likes of the Mighty Mighty Bosstones and Morphine. After you've passed through security, you can look down on burgeoning glam bands from the spacious balcony or hang out at one of the many bars inside.

# Rock, Pop & Soul

*See also* **Coney Island High** *and* **Don Hill's** *in chapter* **Clubs**.

## Acme Underground

*9 Great Jones Street, at Lafayette Street (420 1934). Subway 6 to Bleecker Street.* **Tickets** $3-$10. **No credit cards.**

The **Great Jones Café** (*see chapter* **Restaurants**) hides this small basement venue. After a year of uncertainty, it's emerged as one of those joints that remind you that NYC is just like any other town: needless 'quirky' grad student bands perform here alongside more worthy acts.

## Arlene Grocery

*95 Stanton Street, between Ludlow & Orchard Streets (358 1633). Subway F to Second Avenue; J, M, Z to Essex Street.* **Tickets** free. **No credit cards.**

Irish-themed rock, hard-boiled folkies and indie fixtures abound here, and it's already a favoured venue for impromptu gigs by artistes like Jeff Buckley and Spacehog.

## Back Fence

*155 Bleecker Street, at Thompson Street (475 9221). Subway A, C, E, B, D, F, Q to West 4th Street.* **Tickets** free-$5. **Credit** MC, V.

With its sawdust-covered floor, checkered tablecloths and, yes, a fence mounted on the back wall, Back Fence is one of the quainter bars among the bustling neighbourhood honky-tonks. It tends to book a rotation of hackish regular locals.

## Baggot Inn

*82 West 3rd Street, between Thompson & Sullivan Streets (477 0622). Subway A, C, E, B, D, F, Q to West 4th Street.* **Tickets** $5. **Credit** AmEx, MC, V.

Formerly the Sun Mountain Café, the Baggot Inn refurbished its interior along with its booking policies: good trad rock can be heard, as well as typical horrid Bleecker Street fare.

## Bitter End

*147 Bleecker Street, at Thompson Street (673 7030). Subway A, C, E, B, D, F, Q to West 4th Street.* **Tickets** $5. **Credit** AmEx, Disc, MC, V.

The *ne plus ultra* of Bleecker Street joints. Now free of looming lease troubles that plagued it for years, the Bitter End will forever feature singer-songwriters and pop-rockers who are quite jazzed to perform where Dylan played all those years ago.

## Bottom Line

*15 West 4th Street, at Mercer Street (228 6300). Subway N, R to 8th Street.* **Tickets** $15-$25. **No credit cards.**

Catch the management on a bad night, or attend a particularly crowded evening, and you find yourself a prisoner at

*Art Deco home to the Rockettes, but for how long?*

the Riker's Island of rock. That said, Allan Pepper's cabaret-style club has persisted for 25 years, longer than any similar venue. Roots music, singer-songwriter stylings, the occasional jazz or fusion gig and Buster-frigging-Poindexter and his Banshees of Blue all find a home here.

## Brownies

*169 Avenue A, between 10th & 11th Streets (420 8392). Subway L to First Avenue.* **Tickets** $6-$8. **No credit cards.**
A loud, basic bar filled with loud, basic bands. Although its sound system doesn't exactly kick ass, in the last couple of years Brownies has been beating CBGB at its own game, booking the finest in upcoming rock, as well as hard-gigging local bands.

## Café Wha?

*115 MacDougal Street, between West 3rd & Bleecker Streets (254 3706). Subway A, C, E, B, D, F, Q to West 4th Street.* **Tickets** $3-$10. **Credit** AmEx, MC, V.
One of the crucial New York City rock venues of the 1960s, the Wha? now typifies the current Bleecker Street experience. Undistinguished bar bands play here to tourists.

## CBGB

*315 Bowery, at Bleecker Street (982 4052). Subway B, D, F, Q to Broadway/Lafayette Street; 6 to Bleecker Street.* **Tickets** $3-$12. **No credit cards.**
CBGB is beloved by every musician who's played there as much for the crystal-clear sound system as the undeniable vibe of playing the birthplace of punk rock. However, it's a little tougher for the average punter, who must contend with horrid sightlines and furnace-like atmosphere when it's crowded, and the most Godforsaken bathrooms known to man. The booking is hit or miss at best.

## CB's 313 Gallery

*313 the Bowery, at Bleecker Street (677 0455). Subway B, D, F, Q to Broadway/Lafayette Street; 6 to Bleecker Street.* **Tickets** $6-$10. **Credit** AmEx, MC, V.
CBGB's more cultivated neighbour. It's just as long and narrow, but is festooned with local artists' work instead of graffiti and layers of posters. The overall effect makes it seem that you're in a club in Toronto, not NYC. Singer-songwriterly fare dominates.

## Continental

*25 Third Avenue, at St Mark's Place (529 6924). Subway 6 to Astor Place.* **Tickets** free-$6. **No credit cards.**
The skies will rain blood; the earth will belch fire; the day of reckoning will come and the Continental will still be there, booking local grease-a-billy, hard rock, punk and garage bands for little or no cover.

## The Cooler

*416 West 14th Street, between Ninth Avenue & Washington Street (229 0785). Subway A, C, E, L to 14th Street/Eighth Avenue.* **Tickets** free-$15. **Credit** AmEx, MC, V.
This spacious former meat locker isn't always climate-controlled – especially in the dead of winter or at a crowded summer show. Monday nights are free, and the bills are usually interesting, mixing indie rock with the more avant-garde.

## Downtime

*251 West 30th Street, between Seventh & Eighth Avenues (695 2747). Subway 1, 9 to 28th Street.* **Tickets** $5-$12. **Credit** AmEx, MC, V.
During the week, run-of-the-mill rock bands play in this vertically spacious bar with an upstairs lounge and pool table. On Saturdays the Bat Cave takes over, and the heavy-black-eyeliner crowd digs industrial bands.

## Fez

*380 Lafayette Street, at Great Jones Street (533 2680). Subway B, D, F, Q to Broadway/Lafayette Street; 6 to Bleecker Street.* **Tickets** $5-$18. **Credit** AmEx, MC, V.
With its gold lamé and red velvet curtains, Fez is one of the city's finest venues for that glittering lounge/cabaret atmosphere. It books a variety of local events including the popular Loser's Lounge series, and international pop stars such as the Divine Comedy, Donovan and Joni Mitchell. There are also 'alternative comedy' happenings. It's a sit-down-dinner-theatre-style venue with little standing room.

## Hotel Galvez

*103 Avenue B, between 6th & 7th Streets (358 9683). Subway F to Second Avenue, 6 to Astor Place.* **Tickets** free. **Credit** AmEx, MC, V.
After you've stuffed yourself on Galvez's fine Southern cooking, you can hear upcoming singer-songwriters in one of the smallest and cosiest spaces in the East Village.

## Lakeside Lounge

*162 Avenue B, between 10th & 11th Streets (529 8463). Subway L to First Avenue.* **Tickets** free. **No credit cards.**
Not only does this year-old bar have an unmatchable country- and blues-intensive jukebox, but appropriately roots-inflected local outfits throw it down regularly here for no cover.

## Le Bar Bat

*311 West 57th Street, between Eighth & Ninth Avenues (307 7228). Subway 1, 9, A, B, C, D to Columbus Circle.* **Tickets** $10-$20; free before 9pm (8.30pm Sat). **Credit** AmEx, MC, V.
A bizarre bar venue set in an old cavelike recording studio. The bands here are usually happy party-time funk and soul providers and the crowd a jolly bunch of after-workers.

## Lion's Den

*214 Sullivan Street, between Bleecker & West 3rd Streets (477 2782). Subway A, C, E, B, D, F, Q to West 4th Street.* **Tickets** $5-$10. **Credit** AmEx.
A cavernous dive catering to the tastes of Bleecker Street regulars and NYU students. Lion's Den books plenty of Deadhead-friendly jam bands, reggae, funk and rock.

## Luna Lounge

*171 Ludlow Street, between Houston & Stanton Streets (260 2323). Subway F to Second Avenue.* **Tickets** free. **No credit cards.**
A nice alternative to the often-overcrowded Max Fish across the street, Luna Lounge offers free rock shows in a comfy environment – meaning old beat-up sofas and chairs in the band room and vinyl booths in the bar room.

## Maxwell's

*1039 Washington Street (1-201 798 4064). PATH train from 33rd, 23rd, 14th, 9th or Christopher Streets to Hoboken/bus 126 from Port Authority Bus Terminal.* **Tickets** $5-$12. **Credit** AmEx, DC, MC, V.
There are more bars per capita in Hoboken, New Jersey, than anywhere in the US, apparently, and Maxwell's has recently become quite like all the others along Washington Street. The days when it rivaled CBGB are gone, but 'Swells still manages to attract a great bill now and again. There's a restaurant and microbrewery in the front.

## McGovern's

*305 Spring Street, between Hudson & Greenwich Streets (627 5037). Subway 1, 9 to Houston Street.* **Tickets** free-$5. **Credit** AmEx, Disc, MC, V.
A narrow bar with unenviable sight lines, McGovern's books small-fry talent on the cheap. Still, it's a decent place for a beer.

## Mercury Lounge

*217 East Houston Street, at Avenue A (260 4700).*
*Subway F to Second Avenue.* **Tickets** $6-$12. **Credit**
AmEx, Disc, MC, V.

With a good ear for booking future faves like Morphine and
Bis, a knack for attracting bands seemingly above its station and unassailable acoustics and sightlines, the Mercury
Lounge is the small venue to beat in NYC. If band X doesn't
sound good here, it's invariably because band X does not
have its shit together.

## Nell's

*246 West 14th Street, between Seventh & Eighth*
*Avenues (675 1567). Subway A, C, E, L to 14th Street-*
*Eighth Avenue.* **Tickets** $10-$15. **Credit** AmEx, MC, V.

With plush interiors modelled after a Victorian gentlemen's
club, this lushly appointed room was the place to be seen
in the late 1980s – if you could get in. The crowd has shifted from international jet-set to the upscale hip-hop set – the
late Notorious B.I.G. shot a video here. On the ground floor
they feature live jazz, blues and reggae. DJs pack the dance
floor downstairs.

## New Music Café

*380 Canal Street, at West Broadway (941 1019). Subway*
*1, 9, A, C or E to Canal Street.* **Tickets** $5-$10.
**No credit cards.**

As progressive as its busy schedule will allow, the NMC
packs in (literally, it can be very cramped) all sorts of music
from the mundane to the inspiring.

## Nightingale Bar

*213 Second Avenue, at 13th Street (473 9398). Subway*
*L to First Avenue.* **Tickets** $5. **No credit cards.**

The stage at this noisy bar is about six inches off the ground
and the mirror behind the stage gives an illusion of space.
But when seeing a band at Nightingale, there's no way to
avoid feeling you're right up there with them.

## Paddy Reilly's Music Bar

*519 Second Avenue, at 29th Street (686 1210). Subway*
*6 to 28th Street.* **Tickets** $5-$10. **Credit** AmEx.

The premier venue in NYC for Irish rock, in that Black 47
plays here every Saturday.

## Prospect Park Bandshell

*9th Street, at Prospect Park West, Park Slope, Brooklyn*
*(1-718 965 8969). Subway F to Seventh Avenue; 2, 3 to*
*Grand Army Plaza.* **Tickets** free.

The Prospect Park Bandshell is to Brooklyn what Central
Park Summerstage is to Manhattan: the place to hear great
music in the great outdoors at no cost. The shows, produced
by Celebrate Brooklyn, mirror the borough's great melting
pot, so you're just as likely to hear Afropop and Caribbean
music and jazz and blues. Past acts have included Philip Glass,
Randy Weston, and King David Rudder & Charlie's Roots.

## Rodeo Bar

*375 Third Avenue, at 27th Street (683 6500). Subway 6*
*to 28th Street.* **Tickets** free. **Credit** AmEx, MC, V.

It looks like any other Murray Hill joint – and half of it is,
actually. But the sawdust-strewn northern half books local
roots outfits and the occasional nascent phenomenon.

## Sidewalk

*94 Avenue A, at 6th Street (473 7373). Subway F to*
*Second Avenue, 6 to Astor Place.* **Tickets** free. **Credit**
AmEx, MC, V.

Behind the front room at this neighbourhood café, you'll find
the world capital of 'antifolk'. In other words, low-mainte-
nance acoustic music rules, whether it's irreverent and ingenious (which describes antifolk guru Lach or perennials the
Humans) or self-important folkie swill.

## Spiral

*244 Houston Street, between Avenues A & B (353 1740).*
*Subway F to Second Avenue; 6 to Astor Place.*
**Tickets** $6. **No credit cards.**

As long as you have a phone, you can play at the Spiral.
Located kitty-corner from the hub of Ludlow Street, this
club has a dank atmosphere that is slightly perked by its
pinball machine. The fare consists of straightahead small-
fry rock bands.

## Tramps

*51 West 21st Street, between Fifth & Sixth Avenues*
*(727 7788). Subway F, N, R to 23rd Street.* **Tickets** $5-
$20. **No credit cards.**

Goddamn those two columns about seven feet in front of
Tramps' stage! Otherwise, we haven't a bad word to say
about this midsize venue, which serves up plenty of alt and
modern rock along with loads of funk, reggae, country,
blues and more.

## Westbeth Theatre Center
## Music Hall

*151 Bank Street, between West & Washington Streets*
*(741 0391). Subway A, C, E to 14th Street; L to Eighth*
*Avenue.* **Tickets** $8-$35. **No credit cards.**

The Westbeth is a 500-capacity space with decent sound that
has seen recent shows from Pavement, the Dirty Three and
Mark Eitzel. It has a nice extra bar area outside in which to
hang if you're not digging the opening act.

## Wetlands

*161 Hudson Street, at Laight Street (966 4225).*
*Subway 1, 9, A, C, E to Canal Street.* **Tickets** free-$15.
**Credit** (bar only) AmEx, MC, V.

Deadheads seeking to keep the vibe alive after Jerry
Garcia's death flock here for the weekly events that feature
either Dead cover bands or musicians peripherally connected to the band. More than that, this club regularly
books ska, funk, reggae, jungle and hardcore marathons.
You can brief yourself on a number of political causes by
perusing the postings.

# Jazz & Experimental

## Birdland

*315 West 44th Street, between Eighth & Ninth Avenues*
*(581 3080). Subway A, C, E to 42nd Street.*
**Tickets** from $10, plus $10 minimum. **Credit** AmEx,
MC, V.

The flagship venue for the recent jazz resurgence in midtown, Birdland presents many of jazz's biggest names in the
neon splendour of Times Square. The dining area's three-
tiered floor plan allows for maximum visibility, so patrons
can enjoy everyone from Pat Metheny to Jon Faddis and
Chico O'Farill while also enjoying the fine cuisine. To compete with the rest of the Monday night big bands in residence, the club has enlisted the Toshiko Akiyoshi Jazz
Orchestra featuring Lew Tabackin.

## Blue Note

*131 West 3rd Street, between MacDougal Street & Sixth*
*Avenue (475 8592). Subway A, B, C, D, E, F, Q to West*
*4th Street.* **Tickets** $7.50-$47.50, plus $5 minimum.
**Credit** AmEx, DC, Disc, MC, V.

'The jazz capital of the world' is how this famous club sub-
titles itself, and the reception that the household names who
play here are given often suggests visiting heads of state.
Recent acts have included the Dave Brubeck Quartet, David
Sanborn, Ray Charles, Lionel Hampton and Grover
Washington Jr. All this comes at a price: dinner runs to
around $24 a head.

### Iridium
*48 West 63rd Street, at Columbus Avenue (582 2121).*
*Subway 1, 9 to 66th Street/Lincoln Center.* **Tickets** $25-
$40, plus $5 minimum. **Credit** AmEx, DC, Disc, JCB, MC, V.
This club's location – across the street from the Lincoln
Center – guarantees that its lineups are generally top-notch.
With a décor that's a little bit Art Nouveau and a little bit Dr
Seuss, Iridium lures the upscale crowds by booking a mix
that is equally split between jazzhold names and household
ones. Monday nights belong to the legendary guitarist-inven-
tor-icon Les Paul, who often ends up sharing the stage with
one of the guitar heroes who swear by his prize invention,
the Gibson solid-body electric guitar.

### Knitting Factory/AlterKnit Theater
*74 Leonard Street, between Broadway & Church Street
(219 3055). Subway A, C, E to Canal Street; 1 or 9 to
Franklin Street.* **Tickets** $5-$20. **Credit** ($15 minimum)
AmEx, MC, V.
The Knitting Factory is recommended for those who like their
music a little off the rails. New York's avant-garde music mall,
it features an up-to-the-minute blend of experimental jazz,
rock, alternative cinema and poetry. The café and bar are
open throughout the day, and the main room holds 250 people. *See also chapters* **Spoken Word** *and* **Dance**.

### Smalls
*183 West 110th Street, at Seventh Avenue (929 7565).
Subway 1, 9 to Christopher Street/Sheridan Square.*
**Tickets** $10. **No credit cards.**
The spot where jazz new jacks rub elbows with their college-
student counterparts and beat era nostalgists, Smalls books
both high profile up-and-comers and established stars such
as Lee Konitz. There's no liquor licence, but you can bring
your own or sample some of the juices at the bar.

### Sweet Basil
*88 Seventh Avenue South, between Bleecker & Grove
Streets (242 1785). Subway 1 or 9 to Christopher Street.*
**Tickets** $17.50 cover, plus $10 minimum. **Credit** AmEx,
MC, V.
Past players here have included Art Blakey and Abdullah
Ibrahim, but the emphasis now is on the traditional. There's
a jazz brunch on Saturdays and Sundays.

### Village Vanguard
*178 Seventh Avenue South, at Perry Street (255 4037).
Subway A, C, L to 14th Street-Eighth Avenue.* **Tickets**
$15, plus $10 minimum. **No credit cards.**
This basement club is still going strong after 60 years. Its
stage – a small but mighty step-up that has seen the likes of
John Coltrane, Bill Evans and Miles Davis – still hosts the
*crème de la crème* of mainstream jazz talent. The Monday
night regular is the 17-piece Village Vanguard Jazz Orchestra,
which has now held the same slot for more than 30 years.

### Visiones
*125 MacDougal Street, at West 3rd Street (673 5576).
Subway A, C, E, B, D, F, Q to West 4th Street/Washington
Square.* **Tickets** $7-$15. **Credit** AmEx, DC, Disc, MC, V.
The food at this popular Village spot may be nouvelle Tex-
Mex, but the jazz is strictly postbop. Mondays belong to the
Gil Evans-inspired orchestra piloted by composer-conduc-
tor Maria Schneider.

### Zinno
*126 West 13th Street, between Sixth & Seventh Avenues
(924 5182). Subway 1, 2, 3, 9 to 14th Street.* **Tickets**
$10 cover, plus $15 minimum. **Credit** AmEx, MC, V.
A supper club for those who want more than mere polite
background noise with their dinner, Zinno is where the mainstream's most accomplished jazzers (Hilton Ruiz, Michael
Moore, Bucky Pizzarelli) get to perform in relaxed, intimate
duos and trios. The cuisine isn't hard on the palate, either.

## Reggae, World & Latin

### S.O.B.s
*200 Varick Street, at Houston Street (243 4940). Subway
1, 9 to Houston Street.* **Tickets** $10-$25. **Credit** AmEx,
DC, Disc, JCB, MC, V.
S.O.B.s' stands for Sounds of Brazil, but that's not the only
kind of music you'll hear at the city's premier spot for musicians from South of the Border. That means reggae, samba
and even Afropop. Mondays belong to La Tropica Nights,
an evening devoted to the biggest names in salsa. Looking
like the safari-style burger joint at Disneyland, S.O.B.'s will
cure your thirst for all things percussive and exotic.

### Zinc Bar
*90 Houston Street, between La Guardia Place &
Thompson Street (477 8337). Subway A, C, E, B, D, F,
Q, to West 4th Street-Washington Square.* **Tickets** $15
cover; $5 minimum. **No credit cards.**
A cosy – and we mean cosy – sub-nook situated where NoHo
meets SoHo, Zinc Bar is the place to catch up with the most
diehard night owls. It's got an after-hours feel that actually
starts well before daybreak, and the atmosphere is enhanced
by the astonishingly cool mix of jazz, Latino, Brazilian and
flamenco bands that gig there nightly.

## Blues, Folk & Country

### Chicago B.L.U.E.S.
*73 Eighth Avenue, between 13th & 14th Streets (924
9755). Subway A, C, E, L to 14th Street/Eighth Avenue.*
**Tickets** free-$20. **Credit** AmEx, MC, V.
When Otis Rush or some other titan of the blues come to town,
they often settle in at this cosy West Village club. While the
opening acts can be startlingly bad, the chance of seeing the
likes of Johnnie Johnson at close range should not be missed.

### Fast Folk Café
*41 North Moore Street, between Varick & Hudson
Streets (274 1636). Subway 1, 9 to Franklin Street; A, C,
E to Canal Street.* **Tickets** free-$15. **No credit cards.**
No local venue wants much to be known as a folk venue, save
for this tiny TriBeCa bastion of intimate acousticism.

### Louisiana Bar & Grill
*622 Broadway, between Bleecker & Houston Streets
(460 9633). Subway B, D, F, Q to Broadway/Lafayette
Street; 6 to Bleecker Street.* **Open** 6pm-midnight Mon-
Thur; 6pm-2am Fri, Sat; 5-10pm Sun. **Tickets** free.
**Credit** AmEx, MC, V.
Apart from the fine Cajun cuisine available here, the Louisiana
is known for booking top-shelf rockabilly, country and blues
acts, including local legends the Harlem All-Stars.

### Manny's Car Wash
*1558 Third Avenue, between 87th & 88th Streets (369
2583). Subway 4, 5, 6 to 86th Street.* **Tickets** free-$15.
**Credit** AmEx, MC, V.
Every evening, authentic Chicago-born blues blares from the
tiny stage of this elongated nightspot on the city's Upper East
Side. Patrons are generally locals and can be tatty, serious
blues lovers or junior Wall Streeters ogling the single women
(women get in free on Monday nights). A blues jam occurs
on Sunday nights when there's mostly standing room only.

### Terra Blues
*149 Bleecker Street, at Thompson Street (777 7776).
Subway A, B, C, D, E, F or Q to West 4th Street.*
**Tickets** free-$15. **Credit** AmEx, MC, V.
Gracing the stage at this otherwise typical Bleecker Street
bar are a wide range of blues-based artists, both local and
imported, ranging from authentic Chicago guitar pickers, to
local blues duo Satan and Adam.

# Theatre

*It's all an act: New York reaches the top in stages, offering world-beating talent in a dramatic choice of venues.*

*Queuing round the block for the latest hot ticket at **TKTS** in Times Square.*

New York is the crowned capital of the stage, with venues throughout Manhattan and even into the outer boroughs. Performance spaces range from those occupying the glittering rejuvenated 'Great White Way' of Broadway to others situated in the intimacy of Theater Row; from the 'not only Greenwich Village' of Off-Broadway to the nooks and crannies of Off-Off-Broadway and the out-of-the-way spaces of some very professional community theatres. Whatever your theatrical tastes you'll find it in New York, where more is always better.

## INFORMATION

The Sunday Arts and Leisure and the Friday Weekend sections of the *New York Times* are reliable sources of information, as are the listings in *Time Out New York*, *New York Magazine*, the *New Yorker* and the *Village Voice*. In addition there are several phone lines offering everything from plot synopses and show times to an agent ready to sell tickets (you'll need a touch-tone phone). The best is **NYC/On Stage** (768 1818), a service of the Theater Development Fund (*see chapter* **Dance**),

which will tell you about performances on Broadway, Off-Broadway and Off-Off-Broadway, as well as classical music, dance and opera events. The **Broadway Show Line** (563 2929) gives similar information, but is restricted to Broadway and Off-Broadway shows, and you must know which show you are interested in before using it. The **Association for a Better New York** (370 5800) service is wide-ranging, detailed and less commercial: useful for smaller productions and one-off events. This service works by venue rather than show name.

## BUYING TICKETS

Provided you have one of the major credit cards, buying Broadway tickets requires little more effort than picking up a phone. Almost all Broadway and Off-Broadway shows are served by one of the city's 24-hour booking agencies. The information lines (*above*) will refer you to ticket agents, often on the same call. **Telecharge** (239 6200) and **Ticketmaster** (307 4100) carve up the bulk of the shows between them, with the smaller **Ticket**

Central (279 4200) specialising in Off-Broadway and Off-Off-Broadway shows. You will have to pay a service charge to the agency, but since most theatres don't take telephone bookings, you don't have much choice, except to buy tickets in person from a theatre's box office.

The cheapest full-price tickets on Broadway are for standing room and cost about $15, though not all theatres offer these. If a show is sold out, it's worth trying for standby tickets just before show time. Tickets are slightly cheaper for matinees and previews, and for students or groups of 20 or more. Look out for 'two-fers' – vouchers that allow you to buy two tickets for slightly more than the price of one. These generally promote long-running Broadway shows and occasionally the larger Off-Broadway ones. Some sell-out shows offer good seats at reduced rates (usually $20) after 6pm on the day of performance. But those in the know start queuing hours beforehand. The best way of obtaining tickets, however, is to go to **TKTS** (*see chapter* **Music**) where you can get as much as 75% off the face value of some tickets. Get there early to avoid the queue, or at around 7pm when most shows are about to start.

## NEW YORK SHAKESPEARE FESTIVAL

The Delacorte Theater in Central Park is sister to The Public (*see page 255*). When not producing Shakespeare under its roof (for a price), it offers the Bard for free out-of-doors in the New York Shakespeare Festival (June to September). If you're in the city during the summer, this is an absolute must. Tickets are free, and are distributed at 1pm on the day of the performance, from both the Delacorte and the Public. Normally, 11.30am is a safe time to get there, but when shows feature box office giants, the queue starts as early as 7am. Two tickets are allotted per person.

### Delacorte Theater
*Central Park at 81st Street (539 8750). Subway B or C to 81st Street; 6 to 77th Street.*

## Broadway

Broadway is booming. In recent years box office takings for newly opened shows have repeatedly broken records and, by putting big-name movie stars in leading roles, Broadway now competes directly with Hollywood for its audiences.

# The New Vaudeville

No matter what you feel about post-modernism, it has definitely left behind a burgeoning form of theatre. New Vaudeville – variety entertainment, dusted down and dosed with adrenalin – has taken New York by storm, with shows such as *Tubes*, *Stomp*, *Tap Dogs* and *Tokyo Shock Boys* playing before sell-out crowds.

These reviews are paced like live MTV, which partly explains their success. Take *Tubes*, an offering by the Blue Man Group, and best described as a messy, colourful audience-participation romp. Opinions vary as to whether the show is utterly insane or truly profound, but it's undoubtedly enormous fun. Take a friend – or better still, an enemy – and watch them get mummified in toilet paper.

New Yorkers were recently invited to watch the epitome of vulgarity when the *Tokyo Shock Boys* grossed out Off-Broadway audiences. The bathroom lunacy included snorting water through the nose until it squirted out of the eyes, or flaunting their genitals. But audiences kept coming. Flash-paced, mindless fun, with young performers who packed more energy than the Manhattan Project.

In *Tap Dogs*, heavy metal met tap, when six flashy super-hunks from Australia womped around in their sweaty boxers. An evening of high-energy gymnastics performed to deafening heavy metal music augmented by hypnotic flashing lights, and with a grand finale in a water trough that drenched the first row of the audience.

*Stomp* flaunts the tap-dancing skills of a dozen or so very aggressive young bang-on-the-can Brits. Fred and Ginger they ain't, but their virtuosity is impressive. The power of rhythm is exploited with such verve it leaves audiences breathless.

It doesn't really matter whether you define such entertainment as 'theatre' or not. What's certain is that New Vaudeville has succeeded in enticing into theatres many people who would otherwise give them a wide berth. Watch out for these and similar shows at one of the Off-Broadway theatres below.

### Astor Place Theater
*434 Lafayette Street, between 4th Street and Astor Place (254 4370). Subway 6 to Astor Place.*

### The Orpheum
*126 Second Avenue, between 7th Street and St Marks Place (477 2477). Subway 6 to Astor Place.*

### Union Square Theater
*100 East 17th Street, at Park Avenue South (307 4100/ 1-800 755 4000). Subway 4, 5, 6 to Union Square.*
*Disabled: toilets.*

*Willem Dafoe (right) and Dave Shelly get to grips with Eugene O'Neill's 'The Hairy Ape'.*

'Broadway' in theatrical terms, is the district around Times Square somewhere between 41st and 53rd Streets. This is where the grand theatres are clustered together, most built in the first 30 years of this century. Officially, there are 38 of them designated as being on Broadway, for which full-price tickets cost up to $75. The big shows are hard to ignore; blockbusters like *Cats, Phantom of the Opera, Les Miserables, Miss Saigon, Rent* and *Grease* declare themselves on vast billboards. However, there's more to Broadway than the undemanding razzle-dazzle of a Cameron Mackintosh production. In recent years, provocative new dramas by such playwrights as Terrence McNally, Horton Foote and Wendy Wasserstein have had resounding successes, as have many revived classics. Other noticeable trends are the revival of old-time musicals and the staging of animated movies.

Look out for the irrepressible **Roundabout Theater** (869 8400), a critically acclaimed home of the classics played by all-star casts, which, as we went to press, was about to move to new quarters.

## Off-Broadway

As a rule, Off-Broadway theatres have fewer than 500 seats and are located in Greenwich Village. But Off-Broadway theatres are also found on the Upper West Side, the Upper East Side, and in midtown.

As Broadway increasingly becomes a place of spectacle-*sans*-substance, those playwrights who would once have opted for a Broadway production now opt for Off-Broadway, where they find

audiences who are interested in plays that have something to say. The runaway cost of mounting a play on Broadway has also led to Off-Broadway being – as is was originally – the place to introduce new works.

So, if it's brainfood you're after, dine Off- or Off-Off-Broadway – but be prepared for considerable variations in standards. Listed below are some of the most reliable theatres and repertory companies. Tickets cost from approximately $10 to $40.

### Atlantic Theater Company

*336 West 20th Street, between Eighth & Ninth Avenues (239 6200). Subway C or E to 23rd Street.*
Created about 15 years ago out of acting workshops taught by David Mamet and William H Macy, this dynamic little theatre (in a former church sanctuary on a lovely Chelsea street) has presented over 80 plays. Productions have included Mamet's *Edmond*, as well as the premieres of Howard Korder's *Boys Life* and Craig Lucas's *Missing Persons*.

### Brooklyn Academy of Music

*30 Lafayette Avenue, Brooklyn (1-718 636 4100). Subway 2, 3, 4, 5, B, D or Q to Atlantic Avenue; B, N or R to Pacific Street.*
Brooklyn's grand old opera house – as well as the associated Carey Playhouse and Majestic Theater – stages the famous Next Wave Festival in the last three months of each year. This is a programme of musical, theatrical and dance pieces by American and international artists. Recent ventures included a much acclaimed Out of Joint production of *The Steward of Christendom* and *The Music of Stephen Sondheim*, an all-star gala attended by the maestro himself. *See also chapter* **Dance**.
*Disabled: toilets. Internet: http://www.bam.org*

### Lincoln Center

*Between Columbus & Amsterdam Avenues, 62nd to 65th Streets (875 5400/programmes & information 546 2656). Subway 1 or 9 to 66th Street.*
The Lincoln Center complex houses two amphitheatre-shaped

drama venues: the recently renovated 1040-seat Vivien Beaumont Theater (considered a Broadway theatre) and the 290-seat Mitzi E Newhouse Theater (considered Off-Broadway). Expect polished productions of new and classic plays, with many a big-name actor.

## La Mama

*74A East 4th Street, between the Bowery & Second Avenue (475 7710). Subway 6 to Astor Place.*
This is where Off-Broadway began. When acclaimed producer Ellen Stewart opened La Mama ('Mama' is her nickname) in 1962, it was New York's best-kept theatre secret. Now, with over 50 Obie (Off-Broadway) Awards to its name, it's a fixture in the city's dramatic life. Extraordinary things are done with the stage in this cavernous space: sometimes it takes up most of the theatre. La Mama isn't for those looking for traditional theatre; it is here that new ground is broken. Harvey Fierstein's *Torchsong Trilogy* started at La Mama.
*Disabled: toilets.*

## Manhattan Theatre Club

*City Center, 131 West 55th Street, between Sixth & Seventh Avenues (645 5590/box office 581 1212). Subway D or E to Seventh Avenue.*
Manhattan Theatre Club has a reputation for sending young playwrights on to Broadway. It first staged *Sylvia* and *Ain't Misbehavin'*. Linda Ayvasian's *Nine Armenians* earned a 1997 Obie Award nomination here. The club's two theatres, in the basement of City Center, are the 299-seat Mainstage Theater, which offers four plays each year by both new and established playwrights, and the more flexible Stage II Theater, an outlet for works in progress, workshops and staged readings. One of the Club's highlights is its Writers in Performance series. Guest speakers have included Isabel Allende, Eric Bogosian and Toni Morrison.
*Disabled: toilets.*

## New York Theater Workshop

*79 East 4th Street, between Second and Third Avenues (505 1892/460 5475). Subway 6 to Astor Place.*
Founded in 1979, this Off-Broadway company produces new plays using young directors who are eager to harness challenging works. Besides initiating plays by such authors as David Rabe (*A Question of Mercy*), Caryl Churchill (*Mad Forest*) and Tony Kuchner (*Slavs!*), it is most noted for premiering *Rent*, Jonathan Larson's Pulitzer Prize-winning musical. The Workshop also offers a home to upstart performance artists through its O Solo Mio festival.
*Disabled: toilets.*

## The Public Theater

*425 Lafayette Street, between Astor Place & East 4th Street (239 6200). Subway 6 to Astor Place; N or R to 8th Street.*
One of the most consistently interesting theatres in the city. Dedicated to the production of New American playwrights and performers, the Public presents new explorations of Shakespeare and the classics. There are five stages, so there's a constant circulation of short-run goodies. There's also a brand new coffee bar. The Public is now under the aegis of George C Wolfe, responsible for the first New York production of Tony Kushner's *Angels in America*.
*Disabled: toilets.*

# Off-Off Broadway

The technical definition of Off-Off Broadway is a show by performers who don't have to be card-carrying pros, at a theatre with less than 100 seats. It's here that the most innovative and daring writers and performers are willing to experiment.

Pieces may combine various media, including music, dance, mime, film, video and – typical of New York – performance monologue, a strange combination of theatre and psychotherapy.

But Off-Off Broadway is not restricted to experimental work. At venues like the Theater for the New City, and from companies such as the Jean Cocteau Repertory Company, you'll also see classical works and more traditional contemporary plays. Tickets cost roughly $15 to $25. *See also chapters* Dance *and* Cabaret.

## Bouwerie Lane Theater

*330 the Bowery, at Bond Street (677 0060). Subway F to Second Avenue; 6 to Bleecker Street.*
Housed in the old cast-iron German Exchange Bank, this is the resident theatre of the Jean Cocteau Repertory Company, which is devoted to producing the classics in rep. Recent works include Brecht's *Mother Courage*, Shakespeare's *Othello* and Orton's *What the Butler Saw.*

## CBGB's 313 Gallery

*313 the Bowery, at Bleecker Street (677 0455). Subway 6 to Bleecker Street.*
Next door to the famous punk venue is this multi-purpose space which has proved a consistently good bet for a wide range of unusual theatre and other small-scale performances.

## En Garde Arts

*(941 9793/fax 343 1177).*
A company that presents site-specific theatre throughout the city. It gave us *Stonewall 25* on the scene of the original riots, *JP Morgan Saves the Nation* smack in the middle of Wall Street, *The Trojan Women* at a graffiti-inflicted abandoned amphitheatre on the East River, and Fiona Shaw's startling rendition of TS Eliot's *The Wasteland* at the Liberty Theater, each evening after the demolition squad had completed a day's work before the theatre's re-opening.

## Irish Repertory Theater

*132 West 22nd Street, between Sixth & Seventh Avenues (727 2737). Subway 1 or 9 to 23rd Street.*
Dedicated to performing works from both master and contemporary Irish playwrights, this company in Chelsea has produced some interesting sell-out shows. Notable are the revival of Wilde's *The Importance of Being Ernest* and Hugh Leonard's *Da* starring the dynamic Brian Murray. There's no blarney here.
*Disabled: toilets.*

## The Kitchen

*512 West 19th Street, between Tenth & Eleventh Avenues (255 5793). Subway A, C, E or L to 14th Street.*
A small, experimental theatre with a season running from September to May. It presents an eclectic repertoire of video, readings, music, dance and performance art. A good place to see edgy New York experimentation.
*Disabled: toilets.*

## Naked Angels Theater Company

*311 West 43rd Street, between Eighth & Ninth Avenues (397 7841). Subway A, C or E to 42nd Street.*
This co-operative company of nearly 40 actors and playwrights (including Joe Mantello and Jon-Robin Baitz) stages moderately experimental theatre and performance events.

## Pearl Theater Company

*80 St Mark's Place, between Second & Third Avenues (505 3401). Subway 4 or 5 to Astor Place; N or R to 8th Street.*
Newly housed on the punk promenade of the East Village, this troupe of resident players relies primarily on its

actors' ability to present the classics clearly. Besides Shakespeare and the Greeks, Pearl has successfully produced the works of Ionesco, Sheridan, Molière and Shaw, plus lesser known authors like Ostrofsky and Otway – all on a minimally dressed small stage, with actors in the simplest of costumes.

### The Performing Garage

*33 Wooster Street, between Broome & Grand Streets (966 3651). Subway A, C or E to Canal Street.*
The Performing Garage features the works of the Wooster Group, whose members include Richard Foreman, Willem Dafoe and Spalding Gray. Gray developed his well-known monologues here, among them *Swimming to Cambodia*; Dafoe once played the lead in Eugene O'Neill's *The Hairy Ape*. As well as presenting deconstructed versions of theatre classics, the company hosts a visiting artists series, dance performances and monthly readings.

### PS 122

*150 First Avenue, at East 9th Street (477 5288). Subway 6 to Astor Place; N or R to 8th Street.*
One of New York's most exciting venues, housed in an abandoned school on the Lower East Side. It's a non-profit-making arts centre for experimental performance, with two theatres presenting dance, performance, music, film and video. Artists develop, practise and present their work here; it has provided a platform for Whoopi Goldberg, Meredith Monk and Phillip Glass.

### Playwrights Horizons

*416 West 42nd Street (564 1235). Subway A, C or E to 42nd Street.*
This power-packed company can boast over 300 premieres of important contemporary plays, including dramatic offerings like *The Substance of Fire*, *Driving Miss Daisy* and *The Heidi Chronicles*, and musicals such as *March of the Falsettos*, and *Sunday in the Park with George*. More recently the works of newcomers Adam Guettel, Tina Landau (*Floyd Collins*), Jeanine Tesorie and Brian Crawkey (*Violet*) have been staged.

### Ridiculous Theatrical Company

*(594 7704).*
Picture *Hush, Hush Sweet Charlotte* and *Whatever Happened to Baby Jane* performed by Bette Davis as if she were a male crossdresser: that's Everett Quinton's Ridiculous Theatrical Company. Founded in 1967, this reckless group of actors reach for the top of parody, farce and buffoonery, and go right over it every time – usually in full drag. Notable productions include founding father Charles Ludlum's tongue-in-cheek adaptations of *Camille* and *Medea*, and the Wagner parody, *Der Ring Gott Farblonjet*. Got the picture?

### Second Stage Theater

*2162 Broadway, at 76th Street (873 6103). Subway 1, 2 or 3 to 72nd Street.*
Created as a venue for American plays that didn't get the critical reception it was thought they deserved, Second Stage now also produces the works of new American playwrights. It staged the premiere of Lanford Wilson's *Sympathetic Magic* and the revival of his *London Sky*, as well as the premieres of Tina Howe's *Painting Churches* and *Coastal Disturbances* and David Mamet's *The Woods*.

### Signature Theater Company

*424 West 42nd Street, between Ninth & Tenth Avenues (967 1913). Subway A, C or E to 42nd Street.*
Each season this unique award-winning company focuses on the works of a single playwright in residence. Notable among its achievements was the introduction of Edward Albee's *Three Tall Women* and Horton Foote's *Young Man from Atlanta* which went on to win the Pulitzer Prize. The 1997/98 playwright in residence is Arthur Miller.

### Theater for the New City

*155 First Avenue, between 9th and 10th Streets (875 7792/254 1109). Subway L to First Avenue.*
Hard-hitting political dramas are performed by the Living Theater group in one of the building's four theatres. Recent productions have included *Caprichos*, as well as *Already Seen*, *Rite of Passage* and *My Name Is* as part of the Out on the Edge Festival of Lesbian and Gay Theater.

# Dance

*From perennial favourites like 'The Nutcracker' to avant-garde events at The Kitchen, New York has it choreographed.*

Even though money is tight, the New York dance scene is as vital as ever. There is no other city in the world that boasts such a high calibre of established companies and emerging choreographers. Of the two major seasons – from October to December, and from March to June – the spring stretch is decidedly the richer. Not only are both the New York City Ballet (NYCB), the George Balanchine-founded neo-classical company extraordinaire, and the American Ballet Theatre (ABT), which presents full-length classics, in full swing, but there is also an abundance of modern dance.

Both ballet companies are equally dazzling. At ABT, it's all romance, with captivating productions of classic ballets such as *Romeo and Juliet* and *The Sleeping Beauty*. Here the dancers are what keep devoted fans in awe; currently, Paloma Herrera and Angel Corella deservedly hold court as young stars, but one can also catch the elegance and mature partnering of dancers such as Susan Jaffe and Jose Manuel Carreño. At NYCB, it's the stunning choreography that matters. Unlike at the ABT, the dancers aren't publicised (although cast lists are posted inside the door of the New York State Theater each week). You're likely to see a star or two, but equally exciting is to watch a corps dancer make a grand début in a principal's role.

Other classical companies include the Dance Theatre of Harlem, founded by former NYCB dancer Arthur Mitchell. In 1968, motivated by news of Martin Luther King's assassination, Mitchell decided to give the children of Harlem the same opportunities he had been given and began teaching out of a remodelled garage. With Karel Shook, his teacher and mentor, he founded Dance Theatre of Harlem a year later, as both a school and a professional company. New York performances are rare these days; the troupe makes more appearances at the Kennedy Center than the City Center, but there are occasional informal performances. Another small but respected ballet company is Eliot Feld's Ballet Tech, a group comprised of students from his school, many of whom were plucked as children from auditions held in New York City public schools. Regional ballet companies, such as the Pacific Northwest Ballet, which is led by former NYCB dancers Kent Stowell and Francia Russell, perform at City Center or the Joyce Theater. International companies, such as the Paris

Opera Ballet or the Kirov, usually grace the stage of the Metropolitan Opera House.

Modern dance is unique to New York, having been popularised throughout the world by divas Martha Graham and Doris Humphrey. Although neither choreographer is alive, the Martha Graham Company and the José Limón Company perform more or less every year at City Center and the Joyce Theater respectively. Established modern choreographers Paul Taylor, Merce Cunningham, Trisha Brown, Bill T Jones and Mark Morris present their companies fairly regularly at the Brooklyn Academy of Music, City Center and the Joyce, but if you really want to appreciate the community, it's best to take a trip to one of the city's downtown, experimental venues such as PS122, the Danspace Project at St Mark's Church or the Dance Theater Workshop. These are excellent spaces in which to view the unexpected – tickets are inexpensive, and, even though the choreographers are taken quite seriously, the crowds are more laid-back.

The Theater Development Fund's NYC/On Stage service (*see page 260*) offers information on all theatre, dance and music events in town. For information on weekly performances, see *Time Out New York*, which covers all types of dance, from ballet to tap or modern dance, and features 'preview' columns on a selective basis as well as a listing of classes for beginner and advanced dancers. The *Village Voice* covers the downtown scene well; and the Sunday *New York Times* occasionally carries a box of dance listings for the week. *Dance Magazine* ($3.95, monthly) is a good way to find out about a performance ahead of time.

## Major Venues

### Lincoln Center

It's somehow very satisfying to stand in the middle of all this dance history. Along with the New York State Theater and the Metropolitan Opera House, there are dance performances on occasion at the Clark Studio Theater, located in the David Rose Building, which is also home to Balanchine and Lincoln Kirstein's School of American Ballet (SAB). Each June, students from SAB present workshop performances. For balletomines, it's an exciting weekend, open to all sorts of possibilities. The next Darci Kistler is waiting to be discovered.

*The Paul Taylor Dance Company in 'Man is a Social Animal' from Cloven Kingdom.*

## New York State Theater

*Broadway, at 63rd Street (870 5570). Subway 1 or 9 to 66th Street.* **Tickets** $10-$82. **Credit** (telephone bookings only; $1 surcharge) AmEx, MC, V.

Otherwise known as the House of Balanchine, this rich theatre was built for the New York City Ballet in 1964 and continues to present works by its founder George Balanchine, founding choreographer Jerome Robbins and current ballet master-in-chief Peter Martins. The company is renowned for its neo-classical roots, the dancers for their exquisite technique. Even from the inexpensive fourth ring seats, the view is unobstructed, but the best seats in the house are in the first ring, where not only is the music best appreciated, but one is able to enjoy all of the dazzling patterns that Balanchine choreographed. There are two seasons: winter begins just before Thanksgiving, featuring over a month of *Nutcracker* performances, and runs until the beginning of March; the spring season usually begins in April or May and lasts for eight weeks.
*Disabled: toilets.*

## Metropolitan Opera House

*Broadway, at 64th Street (362 6000). Subway 1 or 9 to 66th Street.* **Tickets** $24-$145. **Credit** AmEx, MC, V.

During the autumn and winter, the Opera House is the land of the Metropolitan Opera; spring belongs to American Ballet Theatre. Founded in 1939 by Mikhail Mordkin as Ballet Theatre, the company offered classics and new works created by Mordkin in a traditional Russian style. The focus of ABT is still classical; along with ballet staples such as *La Bayadere* and *Swan Lake*, artistic director Kevin McKenzie presents pieces by Twyla Tharp, Anthony Tudor and Lar Lubovitch. For those who fret that there isn't an autumn season to showcase these first-class dancers, one has been added (3-15 November at City Center). Apart from ABT, the Met hosts a range of top international companies. The acoustics are wonderful, but the theatre is vast – from the top tiers the dancers sometimes look like scurrying ants, so sit closer if you can afford it.
*Disabled: toilets. Internet: http://www.metopera.org*

## Other Major Venues

### Brooklyn Academy of Music

*30 Lafayette Avenue, Brooklyn (1-718 636 4100). Subway 2, 3, 4, 5, B, D or Q to Atlantic Avenue; B, N or R to Pacific Street.* **Tickets** $15-$50. **Credit** AmEx, MC, V.

Don't let the fact that this is in Brooklyn scare you off. BAM, as it's affectionately known, showcases many superb modern and out-of-town companies. BAM's Opera House, with its old columns and carved marble, is one of the most beautiful stages for dance to be found in the city. The annual Next Wave Festival each autumn showcases experimental and established dance and music groups, and during the spring, short festivals that focus on ballet, tap, hip-hop and modern dance are presented.
*Disabled: toilets. Internet: http://www.bam.org*

### City Center Theater

*131 West 55th Street, between Sixth & Seventh Avenues (581 7907). Subway B, D or E to Seventh Avenue.* **Tickets** $25-$50. **Credit** AmEx, MC, V.

Before the creation of the Lincoln Center changed the cultural geography of New York, this was the home of the New York City Ballet, the Joffrey Ballet and American Ballet Theatre. The lavish décor is all gold; so are the companies that pass through, including those of Paul Taylor, Merce Cunningham and Martha Graham, as well as international troupes including the Whirling Dervishes of Turkey.
*Disabled: toilets.*

### Joyce Theater

*175 Eighth Avenue, at 19th Street (242 0800). Subway 1 or 9 to 18th Street; A, C or E to 23rd Street.* **Tickets** $7-$35. **Credit** AmEx, DC, Disc, MC, V.

The Joyce – once a seedy repertory cinema called the Elgin – is one of the finest theatres in which to see dance. It's intimate, but hardly a box: out of the 472 seats, there's not a bad one in the house. Choreographers, both emerging, like David Dorfman, and established, as in the case of Bill T Jones, have performed over the last year. In residence is Eliot Feld's company, Ballet Tech (formerly Felt Ballets/NY). Feld, who began his performing career in Balanchine's *The Nutcracker* and Robbins's *West Side Story*, presents his company in two seasons (one in March, one in July). The Joyce also plays host to a variety of out-of-town ensembles, along with a few staples, including the Pilobolus Dance Theatre in June and the Altogether Different Festival in January. During the summer, when many theatres are dark, the Joyce schedule often includes close to a dozen companies. The Joyce Soho showcases emerging artists.

*Disabled: toilets. Internet: http://www.joyce.org*
**Branch**: Joyce Soho 155 Mercer Street (431 9233).

## Other Venues

### Aaron Davis Hall at City College
*135th Street, at Convent Avenue (650 6900). Subway 1, 9 to 137th Street.* **Tickets** $15-$100. **No credit cards**.
It's a trek, but well worth it. Troupes here often celebrate African-American life and culture. Choreographer Donald Byrd presented *The Harlem Nutcracker* here before taking it to BAM.
*Disabled: toilets.*

### Context Studios
*28 Avenue A, between 2nd & 3rd Streets (777 3394). Subway F to Second Avenue, 6 to Astor Place, L to First Avenue.* **Tickets** $10-$15. **No credit cards**.
An intimate theatre that specialises in downtown choreographers and musicians.
*Disabled: toilets.*

### Merce Cunningham Studio
*55 Bethune Street, between Washington & West Streets, 11th Floor Studio (691 9751). Subway A, C or E to 14th Street; 1 or 9 to Christopher Street.* **Tickets** $5-$30.
**No credit cards**.
Located in the Westbeth Complex, on the edge of Greenwich Village (no matter which subway you take, be prepared for a good walk), the Cunningham Studio is rented to individual choreographers for performances. The stage is a studio in Cunningham's school, so be prepared to take off your shoes. It's informal and casual, but arrive early for a seat or you might just end up on the floor. For more details, contact the Cunningham Dance Foundation on 255 8240.

### Dance Theater Workshop
*Bessie Schonberg Theater, 219 West 19th Street, between Seventh & Eighth Avenues (691 6500/box office 924 0077). Subway 1 or 9 to 18th Street; C or E to 23rd Street.* **Tickets** $12-$15. **Credit** AmEx, MC, V.
You won't find a pair of pointe shoes here, rather an abundance of experimental dance and theatre, which is presented in a small, intimate space. During popular shows, cushions are tossed on the floor for those without a seat (if you pay in advance, you get one). Drop by the theatre for a schedule. It's one of the most user-friendly and best organised of the downtown venues, and a must-see if you're interested in exploring the full range of New York dance. You probably won't see anyone famous performing – but they might be in time. DTW has launched the careers of dozens of acclaimed artists, including Bill T Jones, Mark Morris and Whoopi Goldberg.

### Danspace Project
*St Mark's in the Bowery Church, Second Avenue & 10th Street (674 8194). Subway 4, 5, 6, N or R to Union Square; L to Third Avenue.* **Tickets** $12.
**No credit cards**.
A gorgeous place to see dance that is even more heavenly when the music is live. Downtown choreographers are selected by the director, Laurie Uprichard, whose standards are, thankfully, high.

### Florence Gould Hall
*Alliance Française, 55 East 59th Street, between Park & Madison Avenues (355 6160). Subway 4, 5 or 6 to 59th Street; N or R to Fifth Avenue.* **Tickets** $10-$15. **Credit** AmEx, MC, V.
In 1996, the Pascal Rioult Dance Theatre was named resident choreographer of the Alliance Française; his company presents two seasons at Florence Gould Hall, one in early November, the other in May. Rioult, former principal dancer with the Martha Graham Company, choreographs engaging dances, beautifully performed. The theatre also hosts performances by other companies throughout the year, such as Battery Dance Company and the New York Theater Ballet.
*Disabled: toilets.*

### The Kitchen
*512 West 19th Street, between Tenth & Eleventh Avenues (255 5793). Subway A, C, E or L to 14th Street.* **Tickets** $8-$25. **Credit** AmEx, MC, V.
Best known as an avant-garde theatre space, the Kitchen's programming includes the most experimental dance events, of a kind you're unlikely to see at the Lincoln Center. A downtown fixture.

### Knitting Factory/AlterKnit Theater
*74 Leonard Street, between Broadway & Church Street (219 3055). Subway A, C, E to Canal Street; 1 or 9 to Franklin Street.* **Tickets** $5. **Credit** ($15 minimum) AmEx, MC, V.
The Knitting Factory is better known for its funky music programming, but it also offers dance on occasion in its AlterKnit Theatre. Expect funky, experimental work.

### Marymount Manhattan Theater
*221 East 71st Street, between Second & Third Avenues (517 0475). Subway 6 to 68th Street.* **Tickets** $5-$10.
**No credit cards**.
Owned by the school of the same name, this theatre features contemporary dance performances as well as theatre and opera productions.
*Disabled: toilets.*

### Movement Research
*Judson Church, 55 Washington Square South (477 6854). Subway A, C or E to West 4th Street.* **Tickets** free.
Directors Audrey Kindred and Anya Pryor carry on the tradition of free Monday night dance at the Judson Church, a custom started in the 1960s by avant-garde choreographers Yvonne Rainer, Steve Paxton and Trisha Brown. At least two choreographers perform a night; the artists tend to be both established and emerging. The series runs from September to June and is highly recommended. Book first.
*Disabled: toilets.*

### Ohio Theater
*66 Wooster Street, between Spring & Broome Streets (966 4844). Subway C, E to Spring Street.*
**Tickets** $10-$20. **No credit cards**.
Weekend performances by capable companies. The glorious Neo Labos Dancetheater performs each autumn.

### PS 122
*150 First Avenue, at 9th Street (477 5288). Subway 6 to Astor Place; F to Second Avenue.* **Tickets** $9-$15.
**Credit** AmEx, MC, V.
Located in the East Village, PS 122 was once a Public School (hence PS) and is now a Performance Space. It's dedicated to staging new and unconventional works.

### Symphony Space
*2537 Broadway, at 95th Street (864 1414). Subway 1, 2, 3 or 9 to 96th Street.* **Tickets** $10-$20. **Credit** AmEx, MC, V.

Located in an ungentrified part of upper Broadway, this is a centre for all the performance arts, where the World Music Institute produces many international dance troupes. Different from the norm.
*Disabled: toilets.*

### Town Hall
*123 West 43rd Street (840 2824). Subway 1, 2, 3, 7, 9, N or R to 42nd Street/Times Square.* **Tickets** *$10-$25.* **No credit cards.**
An attractive house on a rather seedy side street in the theatre district, the Town Hall presents a variety of music and dance events, including Dance Brazil and the American Tap Dance Orchestra. It's also the New York home of trendy guru Marianne Williams.
*Disabled: toilets.*

## Summer Performances

### Central Park SummerStage
*Central Park, Rumsey Playfield, at 72nd Street (360 2777). Subway B, C to 72nd Street; 6 to 68th Street.* **Tickets** *free.*
This outdoor dance series runs on Fridays in July and the first couple of weeks in August. Temperatures can get steamy, but the choreographers are well worth watching.

### Dances for Wave Hill
*West 249th Street, at Independence Avenue, Riverdale, Bronx (989 6830). Subway 1, 9 to 231st Street, then Bx7,*

# The Nutcracker

There are many versions of this essential Christmas tale that buzz around the city in the month of December, but perhaps Balanchine's 1954 classic is the most beloved – sweet but not cloying, and chock full of glorious dancing. It is performed at the State Theater from late November to early January, and though it's a hot ticket, a trip to the box office will often turn up seats.

As always, there are alternative Nutcrackers: Mark Morris's *The Hard Nut* is a kitsch variation on the theme, featuring sets and costumes from the 1960s. Donald Byrd's *The Harlem Nutcracker* is even more tempting. Set to Duke Ellington's arrangement of Tchaikovsky's *Nutcracker Suite* – grooves and all – it tells the poignant story of a widow, Clara, who grieves for her husband on Christmas Eve. It's all heart. See both at BAM.

New York Theater Ballet (679 0401) presents a condensed version geared to the attention spans of small children. Even the Rockettes get into the act at Radio City Music Hall (*see chapter* **Music**), doing their precision drill thing to excerpts from Tchaikovsky's great score. ABT has its own *Nutcracker*, available on video, but doesn't perform it in New York during the Christmas season.

*Bx10 or Bx24 bus to 252nd Street.* **Tickets** *$4.* **No credit cards.**
A gorgeous setting for outdoor dance. The series, sponsored by Dancing in the Streets, runs in July.

## Bargains

### Theater Development Fund
*1501 Broadway, between 43rd & 44th Streets (221 0013). Subway 1, 2, 3, 7, 9, N or R to 42nd Street/Times Square.* **No credit cards.**
TDF offers a book of four vouchers for $28, which can be purchased at the TDF offices by visitors who bring their passport or out-of-state driver's licence. Each voucher is good for one admission at off-off-Broadway music, theatre and dance events, at venues such as the Joyce, the Kitchen, Dance Theater Workshop and PS 122. TDF also provides information by phone on all theatre, dance and music events in town with its NYC/On Stage service (768 1818).

## Dance Shopping

Both the New York City Ballet and American Ballet Theater have gift shops, open during intervals, selling everything from autographed pointe shoes to ballet-themed T-shirts and jewellery.

### Ballet Company
*1887 Broadway, between 62nd & 63rd Streets (5246 6893/1-800 219 7335). Subway 1 or 9 to 66th Street.* **Open** *10am-7pm Mon-Sat; 11am-6pm Sun.* **Credit** *AmEx, DC, MC, V.*
This small but densely packed emporium, where just about everything is pink, carries dance books, videotapes and memorabilia.

### Capezio Dance-Theater Shop
*1650 Broadway, at 51st Street (245 2130). Subway C or E to 50th Street.* **Open** *9.30am-6.30pm Mon-Wed, Fri; 9.30am-7pm Thur; 9.30am-6pm Sat; 11am-5pm Sun.* **Credit** *AmEx, MC, V.*
Capezio carries a good stock of professional-quality shoes, practice and performance gear as well as dance duds that can be worn on the street.
**Branches:** 136 East 61st Street (758 8833); 2121 Broadway (799 7774); 1776 Broadway (586 5140).

### KD Dance
*339 Lafayette Street, at Bleecker Street (533 1037). Subway B, D, F or Q to Broadway/Lafayette Street; 6 to Bleecker Street.* **Open** *noon-8pm Mon-Sat.* **Credit** *AmEx, MC, V.*
This shop owned by Tricia Kaye, former principal dancer and ballet mistress of the Oakland Ballet, and dancer David Lee, features the softest, prettiest dance knits available.

## Dance Schools

Most major companies have their own schools. Amateurs are welcome at the following (classes for beginners start at $10):

### Alvin Ailey American Dance Center
*Third Floor, 211 West 61st Street (767 0940). Subway A, B, C, D, 1 or 9 to 59th Street.*

### American Ballet Theatre
*Third Floor, 890 Broadway, at 19th Street (477 3030). Subway N, R to 23rd Street; L to Sixth Avenue.*

# Alvin Ailey American Dance Theater

Perhaps no New York company is as revered as Alvin Ailey American Dance Theater, a troupe of exquisite and powerful dancers who reign over City Center every December. Along with the works of Ailey, the company presents dances by former dancer and current artistic director Judith Jamison, as well as Lar Lubovitch, Ulysses Dove, Hans von Manen and George Faison.

Ailey, who died of AIDS in 1989, founded the company in 1958. He was born in Texas and later moved to Los Angeles. Inspired by performances of the Katherine Dunham Company and Ballet Russes de Monte Carlo, he studied with Lester Horton and began to choreograph while dancing in that company. He created 79 works in his lifetime, and maintained that the Ailey company should be a repertory company, dedicated to the preservation and enrichment of the American modern dance heritage and the uniqueness of black cultural expression.

His works – such as *Blues Suite, Night Creature* and the breathtaking 1960 *Revelations* – still warrant standing ovations. Jamison has continued the journey begun by Ailey with grace, poise and the polish she brought to her own performances. The audience can't help but be transformed. 'I want their minds and their spirits to be jarred, and I want them not necessarily to be happy all the time,' explains Jamison. 'That's not the point of the excursion.

The excursion is to have you leave differently than when you came in, to have your perspective change – so you think differently about yourself in relationship to the rest of the world.'

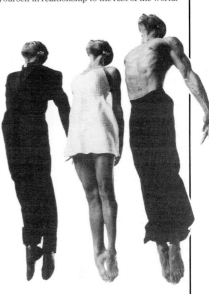

### Dance Space
*Sixth Floor, 622 Broadway, between Bleecker & Houston Streets (777 8067). Subway B, D, F, Q to Broadway/Lafayette Street; 6 to Bleecker Street.*

### 550 Broadway Dance
*Third Floor, 550 Broadway, between Prince & Spring Streets (925 1466). Subway N or R to Prince Street; 6 to Spring Street; B, D, F, Q to Broadway/Lafayette Street.*

### Martha Graham School
*316 East 63rd Street (838 5886). Subway 4, 5 or 6 to 59th Street; N or R to Fifth Avenue.*

### Limon Institute
*Ninth Floor, 611 Broadway, between Houston & Bleecker Streets (777 3353). Subway B, D, F, Q to Broadway/Lafayette Street; 6 to Bleecker Street.*

### Merce Cunningham Studio
*55 Bethune Street, near Washington Street (691 9751). Subway A, C, E, 1, 2, 3, 9 to 14th Street; L to Eighth Avenue.*

### Paul Taylor School
*Second Floor, 552 Broadway, between Prince & Spring Streets (431 5562). Subway B, D, F, Q to Broadway/Lafayette Street; 6 to Bleecker Street.*

### Peridance Center
*Second Floor, 132 Fourth Avenue, between 12th & 13th Streets (505 0886). Subway 6 to Astor Place, L to Third Avene.*

## Other Dance

### Ballet Hispanico School of Dance
*167 West 89th Street, between Columbus & Amsterdam Avenues (362 6710). Subway 1 or 9 to 86th Street.*
All styles of Latin and Spanish dance, including Flamenco.

### Fareta School of Dance and Drum
*622 Broadway, at Bleecker Street (677 6708). Subway B, D, F or Q to Broadway/Lafayette Street.*
Traditional African dance, as well as Cuban, Brazilian and Haitian styles.

### Paul Pellicoro's DanceSport
*1845 Broadway, at 60th Street (307 1111). Subway A, B, C, D, 1 or 9 to Columbus Circle.*
The man who taught Al Pacino to dance in *Scent of a Woman*. All styles of ballroom and Latin dancing.

# Sport & Fitness

*Watch it or do it – and give yourself a sporting chance in a sports-crazy city.*

Because New Yorkers come from everywhere and nowhere they are passionately devoted to their local heroes. They may grouse about the players and condemn the owners but when the home team is in contention for a championship, all ears are open for the latest score. And if the team wins, it's ticker-tape parades and pandemonium in the streets.

Baseball, the national pastime, is very much a product of the five boroughs. The basic rules of the game were drawn up by a New York team in 1846 and the first professional leagues originated in the city during the 1870s. Babe Ruth and the Yankee's 'Murderer's Row' of the 1920s cemented the game's grip on the popular imagination. Joe DiMaggio did likewise in the 1930s. During the 1950s three of New York's boroughs had great teams; there were endless debates on the relative merits of the Yankees' Mickey Mantle, the (Manhattan-based) Giants' Willie Mays and the Brooklyn Dodgers' Duke Snider. The colour line in American professional sport was broken in New York when Jackie Robinson stepped onto the field for the Brooklyn Dodgers.

For a time, when 'Broadway' Joe Namath stood at the helm of the New York Jets, it seemed as though the gridiron of American football might supplant the baseball diamond in the hearts of New Yorkers. But it is basketball that grips the city now. (Though some devotees will argue for ice hockey, which mimics the big town with its institutionalised violence. And it was heaven when the New York Rangers, after 50 years of drought, reclaimed hockey's crown, the Stanley Cup.)

## Spectator Sports

'How about those Mets?' Mention 'sports' (never sport) and the average New Yorker will turn into an experienced team manager and offer a barrage of educated opinion. This is a town where people read the tabloids from the back to the front and where arguments over half-remembered sporting trivia are far more vociferous than any disputes about politics, sex or religion. Sport is one of life's essentials here.

### INFORMATION

All the daily papers carry a massive amount of sport analysis and give listings of the day's events and TV coverage. On Mondays they list the coming week's schedule for local teams in Major League baseball, NBA basketball, NFL football and NHL hockey. *New York Newsday* also includes full league results for British football (under 'soccer'). *The New York Times'* excellent Sports supplements appear on Sundays and Mondays. Buy the weekly *Sports Illustrated* ($2.95) to get a feel for things. For news of special events contact the New York Convention & Visitors Bureau on 397 8222.

### TICKETS

Your first call for tickets should be to the team itself. You may be referred to Ticketmaster (307 7171), which sells the same tickets with a booking fee added. For many events, however – especially football and basketball – demand for tickets far outstrips supply. If you are certain that neither the team nor Ticketmaster can help, you have two options: touts or ticket brokers. If you're staying in a hotel, it's worth having a word with the concierge, as they often have wily connections.

### TOUTS

If you buy from a ticket tout, known as 'scalpers', you won't be able to get your money back if you're

# The baskets

They don't call it 'the city game' for nothing. It may be the invention of a New England WASP, Dr James Naismith, but it was black inner city youth who perfected it. Basketball's minimal demands on space and equipment make it ideal for an urban environment. The level of play in the street courts of the city today is good enough to draw in the pros on their days off. Check out any of the public courts listed below.

New York is basketball crazy. The hottest ticket in town today is courtside for the New York Knickerbockers at Madison Square Garden, where a mix of trendies and loyalists rub shoulders with fixtures Spike Lee and Woody Allen. What draws them is the sight of teams of tall (usually black) men in skimpy outfits defying the laws of gravity. The moments of pure athleticism, intuition and improvisation – both by team and individual – are beyond those found in any other sport. The intimate space of the contest brings out real individual expression: players have character and sass. If you can't find (or afford) tix, get down to a good sports bar and drink in the atmosphere with a friendly sixpack.

Unfortunately, the current Knicks team seems doomed to eternal bridesmaidhood. The sublime Michael Jordan rules the roost with his Chicago Bulls. New York's second-place status is a bitter pill for a town that not-so-secretly believes itself the navel of the world. The team today is like the city – richly talented and neurotically insecure. Both are slightly unsettling and incredibly exciting to watch.

## Hottest Street Games

**Asphalt Green** *East 90th Street, at East End Avenue. Subway 4, 5 or 6 to 86th Street.*
**The Battlegrounds** *151st Street, at Amsterdam Avenue. Subway 1 or 9 to 145th Street.*
**Goat Park** *99th Street, at Amsterdam Avenue. Subway 1, 2, 3 or 9 to 96th Street.*
**Marcus Garvey Park** *121st Street, at Madison Avenue. Subway 4, 5 or 6 to 125th Street.*
**West 4th Street Courts** *Sixth Avenue, at West 4th Street. Subway A, B, C, D, E or F to West 4th Street/Washington Square.*

---

tricked but, provided you're careful, this can be a reliable way of buying seats. Before you part with any cash, check that the ticket has the correct details, and make sure you know where your seats will be. Diagrams of stadium seating arrangements are printed in the front of the *Yellow Pages*. Sometimes (though rarely) touts will over-estimate demand and as game time nears will try to off-load their tickets at bargain prices.

### TICKET BROKERS

Ticket brokers offer much the same service as touts, although their activities are more regulated. It's illegal in New York State to sell a ticket for more than its face value plus booking fee, so these firms operate from other states by phone. They can almost guarantee tickets for 'sold out' events, and tend to deal in the better seats. Not surprisingly, this is a service you pay for. Good seats for the

NBA basketball play-offs run close to $1,000 and tickets for most Giants football games *start* at $100. Look under 'Ticket Sales' in the *Yellow Pages* for brokers. Three of the more established are Prestige Entertainment (1-800 2 GET TIX), Ticket Window (1-800 SOLD OUT) and Union Tickets (1-800 CITY TIX).

## Baseball

Baseball is 'America's favourite pastime', and enthusiasm for the game runs to religious proportions, though the long 1995 players' strike weakened support. Local teams are the Yankees and the Mets. The season runs from April to October; tickets for the average game are easy to get hold of.

### The Mets

*Shea Stadium, 126th Street & Roosevelt Avenue, Flushing, Queens (information 1-718 507 8499). Subway 7 to Shea*

# Big screens & beer nuts

The great American sports fan needs two things: a ready supply of beer (essential if you are to find baseball interesting), and a nearby audience for his illuminating match-play insights. These elements are readily available in that favourite American institution: the sports bar.

Hundreds of New York bars provide TV sport as a drinking companion, but some go to extremes to take you to big-screen sports heaven. **Mickey Mantle's**, 42 Central Park South, near Sixth Avenue (688 7777), projects the action onto ten huge screens. The **Sporting Club**, 99 Hudson Street, at Franklin Street (219 0900), has nine giant screens plus digital score-

boards and quiz/betting machines at the bar.

Taking the sports bar theme to its limits and beyond is **Hackers Hitters & Hoops** (*above*), 123 West 18th Street, between Sixth & Seventh Avenues (929 7482), which is a bar with a sporting club attached, boasting one basketball court, two baseball batting cages, a golf simulator, a mini-golf game and two giant screens.

But if you get tired of the televisual glitz of US franchise sports, there's always **McCormack's**, 365 Third Avenue, at 27th Street (683 0911), the best place if you just want to watch British football in the company of some ex-pat hooligans.

---

*Stadium.* **Open** for information 9am-5.30pm Mon-Fri. **Admission** $7-$18. **Credit** AmEx, MC, V. *Disabled: toilets.*

### New York Yankees
*Yankee Stadium, River Avenue & 161st Street, Bronx (information 1-718 293 4300/ticket office 1-718 293 6000). Subway 4, C or D to 161st Street.* **Open** for information 9am-5pm Mon-Fri; 10am-3pm Sat and during games. **Admission** $12-$21. **Credit** AmEx, Disc, MC, V. *Disabled: toilets.*

## Basketball

The season runs from October to July. Local players include the famous professionals of the Knicks and

the Nets, the two NBA teams, as well as the rising stars of the region's college squads. Tickets for most NBA games, however, range from expensive to unobtainable. If you miss out, exciting basketball action can be had for free by watching the hustlers play pick-up games on street courts (*see page 263*).

### New Jersey Nets
*Continental Airlines Arena (Meadowlands Arena), East Rutherford, New Jersey (information 1-201 935 8888/ tickets 1-201 935 3900). Bus from Port Authority Bus Terminal, 42nd Street at Eighth Avenue, $3.25 each way (564 8484 for information).* **Open** for information 9am-6pm Mon-Fri; 10am-2pm Sat. **Admission** $16-$44.50. **Credit** AmEx, MC, V.

### New York Knickerbockers (Knicks)

*Madison Square Garden, Seventh Avenue at 33rd Street (information 465 5867). Subway A, C or E to 34th Street.* **Open** for information 9am-6pm Mon-Fri; 10am-3pm Sat. **Admission** official prices are fairly meaningless. Ticket information is usually restricted to 'this game is sold out'.

## Boxing

### Golden Gloves Boxing Championships

*The Paramount, Madison Square Garden, Seventh Avenue at 33rd Street (information 465 6741). Subway A, C or E to 34th Street.*
The Championships, a long-running New York tradition and amateur boxing's most prestigious competition, take place every January.

## Cricket

Cricket, although considered incomprehensible by most Americans, is played by about a million people in the US. New York, with large populations of Indians, Pakistanis and West Indians, not to mention Brits, has about 20 teams and at least two parks where the sound of leather on willow can be heard during the season, which runs from April to October.

### Van Cortlandt Park

*Van Cortlandt Park, Park South & Bailey Avenue, Bronx Subway 1 or 9 to 242nd Street.*
There are six or seven pitches here. The New York Cricket League (1-201 343 4544) arranges Sunday matches.

### Walker Park

*50 Bard Avenue, at Delafield Court, Staten Island. Ferry to Staten Island, then S61 or S74 bus to Bard Avenue.*
The Staten Island Cricket Club (1-718 447 5442) plays here most weekends during the season.

## Football

American football, a cross between chess and war, provides some spectacular action. The season runs from August to December and is followed by the play-offs for the Superbowl, which takes place on the third Sunday in January. There are two local teams, both of which play at Giants Stadium.

### Giants Stadium

*Meadowlands Sports Complex, East Rutherford, New Jersey (1-201 935 3900). Bus from Port Authority Bus Terminal, 42nd Street at Eighth Avenue, $3.25 each way (564 8484 for information).*

### New York Giants

*(Information 1-201 935 8222).*

### New York Jets

*(Information 1-516 560 8100/single tickets 1-516 538 7200).*
The Giants have a 20-year waiting list for season tickets, so the only way to see a game is to know someone with a season ticket or pay blood money to a broker. The Jets are slightly more accessible. They have a waiting list of 13,000 but sell scattered single seats for $25 on a first-come, first-served, cash-only basis from the New York Jets office, 1000 Fulton Avenue, Hempstead NY, and via Ticketmaster.

## Horse Racing

There are three major race tracks near New York – Belmont, Aqueduct and the Meadowlands. If you fancy a flutter but not the trek to Long Island or Jersey, head for an Off Track Betting Shop ('OTB') and catch the action and atmosphere there instead.

### Aqueduct Racetrack

*110th Street & Rockaway Boulevard, Ozone Park, Queens (1-718 641 4700). Subway A to Aqueduct Racetrack.* **Season** Nov-May. **Admission** clubhouse $3.50; grandstand $2. **No credit cards.**
Thoroughbred flat races are held here five days a week (Wed-Sun) during the season.

### Belmont Park

*Hempstead Turnpike & Plainfield Avenue, Belmont, Long Island (1-718 641 4700). Pony Express from Penn Station to Belmont Park.* **Season** May-Oct. **Admission** clubhouse $4; grandstand $2. **No credit cards.**
Thoroughbred flat racing five days a week (Wed-Sun) in season. The Belmont Stakes, the third leg of the Triple Crown, is usually held on the second Saturday in June.

### Meadowlands Racetrack

*East Rutherford, New Jersey (1-201 935 8500). Bus from Port Authority Bus Terminal, 42nd Street at Eighth Avenue, $3.25 each way (564 8484 for information).* **Season** Jan-Aug trotting; Sept-Dec thoroughbred. **Admission** clubhouse $2, grandstand free. **No credit cards.**
Races five days a week (Tue-Sat) during seasons.

## Ice Hockey

A fast, skillful sport with spectacular violence never far away. Tickets are not too hard to get (with the possible exception of Rangers games, since they are one of the league's strongest teams). Tickets for all fixtures go on sale at the beginning of the season, which runs from October to April.

### New Jersey Devils

*Meadowlands Arena, East Rutherford, New Jersey (Devils information 1-201 935 6050). Bus from Port Authority Bus Terminal, 42nd Street at Eighth Avenue, $3.25 each way (564 8484 for information).* **Open** 9am-6pm and during games. **Admission** $18-$50. **Credit** AmEx, MC, V.

### New York Islanders

*Nassau Memorial Coliseum, Hempstead Turnpike, Uniondale, Long Island (Islanders information 1-516 794 4100). Long Island Railroad (1-718 217 5477) from Penn Station, Seventh Avenue at 32nd Street, to Westbury Station.* **Open** 10.45am-5.45pm daily and during games. **Admission** $19-$60. **Credit** AmEx, MC, V.

### New York Rangers

*Madison Square Garden, Seventh Avenue at 33rd Street (465 6741/Rangers information 465 6486). Subway A, C or E to 34th Street.* **Admission** $18-$65. **Credit** AmEx, Disc, MC, V.

## Soccer

Football, sorry, 'soccer', is very popular in New York, notably among the ethnic teams of the outer boroughs. You can catch matches every weekend, played in full international strip and to a very average standard, in the parks in the Polish, Italian and

Latin American neighbourhoods. A higher standard of play can be seen in the games of the NY/NJ MetroStars, established in the wake of America's hosting of the 1994 World Cup. The team is based at the Meadowlands Arena in New Jersey.

### NY/NJ MetroStars
*Meadowlands Arena, East Rutherford, New Jersey (information 1-201 935 3900). Bus from Port Authority Terminal, 42nd Street at Eighth Avenue, $3.25 each way (564 8484 for information).* **Season** Apr-Aug. **Tickets** $11-$27. **Credit** AmEx, MC, V.

## Tennis

### US Open
*USTA Tennis Center, Flushing, Queens (information and tickets 1-718 760 6200). Subway 7 to Shea Stadium.* **Dates** late Aug to early Sept. **Admission** $25-$50 day tickets. **Credit** AmEx, DC, Disc, MC, V.
Tickets go on sale at the end of May.

### Virginia Slims Championship
*Madison Square Garden, Seventh Avenue at 33rd Street (465 6500). Subway A, C or E to 34th Street.* **Dates** 2nd & 3rd weeks of Nov. **Admission** $15-$45. **Credit** AmEx, MC, V.
The top 16 women's singles players and top 32 doubles compete for megabucks. Tickets go on sale at the end of April.

## Active Sports
## General Information

### Department of Parks & Recreation
*(recorded information 360 3456).*
Information on sports activities in city parks.

### Women's Sports Foundation
*(Information and referral service 1-800 227 3988).* **Open** 9am-5pm Mon-Fri.
Staff here are happy to answer any queries you may have about women's events, facilities and sporting history.

## Bowling

### Bowlmor Lanes
*110 University Place, at 12th Street (255 8188). Subway 4, 5, 6, L, N or R to Union Square.* **Open** 10am-1am Mon-Thur, Sun; 10am-4am Fri, Sat. **Rates** $3.50 per person per game; $2 shoe rental. **Credit** AmEx, MC, V.
A bar, grill, pro shop and a massive 44 lanes.

### Leisure Time Recreation
*625 Eighth Avenue, at the Port Authority Bus Terminal, 42nd Street at Eighth Avenue (268 6909). Subway A, C or E to 42nd Street.* **Open** 10am-11pm Mon-Thur, Sun; 10am-2am Fri, Sat. **Admission** $4 per person per game; $2 shoe rental. **Credit** MC, V.
Let fly a few strikes down one of 30 lanes while you're waiting for your bus. Or sink some shots at the bar.

## Cycling

### AYH Five-Borough Bicycle Club
*AYH Hostel, 891 Amsterdam Avenue, NY 10025, at 103rd Street (932 2300).*
Advice and courses on all aspects of cycling, from risking death in the busy Manhattan streets to scenic mountain biking outside the city limits. The Club also arranges the excellent Annual Five-Borough Bike Tour (in May).

## Cycle Hire
You can rent bikes in and around Central Park (at the Loeb Boathouse), where the 7.2 mile road loop is closed to traffic at the weekends; *see chapter* **Sightseeing**.

### Metro Bicycles
*1311 Lexington Avenue, at 88th Street (427 4450). Subway 4, 5 or 6 to 86th Street.* **Open** 9.30am-6.30pm Mon, Tue, Fri-Sun; 9.30am-7.30pm Wed, Thur. **Rates** $6 per hour, $25 per 8-hour day. **Credit** AmEx, Disc, MC, V.
Leave a driving licence or credit card as security.

## Golf
*See also opposite* **Chelsea Piers**.

### Kissena Park Golf Course
*164-15 Booth Memorial Avenue, at 164th Street, Queens (1-718 939 4594). Subway 7 to Main Street, Flushing, then Q65 bus.* **Open** dawn-dusk daily. **Green fees** $18 Mon-Fri; $20 before 3pm Sat, Sun; $10 after 3pm Sat, Sun. **Club rental** $10 per round. **No credit cards**.
A short 'executive' course with great views of the Manhattan skyline. Pro lessons cost $35 for 30 mins. Book six and get one free. Par 64.

### Richard Metz Golf Studio
*Third Floor, 425 Madison Avenue, at 49th Street (759 6940). Subway E, F or 6 to 51st Street/Lexington Avenue.* **Open** 10am-8pm Mon-Thur; 10am-7pm Fri; 10am-5pm Sat. **Rates** one lesson $60; five lessons $250; ten lessons $350. **Credit** AmEx, DC, Disc, JCB, MC, V.
Practise your swing into a teaching net and then analyse the movement on video. Lessons last half an hour and cater for all levels. There are three nets, putting areas and a golf shop.

### Silver Lake Park
*Victory Boulevard & Clove Road, Staten Island (1-718 447 5686). Ferry to Staten Island, then S67 bus.* **Open** dawn-dusk daily. **Green fees** $16 Mon-Fri; $20 Sat, Sun; $2 booking fee. **Credit** AmEx, MC, V.
The course is difficult, with narrow fairways and hills to negotiate. Console yourself with nature when your golf ball ends in the woods once again – it's a very picturesque setting. Par 69.

### Van Cortlandt Golf Course
*Van Cortlandt Park, Park South & Bailey Avenue, Bronx (1-718 543 4595). Subway 1 or 9 to 242nd Street.* **Open** half an hour before sunrise to half an hour after sunset, daily. **Green fees** $26 Mon-Fri; $28 Sat, Sun. **Club rental** from $20 per round. **Credit** AmEx, MC, V.
The oldest public course in the country, rich in history and easily the most 'New York' of the city's 13 public courses. It's quite short but challenging – narrow with lots of trees and hilly in places. Lessons cost $35 for 30 minutes. Par 70.

## Gyms & Fitness Classes
The following megagyms offer day membership to visitors (some form of photo ID is usually required). Most have more than one branch: phone for more details, as well information about opening times, classes and facilities. *See also page 270* **YMCAs**.

**Asphalt Green** *555 East 90th Street, at York Avenue (369 8890). Subway 4, 5 or 6 to 86th Street.* **Day membership** $15.

**New York Health & Fitness Club** *39 Whitehall Street, at Water Street (269 9800). Subway N or R to Whitehall Street.* **Day membership** $50.

**New York Sports Club** *151 East 86th Street, between Lexington & Third Avenues (860 8630). Subway 4, 5 or 6 to 86th Street.* **Day membership** $25.

**Sports Center at Chelsea Piers** *Pier 60, 23rd Street, at West Side Highway (336 6000). Subway C or E to 23rd Street.* **Day membership** $31.

**World Gym of Greenwich Village** *232 Mercer Street, between Bleecker & West 3rd Streets (780 7407).* **Day membership** $18.

## Horse Riding

### Claremont Riding Academy

*175 West 89th Street, at Amsterdam Avenue (724 5100). Subway 1 or 9 to 86th Street.* **Open** 6.30am-10pm Mon-Fri; 6.30am-5pm Sat, Sun. **Rental** $33 per hour. **Lessons** $38 per 30 min, groups $35 per hour. **No credit cards.**
The academy teaches English-style (as opposed to Western) riding. Beginners use an indoor arena; experienced riders can also trek along the six miles (9.6km) of trails in Central Park.

### Jamaica Bay Riding Academy

*7000 Shore Parkway, Brooklyn (1-718 531 8949). By car via Belt Parkway.* **Open** 9am-5pm Mon, Wed, Sat, Sun; 9am-9pm Tue, Thur. **Guided trail ride** $23. **Lessons** $45 per hour. **No credit cards.**
The trail ride, through the 300-acre Jamaica Bay Wildlife Refuge, lasts 45 minutes. English and Western riding.

## Pool

### Chelsea Billiards

*54 West 21st Street, between Fifth & Sixth Avenues (989 0096). Subway F to 23rd Street.* **Open** 24 hours daily. **Rates** *9am-5pm daily* $4 per hour for first player, $8 for two or more players; *5pm-9am Mon-Thur, Sun* $5 per hour for first player, $10 for two or more players; *5pm-9am Fri, Sat* $6 for first player, $14 for two or more players. **Credit** AmEx, MC, V.
A comfortable and welcoming pool parlour with full-size snooker tables, too. Hot dogs and snacks are available.

## Racquetball

Racquetball is a bit like squash. It's played in a four-sided court, but the ball is softer and the racquet is like a small version of a tennis racquet, with looser strings. A high-energy game.

### Manhattan Plaza Racquet Club

*450 West 43rd Street, between Ninth & Tenth Avenues (594 0554). Subway A, C or E to 42nd Street.* **Open** 6am-midnight daily. **Rates** $19-$28 per court per hour, plus $10 guest fee. **Credit** AmEx, MC, V.
Rates vary according to the time of day. The club also has five hard tennis courts ($28-$38 per court per hour, plus $20 guest fee).

## Rollerblading (In-line Skating)

A familiar sound on New York streets is the quiet skish-skish of insane rollerbladers. It's not unusual to see them on the Avenues, reaching 30mph facing oncoming traffic. A slightly more sane variety can be found whirling around Central Park, either on the road loop (closed to traffic at weekends) or near the bandshell at 72nd Street. The 'coneheads', or slalomers, strut their stuff at Central Park West and 67th Street, across from the Tavern on the Green.

To give it a try yourself, visit Wollman Memorial Rink (*see chapter* **Sightseeing**). If you'd prefer to be indoors, head for the new Chelsea Piers complex (*see below*). If you don't want to be restricted to the rink, you can rent skates from the many rollerblade shops close to the park. Try Blades, 160 East 86th Street (996 1644) and 120 West 72nd Street (787 3911). Stick with the pack and follow the flow of traffic. At weekends there are plenty of people around to rescue you if you wipe out, and even a volunteer force of NYRS skate patrollers (in red T-shirts with white crosses) who run free stopping clinics for beginners. You'll find them on Saturdays and Sundays from 12.30pm to 5.30pm at the 72nd Street entrance near the Rumsey playfield.

### New York Skate Out

*PO Box 1120, NY 10023 (935 1319).*
A non-profitmaking organisation offering group classes ($13), skating tours of the city and more.

## Running

Join the joggers in Central Park, Riverside Park or round Washington Square in the early morning or early evening. It's best, for women especially, to avoid jogging alone. And don't carry anything that's obviously valuable. For the New York City Marathon, *see chapter* **New York by Season**.

# Chelsea Piers

Four of the city's huge abandoned Hudson River piers have been transformed into the most extensive public sports complex in the United States. The 1.7 million square feet of Chelsea Piers boasts an astounding list of facilities: two full-size ice rinks, two open-air roller rinks, indoor soccer pitches, baseball batting cages, basketball and sand volleyball courts, a pool, restaurants, a sun-deck, the state's largest gym, the Northeast's largest rock-climbing wall, the world's longest indoor running track, and a golf driving range so large it seems impossible that it's in Manhattan.

The whole thing is built in the remains of the city's famous maritime passenger terminals – it was here that the *Titanic* was headed when it sank – and also houses film and TV studios, a marina and a sporting goods superstore.

*Piers 59-62, West 17th-23rd Streets, at the Hudson River (336 6666). Bus M23 to Hudson River.*

### New York Road Runners Club

*9 East 89th Street, between Fifth & Madison Avenues
(860 4455). Subway 4, 5 or 6 to 86th Street.* **Open**
10am-8pm Mon-Fri; 10am-5pm Sat; 10am-3pm Sun.
**Membership** from $30. **Credit** AmEx, Disc, MC, V.
Contact the club – the world's largest running – for information on short runs, safety, local runs, children's classes
and marathons.

## Sailing

### New York Harbor Boating

*The Enterprise, North Cove Yacht Harbor, World
Financial Center (recorded information 786 0400).
Subway 1, 9, A or C to Cortland Street/World Trade
Center.* **Open** dawn-dusk daily. **Credit** MC, V.
J24 sailing boats are for rent from $150 for half a day. There
are also larger boats at larger prices, right up to a Beneteau 43.
You need the relevant certification, but a captain can be pro-
vided for an extra fee. The Manhattan Sailing School runs an
ASA-certified sailing school and offers a 'learn to sail' course
for $440, or an introduction to sailing for $40 for three hours.

## Skating

For the Wollman Memorial Rink, *see chapter*
**Sightseeing**.

### Rockefeller Center Ice Rink

*1 Rockefeller Plaza, Fifth Avenue, between 49th & 50th
Streets (recorded information 332 7654). Subway B, D, F
or Q to Rockefeller Center.* **Open** 9am-1pm, 1.30-
5.30pm, 6-10pm, Mon-Thur; 8.30-11am, 11.30am-2pm,
2.30-5pm, 5.30-8pm, 8.30pm-midnight, Fri, Sat; 8.30-11am,
11.30am-2pm, 2.30-5pm, 5.30-10pm, Sun. **Rates** $8 adults,
$7 under-12s, Mon-Thur; $9 adults, $7 under-12s, Fri-Sun.
**Skate hire** $4. **No credit cards**.
The famous outdoor rink, under the giant statue of
Prometheus, is perfect for atmosphere, but a little small. It's
unmissable, however, when the giant Christmas tree is lit.

## Squash

The **West Side YMCA** (*see page 270*) has some
courts and offers a day rate for membership. Court
use is free for members. There are few other places
where you can play squash cheaply.

## Swimming

### Municipal Pools

*(Parks Department hotline 1-800 201 7275).*
An annual membership fee of $25, payable by money order
only (available at post offices) at any of the pools, entitles
you to use all New York's municipal pools, both indoor and
outdoor, free for a year. Outdoor pools are free to all, and
open June-Sept. You need proof of your name, an address in
the New York City area, and a passport-size photograph to
register. Some of the best city-run pools are: Asser Levy Pool,
23rd Street, at FDR Drive (447 2020); Carmine Street
Recreation Center, Clarkson Street & Seventh Avenue South
(242 5228); East 54th Street Pool, 348 East 54th Street, at First
Avenue (397 3154); West 59th Street Pool, 59th Street,
between Tenth & Eleventh Avenues (397 3159).

### Sheraton Manhattan Hotel

*790 Seventh Avenue, at 51st Street (581 3300).
Subway B, D or E to Seventh Avenue.* **Open to non-
residents** 6am-9pm Mon-Fri; 8am-8pm Sat, Sun.
**Admission** $20 for non-residents. **Credit** AmEx, DC,
Disc, MC, V.

# American Zen

In response to New York's omnivorous
appetite for spectator sports, local promoters
serve up events of the most outlandish
variety. Cockfights and dog matches go on
deep in the hinterland, but some of the shows
at mainstream venues, though sanitised for
mass consumption, are just as bizarre.

### NASA for Rednecks:
### Monster Truck Shows

A giddily pointless display of conspicuous consumption, macho posing and techno fetishism, monster
trucks are pure Americana. The vehicles consist of
stock truck bodies installed with gargantuan engines,
reinforced suspensions, 'bigfoot' tyres and paint jobs

in the heavy metal mode. Shows include competitive racing, but the heart of the rallies are the ramp jumps over lines of 'crush cars'. This turbo-charged mechanical version of sumo grew out of stock car racing – America's number one spectator sport – and probably functions as a safety valve for the vestiges of the chivalric code in American male psychology. If a white man can't run amok with a mass of rubber, steel and gasoline, what's the good of it? The Nassau Memorial Coliseum (1-516 794 9300) hosts at least one of these shows yearly.

## Identity Wars: Professional Wrestling

We were shocked, yes, shocked, to hear that the State of New Jersey, just across the Hudson, recently decreed that, for purposes of taxation, professional wrestling is to be considered 'entertainment' rather than 'sport'. The transparently fraudulent cartoon violence of these matches, replete with 'secret' holds and frequent interludes of taunting and posing midbattle, has always been the ultimate in suspension of disbelief.

Pro wrestling evolved on the chitlin circuit of the American South and gained a foothold in the urban North with the advent of commercial television in the 1950s. As the sight of fat, sweaty men in underwear lacked something in showmanship, the heroes and villains of that time

played on various ethnic stereotypes (Bruno Sammartino, the Kalmikoffs, the Wild Samoans) to build fan identification. Names today tend to reflect lifestyle choices (Honky Tonk Man at one pole, Hunter Hearst Helmsley at the other), or simple thuggery (Hit Man, Razor, the Nasty Boys). These guys never step out of character, either. Catch them in a post-match interview and they're still ranting and raving. Madison Square Garden (465 6741) offers these matches on a regular basis.

## Too Much is Not Enough: Extreme Fighting

Despite much politicking and the best efforts of well-connected lobbyists, this combination of boxing, martial arts and free-for-all brawling found itself still restricted to pay-per-view television. New York became the first state to sanction the 'sport' in early 1997 and a match was scheduled for the New York City area. The Giuliani administration, however, feared a stain on the city's budding reputation for renewed gentility, and the ensuing public outcry forced the promoters to move the match first to upstate New York and, ultimately, to a small city in Alabama. What better endorsement could a display of brutality get than 'Banned In New York City?' Look for it on the tube.

*For a dose of East Village spiritualism, try the **Jivamukti Yoga Center**.*

Pricier than the municipal pools, but much less crowded. The place to come if you want to swim in peace.

## Tennis

To play on municipal courts, including those in Central, East River and Riverside Parks, you'll need a permit from the Department of Parks (360 8133). They cost $50 ($20 senior citizens, $10 under-18s) and are valid for the season (April to November). *See also page 267* **Manhattan Plaza Racquet Club.**

### HRC Tennis
*East River, at Wall & South Streets (422 9300). Subway 2 or 3 to Wall Street.* **Open** 6am-midnight daily. **Court fees** $50-$120 per hour. **Credit** AmEx, MC, V.
This is part of the New York Health & Racquet Club. There are eight green clay courts, under bubbles on twin piers by the river. Five tennis pros are on hand to give lessons ($28 per hour plus court fees).

### Midtown Tennis Club
*341 Eighth Avenue, at West 27th Street (989 8572). Subway 1 or 9 to 28th Street.* **Open** 7am-midnight Mon-Thur; 7am-8pm Fri; 8am-8pm Sat; 8am-10pm Sun. **Court fees** $35-$70 per hour. **Credit** AmEx, MC, V.
Eight indoor hard courts, four uncovered in the summer.

## YMCAs

There are Ys throughout the five boroughs, all with a wide range of facilities. Three of the Manhattan sites offer day rates for visitors. Membership of a Y in another country may get you discounts; and if you're already paying for accommodation, the sports facilities are free.

### Harlem YMCA
*180 West 135th Street, at Seventh Avenue (281 4100). Subway B or C to 135th Street.* **Open** 6am-10pm Mon-Fri; 6am-6pm Sat.* **Membership** $10 per day; $60 per month; $475 per year. **Credit** MC, V.

Boasts a four-lane swimming pool, basketball court, full gym and a sauna.

### Vanderbilt YMCA
*224 East 47th Street, between Second & Third Avenues (756 9600). Subway 6 to 51st Street.* **Open** 5am-10pm Mon-Fri; 7am-7pm Sat, Sun.* **Membership** $15 per day; $65 per month; $785 per year. **Credit** MC, V.
Two swimming pools, a running track, a steam sauna and a gym with basketball, handball and volleyball – plus yoga and aerobic classes.

### West Side Branch YMCA
*5 West 63rd Street, between Broadway & Central Park West (787 4400). Subway 1, 9, A, B, C or D to Columbus Circle.* **Open** 6.30am-10pm Mon-Fri; 8am-8pm Sat; 9am-7pm Sun.* **Membership** $15 per day; $50 per week; $100 per month. **Credit** MC, V.
Two pools and three gyms with all the equipment you could imagine, plus an indoor track, squash courts and facilities for basketball, volleyball, handball, racquetball, boxing, aerobics and yoga. There is also a full range of classes. Day rate includes access to everything.

## Yoga

### Integral Yoga Institute
*227 West 13th Street, between Seventh & Eighth Avenues (929 0586). Subway A, C, E or L to 14th Street/Eighth Avenue.* **Open** 10am-8.30pm Mon-Fri; 9am-5.30pm Sat. **Rates** $8 per class. **Credit** (not for individual classes) AmEx, MC, V.
A range of classes is offered – phone for a timetable. You don't need to book.

### Jivamukti Yoga Center
*Second Floor, 149 Second Avenue, between 9th & 10th Streets (353 0214). Subway 6 to Astor Place.* **Open** 7am-9.15pm Mon-Fri; 10am-5.45pm Sat; 7.30am-5.45pm Sun. **Classes** no credit cards.
This is Yoga Express: high-impact East Village spiritualism involving much chanting, Hatha yoga and meditation. You can take open, basics, basics II or Astanga classes, all lasting one hour 45 minutes.

# In Focus

# Gay & Lesbian New York

**Come out and take pride in the vibrant world of queer New York.**

While local gay activists still have their battles with New York's current Republican Mayor, Rudolph Giuliani, the fact that he recently appeared at a social function in Marilyn Monroe-esque drag, is some indication that in New York no one is too conservative to demonstrate a little bit of queer sensibility.

From the offices of City Hall to the floor of the Wall Street Stock Exchange, from the media and advertising conglomerates on Madison Avenue to the big business of design and fashion on Seventh Avenue, and from the bright lights of Broadway to the quiet white rooms of museums and art galleries – it is impossible to ignore the fact that openly gay men and women are a powerful part of what makes New York one of America's financial and cultural centres of the world. As the site of the 1969 Stonewall riots and the birthplace of the American gay rights movement, New York City is a queer Mecca and is also home to more than 500 lesbian, gay, bisexual and transgender social and political organisations.

During **Gay & Lesbian Pride**, which takes place annually over the last weekend in June, the Empire State Building is lit up in lavender (*see chapter* **New York by Season**). This amazing celebration draws hundreds of thousands of visitors and tourist dollars into the city. The Pride march, which takes place on the Sunday of Pride weekend, draws between 250,000 and 500,000 spectators, and a number of Manhattan businesses now fly the lesbian and gay-friendly rainbow flag in celebration. Pride is a great time to visit the Big Apple – you'll feel as though everyone here is queer. Another good reason to arrive during the summer months is so you can sample lesbian and gay resort culture on **Fire Island**, which is only a short trip from the centre of town (*see page 274*).

An essential stop for any lesbian or gay visitor to New York is the **Lesbian & Gay Community Center** (*see page 274*), a nexus of information and activity which serves as a meeting place for over 300 groups and organisations. You can pick up copies of New York's free weekly gay and lesbian publications at the centre. And don't miss *Time Out New York*'s Gay & Lesbian listings for the latest happenings around town.

Though the sizeable gay and lesbian population of New York is quite diverse, the lesbian and gay club and bar scenes don't really reflect this, since they are almost entirely gender-segregated, and like their straight counterparts, tend to attract the single, 35-and-under crowd. However, the social alternatives are plentiful, among them the burgeoning queer coffee-bar, bookstore and restaurant scene and the dozens of gay and lesbian films and plays that are shown in mainstream venues (*see chapters* **Theatre**, **Film** *and* **Cabaret**).

There's no doubt about it: New York is a 24-hour non-stop city with a multitude of choices for queer entertainment. Enjoy!

## Information

### Publications

New York's true gay weeklies are *HX* (Homo Xtra), which includes expansive listings for bars, dance clubs, sex clubs, restaurants, cultural events and group meetings, and loads of funny personals, and *HX For Her*, New York's only dedicated lesbian weekly. The *LGNY* (Lesbian & Gay New York) newspaper offers political coverage and serious articles. All three are free at gay and lesbian venues and shops.

National publications include *Out* ($3.95) and *The Advocate* ($3.95), both of which are published monthly. Lesbian magazines include *Girlfriends* ($4.95) and *Curve* ($3.95), a couple of colourful and fun monthly magazines for gay women, with profiles and features about women in the know and in the new; and the rather tacky *Bad Attitude* ($3.95) and the far better, sex quarterly *On Our Backs* ($5.95). Gloria Steinem's stalwart bi-monthly *Ms* ($5.95) is still read for its mainstream feminist features.

*The New York Gayellow Pages* ($4.95), essential for planning a longer stay, provides a wide range of general information covering the greater New York area. It's available at **A Different Light** and the **Oscar Wilde Memorial Bookshop** (*see page 273*).

*He had nothing to declare but his genius: the* **Oscar Wilde Memorial Bookshop**.

## Television

There's an abundance of gay-related broadcasting, though nearly all of it is poorly produced on the public access cable channels. There are confusing regional variations and you may not be able to watch it all on a hotel TV. Some of the funniest programmes are to be found on Channel 35 (in most of Manhattan), which is where the infamous Robin Byrd hosts her *Men For Men* softcore show. Lesbians shouldn't miss *Dyke TV*, at 8pm on Tuesday on Channel 34 (Manhattan only), an entertaining hour of girl goings-on around the country. Manhattan Neighborhood Network (channels 16, 17, 34 and 69 on all Manhattan cable systems) has plenty of gay shows, ranging from drag queens enjoying their 15 minutes of fame, to serious discussion programmes. You might also want to check-out RuPaul's on-going chat show on VH1. *HX* provides the most current TV listings.

## Bookshops

Most New York bookshops have gay sections (*see* chapter **Shopping & Services**), but the following are exclusively lesbian and gay.

### A Different Light Bookstore & Café

*151 West 19th Street, between Sixth & Seventh Avenues (989 4850). Subway 1 or 9 to 18th Street.* **Open** 10am-midnight daily. **Credit** AmEx, Disc, MC, V.
The biggest and best gay and lesbian bookshop in New York. It's great for browsing, and has plenty of free readings, film screenings and art openings. There are also useful bulletin boards with local information, and a cute café.

### Oscar Wilde Memorial Bookshop

*15 Christopher Street, between Sixth & Seventh Avenues (255 8097). Subway 1 or 9 to Christopher Street/ Sheridan Square.* **Open** noon-8pm Mon-Fri, Sun; noon-9pm Sat. **Credit** AmEx, Disc, MC, V.
New York's oldest gay and lesbian bookshop, stocked to the brim, and offering many discounts.

## Centres & Phone Lines

For women's health care, *see page 282*.

### Audre Lorde Project Center

*85 South Oxford Street, at Lafayette Avenue, Brooklyn (1-718 596 0342). Subway C to Lafayette Avenue.*
Properly called the Audre Lorde Project Center for Lesbian, Gay, Bisexual Two-Spirit & Transgender People of Color Communities, this is a new community centre providing resources for queer people of colour. Phone for information about events and group meetings.

### Barnard Center for Research on Women

*101 Barnard Hall, 3009 Broadway, at 117th Street (854 2067). Subway 1 or 9 to 116th Street.* **Open** 9.30am-5pm Tue-Fri; 9.30am-9pm Mon.
An academic centre with a distinctly off-putting name, this is where to explore scholarly feminism, through a calendar of classes, lectures and film screenings. The library has an extensive archive of feminist journals and government reports.

### Gay Men's Health Crisis

*129 West 24th Street, between Sixth & Seventh Avenues (807 6664/AIDS advice hotline 807 6655). Subway 1 or 9 to 23rd Street.* **Open** *advice hotline* 10am-9pm Mon-Fri; noon-3pm Sat; recorded information at other times; *office* 10am-6pm Mon-Fri.
This was the first organisation in the world to take up the challenge of helping people with AIDS. It has a three-fold

mission: to push the Government to increase services; to help those who are sick by providing services and counselling for them and their families; and to educate the public and prevent the further spread of HIV. There are 204 staff and 2,200 volunteers. The support groups meet mainly in the evenings.

### Gay & Lesbian Switchboard
*(777 1800).* **Open** 10am-midnight daily.
A phone information service only. Callers who need legal help can be referred to lawyers, and there's information on bars, restaurants and hotels. The switchboard is especially good at giving advice to people who have just come out, and to those who may be feeling suicidal. There are also apartment and job listings and details of all sorts of other gay and lesbian organisations.

### Lesbian & Gay
### Community Services Center
*208 West 13th Street, between Seventh & Eighth Avenues (620 7310). Subway 1, 2, 3, F or L to 14th Street/Seventh Avenue.* **Open** 9am-11pm daily.
Founded in 1983, the Center provides political, cultural, spiritual and emotional sustenance to the lesbian and gay community. While it principally offers programmes and support for the city's residents, there's plenty to interest the visitor. You'll be amazed at the diversity of groups (more than 300) that meet here. It also houses the National Museum and Archive of Lesbian and Gay History and the Vito Russo lending library.

### Lesbian Herstory Archive
*PO Box 1258, New York, NY 10116 (1-718 768 3953/fax 1-718 768 4663).* **Open** by appointment only.
Newly housed in the Park Slope area of Brooklyn (becoming known as 'Dyke Slope' for its large and growing lesbian population), the Herstory Archives were started by Joan Nestle and Deb Edel in 1974, and have reached massive proportions, now including over 10,000 books (theory, fiction, poetry, plays), 1,400 periodicals and innumerable personal memorabilia. You too can donate a treasured possession (T-shirt, photo album, badge collection) and become part of Herstory.

### National Organisation for Women
*105 East 22nd Street, at Park Avenue South (260 4422). Subway 6 to 23rd Street.* **Open** 10am-5pm Mon-Fri.
NOW is a political campaigning organisation, not a drop-in centre, but you can call in at the Manhattan branch to pick up the bi-monthly newsletter 'NOW-NYC News' or the Chapter Calendar. NOW divides its energies between various support groups for women (especially groups for divorced or separated women) and campaigning for better treatment for women in society.

### NYC Gay & Lesbian
### Anti-Violence Project
*647 Hudson Street, at Gansevoort Street (807 0197). Subway 1, 2 or 3 to 14th Street.* **Open** 10am-8pm Mon-Fri; switchboard open 24 hours daily.
Advice and support for the victims of anti-gay and anti-lesbian attacks. The project also provides advice on going to the police and works with the NYPD Bias Unit. Short- and long-term counselling are available.

## Fire Island

Over the years, Fire Island, a long thin strip of land off the southern coast of Long Island, has become the favourite summer habitat for New York's gay men and a growing number of lesbians. Two particular island locales have become synonymous with sun- and sea-worshipping fags and dykes,

flamboyant parties and general seasonal extravagance: **The Pines** (snotty, affluent and mostly gay) and **Cherry Grove** (tacky, suburban and mostly lesbian). The majority of the accommodation in both the Pines and the Grove is in private houses, which are rented out in timeshares. Make friends with the right person and you could land yourself an invite. Otherwise you might have to settle for a day trip, as there is very little hostel/hotel accommodation, and what there is, is expensive and far from luxurious. For details see *HX* or *HX for Her*.

### GETTING THERE
By car or LIRR train from Penn Station to Sayville, then by passenger ferry. The station is about two miles from the ferry terminal and cabs are always around. There are between eight and 20 sailings a day, depending on the day and season. The ferry costs $10 for the round trip.

### Long Island Railroad (LIRR)
*(1-718 217 5477 for schedules).*

### Sayville Ferry Company
*(1-516 589 0810 for schedules).*

---

# Boy's life

When *New York* magazine ran a cover story lamenting the new homogeneity of gay male culture, the focus of its critique was booming 'Fag Chic' in Chelsea. While the West Village has quaint historical gay sites (such as **The Stonewall** *see page 277*), friendly show-tune piano cabarets, and unpretentious stores full of rainbow knick-knacks and slogan T-shirts, the centre of gay life has shifted slightly uptown to **Chelsea**, and now sports a new attitude that can be daunting.

Chelsea's main drag is **Eighth Avenue**, between 16th and 23rd Streets, which is lined with businesses catering to upwardly-mobile gay men – gyms, sexy clothing and exotic home furnishing stores, tanning and grooming salons, galleries, cafés, bars and mid-range restaurants for brunch, business lunches, and late dinners. Perfectly toned, youngish (25-40), mostly Caucasian, men who might describe themselves as 'straight-acting and appearing' are standard in Chelsea. If you're not one of them, be prepared to be snubbed or possibly ignored. Women too, probably won't feel very welcome in Chelsea's luxurious surroundings – unless they look like supermodels.

Most of Manhattan's **dance clubs** are a hop, skip and jump uptown from Chelsea, and feature a big gay house/techno night during the weekend, when you can spin and twirl with upwards of 500 half-naked men until the wee small hours of the following day.

Somewhat in reaction to Chelsea, a counterculture scene of rock-punk-glitter-fashion boys and theatrical drag queens thrives in the **East Village**, centred on a handful of small dive bars. The scene has an arty, bohemian vibe, and there are many equally lovely men to be found here, ranging from 1970s macho butches to Bowie-type androgynes. The scene tends to be even younger than the Chelsea version (although some men may appear to be younger than they are), but the crowd is more mixed, both racially and sexually. The bars also tend to feature terribly amusing live performances, which draw crowds in by midnight and spit them out by 4am.

Some habitués of Chelsea and the East Village do mix. Men of all ages, shapes and sizes frequent the leather/fetish bars and clubs, such as **The Spike** in Chelsea and **The Lure**, in the West Village, an area known as the Meet Market (*see page 277 for both*). If you're a devotee of the leather scene, you might want to plan your trip around either the **New York Mr Leather Contest**, which takes place in the autumn, or the Black Party at **Saint at Large** – a special all-night leather and S/M-themed circuit party which attracts over 7,000 people and is held annually in late March (*see page 279*).

For open-air and open-market cruising, try the legendary old trucker piers located at the end of Christopher Street along the Hudson River or the Ramble in Central Park, located below the 79th Street Transverse and the lake. And although the city has made every effort to clean up Times Square and turn it into an extension of Disney World, you can still find gay burlesque at the

**Gaiety**, located right off Broadway on 46th Street (221 8868), and the **Eros Theater** on Eighth Avenue and 45th Street (221 2450).

But if you're just an average T-shirt and jeans-type gay man, don't worry. Not only will you be fine in almost any gay space, you'll be surprised at how much cruising happens on the streets while you're walking around town, and how easy it is to turn a glance into a conversation.

## Aaah Bed & Breakfast

*PO Box 2093, New York, NY 10108 (246 4000/fax 765 4229).* **Rates** $60-$150 in private homes; from $60 singles, $85 doubles in hotel. **Credit** (for confirmation fee only) AmEx, MC, V.

A reservation service which places guests in private homes and allows you to request a particular neighbourhood and specify gay or lesbian accommodation. It also has a bed and breakfast hotel on West 58th Street.

## Chelsea Mews Guest House

*344 West 15th Street, NY 10011, between Eighth & Ninth Avenues (255 9174). Subway A, C or E to 14th Street/Eighth Avenue.* **Rates** single $75; double $85-$150. **No credit cards**.

Built in 1840, this guest house has accommodation primarily for gay men, but gay women are also welcome. The rooms are comfortable and well furnished. No smoking is allowed.

## Chelsea Pines Inn

*317 West 14th Street, NY 10014 (929 1023/fax 645 9497). Subway A, C, E or L to 14th Street/Eighth Avenue.* **Rates** doubles and triples $75-$99. **Credit** AmEx, DC, Disc, MC, V.

A central location near the West Village and Chelsea for gay male guests, but lesbians are also welcome. The rooms are clean and comfortable; some have private bathrooms and all have radio, television and air conditioning.

**Stonewall**: *a historic monument with a good pool table. See page 277.*

## Colonial House Inn

*318 West 22nd Street, NY 10011, between Eighth &
Ninth Avenues (243 9669/1-800 689 3779). Subway C
or E to 23rd Street.* **Rates** $65-$99. **No credit cards**.
A beautiful townhouse inn on a quiet street in the heart of
Chelsea. It's run by gay men for a primarily gay clientele,
though lesbians are also welcome. The Colonial House is
a great place to stay in, even if some of the cheaper rooms
are small. There's a lovely living room for coffee and
lounging.

## Incentra Village House

*32 Eighth Avenue, NY 10014, between 12th & Jane Streets
(206 0007). Subway A, C, E or L to Eighth Avenue/14th
Street.* **Rates** $99-$169. **Credit** AmEx, MC, V.
Two cute 1841 historic townhouses perfectly situated in the
West Village, make up this guest house run by gay men primarily for gay men, although lesbians are also welcome. The
rooms are spacious with private bathrooms and kitchenettes.
While interestingly decorated, they aren't always maintained
at the height of cleanliness.

## Bars

Most bars in New York offer themed nights, drinks
specials and happy hours, and the gay ones are no
exception. Don't be shy, remember to tip the bartender and carry plenty of business cards. *See also
chapters* **Cafés & Bars** *and* **Cabaret**.

## Chelsea

### Barracuda

*275 West 22nd Street at Eighth Avenue (645 8613).
Subway C or E to 23rd Street.* **Open** 4pm-4am daily.
**No credit cards**.
A little bit of the East Village has moved into Chelsea with
this cosy, comfy but cruisy neighbourhood hang-out. It
comes complete with 1950s kitsch décor, sofas, pool table
and pinball machine. Theme nights include blacktress drag
diva Mona Foot's Star Search on Thursdays.

### Champs

*17 West 19th Street, between Fifth & Sixth Avenues (633
1717). Subway N or R to 23rd Street.* **Open** 5pm-4am
daily. **No credit cards**.
Spacious, busy and crowded, this gay sports bar combines
the big games on big screens with big guys dancing on the
big bar. Mock-jock heaven.

### g

*223 West 19th Street, between Seventh & Eighth Avenues
(929 1085). Subway 1, 2, 3, 9 to 18th Street/ Seventh
Avenue.* **Open** 4pm-4am daily. **No credit cards**.
This new, classy lounge is the latest Chelsea sensation,
attracting an 'A-List' crowd of hunky men. The space is often
filled to capacity, while outside there's an intimidating queue
of slightly pathetic souls waiting to get in.

### The Spike

*120 Eleventh Avenue, at West 20th Street (243 9688).
Subway C or E to 23rd Street.* **Open** 9pm-4am daily.
**No credit cards**.
The Spike lives up to most visitors' preconceptions of a 1970s
New York gay bar. It's a former hardcore leather venue (a
few old clones still hang around) that has been taken over

*Close encounters at Chelsea's latest
sensation:* **g**.

by a new and more varied generation of cruisers and pre-
clubbers. Weekend evenings retain an easy-going and fairly
traditional leather flavour.

## East Village

### The Bar

*68 Second Avenue, at East 4th Street (674 9714).
Subway F to Second Avenue.* **Open** 3pm-4am daily.
**No credit cards**.
After a decade in business, this is one of the more established gay bars – refreshingly beery and brimming with
pick-up potential. At night, it gets crowded with young
locals. The Bar used to be known as an ACT-UP (Aids
Coalition to Unleash Power) hang-out, and activist types
still abound.

### Beige

*Tuesdays at the Bowery Bar, 40 East 40th Street, at the
Bowery (475 2220). Subway 6 to Bleecker Street.*
**Open** 11.30am-4am Fri; 10am-4am Sat, Sun.
**Credit** AmEx, DC, MC, V.
A respected gay promoter and his lesbian associate take
over this glam restaurant and model hang-out on
Tuesdays. They fill it with a mixed, discriminating after-
dinner crowd of sophisticated, slightly older downtown
types primed for heady nights of lounge music, spectacle
and conversation.

### Wonder Bar

*505 East 6th Street, at Avenue B (777 9105). Subway F
to Second Avenue.* **Open** 6pm-4am daily. **No credit
cards**.
No longer a campy, white-trash dive, Wonder Bar has been
turned into a sexy lounge by its new owners, and now features quality soul and trip-hop DJs. It is also the only fully
mixed lesbian and gay bar in the city, drawing attractive
men and women who come to kick-back and relax.

## West Village

### hell

*59 Gansevoort Street, between Ninth Avenue and
Washington Street (727 1666). Subway A,C or E to 14th
Street.* **Open** 7pm-4am daily. **Credit** AmEx, MC, V.
Branching out of Chelsea into the new nightlife hot-spot –
the Meat Market – the owners of the Big Cup present this
naughty red and black lounge. This West Village venue
attracts an adventurous crowd tired of the old and hungry
for something new.

### The Lure

*409 West 13th Street, at Ninth Avenue (741 3919). Subway
A, C or E to 14th Street/Eighth Avenue.* **Open** 8pm-4am
Mon-Sat; 5pm-4am Sun. **No credit cards**.
A lively fetish bar that attracts a broad and energetic
bunch. On Wednesdays it hosts **Pork**, a fun and sexy occasion when the raucous music and the hot bodies encourages the crowd to act like pigs. A strict dress code (leather,
rubber, uniforms and no cologne) ensures no casual
hangers-on.

### Stonewall

*53 Christopher Street, at Seventh Avenue (463 0950).
Subway 1 or 9 to Christopher Street/Sheridan Square.*
**Open** 2.30pm-4am daily. **No credit cards**.
A landmark bar, where the 1969 gay rebellion against police
harassment took place. Back then, the Stonewall was actually in the building next door. Ask the bartender to talk you
through the story. There's a good pool table and friendly customers, but these days Stonewall is more a historical monument than an exciting bar.

### Uncle Charlie's

*56 Greenwich Avenue, between Sixth & Seventh Avenues (255 8787). Subway 1 or 9 to Christopher Street/ Sheridan Square.* **Open** 3pm-3am Mon-Thur, Sun; 3pm-4am Fri, Sat. **No credit cards.**

The Big Mac of gay bars, Uncle Charlie's attracts a diverse group of men from all over New York. It's one of the best places to go after work and is usually busy during the week. A good place to start your night crawl.

## Uptown

### The Works

*428 Columbus Avenue, between West 80th & West 81st Streets (799 7365). Subway B or C to 81st Street.* **Open** 2pm-4am daily. **No credit cards.**

The major hang-out for young gay men on the Upper West Side attracts a decidedly yuppity, thirtysomething crowd. On Sunday afternoons there's a popular beer blast: between 6pm and 1am you pay $5 to drink all the beer you can manage. All contributions go to the Gay Men's Health Crisis.

## Clubs

Almost all New York clubs have gay nights; many of those we list are one-nighters rather than permanent venues. There's also a large number of fund-raising parties and other one-off events worth looking out for. For more clubs, the majority of which are gay-friendly, plus more information about some of those below, *see chapter* **Clubs.**

## Dance Clubs

### Columbia Dance

*Earl Hall, Columbia University, Broadway, at 116th Street (854 1488). Subway 1 or 9 to 116th Street.* **Open** 10pm-2am first Fri and third Sat of the month.

On the first Friday and third Saturday of every month in the autumn and winter, the prestigious Ivy League university hosts the Columbia Dance. Hang out with the thousands of graduate and undergraduate students who enjoy this ever-popular venue and maybe even help one of them with his homework.

### Escuelita

*301 West 39th Street, at 8th Avenue (631 0588). Subway A, C or E to 42nd Street.* **Open** from 10pm Thur-Sun.

Extravagant, not-to-be missed drag follies are staged nightly here and feature a bevy of Latin talents. There's also sweaty dancing to salsa, merengue and house. Customers are friendly and almost all Latin.

### Mother

*432 West 14th Street, at Washington Street (677 6060). Subway A, C or E or L to 14th Street/Eighth Avenue.* **Open** from 10.30pm Tue-Sun.

One of the only vestiges of true twisted New York nightlife left. Queer, but not necessarily gay revellers gather here every week for clever fetish, dress-up and performance oriented theme nights such as the annual **Night of A Hundred Stevies** (a tribute to Stevie Nicks) or Saturday night's **Click & Drag** (cyber fetish). The dyke-oriented performance cabaret **Bra Bar** also happens here one Saturday a month.

*Count those reps at the* **Chelsea Gym** *and remember: no pain, no gain. See page 279.*

### Saint at Large

*Information (674 8541).*
The legendary Saint, with its huge aluminium domed interior, was one of the first venues where New York's gay men enjoyed dance-floor freedom. It was also where they felt the initial impact of AIDS. The club closed, but the decadent clientele keeps its memory alive with a series of four huge circuit parties each year. These attract legions of gay men from around the US: the Black Party, White Party (referring not to skin colour, but to the mood of the event), Hallowe'en and New Year's Eve.

### Sugar Babies

*Mondays at Plush, 431 West 14th Street, between Ninth Avenue & Washington Street (367 7035). Subway A, C or E to West 14th Street.* **Open** from 10pm Mon.
Live drumming on the dance-floor by Fred 'the Animal' spices, alternates with DJs Tedd Patterson and Ken Carpenter's deep house sounds, as a young mixed bunch of art student types gyrates. Although relocated from the East Village, this long-running night remains a weekly favourite.

### Saturdays at Twilo

*530 West 27th Street, between Tenth & Eleventh Avenues (268 1600). Subway C or E to 23rd Street/ Eighth Avenue.* **Open** from 10pm Sat.
Crowds of gay men who flocked to the Roxy on Saturday night for almost a decade, now head here for ecstatic nights of frenzied dancing. Cavernous and always bursting at the seams, this is a sure bet every week.

### SqueezeBox

*Fridays at Don Hill's, 511 Greenwich Street, at Spring Street (334 1390). Subway 1 or 9 to Houston Street.* **Open** from 10pm Fri.
Gay but sick and tired of disco? Join the all-ages, pansexual, celebrity-studded crowd of twisted sisters and queer headbangers at this unique punk-glitter-glam-rock club. Live bands each week plus an impromptu mosh pit.

## Sex Clubs

Even with Mayor Giuliani's crackdown, New York still has several active sex clubs. For more details, consult HX magazine's 'Getting Off' section.

## Restaurants

Few New York restaurants would bat an eye at same-sex couples enjoying an intimate dinner. The neighbourhoods mentioned above have hundreds of great eating places that are *de facto* gay restaurants, and many that are gay-owned and operated. Below are a few of the most obviously gay places in town. *See also chapter* **Restaurants**.

### Candy Bar & Grill

*131 Eighth Avenue, between 16th & 17th Streets (229 9702). Subway A, C or E to 14th Street.* **Brunch** from noon Sat, Sun. **Dinner** 6pm-midnight daily. **Average** $16. **Credit** Disc, DC, MC, V.
Unique cocktails like the Tina Louise and the Vampire's Kiss are the speciality of this trendy, mixed, see-and-be-seen restaurant and late-night hang-out. The adequate cuisine is a mix of American and pan-Asian. Drinks are served until 1am. The Candy is owned by a lesbian and gay partnership.

### Eighteenth & Eighth

*159 Eighth Avenue, at 18th Street (242 5000). Subway 1 or 9 to 18th Street.* **Meals** 9am-midnight Mon-Thur, Sun; 9am-12.30am Fri, Sat. **Average** $10. **Credit** MC, V.

Health conscious, own-made food make this small restaurant one of the great success stories of Chelsea. It's always full of cute, cruisy boys, so be prepared to wait.

### Food Bar

*149 Eighth Avenue, between 17th & 18th Streets (243 2020). Subway A, C or E to 14th Street.* **Lunch** noon-4pm, **dinner** 5pm-midnight, daily. **Average** $12. **Credit** MC, V.
Jam-packed with big, beefy guys (and that's only the waiters), the Food Bar provides the ultimate experience in cruising while dining. The food is not the main selling point of this Chelsea hot-spot.

### Lips

*2 Bank Street, at Greenwich Avenue (675 7710). Subway 1, 2, 3 or 9 to 14th Street.* **Brunch** noon-6pm Sat, Sun. **Dinner** 6pm-midnight Mon-Thur, Sun; 6pm-2am Fri, Sat. **Average** $16. **Credit** AmEx, DC, MC, V.
The most original of Manhattan's theme restaurants, Lips pays homage to New York drag queens with memorabilia and (delicious) entrées named after the local favourites. With drag waitresses, loud showtime music and Auntie Mame playing on video monitors in the background, the effect may be a bit too gay for some tastes.

### Townhouse Restaurant

*206 East 58th Street, at Third Avenue (826 6241). Subway 1 or 9 to Christopher Street.* **Brunch** noon-4pm Sun. **Lunch** noon-3.30pm Mon-Sat. **Dinner** 5-11pm Mon-Thur; 5pm-midnight Fri, Sat; 6-11pm Sun. **Credit** AmEx, DC, MC, V.
A very elegant uptown haunt for true gentlemen and their gentlemen friends. Very gay, but somehow full of old-world discretion at the same time. The food is continental, decent and affordable.

### Universal Grill

*44 Bedford Street, at Seventh Avenue South (989 5621). Subway 1 or 9 to Christopher Street.* **Brunch** 11am-3.30pm Sat, Sun. **Lunch** 11.30am-3.30pm Mon-Fri. **Dinner** 6pm-midnight daily. **Average** $20-$25. **Credit** AmEx.
Great music and delicious food – from Californian healthy grills to filet mignon. Tell the staff it's your birthday and you'll be in for a big, fun surprise.

## Gyms

*See chapter* **Sport & Fitness** for more fitness facilities, including YMCAs.

### American Fitness Center

*128 Eighth Avenue, at 16th Street (627 0065). Subway A, C, E or L to 14th Street/Eighth Avenue.* **Open** 6am-midnight Mon-Fri; 8am-9pm Sat, Sun. **Membership** $749 per year; $155 per month; $15 per day. **Credit** AmEx, DC, MC, V.
This fully equipped über-gym is barbell-bunny heaven. It's vast and spotless, with 15,000sq ft/1,400 sq m of free-weight space, acres of cardiovascular machines and endless aerobics classes.

### Chelsea Gym

*267 West 17th Street, at Eighth Avenue (255 1150). Subway A, C, E or L to 14th Street.* **Open** 6am-midnight daily. **Membership** $399-$499 per year; $80 per month; $35 per week; $12 per day. **Credit** MC, V.
There are hundreds of gyms in New York, but this men-only gym is by far the gayest. The modestly-sized gym has three Nautilus machines, loads of free weights and very active sauna, steam room and showers.

# Dyke life

The most exciting aspect of lesbian life in Manhattan is that the women you'll see out and about in bars, clubs, restaurants, bookshops, community meetings and at lesbian cabarets will truly defy all stereotypes. While lesbian culture is not as visible or as geographically concentrated as gay men's social venues, it is also far less segregated, either by age or race, and is far more friendly and welcoming.

If you're into community activism, you'll find plenty to spark your interest (although the glory days of outrageous civil disobedience from WHAM – Women's Health Action Mobilisation – and the Lesbian Avengers are no more). Just check in at the **Lesbian & Gay Community Services Center** (*see page 274*). The centre also offers a wide range of support groups and 12-step meetings for people in recovery. But if one of your main complaints has always been that you're not into the activist or recovery scene, and you're a dyke who just wants to have some unbridled fun, New York City has plenty to offer.

The East Village is experiencing a bit of a dyke renaissance, focused on a new full-time lesbian bar called **Meow Mix**. Its success has encouraged some one-off performance nights, such **Wow Wednesdays** (*see page 282*), the **Bra Bar** and weekly venues such as drag king cabaret at **Club Casanova**. The idea that lesbians want more for their money has also given old standard bars in the West Village a reason to try a little harder. Meanwhile, lesbian discos are getting progressively larger and are no longer held only in funky, out of the way dives. One long-running weekly night had been attracting upwards of 800 women a night. Unfortunately, the rising popularity of these clubs doesn't guarantee they'll be around for long, so check the dedicated lesbian bar guide *HX for Her* or *Time Out New York* for the most current information. As a rule, your male friends, even if they are gay, will not be welcome in most women's bars and clubs unless the venue or the night is specifically stated as being mixed.

Outside Manhattan, Park Slope in Brooklyn (also known as Dyke Slope) remains a sort of lesbian residential hub, but beyond visiting the **Lesbian Herstory Archives** or **The Audre**

Lorde Project (*see page 273*), or just hanging-out in the park, there isn't much to see.

If you're staying with friends in Brooklyn and plan to travel into Manhattan to take advantage of dyke nightlife, take a taxi back to Brooklyn instead of riding the subways late at night. Though stories of how dangerous New York is at night are greatly exaggerated, it isn't a good idea to travel alone in any city after hours (*see page 282* **Safety**).

## Accommodation

*See also page 277* **Colonial House Inn** *and* **Incentra Village House**.

### Allerton Hotel for Women

*130 East 57th Street, at Lexington Avenue (753 8841). Subway 4, 5 or 6 to 59th Street; N or R to Lexington Avenue.* **Rates** from $50 single. **Credit** AmEx, MC, V.
This is an unfashionably decorated, clean, cheap and safe women-only hotel in a respectable but dull area. It's good for those on a budget or for cautious students.

### East Village Bed & Breakfast

*Apt 6, 244 East 7th Street, at Avenue C (260 1865). Subway F to Second Avenue.* **Rates** single $50, double $75, incl breakfast. **No credit cards.**
A small, friendly, women-only B&B deep in the bowels of the East Village, run by women. There are only two rooms, so early reservations are essential.

### Markle Residence for Women

*123 West 13th Street, between Sixth & Seventh Avenues (242 2400). Subway F or L to 14th Street/Sixth Avenue.* **Rates** $118-$210 per week, incl two meals (one month minimum). **Credit** MC, V.
Offering women-only Salvation Army accommodation in a pleasant Greenwich Village location, the Markle has clean, comfortable rooms all of which have telephone and ensuite bathrooms.
*Disabled: rooms.*

## Bars & Lounges

*See also page 277* **Beige** *and* **Wonder Bar**.

### Bra Bar

*One Saturday a month at Mother (see p277 for listings).*
This on-off grrl power cabaret provides entertaining shows which can include anything from nude spoken word events to experimental dance or drag king game shows. Always infused with a wry intelligence and an outrageous sense of humour, Bra Bar attracts a smart, arty crowd. Phone the Bra Line for more information on forthcoming events (539 8882).

### Crazy Nanny's

*21 Seventh Avenue South, corner of Leroy Street (366 6312). Subway 1 or 9 to Christopher Street.* **Open** 4pm-4am daily.
An old faithful. There's a loud neon-decorated bar and disco with TV screens and a pool table downstairs, with DJ, dancing and a big-screen TV upstairs. Nanny's has started to stage theme nights; depending on who is DJ-ing, the crowd might be predominately of black women, or a mixed, trendy bunch of fags and dykes. This is still a place to hang-out and have a frosty cold one, after a softball game on a weekend afternoon.

### Henrietta Hudson

*438 Hudson Street, at Morton Street (243 9079). Subway 1 or 9 to Christopher Street.* **Open** 3pm-4am Mon-Fri; 1pm-4am Sat, Sun.
A watering hole for preppy, middle-class suburban girls with lots of hair. Women love it for cruising; it's laid out so you can eye everyone up at once, then make your choice and make a move. Special themed evenings include a dyke stand-up comedy night on Tuesdays.

### Julie's

*204 East 53rd Street, between Second & Third Avenues (688 1294). Subway 6, E or F to Lexington Avenue/51st Street.* **Open** from 5pm daily.
An incredibly discreet, elegant bar for mature professional and often closeted women in search of the same. Julie's stays open as late as 4am if business is good. Hors d'oeuvres are served from 5pm to 8pm.

### Meow Mix

*269 Houston Street, at Suffolk Street (254 1434). Subway B, D, F or Q to Broadway/Lafayette Street.* **Open** 8pm-4am Tue-Sun.
The latest lesbian bar features dancing to classic rock and soul, go-go dancers and performances from girl bands such as punk-and-roll-sensations Sleatee-Kinney and Phranc, along with the usual political fund raisers, comedy nights and poetry readings.

## Clubs

Great club nights are the holy grail of New York City. Something that's fabulous one week sucks or is closed down the next, and so the search continues. These are the current lesbian hot spots, but don't panic if they're not around in a few months' time – there are bound to be new nights and venues blossoming in their place.

### Clit Club

*Fridays at Mother (see p278 for listings).* **Open** 10pm-5am Fri.
The longest-running lesbian night (six years and counting) is still going strong, with new weekly midnight performances ranging from sexy strip-teases to obscure performance art. Banging DJs and bodacious go-go girls are still a standard here. New renovations have transformed this once dark dive into a larger, more user-friendly space. Under the auspices of Mother, the club no longer has a restrictive policy discouraging men, but the only males who come by are the Mother regulars – gays and cross-dressers, who hang-out here other nights of the week. Similarly, dykes are welcome at Mother any night.

### Club Casanova

*Sundays at Velvet, 167 Avenue A, between 10th & 11th Streets (475 2172). Subway L to First Avenue.* **Open** from 10pm Sun.
The only dedicated Drag King club in New York (and perhaps the world) has been the centre of major media frenzy. What could be worthy of such attention? Exposing the unlimited potential for humour and parody when women dress-up as men like KISS and The Village People, or re-enact scenes from *Shaft* and *Crusin'*. Fabulous! Gay men are also welcome and there are usually plenty of straights, too.

### SqueezeBox

*See p279 for listings.*
Squeezebox is New York's hippest, hottest drag/dyke rock and roll party. With great bands like Lunachicks and Sexpod performing, and tattooed go-go boys and girls gyrat-

ing on the bar, amid a super-mixed, celebrity-peppered crowd, you can count on seeing plenty of the hottest down-town dykes around.

### Wow Wednesdays
*Rebar, 127 Eighth Avenue, at 16th Street (631 1102)*
*Subway A, C, E, 1, 2, 3 or 9 to 14th Street.*
**Open** 6.30pm-2am Wed.
Wow Wednesdays at Rebar is the perfect place in which to bridge the gap between Happy Hour and disco time. Drop by early for a drink with friends, or swing by late and expect to shake some serious butt.

## Restaurants & Cafés

*See also page 279* **Candy Bar & Grill**.

### Big Cup
*228 Eighth Avenue, at 21st Street (206 0059). Subway C or E to 23rd Street.* **Open** 7am-2am Mon-Thur, Sun; 7am-3am Fri, Sat. **No credit cards**.
A big, colourful bustling coffee joint with a modest selection of sweets and sandwiches. Big Cup's charm lies in its mis-matched chairs, quippy staff and friendly, flirtatious clien-tele. Hang-out for hours during the day, but at night, the throng can be overwhelming.

### Cowgirl Hall of Fame
*519 Hudson Street, at 10th Street (633 1133).*
*Subway 1 or 9 to Christopher Street.* **Lunch** noon-4pm, **dinner** 5-11pm, daily. **Average** $20. **Credit** AmEx.
In name and spirit, this is a great girl place in which to eat. Though it's not known as a particularly lesbian or gay joint, it's definitely camp with its Tex-Mex and C&W music drifting from the jukebox and cowgirl memorabilia all over the walls. Women with kids come again and again because their high-chair and entertainment needs are amply met by the sympathetic single-parent owner, Sherri. The pre-club scene revs up on frozen margaritas at the steerhorn-decorated bar.

### Rubyfruit
*531 Hudson Street, at Charles Street (929 3343).*
*Subway 1 or 9 to Christopher Street.* **Open** 3pm-2am Mon-Thur; 3pm-4am Fri, Sat; 11.30am-2am Sun.
**Average** $20. **Credit** AmEx, DC, Disc, MC, V.
A warm and energetic band of dykes patronise Rubyfruit – the only lesbian bar and restaurant in town. Though the food is solidly good, it's not the main selling point. The congenial customers and a varied programme of cabaret and music make this a good place for old-school but fun-loving dykes.

## Health

The public healthcare system is practically non-existent in the United States and costs of private healthcare are exorbitant, so make sure you have comprehensive medical insurance when you travel to New York.

### Community Health Project
*(675 3559).* **Open** 10am-10pm Mon-Thur.
CHP, based at the Lesbian & Gay Community Center (*see p274*), is the place for lesbian women to go for cheap health check-ups.

### Lesbian Aids Project
*(337 3532).* **Open** 10am-6pm Mon-Fri
Gay Men's Health Crisis information/counselling initiative for lesbians (*see p273*).

### Planned Parenthood
*Margaret Sanger Centre, 380 Second Avenue, between 21st & 22nd Streets (677 6474). Subway 6 to 23rd Street.* **Open** 8.30am-4pm Mon-Fri.
This is the main branch of the best known, most reason-ably priced network of family planning clinics in the US. Counselling and treatment is available for a full range of gynaecological needs, including abortion, treatment of STDs, HIV testing and contraception. Phone for an appointment and more information about their services.

## Safety

New York women are used to the brazenness with which they are stared at by the city's pop-ulation of dubious male streetlife and develop a hardened or dismissive attitude towards it. If your unwelcome admirers ever get verbal or start following you, unless you are confident about your acid-tongued retorts, ignoring them is better than responding. Walking into the near-est shop is your best bet to get rid of really per-sistent offenders.

As for more serious safety issues, with a mini-mum of awareness and common sense you can reduce the chances of anything happening to you to almost zero. Take the usual big-city precautions: stay in areas where there are people, don't carry or wear anything that could catch a thief's eye and as far as possible try not to look lost or vulnera-ble. Look as if you know where you are going and you will probably get there safely. Advice issued by the Crime Prevention Department of the police includes: never carry anything you'd fight for; don't carry a separate wad of 'mugger's money', simply hand over all the money you have on you (if you're found to have kept money back, you'll be in worse trouble); and, while resisting is rarely a good idea, you should never ever resist when a weapon is involved. For further safety advice, *see chapter* **Essential Information**. For the **NYC Gay and Lesbian Anti-Violence Project** *see page 274*.

### Brooklyn Women's Martial Arts Center for Anti-Violence Education
*421 Fifth Avenue, between 7th & 8th Streets, Brooklyn (1-718 788 1775). Subway F or R to Fourth Avenue/9th Street.* **Open** 11am-8pm Mon-Fri.
**No credit cards**.
A centre dedicated to martial arts training for women and children. Its programmes teach defensive techniques for real-life situations, including both physical and non-physical methods of dealing with aggression or attack. Free childcare is offered, and classes are in the evenings or at weekends. Classes in karate and tai chi are also offered.

### Rape Hotline
*Sex Crimes Report Line of the New York Police Department (267 7273).* **Open** 24 hours daily.
Reports of sex crimes are handled by a female detective from the New York Police Department, who will inform the appro-priate precinct, send an ambulance if requested and provide counselling and medical referrals. A detective from the Sex Crimes Squad will interview the victim. You can request to be seen in your own home.

# Children

**There's only one thing missing from New York's vast range of facilities and opportunities for youngsters – and that's where to dump the folks.**

New York is a noisy, non-stop, loud-mouthed, horn-honking, in-your-face city where anything goes and everything seems possible – which could be why so many kids think it was made for them. It's the perfect environment for short attention spans and experience-hungry spirits; possibly the only place in the world where a child can work in a Nigerian garden in the morning, take a class in an obscure Indian dance form in the afternoon, sleep overnight at the zoo and wake up in time to catch a participatory jazz concert. Kids don't get bored in New York. They get 'overscheduled'.

Luckily, besides a stream of children's events and activities – from family-orientated dance and music performances by top companies, to stand-up comedy by kids, puppet shows, interactive science exhibits, ice-skating and much more – there are the totally unscheduled pleasures of the street. If you let them (and remember: 'well behaved' is a culture-bound term), kids will have a ball running up and down industrial loading bays, checking out street performers, swinging on subway poles, or just wandering around taking it all in. Especially during the warmer months, street life in New York satisfies all of a child's senses and will provide yours with endless stories to take home.

Friday's *New York Times* and the weekly *Time Out New York* and *New York* magazines have good listings of children's activities. Also read the monthly *Parentguide Magazine* distributed free in libraries, toy shops, playcentres and other children-intensive places. Pick up a copy of *Events for Children* from any branch of the New York Public Library for extensive listings of free storytellings,

puppet shows, films and workshops in libraries. The Donnell Library, home of the Central Children's Room, is the best place for events; it also houses the real Winnie the Pooh and other toys that belonged to Christopher Robin (*see chapter* **Museums**).

All branches of Barnes & Noble bookshop have regular, free story-reading hours and special events; pick up a calendar in any of their branches. You might also want to invest in a copy of Alfred Gingold and Helen Rogan's invaluable, slim paperback, *The Cool Parents' Guide to All of New York* (City Books). It offers some unusual suggestions for excursions that can be enjoyed by both children and adults. The New York Citysearch web site (http://www.city-searchnyc.com) has well-organised family listings; search by age, location, date or subject.

Though there's no end of events and activities designed specifically for kids, don't pass by some of the exciting, cutting-edge stuff for adults; some of the zany off-Broadway shows are sure hits with children, as are most 'new media' art shows.

For more ideas, *see also chapters* **Sightseeing**, **New York by Season**, **Trips Out of Town** *and* **Sport & Fitness**.

## Amusement Parks

*See also chapter* **Trips Out of Town**.

### Astroland
*1000 Surf Avenue, at West 8th Street, Coney Island, Brooklyn (1-718 372 0275). Train B, D, F or N to Stillwell Avenue-Coney Island.* **Open** *winter* phone for details; *summer* noon-late daily (weather permitting). **Admission** $1.75 single rides. **No credit cards.**
The famous Coney Island amusement park is rather run-down and tacky now, but a delight to children nonetheless. In the summer months you can still ride the frightening Cyclone rollercoaster (younger children like the Tilt-a-Whirl), watch a snake-charmer, get sticky candy-floss fingers, bite into a Nathan's famous hotdog and, if you don't mind boom-boxes and broken glass, enjoy the sun and sand.

## Circuses

Check the press for details of when the unmissable French-Canadian **Cirque du Soleil** is in town (usually April). The music, costumes and staging are pure fantasy; though younger children might find the stylish clowns a little grotesque. Tickets are snapped up fast.

### Big Apple Circus

*(information 268 0055/offices 268 2500/Ticketmaster 307 4100).* **Tickets** prices vary.

New York's own travelling circus was founded ten years ago as a more traditional, one-ring alternative to the Ringling Brothers' three-ring wonder. It prides itself on being a true family affair, with acts by the founder's two children; Grandma, Big Apple's beloved clown and the real glue of the theme-based show, is not a family member. The circus has a regular winter season (Oct-Jan) in Damrosch Park at the Lincoln Center; watch out too for spring dates in various parks.

### Ringling Brothers and Barnum & Bailey Circus

*Madison Square Garden, Seventh Avenue, between 31st & 33rd Streets (465 6741). Subway A, C or E to Penn Station.* **Season** April. **Tickets** $8.50-$25. **Credit** AmEx, DC, Disc, MC, V.

The original American circus, this has three rings, lots of glitz and plenty to keep you glued to your seat. It's extremely popular, so reserve seats well in advance.

## Museums & Exhibitions

Check the **By Neighbourhood** and **Museums** chapters for plenty more museum options, including the revamped dinosaur halls at the American Museum of Natural History, the Liberty Science Center (don't miss the touch tunnel), the New York Transit Museum and the Sea, Air & Space Museum, which is a fabulous collection of military and maritime junk housed on an aircraft carrier. Most of these museums offer weekend workshops for children. In addition the following are especially suitable for children.

### Brooklyn Children's Museum

*145 Brooklyn Avenue, at St Mark's Avenue, Brooklyn (recorded information 1-718 735 4432). Subway 3 to Kingston Avenue; B43, B45, B47 or B65 bus.* **Open** *winter* 2-5pm Wed, Thur, Fri; noon-5pm Sat, Sun; *summer* noon-5pm Mon, Wed-Sun. **Admission** suggested donation $4. **No credit cards**.

Founded in 1899, this was the world's first museum designed specifically for children. You reach the exhibits via a walkway leading through a long, water-filled tunnel. In the music studio children can dance on the keys of the walk-on piano and play around with synthesizers. Special workshops are offered, mostly of a multicultural nature.

### Brooklyn Museum of Art

*See chapter* **Museums** *for listings.* **Times** 11am, 2pm Sat. **Admission** free with museum ticket.

'Arty facts' is a lively drop-in programme focusing on a different theme each month. Children aged five to ten examine in depth three or four works in the museum's galleries, learn about the people who made them and then go make their own in the art studio.

### Children's Museum for the Arts

*72 Spring Street, between Broadway & Lafayette Street (941 9198). Subway C, E to Spring Street.* **Open** 11am-5pm daily. **Admission** $4 Mon-Fri; $5 Sat, Sun. **Credit** AmEx, MC, V.

A favourite hang-out for the under-sixes, this is less a museum than an art playground, with a floor-to-ceiling chalkboard, art computers and vast stores of art supplies – perfect for young travellers pining for their crayons. Children must be accompanied by an adult.

### Children's Museum of Manhattan

*212 West 83rd Street, between Broadway & Amsterdam Avenue (721 1234). Subway 1 or 9 to 86th Street.* **Open** 10am-5pm Tue-Sun. **Admission** $5; $2.50 concessions. **Credit** AmEx, Disc, MC, V.

*Young artists-in-the-making at the* **Brooklyn Children's Museum.**

The star exhibits include 'Sounds Fun', a kind of playground about acoustics at the centre of which is a jungle gym that replicates the human ear; and 'Seuss!', an interactive environment for pre- and beginner readers based on the books of Dr Seuss. There are no eating facilities, but you may leave for lunch and return on the same ticket.

## Metropolitan Museum of Art
*See chapter* **Museums** *for listings.*
Any child who's read EL Konigsburg's *From the Crazy, Mixed-Up Files of Basil E Frankweiler* will want to visit the museum in which the story's young protagonists squatted when they ran away from home. Like them, most kids will want to head straight for the Egyptian galleries for a look at mummies and, most impressively, the awesome temple of Dendur. But what really sets the Met apart for young visitors is its range of self-guided children's tours or 'art hunts' designed with an unusually acute sense of what makes kids tick. From 'Mummies' to 'Colonial Children' and 'Food for Thought', each tour is printed in large type with very cool graphics, a simple floor map, step-by-step directions so children can go hunting by themselves plus playful questions and tidbits of information to engage their interest. A tour takes about an hour to complete.

## Museum of Modern Art
*See chapter* **Museums** *for listings.*
Guided family tours, with a different slant each week, introduce children to the highlights of MoMA during pre-public hours in winter months. The museum's *Art Safari* (available from its bookshop) is a self-guided family tour focussing on animals in the collection's artworks. The entrance is at the John Noble Education Center, 18 West 54th Street. Highly recommended for ages five to ten.

## Socrates Sculpture Park
*Broadway, at the East River, Queens (1-718-956-1819). Subway N to Broadway/Long Island City.* **Open** 10am-sunset daily. **Admission** free.
Unlike most art exhibitions, this one, an outdoor, city-owned spread of large-scale contemporary sculpture by local artists, is utterly devoid of snarling guards and 'don't touch' signs. Without even risking an adult's glare, children climb on, run through, sit astride and generally interact with the works that seem to have been plopped haphazardly around the five-acre, waterside park.

## Sony Wonder Technology Lab
*550 Madison Avenue, between 55th & 56th Streets (833 8100). Subway 4, 5 or 6 to 51st Street.* **Open** 10am-6pm Tue, Wed, Fri, Sat; 10am-9pm Thur; noon-6pm Sun (schools groups have priority 10am-noon Tue-Fri). **Admission** free.
Most children think this is the coolest place on earth, not least because of the personalised log-on cards that cause your name and image to be flashed on monitors as you move between six digital workstations. Visitors can play at being medical diagnosticians, remix a Celine Dion song, design computer games, edit a music video or crisis-manage an earthquake. Best of all is the High Definition Interactive Theater, where the audience directs the action in an exciting video adventure. Get here early – by 2.30pm at weekends – or you might not get in.

# Music

## Growing Up With Opera
*John Jay Theater, 899 Tenth Avenue, at 59th Street (769 7008). Subway A, B, C, D, 1, 9 to 59th Street/Columbus Circle.* **Tickets** $15-$25. **Credit** AmEx, MC, V.
Short operas sung in English by the Metropolitan Opera Guild, some especially commissioned for young audiences.

## Jazz for Young People
*Alice Tulley Hall, Lincoln Center, Broadway at 65th St (information 875 5299/tickets 721 6500).* **Tickets** $8-$12. **Credit** AmEx, MC, V.
Interactive concerts with Wynton Marsalis, who helps children figure out answers to questions such as 'What is Jazz?'

## Little Orchestra Society
*Florence Gould Hall, 55 East 59th Street, between Park & Madison Avenues (704 2100). Subway 4, 5 or 6 to 59th Street.* **Tickets** $15-$32. **Credit** AmEx, MC, V.
'Lollipop' orchestral concerts for children aged three to five, combining classical music with dance, puppetry, theatre and mime. In addition, *Amahl and the Night Visitors* is presented every Christmas. 'Happy Concerts' for six- to 12-year-olds are presented at Avery Fisher Hall.

## New York Philharmonic Young People's Concerts
*Avery Fisher Hall, Lincoln Center Plaza, Broadway and 64th Street (875 5030). Subway 1 or 9 to 66th Street.* **Tickets** $8-$20. **Credit** AmEx, MC, V.
Initiated by Leonard Bernstein, these educational concerts, in which the musicians address the audience directly, are preceded by hour-long 'Children's Promenades' during which kids meet orchestra members and try out instruments.

# Puppets

## International Festival of Puppet Theater
*Information 439 7529 ext 1998.* **Shows** September 1998.
This biennial festival of puppet theatre is produced by the Jim Henson Foundation. Although its central component is cutting-edge productions for adults, children can enjoy a rich blend of offerings from several continents. Also watch out for festival-piggybacking puppet activity around town.

## Lenny Suib Puppet Theater
*Asphalt Green, 555 East 90th Street, at York Avenue (369 8890). Subway 4, 5 or 6 to 86th Street.* **Shows** 10.30am, noon, Sat, Sun. **Admission** $8; $6 children. **No credit cards.**
A wide variety of puppeteers from around the country perform here, most of them well-respected members of the puppetry community. Shows last around an hour and are suitable for children aged three to eight.

## Puppet Company
*31 Union Square West, at 16th Street, loft 2B (741 1646). Subway 4, 5, 6, B, D, L, N or R to 14th Street.* **Shows** Oct-April 1pm, 3pm, Sun. **Tickets** $7.50. **No credit cards.**
Three- to seven-year-olds cram on to benches in this intimate loft space, to watch the company's perennial hand-puppet host, the debonair Al E Gator, introduce the season's puppet play. Each play is augmented with a humourous, inventive puppet revue and a short puppet-making demonstration. Performances last about 50 minutes; reservations are essential.

## Puppetworks
*338 Sixth Avenue, at 4th Street, Brooklyn (1-718 965 3391). Subway M, N or R to Union Street.* **Shows** 12.30pm, 2.30pm, Sat, Sun. **Tickets** $7; $5 2-18s. **No credit cards.**
The company, established back in 1938, offers two different plays a season alternating weekly. Usually performed with marionettes, the plays are based on classic tales, such as *Beauty and the Beast* or *Alice in Wonderland*, and are exquisitely produced.

*Don't forget to make a wish... Al E Gator and guest at the* **Puppet Company**, *page 285.*

## Swedish Cottage Marionette Theater

*Central Park, at 81st Street (988 9093). Subway B or C to 81st Street.* **Shows** *Dec-Aug* 10.30am, noon, Tue-Fri; noon, 3pm, Sat. **Tickets** $5; $4 2-12s. **No credit cards**.
Run by New York's Department of Parks and Recreation, the company opened this intimate theatre in 1972 after touring New York's parks and boroughs since 1938. Performances run from December to June and include such classics as *Rumpelstiltskin* and *The Magic Flute*. Booking is essential.

## Theatres

### Kids' Theater at the Knitting Factory

*See chapter* **Dance** *for listings.* **Shows** *Sept-April* 1pm Sat. **Tickets** $8.50. **Credit** AmEx, MC, V.
West End Kids' Productions programmes a variety of acts at one of downtown's homes of the avant-garde, including puppetry, magic, variety and some acts that defy description. Most are geared to kids aged three to nine. Phone the company for a schedule of events (877 6115).

### New Victory Theater

*209 West 42nd Street, between Broadway and Eighth Avenue (563 5444/382 4020). Subway A, C, E, N, R, 1, 2, 3, 9 to 42nd Street.* **Tickets** $10-$30. **Credit** AmEx, MC, V.
New York's first and only year-round, full-scale children's theatre – and the first of the New 42nd Street theatres to be reclaimed from porndom when it opened, fully renovated, in 1995 – the New Victory is a gem that shows the very best in international theatre and dance for young audiences. Productions tend toward the sophisticated, with many being targeted for the over-ten set.

### TADA! Youth Ensemble

*120 West 28th Street, between Sixth & Seventh Avenues (627 1732). Subway 1 or 9 to 28th Street.* **Shows** *Jul, Aug* noon, 2pm, Mon-Fri; 1pm, 3pm Sat, Sun. **Tickets** $12; $6 under-17s. **No credit cards**.

Musicals performed by and for children. The ensemble cast is made up of kids aged eight to 17, drawn from auditions of young hopefuls from city schools. The shows are usually musical comedies, specially commissioned by TADA! They are extremely well presented and very popular. Booking advisable; phone for details of workshops.

### Thirteenth Street Repertory Company

*50 West 13th Street, between Fifth & Sixth Avenues (675 6677). Subway 4, 5, 6, L, N or R to Union Square.* **Shows** 1pm, 3pm Sat; 1pm, 3pm, Sun. **Tickets** $7. **No credit cards**.
Four year-olds and up enjoy musicals and fairytales lasting about 45 to 50 minutes. Booking advisable.

## Outdoor Activities

### Brooklyn Botanic Gardens

*1000 Washington Avenue, Brooklyn (1-718 622 4544). Subway 2 or 3 to Eastern Parkway/Brooklyn Museum.* **Open** *winter* 8am-4.30pm Tue-Fri; 10am-4.30pm Sat, Sun; *summer* 8am-6pm Tue-Fri; 10am-6pm Sat, Sun. **Admission** $3; $1 concessions. **No credit cards**.
In the indoor Discovery Center, children learn about plants and nature through some inventive exhibits, such as a synthetic oak tree which has doors and holes hiding creatures that live in a real tree trunk. Potting benches are at child height. The garden's highlight, a 13,000 sq ft (1,200 sq m) 'Discovery Garden', lets children play botanist, make toys out of natural materials, weave a wall and get their hands dirty.

### New York Botanical Gardens

*Southern Boulevard, at 200th Street, Bronx (1-718 817 8705). Subway 4, C or D to Bedford Park, then BX26 bus.* **Open** *April-Oct* 10am-6pm Tue-Sun; *Nov-Mar* 10am-4pm Tue-Sun. **Admission** $3; $1 concessions; free under-6s; free 10am-6pm Wed, 10am-noon Sat. **No credit cards**.
Due to open in spring 1998, the immense Children's Adventure Garden promises to be a 'museum of the natural

world' where children interact with exhibits in a variety of 'galleries', both indoor and outdoor, that show how plants live. In addition, children can run under 'Munchy', a giant topiary; poke around in a touch tank; and plant, weed, water and harvest in the Family Garden.

### Nelson Rockefeller Park
*Hudson River at Chambers Street (information 267 9700). Subway C or E to World Trade Center.* **Open** 10am-sunset daily. **Admission** free.
River breezes always make this park several degrees cooler than most of the city, a big plus in the summer. There's plenty for children to do here besides watch the boats (Saturday's a good day for ocean liners): they can play on Tom Otterness's amazingly quirky sculptures in the picnic area (near Chambers Street entrance); enjoy one of New York's best playgrounds; and participate with local children in art, sports or street-game activities (Mon-Thur afternoons, May to Oct; call for specific locations). Special events such as kite-flying or fishing are planned throughout the summer. In addition, two blocks north on Pier 25 is a mini-golf course as well as a sand-and-sprinkler area for overheated tots. The River Project (941 5901) on Pier 26 opens its doors to children at weekends, when they can help set river traps, examine small creatures under microscopes and feed the aquarium fish.

## Central Park

Manhattanites don't have gardens; they have Central Park, which like the rest of the city is over-populated with people doing all sorts of things, some of which are fun to watch. There are plenty of places and programmes specially aimed at children; phone 360 8236 for details. **Arts in the Park** (988 9093) organises an extensive programme of children's summer arts events here and in other parks throughout the city. In addition, the **Urban Park Rangers** (360 2774) arrange guided walks, nature-related activities and school vacation programmes. The **Parks Department** events hotline (360 3456) provides a huge menu of events and activities in all the New York parks. Stop by the Dairy, an information centre with an interactive exhibition on the history of the park; nearby are the beautiful **antique carousel** (90¢ a ride) and the **Heckscher Playground**, which has handball courts, horseshoes, several softball diamonds, a puppet theatre, a wading pool and a crèche. *See also chapter* **Sightseeing**.

### Charles A Dana Discovery Center
*Central Park, at 110th Street, near Fifth Avenue (860 1370). Subway 2 or 3 to 110th Street.* **Open** mid Feb-mid Oct 11am-5pm Tue-Sun; mid Oct-mid Feb 11am-4pm Tue-Sun. **Admission** free.
Now Harlem Meer has been restored and stocked, you can take the kids fishing here. Poles and bait are given out (with parental ID) to children over five until 90 minutes before closing; staff members are available to help. Other activities include birdwatching and workshops – mostly park-related (for instance, kite-making or sun printing) and often environmental in nature (1-3pm weekends).

### Conservatory Water
*Central Park, at 77th Street, near Fifth Avenue. Subway 6 to 77th Street.*
Known as Stuart Little's Pond after EB White's storybook mouse, this ornamental pond is the place to watch model yacht races; when the boatmaster is around you can hire one

of the remote-controlled vessels for $7-$10 an hour and have a go at some wind-powered fun. Be warned – it's not as speedily responsive as Nintendo. Nearby is a large bronze statue of Alice in Wonderland, into whose lap and over whose head children climb.

### Henry Luce Nature Observatory
*Belvedere Castle, Central Park, at West 79th Street (772 0210). Subway B or C to 81st Street.* **Open** Oct-Feb 11am-4pm Tue-Sun; Feb-Oct 11am-5pm Tue-Sun. **Admission** free.
The newest children's hotspot in Central Park, with telescopes, microscopes and simple hands-on exhibits that teach about the plants and animals living (or hiding) in the surrounding area. Workshops are held on weekend afternoons (1-3pm), and kids (with parental ID) can borrow a 'discovery kit' – a backpack containing binoculars, a birdwatching guide and everything they need to watch, classify and document the world outside the observatory.

### North Meadow Recreation Center
*Central Park, at 79th Street (348 4867).*
Borrow (with ID) a fun-in-the-park kit bag containing a frisbee, hula hoop, whiffle ball and bat, jump rope, kick ball and various games.

### Stories at the Hans Christian Andersen Statue
*Central Park, at Conservatory Water (929 6871/340 0906).*
A real New York tradition, not to be missed. For generations, children have gathered at the foot of the statue for stories read by master storytellers from all over America. Besides the classics, including favourites by Andersen, children can hear myths and tales from around the world.

### Wildman's Edible Park Tours
*Various city parks, including Central and Prospect Parks. Phone for meeting place and instructions (1-718 291 6925).*
The irrepressible urban forager and naturalist, 'Wildman' Steve Brill, was offering eat-as-you-go foraging tours of city parks long before his illegal activities (he was arrested for eating Central Park's dandelions) were sanctioned by the parks commissioner in 1986. Though his tours are not geared specifically for children, he pays them special attention, pronouncing them mushroom hunters 'because you're close to the ground', letting them play Brillaphone – a musical 'instrument' invented by his father – and thrilling them with his non-stop, joke-laden edubanter. Bring a paper bag for the vegetable matter you pick or dig up.

## Zoos

### Central Park Wildlife Conservation Center
*See chapter* **Sightseeing** *for listings.*
This small but perfectly formed zoo is one of the highlights of the park. You can watch seals frolic above and below the waterline, crocodiles snapping at monkeys swinging on branches and huge polar bears swimming endless underwater laps like true neurotic New Yorkers. The chilly penguin house is a favourite summer retreat for overheated kids.

### International Wildlife Conservation Park (Bronx Zoo)
*See chapter* **Sightseeing** *for listings.*
Over 4,000 animals and 543 species live in reconstructed natural habitats, in one of the world's largest and most magnificent zoos. Inside is the Bronx Children's Zoo, scaled to the needs of the very young, with lots of domestic animals to pet plus wonderful exhibits which let the viewer see the world from the viewpoint of the animal – whether it's perching or climbing. Camel and elephant rides are organised from April to October. Don't miss the sea-lion-feeding spectacle (daily at 3pm).

### New York Aquarium for Wildlife Conservation

*Surf Avenue & West 8th Street, Brooklyn (1-718 265 3405). Subway D, F to West 8th Street.* **Open** 10am-6pm daily. **Admission** $7.75; $3.50 concessions. **No credit cards.**
Though the aquarium is rather funky, kids enjoy seeing the famous Beluga whale family. There's also a re-creation of the Pacific coastline and an intriguing glimpse of the kind of things that manage to live in the East River, plus the usual dolphin show and some truly awesome sharks. Watch the dolphins being fed daily at 11.30am and 3pm. It's right by the sea and a mere stroll from the action of Coney Island.

## Play Spaces

### Playspace

*2473 Broadway, at 92nd Street (769 2300). Subway 1, 2, 3, 9 to 96 Street.* **Open** 9.30am-6pm Mon-Sat; 10am-6pm Sun. **Admission** $4.50. **No credit cards.**
Children build in the immense sandbox, ride on toy trucks, dress up and climbing on the jungle gym, while parents take in the views through huge plate-glass windows.

### Rain or Shine

*115 East 29th Street, between Park & Lexington Avenues (889 2144). Subway 6 to 29th Street.*
**Open** 9am-6pm Mon-Fri; 10am-6pm Sat, Sun.
**Admission** $8.95 child, $1 discount for siblings; free parents. **No credit cards.**
A parent-accompanied play space in a rain forest setting, filled with activity areas and toys designed to encourage imaginative play, including a giant sandbox and a tree house There's also a stage and dressing-up area, an art room and a baby area. Suitable for children aged six months to six.

### WonderCamp Entertainment

*27 West 23rd Street, between Fifth & Sixth Avenues (243 1111). Subway F, N or R to 23rd Street.*
**Open** 11am-6pm Tue-Thur, Sat, Sun; 11am-8pm Fri.
**Admission** $6.50. **Credit** MC, V.
Indoor entertainment with an American camp theme and a highly commercial edge, for children aged one to ten. An adult has to accompany them, but once inside they are kept thoroughly busy. Bookings not accepted.

## Babysitting

### Baby Sitters' Guild

*(682 0227).* **Open** 9am-9pm daily. **No credit cards.**
Long- or short-term babysitters cost $10-$20 an hour and speak 16 languages between them. If you tell the agency you'll need a babysitter more than once during your stay, they'll do their best to book the same sitter for you each time.

### Avalon Nurse Registry & Child Service

*(245 0250).* **Open** 8.30am-5.30pm Mon-Fri; 9am-8pm Sat, Sun. **No credit cards.**
Get yourself a full- or part-time nanny or a casual babysitter from Avalon. Casual babysitting (four hours minimum) costs $10 an hour plus $2 for each additional child, with travelling expenses on top.

### Pinch Sitters

*(260 6005).* **Open** 7am-5pm Mon-Fri. **No credit cards.**
Pinch Sitters specialises in emergency childcare, mainly by creative types moonlighting between engagements, and mainly for creative types with unpredictable freelance schedules. The agency will try to get you a sitter within the hour; to be safe, call in the morning for an evening sitter or the previous afternoon for a daytime sitter. Charges are $10 an hour, (minimum four hours).

# Media mania

New York being media city, it makes sense that children should not only watch television but make it too. Tune in to either of the city's public access TV stations most evenings, and you're likely to catch a zero-budget, teen-produced show featuring a panel of giggling girls or some gangly adolescent playing talk-show host in his or her bedroom.

On the principle of 'if you can't beat them, join them', several museums have set up state-of-the-art television and radio labs and workstations designed to promote media literacy among the square-eyed, boom-boxed young. Whether or not the literacy plan is working, kids are having a great time getting behind cameras, rolling tape, operating lighting, sound and special effects, taking charge in the editing room and, if they're extrovert types, getting in front of the cameras too.

**CMOM-TV**, at the **Children's Museum of Manhattan** (721 1234) operates from the Time Warner Media Center where there are regular weekend workshops for ages six and up. Though some workshops have a circumscribed theme – an interview with Columbus on Columbus Day or Sports News during the Olympics – generally children can choose among themselves between several options. They might produce the daily newscast or weather report; a news magazine, in which they develop the feature story, anchor the programme and report 'on location'; or the station's own talk show, Motor Mouth.

The **Staten Island Children's Museum** (1-718-273-2060) has both a radio and TV studio where children ages six and up can create whatever kind of programme they choose – from commercials to newscasts – and take home a video or audio tape of their production. At the Museum of Television & Radio (*see chapter* **Museums**) groups of children aged eight and up use original scripts and authentic sound-effect machines as they tape vintage radio shows such as *Superman* and there are some exciting workstations at the American Museum of the Moving Image (*see chapter* **Museums**), where kids can create their own animations or re-edit movie footage.

# Business

**Welcome to the world capital of capitalism, where you can go to the Wall (Street) and still make millions.**

New Yorkers have always promised to get it for you wholesale. The first European immigrants came for fur trading, not farming, and the city thrived as the gateway, via the Erie Canal and the Hudson River, to the North American interior. No wonder that Laurie Anderson once remarked that American men have only two role models: the salesman and the cowboy. It's the first lesson in doing business in New York. Everyone you'll deal with is one part foot-in-the-door, fast-talking encyclopaedia seller, and in equal measure a maverick, self-interested pioneer.

American selling culture is deeply ingrained in the society, so even the most timid-seeming person will be able to switch on all the convincing bluster of a PT Barnum at a moment's notice. The need for cutting through the patter is learnt fast. When it comes to the cowboy, it's that fierce individualist streak which explains why everyone is so ambitious. People work hard here – very hard – but only because they want to reach the top rung and kick their boss off the ladder. Most people's dreams are of financial autonomy, and even the most deeply embedded corporate cog is only turning up at the office in the hope of one day running the whole machine.

What's more, all are awarded a grandiose title. There may be only three people in a company, but rest assured, one is President and CEO, another is Chairman and the office boy is Vice President, Caffeine Distribution.

Corporate hospitality may be impressive, but don't think it runs wild. Nowhere more so than in New York is the chestnut about free lunches to be heeded. And note that New Yorkers will generally avoid drinking at lunchtime.

Business language is full of metaphors of sport and war. There are winners and losers, negotiations are the battlefield or the ballpark, and a scream of triumph is released after a deal is made (and the 'opponent' lies 'defeated'). The lesson is that there's no room for 'understandings'. If something has gone unmentioned, don't assume it will be done as you'd like. Specifically, don't be embarrassed about talking 'bottom-line' terms. No one is ashamed to talk about money. If *you* are, they will stiff you – get it in writing. Equally, brag loud and long about what you can offer, otherwise they'll listen to someone else. As any salesperson will tell you – it's as easy as ABC: Always Be Closing.

*The land of opportunity – and fake Rolexes.*

## Information

The business world's bible, the *Wall Street Journal* (75¢), contains all the up-to-date facts and figures on US and worldwide commerce. In-depth business profiles are published in *Fortune* ($4.50) and *Forbes* ($5) magazines; *Inc* ($3) is a glossy, monthly mag which makes business seem like fun. You'll find many more business mags at newsstands.

### Dow Jones Report
*(24-hour recorded information 976 4141).*

### New York Partnership & Chamber of Commerce
*Battery Park Plaza, between State & Whitehall Streets (493 7500). Subway 6 to 33rd Street.* **Open** 8.30am-5.30pm Mon-Fri.
The Chamber gives advice on local needs and provides market information. The NYC Partnership organises training programmes.

### NYC Department of Business Services

*110 William Street, near Fulton Street (696 2442).*
*Subway 2, 3, 4, 5, J or M to Fulton Street.* **Open** 9am-
5pm Mon-Fri.
Free advice on starting and running a business, plus information about grants or loans the city may be able to offer.

## Stock Exchanges

### Commodities Exchange Center

*9th Floor, 4 World Trade Center, off Liberty Street*
*(748 1000). Subway 1, 9, N or R to Cortlandt Street.*
**Open** 10.30am-3pm Mon-Fri. **Tours** 11am, 1pm, 2pm,
Mon-Fri.
There are four exchanges here: the New York Mercantile
Exchange, the Coffee, Sugar, and Cocoa Exchange, the New
York Cotton Exchange, and the Commodities Exchange. The
Visitors' Gallery is on the ninth floor. Book two weeks in
advance for tours.

### International Monetary Market

*67 Wall Street, near William Street (363 7000). Subway*
*4 or 5 to Wall Street.* **Open** 9am-5pm Mon-Fri.
This is the marketing division of IMM; the head office is in
Chicago. No trading is done here but the office will help anyone from brokers to institutional users and give advice on
applications for futures and options.

### New York Stock Exchange

*11 Wall Street, at Broad Street (656 3000). Subway 4 or*
*5 to Wall Street.* **Open** 9.30am-4pm Mon-Fri.
The New York Stock Exchange still operates as an auction
house: specialist market makers and brokers trade on the
floor trying to make a megabuck. More than 10,000 institutions with $3 trillion in securities under management have
access to and use the Exchange's market system. The visitors' centre is at 20 Broad Street (*see chapter* **Sightseeing**).

## Libraries

*See also chapter* **Museums**.

### Brooklyn Public Library (Business Branch)

*280 Cadman Plaza West, at Tillary Street (1-718 722*
*3333). Subway 2 or 3 to Court Street/Borough Hall.*
**Open** 10am-8pm Mon; 1-8pm Tue; 10am-6pm Wed, Fri;
1-6pm Thur; 10am-5pm Sat. **Admission** free.
This library, which is separate from the NYPL (*see below*),
is a great resource for all sorts of US business information.

### NYPL Science, Industry
### & Business Library

*188 Madison Avenue, at 34th Street (592 7000). Subway*
*6 to 33rd Street.* **Open** 10am-6pm Mon, Fri, Sat; 11am-
7pm Tue-Thur. **Admission** free.
The New York Public Library's state-of-the-art business
library. It opened in May 1996 at a cost of $100 million, and
contains a vast range of business and industry resources.
Many of these are accessible online either on terminals within the building or by phoning in.

## Importing & Exporting

### US Customs Service (New York Region)

*6 World Trade Center, off Vesey Street (customs*
*information 466 4547/recorded information 1-800 697*
*3662). Subway 1, 9, N or R to Cortlandt Street.*
**Open** 8am-4.30pm Mon-Fri.
The source of all information on importing goods and merchandise. Staff deal with enquiries on import duty, licences

and restricted goods. There's a useful magazine, *Importing*
*into the US* ($6.50).

### US Department of Commerce

*Suite 635, 6 World Trade Center, off Vesey Street*
*(466 5222). Subway 1, 9, N or R to Cortlandt Street.*
**Open** 9am-5pm Mon-Fri.
Regulates and encourages exports from the US.

### Governor's Office of Regulatory Reform

*17th Floor, Alfred E Smith Building, PO Box 7027,*
*Albany, NY 12225 (1-518 486 3292/1-800 342 3464).*
**Open** 9am-5pm Mon-Fri.
Free information on which – if any – New York State per-
mits are necessary for starting up a particular business.
Topics covered include incorporation, employment, taxes,
and business standards.

## Services
### Air Couriers

### DHL Worldwide Express

*2 World Trade Center, off Liberty Street (1-800 225*
*5345). Subway E to World Trade Center.* **Open** 8.30am-
8.30pm daily. **Credit** AmEx, DC, Disc, MC, V.
DHL will send a courier to pick up from any address in New
York City, or you can deliver packages to its offices and drop-
off points in person. No cash transactions are undertaken.
As well as its international services, DHL also operates a
messenger service within New York.

### Federal Express

*Various locations throughout the city, phone with your zip*
*code for the nearest; or, for free pick-up at your door*
*(777 6500/1-800 247 4747 international).* **Open** 24
hours daily. **Credit** AmEx, DC, Disc, MC, V.
An overnight letter to London costs about $28.50. Next-day
delivery in the US by 10.30am is $15.81; by 3pm it's $13.77.
You save $2.50 off the cost of the package if you deliver it to
a Federal Express office. Packages for overseas should be
dropped off by 3pm, packages for most destinations in the US
by 8pm (some locations have a later time, phone to check).

### Cellular Phones

### InTouch USA

*(391 8323/1-800 872 7626).* **Open** 9am-5pm Mon-Fri.
**Credit** AmEx, Disc, MC, V.
The city's largest cellular communication rentals company,
InTouch rents out phones by the day, week or month. It also
hires out (and can deliver) satellite pagers (with nationwide
coverage), portable faxes, and walkie talkies.

### Computers

There are hundreds of computer dealers in
Manhattan. If you are considering a purchase you
should buy from out of state to avoid sales tax.
Many out-of-state dealers advertise in New York
papers and magazines.

### Kinko's

*24 East 12th Street, between University Place & Fifth*
*Avenue (924 0802). Subway 4, 6, L, N or R to Union*
*Square.* **Open** 24 hours daily. **Credit** AmEx, Disc, MC, V.
A very efficient and friendly place to use computers and
copiers. Kinko's has several workstations and design stations, including IBM and Macintosh, plus all the major programs. Colour output is available. There are many branches
throughout Manhattan.

### User-Friendly
*139 West 72nd Street, between Columbus & Amsterdam Avenues (580 4433). Subway 1, 2, 3 or 9 to 72nd Street.* **Open** 9am-10pm Mon-Thur; 9am-6pm Fri; 11am-7pm Sat; noon-8pm Sun. **Credit** AmEx, MC, V.
Macs and PCs with all the big programs are for hire at User-Friendly's three locations.
**Branches**: 1477 Third Avenue (535 4100); 401 Sixth Avenue (675 2255).

### USPC
*360 West 31st Street, between Eighth & Ninth Avenues (594 2222). Subway A, C or E to 34th Street.* **Open** 9am-5pm Mon-Fri. **Credit** AmEx, MC, V.
Rent by the day, week, month or year from a range of computers, systems and networks from IBM, Compaq, Macintosh and Hewlett Packard for use on your premises. Delivery within one hour is possible.

## Desktop Publishing

### Fitch Graphics
*130 Cedar Street, near World Trade Center (619 3800). Subway 1, 9, N or R to Cortlandt Street.* **Open** 8am-11pm Mon-Fri. **Credit** (until 5pm only) AmEx, MC, V.
A full-service desktop publishing firm, with colour laser output and all pre-press facilities. Fitch works with both Apple Mac and IBM platforms and has a bulletin board for customers to deal with them online.
**Branch**: 25 West 45th Street (840 3091).

## Mailbox Rental

### Mail Boxes Etc USA
*1173A Second Avenue, between 61st & 62nd Streets (832 1390). Subway 4, 5 or 6 to 59th Street; N or R to Lexington Avenue.* **Open** 9am-7pm Mon-Fri; 10am-5pm Sat. **Credit** AmEx, MC, V.
Mailbox rentals, mail forwarding, overnight delivery, packaging and shipping are undertaken. There's also a phone-message service, photocopying and faxing, telexing, typing and business printing. There are nearly 30 other locations in Manhattan, many offering 24-hour access to mailboxes.

## Messenger Services

### A to Z Couriers
*(633 2410)*
Cheerful couriers deliver to all neighbourhoods, including the Bronx, Brooklyn, Queens and Long Island.

### Breakaway
*43 Walker Street, at Church Street (219 8500). Subway A, C or E to Canal Street.* **Open** 7am-9pm Mon-Fri; by arrangement Sat, Sun. **Credit** AmEx, Disc, MC, V.
A highly recommended city-wide messenger service with 25 messengers who promise to pick up within 15 minutes of a request and deliver within the hour.

### Jefron Messenger Service
*141 Duane Street, between West Broadway & Church Street (964 8441). Subway 1, 2, 3 or 9 to Chambers Street.* **Open** 7am-6pm Mon-Fri. **No credit cards**.
Jefron specialises in import/export documents.

## Office Rental

### Bauer Business Communications Center
*New York Hilton, 1335 Sixth Avenue, at West 54th Street (262 1329). Subway B, D, F or Q to Rockefeller Center.* **Open** 7am-5pm Mon-Fri. **Credit** AmEx, Disc, MC, V.

Rent fully equipped desk space here, with full back-up office services. Workstations have a PC or Mac, printer and a selection of useful software. Office services include word-processing, faxing, photocopying, transcription, office equipment rental and a reference library.

### World-Wide Business Centers
*575 Madison Avenue, between East 56th & East 57th Streets (605 0200). Subway 4, 5 or 6 to 59th Street; N or R to Lexington Avenue.* **Open** 9am-5.30pm Mon-Fri. **Credit** AmEx, MC, V.
The company provides furnished, staffed offices, from half a day to long term, equipped with fax, computers and phones. Fax and secretarial services are available without rental of office space.

## Photocopying

### Servco
*130 Cedar Street, opposite 2 World Trade Center (285 9245). Subway 1, 9, N or R to Cortlandt Street.* **Open** 8.30am-5.30pm daily. **No credit cards**.
Photocopying, offset printing, blueprints and binding services are available.
**Branch**: 56 West 45th Street (575 0991).

### Kinko's Copy Center
*24 East 12th Street, between Fifth Avenue & University Place (924 0802). Subway 4, 5, 6, L, N or R to Union Square.* **Open** 24 hours daily. **Credit** AmEx, Disc, MC, V.
Copying, faxing and passport photos, plus on-site use of Apple Macs ($12 per hour, $24 for big graphics machines, charged by the minute). Phone for your nearest branch.

## Postal Service

### US General Post Office
*380 West 33rd Street, at Eighth Avenue (330 4000/ Postal Information Line 967 8585). Subway A, C or E to Penn Station.* **Open** 24 hours daily, for all services except money orders, registered mail and passports (8am-7pm daily).
This is the city's main post office. Call to find out your nearest branch office, or dial the information line to hear a vast menu of recorded postal information.

## Printing

### Dependable Printing
*Flatiron Building, 175 Fifth Avenue (533 7560). Subway N or R to 23rd Street.* **Open** 8.30am-6pm Mon-Fri; 10am-4pm Sat. **Credit** MC, V.
Offset and colour printing, large-size Xerox copies, colour laser printing, binding, rubber stamps, typing, forms, labels, brochures, flyers, newsletters, manuscripts, fax service, transparencies and more.
**Branch**: 257 Park Avenue South (982 0353).

### Directional Printing Services
*280 Madison Avenue, between 39th & 40th Streets (213 6700). Subway 4, 5 or 6 to 42nd Street.* **Open** 9.30am-5.30pm Mon-Fri. **No credit cards**.
Specialises in assisting international firms and offers foreign-language typesetting and printing, as well as graphic design, brochures and reports, and more.

## Telegrams

### Western Union
*(1-800 325 6000).* **Open** 24 hours daily. **Credit** MC, V.
Use the number to arrange telegrams at any time of day or night; the service is charged to your credit card. If you want

# Follow the money

Numismatics you probably knew about, but scripophily? The collection and study of financial documents (stock and bond certificates) could be a curiously anal affair, you might think. And it is, it is. The nineteenth-century issues particularly, Standard Oil and the other industrial giants, are rich in painful, self-important detail. But a visit to the Museum of American Financial History places these ornate pieces of paper in context and illuminates a great deal about the making of America.

The museum's permanent collection focuses on the paraphernalia of corporate transactions: old mechanical price boards, ticker tape machines and paper certificates that electronic trading has nearly made extinct. Special exhibits link these objects to specific topics in the 'history of America's capital markets'.

A show devoted to the growth of American railroads evokes a panorama of social history. It ranges from sketches of the private cars and palatial houses of the robber barons of the day, to photos of green Italian immigrants digging the first tunnels of the New York subway. A glass case of dining car china decorated with company insignia is startlingly elegant. Great lithographs of sprawling industrial complexes – then new – that once graced the walls of corporate offices, summon up the smug optimism of big money in the Brown Decades. The sheer

profusion of railroad issues in pre-Civil War days speaks volumes about the energy of the age. The documentation of fraud and scandal do, too. The artefacts bring to life just where the money went.

Other shows have dealt with the history of the American Banknote Company, long one of the world's premier printers of currency, and with the financing of the American Civil War, when American finance began to come of age. A forthcoming show on mutual funds should have a great deal of contemporary resonance. However you feel about capitalism, the museum makes a thought-provoking stop on your Wall Street tour. Marx would have loved it.

**Museum of American Financial History**
*26 Broadway, Room 200 (908 4519).* **Open** 11.30am-2.30pm Mon-Fri, or by appointment.

---

to write the message in person, or don't have a credit card, go to one of the branches (phone the number above to find your nearest). Western Union can also organise international money transfers.

## Telephone Answering Service

### Messages Plus
*1317 Third Avenue, between 75th & 76th Streets (879 4144). Subway 6 to 77th Street.* **Open** 24 hours daily. **Credit** AmEx, MC, V.
Messages Plus provides telephone answering services, with specialised (for example medical, bilingual) receptionists if required, and plenty of ways of delivering your messages. It will also provide credit card order-taking services with the option of a number, call-forwarding, database generation and pager rental. Faxes and telexes can be sent and delivered.

## Translation

### All Language Services
*545 Fifth Avenue, at 45th Street (986 1688/fax 986 3396). Subway 4, 5, 6, or 7 to Grand Central.* **Open** 24 hours daily. **Credit** MC, V.
Will type or translate documents in any of 59 languages and provide interpreters.

## Writers

### Dial-A-Writer
*Suite 302. 1501 Broadway, between 43rd & 44th Streets, (24-hour answering service 398 1934).* **No credit cards**.
A referral service for professional writers, researchers, editors and publicists. Phone, leave a message and a representative will get back to you.

## Trade Conventions

For further information get in touch with the **New York Convention & Visitors Bureau** (397 8222). New York's two principal convention centres are:

### Jacob K Javits Convention Center
*655 West 34th Street, at Eleventh Avenue (216 2000). Subway 1, 2, 3, 9, A, C or E to Penn Station, then take the M34 crosstown bus to the Center.*

### New York Passenger Ship Terminal
*711 Twelfth Avenue, near 55th Street (246 5451). Subway C or E to 50th Street.*

# Students

*Tips for living, working and studying in the Big Apple.*

New York would miss them if they weren't here, but students don't figure very largely in the life of the city. There is little of the student-only entertainment culture familiar on European campuses. One reason is that American scholars tend to be too busy working to pay for their education to have much fun – in addition to their studies, most are compelled to hold down jobs to support themselves. But a better explanation is simply that there is such a vast range of accessible entertainment possibilities throughout the city that there is no need for students here to segregate themselves.

The *Time Out New York Student Guide* is an essential source of information, covering details of where to get work or entertain the folks, what to do if you get arrested, locked out or robbed, as well as where to shop, eat, drink and generally paint the town red. Published annually in the autumn, it's available free from colleges and some stores.

There are few more exciting places to study than New York, and its colleges and universities attract people from all over the world. Most vocational courses here have strong links with the city's businesses and are consequently well-equipped to launch graduates into employment. Interning (working for free) at a major company is an essential part of many students' time in the city.

The admissions offices of most US educational institutions accept applications directly from international students and can also supply details about visas, fees, student housing (on- or off-campus) and other information. The **Institute of International Education (IIE)** has an information centre and holds a directory of US educational institutions and course catalogues, as well as information on financial aid. It's at 809 United Nations Plaza, New York, NY 10017 (883 8200). UK students can contact the Educational Advisory service of the **Fulbright Commission**, 62 Doughty Street, WC1N 2LS (0171 404 6994) or the US International Commission Agency at any US embassy for information on study in the US. The **Council on International Educational Exchange** (CIEE), 52 Poland Street, London W1V 4JQ (0171 478 2000) can arrange places and visas for summer courses at a clutch of Stateside colleges and smooth the bureaucracy for sandwich-course students looking for internships.

## Immigration

On entering the US as a student, you will need to show a passport, a special visa (*see below*) and proof of your plans to leave (a return airline ticket). Even if you have a student visa, you may be asked to show means of support during your stay (cash, credit cards, travellers' cheques, etc).

If you must bring prescription drugs to the US, make sure the container is clearly marked and that you bring your doctor's statement or a prescription. Of course, marijuana, cocaine and most opiate derivatives and other chemicals are not permitted and possession of them is punishable by stiff fines and/or imprisonment (*see chapter* **Survival** for more on this). Check with the **US Customs Service** before you arrive if you have any questions about what you can bring to the US. Customs allows you 200 cigarettes, $100 worth of gifts and all your personal belongings duty free. If you carry more than $10,000 worth of currency, you will have to fill out a report. If you lose, or need to renew your passport once in the US, contact your country's embassy (*listed in chapter* **Survival**).

## Visas

Non-nationals who want to study in New York (or anywhere else in the US) must obtain an I-20 Certificate of Eligibility from the school or university with which they have enrolled for study, before they can apply for a visa. If you are enrolling in an authorised exchange visitor programme – including a summer course or programme such as BUNAC (*see below* **Work**), wait until you have been accepted on the course or programme before worrying about immigration. You will be guided through the process by an official from the school in question.

You are admitted as a student for the length of your course, plus a limited period of any associated (and approved) practical training, plus a 60-day grace period. After this you must leave the country or apply to change or extend your immigration status. Requests to extend a visa must be submitted 15 to 60 days before the initial departure date. The rules are strict and you risk deportation if you break them.

Information on these, and all other immigration matters, is available from the **US Immigration and Naturalisation Service** (INS). Its New

York office is in the Jacob Javits Federal Building, 26 Federal Plaza, New York, NY 10278. The 'Ask Immigration' hotline (206 6500) is a vast menu of recorded information in English and Spanish. It is available 24 hours daily and is clear and helpful. Advisors are available on 1-800 375 5283 from 8am to 5.30pm Mon-Fri. If you already know what forms you need, you can order them by calling 870 3676. You can visit INS between 7.30am and 3.30pm Mon-Fri.

In the UK, the **US Embassy Visa Information Line** (0891 200 290) provides more information on obtaining student visas. Alternatively, you can write to the Visa Branch of the Embassy of the United States of America, 5 Upper Grosvenor Street, London W1A 2JB.

## Work

When you apply for your student visa, you will be expected to prove your ability to support yourself financially (including the payment of school fees), without working, for at least the first nine months of your course. After the first nine months, you may be eligible to work part-time, though you must have specific permission to do so.

If you are a British student wanting to spend a summer vacation working in the States, contact **BUNAC** at 16 Bowling Green Lane, London EC1R 0BD (0171 251 3472), which can help arrange a temporary job and the requisite visa.

## Student Identification

Foreign students should get themselves an **International Student Identity Card** (ISIC) as proof of student status and to secure discounts. These can be bought from your local student travel agent (ask at your students' union). If you buy the card in New York, you will also get basic accident insurance – a bargain. The New York branch of the Council on International Educational Exchange can supply one on the spot. It's at 205 East 42nd Street, New York, NY 10017 (661 1414) and is open from 9am-5pm Mon-Fri.

Note that a student identity card may not always be accepted as proof of age for drinking (you must be 21).

## Accommodation

Medium- to long-term accommodation is expensive and hard to find in Manhattan. However, if you're studying as part of a US college or university programme, the institution will help you out. The larger colleges have many residential properties and usually provide very nice hall of residence-type accommodation for foreign students (they often lump together the non-Americans in an

'International House'). If somewhere like this is unavailable, or if you'd prefer to share an apartment, many institutions also run a flat- or room-mate-finder operation.

If you'd like to live with a US family for an extended period, the IIE (*see page 293*) publishes the Homestay Information Sheet, listing homestay programmes in which you live with an American host, and so get a realistic exposure to US culture. Phone or write to them for details.

Several of the hostels listed in *chapter* **Accommodation** offer special rates for long-term residents. They include:

### YMHA (de Hirsch Residence at the 92nd St Y)

*1395 Lexington Avenue, NY 10128, at 92nd Street (415 5650/1-800 858 4692/fax 415 5578). Subway 6 to 96th Street.* **Rates** *for stays less than two months* $49 nightly, $343 per week, single occupancy; $35 nightly, $245 per week, double occupancy; *for stays greater than two months* $550 per person per month double occupancy, or $685 per month in private rooms. **Credit** AmEx, MC, V. Although this is nominally a Hebrew organisation, people of all (or no) religion can stay. It's close to many of New York's finest museums, as well as Central Park's jogging track. For long stays you must submit an application and go through a screening process to gain admittance. Applicants will have to attend an interview, although special procedures can be arranged for foreign students. A special emphasis is placed on your interest in learning from a 'group living situation'. Indeed, there are no private baths.
**Hotel services** *Air-conditioning (extra charge). Disabled: rooms. Fitness centre with pool, steam room & sauna. Laundry. Library. Multi-lingual staff. TV lounge.*
**Room services** *Refrigerator on request.*

## Travel

Most agents do discount fares for under-26s; UK specialists in student deals include Council Travel, 28A Poland Street, London W1V 3DB (0171 287 3337) and 205 East 42nd Street, NY 10017 (822 2700), and STA Travel, based in the UK but with more than 100 offices worldwide. In London, contact them at 86 Old Brompton Road, London SW7 3LQ (0171 937 9971); in the US, call 1-800 777 0122 for your nearest office.

## Medical Care

If you're enrolled in a course of study with a US college or university, you are usually eligible for treatment at the campus clinic. It may still be advisable to obtain medical insurance: ask your college authorities for advice.

If you need dental treatment, the NYU Dental Center, 345 East 24th Street, at First Avenue (998 9800) gives 25 per cent student discounts on top of its already low fees (about half of commercial rates). Your treatment will be by an about-to-graduate student, under supervision.

For further healthcare information *see chapter* **Survival**.

# Trips Out of Town

# Trips Out of Town

*Exit Manhattan, find the USA: there are beaches, mountains, and cities full of real Americans.*

The residents of New York City only live here so they can earn enough money to leave town as often as possible. The astonishing weekend congestion at all points of exit is testimony to New Yorkers' overwhelming desire to escape. They do so to engage in those activities for which the concrete pressure cooker of Manhattan is not suitable: to connect with nature, open spaces and normal people.

## GENERAL INFORMATION

Some of the larger magazine stores carry a number of the periodicals specific to resort towns (there are lots of these, especially for the more affluent vacation communities). The *New York Times* is always worth consulting for articles on nearby attractions, and its Sunday travel section is crammed with getaway suggestions and advertising for resorts and guest-houses. Watch out, too, for late specials on flights to nearby cities, which are usually advertised in the midweek editions.

## GETTING THERE

For all of the places listed below, we've included information on how to get there from New York. *See chapter* **Getting Around** for a list of suggested car hire companies. New York rates are exorbitant and you can save up to 50 per cent by renting a car from somewhere outside the city – even if it's from the same firm. Hoboken or Jersey City in New Jersey, or Greenwich in Connecticut are good bets for this, but you should book as far in advance as you can to get the best price.

Metro-North (532 4900) and the Long Island Rail Road, or LIRR (1-718 217 5477), are the two main commuter rail systems. Both offer themed tours in the summer. Amtrak (582 6875/1-800 USA RAIL) is the national rail service for inter-city travel. Call the Port Authority Bus Terminal (564 8484) for information on all bus transport from the city. For airport information, *see chapter* **Getting Around**.

## Beach Life

You can get sand between your toes for a minimum outlay ($1.25) by visiting the three beach areas accessible on the subway. These are **Coney Island** (*see chapter* **New York by Neighbourhood: The Outer Boroughs**), **Rockaway Beach** (subway A, C, or H to Rockaway Park Beach) and **Orchard Beach**, a little slice of Puerto Rico in the Bronx (subway 6 to Pelham Bay Park). These are usually noisy and crowded and often dirty (Pelham Park is the current favourite place for dumping murder victims), but for a slightly larger investment you can find yourself on some very pleasant stretches of ocean front.

## Long Island

Escaping to the small towns and vast beaches that comprise Long Island, the appendage that lies to the east of Manhattan Island, is relatively quick and easy. The beaches improve the further you travel from Manhattan and some, like those in the Hamptons, are among the most unspoilt in the USA. You can reach sea and sand by hopping on a train on the Long Island Rail Road (LIRR), which leaves from Penn Station. In the summer, there are shuttle buses from the train stations to various beaches.

If you want an easy beach experience, take the LIRR to **Long Beach**. The Atlantic, which is warm enough to swim in from July to September, is a few short blocks away from the station. The beach can be absolutely packed in the summer.

Next is **Jones Beach**, where some of New York's biggest summer concerts are staged.

**Robert Moses Beach** is the farthest of the three, but is to be recommended for its white sand and the boardwalks which wind through the shrubs of the endless dunes.

In the summer season between Memorial Day (late May) and Labor Day (early September), harried New Yorkers scramble over each other to get out to their beachside rental homes in the Hamptons (West, East and South), Fire Island (*see chapter* **Gay & Lesbian New York**), Sag Harbor, Bridgehampton, Shelter Island and Montauk.

The **Hamptons** are the perfect backdrop for the socialites, artists and celebrities who drift from benefit bash to benefit bash throughout the summer season. Their homes, wonderful as some are, can't help but be upstaged by the spectacular beaches.

**Montauk Point** is Long Island's furthest tip – remote and not too crowded, and is probably the least commercialised and crowded spot in the Hamptons. It's too far for a day trip but is full of holiday cottages and motels. These can be fairly expensive at the height of the season, but pre- and post-season deals abound.

*New Jersey lifeguards ride the Atlantic surf.*

Try Fort Pond Lodge, Second-House Road, Montauk (1-516 668 2042), a quiet, old-style motel set on a lake, just minutes from the ocean (from $70 a night). Rent a bike and you're all set. Although Montauk is decidedly unpretentious, it attracts its share of celebrities, including Mick Jagger and Keith Richards.

### East Hampton Chamber of Commerce
*79A Main Street, East Hampton, NY 11937 (1-516 324 0362).*

### Montauk Chamber of Commerce
*Box 5024, Montauk, NY 11954 (1-516 668 2428).*

### Southampton Chamber of Commerce
*76 Main Street, Southampton, NY 11968 (1-516 283 0402).*

## Shelter Island

The fact that this tiny island can only be reached by ferry from Long Island, combined with its lack of commercialisation, keeps it free from crowds. There are a few gift shops and an ice-cream parlour but little else to distract you from sailing, cycling, fishing or just relaxing on the beach. About a third of its area, **Mashomack Preserve**, is unpopulated except for birds.

The first house was built here in 1652 and the island gained a reputation as a refuge for pirates (Captain Kidd is thought to have buried treasure here). Quakers who were driven out of Boston settled here; you can visit the **Quaker Cemetery** on the outer boundary of **Sylvester Manor**. Other historic destinations are the **Shelter Island Historical Society Museum, Manhasset Chapel Museum** and **Haven House**.

If you have time, take the four-minute ferry ride to **Sag Harbor**. The information centre on Main Street will tell you what you can do. Try to see the **Sag Harbor Whaling Museum** (1-516 725 0770).

There aren't many hotels on Shelter Island, but the following are worth a try. The Chequit Inn (Shelter Island Heights; 1-516 749 0018) costs $72-$195 a night. The Pridwin Hotel and Cottages at Crescent Beach (81 Shore Road, Shelter Island; 1-516 749 0476) is $66-$199 a night for rooms, $229 for a cottage, but is only open from April to January. The Ram's Head Inn (1-516 749 0811) is open all year round. It costs $110-$150 a night (including breakfast).

### Shelter Island Chamber of Commerce
*Box 598, Shelter Island, NY 11964 (1-516 749 0399).*

### Getting There
Sunrise Express Bus Service from New York City (departs from 44th Street, between Lexington & Third Avenues) to Greenport (1-516 477 1200; $29 return) or Long Island Rail Road from Penn Station to Greenport; then take the ferry (75¢).

## The Jersey Shore

A prime target for New Yorkers' scathing wit is New Jersey and everyone in it. So the Jersey shore will not be high on their list of recommended

destinations. But Jersey's hundred miles of Atlantic seafront includes some splendid beaches and places worth a visit for an insight into American ocean-side culture. In general, the places closest to New York are the least worth visiting. The best beaches are often private (definitely the case in **Long Beach** and **Ocean Beach**); the public ones are usually choked with noisy crowds from northern Jersey's industrial cities. If you're a Bruce Springsteen fan you might want to make the pilgrimage to **Asbury Park**, a remarkably unpleasant stretch of coastline.

At the opposite end of the shore, **Cape May** (*see below*), on the southernmost tip of New Jersey, is the country's oldest seaside resort and has a delicate nineteenth-century feel to it. Just north is **Wildwood**, home to a monstrous boardwalk – a wooden promenade filled with fairground rides, sideshows and food stalls. Coney Island pales into insignificance beside this enormous fun palace. Try some saltwater taffy, or maybe frozen custard, a pork roll or an elephant ear – all local delicacies. Ride on the roller-coasters or the huge Ferris wheel, have an old-time photo taken, or just stroll along the boardwalk, watching real-life Americans at play. The beaches here are suitably enormous.

The beaches north of Wildwood, at **Avalon, Sea Isle City** and **Strathmere** are very pleasant and less commercialised. The town centres still have their share of amusingly awful nightspots, however, where you can watch tribal masses of twentysomethings get ecstatic as cover bands play Billy Joel songs. The area just inland is a mass of tiny islands, bays and inlets. These connect the different beaches and provide the perfect setting for sailing, fishing, windsurfing and jet-skiing.

**Atlantic City** has little in the way of attractive coastline. What draws people here is gambling – and lots of it (*see page 304* **The Bright Lights**). Further up the coast, however, are some beautiful spots, such as **Island Beach**, which is a National Park. The comparatively limited access here means unspoilt beaches, and the natural scenery is quite beautiful.

### New Jersey Department of Parks
*501 East State Street, Trenton, New Jersey 08625 (1-609 292 2797).*

### New Jersey Division of Tourism
*CN 826, Trenton, New Jersey 08625 (1-609 292 2470/ 1-800 537 7397).*

## Cape May

Cape May in southern New Jersey, 160 miles out of New York City, is the nation's oldest seaside

*The Vanderbilt's modest place in the country overlooks the Hudson River.*

resort. Its 600 Victorian 'gingerbread' homes make the entire town a national landmark. The best time to go is early September, when the crowds have thinned but the water is still warm enough to swim in. Rent a bike and visit **Cape May Point**, where the Atlantic meets **Delaware Bay** and visitors sift through the sand for pieces of polished quartz known as Cape May diamonds. **Cape May Point State Park** has a lovely bird sanctuary and one of the country's oldest lighthouses, built in 1744.

Cape May was the prime vacation spot until a fire ravaged the town in 1878. US presidents and colonial luminaries were among those who came here for relaxation. Later visitors included the young Wallis Warfield, better known as the Duchess of Windsor, who came to the Columbia Hotel in 1917 to plan her coming-out party.

The **Physick Estate**, at 1048 Washington Street (1-609 884 5904), is a Victorian mansion built in 1859 which now operates as a museum of Victorian life.

If you want to stay, note that in the summer and during October's Victorian Week most hotels have a two- to four-night minimum stay. The Chalfonte Hotel at 301 Howard Street (1-609 884 8409) includes breakfast and dinner in its $69-$169 room rate.

### Greater Cape May Chamber of Commerce
*PO Box 556, Cape May, NJ 08204 (1-609 884 5508).*

### Mid-Atlantic Center for the Arts
*PO Box 340, Cape May, NJ 08204 (1-609 884 5404).*

### Getting There
New Jersey Transit bus from Port Authority Terminal. By car, take the Garden State Parkway (from the Lincoln or Holland tunnel) south to the last exit.

## Mountain Ranges

Nearly half the population of New York State is crammed into the five boroughs of New York City. This leaves the other 47,000 square miles (122,000sq m) relatively unpopulated. Hikers and skiers will be pleased to hear that this area includes some of the most dramatic mountain scenery in the United States.

## Bear Mountain

For a fine day-trip alternative to the beaches, Manhattan's closest wilderness is to be found at **Bear Mountain State Park**, Palisades Parkway and Route 9W (1-914 786 2701). It's only an hour by bus (Short Line Buses 736 4700; $19.20 round-trip from Port Authority Terminal).

The bus will drop you at an appalling visitors' centre with really gross fast food and hundreds of unadventurous families picnicking in the car park, but a ten-minute walk along one of the many trails will put you right out there away from it all.

**Lake Champlain** – *the largest in Adirondack Park.*

If you have a car, head off to the area around **Cranberry Lake**, where there's a campsite and a trail lodge and things are organised less for the day-tripping hordes and more for the serious hiker.

## The Catskills

The Catskills mountain range, an offshoot of the **Appalachian Mountains**, just 90 miles from the city, is New York's nearest major forest and park area. The landscape is magnificent. There are hiking and cycling trails, trout-filled streams, whitewater rapids for canoeing, golf courses, tennis courts, campsites, ski resorts and lakes.

As well as the Catskills' natural beauty, there are other attractions. You can explore mountain caverns at **Ice Caves Mountain** in Ellenville (1-914 647 7989) and go on organised canoe trips on the Delaware and other rivers running through the park. **East Durham** is home to the **Zoom Flume Water Park** (1-518 239 4559; open June-Labor Day), although this is something of a tourist trap.

A taste of local history can be found at the **Hurley Patentee Manor** (1-914 331 5414; open June-Labor Day) in Hurley, the **Tulthilltown Grist Mill** (1-914 255 5695) in Gardiner and **Fort Delaware Museum of Colonial History** (1-914 252 6660; closed in winter) in Narrowsburg.

**Kingston**, the largest town in the Catskills, is home to the **Hudson River Maritime Museum** (1-914 338 0071) and a well-stocked **Trolley Museum** (1-914 331 3399; closed in winter). The

**Rhinebeck Aerodrome** (1-914 758 8610), in Rhinebeck, has vintage World War I aeroplane displays.

There are several ski resorts in the Catskills. The most famous of these is **Hunter Mountain**, where the 46 trails are usually packed with New Yorkers during the season. The snow at **Ski Windham**, another large mountain resort, is 100 per cent machine-made (as at most of the mountains in the area) and the facilities are similar to those at Hunter. *See page 303* **Skiing & Snowboarding** for more information.

The Catskills have a good range of accommodation. The Mohonk Mountain House Hotel (1-914 255 1000/1-800 772 6646) is a lavish castle on a secluded lake where rooms cost $280-$505 a night (full board for two people). A more economical option is Jingle Bells Farms (1-914 255 6588), an intimate bed and breakfast costing $100 a night.

There are some great wineries in the area, including **Benmarl Winery** (1-914 236 4265) and **Brotherhood Winery** (1-914 496 9101).

The only thing you can't escape in this wilderness is New Yorkers: from Friday night to Sunday evening the Catskills is packed with them. At the weekends, the road between the Catskills and New York City is backed up for miles. If you possibly can, plan your trip to avoid the traffic jams.

### Delaware County Chamber of Commerce

*97 Main Street, Delhi, NY 13753 (1-607 746 2281/ 1-800 642 4443).*

**Greene County Promotion Department**
*Box 527, Catskill, NY 12414 (1-518 943 3223).*

**National Park Service, Upper Delaware National Scenic & Recreational River**
*PO Box C, Narrowsburg, NY 12764 (1-914 252 3947).*

**Sullivan County Office of Public Information**
*(1-914 794 3000).*

**Ulster County Public Information Office**
*County Office Building, Box 1800, Kingston, NY 12401 (1-914 331 9300/1-800 UCO).*

**Ulster County Chamber of Commerce**
*7 Albany Avenue, Suite 93, Kingston, NY 12401-2998 (1-914 338 5100).*

## The Adirondacks

The largest area of untouched beauty in the state is **Adirondack Park**, in the north-east. At least 40 per cent of the park is officially classified as a wilderness – the largest in the US outside Alaska. Route 87 runs north through the eastern side of the park and is the best road from the city (the journey takes about four hours). The park is suitable for all the usual outdoor activities, and, despite some nine million visitors each year, remains relatively unspoilt.

**Lake George** is a long, thin lake, dotted with tiny islands and surrounded by mountains, which runs along the south-eastern side of the park. **Glens Falls**, at the south end, is a booming tourist town. North of Lake George is **Lake Champlain**.

Straddling the Vermont/New York state border and continuing north beyond the Canadian border into Quebec, it is the largest lake in Adirondack Park and a popular vacation spot. **Port Kent** and **Plattsburgh** are the two major towns on Lake Champlain. For people who enjoy feeling terrified, **Ausable Chasm** (1-518 834 7454) is a narrow (20 feet/6m) gorge in Lake Champlain where you can ride the roaring rapids, *Deliverance*-style. This hair-raising excursion runs daily from mid-May until mid-October ($13.95 adults, $8.95 under-12s, free for the under-sixes).

**Saranac Lake** (1-518 891 1990/1-800 347 1992) and **Tupper Lake** (1-518 359 3328) are two gorgeous spots, with a full complement of hotels, campsites and other outdoor facilities. Robert Louis Stevenson rented a house on Saranac Lake; he called the area 'Little Switzerland' and wrote *The Master of Ballantrae* there.

The three highest mountains in the park are Whiteface, Marcy and Jo. Marcy, at 5,344 feet (1,036m) above sea level, is the highest in New York State. Whiteface, replete with alpine glacier, has some of the most challenging ski slopes in the east, as well as gentler runs for the novice, and high-speed lifts. For more information, phone (1-518 946 2223).

The nearby town of **Lake Placid** was the scene of the 1932 and 1980 Winter Olympics. It has a long tradition of hospitality towards visitors and some very European architecture, with small chalet-style shops, bars, clubs, restaurants and hotels. In the summer months, golfing, boating,

*For deep-sea fishing trips, see page 303.*

fishing, camping and hiking are all available. Phone (1-800 462 6236) for more information.

Other big ski resorts in the Adirondacks include **Gore Mountain** (1-518 251 2411/1-800 342 1234) and **Big Tupper** (1-518 359 3651). These raw and beautiful peaks can be dangerous. Winds can get up to 60 miles an hour (96k/h) and the temperature down to −60°F (−15°C).

Besides nature, there are other things that draw people to the Adirondacks. The **Hyde Collection** (1-518 792 1761) in Glens Falls, the **Adirondack Museum** (1-518 352 7311) at Blue Lake Mountain and North River's **Barton Mines Corporation** (1-518 251 2296), the largest garnet mine in the world, are just a few of the cultural nuggets in this massive wilderness.

### Central Adirondack Association & Tourist Information Center

*Old Forge, NY 13420 (1-315 369 6983).*

### Lake Placid Chamber of Commerce & Visitor Center

*216 Main Street, Lake Placid, NY 12946 (1-518 523 2445).*

## Outdoor Pursuits

If you're windswept and outdoorsy you needn't leave your adventuresome pastime behind just because you're in New York. There are few activities which aren't possible in the region. Here are just some that are. For more, see *chapter* **Sport & Fitness**.

## Boating

Boating, canoeing and white-water rafting are popular sports in the many rivers, waterways, lakes, sounds, bays and ocean within reach of New York. The network of canals instrumental in the industrialisation of America, though still used commercially, is a prime leisure resource, with access free to everyone. The Erie Barge Canal links east with west by joining the Atlantic Ocean and Hudson River to the St Lawrence River and the Great Lakes. The Champlain Canal connects the 110-mile (176 kilometre) Lake Champlain with the Hudson River.

### Batenkill Sports Quarters

*Route 313, Box 143, Cambridge, NY 12816 (1-518 677 8868).*
This company offers canoe, kayak and tubing trips.

### McDonnell's Adirondack Challenges

*Box 855, Saranac Lake, NY 12983 (1-518 891 1176).*
McDonnell's arranges canoeing and kayaking, as well as hiking, fishing and camping for individuals and groups.

### Middle Earth Expeditions

*HCRO1 Box 37, Lake Placid, NY 12946 (1-518 523 9572).*
Outdoor pursuits for groups and individuals.

### NYS Passenger Vessel Association

*PO Box 95, Rifton, NY 12471 (1-800 852 0095).*
Offers information on the many boating operators throughout New York State.

### Port Jervis Tri-State Chamber of Commerce

*10 Sussex Street, PO Box 121, Port Jervis, NY 12771 (1-914 856 6694).*
Information on several operators that offer trips down the Delaware River, including white-water rafting.

### Rivett's Marine

*PO Box 601, Lake Trail, Old Forge Lake, Old Forge, NY 13420 (1-315 369 3123).*
Boat rental, sale and service.

### Wild & Scenic River Tours

*166 Route 97, Burryville, NY 12719 (1-914 557 8783/ 1-800 836 0366).*
Canoeing, kayaking and white-water rafting.

## Camping

There are 500 public and privately owned campsites (or 'campgrounds', as they are called) throughout New York State. Some are deep in the wilderness and only accessible by boat; others are relatively close to a town or city. Reservations are recommended, but not always necessary. For more information, contact:

### New York State Office of Parks, Recreation & Historic Preservation

*Empire State Plaza, Albany, NY 12238 (1-518 474 0458).*
Information on all parks and park activities within the state.

### New York State Campgrounds

*(1-800 456 CAMP).*
Call to make campsite reservations.

## Climbing

The **Shawangunks**, or 'Gunks', in the Catskills offer some of the best climbing in the country, with sheer limestone cliffs over 300 feet (95m) high. You need to buy a day pass ($5) from the Mohonk Preserve, 1000 Mountain Rest Road, Mohonk Lake, Newpaltz (1-914 255 0919). The local equipment store, Rock and Snow, at 44 Main Street, Newpaltz (1-914 255 1311) will be happy to give advice.

### Tents & Trails

*21 Park Place, between Church Street & Broadway (227 1760). Subway A or C to Chambers Street.* **Open** 9.30am-6pm Mon-Wed, Sat; 9.30am-7pm Thur, Fri; noon-6pm Sun. **Credit** AmEx, MC, V.
Apart from the supermarket-style chain Eastern Mountain Sports, this is the only specialist climbing equipment store in Manhattan. Full of colourful ropes and friendly advice.

## Cycling

A choice of landscapes in the area surrounding New York City means there's something for all cyclists, from recreational to racing, and from touring to mountain biking. Drop into one of New York's bike stores and look out for cycling mags.

For information on cycling in a particular area, contact the local Chamber of Commerce.

For more information, contact the New York State Office of Parks, Recreation & Historic Preservation (*see above* **Camping**), or the League of American Bicyclists (Suite 120, 190 West Ostend Street, Baltimore, Maryland 21230; 1-410 539 3399).

## Fishing

With a licence, you can fish in New York State's 70,000 miles (112,000 kilometres) of streams and rivers and 4,000 lakes and ponds. The first day of the fishing season (check the dates with the DEC, *below*) is a big day in the New York social/sporting calendar. Check the newspapers the day before for stock reports.

The favourite fishing spots in New York State are Lakes Erie and Ontario (two of the Great Lakes), Chitauqua Lake, the St Lawrence River, the Finger Lakes, Oneida Lake, Lake Champlain and Lake George and the Delaware, Hudson and Allegheny rivers. Burr Pond and Kent Fall State Parks, both in Connecticut, are also favoured spots for freshwater fishing, as are Caleb Smith and Connetqout River State Parks, both of which are in Long Island.

There are plenty of coastal areas where sea fishing is permitted. The resorts on Long Island and the Jersey shore have companies which charter boats and equipment. These operators can usually also take care of licensing requirements (sea-fishing requires a different licence from inland).

For freshwater fishing you must get a fishing licence ($14 resident; $35 non-resident, for the season, 3- and 5-day passes available) if you are aged between 16 and 69. People over 65 get a discount. Licences can be purchased at most fishing tackle stores. For information on licences for New York call 1-518 457 3521; for New Jersey, 1-609 292 2965; for Connecticut, 1-860 424 3105. To get a licence by post, or for other fishing information, contact the DEC (*see below*).

### Capitol Fishing
*218 West 23rd Street, between Seventh & Eighth Avenues (929 6132). Subway 1 or 9 to 23rd Street.*
**Open** 9am-6pm Mon-Wed, Fri; 9am-7pm Thur; 9am-5pm Sat. **Credit** AmEx, Disc, MC, V.
Both saltwater and freshwater equipment is sold here. It's also possible to hire equipment, depending on what you need.

### Department of Environmental Conservation (DEC)
*50 Wolf Road, Albany, NY 12233 (1-518 474 2121/ 1-518 457 3521).*

### Urban Angler
*118 East 25th Street, 3rd Floor, between Lexington & Park Avenues (979 7600). Subway 6 to 28th Street.*
**Open** 10am-6pm Mon, Tue, Thur, Fri; 10am-7pm Wed; 10am-5pm Sat. **Credit** AmEx, MC, V.
This is the best fly-fishing store in New York. For licences,

equipment and friendly information on the best places to fish in the region, both surf casting (saltwater) and freshwater – this is the place to come.

## Hiking

Some of the most spectacular and challenging trails in the country can be found in New York State. The most famous, and popular, of these is the **Appalachian Trail**. Stretching from Maine to Georgia, this 2,100 mile (3,360 kilometre) trek is tackled by four million hikers annually. For more information about hiking in the region, contact:

### Adirondack Mountain Club
*814 Goggins Road, Lake George, NY 12845 (1-518 668 4447/fax 1-518 668 3746).*

### Appalachian Mountain Club
*New York-North Jersey Chapter, 5 Tudor City Place, East 41st Street, New York, NY 10016 (986 1430).* **Open** 8.30am-5.30pm Wed-Fri.

### Finger Lakes Trail Conference
*PO Box 18048, Rochester, NY 14618-0048 (1-716 288 7191).*

### Long Island Greenbelt Trail Conference
*23 Deer Path Road, Center Islip, New York 11722 (1-516 360 0753).*

## Horse Riding

New York has some splendid countryside for horse riding, with miles of horse-trails and special facilities for riders and horses as well as parks, campsites and riding stables where you can hire horses. For information on these, contact the local Chamber of Commerce. Check whether or not you will be covered by the stable's insurance; some only insure experienced riders and only if they go no faster than a walk.

Forty-one of New York State's counties have county fairs, almost all with equestrian events. They are usually held during the summer. For information on these, contact the NYS Department of Agriculture and Markets, Winners Circle, Capital Plaza, Albany, NY 12235 (1-518 457 0127).

The following address is useful for all equestrian enquiries:

### American Horse Show Association in NYS
*Suite 409, 220 East 42nd Street, NY 10017 (972 2472).*

## Skiing & Snowboarding

For information on the excellent skiing in the area, search out some of the specialist ski magazines and consult the Sunday travel supplement of the ubiquitous *New York Times*. As well as the **Catskills** and **Adirondacks**, there are challenging ski resorts nearby in the **Berkshires**, 110 miles (177km) from New York City on the Massachusetts border.

Some of the larger sports stores arrange all-inclusive day-trips by bus during the season, usually to Hunter Mountain, for both skiing and snowboarding, including equipment rentals and tuition if necessary. Day trips cost around $60. Some of the best-organised are run by Blades, Paragon and Scandinavian.

### Blades
*659 Broadway, at Bleecker Street (477 7350). Subway 4, 5, 6, B, D, F or Q to Broadway/Lafayette.* **Open** 11am-9pm Mon-Fri; noon-9pm Sat; 11am-7pm Sun. **Credit** AmEx, MC, V.
The emphasis is on snowboarding, and the Blades trips usually consist of noisy bus loads of young board-rats, with lots of sponsorship freebies (stickers, CDs, sports drinks) given away.

### New York Ski Club
*AYH, 891 Amsterdam Avenue, at 103rd Street (932 2300).*
Trips and advice for anyone skiing on a budget.

### Paragon Sports
*867 Broadway, at 18th Street (255 8036). Subway 4, 5, 6, L, N, R to Union Square.* **Open** 10am-8pm Mon-Sat; 11am-6.30pm Sun. **Credit** AmEx, Disc, MC, V.
Paragon's trips are slightly more adult than Blades, with a more even blend of skiers and boarders.

### Scandinavian
*40 West 57th Street, between Fifth & Sixth Avenues (757 8524). Subway B or Q to 57th Street.* **Open** 10am-7pm Tue, Wed, Fri; 10am-6.30pm Thur; 10am-6pm Sat; 11am-5pm Sun. **Credit** AmEx, MC, V.
A ski shop with a wide range of equipment, as well as information leaflets and a great deal of helpful advice. Though board rentals are available, the emphasis here is definitely on skiing.

### Snow Conditions & Information
**Adirondacks**: Whiteface (1-518 946 2223/1-800 462 6236); Lake Placid (1-800 462 6236); Gore Mountain (1-518 251 2411/1-800 342 1234); Big Tupper (1-518 359 7902). **Berkshires** Catamount (1-518 325 3200/1-413 528 1262). **Catskills** Hunter Mountain (1-518 263 4223/1-800 FOR SNOW). **Ski Windham** (1-518 734 4300/1-800 729 4SNO).

## Whale Watching

### Riverhead Foundation for Marine Research & Preservation
*431 East Main Street, Riverhead, NY (1-516 369 9840).* **Credit** Disc, MC, V.
Daily whale watching trips run between 1 May and Labor Day, after which there are weekend trips and seal and bald eagle cruises. Excursions last between four and seven hours.

## The Bright Lights
## Gambling

Because it is largely illegal in most states, gambling is as exciting to the average American as alcohol is to a 15 year-old. If you're not content with New York's various city and state lotteries, and the heavily-promoted Off Track Betting fails to turn you on, you'd better leave town. Las Vegas is a continent away but you can hop on a bus and be haemorrhaging money on the blackjack tables in **Atlantic City** or **Verona** within a couple of hours.

### Atlantic City
*New Jersey.* **Getting There** Greyhound bus from Port Authority Bus Terminal to various casinos; return bus picks you up at the Atlantic City Bus Terminal, two blocks from Boardwalk. **Fare** $23 return.
The trip to Atlantic City takes about two and a half hours. The town is famous for its faded glamour, its Mafia connections and its casinos. While many New Yorkers disparage the place, anyone who's never encountered organised, excessive gambling before will find it amazing. The most famous of its many casinos are **Trump Plaza**, **Caesar's Palace** and Donald Trump's latest, the **Taj Mahal**. Once you're inside one casino, you can get to the others by way of the **Boardwalk**, which runs along the edge of the Atlantic Ocean, or take the Pacific Avenue bus. Bring your own spending money, or just watch the crazed antics of the frenzied crowd. Besides bars, restaurants and gift shops, there are floor shows and, at some casinos, concerts (the Rolling Stones played the live telecast of the Steel Wheels tour at the arena attached to Trump Plaza). The annual Miss America Pageant is held in the **Atlantic City Convention Center** at 2314 Pacific Avenue. Shoppers should head for **Ocean One**, a vast shopping mall set right on the water. Phone the **Atlantic City Convention & Visitors Authority** (1-609 348 7130) for more information.

### Turning Stone Casino
*Verona, New York (1-315 361 7711).* **By car** Take Route 90 past Utica to exit 33 (about 300 miles). **Open** 24 hours daily. **Credit** AmEx, DC, MC, V.
The various Indian Nations, independent from state gambling laws, are free to make their own rules about games of chance. Since they can turn a huge profit, many fast growing gambling resorts are the result. Turning Stone, in beautiful countryside east of the Finger Lakes, was recently opened by the Oneida Indian Nation. In terms of the number of games tables, it's the largest casino in the world. There are 16 roulette wheels, 122 blackjack tables, 24 crapshoots (dice), 10 baccarat tables and eight big six (poker) tables. It was completed in September 1993, and little in the way of sleazy resort services have sprung up to help you fritter away your winnings. If you break the bank, head to Syracuse and book into the king size suite at the **Embassy** (1-800 EMBASSY) for $136 a night. If you lose everything, there's a **Super 8 Motel** (1-315 363 5168) in Oneida for $51 a night (summer) or $37.69 a night (winter).

## Theme Parks

### Action Park
*Vernon, New Jersey, on Route 94, 48 miles/72km from Manhattan (1-201 827 2000).* **Getting There** *by car* take Route 80 west, then Route 23 north, and Route 94 north; *by bus* NJ Transit (1-201 762 5100). **Open** *June 14-Sept 1* 10am-11pm daily. **Admission** $27 adult Mon-Fri; $28 Sat, Sun; $15 children under 4ft tall; group discounts. **Credit** AmEx, CB, DC, JCB, V.
Bungee jumping, go-kart racing, the terror of the Slingshot, which propels you 14 storeys into the air, and the world's largest water park are among the attractions here. The setting is beautiful – 200 acres of woods and hills – and there's a cablecar ride to the top of nearby Mount Hamburg. Don't forget your swimming gear because the best rides are definitely the wet ones. You can save plenty of cash (up to $9 per person) by redeeming vouchers offered in cross-promotions

**Sunnyside** – *Washington Irving's house near Sleepy Hollow. See page 308.*

with companies like Coca Cola, McDonald's, Burger King and Shoprite. Call up the park and ask where to find the latest discount vouchers.
*Disabled: toilets.*

### Playland
*Rye, New York (Amusement Park 1-914 967 5230/ ice-skating rinks 1-914 967 2040).* **Getting There** Metro-North from Grand Central to Rye, then connecting bus. **Open** *summer* noon-11pm Tue-Thur, Sun; noon-midnight Fri, Sat; phone for details of winter hours. **Admission** free. **Tickets** $17 for 36; $13 for 24 (rides 'cost' 3-5 tickets). **Credit** MC, V.
An old-fashioned amusement and theme park, set on the banks of the Long Island Sound. It is known for its new and historic amusement rides and attractions, including the Derby Racer and the Dragon Coaster, as well as the new Magic Carpet. There's a separate Kiddie Land for little children. There are also picnic grounds, a pool and, of course, the beautiful beach. A firework display is held on Wednesday and Friday nights during July and August. You may recognise Playland from a scene in the film *Big*.

### Six Flags Great Adventure & Safari Park
*Jackson, New Jersey, on Route 537, 50 miles (80km) from Manhattan (1-908 928 1821).* **Getting There** *by car* take exit 7A off the New Jersey turnpike or exit 98 off the Garden State Parkway to Interstate 195, exit 16; *by bus* NJ Transit (1-201 762 5100) from Port Authority Bus Terminal ($39 return, incl admission). **Open** *May-Sept* 10am-10pm daily; *Oct-April* 10am-8pm Sat, Sun.

**Admission** $35 adults; $25 children under 4ft tall; $18 senior citizens. **Credit** AmEx, Disc, MC, V.
'Bigger than Disneyland and a whole lot closer' is the slogan with which this theme park entices Manhattanites. There's a huge drive-through safari park, a massive collection of top-of-the-range rides and the obligatory fast food and junky souvenirs. Not to be missed is the Great American Scream Machine, the reputedly world's highest/fastest roller-coaster, and the Batman ride, a particularly scary roller-coaster which, instead of the normal carriages, has you hanging down from the track with your legs dangling in the breeze. As with Action Park, call to find out about promotional discounts.
*Disabled: toilets.*

## On the History Trail

If you're keen on history or just enjoy scenery, you'll get both with a trip up the **Hudson Valley**. Beautiful summer residences of famous New Yorkers line the river (*see below*). Most are open from March until the end of the year. You can get information from **Historic Hudson Valley**, 150 White Plains Road, Tarrytown, NY 10591 (1-914 631 8200/reservations 1-800 533 3779), which also offers boat trips from Manhattan or New Jersey up the Hudson to several of the historic houses.

*The formal gardens at **Old Westbury** in New York State.*

*A long way from New York City, but worth the trek:* **Niagara Falls**.

Another way to see them is by car. The Historic Hudson Valley office and any of the sites listed below can provide you with detailed driving instructions.

Metro-North, the commuter railway that leaves Manhattan's Grand Central Terminal, is a fast, easy and scenic way to get to towns near these sights, and themed tours are often available. Or you can take an Amtrak train from Penn Station. *See chapter* **Getting Around** *for more information.*

### Cold Spring

*New York.* **Getting There** Metro-North Hudson Line to Cold Spring. **Fare** $14.

Any time of the year, Cold Spring offers spectacular close-up views of the Hudson River. It's only 50 miles (80km) from Manhattan, but it seems like more. If you arrive by train, walk through the underpass to get to Main Street, where a number of narrow-frame houses with porches and shutters sit alongside the four-storey commercial buildings. The place is tiny but has plenty of shops. For nearly a century life centred around the **Cold Spring Foundry**, an ironworks which opened in 1817 making gun tubes and steam engines. Head down to the water where you'll find a gazebo, the town dock and a tiny beach. You'll get a great view of the lush, green **Hudson Highlands** across the way. The **Main Street Café** (129 Main) sells fresh-baked buns for breakfast, good sandwiches and own-made fruit pies. **Hudson House** (2 Main), a landmark 1832 inn, serves American food; **Dockside Harbor** (1 North Street), which is on a grassy point by the water, has a seafood menu and a play area for children. Cold Spring is very popular with New Yorkers in the autumn.

### Montgomery Place

*River Road, Annandale-on-the-Hudson, New York (1-914 758 5461).* **Getting There** Amtrak to Rhinecliff Station, then call the Blue Coach cab service when you arrive (1-914 876 2900). **Open** *April-Oct*

10am-5pm Mon, Wed-Sun; call for out-of-season hours. **Admission** $6 adults; $3 children over 6. **Credit** AmEx, V.

A fabulous mansion in lush grounds about 100 miles (160km) from Manhattan. It was built in 1804 for Janet Livingston Montgomery, the widow of a Revolutionary War patriot, and is set in 434 acres along the Hudson River. There are formal gardens, woodlands, views of the Catskill Mountains and a lawn where games are played and lemonade is served. Visitors can pick their own raspberries in July and peaches in August.

### Museum Village

*Monroe, New York (1-914 782 8247).* **Getting There** *by car* take the New York State Thruway (I-87) north to exit 16 at Harriman. Go four miles (6.4km) west along Route 17 to exit 129; *by bus* Shortline bus from Port Authority to Museum Village (fare and schedule information 1-800 631 8405). **Open** *first weekend in May-first weekend in Dec* 10am-5pm Wed-Fri; noon-5pm Sat, Sun. **Admission** $8 adults; $5-$6 concessions. **Credit** MC, V.

About 55 miles (89km) outside Manhattan lies a 17-acre replica of a nineteenth-century village, dedicated to the re-creation of the lives of American Civil War troops. There are about 25 exhibition buildings, all with authentic details, some of which are staffed by guides and craft workers dressed in period costume. On Labor Day, the last weekend in August, historical re-enactors march in and recreate life circa 1864 for the annual Civil War Weekend. They sleep in Union and Confederate 'dog' tents, cook on open fires, participate in mock battles and trot around on horseback. Women in hoop skirts mourn the 'dead' and a blacksmith hammers in his shop. Children can join drill sergeants or help make craft items.

### Old Westbury Gardens

*Old Westbury, NY 11568 (1-516 333 0048).* **Getting There** *by car* take the Long Island Expressway east to exit 39S, Glen Cove Road; follow service road east for 1.2

miles to Old Westbury Road; *by train* LIRR to Old Westbury; *by train* LIRR to Westbury, then cab.
**Open** *April-Dec* 10am-5pm Mon, Wed-Sun. **Admission** $6 gardens; $10 house & garden. **No credit cards.**
Carnegie loot was behind this eclectic pile created by the English designer George Crawley for the Phipps family in 1904. The house is built in Restoration style, and has pieces by Chippendale and Reynolds, among others, inside. The wonderful grounds are huge and contain examples of just about everything from formal alleys to Japanese gardens and sweeping parkland.
*Disabled: toilets.*

### Phillipsburg Manor

*Upper Hills, Tarrytown, NY (1-914 631 3992).*
**Getting There** *by car* north on New York State Thruway (I-87), take exit 9 for Tarrytown and the sign is 2 miles (3km) on the left; *by train* Metro-North to Tarrytown, then 5-mile (8km) cab journey.
**Admission** $8 adults; $4-$7 concessions.
**Open** *Mar-Dec* 10am-5pm Mon, Wed-Sun.
**Credit** AmEx, MC, V.
The manor was once the home of Frederick Flypse (later called Flypsen, then Philipse), who came to the New World in the early 1650s as Governor Peter Stuyvesant's carpenter. Through business acumen and some shrewd marriages, Frederick managed to elevate his landholding of about 52,500 acres to the status of 'Lordship or Mannour of Philpsborough'. At the Upper Mills, which was just a small portion of his holding, Frederick constructed a dam, grist mill and manor house, with a Dutch church adjacent to the property. A lively film explains the manor's history up to the 1940s, when John D Rockefeller bought the property to preserve it as a historical site. It was officially declared a protected site in 1969 (even though it only covers 20 acres now). The grist mill still works and the Dutch barn is filled with animals. Guides wear period costumes. It's a charming place.
*Disabled: toilets.*

### Sunnyside

*Tarrytown, New York (1-914-591 8763).* **Getting There** *by car* north on New York State Thruway (I-87), take exit 9 for Tarrytown and go one mile south on Route 9; *by train* Metro-North to Irvington, NY, then a 20-minute walk, or call (1-914 631 0031) for a cab.
**Admission** $8 adults; $4-$7 concessions. **Open** *Mar-Dec* 10am-5pm Mon, Wed-Sun. **Guided tours** 10.30am-4pm.
**Credit** AmEx, MC, V.
This is the delightful home of Washington Irving, author of *Rip Van Winkle* and *The Legend of Sleepy Hollow.* Sunnyside was built on the banks of the Hudson in 1835. Chatty guides in period costume lead you through the home; you can escape them by strolling through the lovely grounds. Irving is buried in Sleepy Hollow Cemetery, between Sunnyside and Phillipsburg Manor (*see above*). Ask for directions.
*Disabled: toilets.*

### Van Cortlandt Manor

*Croton-on-Hudson, New York (1-914 271 8981).*
**Getting There** *by car* north on New York State Thruway (I-87), take exit 9 for Tarrytown then go 9 miles (15km) north; *by train* Metro-North to Croton-on-Hudson, then 10-minute walk. **Open** *March-Oct* 10am-5pm Mon, Wed-Sun; *Nov, Dec* 10am-5pm Sat, Sun.
**Admission** $8 adults; $4-$7 concessions. **Credit** AmEx, Disc, MC, V.
Set into a hillside overlooking the Croton and Hudson Rivers, the mansion was once home to Pierre Van Cortlandt, the state's first Lieutenant Governor, and his son Phillip, who served both as an officer under General Washington and a US Congressman. Now, there's a gift shop and picnic area on his estate.

Surrounding the cast-iron and concrete grandeur of the city, New York State offers scenery of stupendous natural beauty. The best time to admire its grandeur is in the autumn, when the trees turn deep scarlet, flaming orange and soft gold. Against a backdrop of crashing waterfalls, soaring mountain peaks and seemingly endless forests, visitors can appreciate the less frenetic charms of the United States.

In addition to the regions covered below, and elsewhere in this chapter, there are a number of other places that should be seen if you're driving through the state.

The **Thousand Islands Region** on the St Lawrence Seaway is a favourite vacation spot for New Yorkers and Canadians. Boating and fishing are the main interests. Glaciers carved gouges right through the middle of the state and left long bony indentations called the **Finger Lakes**. This area has become popular for any outdoor activity, for its vineyards and wineries, and for **Watkin's Glen** gorge and raceway. **Rochester** and **Syracuse** are the biggest local cities. One highlight in Rochester is the **Kodak Factory** tour and museum. **Alleghany State Park** and **Chautauqua Lake** are huge natural refuges in the very southwestern corner of the state near Jamestown. Throughout the state, wonders can be found in the most unlikely places. For instance, **Elmira**, near the southern border of New York, where Mark Twain summered and wrote much of his best work, or **Corning**, where you can go on the Corning Glass Factory Tours.

### Hostelling International

*891 Amsterdam Avenue, at 103rd Street, NY 10025 (932 1860).*
The American Youth Hostels organisation is an excellent source of information on all outdoor activities, state- and nationwide.

### New York State Tourist & Travel Information Center

*(1-518 474 4116/1-800 225 5697).*

## Albany

Although overshadowed by New York City, **Albany** is the capital of the Empire State, and the nation's oldest chartered city (1686). The **Empire State Plaza**, overlooking the city, is where many of the state government buildings are located. The imposing **Corning Tower** is open from 9am until 4pm every day, and there are daily tours of the **State Capitol** building. The **Albany Institute of History and Art** (1-518 463 4478) is the elegant home of a wonderful collection of locally made silver and furniture. Other places near Albany worth a visit include **Schenectady**, **Saratoga** and **Cooperstown**.

*The 1798 Boston **State House** is still the seat of Massachusetts' government. See page 311.*

Just 70 miles (112km) west of Albany, in Cooperstown, is the most important baseball diamond in the world. This is where Abner Doubleday invented baseball in 1839 and where you will find the **Baseball Hall of Fame** (1-607 547 7200), filled with memorabilia of the national pastime. Next to the museum is the **Abner Doubleday Memorial Field** where Abner worked out the finer points of the game.

For more information about the Greater Albany area, contact the **Albany County Convention & Visitors Bureau** at 52 South Pearl Street, Albany, NY 12207 (1-518 434 1217/1-800 258 3582).

## Niagara Falls

**Niagara Falls** may be a long way from New York City, but good things are worth travelling for and this is one of the best. No matter what is done (and plenty is) to make a buck off this natural wonder, its beauty and power remain undiminished.

. The Falls, which are part of the Niagara River, separate the United States from Canada and Lake Erie from Lake Ontario. **American** and **Bridal Veil Falls** are in the United States and **Horseshoe Falls** are in Canada.

The 182-foot (55-m) high falls span 3,175 feet (953m) and throw three quarters of a million gallons of water over the edge per second. A bridge out to **Goat Island**, which separates the two countries' waterfalls, provides an impressive view of the cascades. You can see the mist and rainbows produced by the falls and hear the loud

thunder especially well from there. The **Cave of the Winds** is where raincoats are an absolute must. Visitors go down in the lift to the bottom of the American falls, travel a short way and look out through the falls while standing under and behind them. The water acts as a prism when there is sufficient light, so it can be like standing in a rainbow.

Other attractions on the American side are the observation tower on **Prospect Point**, which provides a panoramic view of the falls, and the **Maid of the Mist** boat trips, which get close enough to the falls for all and sundry to be tossed around and thoroughly drenched. Further down the gorge are the infamous whirlpools, the **Schoelkopf Geological Center**, the **Robert Moses Niagara Power Plant**, which supplies much of the East Coast with electricity, and **Old Fort Niagara**. The Canadian side of the falls (accessible by bus from Buffalo) has the best views of the water, and some incredibly kitsch honeymoon hotels. The biggest attraction, apart from the water, is the **Native American Center**, a fascinating collection of artefacts housed in a turtle-shaped building.

The area has more to offer than the falls. **Buffalo**, New York State's second largest city, is one of the most attractive renovated old industrial cities of America. Buffalo has a professional football and hockey team and a new major league baseball team and field. In addition to the attraction of high-class spectator sports, there are the Erie Canal, Lakes Erie and Ontario, and the fabulous Albright-Knox Museum of Art.

### Greater Buffalo Convention & Visitors Bureau
*617 Main Street, Buffalo, NY 14203 (1-800 283 3256).*

### Niagara County Convention & Visitors Bureau
*139 Niagara Street, Lockport 14094 (1-800 338 7890).*

### Niagara County Tourism & Fishing Office
*139 Niagara Street, Lockport 14094 (1-716 439 7300).*

## Saratoga

Located about 175 miles (282km) north of Manhattan, **Saratoga** gained fame for its mineral-water baths and racetrack. Its heyday was in the 1870s but it's still a deservedly popular tourist destination. Visit it from July to September when the **Saratoga Race Course** (1-518 584 6200) – the country's oldest and loveliest – has its season.

From June to early September the **Saratoga Performing Arts Center (SPAC)** formed in 1966, attracts lovers of classical, pop music and jazz, ballet and opera. In July, the New York City Ballet takes up residence here for three weeks, followed by the Newport Jazz Festival. The New York City Opera and Philadelphia Orchestra continue the season.

The wealthy built beautiful homes here and the highest concentration of them is along Union Avenue, North Broadway and Caroline Street. There is also the **National Museum of Racing**, Union Avenue and Ludlow Street (1-518 584 0400), and the **National Museum of Dance** (1-518 584 9330), part of SPAC.

You should also visit the mineral bath and get a massage at the **Lincoln Mineral Baths** in Saratoga Spa State Park (1-518 584 2011). View the area, plus the Green Mountains of Vermont, from a hot air balloon, on a tour with Adirondack Balloon Flights (*see below*).

While the cost of a stay at the Adelphi Hotel on Broadway (1-518 587 4688) may be steep for the average tourist (from $125), you should at least take a look at its lobby. Built in 1877, it's the only remaining grand hotel in town. Most of the fine restaurants and bars seem to be on Broadway. For nightlife, make a reservation at Caffe Lena on Phila Street (1-518 583 0022): everybody's played here, including Bob Dylan back in 1962. For more information about Saratoga, contact the Chamber of Commerce.

### Adirondack Balloon Flights
*PO Box 65, Glens Falls, NY 12801 (1-518 793 6342).*
**Price** $175 per person. **Credit** AmEx, Disc, MC, V.
A breathtaking way to see the beauty of the Adirondacks and the Lake George region, as well as the Green Mountains of Vermont. The one-hour balloon ride is especially beautiful during the autumn. Flights are scheduled around sunrise and three hours before sunset and may be cancelled if the weather's bad.

### Saratoga County Chamber of Commerce
*28 Clinton Street, Saratoga Springs, NY 12866 (1-518 584 3255/584 4471).*

### Saratoga County Promotion Department
*County Municipal Center, Ballston Spa, NY 12020 (1-800 526 8970).*

### Saratoga Performing Arts Center (SPAC)
*Saratoga Springs, NY 12866-0826 (1-518 584 9330/ credit card reservations 1-518 587 3330).* **Open** *June-first week Sept* 10am-5pm Mon-Sat; 1-5pm Sun. **Tickets** $13-$47.50. **Credit** AmEx, MC, V.
Tickets for New York City Opera events range from $13 for a seat on the lawn to $42 for an orchestra box; Newport Jazz Festival day tickets cost $29 for a lawn seat bought in advance and $40 for an orchestra seat. Tickets for the New York City Ballet or the Philadelphia Orchestra cost from $13 to $30.50, and you will pay up to $70 for the Ballet's gala performance at the end of the season in July.
*Disabled: toilets.*

### Getting There
By Amtrak train, the journey takes roughly 3½ hours, and costs around $65 return; by Greyhound bus, it takes 4 hours and costs roughly $50 return.

## General Information

For more information on areas worth visiting within New York State contact:

### Allegheny State Park, Recreation & Historic Preservation Region
*2373 Aspi, Salamanca, NY 14779 (1-716 354 9121).*

### Allegheny Historical Society County Museum
*Court Street, Belmont, NY 14813 (1-716 268 9293).*

### Central New York State Park Region
*6105 East Senaca Turnpike, Jamesville, NY 13078 (1-315 492 1756).*

### Economic Development & Tourist Information
*(1-716 268 9229).*

### Finger Lakes Association
*309 Lake Street, Penn Yan, NY 14527 (1-315 536 7488).*

### Greater Rochester Visitors' Association
*126 Andrew Street, Rochester, NY 14604 (1-716 546 3070).*

### Mark Twain Country Information Office
*215 East Church Street, Elmira, NY 14901 (1-607 734 5137).*

### Northern Chautauqua County Chamber of Commerce
*212 Lakeshore Drive West, Dunkirk, NY 14048 (1-716 366 6200).*

### Syracuse Convention & Visitors Bureau
*572 South Salina Street, NY 13202 (1-315 470 1800).*

### Thousand Islands State Park & Recreation Region
*Keewaydin State Park, Alexandria Bay, NY 13607 (1-315 482 2593).*

## City Life

New York is hardly representative of American cities. In fact most Americans think of it as another planet entirely. If you'd like to step out of Manhattan's whirling maelstrom for a few days and see the sights of a more typical urban US, three of the country's most important cities are within four or five hours' drive.

## Boston

The city of Boston was the birthplace of the United States as an independent nation. Its antique architecture and winding streets tell the story of the early colonists leading up to their violent rebellion against British rule. Until 1755 it was the biggest city in America, destination of the country's earliest waves of immigration, and throughout the colonial period it remained the busiest foreign port in the British Empire. This early and rapid growth in the seventeenth and eighteenth centuries has left it with a refreshingly human scale. Its preserved gentility and the noticeably low impact of the automobile make it a real contrast to New York and most American cities.

Walking the **Freedom Trail**, marked throughout its length by red bricks set in the street, is the easiest way to take in the city's history. Start at the Visitor Information Center on **Boston Common**, once an area of grazing land bordering the sea, until nineteenth-century landfill turned the estuary into the residential area of the Back Bay. Follow the trail past the gilded dome of the **State House** (1798), still the seat of Massachusetts' government, and the **Park Street Church**, where William Lloyd Garrison announced his campaign to abolish slavery in 1829.

King's Chapel **Burying Ground** and **Old Granary Burying Ground** are the resting places of the city's first colonists and such famous American patriots as Samuel Adams, Paul Revere and John Hancock. The **Old State House**, lovingly restored to its original 1712 condition, was where the Declaration of Independence was read, on 18 July 1776. A ring of stones outside marks where five people were killed when soldiers fired on an angry crowd during the 1770 Boston Massacre.

**Old North Church** and **Copp's Hill Burial Ground** were the two places lit by signal lanterns to alert Paul Revere that the British were coming. Revere entered the history books by riding several miles at a furious pace to carry the warning to nearby Lexington and the massed Patriot forces. The **USS Constitution** ('Old Ironsides') is the world's oldest warship still afloat – you can take a ferry from Long Wharf to Charlestown Navy Yard to see it. If you would prefer a more rapid look at the city, there are numerous trolley bus companies operating a sightseeing circuit. These allow you to step on and off at a number of strategic places.

Competing tourist trails include the **Harborwalk**, with a maritime theme, starting at the National Park Service Visitors Center (*see below*); and the **Black Heritage Trail**, at the Boston African-

The **Jefferson Memorial** in East Potomac Park, Washington DC. See page 312.

American National Historic Site, 46 Joy Street (1-617 742 5415/1-617 742 1854). The waterfront is where you'll find the excellent **New England Aquarium**, **Central Wharf** (1-617 973 5200), the **Children's Museum**, 300 Congress Street (1-617 426 6500), and the **Computer Museum** (1-617 426 2800). The **Boston Tea Party Ship and Museum**, Congress Street Bridge (1-617 338 1773), is based around the event which provoked the rejection of British rule: the dumping, in 1773, of a British cargo of tea into the harbour.

Boston has a thriving stand-up comedy scene, and is also home to TV's *Cheers*, or at least the Bull and Finch Bar, 84 Beacon Street, Beacon Hill (1-617 227 9605), where the exterior shots were filmed.

The Boston Symphony Orchestra, Symphony Hall, 301 Massachusetts Avenue (1-617 266 1492), gives its famous Boston Pops concerts in May and in June. Over the river in Cambridge is where you'll find the hushed lawns and studious cloisters of Ivy League academia that is **Harvard University**.

### GETTING THERE

If you're driving, take I-95 through Connecticut and Rhode Island. The trip can be made in under four hours. Greyhound buses leave from the Port Authority Bus Terminal in New York City every hour, take about 4½ hours and cost from $50 return. Amtrak runs trains nearly as frequently ($80-$90 return). If you look out for bargains, off-peak discounts and student reductions, it will cost you around the same to fly, especially if you book early in advance. Both Delta (239 0700/1-800 325 1999/www.delta-air.com) and USAir (1-800 428 4322) run regular air shuttles from New York. Phone (1-800 235 6426) for Logan Airport information.

### ACCOMMODATION

#### Bed & Breakfast Agency of Boston
*47 Commercial Wharf, Boston, MA, 02110 (1-617 720 3540/1-800 248 9262/from UK 0800 895128).*

#### Boston International AYH Hostel
*12 Hemenway Street (1-617 536 9455).*
A bed in a dorm costs $18 for members; $21 for non-members.

#### Newbury Guest House
*261 Newbury Street, Boston, MA 02116 (1-617 437 7666).* **Credit** AmEx, MC, V.
Doubles from $95, suites from $125.

#### Regal Bostonian
*Fanieul Hall, Marketplace, Boston, MA 02190 (1-617 523 3600).* **Credit** AmEx, Disc, MC, V.
Doubles from $245, suites from $335.

## Useful Addresses

#### Greater Boston Chamber of Commerce
*Fourth Floor, 1 Beacon Street, Boston, MA 02108 (1-617 227 4500/1-888 733 2678).*

#### Greater Boston Convention & Visitors Center
*Suite 400, 800 Boylston Street, Prudential Tower, Boston, MA 02199 (1-617 536 4100/1-800 888 5515).*

#### National Park Service Visitors Center
*15 State Street, Boston MA 02129 (1-617 242 5667/ 1-617 242 5642).*

## Washington DC

The seat of government and the nation's capital city was moved to Washington in the uninviting swamplands of DC – 'District of Columbia' – with the express purpose of dissuading politicians from staying there too often. The city was built during the nineteenth century to a plan drawn up in 1800 by Frenchman Pierre L'Enfant and the African American Benjamin Manneker. It is full of gracious avenues and imposing buildings, site not only of the various government offices but also an abundance of national cultural institutions. There is also a heavy corporate presence here.

Washington is a city with a double life, however. Beyond the formal grandeur there are neighbourhoods of extreme poverty where guns and crack are the tools of the local economy. Although it was the first city to have a black majority (it was proudly christened 'Chocolate City'), as in all of urban America, the wealth here is very clearly divided along racial lines. Come and see the high-powered wheels of government in action, but don't forget that Washington is also the scene of appalling violence, a place where the world's surgeons are sent to learn about bullet-wounds.

Take a free tour around the **US Capitol**, the famous white-domed home of the Senate and the House of Representatives. Other government attractions include the **US Supreme Court**, where you can oversee proceedings as the laws of the land are tossed around; and of course the **White House**, home and office of the President. The largest library in the world, the **Library of Congress**, grew from Thomas Jefferson's private collection and now contains over 100 million books.

Monuments to various leaders and visionaries abound. The simple obelisk of the **Washington Monument**, at 555 feet (169m) the world's tallest masonry structure, lies at the centre of the large formal park known as **The Mall**. In The Mall's western corner Abraham Lincoln is immortalised in the **Lincoln Memorial**, a colonnade containing his huge bronze statue. The **Jefferson Memorial** lies among the flower trees of East Potomac Park.

Also in the Mall, don't miss the moving sculptural symbolism of the **Vietnam Veterans' Memorial**. The other great monument of war, the **Iwo Jima Memorial**, the famous sculpture of World War II GIs erecting a flagpole, is on the other side of the Potomac River, to the north of

**Arlington National Cemetery**, which is full of the country's most famous dead people.

If a location begins with 'National', the chances are you'll find it in Washington DC. The **National Museum of Natural History** is at the north of the Mall at 10th Street & Constitution Avenue NW (1-202 357 2747); the **National Museum of American History** is at the north of the Mall between 12th Street & Constitution Avenue NW (1-202 357 1481); and the **National Air & Space Museum**, on the south side of the Mall, between 4th & 7th Streets (1-202 357 1400), is the city's most popular destination.

The **National Museum of African Art** is on the south side of The Mall at 950 Independence Avenue SW (1-202 357 4860); the **National Museum of American Art** is on 8th & G Streets (1-202 357 3111); the **National Gallery** is on the north of The Mall between 3rd & 7th Streets (1-202 737 4215).

The **National Archives**, north side of The Mall at 7th Street & Constitution Avenue (1-202 501 5400), not only houses the Declaration of Independence, the Bill of Rights and the US Constitution, it also contains a 1297 copy of the Magna Carta and the infamous Watergate tapes. The latest addition is the **US Holocaust Memorial Museum** 14th Street & Independence Avenue SW (1-202 488 0400).

Other galleries include the **National Portrait Gallery**, F Street between 7th & 9th Streets (1-202 357 2920); the **Sackler Gallery**, on the south side of the Mall at 1050 Independence Avenue SW (1-202 357 4880) with its oriental collections; the **Corcoran Gallery**, 500 17th Street NW, between E Street & New York Avenue (1-202 639 1700); and the **Phillips Collection**, 1600 21st Street at Q Street (1-202 387 2151/phillipsco@aol.com) with its excellent modern art. Finally, the **National Museum of Women in the Arts** is at 1250 New York Avenue (1-202 783 5000).

Many of these galleries and museums are part of the **Smithsonian Institute** (1-202 357 2700), 'the nation's attic'. The visitor centre for the institute is at the Castle, halfway down the Mall: it's the place to go for details on all the various attractions in the area.

Don't miss the hour-long tour around the **FBI Headquarters**, Pennsylvania Avenue, between 9th & 10th Streets (1-202 324 3000/tour information 1-202 324 3447). Crime detection techniques are explained, and the tour ends with a blazing display of automatic gunfire.

Other insights into America's power structures can be gained at the **Bureau of Printing and Engraving**, 14th Street at C Street (1-202 622 2000), where ordinary paper rolls through some inky presses and emerges as millions of dollars. The club and bar scene is fairly unimpressive.

Head to the **Kennedy Center** (1-202 467 4600) instead for more highbrow entertainment.

## GETTING THERE

If you're driving, take I-95 south through New Jersey and Pennsylvania. The trip can be made in about five hours. Greyhound buses leave from the Port Authority Bus Terminal every hour (7am-8pm), costing $50 return ($53 Fri-Sun) and taking about 4½ hours. Amtrak runs trains nearly as frequently from $90 return.

Because of the volume of traffic between New York and DC, with off-peak discounts and student reductions it will cost you around the same to fly. Both Delta (239 0700) and USAir (1-800 428 4322) fly regular air shuttles from New York and there's a flight every half hour. Continental (1-800 231 0856), TWA (290 2121) and United (1-800 241 6522) also run services between the two cities.

## ACCOMMODATION

### Bed & Breakfast Accommodation

*PO Box 12011, Washington, DC 20005 (1-202 328 3510/bnbaccom@aol.com).*
This agency will track down B&B accommodation.

### Harrington Hotel

*436 11th Street NW, Washington DC, 20004 (1-202 628 8140).* **Credit** AmEx, Disc, JCB, MC, V.
Doubles from $78.

### Hay-Adams Hotel

*1 Lafayette Square NW, Washington, DC 20006 (1-202 638 2260).* **Credit** AmEx, Disc, MC, V.
Be the president's neighbour for $285 per night (double room).

### Washington International AYH Hostel

*1009 11th Street NW, Washington DC, 20001 (1-202 737 2333).*
Dorm beds $18 per night for members, $21 for non-members.

## USEFUL ADDRESSES

### Washington DC Convention & Visitors Center

*Suite 600, 1212 New York Avenue NW, Washington, DC 20005 (1-202 789 7000).*

# Philadelphia

When Charles II rid himself of a troublesome nonconformist, William Penn, by giving him a chunk of the New World, Pennsylvania was founded. Penn, a Quaker, created the 'holy experiment' of a colony based on tolerance.

The capital was built in 1682 on a grid system of Penn's devising which became the norm for American cities. He called his city Philadelphia, meaning 'City of Brotherly Love', and was unique in signing a treaty for peaceful co-existence with the local American Indians.

Penn's example attracted like-minded settlers, including Catholics, Mennonites from Germany and other Quakers who migrated to the city. Freed from the shackles of discrimination, they put all their efforts into trading and commerce, and built Philadelphia into the British Empire's second largest city.

It was here that the Declaration of Independence was first read, and also where the US Constitution was drawn up. Philadelphia was the emerging nation's capital for many years during the War of Independence and remained so until the grandiose designs of Washington DC were made a reality in 1800.

With its traditions of tolerance, Philadelphia became a key destination in the North for many of the black people freed from slavery after the Civil War, and the city provided America with its first black mayor.

Like Boston, much of the city's history is tied up in the events of the American Revolution. If you visit **Independence Hall** you can see where the Declaration of Independence was drawn up, as well as the Constitution itself. **Congress Hall** next door was the seat of the nation's first government, while the **Old City Hall** was the first home of the Supreme Court.

These buildings are all in the **Independence Hall National Park**, which also includes the **Franklin Museum**, commemorating the wit and wisdom of Benjamin Franklin; the **Free Quaker Meeting House**; the **Franklin Post Office** postal museum; and the **Philosophical Hall** which Franklin founded as a debating arena. In fact the whole city is full of places where Franklin, Jefferson, Washington and chums ate, slept, worked and worshipped.

You can't miss seeing the **Liberty Bell**, the famous cracked bell which rang out for each Patriot victory and was later adopted as an anti slavery symbol. It can be found in a small purpose-built museum on Market Street.

The importance of Philadelphia as a port is emphasised in the **Independence Seaport Museum**, 211 South Columbus Boulevard, at Walnut Street (1-215 925 5439). Art hotspots include the **Philadelphia Museum of Art**, Franklin Parkway at 26th Street (1-215 763 8100), not only a world-class art gallery but also a featured location in the film *Rocky*; the **Rodin Museum**, Franklin Parkway at 26th Street (1-215 763 8100); and the **Museum of American Art**, Broad Street and Cherry Street (1-215 972 7600/pafa@pafa.org).

Other museums worth a visit include the **Franklin Institute Science Museum**, 20th Street and Franklin Parkway (1-215 448 1208), with its truly amazing **Planetarium**, **Futures Center** and **Omniverse** movie screen. The literary **Rosenbach Museum** at 2010 Delancey Place (1-215 732 1600) keeps Joyce's manuscript of *Ulysses*.

There's also the **University Museum of Archaeology and Anthropology**, Spruce Street and 33rd Street (1-215 898 4000); the

**Institute of Contemporary Art**, 118 South 36th Street and Sansom Street (1-215 898 7108); the **Academy of Natural Sciences**, 19th Street & Franklin Parkway (1-215 299 1020); and the wonderful **Mutter Museum**, 19 South 22nd Street (1-215 563 3737), which is full of strange medical exhibits and other gruesome things in pickle-jars.

While you're in Philadelphia, don't forget this is the cheese capital of the nation. Enjoy some cheese fries, grab a slice of cheesecake, and wander down to the southside of town where the Italian neighbourhood provides visitors with the best cheese steaks in town – the essential Philly dish.

The city's nightlife is centred around **South Street**, a yuppified strip of bars and restaurants. For more low-brow entertainment head to any of the music bars catering to the large and influential student population, but be warned that this is a college town, and the over-21 drinking rule is rigorously enforced. You won't get into a bar without ID – even if you look positively middle-aged.

## GETTING THERE

It'll take you about two and a half hours by car to get to Philadelphia from New York on I-95. The Greyhound company runs buses every hour (7am-8pm) at a return price of $23-$25; it will cost around $50 return by train. Almost all domestic airlines operate between the two cities for around $80 return. Call Philadelphia International Airport (1-215 937 6937) for details of airlines.

## ACCOMMODATION

### Bed & Breakfast Center City

*1804 Pine Street, Philadelphia, PA 19103 (1-215 735 1137).* **Credit** MC, V.
B&B can be arranged for $50-$90 a night.

### Chamounix Mansion International AYH Hostel

*West Fairmount Park, Philadelphia, PA 19131 (1-215 878 3676/chmounix.libertynet.org).* **Credit** MC, V.
Dorm beds cost $11 for members, $14 for non-members.

### Comfort Inn

*100 Christopher Columbus Boulevard, Philadelphia, PA 19106 (1-215 627 7900).* **Credit** AmEx, DC, Disc, MC, V.
Rooms cost $89-$139 a night, including breakfast.

## USEFUL ADDRESSES

### Independence Hall National Park

*Visitor Center at 3rd & Chestnut (1-215 597 8974/ line for the hearing impaired 1-215 597 1785).*

### Philadelphia Convention & Visitors Bureau

*Suite 2020, 1515 Market Street, Philadelphia, PA 19102 (1-215 636 3300).*

### Visitor Center

*1525 JFK Boulevard, at 16th Street (1-215 636 1666/ 1-800 537 7676).*

# Survival

# Survival

**A directory of New York resources and helplines.**

All 1-800 numbers can be called toll-free from within the US.

## Emergencies

### Ambulances
In an emergency, **dial 911** for an ambulance or call the operator on 0. To complain about slow service, non-attendance or poor treatment, call the Department of Health Emergency Medical Service (1-718 416 7000).

### Fire
In an emergency, dial **911**.

### Police
In an emergency, **dial 911**. For the location of the nearest police precinct or for general information about police services, call 374 5000.

## Helplines & Agencies

### Better Business Bureau
*(533 6200).* **Open** 9am-5pm Mon-Fri.
Advice on consumer-related complaints: shopping, services etc. Each enquiry costs $3.80 plus New York City tax.

### Center for Inner Resource Development
*(734 5876).* **Open** 24 hours daily.
Trained therapists will talk to you day or night, and deal with all kinds of emotional problems, including the consequences of rape.

### Childhelp's National Child Abuse Hotline
*(1-800 422 4453).* **Open** 24 hours daily.
Trained psychologists provide general crisis counselling and can help in an emergency. Callers include abused children, parents having problems with children and runaways.

### Community Action for Legal Services
*(431 7200).* **Open** 9am-5pm Mon-Fri.
A government-funded referral service for people with any kind of legal problem.

### Con Ed Emergency Line
*(Gas emergency 683 8830/Electrical or steam emergency 683 0862).* **Open** 24 hours daily.
Call these numbers if you smell gas or spot a steam leak, or if your electricity fails. Gas leaks are dealt with quickly. Other problems tend not to be.

### Help Line
*(532 2400).* **Open** 9am-10pm daily.
Trained volunteers will talk to anyone contemplating suicide, and can also help with other personal problems and practical things like problems with health insurance.

### Legal Aid Society
*(577 3300).* **Open** 9am-5pm Mon-Fri.
Free advice and referral on legal matters.

### New York City Department of Consumer Affairs
*(487 4444).* **Open** 9.30am-4.30pm Mon-Fri.
Report complaints on consumer-related affairs.

### St Lukes/Roosevelt Hospital Rape Crisis Center
*(523 4728).* **Open** 9am-5pm Mon-Fri, recorded referral message at other times.
Provides a trained volunteer who will accompany you through all aspects of reporting a rape and getting emergency treatment.

### The Samaritans
*(673 3000).* **Open** 24 hours daily.
People thinking of committing suicide or suffering from depression, grief, sexual anxiety or alcoholism can call this organisation for advice.

### Sex Crimes Report Line of the New York Police Department (NYPD)
*(267 7273).* **Open** 24 hours daily.
Reports of sex crimes are handled by a female detective from the NYPD's Bureau. She will inform the appropriate precinct, send an ambulance if requested and provide counselling and medical referrals. A detective from the Sex Crimes Squad will interview the victim, and you can request to be seen in your own home. Matters relating to violence against gay people, child victimisation and referrals for the family and friends of victims are also handled.

### Victim Services Agency
*(577 7777).* **Open** 24 hours daily.
Telephone and one-to-one counselling for any victim of domestic violence, personal crime or rape, as well as practical help with court processes, compensation and legal aid.General Information

## General Information

The Yellow and White Pages have a mine of useful information at the front, including theatre seating diagrams and maps. Hotels will have copies; otherwise, try libraries or Nynex (the phone company) payment centres.

### Recorded Information Phonelines
These 24-hour information lines add extra weight to your phone bill. An opening message should tell you how much per minute you are paying.

**Sports scores** *(1-900 976 1313).*
**Stock market prices** *(1-900 976 4141).*
**Time** *(1-900 976 1616).*
**Weather forecast** *(1-900 976 1212).*

## Auto Services
### Breakdowns/Car Towing
Towing prices are regulated by the city and everyone charges the same – that is, the maximum.

## Citywide Towing

*522 West 38th Street, between Tenth & Eleventh
Avenues (924 8104).* **Open** 24 hours daily.
**No credit cards.**
All types of repairs done on foreign and domestic autos. Free
towing is offered if the firm gets the repair job.

# Car Wash

## Carzapoppin'

*610 Broadway, at Houston Street (673 5115).* **Open**
24 hours daily. **No credit cards.**
It's still only $5 to give the exterior of your car a shampoo.
Interior cleaning costs extra.

# 24-hour Gas Stations

## Downtown

*Amoco, 610 Broadway, at Houston Street (473 5924).*
**Credit** AmEx, DC, Disc, JCB, MC, V. No repairs.

## Midtown

*Gulf, FDR Drive & 23rd Street (686 4784).* **Credit**
AmEx, Disc, Gulf, MC, V. Some repairs.

## Uptown

*Shell, Amsterdam Avenue & 181st Street (928 3100).*
**Credit** AmEx, Disc, MC, V. Repairs.

# Communications

For information about telephones, *see chapter*
**Essential Information.**

## New York Post Office

*380 West 33rd Street, at Eighth Avenue (967 8585/
postal information line 330 4000). Subway A, C or E to*

*Penn Station.* **Open** 24 hours daily; midnight-6pm daily
for money orders and registered mail.
This is the city's main post office. Phone to find out your
nearest branch office, or call the information line to hear a
vast menu of recorded postal information. There are 59 full-
service post offices in New York; queues are invariably long,
but stamps are available from self-service vending machines
at face value. Post offices are usually open 9am-5pm Mon-
Fri; Sat opening hours vary from office to office.

## Express Letters

*(967 8585).*
Phone this central number for information. You need to
use special envelopes and fill out a form, which can be done
either at a post office or by organising a pick up. You are
guaranteed 24-hour mail delivery to major US cities.
Letters – both domestic and international – must be sent
before 5pm.

## Poste Restante

*c/o General Delivery, General Post Office, 421 Eighth
Avenue, New York, NY 10001.*
Poste restante is called 'general delivery' in the US. You will
need to show some form of identification – a passport or ID
card – when picking up letters.

## Stamps

Stamps are available at all post offices and from vending
machines in most drugstores (where they cost more). Airmail
letters cost 60¢ for the first 0.5oz (14g) and 40¢ each additional 0.5oz to anywhere in the world. It costs 32¢ to send a
letter within the US, and 50¢ to send a postcard anywhere in
the world.

## Western Union Telegrams

*(1-800 325 6000).* **Open** 24 hours daily.
Telegrams to addresses worldwide are taken over the phone,
24 hours daily, and charges added to your phone bill. Not
available from pay phones.

## Foreign Consulates

Check the Yellow Pages for a complete list of consulates and embassies.

**Australia** *(408 8400)*.
**Canada** *(596 1700)*.
**Great Britain** *(745 0200)*.
**Ireland** *(319 2555)*.
**New Zealand** *(832 4038)*.

## Disabled

### Mayor's Office for People with Disabilities
*52 Chambers Street, near Broadway, Room 206 (788 2830). Subway 1, 2, 3, A or C to Chambers Street.* **Open** 9am-5pm Mon-Fri.
The office organises services for disabled people and offers help and advice.

### Lighthouse Incorporated
*111 East 59th Street, between Park & Lexington Avenues (821 9200/1-800 334 5497). Subway 4, 5 or 6 to 59th Street/N or R to Lexington Avenue.* **Open** 9am-5pm Mon-Fri.
In addition to running a store selling handy items for sight-impaired people, this organisation provides help and information for the blind dealing with life – or a holiday – in New York City.

### New York Society for the Deaf
*817 Broadway, at 12th Street (777 3900). Subway 4, 5, 6, L, N or R to Union Square.* **Open** 9am-5pm Mon-Thur; 9am-4pm Fri.
Advice and information on facilities for the deaf.

## Medical Treatment

## Emergency Rooms

You will have to pay for emergency treatment. If you can, contact the emergency number on your travel insurance before seeking treatment. They will direct you to an emergency room that will deal directly with your insurance company. Emergency rooms are always open at:

### Cabrini Medical Centre
*227 East 19th Street, between Second & Third Avenues (995 6120). Subway 4, 5, 6, L, N or R to Union Square.*

### Mount Sinai Hospital
*Madison Avenue & West 100th Street (241 7171). Subway 4, 5 or 6 to 96th Street.*

### Roosevelt Hospital
*428 West 59th Street, off Ninth Avenue (523 4000). Subway 1, 9, A, B, C or D to Columbus Circle.*

### St Luke's Hospital Centre
*West 113th Street & Amsterdam Avenue (523 3335). Subway 1 or 9 to 116th Street.*

### St Vincent's Hospital
*Seventh Avenue at 11th Street (604 7998). Subway 1, 2, 3, 9 or F to 14th Street/L to Sixth Avenue.*

## Clinics

Walk-in clinics offer treatment for minor ailments. Most require immediate payment, although some will send their bill directly to your insurance company. You will have to claim back the cost of any prescription medicines yourself.

### Eastern Women's Center
*44 East 30th Street, between Park & Madison Avenues (686 6066). Subway 6 to 33rd Street.* **Open** 9am-5pm Tue-Sat. **Credit** AmEx, MC, V.
Pregnancy tests cost $20; counselling and gynaecological tests are also available.

### Doctors Walk-in
*57 East 34th Street, between Park & Madison Avenues (252 6000). Subway 6 to 33rd Street.* **Open** 8am-5.30pm Mon-Fri; 10am-1.30pm Sat. **Basic fee** $75. **Credit** AmEx, MC, V.
If you need X-rays or lab tests, go as early as possible and no later than 4pm Mon-Fri. No lab work is done on Saturday.

## Dentists

### Emergency Dental Associates
*(1-800 439 9299)*. **Open** 24 hours daily.

### New York University College of Dentistry
*(998 9800)*. **Open** 8.30am-8pm Mon-Thur; 9am-6pm Fri. **Credit** MC, V.
If you need your teeth fixed on a budget, you can become a subject for final-year students. They're slow but proficient and an experienced dentist is always on hand to supervise. The basic fee is $65.

## Doctors: House Calls

If you want to complain about misconduct or excessive charges, call the Department of Health's Professional Medical Conduct Division (613 2650).

### BLT Answering Service
*(1-718 238 2100)*. **Basic fee** *private address* from $80; *hotel* from $125. **Credit** (private addresses only) MC, V.
Doctors will make house calls round the clock. Expect to wait about two hours.

## Drugstores

*See also chapter* **Shopping & Services**.

### Kaufman Pharmacy
*Beverly Hotel, 557 Lexington Avenue, at 50th Street (755 2266). Subway E, F or 6 to 51st Street/Lexington Avenue.* **Open** 24 hours daily. **Credit** AmEx, MC, V.
Manhattan's only round-the-clock full-service pharmacy. Delivery is free within a ten-block radius.

## Health Advice

For advice on AIDS and HIV, *see chapter* **Gay & Lesbian New York**.

### Alcoholics Anonymous
*(647 1680)*. **Open** 24 hours daily.

# Sex, drugs 'n' the slammer

There was a time, not long ago, when New York's social life resembled nothing so much as that of Caligula's Rome. Anything went at the gay bars and bathhouses of the 1970s, and consensual sex in the straight community, while less overt, was casual in the extreme. Drug trafficking and consumption in public spaces was a given and enforcement was lax. That was then. HIV and a resurgence of America's puritan streak turned out the party lights.

For those who prefer their flesh the old-fashioned way, the back pages of the *Village Voice* and most of Al Goldstein's ancient and honoured *Screw* contain the whole range of escort, dating and role-playing services. The much-touted renovation of Times Square is well under way, but peep shows and X-rated cinemas can still be found on nearby Eighth Avenue and topless bars and strip clubs of all gender orientations reach from the East Village to Queens Boulevard.

What was formerly the official bird of the city – the common streetwalker – is clearly an endangered species, driven from its nests along the far western avenues. These days, you're more likely to be approached in the east side hotel district. But, though AIDS mortality rates have dropped in the past few years, rates of infection still hold steady – and are by no means limited to the gay population. And those who engage the services of prostitutes are liable to felony indictments for 'criminal solicitation', bringing jail-time of one to 15 years.

Recreational drug use is highly problematic. Pills and powders are still proffered in a good number of clubs but purity is unreliable and police raids frequent. Nickel bags and loose joints are still sold in the downtown parks but such transactions require fine street sense. Official NYPD policy is to focus on upper-level drug dealers but some 150 busts for simple possession occur every day and New York State's drug laws are severe. Possession of even trace amounts of illegal substances can put a big dent in your visit.

Jail time for simple possession, as stated in the legal code, ranges from three months to one year for marijuana (not a 'controlled substance', legally speaking) to up to 15 years for more than an ounce of hashish – not that you're likely to find any in this town, or this country, for that matter. Up to 1,000 microgrammes of LSD can get you a year – and with the quality of acid on the street these days, you'll be lucky if 10 hits adds up to that much (and there's no telling what other active ingredients are soaked in that blotter). Any more than that puts you in felony country, which is a very nasty place indeed. And as for coke, heroin and ecstasy – don't even think about it. Even in New York, decadence ain't what it used to be.

## Cocaine Anonymous

*(262 2463)*. **Open** 24-hour recorded information.

## Drug Abuse Information Line

*(1-800-522 5353)*. **Open** 24 hours daily.
This state-run programme refers callers to recovery programmes throughout New York city and state.

## NYC Department of Health Bureau of Maternity Services & Family Planning

*2 Lafayette Street, 18th floor, at Reade Street*
*(442 1740)*. *Subway N or R to City Hall*. **Open** 8am-5pm Mon-Fri.
Leaflets and advice; phone for an appointment. Contact the Women's Health Line (230 1111) on the 21st floor of the same building for contraceptive advice.

## NYC Department of Health VD Information Hotline

*(427 5120)*. **Open** 8am-4pm Mon-Fri.
Information, and referral for treatment and counselling.

## Pills Anonymous

*(874 0700)*. **Open** 24-hour answering service.
Information on drug-recovery programmes for users of marijuana, cocaine, alcohol and other addictive substances, as well as referrals to DA meetings.

## Law

### Sandback, Birnbaum & Michelen Criminal Law

(517 3200/1-800 766 5800). **Open** 24 hours daily.
This is the number to have in your head when the cops read you your rights in the middle of the night.

## Left Luggage

Left-luggage lockers appear to be a thing of the past, for security reasons. However, there are baggage rooms at Penn Station, Grand Central Station and the Port Authority Bus Terminal.

## Lost Property

For property lost in the street, contact the police. For lost credit cards, *see page320* **Money**.

### Buses & Subways

*New York City Transit Authority, Eighth Avenue/34th Street subway station, near the A train platform*. **Open** 8am-noon Mon-Wed, Fri; 11am-6.45pm Thur.

### Grand Central Station

*(532 4900).*
For items left on Metro-North.

### JFK

Contact the airline on which you're travelling, or phone 1-718 244 4444 for further information.

### LaGuardia

Contact your airline or phone 1-718 476 5115.

### Newark

Contact your airline or phone 1-201 961 6000.

### Penn Station

*(630 7389).*
For items left on Amtrak, New Jersey Transit and the Long Island Rail Road.

### Taxis

*(221 8294).*
Phone this number if you leave anything in a taxi: it worked for Wallace and Gromit recently.

## Money

If you do run out of cash, don't expect your embassy or consulate to lend you money – they won't, although they may be persuaded to repatriate you. In an emergency, you can have money wired to **Western Union**; phone 1-800 325 6000 for the location of their nearest office. Another service is **MoneyGram**, which has 1,300 different locations in Manhattan alone (phone 1-800 926 9400 for information and the whereabouts of their nearest office). For more information on currency, *see chapter* **Essential Information**.

## Banks

Normal banking hours are 9am-3.30pm Monday to Friday (some banks stay open later on Fridays).

## Lost Credit Cards

### American Express Travellers' Cheques

*(1-800 221 7282).*

### American Express Card

*(1-800 528 2121).*

### Diners Club

*(1-800 234 6377).*

### Discover

*(1-800 347 2683).*

### Mastercard/Access

Contact the issuing bank.

### Visa Travellers' Cheques

*(1-800 227 6811).*

### Visa

Contact the issuing bank.

## Restrooms

Public toilets are rare in New York. You will find some at the Port Authority Bus Terminal, Penn Station and Grand Central Station; otherwise, you will always find toilet facilities in cafés and bars, department stores and the public lobbies or atriums of large buildings. Fast-food outlets also have readily accessible toilets. We recommend any of those listed below, all of which are centrally located.

### Waldorf-Astoria
*301 Park Avenue, at 50th Street. Subway 6 to 51st Street.* **Open** 24 hours daily.

### Citycorp Centre
*52nd Street & Fifth Avenue. Subway E or F to Fifth Avenue.* Open 7am-midnight Mon-Fri; 8am-midnight Sat, Sun.

### Park Avenue Plaza
*Park Avenue, between East 52nd & East 53rd Streets. Subway E or F to Fifth Avenue.* **Open** 8am-10pm daily.

### Trump Tower
*725 Fifth Avenue, near 57th Street. Subway N or R to Fifth Avenue.* **Open** 8am-10pm daily.

### GE Building
*30 Rockefeller Plaza. Subway N or R to Fifth Avenue.* **Open** 8am-7pm Mon-Fri.

## Security

The following emergency locksmiths are open 24 hours daily. Both require proof of residency or car ownership plus ID.

### Champion Locksmiths
*16 locations in Manhattan (362 7000).* **Rates** $15 call-out charge day or night plus minimum of $35 to fit a lock. **Credit** AmEx, MC, V.

### Elite Locksmiths
*470 Third Avenue, between East 32nd & 33rd Streets (685 1472).* **Rates** $35 during the day; $75-$90 at night. **No credit cards**.

## Transport

For information on travel to and from the three major airports and general transport information, *see chapter* **Getting Around**. For a complete list of foreign airlines, consult the Yellow Pages.

## US Airlines

### Central Airlines Ticket Office
*100 East 42nd Street, at Park Avenue (986 0888).* Issues tickets for Delta, Northwestern, Continental, Virgin Atlantic, American and Scandinavian airlines.

**Alaska Airlines** *(1-800 426 0333).*
**America West** *(1-800 235 9292).*
**American** *(1-800 433 7300).*
**Continental** *(319 9494/1-800 231 0856).*
**Delta** *(239 0700).*
**Kiwi International Airlines** *(1-800 538 5494).*
**Northwest** *(domestic 1-800 225 2525/international 1-800 447 4747).*
**Tower Air** *(1-718 553 8500).*
**United** *(1-800 241 6522).*
**US Air** *(1-800 428 4322).*

# Size conversion chart for clothes

| Women's clothes | | | | | | | | | |
|---|---|---|---|---|---|---|---|---|---|
| British | 8 | 10 | 12 | 14 | 16 | • | • | • | • |
| American | 6 | 8 | 10 | 12 | 14 | • | • | • | • |
| French | 36 | 38 | 40 | 42 | 44 | • | • | • | • |
| Italian | 38 | 40 | 42 | 44 | 46 | • | • | • | • |
| **Women's shoes** | | | | | | | | | |
| British | 3 | 4 | 5 | 6 | 7 | 8 | 9 | • | • |
| American | 5 | 6 | 7 | 8 | 9 | 10 | 11 | • | • |
| Continental | 36 | 37 | 38 | 39 | 40 | 41 | 42 | • | • |
| **Men's suits/overcoats** | | | | | | | | | |
| British | 38 | 40 | 42 | 44 | 46 | • | • | • | • |
| American | 38 | 40 | 42 | 44 | 46 | • | • | • | • |
| Continental | 48 | 50/52 | 54 | 56 | 58/60 | • | • | • | • |
| **Men's shirts** | | | | | | | | | |
| British | 14 | 14.5 | 15 | 15.5 | 16 | 16.5 | 17 | • | • |
| American | 14 | 14.5 | 15 | 15.5 | 16 | 16.5 | 17 | • | • |
| Continental | 35 | 36/37 | 38 | 39/40 | 41 | 42/43 | 44 | • | • |
| **Men's shoes** | | | | | | | | | |
| British | 8 | 9 | 10 | 11 | 12 | • | • | • | • |
| American | 9 | 10 | 11 | 12 | 13 | • | • | • | • |
| Continental | 42 | 43 | 44 | 45 | 46 | • | • | • | • |
| **Children's shoes** | | | | | | | | | |
| British | 7 | 8 | 9 | 10 | 11 | 12 | 13 | 1 | 2 |
| American | 7.5 | 8.5 | 9.5 | 10.5 | 11.5 | 12.5 | 13.5 | 1.5 | 2.5 |
| Continental | 24 | 25.5 | 27 | 28 | 29 | 30 | 32 | 33 | 34 |

**Children's clothes**

In all countries, size descriptions vary from make to make, but are usually based on age or height.

# Further Reading

**Allen, Irving Lewis**: *The City in Slang*. How New York living has spawned hundreds of new words and phrases.
**Federal Writers' Project**: *The WPA Guide To New York City*. A wonderful snapshot of 1930s New York, by the writers employed by FDR's New Deal.
**Fitch, Robert**: *The Assassination of New York*. Essay on the economic death of New York in the 1980s.
**Hood, Clifton**: *722 Miles*. History of the subway.
**Koolhaas, Rem**: *Delirious New York*. New York as terminal city. Urbanism and the culture of congestion.
**Lewis, David Levering**: *When Harlem was in Vogue*. A study of the 1920s Harlem renaissance.
**Liebling, AJ**: *Back Where I Came From*. Personal recollections from the famous *New Yorker* columnist.
**O'Connell, Shaun**: *Remarkable, Unspeakable New York*. History of New York as literary inspiration.
**Pye, Michael**: *Maximum City: The Biography of New York*. Uniquely angled and unmissably stylish history.
**Riis, Jacob**: *How the Other Half Lives*. Pioneering photo-journalist record of gruesome tenement life.
**Rosenzweig, Roy, & Blackman, Elizabeth**: *The Park and its People*. A lengthy history of Central Park.
**Sante, Luc**: *Low Life*. Opium dens, brothels, tenements and suicide salons in 1840-1920s New York.
**Schwartzman, Paul, & Polner, Rob**: *New York Notorious*. New York's most infamous crime scenes.
**Stern, Robert M**: *New York 1930*. A massive coffee-table slab with stunning pictures.
**Stern, Robert M**: *New York 1960*. Another.
**Still, Bayrd**: *Mirror for Gotham*. New York as seen by its inhabitants, from Dutch days to the present.

**Chauncey, George**: *Gay New York*. New York gay life from the 1890s on.
**Cole, William** (ed): *Quotable New York*. Hundreds of hilarious quotes about the city.
**Donaldson, Greg**: *The Ville: Cops and Kids in Urban America*. Gripping sociology of Brownsville, Brooklyn.
**Friedman, Josh Alan**: *Tales From Times Square*. Sleaze, scum, filth and depredation in Times Square.
**Kinkead, Gwen**: *Chinatown: A Portrait of a Closed Society*.
**Toop, David**: *Rap Attack 2; African Rap to Global Hip Hop*. The best cultural history of hip-hop.
**Cooper, Martha, & Chalfant, Henry**: *Subway Art*.
**Torres, Andrés**: *Between Melting Pot and Mosaic*. African Americans' and Puerto Ricans' role in the city's life from 1945 to 1995.
**Trebay, Guy**: *In the Place To Be*. Wonderfully observed essays by a leading *Village Voice* writer.
**Wyatt Sexton, Andrea** (ed): *The Brooklyn Reader*. Thirty writers celebrate America's favourite borough.

**Wolfe, Gerard R**: *A Guide to the Metropolis*. Historical and architectural walking tours.
**Gayle, Margaret**: *Cast Iron Architecture in New York*.
**Goldberger, Paul**: *The City Observed*. The *New York Times'* architecture critic leads you round the city.
**Klotz, Heinrich**: *New York Architecture 1970-90*. A vast and beautiful full-colour volume.
**Sabbagh, Karl**: *Skyscraper*. How a skyscraper is built.
**Willensky, Elliot, & Norval White**: *American Institute of Architects Guide to New York City*. A comprehensive directory of important buildings.

**Bell, Trudy**: *Bicycling Around New York City*.
**Berman, Eleanor**: *Away for the Weekend*. Trips within a 250 mile radius of New York.
**Brown, Arthur S, & Holmes, Barbara**: *Vegetarian Dining in New York City*. Includes vegan places.
**Freudenheim, Ellen**: *Brooklyn*. Subtitled 'where to go, what to do, how to get there'.
**Leon, Ruth**: *New York's Guide to the Performing Arts*. Astonishingly detailed directory of performance venues.
**Marden, William**: *Marden's Guide to New York Booksellers*. Over 500 dealers and stores.
**Michel, John & Barbara**: *Antiquing New York*. Over 1000 antique dealers, markets and fairs listed.
**Miller, Bryan**: *NY Times Guide to Restaurants in New York City*. By the famous food critic.
**Orky, Pollan** *Shopping Manhattan: the Discriminating Buyer's Guide to Finding Almost Anything*. The title says it all.
**Rovere, Vicki**: *Worn Again, Hallelujah!* Guide to NYC's thrift stores and treasure troves.
**Sandvick, Victoria, & Bergman, Michael Ian**: *Single in New York*.
**Steinbicker, Earl**: *Daytrips From New York*.
**Zagat**: *New York City Restaurants*. The leading, and bewildering, comprehensive guide.

**Auster, Paul**: *New York Stories*. Walking the Manhattan grid in search of the madness behind method.
**Baldwin, James**: *Another Country*. Racism under the bohemian veneer of the 1960s.
**Barnhardt, Wilton**: *Emma Who Saved My Life*. Big ambitions set against colourful 1970s NYC.
**Carr, Caleb** *The Alienist*. Hunting a serial killer in New York's turn-of-the-century *demi-monde*.
**Ellison, Ralph**: *Invisible Man*. Coming of age, black and in 1950s New York.
**Friedman, Kinky**: *Kinky Friedman Crime Club*. Cigar-chomping cowboy 'tec wisecracks through '90s NYC.
**Janowitz, Tama**: *Slaves of New York*. Satirical stories of 1980s NYC bohemia.
**Kramer, Larry**: *Faggots*. Hilarious gay New York.
**Miller, Henry**: *Crazy Cock*. Most of Miller's novels are set in Brooklyn; this is 1920s Greenwich Village.
**Price, Richard**: *Clockers*. Cops, kids and crack in urban Jersey City, but just as easily the South Bronx.
**Runyan, Damon**: *On Broadway*. Inimitable tales of guys and their dolls in 1930s New York.
**Selby, Hubert Jr**: *Last Exit to Brooklyn*. Tale of 1960s Brooklyn dockland degradation.
**Smith, Betty**: *A Tree Grows in Brooklyn*. An Irish girl in 1930s Brooklyn.
**Wharton, Edith**: *Old New York*. The novellas here include *The Age Of Innocence*.
**Wolfe, Tom**: *Bonfire of the Vanities*. Rich/poor, black/white. An unmatched slice of 1980s New York.

# Index

# Advertisers' Index

Please refer to the relevant sections for addresses/telephone numbers

Section sponsored by
**AT&T**

# Maps

Place of Interest and/or Entertainment . . . . . . . .

Parks . . . . . . . . . . . . . . . . . . . . . . . . . . . . . . . . . . . . . . .

Railway Station . . . . . . . . . . . . . . . . . . . .

Area Name . . . . . . . . . . . . . . . . . . . . . . **SOHO**

Soldiers' & Sailors' Monument

Riverside Church

Park

Riverside

CLAREMONT AVE

W 115TH ST

W 121ST ST

W 118TH ST

Symphony Space

WEST END AVE

BROADWAY

AMSTERDAM AVE

W 98TH ST

W 100TH ST

W 102ND ST

W 103RD ST

Verdi Square

W 109TH ST

W 111TH ST

W 113TH ST

Columbia University

Morningside Park

MORNINGSIDE DRIVE

UPPER WEST SIDE

W 86TH ST

W 84TH ST

W 90TH ST

W 92ND ST

W 94TH ST

W 96TH ST

W 105TH ST

W 107TH ST

COLUMBUS AVE

Cathedral of St. John the Divine

MANHATTAN AVE

FREDERICK DOU

ADAM CLAYTON POWELL JR BLVD

ST NICHOLAS AVE

LENOX AVE

WEST DRIVE

Central Park

97TH ST TRANSVERSE RD

86TH ST TRANSVERSE RD

The Reservoir

The Pool

WEST DRIVE

Harlem Meer

Great Lawn

EAST DRIVE

EAST DRIVE

Conservatory Garden

Harlem Meer

FIFTH AVE

Marcus Garvey Park

Goethe House

E 86TH ST

YORKVILLE

E 84TH ST

E 88TH ST

E 90TH ST

E 92ND ST

E 94TH ST

E 96TH ST

E 98TH ST

Guggenheim Museum

National Design Museum

Jewish Museum

International Center of Photography

Museum of the City of NY

El Museo del Barrio

SPANISH HARLEM

E 105TH ST

E 109TH ST

E 111TH ST

E 113TH ST

E 121ST ST

MADISON AVE

PARK AVE

LEXINGTON AVE

THIRD AVE

SECOND AVE

FIRST AVE

E 103RD ST

E 102ND ST

E 100TH ST

E 107TH ST

E 115TH ST

E 117TH ST

E 119TH ST

E 113TH ST

Jefferson Park

EAST END AVE

FRANKLIN D ROOSEVELT DR

Carl Schurz Park

Gracie Mansion

| O | N | M | L | K | J | H | G | F | E | D | C | B | A |

1

2

3

**Subway** .......................... Ⓜ

0

0.5 mile

© Copyright Time Out Group 1997

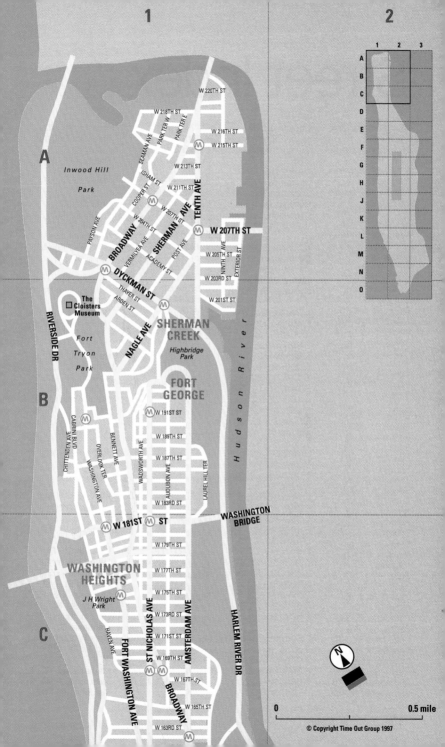

# Street Index

65th St Transverse
  Rd - H2
79th St Transverse
  Rd - H2
86th St Transverse
  Rd - G2
97th St Transverse
  Rd - G2

Academy St - A1
Adam Clayton Powell
  Jr Blvd - D2, F2
Albany St - N2
Allen St - M3
Amsterdam Ave - C1-
  G1
Ann St - N2
Arden St - B1
Audubon Ave - B1
Audubon Terr - D1
Ave of the Americas -
  L2

Bank St - L1
Barclay St - N2
Barrow St - L1
Battery Pl - N2
Baxter St - M2
Beach St - M2
Bedford St - L2
Beekman St - N2
Bennett Ave - B1
Bethune St - L1
Bleecker St - L2
Bridge St - N2
Broad St - N2
Broadhurst Ave - D1
Broadway - A1-H1
Broadway - K2-M2
Brooklyn Bridge - N3
Brooklyn-Battery
  Tunnel - O2
Broome St - M2, 3

Cabrini Blvd - B1
Canal St - M2
Catherine St - M3
Centre St - M2
Chambers St - M2
Charles St - L1
Charlton St - M2
Cherry St - M3
Chittenden Ave - B1
Christopher St - L1

Chrystie St - M3
Church St - M2
Claremont Ave - E1,
  F1
Clarkson St - M2
Clinton St - M3
Columbus Ave - F1
Convent Ave - E1
Cooper St - A1
Crosby St - M2

Delancey St - M3
Desbrosses St - M2
Dominick St - M2
Duane St - M2
Dyckman St - A1, B1

E 2nd St - L2, 3
E 4th St - L2, 3
E 6th St - L2, 3
E 8th St - L2, 3
E 8th St - L3
E 10th St - L2, 3
E 12th St - L2, 3
E 14th St - L2, 3
E 16th St - L2
E 18th St - L2
E 20th St - L2
E 22nd St - K2
E 23rd St - K2, 3
E 26th St - K2
E 28th St - K2
E 30th St - K2, 3
E 32nd St - K2
E 34th St - K2, 3
E 36th St - K2, 3
E 38th St - K2, 3
E 40th St - K2
E 42nd St - J2, 3
E 44th St - J2, 3
E 46th St - J2, 3
E 48th St - J2, 3
E 50th St - J2, 3
E 52nd St - J2, 3
E 54th St - J2, 3
E 56th St - J2, 3
E 58th St - J2, 3
E 60th St - J2, 3
E 62nd St - J2, 3
E 64th St - H2, 3
E 66th St - H2, 3
E 68th St - H2, 3
E 70th St - H2, 3

E 72nd St - H2, 3
E 74th St - H2, 3
E 76th St - H2, 3
E 78th St - H2, 3
E 79th St - H2, 3
E 80th St - H2, 3
E 82nd St - H2, 3
E 84th St - G2, 3
E 86th St - G2, 3
E 88th St - G2, 3
E 90th St - G2, 3
E 92nd St - G2, 3
E 94th St - G2
E 96th St - G2
E 98th St - G2
E 100th St - G2, 3
E 102nd St - G2, 3
E 103rd St - F2
E 105th St - F2
E 107th St - F2
E 109th St - F2
E 111th St - F2
E 113th St - F2
E 115th St - F2, 3
E 117th St - F2, 3
E 119th St - F2, 3
E 121st St - F2
E 131st St - E2
E 135th St - E2
E 145th St - D2
East Broadway - M3
East Drive - G2, H2
East End Ave - G3
East Houston St - L3
Edgecombe Ave - D1
Eighth Ave - J1, K1
Eldridge St - M3
Eleventh Ave - J1, K1
Elizabeth St - M2
Entrance St - M2
Essex St - M3
Exchange Pl - N2
Exterior St - A1

Fifth Ave - E2-L2
First Ave - F3-K3
First Pl - N2
Forsyth St - M3
Fort Washington Ave -
  C1
Frankfort St - N2
Franklin D Roosevelt
  Dr - G3, K3, L3,
  N2, 3

Franklin St - M2
Frederick Douglas
  Blvd - D1, E1
Freedom Pl - H1
Front St - N2
Fulton St - N2

Gold St - N2
Grand St - M2, 3
Greene St - M2
Greenwich Ave - L2
Greenwich St - L1,
  M2, N2

Hamilton Place - E1
Harlem River Dr - C1,
  D1, 2
Haven Ave - C1
Henry Hudson Pkwy -
  D1-H1
Henry St - M3
Hester St - M2
Horatio St - L1
Howard St - M2
Hubert St - M2
Hudson St - L1, 2,
  M2

Isham St - A1

Jackson St - M3
Jane St - L1
John St - N2

Kenmare St - M2
King St - M2

Lafayette St - L2, M2
Laight St - M2
La Salle St - E1
Laurel Hill Ter - B1
Lenox Ave - D2, F2
Leonard St - M2
Lexington Ave - F2-K2
Liberty St - N2
Lincoln Tunnel - K1
Lispenard St - M2
Little W 12th St - L1
Ludlow St - M3

Madison Ave - E2-J2
Madison St - M3
Maiden Lane - N2

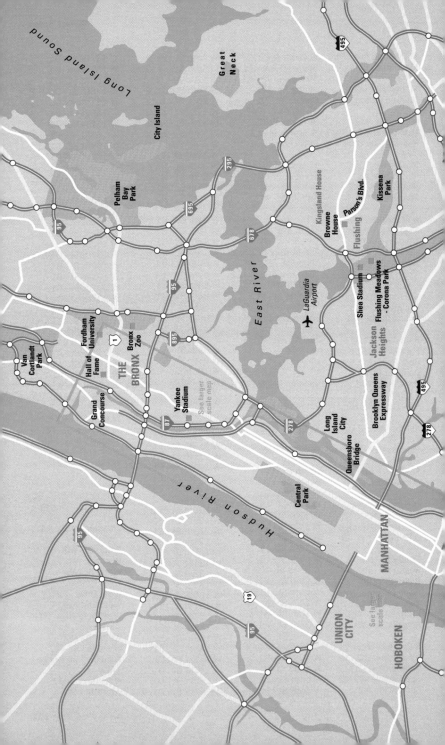

# New York City

**ATLANTIC OCEAN**

**QUEENS**

*J.F.K. Airport*

**Jamica Bay**

**Wildlife Refuge**

BUSHWICK AVENUE

**Williamsburg**

LINDEN BOULEVARD

Soldiers' & Sailors'
Memorial Arch

Brooklyn
Museum &
Botanic
Gardens

**BROOKLYN**

FLATBUSH AVENUE

**Marine
Park**

Prospect
Park

Brooklyn Heights
Promenade

OCEAN PARKWAY

**Bensonhurst**

**Brighton Beach**

4TH AVENUE

**Brooklyn
Bridge**

FORT HAMILTON PARKWAY

**Coney Island**

Ellis Island

Liberty
State
Park

Liberty
Island

**U p p e r**

**B a y**

**Bay
Ridge**

**L o w e r**

**B a y**

**JERSEY
CITY**

Snug Harbour
Cultural Center

**BAYONNE**

**STATEN
ISLAND**

0     5 km

© Copyright Time Out Group 1997

**How to get from Peoria to Pretoria.**

 AND **1 800 CALL ATT**® GETS YOU FROM THE U.S. TO THE WORLD.

It's all within your reach.

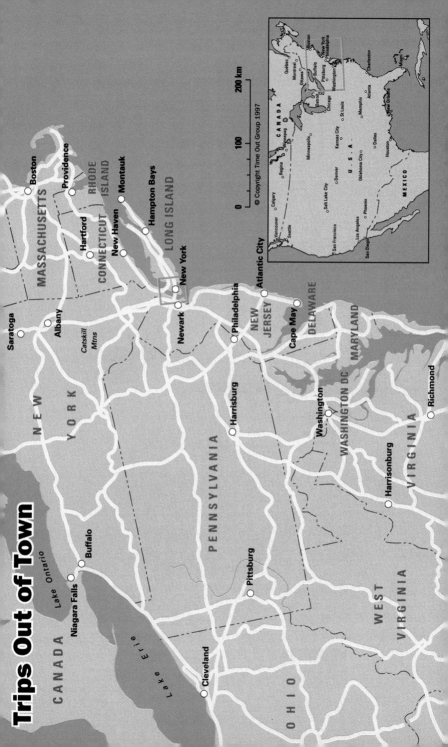

# Trips Out of Town

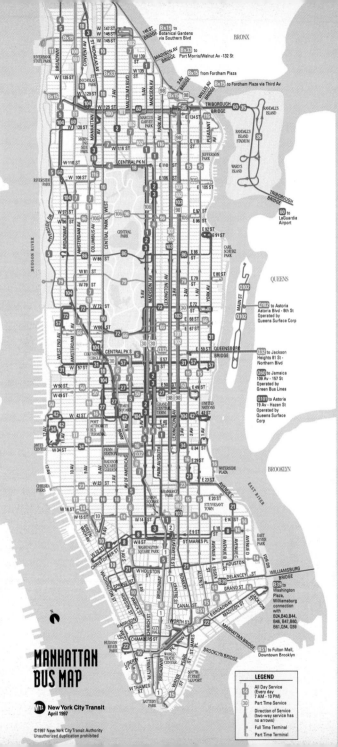

# MANHATTAN BUS MAP

**MTA** New York City Transit
April 1997

©1997 New York City Transit Authority
Unauthorized duplication prohibited

**LEGEND**

| | |
|---|---|
| **14** | All Day Service (Every day) 7 AM - 10 PM |
| **30** | Part Time Service |
| | Direction of Service (two-way service has no arrows) |
| | Full Time Terminal |
| | Part Time Terminal |

# MANHATTAN SUBWAY MAP

**MTA** New York City Transit
April 1997

# Let us know what you think about the *Time Out New York Guide*

## About this guide...

### 1. How useful did you find the following sections?

| | Very | Useful | Fairly | Not very |
|---|---|---|---|---|
| Accommodation | ☐ | ☐ | ☐ | ☐ |
| Sightseeing | ☐ | ☐ | ☐ | ☐ |
| History | ☐ | ☐ | ☐ | ☐ |
| New York by Neighbourhood | ☐ | ☐ | ☐ | ☐ |
| Eating & Drinking | ☐ | ☐ | ☐ | ☐ |
| Shopping & Services | ☐ | ☐ | ☐ | ☐ |
| Museums & Galleries | ☐ | ☐ | ☐ | ☐ |
| Arts & Entertainment | ☐ | ☐ | ☐ | ☐ |
| In Focus | ☐ | ☐ | ☐ | ☐ |
| Trips Out of Town | ☐ | ☐ | ☐ | ☐ |
| Survival | ☐ | ☐ | ☐ | ☐ |

### 2. Is there anything you'd like us to cover in greater depth?

_____

## About other *Time Out* publications...

### 3. Are you a *Time Out* magazine reader?   Yes ☐   No ☐

### 4. Have you bought other *Time Out* guides? If so, which ones?

| | | | |
|---|---|---|---|
| Amsterdam Guide ☐ | Barcelona Guide ☐ | | |
| Berlin Guide ☐ | Brussels Guide ☐ | | |
| Budapest Guide ☐ | Florence Guide ☐ | | |
| Los Angeles Guide ☐ | Madrid Guide ☐ | | |

| | |
|---|---|
| Miami Guide ☐ | Paris Guide ☐ |
| Prague Guide ☐ | Rome Guide ☐ |
| San Francisco Guide ☐ | Sydney Guide ☐ |
| London Visitors' Guide ☐ | Shopping & Services Guide ☐ |
| Student Guide ☐ | Film Guide ☐ |
| The Book of Country Walks ☐ | Eating & Drinking in London Guide ☐ |

## About you...

### 5. Did you travel to New York:

| | | | |
|---|---|---|---|
| Alone? ☐ | | With partner? ☐ | |
| As part of a group? ☐ | | With children? ☐ | |

### 6. How long is/was your trip to New York?

| | |
|---|---|
| Less than three days ☐ | Three days-one week ☐ |
| One week-two weeks ☐ | Over two weeks (please specify) ☐ |

### 7. Name: _____

### Address: _____

### 8. Age: up to 19 ☐   20-24 ☐   25-29 ☐   30-34 ☐   35-44 ☐   45+ ☐

### 9. Nationality: _____

### 10. Occupation: _____

### 11. Would you like to receive information about new titles? Yes ☐   No ☐